HISTORY OF THE POPES

VOL. XXIX.

PASTOR'S HISTORY OF THE POPES

THE HISTORY OF THE POPES. Translated from the German of LUDWIG, FREIHERR VON PASTOR. Edited, as to Vols. I.–VI. by the late FREDERICK IGNATIUS ANTROBUS, and, as to Vols. VII.–XXIV. by RALPH FRANCIS KERR, of the London Oratory, and Vols. XXV.–XXIX. by DOM ERNEST GRAF, of Buckfast Abbey. In 29 Volumes.

Vols. I. and II.	A.D. 1305–1458
Vols. III. and IV.	A.D. 1458–1483
Vols. V. and VI.	A.D. 1484–1513
Vols. VII. and VIII	A.D. 1513–1521
Vols. IX. and X.	A.D. 1522–1534
Vols. XI. and XII.	A.D. 1534–1549
Vols. XIII. and XIV.	A.D. 1550–1559
Vols. XV. and XVI.	A.D. 1559–1565
Vols. XVII. and XVIII.	A.D. 1566–1572
Vols. XIX. and XX.	A.D. 1572–1585
Vols. XXI. and XXII.	A.D. 1585–1591
Vols. XXIII. and XXIV.	A.D. 1592–1604
Vols. XXV. and XXVI.	A.D. 1605–1621
Vols. XXVII. to XXIX.	A.D. 1621–1644

The original German text of the *History of the Popes* is published by Herder & Co., Freiburg (Baden).

THE HISTORY OF THE POPES

FROM THE CLOSE OF THE MIDDLE AGES

DRAWN FROM THE SECRET ARCHIVES OF THE VATICAN AND OTHER ORIGINAL SOURCES

FROM THE GERMAN OF

LUDWIG, FREIHERR VON PASTOR

TRANSLATED BY

DOM ERNEST GRAF, O.S.B.

MONK OF BUCKFAST

VOLUME XXIX.

GREGORY XV. AND URBAN VIII. (1621–1644)

LONDON

KEGAN PAUL, TRENCH, TRUBNER & CO., LTD.

BROADWAY HOUSE: 68–74 CARTER LANE, E.C.

1938

Imprimi potest

Sublaci, ex Proto-Coenobio Stae Scholasticae,
die 29 Decembris 1937.

D. Emmanuel Caronti, O.S.B., Abbas Generalis.

PRINTED IN GREAT BRITAIN BY
STEPHEN AUSTIN AND SONS, LTD., HERTFORD.

CONTENTS OF VOLUME XXIX.

	PAGE
Table of Contents	vii–xi
List of Unpublished Documents in Appendix . .	xv
Church Reforms by Urban VIII.—The Jubilee of 1625—Reform of the Breviary—Religious Orders—The Roman Inquisition and the Trial of Galileo—Beginnings of Jansenism—Its rôle in the History of the Church	1–156
Creations of Cardinals by Urban VIII.—Relations with Poland—Struggle against the Cæsaro—Papalism of the small Italian States, of Venice and Spain—The Portuguese Revolution	157–211
Propaganda and the Missions	212–264
The Situation of Catholics in Switzerland, Holland, Denmark, Sweden, England, Ireland, and Scotland	265–359
The States of the Church and the War of Castro .	360–407
Urban VIII. as Patron of Literature and Arts—Rome a Baroque City	408–544
Appendix of Unpublished Documents	545–590
Index of Names	591–606

For Bibliography, see Volume XXVII.

TABLE OF CONTENTS OF VOLUME XXIX.

URBAN VIII. 1623–1644.

CHAPTER I.

CHURCH REFORMS BY URBAN VIII.—THE JUBILEE OF 1625—REFORM OF THE BREVIARY—RELIGIOUS ORDERS—THE ROMAN INQUISITION AND THE TRIAL OF GALILEO—BEGINNINGS OF JANSENISM—ITS RÔLE IN THE HISTORY OF THE CHURCH.

A.D.		PAGE
1623	Church reforms	1
1625	The year of Jubilee	4
	Beatifications by Urban VIII. and Canonizations	8
	Measures relating to Church music	11
	Reform of the Breviary	12
1634	Revision of the Missal	18
	Regulation of Feasts and	19
	The Religious Orders	20
1639	The Centenary of the Society of Jesus	22
	Mary Ward	24
	Her attempt to found a religious Order	25
	The Society of the " English Ladies "	27
	Opposition to the Society	29
1645	Death of Mary Ward	32
	Her influence	33
	The Congregation of the Inquisition	34
	Its activities	35
	Its dealings with Galileo Galilei	42
1633	His condemnation	58
	The Congregation of the Index	62
	Foundation of new religious associations	63
	Religious revival frustrated by the teaching of	66
	Baius	67
	Jansenius and	68
	Du Vergier de Hauranne	69
	The Heresy of Jansenius	71
	St. Cyran's propaganda	76

A.D. PAGE

His influence on the Arnauld family . . . 78
The Abbesses of St. Cyr and Port Royal . . . 79
The Abbey of Port Royal 83
Accusation of heresy at Port Royal . . . 83
St. Cyran's influence and teaching 87
1638 His imprisonment 91
Death of Jansenius 93
The publication of his book *Augustinus* . . . 94
His heresy set forth 97
Suppression of *Augustinus* by Rome . . . 105
Polemical writings and disputations . . . 107
1643 Bull condemning Jansenius published . . . 120
It is defied by Antoine Arnauld and . . . 123
Opposed in Flanders and Paris 124
The Pope's decision 125
Antoine Arnauld, joint founder of Jansenism . . 132
His teaching 133
Opinions on his writings 138
He is summoned to Rome 145
Jansenist tenets and 146
Publications 153
Its temporary triumph 155

CHAPTER II.

CREATIONS OF CARDINALS BY URBAN VIII.—RELATIONS WITH POLAND—STRUGGLE AGAINST THE CÆSARO—PAPALISM OF THE SMALL ITALIAN STATES, OF VENICE AND SPAIN—THE PORTUGUESE REVOLUTION.

1623–24 Creation of Cardinals 157
Definition of Cardinalitial dignities 161
1633 Further creations of Cardinals 162
1643 Final Creation by Urban VIII. 163
His difficulties in selection 165
1632 Polish Embassy to Rome 167
Urban's support of the Union 169
His defence of the independence of the Church . 171
Leads to disputes with Savoy, Tuscany, and . . 173
Lucca 174
Still greater difficulties caused by Venice . . . 175
The policy of Venice 176
A new nuncio, Vitelli, sent there 181
1638 The so-called " Inscription trouble " . . . 183
Relations between Rome and Spain . . . 184
1637 Sudden illness of the Pope 192
Disaffection of Spain 194
Attack on the Church in Portugal 196

A.D. PAGE

The pretensions of Spain 198
1640 Insurrection in Catalonia 201
Compromise between Rome and Spain . . . 203
1642 Demands of the Spanish Envoy 207
Who leaves Rome in indignation 209
The fall of Olivares makes for peace . . . 211

CHAPTER III.

PROPAGANDA AND THE MISSIONS.

The foundation of the Urban College 212
1637 Bull confirms the establishment of Propaganda . 213
The scope of Propaganda 214
Reports to and from Propaganda 217
Mission work in Turkey 220
1625 The situation in Albania and 222
In Bulgaria 223
The organization of French Missions 225
Jesuit work in the Levant hindered by Cyril Lukaris 227
His treachery 228
The " affair Lukaris " 231
1638 He is finally deposed and strangled 240
The Latins attempt to recover the Holy Places in Palestine 241
The Pope's solicitude for the Missions 243
Faculties granted to Carmelites and Capuchins . 244
Jesuit Missions in Madeira, Siam, Cochin China, and 247
China 248
Divergences of opinion among the Missionaries . 250
1632 Martyrdoms in Japan 253
The Church in Ethiopia, in 254
East Africa, and 258
The Congo 259
1631 Conversions in Mexico 261
Missions in East and West Indies 262

CHAPTER IV.

THE SITUATION OF CATHOLICS IN SWITZERLAND, HOLLAND, DENMARK, SWEDEN, ENGLAND, IRELAND, AND SCOTLAND.

Catholicism in Switzerland and in 265
The Netherlands 270
Difficulties in Holland 273
Effects of the reformation in Sweden and Denmark . 274
Relations between the Holy See and England . . 276

A.D.		PAGE
	Prospective marriage alliance of Prince of Wales with	279
	Spain	281
	Its failure leads to.	285
	Persecution of English Catholics	287
	Renewal of the negotiations	289
1624	The marriage treaty signed	293
	Postponement of the wedding.	295
	Protestant attitude of Pashanicut	296
	Further persecution of Catholics	299
	A Bishop appointed for England	303
	His imprudences and resignation	305
	Attacks on the Jesuits in England	309
	Charles I.'s comparative leniency towards Catholics .	310
	The so-called Papal Envoy, Panziani	312
	His misapprehensions and optimism	314
	Consent as Papal Envoy	318
	His Counsel to Queen Henrietta Maria	321
	Report to Rome on the Puritans	323
1639	The Catholic support of King Charles	325
	Puritan tumults and violence	326
1640	Extreme danger of the Catholics	327
1642	Civil war in England	333
	The state of Ireland	339
	Cruel treatment of the Irish	341
	The Assembly at Kilkenny	345
	The Papal Envoy Scarampi arrives in Ireland . .	346
	A twelve months' truce concluded	347
	Displeasure of the Pope	348
	The Catholics in Scotland	349
	The Faith in N. America	352
	The work of the Jesuits in Maryland	356
	The end of their mission there	359

CHAPTER V.

THE STATES OF THE CHURCH AND THE WAR OF CASTRO.

A.D.		PAGE
	The military weakness of the States of the Church .	360
	Urban VIII.'s plans for defence	361
1629–30	The Plague in Italy	366
	Successful precautions in Rome	368
	The Pope's forethought for the Poor	371
	The question of precedence	375
	The population of Rome and	376
	The noble families of the period	377
	Plans for the Campagna.	379
	Papal expenditure	380
	Relations between the Holy See and the Duke of Parma	382
	The aggressions of the latter lead to	385

A.D.		PAGE
1640	War—and the	387
	Excommunication of the Duke	389
	The fruitless invervention of France	391
	Negotiations	395
1644	Farnese finally yields	398
	The impoverishment caused by the war	399
1639	The Illness of Urban VIII. and his recovery	401
1644	A further attack of weakness	402
	His last Consistory	403
	Death of Urban VIII., July 29, 1644	404
	His virtues overshadowed by his weakness	406

CHAPTER VI.

URBAN VIII. AS PATRON OF LITERATURE AND ART—ROME A BAROQUE CITY.

A.D.		PAGE
	Urban as Patron of Literature	408
	His poetry	409
	The intimates of the Pope	423
	Poets of the period	427
	The Pope as Antiquarian and	433
	Student of history	435
	Francesco Barberini	437
	The career of Luke Holste	440
	Cardinal Barberini's support of literature	444
	The Vatican Library	448
	Urban VIII.'s care of the Roman Archives	451
	Baroque art	455
	The works done by Bernini	456
	High Altar in St. Peter's	457
1633	Unveiled on the Feast of St. Peter	464
	The lavish liberality of the Pope	465
	The Baldacchino in St. Peter's	466
1638	The Loggias completed	471
	Further embellishments of the Basilica	472
	The Monument to Urban VIII.	478
	The Restoration of other churches in Rome	482
	The Munificance of the Cardinal Nephews	489
	Artists of the period	495
	The building of the Palazzo Barberini	498
	Other Barberini buildings and restorations	507
	The Fountains of Rome	513
	Guides to the City	515
	A description of the *Rioni*	519
	The markets in Rome	533
	Foreign Artists in Rome	535
	The Patronage of Urban VIII.	543
	Rome a baroque city	544

LIST OF UNPUBLISHED DOCUMENTS IN APPENDIX.

		PAGE
1	Nuncio Sacchetti to the Cardinal Legate, Fr. Barberini	547
2	Pope Urban VIII. to Cardinal Richelieu	547
3	Pope Urban VIII. to Wallenstein, Duke of Friedland .	548
4	The French Ambassador Béthune to (D'Herbault) .	548
5	The French Ambassador Béthune to (D'Herbault) .	551
6	Cardinal Francesco Barberini to the French Nuncio Guido Del Bagno	554
7	The French Nuncio G. Del Bagno to Cardinal Francesco Barberini	556
8	Cardinal Francesco Barberini to the French Nuncio G. Del Bagno	557
9	Cardinal Francesco Barberini to Ciriaco Rocci, Nuncio in Germany	557
10	Pope Urban VIII. to Tilly	557
11	The French Nuncio Alessandro Bichi to Cardinal Francesco Barberini	559
12	Cardinal Francesco Barberini to the French Nuncio Alessandro Bichi	559
13	Cardinal Fr. Barberini to the French Nuncio Alessandro Bichi	560
14	Cardinal Fr. Barberini to the Spanish Nuncio Monti .	560
15	P. Savelli to Emperor Ferdinand II.	564
16	Instruction of Cardinal Barberini for the Nuncios Ceva and Grimaldi	565
17	Draft of a Brief of Urban VIII. to Emperor Ferdinand II.	569
18	Pope Urban VIII. to Emperor Ferdinand II. . . .	570
19	Protocol of Cardinalitial Congregation "De Redditibus Ecclesiasticis" of 1642/3	571
20	The Nuncio Extraordinary F. Chigi to Cardinal Fr. Barberini	572
21	The Nuncio Extraordinary F. Chigi to Cardinal Fr. Barberini	572
22	Avviso di Roma of July 30th, 1644	573
23	Writings dedicated to Urban VIII.	573
24	Writings dedicated to Cardinal Fr. Barberini . .	577
25	The Elogia and Avvisi of Theodore Ameyden . .	579
26	Andrea Nicoletti's Life of Urban VIII.	584

CHAPTER I.

Church Reforms by Urban VIII—The Jubilee of 1625—Reform of the Breviary—Religious Orders—The Roman Inquisition and the Trial of Galileo—Beginnings of Jansenism—Its Rôle in the History of the Church.

(1)

Both as nuncio in France and subsequently as Bishop of Spoleto, Urban VIII. had shown himself penetrated with the spirit of the Catholic reform and as Pope he never lost sight of that all-important matter. Soon after his election it became evident that he was determined to adhere strictly to the decrees of the Council of Trent.[1] In September, 1623, the reform began with the persons of his entourage,[2] and in December he announced that the prescriptions concerning the duty of residence would be applied more rigidly.[3] To this end special decrees were issued.[4] In a consistory of March 18th, 1624, he insisted on this obligation for all Bishops and Archbishops and laid stress on the fact that the Cardinals were likewise subject to it.[5] In the consistory of January 29th, 1625, he reminded the Cardinals of their duties, more especially of that of defending the faith and the Church's liberty and of

[1] See *Avviso of August 19, 1623, *Urb.* 1093, Vatican Library. The necessities of the time repeatedly compelled Urban VIII. to bestow more than one benefice upon single individuals, in opposition to the decrees of the Council of Trent.

[2] *Cf.* the *report of the envoy of Este of September 23, 1623, State Archives, Modena.

[3] See Possevino's *report of December 16, 1623, Gonzaga Archives, Mantua.

[4] See *Bull.*, XIV., 457, 477.

[5] See **Acta consist.*, *Barb.*, 2933, Vatican Library.

showing liberality to the poor.[1] In the following year he again reverted to the duty of residence,[2] and he sought to enforce it wherever it was being infringed as, for instance, at Naples.[3] In the last years of his pontificate it was particularly the Spanish Bishops, including the Cardinals, whom he reminded of their obligations in this respect.[4] Rules were laid down for the examination of Bishops in 1591, in a special Instruction based on Gregory XIV.'s Bulls of 1627 on the same subject.[5] One of Urban VIII.'s most useful measures was the thorough revision ordered by him in 1633 of the dispositions of the Code concerning episcopal faculties. These were in a state of great confusion and needed to be adjusted to altered conditions. To this end a special Congregation was instituted, composed of members of the Inquisition and Propaganda,[6] and on their advice an entirely new Code of faculties was created in 1637.[7]

In April, 1624, the Pope ordered a visitation of all the churches and monasteries of Rome, he himself undertaking that of the Lateran, St. Peter's and St. Paul's.[8] His

[1] *Ibid.* [2] See KHEVENHÜLLER, X., 1309.

[3] See the **Instruttione a Msgr. Bichi, vescovo dell'Isola, destinato Nunzio ordin. in Napoli*, of May 30, 1628, MS. in my possession.

[4] See the *Constitution of December 12, 1634, *super residentia episcop., archiepiscop., metropol., etiam S.R.E. cardinalium* (*nec ad alios actos se divertant*), State Archives, Vienna; *Brief to the Spanish episcopate of November 20, 1636, *Epist.*, XIII., Papal Secret Archives. [5] See *Bull.*, IX., 419; XIII., 581.

[6] The *Acts are kept in the Archives of the Roman Inquisition, but are not available.

[7] See MERGENTHEIM, II., 62 *seq.*, 71 *seq.*, who shows that the formula which later on became general at the granting of the quinquennial faculties was first used for Cologne in 1640.

[8] See *Bull.*, XIII., 125 *seq.*, 126 *seq.*, 129 *seq.*; XIV., 8 *seq.* In the Papal Secret Archives, *Arm.* 7, vol. 3, **Decreta visit. eccl., etc., sub Urbano VIII. Cf.* besides CIACONIUS, IV., 500; *NICOLETTI, II., 582 *seq.*, Vatican Library; *Avvisi of April 3 and November 13, 1624, *Urb.*, 1094 *ibid.*; **Diarium P. Alaleonis* of April 14, 1624, *ibid.* See also *Catalogue de quelques manuscrits de la Bibl. Corsini p.* L. G. PÉLISSIER.

example was followed by the Cardinals in their titular churches.[1]

Various prescriptions for the reform of the Roman clergy date from 1624. Religious were forbidden to ride in carriages and all ecclesiastics were ordered to wear clerical dress[2]; at the same time further decrees were issued for the reform of Regulars[3] and for the moral reform of Rome.[4] A stern decree of 1625 dealt with abuses that had crept in with regard to Mass stipends.[5] The Pope had greatly at heart the Roman

[1] See **Acta visit. eccl. Portuen.*, by Cardinal Fr. Barberini and by Cardinal Deto, 1626, *Barb.* 2438, Vatican Library. **Decreta visit. colleg. S. Laurentii in Damaso a card. L. Ludovisio peractae die* 25 *Maii*, 1625; *Cod.* E. 88 of the Boncompagni Archives, Rome; **Visitatio abbatiae Sublacensis per d. Aemilium de Altieriis ep. Camerin. visit. deput., a card. Ant. Barberini*, 1640. Library of the Abbey of Subiaco A.F., II., 5. The Pope *admonished the Cardinals in the Consistory of August 20, 1629, to fulfil their pastoral duties in the suburban dioceses, **Acta consist., loc. cit.*

[2] See *Avviso, January 20, 1624, *loc. cit.*, and *Anal. iuris pontif.*, 1895, 168 *seq.*

[3] See *Avviso of December 25, 1624, *loc. cit.* Prohibition of hearing confessions in private houses, see *Avviso, June 19, 1625, *loc. cit.*

[4] See *Avviso of November 30, 1624, *loc. cit.* An ordinance against bigamy is in *Bull.*, XIV., 595 *seq.*

[5] *Cf.* Barbier de Montault, IV., 23 *seq.* See the work by the same author: *La question des messes sous les Papes Urbain VIII., Innocent XII. et Clement XI.*, Rome, 1864; and Chaillot, *Du commerce des messes et des livres*, Paris, 1866. The abuse of smoking in churches had necessitated severe measures by several synods in Spanish America in 1575, 1588 and 1589. (*Cf.* Moroni, LXXII., 176 *seq.*) When this abuse also spread to Spain, Urban VIII., at the request of the Chapter of Seville, issued a decree forbidding under pain of excommunication all smoking or taking of snuff in the churches of the diocese. The reason given for the measure was that the Pope had been told that: "Pravus in illis partibus sumendi ore vel naribus tabaccum vulgo nuncupatum usus adeo invaluit, ut utriusque sexus personae ac etiam sacerdotes et clerici tam saeculares quam regulares clericalis

Seminary.[1] In 1628 he issued fresh regulations for the Pontifical Seminaries in Germany.[2] In 1636 he established a special Seminary near St. Peter's, chiefly for the purpose of training clerics for the service of the basilica.[3]

In 1625 Urban VIII. was able to celebrate the thirteenth Jubilee. The preparations began as early as the end of September, 1624.[4] On November 13th, the Cardinals were exhorted to see to it that their titular churches were in good condition and to take care that the persons in their service gave the pilgrims an edifying example.[5] Special edicts dealing with the conduct of religious were likewise issued.[6] The Pope was indefatigable ; he took measures for the importation of food, pleaded for support of the hospices of the pilgrims, especially of Trinità de' Pellegrini,[7] and provided special lodgings near St. Peter's for foreign prelates. Cardinal Francesco Barberini, in his capacity of Protector of England,

honestatis immemores illud passim in civitatis et diocesis Hispalen. ecclesiis, ac quod referre pudet, etiam sacrosanctum missae sacrificium celebrando sumere linteaque sacra foedis quae tabaccum huiusmodi proiicit excrementis conspurcare ecclesiasque praedictas tetro odore inficere magno cum proborum scandalo rerumque sacrarum irreverentia non reformident" ; see *Bull.*, XV., 157 ; BENEDICT, XIV., *De synodo dioec.*, lib. 10, cap. 3, no. 2 (*Opp.*, XII., Bassano, 1767, 7). *Cf.* also *Der Tabak in Kultur und Geschichte*, Köln, 1911 ; B. DUHR in the *Abhandlungen der Görres-Gesellschaft*, Köln, 1918, 61–4.

[1] See *Bull.*, XIV., 79 *seq.*, and the *documents on the visitation of the Roman Seminary in the archives of that institution. *Cf.* *Cenni storici del Pontificio Seminario Romano*, Roma, 1914, 21.

[2] *Cf.* *Ius pontif.*, I., 105 *seq.* ; DUHR, II., 1, 624 *seq.*

[3] See *Bull. Vat.*, III., 249. *Cf.* CANCELLIERI, *Lettera sopra il Tarantismo*, 314.

[4] See the *Briefs to the Catholic Princes, which begin on September 29, 1624, in the *Epist.*, II., Papal Secret Archives. *Cf.* also *Avviso of October 30, 1624, *Urb.* 1094, Vatican Library.

[5] See **Acta consist.*, *Barb.* XXXVIII., 2, Vatican Library.

[6] See *Avviso of December 25, 1624, *loc. cit.*

[7] See **Acta consist.* of December 2, 1624, *loc. cit.*

Scotland, and Ireland established a separate hospice for pilgrims from those countries.[1]

In accordance with custom, all plenary Indulgences and the faculties of confessors outside Rome to absolve from sins reserved to the Sovereign Pontiff, were suspended and limited to Rome, though exceptions were made for religious women, the sick and prisoners, and the Portinucula Indulgence was likewise maintained.[2] Wladimir, son of Sigismund, King of Poland, was present at the opening of the Holy Door at Christmas, 1625.[3] The conqueror of the Turks and the Tartars was received with the greatest honours and on his return

[1] See *NICOLETTI, II., 884 *seq.*, 886, *loc. cit.*

[2] See *Bull.*, XIII., 143 *seq.*; MANNI, 178 *seq.*, 183.

[3] The hammer which Urban VIII. used on this occasion was afterwards presented by him to his brother Carlo. In a Brief of June 10, 1625, the hammer is thus described: "Est igitur malleus totus argenteus undique inauratus, variis foliorum ornamentis interstinctus, ponderis librarum 4 cum semissae vi palparis longitudinis, cuius apici duae apes maiores hinc inde insculptae sunt. Altera pars in acumen parumper deflectitur, altera in planam desinit superficiem, ubi portae sanctae quam aperimus simulacrum leviter incisum licet leviter intueri. Utramque partem Barberinae gentis insignia pontificio diademate coronata interiacent, in extremis autem eius oris Nostrum ex apost. dignitate nomen hinc inde inscriptum est: Urbanus VIII. anno iubilaei 1625, senas interiecto utrinque spatio apiculas complectente. Paulo inferius nodus occurrit, cui solis effigies ab utroque latere efformata subicitur. Post haec apostolorum Petri et Pauli statuae, altera quidem in dextero, altera vero in sinistro latere, suis aediculis collocatae conspiciuntur, tum alio nodo interiecto binae lauri, quarum frondes binae apes delibant, artificiose exprimuntur, totidem paulo inferius capulum decorantibus." Private archives of Prince Barberini (now in the Vatican), *Donaz.*, no. 27. *Ibid.*, no. 42, **Donatione della Trulla ossia Cocchiara da muratore*, used by the Pope in closing the door, dated December 29, 1626. The silver hammer is no longer extant, but Prince Barberini possesses the two hammers of gilt bronze with which the Holy Doors of the other two basilicas were opened. A picture of the Porta Santa of St. Peter is in *Barb.* 4409, p. 19, Vatican Library. *Cf.* HEMPEL, 11.

from Naples the Pope presented him with a consecrated sword and hat.[1]

Urban VIII. repeatedly visited the churches designated for gaining the jubilee; several times also he took his place in the confessional at St. Peter's; he remained in it for an especially long time on Holy Saturday; twelve pilgrims were daily entertained at the Vatican; he distributed abundant alms, especially to the Confraternity of Trinità de' Pellegrini. Twice he repaired thither to wash the feet of poor pilgrims.[2] Like the Pope himself, his family also, especially Cardinal Francesco and Costanza Barberini, were particularly unwearied in their attention to the pilgrims,[3] and the Romans vied with them in works of benevolence and piety.[4] Among the Cardinals, Ludovisi especially distinguished himself in this respect.[5]

The precautionary measures against a possible outbreak of the plague[6] as well as those for the provisioning of the city, proved most effective.[7] Notwithstanding the wars of

[1] See *NICOLETTI, II., 893 *seq.*, *loc. cit.*; THEINER, *Mon. Pol.*, III., 375 *seq.*; CIAMPI, III., 4 *seq*; CHLEDOWSKI, II., 115 *seq*; MANNI, 175, 180; *Jahrbuch der kunsthist. Samml. des österreich. Kaiserhauses*, XXII., 138.

[2] See *NICOLETTI, II., 882 *seq*, *loc. cit*; *Avvisi of May 29 and November 26, 1625, *Urb.* 1095, *loc. cit.*; **Diarium P. Alaleonis*, *Barb.* 2818, Vatican Library; MANNI, 185; PRINZIVALLI, *Gli anni santi*, Roma, 1925, 122 *seq.*

[3] See PRINZIVALLI, 111 *seq.*

[4] *Cf.* AMEYDEN, *De pietate Romana*; see SCHMIDLIN, 476.

[5] See GIUNTI, **Vita del card. Ludovisi*, Corsini Library, Rome.

[6] See the *Avvisi of February 15, May 31, July 30 and August 6, 1625, *Urb.* 1095, *loc. cit.* *Cf.* PRINZIVALLI, 113. When the danger of infection from the plague increased, three churches within the city were appointed as jubilee churches (S. Maria in Trastevere, S. Lorenzo in Lucina and S. Maria del Popolo), instead of the three without the walls. Inscriptions can still be seen in these recording the fact; see PRINZIVALLI, 115.

[7] See *Avviso of December 27, 1625, *loc. cit.*

the period, the number of pilgrims was relatively high—among them there were even a few eastern Bishops.[1] Of personages of distinction, besides the Polish Prince, there also came the Landgrave George of Hessen and his brother, as well as several German noblemen.[2] The end of the Holy Year witnessed the arrival of the Emperor Ferdinand II.'s brother, Archduke Leopold, who wished to lay aside his ecclesiastical dignities in order to marry; the Borgia apartments were assigned to him for a lodging.[3]

For the benefit of the pilgrims the Pope had summoned eminent preachers to Rome, such as the Capuchin Francesco del Nero, the Jesuit Luigi Albricio and the Dominicans Niccolò Riccardi and Francesco Maria Campana.[4] The conduct of the pilgrims was exemplary and the frequentation of the Sacraments very great.[5] "In our visits to the churches,"

[1] See the *Avvisi of March 26 and 29, May 14 and November 26, 1625, *loc. cit.*, MANNI, 183. According to these (*cf.* also CANCELLIERI, *Lettera sopra il Tarantismo*, 306 *seq*; PRINZIVALLI, 115), the visitors were not so few as KHEVENHÜLLER (X., 992 *seq.*, 995) and GIGLI (in CANCELLIERI, *S. Maria in Julia*, 46) thought. Guides for pilgrims appeared by P. FELINI, O. PANCIROLI, H. BAVINCK (see SCHUDT, *Mancini*, 123). To these must be added: F. M. TORRIGIO, *Pelegrinaggio d. 4 chiese* (1625), and F. J. H. VON PFLAUMERN, *Mercurius italicus*, Aug. Vind., 1625. MAGNO PERNEO dedicated to Urban VIII. his **Guida Romana del anno santo* 1625, *Barb.* 3260 (*cf.* 3300), Vatican Library. ANT. SANTARELLI published a *Trattato del giubileo* (1624 and 1625), ANDR. VITTORELLI dedicated to Cardinal Barberini a *Hist. de'giubilei pontif.* (Roma, 1625). *Cf.* other works in NOGARA, *Cronista dell'Anno santo*, 1925, Roma, 1928, 1087 *seq.*

[2] See DE WAAL, *Das Heilige Jahr in Rom*, Münster, 1900, 51, 60; *Avviso of April 17, 1625, *Urb.* 1094, *loc. cit.*; CARAFA, *Relazione*, 387; **Diarium P. Alaleonis* for December 6 and 23, 1625, *loc. cit.*

[3] See the *Avvisi of December 10 and 20, 1625, *loc. cit.*; *NICOLETTI, II., 895 *seq.*, *loc. cit*; DE WAAL, 51; GROTTANELLI, *Claudia de'Medici*, 107 *seq.*

[4] See *NICOLETTI, II., 883, *loc. cit.*

[5] See the *Avvisi of April 30 and December 27, 1625, *loc. cit.*

Jerome Marchstaller, Benedictine Abbot of St. Paul in Carinthia, notes in his account of his pilgrimage, "we were specially struck with the devotion of the foreigners; we saw them praying fervently and with many tears. Nor were there wanting members of the nobility and the clergy of Rome, more especially noble ladies, who visited the sacred shrines on foot, bathed in perspiration, so that it would not be fair to generalize and to say 'the nearer to Rome so much the worse', for there was a devil among the Angels in heaven and a Judas among the Apostles, but their impiety injured neither the Angels nor the Apostles. For my part I not only saw nothing scandalous in Rome, but, on the contrary, beheld very great piety."[1] The Dutch pilgrim van den Vondel summed up his impressions of the Holy Year in a Latin poem which was translated by his famous brother Joost. It concludes thus: "This is the great key-bearer of heaven's gate. Hush! Seek not to know more: On your knees! Kiss those feet which so many come to honour."[2]

During his long pontificate Urban VIII. received countless requests for canonizations. Philip III., the Emperors Ferdinand II. and Ferdinand III., the Duke of Bavaria, Maximilian, King Sigismund of Poland, the Grand-Duke of Tuscany, Archduke Leopold, the authorities of Lucca, Genoa and Palermo, the cathedral Chapter of Liège and the Catholics of Switzerland, all made requests of this kind.[3] Urban VIII.,

[1] See *Carinthia*, LXXI. (1881), 302; F. M. Turrigius, **Diarium de rebus in Basil. Vat. atque alibi gestis anno s. iubilaei* 1625, in *Barb.* 2293, Vatican Library. For the Roman hotels of the time see *Studi e docum.*, XIV., 393 *seq.* According to this the celebrated Albergo del Orso was no longer frequented in 1628, and in 1630 it had lost all its prestige; but the Albergo di Monte Brianza was in great favour. For the Jubilee coins and medals see Martinori, 30 *seq.*, 71.

[2] See Baumgartner, *J. v. d. Vondel*, Freiburg, 1882, 78.

[3] *Cf.* besides Hurter, *Ferdinand II.*, XI., 600 *seq.*, and the *Sitzungsber. der Münchener Akad.*, Phil. Kl., 1880, 361, the *Briefs to Philip III. of January 4, 1625, to Ferdinand II., i.e., III. of July 14, 1630, and March 3, 1640, to Maximilian of

as a matter of fact, had a number of processes introduced,[1] but he invariably insisted that questions of this nature must be subjected to a most searching investigation.[2] How much he had this principle at heart is shown by the fact that he only carried out one canonization, viz. that of Andrew Corsini, on April 22nd, 1629.[3] He beatified Giacopo della Marca, Francis Borgia, and Andrew Avellino in 1624,[4] and in 1625 the Capuchin Felix of Cantalice,[5] and Elizabeth, Queen of

November 30, 1624, and June 23, 1626, to Sigismund III. of July 17, 1627, to Archduke Leopold of December 17, 1629, to Lucca, March 4, 1629, one on the same day to the Grand-Duke of Tuscany, to Palermo, January 26, 1630, to Genoa, February 2, 1630, to the cathedral Chapter of Liège, March 3, 1629, to the Swiss, September 13, 1625. *Epist.*, Papal Secret Archives.

[1] See the *Relations of the Rota in *Barb.* 2678 (Vatican Library) on the subject of Gregory X., 2692 on F. of Cantalice, 2757 on Franc. Borgia, 2758 on Juliana of Liège, 2759 on Cat. Fieschi, 2760 and 2773 on A. Avellino, 2762–3 on Josaphat Kuncevic, 2775 on M.M. de Pazzi, 2777 and 2778 on the Japanese Franciscan Martyrs, 2779 on Pius V., 2782 on Ph. Benizzi, 2784 on John of God, 2785 on Peter Regulatus and Cat. Ricci, 2788 on Gaetano di Tiene, 2789 on John of the Cross; *reports of the Congr. of Rites, *ibid.*, 2766 on Gregory X., and 2783 on Ph. Benizzi. According to the *Avviso of June 11, 1637 (*Urb.* 1105, Vatican Library) the beatification of Robert Nobili was discussed at the time. **Atti orig. mand. a Urbano VIII.* 1637 *per la beatif. del P. Honorato de Champigny ord. Capuc.* in *Barb.* 3596, *loc. cit.*; **Processus canonizationis S. Francisci de Paula,* 1636, in *Cod.* VI., E. 5 of the Library at Olmütz.

[2] *Cf.* especially the *Briefs to Archduke Leopold and to Mayence, of March 3, 1629, concerning the beatification of Peter Canisius, *Epist.*, VI., Papal Secret Archives. See also Morus, III., 36 *seq.*

[3] See *Avvisi of April 4 and 25, 1629 (decorations for the feast by Bernini), *Urb.* 1099, *loc. cit.*; *Nicoletti, III., ch. 16, *loc. cit.*; Venuti, *Numismata,* 233; Bonanni (1699), 571.

[4] See *Bull.*, XIII., 192 *seq.*, 255 *seq.*, 331 *seq.*; *cf.* 368.

[5] *Ibid.*, 371 *seq.*

Portugal,[1] a relative of St. Elizabeth of Thüringen. The whole of the beautiful Office of the above-named Saints was drafted by Urban VIII. himself, just as he composed the proper hymns of the feasts of St. Martina and St. Hermenegild established by him.[2] In 1626 he beatified Mary Magdalen de' Pazzi,[3] in 1629 Gaetano da Tiene,[4] in 1630 John of God.[5] The Pope also approved the cult of the Japanese Martyrs of the Franciscan and Jesuit Orders [6] and that of Colomba of Rieti.[7] A decree of January 27th, 1631, laid down certain rules for the sermons preached at canonizations,[8] and a constitution of July 5th, 1634, renewing a decree of the Inquisition of the year 1625, declared that the right to pronounce beatifications and canonizations belonged exclusively to the Supreme Head of the Church. Accordingly, henceforth it was to be unlawful to introduce the cult of any Saint without leave of the Pope, except in the case where a holy personage had been publicly honoured from time immemorial, or at least for a hundred years and with the toleration of ecclesiastical authority, or whose public cult was based either on a decree of a Pope, the Congregation of Rites, or the writings of the Fathers and other holy men.[9]

[1] See **Acta consist.*, *Barb.* 2986, Vatican Library; F. Testi, *Opere II.*, Modena, 1817, 18; *Avviso, May 20, 1625, *Urb.* 1096, *loc. cit.* The decorations for the celebration (teatro) were also by Bernini.

[2] See Bäumer, 510.

[3] See *Bull.*, XIII., 456 *seq.*; Ph. M. Pitovanni, **De sanctitate Magd. de Pazzis ad Urbanum VIII.*, *Cod.* 47 of the Library of S. Maria della Vittoria (Vittorio Emmanuele Library, Rome).

[4] See *Bull.*, XIV., 110 *seq.* *Cf.* *Avviso of October 6, 1629, *Urb.* 1099, *loc. cit.*

[5] See *Avviso of September 11, 1630, *Urb.* 1100, *loc. cit.* *Cf. Bull.*, XIV., 174.

[6] See *Avviso of October 9, 1637, *Urb.* 1097, *loc. cit.* *Cf.* Novaes, IX., 230 *seq.*

[7] See *Avviso of July 19, 1628, *Urb.* 1098, *loc. cit.* *Cf.* Novaes, IX., 217 *seq.*

[8] See **Acta consist.*, *loc. cit.*

[9] See *Bull.*, XIII., 308 *seq*; XIV., 436 *seq*; *Freib. Kirchenlex*, II.², 145. For the execution of the decree see *Hist. Jahrb.*, XII., 64. F. Contelori wrote: *Tractatus et praxis de canonizat. Sanctorum*, Lugduni, 1634.

In accordance with the Canons of Trent, a decree of March 15th, 1642, forbade all representations of Christ and the Saints which, by their form or apparel, departed from ancient usage, as well as the putting up on the façades of churches or in their porches of worldly or other unsuitable paintings.[1] As early as August 11th, 1628, the Pope had forbidden, as unbecoming, the then fairly common representation of the Most Holy Trinity by three heads.[2]

Urban VIII. likewise kept watch on Church music. More than once he took measures against compositions devoid of religious dignity and forbade under severe penalties such as altered the words of Holy Writ, for it was his will that music should be serious and such as to call forth holy, not worldly, thoughts.[3]

Rome, which faithfully preserved the traditions of Palestrina, the mightiest Catholic musician of all time, was just then well provided with great composers. The list is headed by Gregorio Allegri whom Urban VIII. made a member of the papal choir in 1629. He is one of the greatest musical celebrities. After he had become a member of the papal choir, his aspirations rose still higher. He composed several Masses which met with Urban VIII.'s approval. He attained the summit of his fame with his *Miserere* for double choir which for a long time passed for a kind of wonder of the world. Those who have heard it on Good Friday in the Sistine Chapel can never forget the impression made on them; few musical compositions give such powerful expression to deepest grief, yet such as transfigures and sanctifies.[4] The prohibition to copy it imparted to it a peculiar fascination. Mozart was the first to write it down after one hearing and he published it in 1771.

Another remarkable post-Palestrinian Master, Agostino Agazzari, had been choir-master at the Lateran basilica since

[1] See *Bull.*, XV., 170 *seq.*

[2] See Zibrt in the *Sitzungsber. der böhm. Gesellsch. der Wissensch., Phil.-hist. Kl.*, 1894.

[3] See *Nicoletti, LII., 7, p. 874, *loc. cit.*

[4] See Ambros, IV., 92 *seq.*

1626 and from there he went to S. Lorenzo in Damaso, Domenico Allegri had held a similar post at St. Mary Major up till 1629. The organist of St. Peter's was the famous virtuoso Girolamo Frescobaldi who, through his pupils Froberger and Kapsberger exercised a decisive influence on the technique of German instrumental music.[1]

Yet another contemporary musician who rose to high fame was Paolo Agostini. He became choir-master of St. Peter's in 1629 but died in the following year. It is related that on one occasion Urban VIII. stood listening in the middle of the basilica of the Prince of the Apostles whilst Agostini was filling the mighty space with the massed harmonies of a Mass in forty-eight parts and that at the end the Pope bowed with admiration before the master. This piling up of musical effects constitutes a parallel to the enormous and sumptuous churches and the gigantic frescoes of Baroque art.[2]

Starting from the principle that "the psalmody of the Church militant is the daughter of the heavenly hymnody which resounds for ever before the throne of God and that for this reason it should become more and more like that heavenly model and should not, because of any flaws, distract the mind of worshippers from God and the things of God",[3] Urban VIII., in 1629, ordered the resumption of the reform of the Breviary. He instituted a special Congregation for the purpose, Cardinal Caetani being appointed president and Tegrimio Tegrimi, Bishop of Assisi, secretary. Besides Girolamo Lanuvio, referendary of both *Segnaturas*, the Pope nominated

[1] See *ibid.*, 99 *seq*; 435 *seq*. *Cf.* CAMETTI, *G. Frescobaldi*, in the *Riv. musica*, XV. (1908); BÖHN, *Bernini*, 42 *seq*. Frescobaldi's selected works ed. by Haberl (1889).

[2] See AMBROS, IV., 105–6, who remarks: "The church of St. Peter was the proper place. If one wishes to insist on the frequently emphasized analogy between music and architecture, one might say that this kind of music was to music, what the church of St. Peter was to architecture."

[3] See the Constitution "*Divinam psalmodian*", dated January 25, 1631 (to be found in the editions of the Breviary though it is missing in *Bullarium Taurin.*).

to the commission a number of learned religious such as the Augustinian Fortunato Scacchi, the Dominican Niccolò Riccardi, the Cistercian Abbot Ilarione Rancati, the Oratorian Jacopo Vulponi, the Franciscan Luke Wadding, the Barnabite Bartholomeo Gavanti and the Jesuit Terenzio Alciati. The last named having fallen ill in the summer of 1629 his place was taken by a fellow Jesuit, Girolamo Petrucci.[1]

The commission entered upon its task on July 12th, 1629, at the palace of its president and by December 18th, 1631, sixty-six sessions had been held there.[2] The members proceeded with great thoroughness and repeatedly consulted the manuscripts not only of the Vatican Library [3] but those of other collections as well, for instance, the one attached to the Pantheon.[4] More than once other scholars of repute were consulted, for instance, Felice Contelori and Suarez, Cardinal Barberini's librarian.[5] Often enough opinions

[1] See the *protocols of the commission in *Vat.* 6098 and *Barb.* 1185, Vatican Library, first used by BÄUMER (503 *seq.*) together with the remaining MS. material of the same kind. I had access to the extracts from *Vat.* 6098 made by a friend who died all too soon and who had planned a book on the reform of the Breviary, *viz.* the REV. A. SAUER. The Codex is entitled : **Acta in congregatione super emendatione Breviarii de mandato S[mi] D. N. Urbani I. Papae VIII. ordinata, scripta, et subscripta manu propria per me Tegrimium Tegrimium, episc. Assisiensem secret. ab eodem S[mo] specialiter deput.*, pp. 1–12, contain the protocols of the first seven sittings (July 12 and 26, August 9 and 23, September 6 and 20, and November 8, 1629), in Vulponi's hand. On p. 14 the protocols written by Tegrimi begin ; they are numbered (1–55). This numeration is given in what follows.

[2] In BÄUMER, who was prevented by death from finally revising the proofs of his work, it is erroneously stated (p. 502) that there had been " about 45 or 50 meetings ". There had been 7 + 55, and after Tegrimi's illness a further 4 (*Vat.* 6098, p. 274, 276, 282, *loc. cit.*).

[3] See the *protocols of May 23 and July 27, 1630.

[4] See the *protocols of the 35th and 36th meeting.

[5] See the *protocols of the 46th meeting on December 19, 1630, the 48th on January 26, 1631, and the 50th on March 22, 1631.

were sharply divided, thus giving rise to lively discussions.[1] Urban VIII. who intervened personally in these debates,[2] himself revised the draft of the Bull which was to introduce the new Breviary, a fact which Cardinal Caetani reported at the forty-third session on November 28th, 1630.[3] On January 4th, 1631, it was decided to print the new Breviary and by August the work was completed.[4] It was at once put in circulation, for on November 29th, 1631, Cardinal Pázmány received a Brief praising him for having introduced it in Hungary.[5] On December 18th, by order of the Pope, the Congregation gave permission to the Roman printers Ludovico Grignano, Francesco Caballo and their associates, to print and sell the new Breviary on condition that they corrected the mistakes of the first edition which had been printed in the *officina* of the Camera Apostolica.[6] With this

[1] Thus on August 22 and December 19, 1630. *Cf.* also the *protocol of the 49th meeting.

[2] See the *protocols of September 20 and November 28, 1630.

[3] See the *protocols in *Vat.* 6098, p. 175. A first draft of the *Brief dated April 22, 1630, is in *Cod.* S. 3, 1, p. 179 *seq.*, of the Angelica Library, Rome. *Cf.* Lämmer, *Kirchengesch.*, 105.

[4] See the *protocols of the 47th meeting on January 4, 1631, and the 55th on August 16, 1631.

[5] This *document, unknown until now (*Epist.*, IX., Papal Secret Archives) refutes Bäumer's view (p. 502) that the first authentic edition of Urban VIII.'s Breviary was not published until 1632; on the other hand the same scholar's surmise may be correct, namely that the *Bull. Divinam psalmodiam*, which heads the Breviary and is dated, "1631, Ian. 25," may have been ante-dated.

[6] "De mandato Smi D. N. Urbani Papae VIII. Congregatio super emendatione Breviarii concessit licentiam et facultatem Ludovico Grignano, Francisco Caballo et sociis impressoribus librorum hic in Urbe, quod possint imprimere et impressum ad eorum libitum vendere novum Breviarium ad instar ultimi impressi ab impressione Camerali, emendatis tamen in eo aliquibus erroribus adnotatis in fine dicti Breviarii et aliis qui per presentem congregationem corrigentur iuxta notulam eis dandam per rev. p.d. Lanuvium utriusque signaturae referendarium, Barthol. Gavantum relig. cleric. regul. S. Pauli et Terentium Alciatum S.J." *Vat.* 6098, p. 282, *loc. cit.*

act the Congregation, which since the spring of 1631 had also busied itself with the correction of the Missal,[1] concluded its labours. The protocol expressly states that it had nothing to do with the correction of the hymns of the new Breviary.[2] Now this was precisely the chief and most controverted alteration, for the rest of the corrections were inconsiderable. This is regrettable as regards the legends of the Saints where much might have been corrected.[3] However, it was thought that these compositions had been adequately revised at the time of Clement VIII.'s reform, hence controverted points were left unaltered when they were supported by some writer of weight. The alterations were confined to fifteen Saints' legends which were cast into a better form, one also more in accordance with historical accuracy.[4] The homilies from the writings of the Fathers were likewise subjected to a revision; for this purpose they were compared with existing editions and wherever necessary, corrected and

[1] Fiftieth meeting on March 22, 1631: "*In hac congregatione, quae habita fuit de mandato speciali S^mi^, fuit decretum quod post impressionem novi Breviarii Romani debeat, si S^ti^ Suae placuerit, procedi ad emendationem Missalis." Fifty-second session on April 23, 1631: "*Fuit data cura r.p. de Lanuvio, Gavanto et fr. Lucae corrigendi errata in Missali, dummodo deducantur in congregatione ea quae fuerint maioris momenti."

[2] See Bäumer, 504, who wrongly assigns the conclusion of the meeting to December 11. Both in *Vat.* 5098, p. 282, and in *Cod. Barb.* 1185, used by Bäumer, the final meeting is stated to have been on December 18, 1631.

[3] Later on Benedict XIV. and recently Leo. XIII. recognized the necessity of a further reform; *cf.* P. A. Kirsch, *Die historischen Brevierlektionen*, Würzburg, 1902. The drastic reform of the Breviary by Pius X. shows that the Holy See does not regard every ancient liturgical tradition as intangible; see Vacant, *Diction*, IX., 815.

[4] See Bäumer, 504 *seq.* It is a great mistake when it is stated here (p. 506, note 1) in connexion with the *aide-mémoire of the Spaniards concerning St. James' sojourn in Spain (*Cod.* G., 76, p. 141 *seq.*, of the Vallicelliana Library, Rome) that Urban VIII. was very favourable to the Spaniards.

completed.[1] In all Scripture texts the punctuation of the Vulgate of Clement VIII. was rigidly adhered to; nevertheless, for the purpose of appropriate divisions and necessary pauses in the psalmody, asterisks were introduced by which every psalm verse was divided into two parts.[2]

The text of the new Breviary underwent a profound alteration in consequence of the correction of the hymns which was undertaken by the express command of the Pope. Urban, who had always practised the poetic craft, kept this part of the work as much as possible in his own hands, but he made choice of four classically trained Jesuits to collaborate with him.[3] They were Famiano Strada, famous as a Latin stylist, Tarquinio Galuzzi, Girolamo Petrucci and the Pole Matthias Sarbiewski then staying in Rome.[4] In the memorandum which the above-named presented to the Congregation of

[1] See BÄUMER, *loc. cit.*

[2] See BÄUMER, 507. A proposal to this end was made at the meeting of March 2, 1630. *Vat.* 6098, p. 50, *loc. cit.*

[3] Against the suggestion of BÄUMER, though made with reservations, that the impulse for the correction of the hymns came from these four Jesuits, BLUME has already protested in *Stimmen aus Maria-Laach* (LXXVIII., 257 *seq*). He proves that in the memorandum of the four Jesuits for the Congregation of Rites it was stated that what St. Jerome, "by command of Pope Damasus" had been obliged to do for Holy Scripture, "they had had to do (idem facere coguntur) whose latest task was the correction of the hymns", and that against the words "whose latest task" a contemporary hand has added "de mandato (above this 'de iussu') S.D.N. Urbani VIII.". To this I can add still stronger evidence. In the *protocol of the meetings of the commission in *Vat.* 6098, p. 282, the words quoted by BÄUMER (p. 504): "In correctionibus et mutationibus hymnorum, qui sunt in Breviario, Congregatio praedicta nullam habuit partem," are followed by the remark: "quia S.D.N. Urbanus Papa VIII., quem Deus Opt. Max. diu incolumem conservet, ipsos emendavit et in elegantiorem formam, prout videre est in novo Breviario, restituit."

[4] For the part taken by Sarbiewski see DIEL in *Stimmen aus Maria-Laach*, IV. (1873), 352.

Rites, we read : " The hymns composed by Ambrose, Gregory, Prudentius, Sedulius, Fortunatus, and other poets of renown, remain either wholly unaltered and untouched, or are corrected according to good ancient manuscripts, or completed with words taken from some other hymns by the same authors ; and where there seems to be an error either of latinity or metre, the mistake is corrected in conformity with the rules of prosody by the slightest change possible in the syllable." The reason given is the reverence due to the holiness and the venerable antiquity of the authors.[1] Accordingly, the revisers proceeded with the utmost caution : only the hymns of Paulinus of Aquileia and Rabanus Maurus underwent radical changes. In Venantius Fortunatus' hymns in honour of the holy cross, about one and a half dozen metric licences were treated as " mistakes " and altered accordingly. Of the famous hymns of St. Thomas on the Holy Eucharist the memorandum says that they have been preserved unaltered inasmuch as words that may lack elegance, are enhanced by the loftiness of their content and because the Church cherishes them and the ear has become accustomed to them.[2] The *Ave Maris Stella* also remained unaltered.[3] But the rhythmic hymns of the fifth to the tenth century were subjected to a different treatment in view of their clumsiness and because their seeming lack of style offended the ear. These hymns underwent drastic treatment on the metrical anvil : " The outward form became more classical in expression and metre, but many a strong and original peculiarity disappeared, many a deep, stimulating thought was either weakened or completely eliminated, many a rough or clumsily set jewel fell out and was lost." A comparison between the old hymn for the dedication of a church—*Urbs beata Hierusalem*—and the new form cast in iambic mould, shows this only too plainly. Fortunately only a limited number of hymns have been thus deprived of the primitive charm

[1] See Blume, *loc. cit.*, 253.

[2] *Ibid.*, 253–4.

[3] *Cf.* Gavantus, *Thesaur. sacr. rituum*, Vol. II., sect. 5, ch. 6.

which characterized them, notwithstanding the awkwardness of their form.[1]

The Congregation of Rites approved the proposed changes on March 29th, 1629, after which the revised hymns were printed by the Vatican press and eventually incorporated in the new edition of the Breviary. Subsequently the new text was also printed in plain-chant notation for use in choir; a Constitution of April 27th, 1643, enforced it everywhere[2] and the injunction was renewed in the following year.[3] A letter from Strada to Urban VIII. makes it quite clear that the responsibility for the alterations in the hymns does not rest with the four revisors alone but quite as much with the Pope himself.[4] Many hymns, so we learn from this important document, were personally corrected by the Pope and then submitted to Strada's criticism. The latter raised many objections but, in most cases, Urban VIII.'s metrical changes were retained. On the whole it must be admitted that this inroad into the treasury of ancient hymns, which was prompted by an exaggerated passion for the principle of the classic metre, is as regrettable[5] as the new dress with which the Baroque age loved to array the old and venerable basilicas.

On the completion of the revision of the Missal, which mainly dealt with the rubrics, Urban VIII. published a Constitution on September 2nd, 1634, in which it was laid

[1] See BLUME, *loc. cit.*, 255 *seq.*

[2] *Bull.*, XV., 256 *seq.* BÄUMER'S data (p. 509) on this Bull. are wrong.

[3] *Bull.*, XV., 316 *seq.*

[4] Published by L. VENTURI: *Gli'inni della Chiesa tradotti con comment. da L.V.*, 2nd. ed., Florence, 1879. *Cf. Rassegna settiman.*, 1879, February 16, p. 132, where it is pointed out that Urban VIII. had also wished to "correct" the poems of Petrarch, and BLUME, *loc. cit.*, 258 *seq.*

[5] There is general agreement on this now; see both BÄUMER (509, note 4) who quotes the opinion of Batiffol and Chevalier; and also BLUME, *loc. cit.*, 260 *seq.*; KRAUS-SAUER, II., 2, 1, 180, and CABROL in *The Catholic Encyclop.*, II., 776.

down that the revised text must serve as the authentic model for all subsequent reimpressions.[1] The liturgical book for the pontifical functions, that is, the *Pontificale*, was likewise subjected to a fresh revision. The new edition was published in 1644.[2]

Urban VIII. had already embodied in the new edition of the Breviary the rules of the Congregation of Rites concerning the observance of festivals *in choro*, that is, feasts to be observed by the clergy only. In view of the fact that in course of time the number of feast days had become so great that many people no longer knew which were of obligation, Urban VIII. who, in point of fact, had himself instituted many new feasts,[3] laid down fresh regulations in a Bull of September 13th, 1624. This document gave an authentic list of all feasts of universal obligation and urged the Bishops, for the sake of uniformity in the Church, not to institute new ones. Though on this occasion the Pope considerably reduced the number of feasts of obligation, he maintained those of St. Joseph and St. Anne which had been recently imposed by his predecessor Gregory XV.[4] The devotion of the Forty Hours' Prayer

[1] See *Freib. Kirchenlex.*, VIII.², 1561.

[2] *Ibid.*, X.², 188. The Euchologium, *viz.* the liturgical book of the Greek Church, published in Paris by Goar in 1645, was examined by a special congregation in 1636–1643; see MS. *Borgia lat.*, 46, Vatican Library.

[3] See BÄUMER, 510.

[4] See *Freib. Kirchenlex.*, IV.², 1395, X., 872. The Emperor Ferdinand and Maximilian I. of Bavaria begged Urban VIII. to define the Immaculate Conception of the Mother of God; but Urban held that the time had not come for such action; see *Röm. Quartalschr.*, XIII., 63 *seq.*, 374. *Cf. Hist.-polit. Blätter*, LXVII., 760 *seq.* For Urban VIII's. veneration for St. Thomas Aquinas see his *consistorial address of March 2, 1626, **Acta consist.*, Papal Secret Archives. See also the *Brief to the theologians *Salmanticen. Acad.* of April 29, 1629, who are praised because besides venerating St. Augustine and St. Thomas (" illi magni veritatis magistri ") they had not despised the others and venerated " in controversiis coelestem Rom. cathedrae magistratum " (*Epist.*, VI., Papal Secret Archives). Discussions before Urban VIII's. time *de concept. immaculata* in *Barb.*, XVIII., 67,

received Urban VIII.'s warmest support. For its observance in the Vatican, Bernini sketched the sumptuous decorative scheme of the Cappella Paolina.[1] At first the Pope took part in the procession of Corpus Christi on foot and bareheaded; only after 1639, in view of his age, did he do so in the Sedia Gestatoria and wearing the mitre.[2] To the Bull *In Coena Domini* he gave its definitive form.[3] The question whether in a case of necessity laymen could hear confessions, was decided in the negative.[4] A Bull of December 20th, 1631, revoked all papal verbal directions of a juridical character (*oracula vivae vocis*), even for the *forum* of conscience.[5] Urban VIII. had greatly at heart the development of the old and new Orders and the reform of the old ones. What he accomplished in this respect in France has already been related.[6] But he was no less concerned about the Orders in other countries: thus he approved the Statutes of the Discalced Mercedarians, the Italian *Annunziate* and *Angeliche*, the Franciscan Sisters of Dutch Limburg, the Spanish Discalced Trinitarians and the Discalced Carmelites.[7] The Convents of the Italian Discalced Augustinians were formed into four Provinces, the Custodies of the Reformed Franciscans were erected into a special Province whilst the Ambrosian Brothers were suppressed owing to their lack both of personnel and of means for carrying out the object of their foundation.[8]

Vatican Library. In a *Brief to Sigismund III. of July 13, 1632, the Pope had declared that the time for a dogmatic pronouncement was not yet. (THEINER, *Mon. Pol.*, III., 373 *seq.*)

[1] See DE SANTI, 273 *seq.*; 304 *seq.* (with picture). For the three Masses on All Souls' Day see KNELLER in the *Zeitschr. für kath., Theol.*, 1918, 84 *seq.*

[2] See MORONI, IX., 47.

[3] See *Bull.*, XIII., 530 *seq.*; HINSCHIUS, V., 647; EICHMANN, *Recursus ab abusu*, 105.

[4] See NOVAES, IX., 267. For the indulgences granted by Urban VIII., see *Kirchenlex.*, I.², 112. *Cf.* NICOLETTI in RANKE, III.⁶, 164.*

[5] See REIFFENSTUEL, *Ius can.*, 1, 5, tit. 33, n. 152 *seq.*

[6] *Cf.* XXVIII, 436 *seq.*

[7] See HEIMBUCHER, II.², 75, 216, 270, 287, 506, 553.

[8] *Ibid.*, 189, 243, 384.

Both the *Bullarium* [1] and the Instructions to the nuncios [2] testify to the Pope's great interest in the reform of the Orders. In 1625 he confirmed the Benedictine University of Salzburg [3] as well as the newly-founded Austrian Benedictine Congregation: to both these new creations the Bishop of Passau offered the most determined opposition.[4] In 1630 a plan was proposed for a Congregation of all German Benedictines, together with that of Bursfeld, but it was not realized [5]; on the other hand, at the instigation of the splendid Prince-Bishop Paris Lodron, the Congregation of Salzburg was established in 1640. Its aim was a uniform religious discipline and the promotion of pastoral and scholastic activities.[6] The Servites were appointed confessors of the papal Court [7] whilst the Capuchin Girolamo of Narni (died 1632) retained the post of preacher of the palace.[8] Urban, whose brother was a member of the Order, greatly favoured the Capuchins.[9]

[1] See *Bull.*, XIII., 202 *seq.*; 207 *seq.*; 624 *seq.*; XIV., 1 *seq.*; 203 *seq.*; 241 *seq.* *Cf.* *Jahrbuch für schweiz. Gesch.*, XI., 175 *seq.*; *Anal. Francisc.*, I., 361 *seq.*

[2] *Cf.* especially the *Instruction for Sacchetti in Spain of January 27, 1624, Casanatense Library, Rome, XV., 15, p. 149 *seq.*, and the **Instruttione* for the Neapolitan nuncio Bichi of May 30, 1628, MS. in my possession.

[3] See HEIMBUCHER, I.², 373.

[4] *Cf.* the essays of A. DUNGEL in *Studien und Mitteil. aus dem Benediktinerorden*, IV. (1883).

[5] See *Hist.-polit. Blätter*, CIII., 416.

[6] See the excellent work by B. HUEMER: *Die Salzburger Benediktiner-Kongregation von* 1641–1808, Münster, 1918.

[7] See HEIMBUCHER, II.², 227.

[8] See TIRABOSCHI, VIII., 418; WADDING, *Script. Ord. Min.*, Romae, 1650. G. DA NARNI'S *Prediche fatte nel palazzo Apost.*, published in Rome, 1639; **Prediche fatte nel pal. Apost. nel venerdì della Domenica II. di quaresima*, in *Cod. ital.*, 70, p. 1 *seq.*, of the State Library, Munich.

[9] See PELLEGRINO DA FORLÌ (a continuation of *Boverius* which only goes as far as 1633, but not always reliable). *Annali del Ordine dei frati min. Cappuccini I.*, Milano, 1882, 541 *seq.* *Cf.* also HEIMBUCHER, II.², 516, 522.

In 1643 their Constitutions were revised and confirmed.[1] Just then the Order had a number of distinguished members in Rome.[2] Like the Capuchins, the new reform Orders, such as the Theatines, the Barnabites,[3] the Oratorians and especially the Jesuits, gave proof of the greatest zeal and their undertakings were warmly supported by Urban VIII. However, only the Capuchins and the Jesuits extended their influence beyond Italy,[4] but the sons of St. Ignatius surpassed the former both in regard to the extent and the diversity of their activities.

Urban VIII.'s great esteem for the work of the Society of Jesus was well shown on the occasion of the first centenary of the approval of the Order by Paul III. on September 27th, 1540. The anniversary of the confirmation opened in 1639 with a splendid function in the church of the Roman professed house, the Gesù, which had been magnificently decorated according to a design by Andrea Sacchi.[5] The Pope himself visited the church and his nephew, Cardinal Antonio Barberini, bore the whole of the expenses of the festival. On this occasion, among other incidents, first a hundred and then a thousand poor persons were entertained.[6] Antonio's brother, Don

[1] See Heimbucher, II.[2], 390.

[2] *Cf.* D. da Isnello, *Il convento della s. Conzezione d. padri Cappuccini in Roma.* Viterbo, 1923, 26 *seq.*

[3] *Cf.* Premoli, *I Barnabiti nel Seicento*, Roma, 1922.

[4] The Oratorians made new foundations in the Papal States: 1622 at Città di Castello, 1632 at Fabriano, 1637 at Pesara, Forlì and Urbino, 1640 at Spoleto, 1644 at Montecchio, Cesena, Jesi and Matelica. In Tuscany: in 1632 at Florence. In the territory of Venice: 1624 at Padua. In the Milanese territory: 1640 at Lodi and Cremona, 1629 at Reggio di Lombardia. In Sicily: in 1628 at Patarma, 1632 at Messina; beyond the Alps they made only one foundation in 1626, *viz.* at Douai; see Capecelatro, *F. Neri*, II.[3], 701 *seq.*

[5] See Posse, *Sacchi*, 7 *seq.*, 9 *seq*; Voss, 532 *seq.* *Cf. L'Arte*, XXVII., 66 *seq.*

[6] Iac. Damianus, *Synopsis primi saeculi Soc. Jesu.*, Tornaci, 1641, 358 *seq.* *Relazione della solenne festa fatta dal . . . cardinale Antonio Barberini . . . nella chiesa della casa professa*, Roma, 1639 (with dedication to the nieces of Urban VIII., Innocenza and

Taddeo, made himself responsible for the function which took place during the week following the feast of St. Ignatius in the still unfinished church of the Roman College. On August 8th, 1640, the Pope himself came to view the decorations of the church. Tapestries replaced the vault which was still wanting.[1] In other ways also Urban VIII. showed his

Maria); see SOMMERVOGEL, VII., 52, *cf.* 39, 58; also E. RIVIÈRE, *Corrections et additions*, Toulouse, 1912, 762; on the magnificence displayed, *cf. Imago primi saeculi*, 29: "(Natalis Societatis) ab Urbano VIII., P.M. amplissima maximeque solenni indulgentia cohonestatus, ab eiusdem fratris filio Antonio Barberino cardinali tanto apparatu, impensa, splendore Romae celebratus, quantum negue optare pro sua modestia Societas debuit, neque augere propemodum patronus munificentissimus pro animi sui magnitudine potuit." A painting of the celebration is in *La Canonizzazione dei santi Ignazio de Loiola e Francesco Saverio* (special issue), Roma, 1922, 77.

[1] *Copia di una carta de Roma . . . Roma*, 1640, in SOMMERVOGEL and RIVIÈRE, *loc. cit.*; E. RINALDI, *La fondazione del collegio Romano*, Arezzo, 1914, 120; DAMIANUS, *loc. cit.*; SOMMERVOGEL, VII., 121. In Madrid and Vienna there were also celebrations (Damianus, 360), also in the French houses (FOUQUERAY, V., 196). The Province of Upper Germany refrained from public festivities (KROPF, *Hist. provinciae Soc. Iesu Germaniae superioris*, Pars V. Aug. Vindel., 1754, dec. 10, cap. 64, p. 463). The Flandro-Belgian Province perpetuated the solemnity with an account of the activities of the Order in the first hundred years of its existence: *Imago primi saeculi, Antwerp.*, 1640 (a folio volume of almost 1,000 pages of prose and verse with fine copper plates). The General of the Order felt uneasy when he heard of this publication, prepared by Bollandus, but expressed his satisfaction when he saw it. (*Anal. Boll.*, 1914, 321.) The *Morale Pratique des Jésuites* (ARNAULD, *Oeuvres*, XXXII., 45 to 111) made mock of some of the exaggerations of this publication, not without twisting the sense in doing so; so did Pascal in his *Provinciales*; valuation of the work has suffered in consequence of these attacks. There is no trace of pride in the letter which the General of the Order addressed on November 15, 1639, to the Order on the subject of the jubilee celebration. (*Epistolae Generalium Soc. Iesu*, Ghent, 1847, 387 *seqq.*)

goodwill to the Jesuits. He published the Bull of Loyola's canonization which Gregory XV. had not had time to issue.[1] In this document the Society of Jesus is described as a work of Providence for the spread and the defence of the faith.[2] Urban's *Votum* on the canonization when still a Cardinal, had expressed the same thought.[3] The humanistic formation which the Pope had acquired at the Roman College and which he lovingly cherished for years, bore fruit, among other things, in a poem in praise of an ascetical writing by Cardinal Bellarmine in whose honour, as well as that of Charles Borromeo and Cardinal Nobili, he composed several poems.[4]

The attempt of an English lady, Mary Ward, to found a religious Order of women on the model of that of the Jesuits, compelled Urban VIII. to examine more closely to what extent it might be possible to allow some external activity in the nursing and teaching sphere to religious associations of women, notwithstanding the stringent laws of the Church with regard to the enclosure. Mary Ward's plan was to adopt both the scope and the organization of the Society of Jesus: the scope, that is, the work of teaching, in so far as this was possible for lay persons and women; the organization, inasmuch as the government of the new Society was wholly placed in the hands of a Superior General completely independent of the Ordinaries and subject to the Pope alone and who distributed offices and transferred members at will

[1] See Vol. XXVII., p. 121, n. 4.

[2] Bull of August 8, 1623, *Bull.*, XIII., 25 *seq.*

[3] "Eat inficias nemo, Dei munere nobis esse datum b. Ignatium tempore, quo contra debacchantes et in huius s. Sedis perduelles propugnaculum excitaret, ex quo non ipse solum, sed eius instituti viri religiosi iugiter et fortiter dimicarent. . . . Fuerunt orbi christiano suscepti ab eo pro fide catholica labores maxime salutares. . . . Suscepit illa quidem (the Church) plures a b. Ignatio, qui fuerunt ei clypeus, quo parta tueretur; b. vero Xaverius datus est ut esset gladius, quo novis aucta victoriis christiani fines imperii longe lateque protenderent." *La Canonizzazione, etc.*, 41 *seq.*

[4] *Carmina*, Dilingae, 1640, carm., 84 and 158, p. 208, 260.

from one house to another. Exemption from enclosure, Office in choir and a distinctive religious dress, was a matter of course for the new Institute.[1]

Neither birth nor upbringing had prepared Mary Ward for such innovations. She sprang from a distinguished Yorkshire family of confessors of the faith. Her devout grandmother, who for fourteen years had languished in prison for the faith, had had a very great influence on her upbringing. In 1606, when 21 years old, she entered a convent at Saint-Omer. At that time she had no other thought than to renounce the world and to follow as strict a life as possible, since there could be no question then of a woman taking up social work. Accordingly she became a lay sister with the French Poor Clares of Saint-Omer and as an extern begged alms for the community. Soon, however, she realized that this was not her vocation and that a convent of English Poor Clares was greatly needed. By sacrificing her fortune and with the help of the Court of Brussels, she succeeded in founding such a convent at Gravelines, but she herself, though the house of Gravelines and its filiations at Aire, Rouen and Dunkerque [2] regard her as their foundress, soon realized that the separation from the world she so much longed for, was not to be her lot. The idea came to her to return to England in lay attire, there to do as much good as possible by means of the ordinary intercourse of daily life. She frequently repeated

[1] *Cf.* M. C. E. Chambers, *The Life of Mary Ward*, ed. H. J. Coleridge, S.J., 2 vols., London, 1882. Mother Mary Salome, *Mary Ward*, London, 1901; H. Riesch, *Maria Ward*, Innsbruck, 1922; Heimbucher, III.[2], 364 *seq.*; Joseph Grisar in *Stimmen der Zeit*, CXIII. (1927), 34–51, 131–150. The Bull. of Benedict XIV., dated April 30, 1749, forbidding the "English Ladies" to call Mary Ward their foundress, a prohibition revoked by Pius X., contains many oversights and errors; see Grisar, *loc. cit.*, 34 *seq.*; Coleridge, in Chambers, II., xxxviii. It is much to be desired that the acts of Mary Ward's trials kept in the Archives of the Roman Inquisition, should be made accessible to research; without these sources, much must remain obscure in the life of Mary Ward.

[2] Chambers, I., 198–204.

these visits to England, so much so that Abbot, Archbishop of Canterbury, sought to have her arrested, for he was of opinion that she did more harm to Protestantism than six Jesuits.[1] Returning to Saint-Omer, she took a house of her own where, together with five English companions, she devoted herself to a very austere mode of life as well as to the education of youth. So far she was not clear in her own mind as to the details of the life she was to embrace, but on this point light and certainty were granted to her when, as she always maintained, it came to her during prayer that the Society of Jesus was to be her model—in other words, that it was her mission to found for women an Order based on the model of the Jesuit Order.[2]

The task thus assumed by Mary Ward put her in presence of almost insuperable obstacles. True, there already existed in Flanders certain societies of women for the education of girls [3] popularly styled " Jesuitesses ", but they were of purely local importance and their organization was a loose one, whereas Mary planned a world-wide though rigidly centralized Society. As a matter of fact, it soon looked as if the " English Ladies " were about to secure a footing everywhere. To the first foundation at Saint-Omer there was added one in London in 1640. It was planned as a centre for those of the Sisters who were to go from house to house with a view to working for the Catholic faith. Up till the year 1628 foundations had been made at Liège, Rome, Naples, Cologne, Trèves, Perugia,

[1] *Ibid.*, 407.

[2] M. Ward's own testimony in CHAMBERS, I., 283. The name of " Jesuitesses " was not adopted by the community itself; the members called themselves " Matres Anglae, Signorine Inglesi " (RIESCH, 94).

[3] Thus the Sisters of St. Agnes at Douai, Saint-Omer, Mons, Valenciennes, Brussels and elsewhere (Bishop Blaise of St.-Omer in FOLEY, VII., 1255; *cf.* CHAMBERS, I., 501 *seq.*), and later the Sisters of St. Monica (from 1629) at Bruges (*Annuaire de l'Université cath. de Louvain*, 1913, 459). At Tournai the Jesuit Mortaigne had established a congregation of the same kind (MANARAEUS, *De rebus Soc. Iesu*, 46).

Munich, Vienna, Pressburg and Prague.[1] At the same time the Society gained powerful patrons. The Bishop of Saint-Omer, Blaise, published a special Pastoral Letter [2] to defend them against certain attacks of which they had been the object. Archduke Ferdinand of Bavaria and the Emperor Ferdinand II. showed them great favour, as did the very influential Carmelite, Dominic of Jesus and Mary.

Thus the Pope could not have long remained silent; but it was equally impossible for him to approve the new Institute at once and without reservation. The Council of Trent had enforced the rule of strict enclosure as an essential condition for the reform of convents of nuns and Pius V. had still further tightened these prescriptions. Hence it was not to be expected that the Roman Congregations would so soon make an exception; the Societies founded by St. Francis de Sales, by Jeanne de Lestonnac, and the Ursulines, had experience of it. As for the "English Ladies", the fact of their leaning on the Jesuits was fatal.[3] The hatred of which the Society of Jesus had been the object from the first, had just then reached its climax among a section of the English clergy. That party saw in the new Institute only another organization and a tool of the hated Society,[4] hence it was only too ready to lend ear to every calumny and exaggeration. The Vicar-General, Richard Smith, showed as much opposition to Mary Ward as to the Society of Jesus. This readily accounts for the reserve of the Jesuits, for they feared fresh difficulties, although some of their number lent support to the Society.

[1] *Annuaire, loc. cit.*, 460.

[2] March 19, 1615, in FOLEY, VII., 1252–6.

[3] GRISAR, 39 *seqq.*

[4] "Instromento potentissimo (of the Jesuits) per il loro accrescimento e potere (Nuncio Pallotto, August 5, 1628, in KIEWNING, I., 165). On April 9, 1633, someone informed Bishop Richard Smith that the Fathers were trying to obtain through the "English Ladies" that "both sexes shall have a general dependence of them" (CHAMBERS, II., 412; memorandum of the Archpriest Harrison against the new congregation, *ibid.*, 183–6).

The objections to the English Ladies which came from England were passed on to Propaganda. Now the Secretary of that newly founded Congregation, Francesco Ingoli, was not only a great stickler for the letter of the law, he was also keenly opposed to the Jesuits. To this must be added that there were features in the scheme of the new foundress which were of a nature to create difficulties, such as exemption from the Ordinary and the house to house visiting by the Sisters. Differences of opinion and disputes arose even within the Institute itself. The leader of the malcontents, whom the foundress had to dismiss, joined her enemies and published a libellous pamphlet which provided the opponents with welcome weapons. Difficulties there existed then, but Mary Ward trusted too much in the righteousness of her cause to deem it worth while to refute in detail the accusations of her opponents which were for the most part pure calumnies, or to enlighten the Roman Congregation on the true state of things. She appealed directly to the Pope: if he took her side, so she reasoned, she had gained everything.

Already in 1616 she had sent to Paul V. a statement of the scope of her foundation and the means of realizing it,[1] and she had received an encouraging reply from Cardinal Lancellotti, the President of the Congregation of the Council.[2] On Christmas Eve, 1621, armed with letters of recommendation from the Archduchess Isabella, the King of Spain and the Emperor, Mary arrived in Rome in order personally to forward her business with Gregory XV. and to secure a papal approval which would sweep away every obstacle. She was given leave to open a school in Rome, to the end that the results of her work might be seen. She also established schools at Naples and Perugia. In October, 1624, Mary returned to Rome in order to call on the new Pope at Frascati. Urban VIII. received her with the same kindness as his predecessor: as a matter of fact, notwithstanding all the blows that were about to befall her, Mary never forfeited the

[1] In CHAMBERS, I., 375–385.

[2] April 10, 1616, *ibid.*, 385 *seq.*

personal esteem of ecclesiastical authorities. None the less the Roman school was closed, to the regret of the parents, and the foundress was told that there could be no question of the approval of her Society. Towards the end of 1626 Mary Ward resolved to revisit England. The General of the Jesuits gave her a letter of recommendation and she met with the most friendly reception from the Grand-Duke of Florence and from Frederic Borromeo at Milan. On her way through Bavaria, the Elector Maximilian put a house at her disposal at Munich with a view to her opening a school.[1] The other protagonists of the Catholic restoration also showed understanding for her ideas ; before the end of 1628, the favour of Ferdinand II. enabled her to open a school at Vienna which before long numbered 465 pupils.[2] The Archbishop of Gran and future Cardinal Pázmány gave the English Ladies a house at Pressburg whilst they were negotiating with Cardinal Dietrichstein for a foundation at Nikolsburg and Count Althaun sought to attract them to Prague.[3]

Mary Ward nevertheless found opponents even among the friends of the reform. Cardinal Harrach of Prague was not particularly well disposed towards the English Ladies and Bishop Klesl of Vienna would not hear of a Society not approved by the Pope.[4] Moreover he felt hurt because Mary Ward had not first made arrangements with him before making her foundation in Vienna. He protested in Rome and on July 14th, 1628, the nuncios of the imperial Court, at Brussels and at Naples, were instructed to suppress the establishments of the English Ladies.

However, in view of their numerous and eminent supporters, it was not easy to execute this order. At the end of two years Ingoli had had his way in Naples and, notwithstanding the protests of the Archbishop of Cambrai, in Flanders also. In

[1] RIEZLER, VI., 293 *seq.* ; M. TH. WINKLER, *M. Ward und das Institut der Englischen Fräulein in Bayern*, München, 1926, 14 *seq.*

[2] Klesl to Rome, September 23, 1628, in KIEWNING, I., 243.

[3] KIEWNING, I., 77, 227.

[4] To Cardinal Bandini, August 12, 1628, in KIEWNING, I., 165.

the latter country the fate of the English Ladies affected even other teaching Sisterhoods which went under the name of "Jesuitesses".[1] The nuncio of Vienna, Pallotto, did nothing in the matter beyond advising Mary Ward to return to Rome; this he did probably out of consideration for the Emperor and the Elector of Bavaria whose goodwill he needed in the negotiations concerning the Mantuan succession. In Rome Mary Ward met with a very friendly reception on the part of Urban VIII. She was allowed to plead her cause once more before a congregation of Cardinals when she effectively defended her Society for the space of three-quarters of an hour. But all was in vain: on September 30th, 1629, Propaganda, in presence of the Pope, decreed the suppression of the so-called Jesuitesses.

The nuncio of Cologne, Pier Luigi Carafa, made it his particular business to carry out the decision. At his instigation the establishments at Liège, Cologne and Trèves had been closed in July, 1630, by the respective Archbishops.[2] He found himself in a position to deal a blow to the very existence of the Institute when he met with insubordination among the Sisters of his nunciature. Propaganda's decree of suppression had not been communicated to Mary Ward herself; the first intimation reached her through her companion Winefred Wigmore. On April 6th, 1630, she wrote to her daughters that the decree was a surreptitious one, published by their opponent Cardinal Bentivoglio, and without the knowledge of the Pope and the Congregation of Cardinals. She accordingly exhorted her subjects to hold fast to their mode of life and not to allow themselves to be disconcerted even by the threat of excommunication.[3] For the purpose of encouraging the Sisters in this sense she sent Winefred Wigmore to visit the northern houses. The latter, perhaps against the will of the foundress, urged the Sisters of Liège, Cologne and Trèves, to resume community life, and in this she was successful. Carafa now stepped in: he reported matters to Rome,

[1] GRISAR, *loc. cit.*, 131–140.

[2] *Ibid.*, 141–5.

[3] GRISAR, 143.

despatched thither Mary's letter and suggested that the new Society be everywhere dissolved, that the foundress be put under arrest as the cause of the insubordination and that a papal Bull should declare her Institute suppressed for good. In the course of their interrogatories the Sisters had dropped certain remarks which had roused suspicion. Propaganda transmitted Mary's letter to the Inquisition, leaving to that Congregation the decision of the whole affair.

Thereupon Carafa was instructed to have both Mary Ward and Winefred Wigmore arrested on the same day. Both were seized on February 7th, 1630, Mary Ward at Munich and Winefred Wigmore at Liège.[1] Mary was imprisoned in the convent of the Poor Clares at Munich. Through her Sisters she appealed to the Pope who knew nothing of her arrest. The Pontiff commanded that she should be immediately set at liberty. She was taken home in the carriage of the Elector's wife; soon, however, she was informed of Urban VIII.'s Bull [2] suppressing the Society of the Jesuitesses. The Bull finds fault with Mary Ward's foundation for taking over from existing Orders, without leave of the Pope, all their essential elements as well as a General, Rectors and Visitatrixes; for abolishing the enclosure and pretending to exercise a kind of house to house pastoral ministry, a thing that did not become ladies and young girls and for which they were not qualified. The last two points Carafa had singled out as decisive factors in the previous condemnation.[3] On the other hand neither the Bull nor Carafa condemned the efforts on behalf of the education of female youth. Mary Ward was not slow in perceiving that here was a chance of saving her creation at least as a teaching Society. True, the Bull forbade the one-time "Jesuitesses" to live in community, but it was easy for the Pope to do away with this prohibition. Accordingly in 1632 Mary Ward once more took the road to

[1] *Ibid.*, 147; GINZEL, 57–9.

[2] January 13, 1631, in GINZEL, 187–193.

[3] "Peculiariter vero, cum urbes atque provincias adire, interdum in aetatis ac formae flore, periculosum imprimis iudicetur" (GINZEL, 57).

Rome. Urban VIII. received her as kindly as ever. He personally reassured her with regard to the accusation of heresy which had weighed in the decision to arrest her, and allowed Winefred Wigmore and some of her companions to come to Rome, there to make a foundation under the Pope's patronage.[1] The proceedings against the Jesuitesses before the Inquisition terminated with a declaration that they were not, nor ever had been, guilty of any offence against the faith.[2] In other ways also Urban VIII. showed himself favourably disposed towards Mary Ward[3]; she was nevertheless secretly watched and when she wished to take the waters at San Cassiano, owing to continued ill health, it was intimated to her that for certain reasons of State the Pope desired her not to leave Rome.[4] On her complaining of this measure, the Pope once more gave her full liberty and on her return from the baths, surveillance also ceased. Urban put one of his own carriages at her disposal, as well as his private physician and his pharmacy, and sent her wine from his table.[5] When she decided to seek a cure for her chronic illness at Spa, in the more favourable atmosphere of the north, she was given letters of recommendation to the nuncios.[6] Armed with recommendations to Queen Henrietta Maria and Count Rossetti, she went to England in 1639, where she opened more schools in London and in Yorkshire. Her resolution to return to Rome at an early date was not carried out for she died on January 20th, 1645, at Hawarth, near York.

With Mary Ward there passed away one of the most remarkable women of these latter centuries of the Church's history. At a time when so many of her sisters in the upper classes bought an easy life by sacrificing their religious convictions, Mary Ward, at the early age of 21, renounced all things earthly and voluntarily chose a life of poverty and privation, in order that she might belong to God alone. At the end of

[1] CHAMBERS, II., 405 *seqq.*, 428.

[2] The secretary of the Inquisition to Carafa; *ibid.*, 401 *seqq.* GRISAR, 150.

[3] CHAMBERS, II., 413.

[4] *Ibid.*, 431.

[5] *Ibid.*, 439.

[6] *Ibid.*, 447.

her ten years of sacrifice and anxious search, God Himself, such was her conviction,[1] put the plan into her mind which henceforth was to be the object of all her striving and scheming. To forward it she exerted her whole being, the splendid intellectual gifts which enabled her to be ahead of her time, her tenacious and persevering will, the force of her personality with which she won all hearts [2] and subjugated both Pope and Princes. Thus she went her way, amidst fatigues, privations and habitual and grievous interior trials, almost always ailing yet never thinking of rest, near to death and still full of plans for future journeys, now honoured by Princes and by the Pope only to be once more calumniated and persecuted, cast off by those whom she revered and wished to serve, yet never embittered, possessed with the idea of her divine calling yet full of filial submission to the Church, on the brink of ruin yet convinced that her work would endure until the end of time.[3] One might imagine that this portrait was that of a devout heroine of some medieval legend, but Mary Ward stands in the full light of history.

Like St. Francis before her, Mary Ward also was unable fully to realize her original conception. The plan of a Society of Jesuit nuns proved incapable of execution. Nevertheless she did pioneer work for all female teaching Orders in as much as she paved the way for the organization of these Institutes under a Superior General who, notwithstanding the enclosure, may transfer and distribute at will from one house to another the various members of the Society. True, after Urban VIII.'s Bull, out of 200–300 Sisters, distributed in ten houses, who had attached themselves to Mary Ward up

[1] M. Ward to Urban VIII., November 28, 1630: That which she had practised for twenty-two years was " totally and entirely (as far as human judgment can arrive) ordained and commended to me by the express word of Him Who will not deceive, nor can be deceived " (Chambers, II., 330).

[2] Chambers, II., 435.

[3] God gave her an assurance " that this Institute shall remain in the Church of God until the end of the world " (to Urban VIII., *loc. cit.*, 331).

to 1631,[1] only a few continued faithful to her.[2] However, the establishment at Munich remained, though in an altered form,[3] and from there it spread all over the world, especially after the approval of the Rule by Clement XI.[4]

(2)

The Congregation of the Inquisition maintained its long-established pre-eminence under Urban VIII. It usually met three times a week, once under the presidency of the Pope himself.[5] The most distinguished among the Cardinals, including the two nephews Francesco and Antonio Barberini, were among its members.[6] The powers and the sphere of

[1] CHAMBERS, II., 385 *seq.*

[2] *Ibid.*, 396.

[3] *Ibid.*, 390. The house at Vienna remained open at least until 1638 (WIEDEMANN, II., 263). Cardinal Klesl had ordered a visitation of the house on October 7, 1629, which completely satisfied him (*ibid.*, 262).

[4] A summary of the houses in 1921 in RIESCH, 171–6. For the Bavarian houses see BUCHINGER in the *Oberbayr. Archiv*, XVII. (1857), 140 *seqq.*, 158 *seqq.*

[5] *Cf.* ALV. CONTARINI, *Relazione*, 355. The *domus Inquisitionis* had to be repaired in 1626; *cf.* **Arm.* 42, t. 60, p. 59, Papal Secret Archives.

[6] An *Avviso of June 6, 1624, mentions the nomination of Fr. Barberini, Vatican Library. A *note in the Papal Secret Archives (XI., 42, p. 421) gives the names of the members of the Santo Officio under Urban VIII., *viz. Cardinali*: Roma, Barberino, Ceva, S. Honofrio (Ant. Barberini), Spada, Ginetti, S. Clemente (Scaglia), Panzirola, Lugo, Cecchini, Colonna, Monti, Bichi, Verospi, Falconieri; *Consultori*: Il patriarcha d'Antiochia, Generale di S. Domenico, Maestro del Sacro Palazzo, Monsr Bilio, Pauluzzi Albizzi, il P. Commissario, Sigr. Bartolomeo Oreggio, il P. Consultore di S. Apostoli, il P. D. Hilarione Rameati, il compagno del P. Commissario, Sig^r^ Camillo Piazza Priore de'Rei, Sig^r^ Pietro Seristro, Sustituto fiscale. See also MORONI, XVI., 227 *seq.*, and BERTOLOTTI, *Martiri*, 123, 125. PIETRO CONTARINI (213) complained in 1627, that no Venetian was on the Inquisition; so did ALV. CONTARINI (355) in 1635.

activity, hence also the correspondence, of the Roman Inquisition, were extremely wide.[1] In a collection of letters of the Inquisition between the years 1626–8, now in the Vatican Library (*fondo Barberini*), there are letters to Cardinals, Patriarchs, Archbishops, Nuncios and especially to the local Inquisition in the various Italian cities.[2] Here also one sees with how many different questions the Inquisition had to deal. Besides the determination and expedition of the faculties of Bishops, nuncios and religious Orders,[3] it also concerned itself with the veneration of Saints,[4] marriage dispensations, grave moral delinquencies, sacrileges, the abuse of the Sacrament of Penance, false ecstasies and prophecies, witchcraft, superstition, above all with any teaching or expression of opinion contrary to the faith; hence the Congregation worked in close co-operation with that of the Index.[5]

[1] *Cf. Bull.*, XIV., 248 *seq.* This Constitution, issued in 1631, and dealing with the rights of the Inquisition over the religious Orders, was renewed in 1633; see DIANA, *Coordinatus*, IV., Lugduni, 1667, 537. *Ibid.*, 543 *seq.*, *Ampliatio Clementis VIII.*, dated March 3, 1628, against those who not having received Orders, say Mass or hear Confessions; they are to be handed over to the secular arm.

[2] **Barb.*, 6334/36, Vatican Library.

[3] See MERGENTHEIM, I., 23 *seq.*, 179 *seq.*, 236, note 5; II., 30 *seq.*, 63 *seq.* For the intervention of the Inquisition in the controversy of the English Catholics, see below Ch. IV.

[4] See MORONI, XVI., 226.

[5] *Cf.* **Barb.* 6334/36, *loc. cit.* A decree of the Roman Inquisition against the use of talismans in FUMI, *L'Inquisizione Romana e lo stato di Milano*, Milano, 1910, 266. A scholar who was allowed to use the archives of the Inquisition on the question of mixed marriages, communicated to me a decree of June 6, 1638, to the Guardian of the Franciscans at Jerusalem: "*Excommunicationem latam a P. Hyacintho de Verona, cum esset praeses dictorum locorum, contra catholicos matrimonium cum haereticis contrahentes non esse observandam." A few decrees of the Congregation of the Inquisition are in *Editti*, V., 31, of the Papal Secret Archives.

At this time, apart from the Waldenses in Piedmont, Protestantism had practically vanished from Italy.[1] Nevertheless the Pope, who severely reprimanded Cardinal Spada for rising to his feet whilst a heretic said grace before a meal,[2] watched anxiously over the preservation of religious unity in Italy. In 1639, by dint of remonstrances, he succeeded in obtaining from the Duke of Mantua the expulsion of certain Swiss Protestant merchants from the county of Montferrat, for he feared that they might be the means of Protestant heresies creeping in.[3] In other ways also the dissemination of non-Catholic doctrines was sternly dealt with. At Bologna, in 1628, the heresiarch Francesco de Soldati was executed.[4] At Florence, in 1626, the Inquisition proceeded against Antonio degli Albizzi, founder of the Accademia degli Alterati and consul of the Academy of Florence, but he escaped to Germany. The year 1641 saw the end of the trial of the distinguished Canon Pandolfo Ricasoli who was condemned to lifelong imprisonment for his ascetico-quietistic errors as well as for his moral irregularities.[5]

Like this trial, that of Orazio Morandi, Abbot of S. Prassede in Rome, also caused no small stir. Morandi had published in the news-sheets certain prophesies based on astrological superstitions, and among them the early death of the Pope. He was condemned to imprisonment in the gaol of Tor di Nona.[6]

Urban VIII.'s Bull against astrologers, dated April 1st,

[1] See RODOCANACHI, *La Réforme en Italie*, II., 440.

[2] *Brief of December 22, 1623, *Epist.*, I., 1, Papal Secret Archives.

[3] See BERTOLOTTI, *Martiri*, 118.

[4] *Cf.* RULE, II., 328 *seq.*

[5] See L. PASSERINI, *Generalogia d. famiglia Ricasoli*, 161 *seq.* *Cf. Storia dell'Inquisizione in Toscana*, Firenze, 1783, and REUMONT, *Toskana*, I., 516 *seq.*

[6] See BERTOLOTTI, *Martiri*, 119 *seq.*; *idem. Giornalisti, astrologhi e negromanti in Roma nel sec. XVII.* Firenze, 1878, 7 *seq.*, 15 *seq.* *Cf.* *Avviso of June 12, 1630, Vat. Lib.

1631, was connected with this trial.[1] It did no more than renew the prescriptions of Sixtus V. in his Bull *Coeli et Terrae Creator* of January 5th, 1586, directed against astrologers who claimed the power of knowing the future and of setting in motion certain secret forces for the good or the hurt of the living. Sixtus urged the Inquisition to proceed with the utmost rigour against those who evoked the devil as well as against those who read books treating of such evocations. In the above-named Bull, Urban specially commanded that an eye should be kept on such magical arts as were directed against the life of the Pope and that of his kinsfolk down to the third degree. Those guilty of such offences were to be punished not only with excommunication but with death and confiscation of property. If they were clerics, they were to be handed over to the secular arm, subsequently to the application of ecclesiastical penalties. These dispositions of Urban VIII. were soon to be carried out against Giacinto Centini, a nephew of Felice Centini, Cardinal of Ascoli. Centini was anxious for his uncle to become Pope. In view of the fact that the Cardinal was already 60 years old, he was afraid lest he should not live to see his election. With a view to speeding things up, he resolved to get the reigning Pontiff out of the way. To this end he entered into a conspiracy with the ill-famed hermit Diego Guicciolone of Palermo, the Augustinian Domenico Zancone of Fermo and the Friar Minor Cherubino Seraphino of Ancona. Various attempts between 1633–5 did not lead to the desired result. In course

[1] See *Bull.*, XIV., 211 *seq.* *Cf.* REUSCH., II., 181. *Barb.* 921 (Vatican Library) contains: *"*Petri Antonii de Magistris Galathaei de astrologia narratiuncula, in qua permissa a superstitiosa distinguitur ex diversis auctoribus, ubi verus sensus bullae Sixti V. declaratur, quam postea Urbanus VIII. confirmavit.*" *Ibid.*, 298, p. 10 *seq.*: **In astrologos oratio Ferdinandi Casoli ad S.D.N. Urb. VIII.* *Ibid.*, 4261: CESARE CRIVELLATI, *Nuovo trattato contro l'astrologia giuditiaria,* dedicated to Cardinal Antonio Barberini (attempts to show that astrology is a Manichaean heresy).

of time the secret leaked out. In the hope of impunity for himself, Zancone betrayed the whole plot to the Inquisition. Centini and his accomplices were arrested; Centini was beheaded after a lengthy trial; the two others were hanged (April 23rd, 1635) after they had made a public recantation on the previous day in the basilica of St. Peter.[1]

The same basilica, on June 9th, 1635, witnessed the solemn recantation of eight men condemned by the Inquisition. The spectacle drew an extraordinary concourse of people because among the culprits was the Rector of S. Carlo al Corso who was to be handed over to the secular arm for execution for his sacrileges, immoralities and his practice of necromancy; the rest were condemned either to imprisonment or to the galleys.[2] At a recantation on May 18th, 1642, three out of four men whose guilt had been established, escaped with imprisonment; the fourth, a Franciscan Conventual, who had already served a sentence of ten years' imprisonment for saying Mass though he had never been ordained, was

[1] *Cf.* the *Relation* which LE BRET (*Magazin*, IV., 81 *seq.*) published in a German translation, and which was edited independently by GORINI in his *Archivio*, IV. (1875), 340 *seq.*, and by CARINI in the periodical *Il Muratori*, I. (1892), 49 *seq.*, as well as the report from *Cod. Barb.* 4903 of which M. ROSI (*La congiura di G. Centini*, in *Arch. d. Soc. Rom.*, XXII., 350 *seq.*), has made excellent use and printed (357 *seq.*); on p. 366 *seq.*, he gives the judgmenf of the Cardinals of the Inquisition of April 2, 1635. See also **Avviso di Roma*, April 28, 1635, State Archives, Vienna; BERTOLOTTI in the *Riv. europ.*, V. (1878), 473 *seq.*, 510 *seq.*; BALAN, VI., 742. A broadsheet on the conspiracy in *Zeitschr. für Kulturgesch.*, XIII. (1912), 125 *seq.* In 1640 Spada, the governor of Rome, came upon the traces of a plot for poisoning Urban VIII., which had been hatched by an immoral priest, Francesco Orsolino, at one time secretary to the envoy of Savoy, and the Augustinian Domenico Branza. Both criminals were executed; see DECIO CORTESI, *Un cervellotico attentato contra Urbano VIII.*, in the *Corriere d'Italia*, of November 21, 1926.

[2] *Cf.* BERTOLOTTI, *Martiri*, 122 *seq.*

condemned to be burnt for repeating the same sacrilege as well as for hearing confessions.[1]

On November 25th of the same year 1635, the Roman Inquisition published a very important Instruction on the procedure to be followed at the trials of witches.[2] Its purpose was to do away with the grave abuses which had crept into the conduct of these trials as a result of the allegations made by witches concerning their companions at the witches' assemblies. The Instruction laid it down that, on principle, no attention was to be paid to allegations by the accused concerning their accomplices, whereas it was precisely such information which just then led to a recrudescence of the hunt for witches in Germany. The result was that at the very time when in Germany, during the period of the Thirty Years' War, the most dreadful product of popular superstition, belief in the existence of witches, resulted in the most appalling orgies of cruelty, no witches were burnt in Rome.[3] The Instruction proves in striking fashion that a revulsion of reason and humanity from the horrors of the trials for witchcraft took place in Rome very much earlier than in either the Catholic or the Protestant districts of Germany.

In March, 1640, a man was condemned by the Inquisition and handed over to the Governor of Rome for execution, but in this instance the criminal in question was not a heretic but one who had relapsed into Judaism and who obstinately clung to it, namely a Portuguese of the name of Ferdinand Alvarez.[4] The last execution under Urban VIII., on May 19th,

[1] See the **Relatione delle cose occorse nel governo di Roma in tempo di Msgr. G. B. Spada*, MS. in the Library of the Campo Santo al Vaticano, Rome.

[2] See G. Stutz in the *Kathol. Schweizerblätter für Wissenschaft, Kunst und Leben*, 1881, 601 *seq.*; Paulus, *Hexenwahn*, 273 *seq.*

[3] See Paulus, 276.

[4] See the judgment in Bertolotti, *Martiri*, 123 *seq.* The account of the execution is in Bertolotti, *Liberi pensatori bruciati in Roma dal XVI. al XVII. sec.*, Roma, 1904, 99 *seq.* Reusch (*Bellarmin's Selbstbiographie*, Bonn, 1887, 239), wrongly places the execution in 1643. A similar case of a Jew of the year

1642, was that of a Friar Minor who, though not a priest, had said Mass and heard confessions on several occasions.[1] In like manner Ferrante Pallavicini, the author of many obscene writings, paid with his life for his pasquinades against the Barberini; however, it was not the Inquisition but the papal Legate who had the dissolute *littérateur* executed at Avignon in March, 1644.[2]

More than once inculpated persons were sent to Rome at the request of the Roman Inquisition, as, for instance, in 1626 the English Benedictine John Barnes who was arrested in Paris and condemned to lifelong imprisonment by the Roman Inquisition because of his heretical opinions.[3] The poet and philosopher Tommaso Campanella, who had been sent to Rome from Naples, was set free in 1629 when it became evident that his guilt was of a political nature and if in 1632 all the writings of this Dominican, which had not been printed or approved in Rome, were prohibited, there was question only of carrying into effect an ordinance by the terms of which writers living in Rome could not have anything printed elsewhere without permission.[4] The orientalist Girolamo

1635 in the *N. Antologia*, XXXIV. (1877), 298. Urban VIII. furthered the conversion of the Jews wherever possible; he bestowed gifts on converts (see *Rev. juive*, II., 283) and granted them pensions to which the Jews themselves were obliged to contribute (see RODOCANACHI, *Le St.-Siège et les Juifs*, Paris, 1891, 247 *seq.*; *cf.* also *Bull.*, XIV., 554 *seq.*). For the imposition of other taxes on the Jews, especially during the war of Castro, see RODOCANACHI, *loc. cit.*, 249 *seq.* On one occasion Urban VIII. himself stood sponsor at a Jew's baptism (see *Revue Juive*, III., 96). *Cf.* also BERTOLOTTI in GORI'S *Archivio*, V. (1879), 273 *seq.*; *Rev. juive*, II., 289 *seq.*; RIEGER-VOGELSTEIN, vol. 2; *Archiv. für kath. Kirchenrecht*, LIII. (1885), 65 *seq.* A humane ordinance for the Jews who were in custody for debt is found in *Bull.*, XIV., 500 *seq.* A Brief to the King of Spain against the avaricious Jews of Portugal, dated January 15, 1628, is in *Epist.*, V., Papal Secret Archives.

[1] See BERTOLOTTI, *Liberi pensatori*, 105 *seq.*

[2] See REUSCH, *Index*, II., 397, 409.

[3] *Ibid.*, 404 *seq.*

[4] *Ibid.*, 396, 401.

Vecchietti, who had been called to account because of his views on the Last Supper, was eventually set at liberty by the Inquisition and he lived undisturbed in the Eternal City until his death, some time after 1632.[1] The philosopher, Cesare Cremonini of Padua and the Archbishop of Spalato, Marcantonio De Dominis, had occupied the attention of the Roman Inquisition already under Paul V.[2] In 1626 Cremonini was accused of denying the immortality of the soul and of maintaining that the world was eternal. Rome was perturbed by a report that these opinions were gaining ground in Venice[3] but it was not possible to take any steps in the matter because of the opposition of the Venetian Government.[4] It is characteristic of the attitude of the City of the Lagoons that when Paolo Sarpi died on January 15th, 1623, without having been reconciled with the Church, it was proposed to erect a marble monument in his honour, adorned with his bust. Urban VIII. at once instructed his nuncio in Venice, Agucchi, to protest against the scheme. Cardinal Barberini also took energetic action, declaring to the Venetian ambassador in Rome that Rome's reply to the erection of the monument would be the burning of Sarpi's portrait in the Campo de'Fiori. When the French Government also condemned the project, Venice ended by dropping it.[5]

Under Gregory XV. Marcantonio De Dominis had abjured his errors and, accordingly, had been set at liberty. Under

[1] See TIRABOSCHI, VIII., 183 *seq.*; REUSCH, II., 407.

[2] See our account, Vol. XXV., 302 *seq.*

[3] "*Si è inteso che in Venetia vi siano scuole et Accademie nelle quali publicamente si tratta della mortalità dell'anima, effetto della mala dottrina del Dr. Cremonini in Padua." The nuncio is to suggest what should be done (Letters to the nuncio in Venice, January 10, 1626, *Barb.* 6334, Vatican Library). *Ibid.* a letter of the Inquisitor of Ceneda, dated May 23, 1626, stating that P. Veglia was going to write against Cremonini on the immortality of the soul.

[4] *Cf.* REUSCH, II., 397, 409.

[5] See *NICOLETTI, II., 624, 631, Vatican Library. *Cf. Carte Strozz.*, I., 2, 83 *seq.*

Urban VIII. the Inquisition had to take up his case once more in as much as he was accused of having attacked the doctrine of Indulgences and of Transubstantiation, as well as the authority of the Pope and the Councils whilst expounding some ill-defined plans for reunion. In May, 1624, he was taken to the Castle of S. Angelo for examination.[1] It became evident that he had relapsed into many of his former errors.[2] In the course of the trial De Dominis was suddenly seized with mortal sickness. He now changed his attitude and recanted his errors by word of mouth, so that it became possible to give him the Last Sacraments before he expired on September 8th, 1624. A rumour having spread in the City that De Dominis had been poisoned, Urban VIII. had the corpse examined by four physicians, viz. a Spaniard, a Frenchman, a German and an Italian, who found that the Archbishop had died from natural causes.[3] But in view of the fact that he had been accused of the grave crime of recidivism into heresy, the body was not buried and the trial was carried to its conclusion. On December 21st, 1624, De Dominis was condemned in the church of the Minerva as a relapsed heretic, whereupon his corpse, together with his portrait and his writings, was burnt in the Campo de'Fiori.[4]

More famous and much more important than these proceedings of the Inquisition were those against Galileo Galilei. During the first years following the condemnation of the

[1] See the *Avvisi of May 25 and June 8, 1624, Vatican Library. A *retraction of De Dominis addressed to Urban VIII., begun on February 12, 1624 (*Retractationum M. Ant. de Dominis archiep. Spalat. libri X in totidem ipsius de republica ecclesiastica libros*) is in *Barb.* 969, *ibid.*

[2] *Cf.* *NICOLETTI II. 611 *seq.*, *loc. cit.*

[3] *Ibid.*

[4] See REUSCH, II., 404, note 1. The decision of the Inquisition was already announced in an *Avviso of October 19, 1624 (Vat. Lib.), publication of the sentence was made, according to the **Diarium P. Alaleonis*, at the same time as that of the recantation of some heretics, on December 21, 1624 (*Barb.* 2818).

Copernican system of the world under Paul V.,[1] the famous astronomer and physicist had led a peaceful and studious life at Florence, without, however, publishing any scientific work of importance. The only thing he published was some controversial pamphlets against the Jesuits, Grassi and Schreiner, of which an unbiased critic can only say that on this occasion the great scientist was wrong on the main point in dispute.[2] He still held the Copernican system. When the occasion presented itself he sent to the Archduke Leopold of Austria his essay on the tides which he had written in its support during his stay in Rome in 1616.[3] In the covering letter which accompanied it he displayed extraordinary skill in evading the ecclesiastical prohibition. He still cherished the idea of publishing in the same way a larger work in defence of the new system when Urban VIII.'s accession unexpectedly held out to him the most favourable prospects in this respect.

The Barberini Pope was no stranger in the sphere of astronomy.[4] As a Cardinal he had shared the universal enthusiasm for Galileo [5] and he followed with keenest interest the discoveries of the famous scientist which at that time stirred the learned world as much as the discovery of some new work of Cicero or Tacitus would have moved it a century earlier. During his legateship at Bologna he had exchanged letters with Galileo, had asked for a copy of his book on

[1] *Cf.* our account, Vol. XXV., 286 *seqq.*; C. Bricarelli, S.J., *Galileo Galilei e il card. Roberto Bellarmino* (reprint from the *Civ. Catt.*), Roma, 1923; the same, *La figura morale di G. Galilei*, in the *Civ. Catt.*, 1916, III., 685 *seqq.*; IV., 261 *seqq.*, 416 *seqq.* I. del Lungo e A. Favaro, *La prosa di G. Galilei*, Firenze, 1911.

[2] Müller, *Galileiprozess*, 9–39, 68–78. As against Grassi, Galileo wished to show that the comets could move within the orbit of the moon. Schreiner, who was attacked by Galileo for his observations on the sun-spots, defended himself victoriously,

[3] *Cf.* our account, Vol. XXV., 295.

[4] "Astronomicarum rerum scientissimus," he is called by J. B. Riccioli (*Almagestum*, t. I., P. II., Bonon., 1651, 488).

[5] Sante Pieralisi, *Urbano VIII. e Galileo Galilei*, Roma, 1875, 40 *seqq.*

sun-spots,[1] and had exalted the genius and the writings of his great fellow-countryman in the most emphatic language.[2] In his replies Galileo speaks of the "many" favours he had received from the Cardinal, the most flattering of which, he asserts, was that in the course of his journey from Bologna to Rome, Barberini had defended him against Cardinal Gonzaga during a learned discussion at the table of the Grand-Duke.[3] The fact that Galileo's person was left out of the sentence of condemnation of the Copernican system in 1616, may well be due to the influence of Cardinal Barberini,[4] and in 1620, that is, after the above mentioned condemnation, the Cardinal addressed to him both a flattering letter [5] and one of his Latin odes which describes poetically the recent discoveries in Jupiter and Saturn and the discovery of the sun-spots.[6] Galileo could even take the liberty, in his letters to the Cardinal, to poke fun with impunity at the peripatetic philosophers for maintaining that the sun and the stars consisted of incorruptible matter which was both unalterable

[1] To Galileo, June 5, 1612, in FAVARO, XI., 317. "Mi sarà accettissimo di sapere tutto quello che passa in questa materia," he adds.

[2] During an indisposition of the scientist he urges him to take care of his health, "perchè gl'huomini come ella è di gran valore meritano di vivere longo tempo, a benefitio publico, oltre che a ciò mi muove ancora il mio particolare interesse dell'affettione che le porto et le comprobarò sempre, come me le offero con tutto l'animo." To Galileo, October 11, 1610, in FAVARO, XI., 216.

[3] To Barberini, June 2, 1612, *ibid.*, 304 *seq.*

[4] Urban VIII. himself, speaking of Galilei, said to the Florentine ambassador in 1632: "che Dio le perdonasse l'errore d'esser entrato in un intrigo come questo, dopo che S. S[tà] medesima, mentr'era cardinale, ne l'haveva liberato." Niccolini to Cioli, November 13, 1632, in FAVARO, XIV., 428.

[5] "La stima che ho fatta sempre della persona di V. S. et delle virtù che concorrono in lei, ha dato materia al componimento che viene incluso . . . picciola dimostrazione della volontà grande." To Galileo, August 28, 1620, *ibid.*, XIII., 48.

[6] Printed by PIERALISI, 22–5.

and indestructible. The recent discoveries, he wrote,[1] were a kind of Last Judgment for these assertions since already there appeared " signs in the sun, the moon and the stars " (Luke xxi, 25).

After Barberini's election, Galileo's prospects seemed to take on even rosier hues. Virginio Cesarini, to whom Galileo had quite recently dedicated his reply to Grassi, was appointed Maestro di Camera whilst Ciampoli, Galileo's best friend, became Cameriere Segreto.[2] Best of all, the Florentine scientist was even allowed to dedicate his polemical pamphlet against Grassi to the Pope. It appeared in 1623, with Urban VIII.'s arms on the title page and Florence was informed that rumour had it that the Pope had read it in its entirety.[3] If at the accession of Gregory XV. it was believed that henceforth a more favourable wind would blow for science than under Paul V.,[4] with Urban VIII. the hopes of scientists rose higher still.

We can understand how it was that Galileo conceived the hope, notwithstanding all that had happened before, of publishing a defence of the new system. With this idea in mind he decided to go to Rome in order to ascertain on the spot how matters stood. The manner in which the Pope received the news of his plan could only strengthen his expectations. His friend Rinucci wrote to him after an audience in

[1] June 2, 1612, in FAVARO, XI., 311.

[2] Stelluti to Galileo, August 12, 1623, *ibid.*, XIII., 121.

[3] Th. Rinuccini, December 2, 1623, *ibid.*, 154. *Cf.*, however, MÜLLER, note 26.

[4] " Io assicuro V.S.," Rinuccini wrote at that time to Galileo, March 27, 1621 (FAVARO, XIII., 59), " che quanto alle lettere non popolari siamo migliorati in estremo, conietturando io quello che sia per essere nella geometria e scienze più sode, da quello che apparisce fin qui nelle lettere d'humanità che ancor loro nel pontificato passato erano ridotte a termini che apena potevano passare per una buffoneria. Anzi veggo le cose incaminate di maniera, che moralmente si può giudicare che siano per andar rihavendosi sempre più, perchè i cardinali che si farrano, e quei che correranno risico di succedere nel papato, son huomini d'altra stampa che di quella de'lustri passati."

which he had offered his homage to the new Pope, that nothing had given Urban VIII. so much joy as when the conversation turned to Galileo.[1] Galileo's visit to Rome would give him great pleasure, the Pope had declared, provided the journey did not injure his health, for the lives of great men must be preserved as long as possible. Prince Cesi also wrote [2] that the Pope had inquired whether, and when, Galileo was coming ; " in a word, he showed that he loves and esteems you more than ever." Mario Guiducci confirmed this information.[3] In point of fact on his arrival in Rome, towards the end of April, 1624, the famous scientist was received with the greatest honours. On one occasion he was able to converse with the Pope for a whole hour and on the next day for the same space of time with Cardinal Francesco Barberini,[4] and subsequently with other Cardinals, such as Cobelluzio, Boncompagni and Frederick of Hohenzollern.[5] Towards the end of his stay in Rome he was able to write that the Pope had shown him the highest marks of honour and goodwill. On no less than six separate occasions he had had long conversations with him ; he had also been presented with a beautiful painting and two medals in gold and silver and was promised a yearly pension for his son. Galileo took with him to Florence a glowing papal Brief written by his friend Ciampoli, recommending him to the Grand-Duke of Tuscany.[6] The Brief spoke of him as " a man whose fame shines in the sky and is spread over the whole world ".

For Galileo the most valuable result of his Roman journey was the acquaintance he there made of Cardinal Hohenzollern, Bishop of Osnabrück, and that of the Dominican Niccolò Riccardi whose duty it became, at a later date, as Master of the Apostolic Palace (from 1629), to authorize the

[1] " Giuro a V.S. che di niente la veddi tanto rallegrare che quando li nominai lei." October 20, 1632, in FAVARO, XIII., 139.

[2] October 31, 1623, *ibid.*, 140.

[3] December 18, 1623, *ibid.*, 175.

[4] Galileo to C. Picchena, April 27, 1624, *ibid.*, 175.

[5] To Cesi, June 8, 1624, *ibid.*, 182.

[6] June 8, 1624, *ibid.*, 183 ; translation in MÜLLER, 46.

publication of books. Hohenzollern promised Galileo to discuss the Copernican question with the Pope before his return to Germany.[1] As a matter of fact he did represent to the Pope that the German Protestants were all in favour of the new system which they considered as a proved fact; hence it was necessary to proceed with the utmost caution if anything was defined. The Pope replied that the Church had never declared the view of Copernicus to be heretical and would not do so, but that there was no reason to fear that a proof of its truth would ever be forthcoming.[2] Riccardi, too, was of opinion that the system had nothing to do with the faith and that Holy Scripture could be kept out of the whole affair.[3]

On the whole his Roman experiences were calculated to strengthen the somewhat hasty Galileo in the conviction that, with a certain amount of caution, he would be able, notwithstanding everything, to defend Copernicus openly. The information which reached him from Rome after his return to the Court of Florence was not likely to undeceive him. The Jesuit Grassi, Galileo's opponent, so the latter was informed, had declared that if proof of the earth's rotation was discovered, the Scripture texts which speak of the fixity of the earth and the motion of the heavens, would have to be differently interpreted, and that this was also the view of Cardinal Bellarmine.[4] Another correspondent told him of an *accademia* at the house of Cardinal Maurice of Savoy in which the Aristotelians had been severely castigated, amid

[1] Galileo to Cesi, May 15, 1624, in FAVARO, XIII., 179; *cf.* 181.

[2] Galileo to Cesi, June 8, 1624, *ibid.*, 182.

[3] "Che questa non sia materia di fede, nè convenga in modo impegnarci le scritture." *Ibid.*, 183.

[4] "Che quando si trovasse una demostrazione per detto moto, che converebbe intrepretare la Scrittura sacra altrimenti che non s'è fatta ne'luoghi dove si favella della stabilità della terra o moto del cielo: e questo ex sententia card. Bellarmini (M. GUIDUCCI, September 8, 1624, *ibid.*, 203). In his reply to Galileo's pamphlet Grassi also says: "Terrae . . . cuius tamen quies inter fidei nostrae capita expressa non habetur (*Ratio ponderum librae exam.*, 48, in FAVARO, VI., 487).

the applause of the Cardinals.[1] He was informed that his reply to Grassi had been denounced to the Inquisition, but that Guevara, the General of the Regular Minor Clerics, had praised it in his report; the doctrine of the rotation of the earth, Guevara was reported to have said, did not seem to him to deserve condemnation.[2] Guiducci, who supplied these details, added indeed that for the time being the topic should be left alone because Cardinal Barberini, who had hitherto protected them, was away in France as nuncio, and the Pope was preoccupied with the troubles of the war and did not want to be bothered with matters of this kind, so that they would only have to deal with the friars.[3] On the other hand Galileo was assured again and again that the Pope had spoken of him in the kindest terms,[4] and that Cardinal Barberini had stated that Galileo had no greater friend than the Pope and himself.[5] When the Dominican Campanella mentioned to Urban VIII. the case of some German noblemen who were inclined to join the Catholic Church but felt rebuffed by the decree against Copernicus, Urban was reported to have replied that if it had depended on himself, the decree would never have been issued.[6] Galileo probably attached as much importance to the judgment of his friend Riccardi as to the view of the Pope. Though the former only became Master of the Apostolic Palace in 1629, his word carried weight even before that time because of his being likewise a Consultor of the Inquisition. Riccardi,

[1] M. Guiducci, February 8, 1625, in FAVARO, XIII., 253. *Cf.* above p. 45.

[2] The same, April 18, 1625, *ibid.*, 265.

[3] *Ibid.*

[4] "N.S. mi parla della persona sua con singolare affetto (Ciampoli, August 30, 1625, *ibid.*, 279). When the name of Galileo was mentioned, "subito S. Stà mi dimandò di lei e del suo stato con molto affetto (CASTELLI, March 21, 1626, *ibid.*, 313).

[5] BUONARROTI, June 3, 1630, *ibid.*, XIV., 111.

[6] "Non fu mai Nostra intentione, e se fosse toccato a Noi non si sarebbe fatto quel decreto." Castelli to Galileo, March 16, 1630, *ibid.*, 88.

according to the reports that reached Florence, was convinced that Galileo's opinions, since they were confined to the sphere of philosophy, did not offend against the faith ; he was ready to serve him but held back for the time being in order that his intervention might be all the more effective later on, should the Inquisition raise any objections.[1]

All these statements led Galileo to imagine that there was in Rome a strong feeling in favour of Copernicus, so that he might very well take a risk, notwithstanding the decree of the Index, provided he was in a position to furnish the desired proof in support of the new system of the world. More and more he persuaded himself that he had that proof in the phenomenon of the tides. For years he had thought of elaborating it and of using it, in conjunction with other proofs, so as to deal a decisive blow to the Ptolemaic system. Not one of his friends would draw his attention to the obvious futility of his arguments, on the contrary, their letters applauded every one of his assertions and the incense of so much adulation might well have turned the head of a man less sensible to praise and admiration and thus blinded his judgment.

A first move was attempted by the Florentine scientist in the year 1624. In 1616, at his request, the Roman Prelate Ingoli had collected in a small pamphlet all the objections against Copernicus.[2] Galileo now used that work as a peg on which to hang his refutation of these objections[3]; a reply by Kepler to Ingoli's book gave him many hints in this

[1] Castelli on February 26, 1628, *ibid.*, XIII., 393 *seq.* Magalotti reports to Guiducci on September 4, 1632 (*ibid.*, XIV., 380) on a conversation he had had with Riccardi : " che io non era lontano dal credere che se gli anni addrieto fosse stato ben ponderato tutto ciò che si poteva considerare in questa materia, non si sarebbe forse proceduto al far quel decreto (e questo in altro ragionamento me l'ha confessato il Padre Rev.mo, e dettomi di più asseverantemente che si egli fosse stato all'ora in Congregazione, quanto a sè l'arebbe mai permesso).

[2] Favaro, V., 403–412.

[3] *Ibid.*, VI., 501–561.

respect. Once again Galileo represented the Copernican system as an established fact, though some people claimed that supernatural sources proved it to be false. For this reason his friends in Rome could only dissuade him from printing his book, even though Ciampoli [1] had read extracts from it to the Pope himself and these had met with his approval.[2]

For three whole years Galileo had put on one side his book on the tides [3] when Riccardi's appointment as Master of the Palace inspired him with fresh courage and induced him to finish the work.[4] He resolved to print it in Rome itself. Castelli wrote to him that he felt certain that the Master of the Palace would raise no difficulty, but in order to remove all opposition Galileo himself came to Rome in May, 1630.

In the struggle for permission to print which now opened Riccardi played a pitiable and fatal rôle. Since he did not make the papal laws but was merely charged with their execution, he should not have allowed considerations of friendship and his own personal views to interfere with his official duty; hence he should have resolutely refused to approve Galileo's Dialogues. Instead of this he wavered irresolutely between duty and consideration for the famous scientist, for his kinsman, the Tuscan ambassador and for the Grand-Ducal Court which had thrown its weight into the scales in favour of the book, under pressure of the opposition he yielded step by step, thereby encouraging Galileo's friends to insist all the more, until he himself was horrified at the mischief he had done and the calamity that threatened Galileo.[5]

Riccardi entrusted the delicate task of the revision of the

[1] To Galileo, December 28, 1625, *ibid.*, XIII., 295.

[2] *Cf.* MÜLLER, 49–59.

[3] Galileo to Diodati, October 29, 1629, in FAVARO, XIV., 49.

[4] Castelli (to Galileo, February 9, 1630, *ibid.*, XIV., 77) said to Riccardi, that Galileo had decided to write "dopo che sua P. Rev^ma^ era stata deputata nell'officio di Maestro di S. Palazzo, perchè era sicuro che non sarebbero le cose passate e guidate di ignoranti." Riccardi answered that he was wholly for Galileo.

[5] *Cf.* the opinion of L. OLSCHIKI, *Galilei und seine Zeit*, Halle, 1927, 333.

new work to his brother in religion, Visconti.[1] The latter was soon able to inform Galileo [2] that the Master of the Palace liked the book and that only a few minor details needed correction. However, Riccardi felt he must personally examine the book. His decision was that a few things should be altered and that the proofs should be submitted to him. Subject to these reservations he actually gave his *imprimatur*. The impatient scientist, who had returned to Florence in order to escape from the summer heat, imagined that it was best to have the book printed in that city. Riccardi granted this also,[3] on condition that a copy with the desired corrections was sent to him. When Galileo objected that owing to the plague which prevailed just then, communications between Florence and Rome were too uncertain, the Master of the Palace agreed that only the beginning and the conclusion should be forwarded to him whilst all the rest would be examined in Florence in accordance with Galileo's proposal. Thereupon Riccardi instructed the Dominican Stefani, a Consultor of the Inquisition in Florence, either to allow or to forbid the impression of the book regardless of any revision by Rome. The tides were not to appear in the title as the main theme; the new system must not be represented as an established truth but as a mere mathematical hypothesis; hence it must be made to appear that the purpose of the book was a defence of the Roman decrees against Copernicus at least in so far as it showed that the state of the question was well understood in Italy and that those decrees were not inspired by ignorance of astronomy.[4] For the rest Riccardi would have preferred some other censor to Stefani, but as Galileo raised objections to him, he yielded on this point also.[5]

This greatly eased Galileo's position with regard to the

[1] For what follows *cf.* the acts of the case in FAVARO, XIX., 325 *seqq.*, and MÜLLER, 81 *seqq.*

[2] June 16, 1630, in FAVARO, XIX., 120.

[3] *Ibid.*, 325.

[4] Riccardi to Stefani, May 24, 1631, *ibid.*, 327 *seq.* The draft of the preamble, *ibid.*, 328 *seqq.*

[5] Niccolini to Cioli, March 16, 1631, *ibid.*, XIV., 224.

Florentine Inquisition. Stefani went on the principle that Rome had already approved the work which he was charged to examine, whilst Galileo protested the submissiveness and respect with which he was ready to qualify as dreams, chimeras, errors, miscalculations, futility, all grounds and proofs which, in the opinion of competent authority, favoured views which it deemed erroneous ; thus all men could see how sincere he was when he attested that on this point he had never held any other opinion or intention than those of the most holy and venerable Fathers and Doctors of the Church. The views which met with disapproval were not his own whilst those he held were no other than those of St. Augustine and St. Thomas and the other spokesmen of the Church.[1] Stefani was moved to tears by so much docility [2] and gave permission to go to press.

Thus in June, 1631, Galileo could rejoice at the happy issue of the affair.[3] At the cost of " infinite trouble " he likewise obtained Riccardi's permission to print the revised Introduction, though to secure this, the Master of the Palace had had " to be dragged by the hair ", but in the end he had allowed himself to be thus dragged.[4] Thereafter he heard no more of the book until a printed copy reached him in Rome when, to his horror, he saw printed above the Florentine *inprimatur* his own approbation.[5]

The new book failed to take into account the demands

[1] " . . . di non haver mai havuto in questa materia altra opinione e intenzione, che quella che hanno i più santi e venerabili Padri e dottori di s. Chisea. . . . Assolutamente le opinioni che non piacciono non son le mie, e le mie sono quelle che tengono S. Agostino, S. Tommaso e tutti gl'altri autori sacri." Galileo to Cioli, May 3, 1531, *ibid.*, 259 *seq.*

[2] Galileo to Cioli, March 7, 1631, *ibid.*, XIV., 217.

[3] Cioli to Niccolini, June 13, 1631, *ibid.*, 276.

[4] Niccolini to Galileo, July 19, 1631, *ibid.*, 284.

[5] Acts of the trial, *ibid.*, XIX., 326. The name of the Master of the Palace, " non ha che fare nelle stampe di fuori," Urban VIII. remarked to Niccolini. Niccolini to Cioli, September 5, 1632, *ibid.*, XIV., 384.

which Riccardi had laid down in his letter to Stefani as the conditions on which the *imprimatur* would be granted. True, the Preface,[1] in complete accordance with the demand of the Master of the Palace,[2] described the book as a defence of the condemnation by the Index of the new system of the world; if the arguments supporting the Copernican system were explained in its pages, so we read, it was done solely in order that everybody may see that they were known in Italy, and that accordingly those prohibitions were not the fruit of ignorance. However, the Preface is wholly unconnected with the ensuing explanations in which the new system is clearly represented as a fact. Galileo develops his ideas in the form of a dialogue in which the objections against the new teaching are placed in the mouth of a certain "Simplicius" whose very name suggests ridiculous narrow-mindedness[3]; moreover it seems extremely probable that Galileo was tactless enough to make Simplicius defend an idea suggested by the Pope himself.[4] The scientific value of the new work is uneven. Of the three arguments in support of Copernicus the second and third, based on the sun-spots and the tides, are of no value; the simplicity with which the intricate movements of the planets were explained in the new system had already been described by Copernicus himself, all that Galileo did was to present it in a more easily intelligible form. Of value in the new explanation is the refutation of the objections against the motion of the earth based on physics, though the difficulty arising out of the centrifugal force of the earth revolving round its axis was only to be solved by the genius of Newton. Another criticism is that Galileo completely ignores the system of Tycho as a third possibility between that of Copernicus and Ptolemy, and that he passes over in silence Kepler's sublime

[1] *Ibid.*, VII., 29 *seq.*

[2] See above, p. 51.

[3] See OLSCHKI, *loc. cit.*, 345 *Ibid.*, 364, *seq.*, a detailed summary of the dialogue.

[4] MÜLLER, 119, note 122, p. 3. *Cf.* H. DE L'ÉPINOIS in the *Rev. des quest. hist.*, III. (1867), 110 *seq.*, FAVARO, XVI., 455, OLSCHKI, *loc. cit.*, 396.

simplification of the Copernican system. He writes as if Copernicus had already managed to do without any auxiliary orbits like those of Ptolemy, whereas Kepler was the first to render these hypotheses superfluous with his demonstration of the elliptic form of the orbit of Mars.[1]

No doubt Galileo had imagined that the always pliant Master of the Palace would on this occasion also bow before the accomplished fact of the printed book. However, the Index had published its decree against Copernicus because the dissemination of the new opinions was calculated to create confusion and doubt with regard to the credibility of Holy Writ in the minds of the uneducated; in fact Galileo himself had been compelled to make a statement to that effect in his preface,[2] and where there was question of dogma, Rome took things very seriously. The immediate sequestration of Galileo's book by Riccardi, by the Pope's command, was the least of his misfortunes,[3] for the incautious author was about to have to deal with the Inquisition itself.[4]

Out of special consideration for the Grand-Duke of Tuscany and for the famous scientist himself, he received no immediate summons. The Pope appointed a special commission of scientists under the presidency of Cardinal Francesco Barberini, a decided friend of Galileo, to report on the book

[1] For the physical difficulties of the Copernican system, see A. Linsmeier in *Natur und Offenbarung*, XXXVI. (1890), 129 *seqq.*; XXXVII. (1891), 321 *seqq.*, for Galileo's Dialogue on the systems of the world, *ibid.*, XLI. (1895), 155 *seqq.*

[2] "Per ovviare a pericolosi scandali dell'età presente," Favaro, XIX, 328.

[3] *Ibid.*, 326.

[4] The acts of the case are in Favaro, XIX.; older publications are: H. de L'Epinois, Paris, 1877, K. v. Gebler, Stuttgart, 1877. The original MS. taken to Paris in 1811, was brought back to Rome, not as Biot says in the *Journal des Savants*, in 1846, but as early as 1843, the widow of Charles X's Majordomo, the Duke Blacas d'Aulps (d. at Kirchberg, November 17, 1839), having returned it through the nuncio Altieri. *Cf.* A. Mercati in the *Atti della Pont. Accad. delle scienze, Nuove Lincei*, LXXX., Roma, 1927, 58–62.

since, in the first instance, Riccardi thought of merely forbidding the work until it should have been revised.[1] The commission summed up its findings under eight headings; all these points, it declared in its summing-up, might perhaps be corrected; for the rest, the book was deemed useful. However, to these eight points one serious allegation came to be added; it was to the effect that in 1616 the author of the book had been ordered not to hold in any way the Copernican opinion nor to teach or defend it, else the Inquisition would proceed against him.[2] Galileo had bowed to that command but had now violated it. This last point proved most fatal.[3] Urban VIII. would have been very willing to settle the affair without any formal judicial process [4] but Galileo's disobedience made this impossible and the further prosecution of the question had to be left to the Inquisition.

That redoubtable tribunal began by taking stock of the existing situation. It was proved that the Dialogue defended the Copernican teaching as true; that there was a strong suspicion that the aged author gave it a mental assent and that he had transgressed the prohibition of 1616. Thereupon, on September 23rd, 1632, the accused was summoned to appear in person in Rome.

Galileo sought to excuse himself on the plea of his advanced age—he was 70—and his infirmities. However, the Inquisition stood by its order though, for the rest, it treated the aged scientist with every consideration. Urban VIII. advised him to make the journey as comfortably as possible and assured

[1] MÜLLER, 130 *seq.* "Sento poi da qualche amico che ci sia pensiero non di proihibirlo, ma sì bene che si accomodino alcune parole." Niccolino to Cioli, August 22, 1632, in FAVARO, XIV., 375, the same to the same, September 5, 1632, *ibid.*, 384 *seq.*

[2] *Cf.* our account, Vol. XXV., 299.

[3] "Da quel che racolgo, la maggior difficoltà deve consistere nel pretendersi da questi Signori che sin dall'anno 1616 le fusse fatto un precetto, che non disputasse nè discorresse di questa opinione." Niccolini to Cioli, February, 27, 1633. FAVARO, XV., 55.

[4] Niccolini to Cioli, September 18, 1632, *ibid.*, XIV., 391, 392.

him that the quarantine enforced on account of the prevalence of the plague would be shortened.[1] Everybody waited patiently until he arrived at last on February 13th, 1633, " in excellent health." [2] From the Grand-Duke of Florence he had letters of recommendation to all the Cardinals in Rome ; he was allowed to lodge in the Firenze and Medici palaces, though on two occasions he was compelled to move into the building of the Inquisition,[3] but there also the Commissary of the Holy Office met him in every way, assigned to him comfortable rooms that remained unlocked, and allowed him to have with him his personal servant whose movements were not interfered with in any way.

At the first interrogatory, on March 12th, 1633, Galileo maintained that he had not defended the Copernican theory in his book but that, on the contrary, he had shown that Copernicus' opinions and arguments were untenable. When it was pointed out to him that the contrary was too evident for anyone to believe him, he resolved to make a confession at the second interrogatory which was fixed for April 30th, 1633. After the lapse of three whole years, he then stated, he had re-read his book ; he now realized that a reader who was not acquainted with his interior feelings, might get the impression that his refutation, as it stood, was calculated to confirm the new system. The fact that he seemed to attach to Copernicus' arguments more weight than they deserved he explained away as no more than a scientist's vanity : he

[1] MÜLLER, 139.

[2] *Ibid.*, 141.

[3] He remained in the Palace of the Inquisition from April 12–30, and again from June 21–24. From June 24–July 6 he lived in the Medici Palace ; the rest of the time, after February 13, in the Firenze Palace. (FAVARO in *Arch. stor. ital.*, 5, series XXXVII. (1906), 381–8, *Hist. Jahrbuch*, XXX., 626.) The concessions made to Galileo were unprecedented : " Non v'è esempio che si sian più fabbricati processi di persone inquisite, che non siano state ritenute anche in secrete. . . . Nè meno si sa che altri, ben che vescovi, prelati o titolati, non siano, subito giunti in Roma, stati messi in Castello." Niccolini to Cioli, April 16, 1633, FAVARO, XV., 95.

had wished to make a show of smartness ![1] On May 10th, he handed in a supplementary explanation with a view to excusing his disobedience to the decree of 1616 which specifically forbade him to defend Copernicus.[2] That prohibition, he claimed, had only been made known to him by word of mouth so that it was not to be wondered at if particular details had slipped his memory. The only thing in writing in his possession was Cardinal Bellarmine's attestation that he had not had to make a recantation[3]; in this document there was no mention of any specific command for himself but only of a general prohibition for each and all to defend the new theory.

It is easy to see that the Inquisitors could not accept Galileo's assertion that he had given no internal assent to the condemned doctrine. Now if he adhered internally to an opinion which competent authority assured him to be contrary to Holy Writ, a suspicion was bound to arise that he doubted the inerrancy of the Scriptures and since this was in itself a heresy, he became suspect of heresy at least from that particular point of view. Accordingly, on June 16th, the Inquisition decided to question the unhappy scientist on this point of his internal opinion, if need be even with a threat of the torture. If Galileo stood by his previous declarations, he would have to purge himself of the suspicion of heresy by making a solemn recantation, after which he would be condemned to imprisonment at the discretion of the tribunal and forbidden ever again to defend the Copernican theory; if he acted otherwise he would incur the penalties inflicted on recidivists; his book would be banned and his condemnation communicated to all the nuncios and Inquisitors and especially to the professors of the physical sciences.

In consequence of this decision, on June 21st, Galileo had to appear once more before the Inquisition. He was asked the precise question whether he had in the past defended, or was now defending, the Copernican doctrine. He replied that

[1] *Ibid.*, 146 *seq.*

[2] *Cf.* our account, Vol. XXV., 299.

[3] *Cf.*, *ibid.*, 300.

until the decree of 1616 he had thought that both Ptolemy's and Copernicus's system might be true, but with that decree every doubt had vanished from his mind and ever since he had adhered to the opinion of Ptolemy. Thereupon he was confronted with the opinions set forth in his book and pressed, even with a hint of the torture, to speak the truth. However, Galileo stuck to his declaration ; he was well aware that septuagenarians were no longer subjected to the torture.[1]

Accordingly on the following day the last act of the pitiable tragedy was enacted, viz. the solemn proclamation of the sentence. The verdict of the judges was to the effect that, in their opinion, Galileo was strongly suspect of heresy inasmuch as there existed a suspicion of his having defended an opinion which was both false and contrary to Scripture, namely that the sun was immovable whilst the earth moved, that the sun, not the earth, was the centre of the universe, and that an opinion might be held as true, and defended as such, even though it had been condemned as contrary to Scripture ; accordingly Galileo had incurred the censures of the Church though he would be absolved from them if he recanted, but his book would remain prohibited and he himself would be sentenced to imprisonment at the discretion of the Inquisition and to the recitation of the seven pentitential psalms once a week for three years.[2] Finally Galileo read aloud the formula of recantation signed by himself. The Inquisition did not inflict the penalty of imprisonment with which it had threatened him, but on the following day Galileo was taken back to the palace of the Grand-Ducal embassy which was to be his gaol.[3]

The Florentine ambassador took immediate steps to obtain a full pardon for the condemned man but Urban VIII. was

[1] *Cf.* L. GARZEND, *Si Galilée pouvait juridiquement être torturé*, in the *Rev. des quest. hist.*, XC. (1911), 353–389 (1912,) 36–67 ; GRISAR, *Galileistudien*, 90 : " Senes sexagenarii debiles arbitrio Inquisitoris non sunt torquendi. *Bordoni* (1648), in GRISAR, *loc. cit.*

[2] MÜLLER, 153.

[3] *Ibid.*, 151.

unwilling to be rushed. At first the Inquisition, by his direction, only allowed Galileo to betake himself to Siena, to his pupil and admirer Archbishop Ascanio Piccolomini, on condition that he did not leave that city. On December 1st, 1633, he obtained leave to retire to his country house at Arcetri, near Florence, but also on condition that, for the time being, he remained there in retirement.[1]

Galileo's trial under Urban VIII. differs greatly from the one under Paul V. In 1616 everything had turned round the question whether or no the new system of the universe could be made to square with Holy Scripture; in the second trial, on the contrary, the question was a personal one, namely, whether Galileo had acted against the general prohibition of the Copernican theory and the special prohibition laid on him personally. On the other hand the reason of the severity of the proceedings must be looked for in the anxiety lest the dogma of the inerrancy of Holy Scripture should be endangered. But it was due to the sensation caused by the punishment of Italy's greatest scientist that the prohibition of 1616 became better known and stressed.

The severity of Galileo's treatment in 1633 strikes us as somewhat strange in view of the fact that Copernicus had been allowed to dedicate his book to Paul III., and as late as 1624 Urban VIII. had declared that the Copernican teaching was not heretical.[2] Many theologians also had expressed the opinion that if the new system was proved to be true, it would be necessary to give a different interpretation of the Scripture texts which seemed to contradict it.[3] The Commissary General who conducted the proceedings against Galileo, Vincenzo Maculano, himself shared that view. In 1633 the Benedictine Castelli, whose admiration for Galileo often carried him to excesses, explained to Maculano that according to St. Augustine it was not the intention of Holy Writ to give men information on the earth's motion since things of that kind had nothing to do with the salvation of souls; that Copernicus had accomplished a Herculean task by which

[1] MÜLLER, 179 *seqq.* [2] See above, p. 47. [3] *Ibid.*

the Church had herself benefited in the correction of the Calendar; accordingly he felt no hesitation in declaring himself a Copernican and many eminent theologians had not blamed him for it. Maculano replied that personally he also thought that the Copernican question could not be decided by the authority of Holy Scripturc [1]; as for Urban VIII., though he had professed his friendship for Galileo even after the publication of the book,[2] at the present time he spoke of it in severe terms: "Galileo," he said, "has dared to meddle with matters beyond his competence and with the most important as well as the most dangerous which it is possible to discuss in these days; it was not merely a question of mathematics but of Holy Writ, religion and the faith." [3] On another occasion he expressed his displeasure with what Galileo had done in the sharpest terms: "it was an injury to religion as grievous as ever there was and of a perverseness as bad as could be encountered." [4]

[1] "Il detto Padre mi rispose, che quanto a lui era del medesimo parere, che questa questione non si dovesse terminare con l'autorità delle Sacre Lettere" (Castelli to Galileo, October 2, 1632, in Favaro, XIV., 401 *seq*). For Maculano's attitude during Galileo's trial, *cf.* St. Fermi in *Bollett. stor. Piacentino*, VI. (1911), 218 *seqq.*

[2] "S. Stá replicò . . . ch'ancora il S. Galileo era suo amico (Niccolini to Cioli, September 18, 1632, in Favaro, XIV., 392: "che il Signor Galileo è stato suo amico, et hanno insieme trattato e magnato più volte domesticamente, e dispiaceli d'haverlo a disgustare, ma trattarsi d'interesse della fede e della religione" (Niccolini to Cioli, March 13, 1633, *ibid.*, XV., 68).

[3] "Tiene (the Pope) che s'incorra in molti pericoli della fede, non si trattando qui di materie matematiche, ma della Scrittura Sacra, della religione e della fide." Niccolini to Cioli, September 11, 1632, Favaro, XIV., 388.

[4] "In materie simili, dove si trattava di apportar alla religione pregiudizi grandi e de'più pessimi che siano stati mai inventati." "Si trattava della più perversa materia che si potesse mai haver alle mani"; "dottrina perversa in estremo grado." "Son materie fastidiose e pericolose, a che questa sua opera in fatti è perniciosa e la materia è grave più di quel che S.A. si persuade." (Niccolini to Cioli, September 5 and 18, 1632, *ibid.*, 384, 392.

We may probably find an explanation of so surprising a contradiction if we study the text of the final verdict against Galileo. He was condemned because he seemed to think that an opinion could still be defended even when competent authority had pronounced it to be opposed to Holy Writ, whilst danger also lurked in the fact that laymen began to make themselves independent of the declarations of ecclesiastical authority and to interpret Holy Scripture for themselves, on the Protestant model. The authorities were determined to oppose from the outset such an infiltration of Lutheranism in Italy—hence this great severity.[1]

It is not so rare an occurrence in the history of the sciences [2] to see eminent scientists derided and persecuted by their colleagues because of their achievements and discoveries; hence, as a rule, no great importance is attached to such incidents. The regrettable thing in the case of Galileo lies in the fact that the mistake was made by representatives of the Church and in the name of religion. Richly embellished with fables and exaggerations even up to our own days,[3] the incident has provided the enemies of the Church for centuries to come with a pretext for triumph and malicious insinuations.

[1] The expression "heresy" is not applied to the Copernican system in the sentence. For L. Garzend, *L'Inquisition et l'hérésie*, Paris, 1912. *Cf.* the unfavourable opinions in the *Rev. d'hist. ecclés.*, XVII. (1911), 417 *seqq.*; *Études*, CLXVIII. (1921), 111 *seqq.*; *Lit. Rundschau*, 1914, 420.

[2] It will be sufficient to remind readers of Julius Robert Mayer (d. 1878), the discoverer of the preservation of energy, and of Ignatius Philip Semmelweis (d. 1863), the forerunner of Pasteur and Lister, who were both at least temporarily driven to madness by their opponents, of Leopold Auenbrugger (d. 1809), the discoverer of the percussion of the pectoral cavity, which was only rediscovered fifty years later by French physicians.

[3] On this point see Müller, 160 *seqq.* For "E pur si muove," *cf.* also Favaro, in the *Atti del R. Istituto Veneto di scienze*, LXX. (1911). See also Prinzivalli's criticisms of this apocryphal saying which the Roman municipality has had inscribed at the entrance of the Pincio in 1888. *Cf. Bollet. dell'Unione Storia ed Arte*, XXI. (1928), no. 123.

However, mistakes are bound to happen wherever men are at work, except in the case of one tribunal endowed with infallibility by Christ Himself. But this may not be claimed for the tribunal of the Inquisition, even when its decisions receive the Pope's approval in the ordinary form.

The deplorable incident was, however, not without some good results, though these had not been intended. For Galileo personally it was no misfortune that he had to stop his literary work for the general public and to return to strictly scientific research, to turn from astronomy to his own proper subject, viz. physics. It may well be that his work on the laws of movement, which constitutes his true title to posthumous fame,[1] would never have seen the light, had not his condemnation and recantation restrained him from the pursuit of the elusive admiration of his contemporaries. For theologians the mistake of 1616 and 1633 proved a constant warning for centuries to come, a warning that they took to heart: there has been no second Galileo case.

(3)

Among the numerous prohibitions of books issued by the Congregations of the Index and the Inquisition at that period[2] and of which some are in force to this day, a decree of August 1st, 1641, is of special interest; it condemned eighteen different works, the "Augustinus" of Jansenius heading the list. Urban VIII. confirmed the decision in the most solemn manner by a Bull dated March 6th, 1642, which gave special

[1] *Discorsi e dimostrazioni matematiche intorno a due nove scienze attenenti alla mecanica e i movimenti locali*, Leyden, 1638, in Favaro, VIII., 39–319.

[2] See Hilgers, 423, *ibid.*, 547 *seq.*, on the insuffïcently explained prohibition by the Inquisition, as early as May 3, 1640, of the twentieth volume of the *Annales Ecclesiasticae*, published only in 1641, of the Dominican Abraham Bzovius, who died in 1637, a prohibition inculcated anew by Urban VIII. in Briefs to the Senate of Cologne and the Bishop of Osnabrück, Franz Wilhelm von Wartenberg, dated May 26, 1640.

weight to the sentence.[1] Jansenius' heresy has a lengthy pre-history and is intimately connected with France's religious development.

After the terrible experiences of the wars of the Huguenots, the majority of the French people had returned with extraordinary fervour to the ancient religion. It was a change which led to a mighty efflorescence of the spiritual life. The more richly endowed spirits became so penetrated with the thought of religion as to devote all their energies to it and when others also became enkindled by their ardour, all the conditions for the creation of new religious associations were forthcoming.[2]

The first of these new foundations arose after 1592 in the south of France where César de Bus (died 1607), and his companion, Jean Baptiste Romillion, set an example of a complete change in their own persons, for previous to his conversion De Bus had been a worldly cleric and his colleague a Huguenot who had fought Catholicism arms in hand.[3] In 1598 Pierre Fourier founded a Congregation for the education of girls and the Spanish Reformed Carmelites were introduced at the same time as the Italian Ursulines, through Barbara Acarie (Mary of the Incarnation).[4] Like the Sisters of the Visitation of the Bishop of Geneva, Francis de Sales, the Ursulines only received their definitive constitution in France. There also arose at that time in France various important Congregations of

[1] The Index only notes five Bulls of this kind; see HILGERS, 96.

[2] *Cf.* our account, Vol. XXIII., 183 *seqq*; XXVI., 40 *seqq.*; L. PRUNEL, *La réforme catholique en France au XVIIe siècle*, Paris, 1921; G. FAGNIEZ, *La renaissance catholique et la dévotion féminine dans la première moitié du XVIIe siècle*, in the *Rev. des quest. hist.*, 1927, 305 *seqq.*

[3] *Cf.* our account, Vol XXIII., 184; MORONI, XX., 254 *seqq.*; *Brief of April 11, 1616, in *Bull.*, XL., 354. For De Bus, see BEAUVAIS' biography (Paris, 1645).

[4] *Cf.* our account, Vol. XXIII., 184. See H. DE LEYMONT, *Mad. de St.-Beuve et les Ursulines de Paris*, 1562–1630, Lyon, 1890.

priests, as in 1611 the Oratorians of Pierre de Bérulle, in 1624 the Lazarists of Vincent de Paul, in 1642 the Sulpicians of M. Olier, in 1643 the so-called Eudists of Jean Eudes.[1] From 1679 onwards the Brothers of the Christian Schools founded by Jean de Lasalle attained very great importance.[2] The Sisters of St. Charles founded at Nancy in 1626 devoted themselves to the care of the sick,[3] as did the Sisters of Charity founded by St. Vincent de Paul in 1633.[4] Important as these Institutes are, they are not the only ones: as if after the Huguenot wars a new religious spring had burst upon France, fresh associations sprang up in every part of the country for the alleviation of spiritual and temporal needs.[5]

In the old Orders also a movement towards a thorough

[1] HEIMBUCHER, III., 419, 428, 442, 450. For the French Oratorians see our account, Vol. XXVI, 56 *seqq.*

[2] HEIMBUCHER, III., 299 *seq.*

[3] *Ibid.*, 370 *seqq.*

[4] See above p. XXVIII., 469 *seqq.*

[5] In the East, besides Fourier's Congregation, which numbered about 4,000 Sisters in 1789, and 90 houses (HEIMBUCHER, II., 85), and the Sisters of St. Charles Borromeo, there were the contemplative nuns of the Holy Sepulchre (*ibid.*, 82). In the North, in 1630, at Dieppe, Sisters Hospitalers were founded, at Tourcoing a Congregation of Sisters for teaching and nursing (*ibid.*, 303, 507), at Senlis in 1627 a similar Order for teaching (ibid., 302). In the West, Susanna Dubois (d. 1626) founded nursing Sisters in Touraine in 1621; so did Marie de la Fère in Anjou, in 1642 (*ibid.*, 302, 304). The South remained the most fruitful soil for such foundations. Congregations were founded to work for young girls by Jeanne de l'Estonnac in 1627 at Toulouse; by Jeanne Marie Chézard de Matel in 1625 at Lyons; at Le Puy, in 1634 (*ibid.*, I., 392; II., 174, 302), while at Bordeaux, in 1638, a Congregation was begun which combined the care of the sick with that of orphans, as had been done at Aix in 1633 (*ibid.*, 303). Several Congregations undertook the care of fallen girls at Paris in 1618, Nancy 1631, Caen 1644 (*ibid.*, 298 *seqq*). Among many others, Paris saw the rise of the Sisters of St. Geneviève and the Daughters of the Holy Cross in 1636 and 1639 (*ibid.*, III., 543 *seqq.*); at Arras, the Sisters of St. Agnes (*ibid.*, 544), at Le Puy, the Sisters of St. Joseph (*ibid.*, 544), etc.

reform made itself felt not only among the Benedictines,[1] but likewise among the Augustinians, the Premonstratensians, the Trinitarians, the Franciscans and the Carmelites.[2]

Antoinette of Orléans, Duchess of Orléans-Longueville and subsequently a Cistercian at Toulouse, was urged by Paul V. to found a formal seminary for nuns who would in turn reform the convents of nuns.[3] The Jesuit school of Pont-à-Mousson, founded in 1572, alone produced up till the end of the century several reformers of Orders in French Lorraine: thus Pierre Fourier, who had already founded an Order of women, reformed the Austin Canons,[4] Servais Lairuels, the Premonstratensians in 1617,[5] Philippe Thibault (died 1638) founded the Discalced Carmelites of Rennees,[6] and Didier de la Cour the Lorrain Benedictine Congregation of St. Vannes and St. Hidulphe.[7]

Moreover the religious revival was by no means confined to the Orders and religious communities. The French Oratorians and the Sulpicians, in conjunction with the Lazarists and the Jesuits, were preparing the way for a renewal

[1] *Cf.* our account, Vol. XXIII., 183.

[2] The Augustinian Congregation of St. Victor and St. Geneviève (HEIMBUCHER, I., 27, 49), the Reformed Premonstratensians of the north of France in 1617 (*ibid.*, 60), the Discalced Trinitarians in 1622 (*ibid.*, 74), Franciscan Tertiaries (*ibid.*, II., 497), Discalced Carmelites in Touraine (*ibid.*, 555).

[3] *Ibid.*, I., 392.

[4] *Cf.* our account, Vol. XXIII., 184. FOURIER BONNARD, *Lettres choisies de St. Pierre Fourier*, Paris, 1918.

[5] HEIMBUCHER, L., 424; E. MARTIN, *Lairuels et la réforme des Prémontrés*, Nancy, 1893.

[6] HEIMBUCHER, II., 555; B. ZIMMERMANN in the *Cath. Encyclop.*, III., 361.

[7] *Cf* our account in Vol. XXIII., 183. HEIMBUCHER, I., 150 *seqq. Bull.*, XII., 533 *seq*, 533 *seq*. XIII., 624 *seq*. E. DIDIER-LAURENT O.S.B., *Dom Didier de la Cour de la Vallée et la réforme des Bénédictins de Lorraine* (1904). CORDARA, *Hist. Soc. Jesu*, P. VI., t. I., 504. P. DENIS O.S.B., *Le card. de Richelieu et la réforme des monastères bénédictins*, Paris, 1913.

of the secular clergy by means of their seminaries.[1] In like manner the influence of Charles Borromeo, whose ordinances and holy life many French Bishops took for their model, made itself felt in the ranks of the episcopate.[2] The laity were called upon to co-operate extensively in the effort for the diffusion and preservation of the faith and the raising of the moral standard by means of the "Company of the Blessed Sacrament" founded in 1627.[3]

However, by the side of the rich fruits which the religious revival thus yielded in France, there also sprung up a seed which confirmed once again in most unhappy fashion the old experience that only that can thrive in Catholic soil which is itself thoroughly Catholic, and that the more a man burns with ardent zeal, the less may he forsake the solid ground of Catholic teaching and the sure guidance of the Church's authority, if the fire with which he is aflame is not to become a destructive conflagration. It was precisely in consequence of such ill-directed exaggerations that one of the reformed monasteries of France became the heart and centre of a movement destined to inflict, for centuries to come, the deepest wounds on Catholic life, and this far beyond the boundaries of France.[4]

[1] A. DEGERT, *Hist. des Séminaires français jusqu'à la Revolution*, Paris, 1912.

[2] Thus Canigiani of Aix (d. 1591), De Joyeuse of Toulouse (d. 1605), De Sourdis of Bordeaux (d. 1628), Camus of Bellay (1629), Zamet of Langres (d. 1655), Alain de Soliminihac of Cahors (d. 1659), etc. See DEGERT in *Bullet. de litt. ecclés.*, 1912, 148 *seqq*. *Cf.* our account, Vol. XXIII., 187 *seq.*

[3] *Cf.* above p. 455 *seq.* For the social reform after the wars of religion, *cf.* also LE PLAY, *La réforme sociale en France I*, Paris, 1867, 102 *seqq.*

[4] For Port-Royal and Jansenism, *cf. Memoires pour servir à l'histoire de Port-Royal, et la vie de la Rev. Mere Marie Angelique de Ste.-Magdeleine Arnauld reformatrice de ce monastere*, 3 vols, Utrecht, 1742; STE.-BEUVE, *Port-Royal*, 7 vols, 4th ed., Paris, 1878; FUZET, *Les Jansénistes du XVIIe siècle et leur dernier historien M. Ste.-Beuve*, Paris, 1876; RICARD, *Les premiers Jansénistes et Port-Royal*, Paris, 1883 (*cf. Bullet. critique*, 1883,

The spark that started the conflagration came from Flanders. At the University of Louvain the anti-Catholic teaching of Baius [1] found keen defenders even after his death in 1589, especially in the person of Jacob Janson, president of the Falcon College and, after 1614, chancellor of the University.[2] Both Pius V. and Gregory XIII. had condemned the novelties of Baius, but the latter's attitude towards Rome was like his teaching—half Catholic and half Protestant. His clandestine followers neither offered any direct opposition to the papal decisions, nor did they sincerely submit to them ; on the contrary, they sought somehow to harmonize the results of their own investigations with them, by means of artful interpretations. This attitude to Rome was characteristic of the whole movement of which Janson was the leading spirit. Pius V.'s Bull against Baius, which Gregory XIII. had confirmed, was stultified by the simple device of moving a comma from its proper place, thereby giving a false meaning to one of its propositions. Pius V. had stated that certain propositions of Baius might be defended in one sense, but that he condemned them in their strict and literal meaning, which was also that of their author. Now according to the followers of Baius, the Pope was supposed to have declared that certain propositions could be defended if taken in their

288) ; M. E. LOWNDES, *The Nuns of Port-Royal as seen in their own narratives*, Oxford, 1909 ; JEAN LAPORTE, *La doctrine de Port-Royal*, vol. I. (St. Cyran), vol. 2 (A. Arnauld), Paris, 1923 ; CLÉMENCET, *Hist. littér. de Port-Royal*, ed. Guettée, Paris, 1868 ; J. PAQUIER, *Le Jansénisme*, Paris, 1909 ; AUG. GAZIER, *Histoire générale du mouvement Janséniste depuis ses origines jusqu'à nos jours*, Paris, 1924. Further bibliography in PETIT DE JULLEVILLE, IV., 626.

[1] *Cf.* our account, Vol. XVII., 367 *seqq.*

[2] That Janson was an adherent of Baianism follows from his remarks on the *Comma Pianum* in IANSENIUS, *Augustinus de Statu nat. lapsae*, lib. IV., ch. 27. It was Janson's desire to be buried next to Baius ; see VERNULAEUS, *Academia Lovaniensis*, Lovanii, 1627, lib. III., cap. 10, p. 283.

strict and literal meaning, which was also that of the author,[1] and since it was nowhere stated which they were, every single opinion of Baius could be included and further maintained.

It was a pupil of Jacob Janson, Cornelius Jansenius, who gave its final shape to the new heresy of Louvain and linked it for ever with his name.[2] Jansenius was not an original thinker, but he was a gifted man, in particular he possessed a prodigious memory. For the son of a poor artisan [2] of the village of Acquoi, near Leerdam, the course of his studies was bound to be one long struggle against want and privation, but it was precisely this constant effort that strengthened not only the eagerness for work and the tenacious endurance which distinguished him, but his grim obstinacy also and, as a result of his successes, his boundless pride. In 1604, at the age of 19, after a two years' study of philosophy, he came out first from among all the scholars of the four University Colleges of Louvain. This same year gave a decisive turn to his career. He began his theological studies in the College of Adrian IV., under Jacob Janson, who filled the keen student of philosophy with his own contempt for Scholasticism and directed him, in the spirit of Baius, to the study of the Fathers of the Church, especially the study of St. Augustine, as to the pure fountains of theological learning.

For the purpose, it would seem, of a change of air which overwork had rendered necessary, Jansenius made a lengthy stay in Paris where he became a close friend of a man of his

[1] LE BACHELET, *Dictionnaire de Théologie catholique*, I., 2546. *Cf.* our account, Vol. XVII., 377, note 3.

[2] A summary of the Jansenist controversy with a bibliography is to be found in J. CARREYRE in the *Rev. d'hist. de l'église de France*, 1924, October–December.

[3] His father, Jan Ottiie, after whom he called himself Jansen (son of Jan), is said to have been a farrier. See CHÉROT in *Précis historiques*, 1890, 221, for an estimate of the sparse accounts of the youth of Jansenius, *cf. ibid.*, 220 *seqq.*, and VANDENPEEREBOOM, 11 *seq.*

own age and in many ways the exact counterpart of the unimaginative artisan's son from the North, but who was to play as great a rôle in the evolution of Jansenism as Jansenius himself. Du Vergier de Hauranne, a hot-blooded Frenchman of the Midi and a scion of a noble family,[1] was no scholar, notwithstanding his extensive studies. Whenever he takes up his pen, Vergier becomes as a rule diffuse and wearisome and often enough eccentric, bizarre and involved.[2] His first publication made him quite ridiculous. One day, by way of a joke, Henry IV. asked some theologians whether a king who, say in the course of a siege, suffered from complete lack of provisions, would be allowed to kill one of his soldiers and eat him. Du Vergier's pamphlet takes the joke seriously and carries it still further: according to him, not only in this case but in a dozen similar ones, it is lawful and even a duty to kill oneself.[3] But though Du Vergier was no writer, he succeeded, by personal intercourse and through the direction of souls, in enkindling in others the sullen ardour which consumed his own interior and in drawing even men of mark into his orbit, as if by a magic power, by the impressiveness of his forceful personality, the mystery in which he shrouded himself and the prophetlike attitude he adopted when, as one enlightened from on high, he delivered his oracles.[4]

[1] LANCELOT, *Mémoires touchant la vie de M. St.-Cyran*, Cologne, 1638; J. LAFERRIÈRE, *Étude sur Jean du Verger de Hauranne, abbé de St. Cyran*, 1581 *à* 1643, Louvain, 1912 (also J. BRUCKER in the *Recherches de science religieuse*, III. (1912), 370; J. BRUCKER, *Lettres inédites de St.-Cyran dans un manuscrit de Munich, ibid.*, 428–445, IV. (1913), 342–381; BREMOND, IV., 36 *seqq.*

[2] BRUCKER, *loc. cit.*, IV., 345.

[3] "Question royale, où il est montré, à quelle extremité principalement en temps de paix le sujet pourrait être obligé de conserver la vie au prince aux dépens de la sienne," Paris, 1709. Some parts are in (PATOUILLET), III., 340.

[4] It is very difficult to give an opinion on the character of this remarkable man. According to *Ste.-Beuve* (I., 272 *seqq.*), he was a great genius and a unique personality; according to *Bremond*

Notwithstanding their many diversities, Jansenius and Du Vergier agreed on one point: they believed that they had a call to cleanse the Church from the errors which, in their opinion, had disfigured it ever since the rise of scholasticism. Jansenius set himself the task of extricating theology from the false path of an alleged philosophism and rationalism, whilst it was Du Vergier's aim to restore the primitive strictness of ecclesiastical discipline. For the youthful scholars the chief cause of the decay of knowledge and Christian conduct was the Society of Jesus towards which they felt a burning hatred and which they meant to fight with all their energy: up to the very end the story of Jansenism remains a fight against the Jesuits.

With a view to equipping themselves for their gigantic programme of reform, the two men withdrew to a country house of the Du Vergier family near Bayonne. There, from 1611 till 1616, in complete isolation from the world, they devoted themselves to a most intensive study of Christian

on the other hand (IV., 49 *seqq.*) he was in all respects mediocre, a sick man in body and soul. Nobody, however, denies the powerful influence which he exercised on those around him (proofs in Bremond, IV., 38 *seqq.*). Characteristics of his method of directing souls in Brucker, *Recherches*, IV. (1913), 362–381. With regard to the extraordinary illuminations which he claimed to have experienced, see *ibid.*, 365 *seqq.*, and Bremond, IV., 42 *seqq.* According to *Denis Petau*, Du Vergier was " un esprit inquiet vain, présomptueux, farouche, se communiquant peu, et fort particulier dans toutes ses manières . . . (in Rapin, *Histoire*, 30). According to Bishop Pallu, Vincent of Paul said of him: " Je vous proteste que vous ne vîtes jamais homme aussi superbe, ni aussi attaché à son propre sens (in Maynard, II., 282 *seq.*, note). *Richelieu* opened thus: " il est Basque, ainsi il a les entrailles chaudes et ardentes par tempérament; cette ardeur excessive d'elle-même lui fait des vapeurs dont se forment ses imaginations mélancoliques et ses rêveries creuses, qu'il regarde après avec des réflexions de spéculatif comme des lumières inspirées, et il fait de ces rêveries-là des oracles et des mysterès " (in Rapin, 344). Hanotaux says that he was devoured by ambition (I., 113).

antiquity, the Fathers and the early Councils. It is said that they often worked from twelve to fifteen hours a day,[1] so that Du Vergier's mother thought that her son would end by killing his Dutch friend with so much study.

What fruits these vigils bore for Jansenius, appears from the letters he wrote to his French friend after his return to his own country.[2] In 1618 the Dutch Protestants held their synod at Dordrecht at which the most rigid Calvinism won the day. According to the decisions of Dordrecht, Christ did not die for all men, it is impossible to resist grace, some men are predestined to eternal damnation, hence it is impossible for them to be saved. Now Jansenius was of opinion that these dreadful propositions were an almost perfect statement of the Catholic doctrine of predestination and reprobation.[3] He likewise reveals to his friend the sources from which he derived his views. On his return to Louvain, so he wrote, he had found someone—without doubt he means Jacob Janson—who opened his eyes to the doctrine of Augustine and that he was making wonderful discoveries in that Father's writing which, one day, would astonish the world.[4] Six months later he wrote [5] that for the last two years he had been reading Augustine with special care and profit, the more important treatises even two or three times. He had completely changed his mind about him, as well as about other writers; for centuries St. Augustine's teaching had been but little known by the learned but then, after the heretics, no one has done more harm to theology than the "scholastic barkers [6]; Jesuits and Thomists alike were a

[1] LANCELOT, *Mémoires*, I., 101 *seq.*; II., 308 *seq.*

[2] After St. Cyran's arrest they fell into the hands of the Jesuit Pinthereau who had them printed as a pamphlet: *La naissance du Jansénisme découverte à M. le Chancelier par le Sieur de Préville*, Louvain-Caen, 1654. The original manuscripts were publicly exhibited. New ed. *Lettres de M. Corn. Jansénius*, par FR. DU VIVIER (Gerberon), Cologne, 1702.

[3] Letter of 1620, in RAPIN, 89 *seq.*

[4] October 14, 1620, *ibid.*, 78.

[5] STE.-BEUVE, I., 292.

[6] "Clabaudeurs d'école," *ibid.*

hundred miles from the truth and if they persevered on the road they had taken, they would stray even further, though they continued their disputations until the end of the world ". However, Jansenius pitted his own personal views, and this with the utmost confidence, not only against those of the Thomists and the Jesuits and the whole of contemporary scholarship, but he even entertained a very low opinion of the teaching of the Holy See. Until everything had matured, he wrote to his friend, he did not dare to tell anyone what—in accordance with the principles of St. Augustine—he thought of contemporary thought, especially concerning grace and predestination, because he feared to be treated by Rome as others had been.[1] Another time [2] he speaks of the ignorance of that Court of those matters and of Rome's fear of giving rise to fresh complications in the handling and understanding of which the officials showed as much skill as they had displayed in the settlement of the case of Machiavelli.

Meanwhile, in 1619 Jansenius had passed his examination for the doctorate in a three days' disputation and had been appointed lecturer in Holy Scripture at the University of Louvain.[3] On his part Du Vergier, after the departure of his friend, placed himself at the disposal of the Archbishop of Poitiers, Henri Louis Chateignier de la Rocheposai, whose goodwill he had won by a new literary work, also of a peculiar kind. De la Rocheposai had fought the Huguenots arms in hand ; Du Vergier now defended this action of a seventeenth

[1] *Ibid.*

[2] January 20, 1622, in Rapin, 121 *seq.*

[3] A small pamphlet : *Mens et sententia Ill. et Rev. Dni Corn. Iansenii de quaestione : An iudicium Rom. Pontificis, cum universae Ecclesiae aliquid sub anathemate tenendum esse definit, sit infallibile necne* ? (Lovanii s.a. (1718)) gives the list of theses which Jansenius defended on October 7, 1617, " pro prima ad gradum doctoralem responsione." On the doctrine of Papal Infallibility, he takes the view that " Supremus est omnium de religione controversiarum index, cuius iudicium rectum, vere et infallibile est, cum universae Ecclesiae aliquid sub anathemate tenendum esse definit " (a copy of the pamphlet in *Cod.* M. 17 on the Vallicelliana Library, Rome).

century Bishop by appealing to the example of Abraham and Samuel and the warrior Bishops of the Middle Ages.[1] To his influence also we must probably ascribe the public declaration from the pulpit that it was a grave obligation for the faithful to hear Sunday Mass in their parish churches, in consequence of which the Archbishop became involved in regrettable disputes with the Jesuits. In other ways also Du Vergier took advantage of the influence he exercised over the people by reason of the strictness of his life, to agitate against the Jesuits and in favour of his friend's teaching on grace. A great impression was created by the fact that his followers renounced every kind of outward pomp, and he himself rose so high in the Archbishop's esteem that in 1620 he appointed him in his place as commendatory Abbot of the Benedictine Abbey of St. Cyran. From now onwards Du Vergier assumed the name by which he has become famous, viz. the Abbé de St. Cyran.

From 1621 onwards, St. Cyran resided continuously in Paris, but before settling there he paid yet another visit to his friend at Louvain and joined him in one of his journeys. After that visit the letters of Jansenius to St. Cyran take on an entirely different complexion—they bear the stamp of the mysterious. Henceforth his communications are in code; of himself, of St. Cyran, St. Augustine, the Jesuits he only writes under assumed names. He speaks mysteriously of roots that are uncovered, of trees that must rise from them, of a house that is building, of a ship that is being freighted, of persons and communities whose co-operation must be secured. The sum of these aims is designated as "Pilmot", "Cumar", "Comir" in his cryptic language. These are obviously names for the plan of reform conceived by Jansenius and St. Cyran; it was, no doubt, fully discussed at their meetings in 1621 as well as on another such occasion at Péronne on May 1st, 1623.[2]

[1] DUPIN, *Hist.*, II., 70–84. Dupin says of the first two works of St. Cyran that they must be regarded "comme les declamations des rheteurs".

[2] STE.-BEUVE, I., 296 *seq.* In 1654 the royal advocate Filleau published a report on a supposed meeting of Jansenius and

For Jansenius in particular " Pilmot " stood for his toil at his great work on St. Augustine's doctrine on grace to which he devoted all his energy, so much so that he would have been glad to resign his professorial chair.[1] Only his hatred for the Jesuits seemed capable of taking him away from his favourite task. He wrote a large work against them which, however, he did not dare to publish.[2] On two occasions, viz. in 1624 and 1626 he went to Spain for the purpose of working against them; these journeys occupied nearly two years.[3] It so happened that just then the Universities of several countries had started a campaign against Jesuit competition in the field of knowledge. At Cracow they were forbidden to teach publicly. In France eleven Universities, headed by Paris, agreed to exclude the Jesuits. In Spain, Alcalá and Salamanca joined forces with a view to opposing Philip IV.'s plan for a Jesuit University in Madrid.[4] Louvain did not lag

St.-Cyran with four others, who were supposed to have prepared, in 1621, at the Charterhouse of Bourgfontaine, a plan to further the introduction of deism, by alienating the faithful from the Sacraments with their demands of exorbitant conditions for their reception, by throwing discredit on the religious Orders and sowing distrust of the Holy See, etc. When, in the 18th century, Jansenism really led many into deism, the Jesuit Sauvage thought that these results of Jansenism proved the genuineness of the " Bourgfontaine plan ". The meeting of the year 1621 may have taken place, but the intention of introducing deism is unlikely and cannot be proved. See FILLEAU, *Relation juridique sur les affairs du Jansénisme* (1634); (SAUVAGE), *La réalite du Projet de Bourgfontaine demontrée par exécution*, Paris, 1755. *Cf.* B. JUNGMANN, *Dissertationes selectae in hist. eccl. VII.*, Ratisb., 1887, 227[6] *seqq.*

[1] Letter, 7 and 8 (*cf.* above, p. 71, note 2).

[2] Jansenius to St.-Cyran, May 19, June 8, July 16, 1627, and March 17, 1628.

[3] R. SCORRAILLE, in the *Recherches de science relig.*, 1917, 187–254; A. PÉREZ GOYANA in *Razón y Fe*, LVI. (1920), 172 *seqq.*, 451 *seqq.*; LVII. (1920), 181 *seq.*, 318 *seq.*

[4] SCORRAILLE, *loc. cit.*, 194. To what pitch excitement rose at that time is shown by what happened at Toulouse. There a

behind: for some time already that University had done its best to prevent at least the public teaching of philosophy by the tiresome competitors. Jansenius was commissioned by the University to go to Spain in 1624 and again in 1626, and during his second journey he obtained his main object which was the exclusion of the Jesuits from the chair of philosophy[1]; on the other hand he failed to persuade the Spanish Universities to join in a collective petition to the Pope against the teaching privileges of the inconvenient religious.[2] A further misfortune befell him at Valladolid; there, because of certain suspicious expressions of opinion, the Jesuits denounced him to the Inquisition. Jansenius deemed it advisable to get out of Spain as fast as possible and he swore never again to set foot in that country.[3]

On his return Jansenius was at last able to inform his friend, on December 31st, 1627, that he had started work on his book.[4] It took up most of his time, even after a pamphlet of his against Richelieu's Protestant alliances (*Mars Gallicus*),[5] had earned for him from the Spanish Government his promotion, in 1635, to the episcopal see of Ypres.[6] The last lines were written shortly before he was carried off by the plague, on May 6th, 1638.

However deeply Jansenius may have been absorbed in his

professor of the Dominican Order called the Jesuits "Pelagians and Semi-Pelagians!", the students booed when a Jesuit theologian was mentioned; shouts of "Down with Molina! Down with Suarez! Away with Loyola!" were heard. (ALPH. AUGUSTE in *Bullet. de littérat. ecclés.*, 1916, 316.)

[1] SCORRAILLE, *loc. cit.*, 215.

[2] *Ibid.*, 216 *seqq.*, 231 *seq.*

[3] *Ibid.*, 239.

[4] RAPIN, 207.

[5] *Cf.* LODGE, *Richelieu*, 201.

[6] At first Jansenius' enthusiasm for Spain was not very great: he was involved in the conspiracy of the Spanish nobility *against* Spain in 1632. *Mars Gallicus* rehabilitated his reputation in the eyes of the Spanish Government. *Cf.* CUVELIER in the *Biogr. nat. Belge*, XX., 64; SCORRAILLE, *loc. cit.*, 242.

learned studies, he never neglected to seek fresh supporters for his plan of reform by word of mouth also. The most distinguished and influential among the men he secured by this means were Henry Calenus (Van Caelen), Archdeacon and confidant of the Archbishop of Mechlin, and Libertus Fromondus (Froidmont), professor of philosophy and after Jansenius' elevation to the episcopate, professor of Holy Scripture at the University of Louvain. On his deathbed Jansenius entrusted to these two men the publication of his chief work. The Irish Franciscan Conrius, who was named to the archepiscopal see of Tuam by Gregory XV., hardly needed to be converted to Jansenist views for he was a keen disciple of Baius and agreed with Jansenius' interpretation of St. Augustine whose writings on grace he was said to have read twenty times and the others seven times. The Irishman's hostility to scholasticism appears plainly in his chief work; in it he maintains against the opinion of almost all the scholastics, that children who die without Baptism are condemned to the flames of hell.[1] Subsequently this book so pleased the Jansenists that they added it as an appendix to the principal work of the master.

However, the brunt of the propaganda on behalf of "Pilmot" had to be borne by St. Cyran. Jansenius told him of his joy that his friend had begun to handle suitable personalities in so skilful a fashion, for this was necessary in order to get the ship under way.[2] Nevertheless, for the time being, he desired him to confine himself to generalities inasmuch as the affair was not yet ripe. Above all he did not want St. Cyran to busy himself with the spiritual guidance of nuns for he feared that this might distract his confederate from the great enterprise which was beginning so happily.[3] However, a year later, he realized that "Pilmot" might be greatly forwarded with the assistance of some religious community inasmuch as religious are wont to be all fire and flame for any

[1] Rapin, 113 *seq.*, 117; Hurter, III., 635 *seq.*

[2] To St.-Cyran, January 20, 1622, in Rapin, 122 *seq.*

[3] February 26, 1622, *ibid.*, 124.

cause they take up: once won over they would go beyond all bounds either for or against their object.[1]

St. Cyran particularly sought to win over for "Pilmot" the newly-founded Oratory of Cardinal Bérulle. The latter offered a point of contact in so far as, like Jansenius, he was an opponent of the Jesuits on the doctrine of grace. Moreover he lacked a really solid theological formation. A formula of profession composed by him for the French Carmelite nuns was condemned in Paris and, notwithstanding every effort of Jansenius, in Louvain also.[2] A similar fate was to be feared for Bérulle's ascetical writings [3]; none the less, at the request of St. Cyran and though he had not seen them, Jansenius allowed his approbation to be printed on the front page, provided his friend ascertained that the book contained nothing contrary to "our aim".[4]

With a view to keeping the Jesuits away from the young students, Jansenius would have welcomed the Oratory in the city. This wish was fulfilled, as he himself testifies, through St. Cyran who was more intimately linked with Bérulle by a long and close friendship than even any one member of his own Congregation.[5] For all that, Jansenius had occasion, at a later date, to complain [6] that he had failed to instil into the Oratory a "hierarchical spirit", that is, to make of it a ready tool. Nevertheless, in 1630, at St. Cyran's prompting, the Oratorian Guillaume Gibieuf published a book on freedom which was sharply criticized by the Jesuits [7] and subsequently extolled by the Jansenists as preparing the way for the work of their master, though Jansenius

[1] June 2, 1623, *ibid.*, 160.

[2] *Ibid.*, 120.

[3] *Ibid.*, 149 *seqq.*

[4] June 3, 1622, *ibid.*, 134.

[5] "Qui ei longa et arctissima necessitudine plus quam ullus domesticorum eius coniunctus est." Jansenius to Calenus, January 23, 1626 (C. van Aken in *Précis hist.*, 1884, 460).

[6] Rapin, 229 *seq.*

[7] De Meyer, 33–9.

himself was not wholly satisfied with it.[1] In the sequel not a few among the Oratorians became supporters of Jansenius.

Of far greater importance than the propaganda in the religious communities, and truly decisive for future developments was St. Cyran's success with certain lay people, namely the Arnauld family.[2] Relations with this family likewise led, as it were naturally, to the longed-for co-operation of a religious community, only it was not a community of men but a convent of nuns that became the heart and centre of Jansenism.

One of the Arnaulds had already attained a certain notoriety. Antoine Arnauld, born in 1560 and a professed Calvinist until the night of St. Bartholomew, had pronounced, in the capacity of a representative of the University, before the Parliament of 1594, the inflammatory discourse against the Jesuits which contributed so powerfully to their being ordered, in 1595, to leave Paris within three days and the rest of France within a fortnight.[3] Of Antoine's twenty children only ten survived; the six daughters, together with their mother, subsequently entered the convent of Port-Royal and gave it its importance; eventually they were also joined by six nieces.[4] Of the four sons one fell in battle in his youth, another became Bishop of Angers, the youngest became the "great Arnauld", and the head of the Jansenists.[5] It was a most important event in St. Cyran's life when he made the acquaintance of the eldest son, Robert Arnauld, usually known as D'Andilly, from his father's estates. D'Andilly was an official in the finance department at Court and that position of itself gave him great

[1] May 23 and December 7, 1629, and January 31, 1631, in RAPIN, 203 *seq.*

[2] For this remarkable family *cf. Généalogie de la famille des Arnauld*, in the *Mém. de Port-Royal*, I., vi.–xx.; STE.-BEUVE, I., 53 *seqq*; VARIN, *La vérité sur les Arnauld, complétée à l'aide de leur correspondance inédite*, Paris, 1847.

[3] FOUQUERAY, II., 360 *seqq.* *Cf.* our account, Vol. XXIII., 115 *seq.*; STE.-BEUVE, I., 69.

[4] STE.-BEUVE, I., 129.

[5] *Ibid.*, II., 11 *seqq.*

influence. He was a clever man and one who took pride in making friends for himself everywhere, from the lowest menial to the Constable of France ; no one, he used to boast, had ever been acquainted and on familiar terms with so many great personages as himself. St. Cyran first met D'Andilly in 1620, at Poitiers [1] but when the latter settled in the capital, he introduced his friend at Court and the Court preacher, Bishop Cospéau of Nantes, became specially interested in him. However, it was of incomparably greater importance that D'Andilly introduced his new friend to his sister, the Abbess of Port-Royal, through whom he turned that abbey into a stronghold of Jansenism.[2]

It goes without saying that it was no small task for D'Andilly to make suitable provision for his many daughters. Church property had to come to the rescue. [3] Accordingly, the maternal grandfather of the girls, the Advocate-General Marion, gave himself no rest until the Abbess of the Cistercian Convent of Port-Royal consented to accept his niece Jacqueline, then exactly eight years old, as her coadjutrix with the right of succession. After that Henry IV. named her five years old sister Agnes, Abbess of the Benedictines of St. Cyr. In order to obtain the papal confirmation the age of the two children was given as twice what it was ; but the Bulls were nevertheless refused.[4]

The upbringing of the two youthful Abbesses was not exactly a preparation for Christian perfection. They began by taking up residence at St. Cyr, but in 1600 Jacqueline passed to the Cistercian convent of Maubuisson whose Abbess, Angélique,

[1] The gushing letters of St.-Cyran to d'Andilly were published in *Le progrès du Jansénisme par le Sieur de Préville* (PINTHEREAU S.J.), Avignon, 1655.

[2] GUILLAUME DALL (Mme Jules Le Baudy), *La Mère Angélique abbesse de Port-Royal d'après sa correspondance*, Paris, 1893 (*cf.* GAZIER, II., 286) ; M.-R. MONLAUR, *Angélique Arnauld*, Paris, 1901.

[3] R. PLUS, *La vocation d'Angélique Arnauld*, in the *Étude* CXXXIII. (1912), 433–459.

[4] STE.-BEUVE, I., 74 *seqq.*

was so worthy a pupil of the notorious Gabrielle d'Estrées that in 1618 she had to be interned in the convent of the Penitents. In 1602 the death took place of the Abbess of Port-Royal, whose coadjutrix Jacqueline was. Thereupon the girl, now eleven years of age, had to be installed as Abbess. In order to secure the papal consent the petition raised her age to seventeen and gave her name as Angèlique, so that Rome never suspected that there was question of the Jacqueline who had been previously rejected. This time the efforts of the French envoy in Rome, Cardinal d'Ossat, were crowned with success: he obtained the papal confirmation. On September 29th, 1602, the General of the Cistercians blessed the Abbess who made her first Communion on the same occasion: her solemn profession had taken place on October 29th, 1600.

In the years which now followed Angélique, as she was henceforth called, found the religious life an unbearable yoke. She thought of escaping, without the knowledge of her parents, to her Huguenot aunts at La Rochelle and of marrying.[1] When fifteen years old she returned to her parents' house because of sickness, but when on the termination of her convalescence, she showed no desire to go back to Port-Royal, her father began to fear the possible loss of the revenues of the abbey. One day, then, he placed before his daughter an illegibly written document which he insisted on her signing at once. Angélique readily grasped that she was meant to bind herself to return to her convent; however, she did not dare to resist the grim old man; "Bursting with inward indignation"[2] she signed the document without reading it.

Of course all the acts by which it had been intended to tie Angélique to Port-Royal were without value in law. The papal Bull of confirmation was invalid because it had been obtained by subreption; her profession was invalid because made before the canonical age; for the same reason her nomination as Abbess was also invalid; so was the promise extorted from her to return to her convent. Angélique was neither a nun nor

[1] Plus, *loc. cit.*, 441.

[2] "Crevant de dépit en moi-même," *ibid.*, 442.

an Abbess and she was free to return to the world at any time.[1] Of a real training for the religious life there was no question at Port-Royal and she herself stated that none of the Sisters knew their catechism.[2]

But this aversion to the religious state did not last. One night a Capuchin friar offered to preach at Port-Royal.[3] Whilst the Father spoke, Angélique experienced a great change within herself. To be a religious appeared to her now as great a happiness as it had at one time seemed a misery.[4] From that moment she embraced her vocation with all the ardour of a soul that was not only highly gifted and resolute, but truly made for great things; henceforth her one desire was to be a true nun and Abbess, to reform both herself and her Abbey.[5] In effect, though not yet twenty years old, she gradually reformed Port-Royal. The Sisters' right of private property was abolished, the enclosure established and the Rule of the Order enforced. As a result of these measures she had most violent scenes with her father; he disapproved of the strictness of her life, but more particularly of the enclosure, for even he was excluded from the convent. The old lawyer opened all the floodgates of his hitherto irresistible eloquence, he raged and stormed and ended by adopting the gentlest of tones in order to gain admission. Angélique fell into a swoon but remained unshaken. He was beaten, notwithstanding his eloquent pleading, and the man who had never known defeat was at last compelled to go—his daughter had shown him that she could prove herself an Arnauld quite as much as he himself. Notwithstanding his opposition to the reform,

[1] *Ibid.*, 436 *seq.*

[2] *Ibid.*, 440.

[3] March 25, 1608 (U. D'ALENÇON in the *Études franciscaines*, 1910, 46 *seqq.*).

[4] PLUS, 443.

[5] For the hopeless condition of things in Port-Royal, see STE.-BEUVE, I., 83 *seqq.* M. LAROS (*Port-Royal und die Anfänge des Jansenismus Festschrift für Merkle*), Düsseldorf, 1922, 186–197) only treats of the mystic movement in France as the precursor of Jansenism.

her father did not neglect to seek Rome's confirmation of his daughter's dignity and he even based his request on her zeal for a reform.

Soon the fame of Port-Royal rose so high that other convents either sent nuns there in order to learn, or begged for Sisters of Port-Royal to teach them the reform. Angélique herself spent five years at Maubuisson in order to raise that convent from its immeasurable decadence.[1] Little could be done with the older Sisters; accordingly she took in thirty novices and when, on Angélique's return to Port-Royal, the new Abbess hesitated to keep such a number, the former took them all with her to the far poorer and smaller Port-Royal.

Up till then Angélique had been chiefly directed by the Capuchins, among whom Fr. Archangel, the former Lord Pembroke, was an outstanding figure. At Maubuisson, in 1619, she became acquainted with Francis de Sales [2] who took charge of her up to his death, which occurred soon after. He exhorted her to calm and soften her impetuous and hard character through the practice of meekness and humility. Angélique was enchanted with the new director and on his part Francis at once recognized her uncommon gifts,[3] even as Madame de Chantal [4] also saw in her a soul richly endowed by God and one whom she revered more than she could say.

In conversation with Angélique, Madame de Chantal had spoken to her in the highest terms of the Bishop of Langres, Sebastian Zamet,[5] who had reformed another Cistercian community, the Abbey of Tart, and transferred it to Dijon. Zamet,

[1] *Katholik*, 1875, II., 483 *seqq*.

[2] Angélique's deposition in the process of beatification of Francis de Sales, ed. L. Macaire in the *Rev. d'hist. et de littérat. relig.*, XI. (1906), 180; *cf.* 177. For Angélique's relations with St. Francis in general, *cf.* R. Plus in the *Études*, CXXII. (1910), 433–464.

[3] He calls her " une âme extraordinaire " (*Oeuvres*, éd. Migne, VI., 1021).

[4] To Bishop Zamet, June 9, 1628 (*Lettres*, II., Paris, 1878, 164).

[5] L.-N. Prunel, *Sébastien Zamet*, Paris, 1912 (also *Lettres spirituelles de Séb. Zamet*, ed. by Prunel, Paris, 1912). For Zamet's dealings with Angélique, *ibid.*, 200 *seqq.*; F.-T. Perrens in the

a pupli of the Jesuits and a friend of Bèrulle, was a zealous Bishop who sought to reform his clergy by means of synods and statutes and his diocesans by means of visitations and popular missions. He was on terms of special friendship with Bérulle's Oratorians to whom he had entrusted his seminary, one of the oldest in France, and whom he had enabled to found two houses, viz. at Langres and Dijon. He likewise furthered the foundations of Jesuit Colleges at Chaumont and Langres as well as the establishment of over twenty convents of nuns, especially such as devoted themselves to teaching and the care of the sick. When Zamet went to Paris to attend the assembly of the clergy of 1626, he consulted Angélique on the subject of the reform; he pleased the Abbess and she chose him for her adviser.[1] Under his influence profound changes came about. The nuns left the monastery situate at the bottom of a damp, unhealthy valley in which they had hitherto lived, to establish themselves at Paris, in the Faubourg St. Jacques. From now onwards there were two Port-Royals, the country one and the town one. Zamet cherished the further plan of uniting the Cistercian convent of Tart at Dijon, which he had reformed, and Port-Royal, in order that the two Abbeys might exchange their inmates. The new foundation was to be withdrawn from the jurisdiction of the Cistercian Order as well as that of the Ordinary of the diocese and placed under the sole authority of the Bishop, whilst the new Superioresses would not be named by the King but elected by the Sisters.[2] After prolonged efforts Zamet and Angélique obtained from Urban VIII. in 1627, that the two monasteries should be subject to the respective diocesans, namely, Gondi of Paris and Zamet of Langres.[3] The Superioresses of Tart and Port-Royal both resigned their offices after which, with the King's

Rev. hist., LI. (1893), 250–274, LII., 1–42; ZAMET's *Mémoire touchant les filles du Port-Royal et l'abbé de St.-Cyran leur directeur*, 1638, *ibid.*, LII., 29–31; DE MEYER, 493–5; PRUNEL, 265–8. Later on Zamet was abused by the Jansenists; Ste.-Beuve follows their accounts.

[1] PERRENS, LI., 265.

[2] PRUNEL, 209.

[3] *Ibid.*, 225.

permission, they were succeeded by Superioresses elected by the Sisters for a term of three years.[1]

Angélique was now a simple Sister but not for long. Zamet was anxious to make of the two united communities of Tart and Port-Royal the basis of a larger association having for its object the perpetual adoration of the Blessed Sacrament.[2] The plan miscarried, but with papal permission a convent for that object was founded at Paris in 1633 with Angélique as first Superioress.[3] The supreme authority over the new establishment was nominally in the hands of the Archbishops of Paris and Sens and the Bishop of Langres, but in reality Zamet exercised it alone.[4]

The new foundation was wrecked after barely five years' existence mainly owing to an incident which reacted also on the history of Jansenism. The cultus of the Holy Eucharist, as practised in the new convent, was taking a most peculiar turn. In a small booklet, the so-called " Secret Rosary of the Blessed Sacrament ", published at first in manuscript and later in print, the convent advocated devotion to sixteen attributes of our Lord in the Holy Eucharist, but among them there was no mention precisely of those which shine forth most conspicuously in the Blessed Sacrament, viz. Christ's humility, condescension and love ; the book only speaks of the sublimest attributes of His Godhead, His holiness, independence, incomprehensibility, unapproachableness and so forth, and the wish is expressed that every other form of being may vanish before Him even as every other luminary fades before the sun ; praise is bestowed on His freedom in virtue of which He need not consider the claims of mercy or men's merits ; nay, with a view to glorifying the sublimity of Christ, the soul should wish to be repelled and forgotten rather than considered by Him.[5] It may be possible to read into these obscure expressions

[1] *Ibid.*, 229. [2] *Ibid.*, 208 ; *Mém. de Port-Royal*, I., 422, 426.

[3] Prunel, 236. [4] *Ibid.*, 238.

[5] *Ibid.*, 242–8 ; Bremond, IV., 202–211 ; Arnauld, *Œuvres*, 575–588. Arnauld seems to say that the booklet was only distributed in MSS. ; *cf.* against this Zamet in Prunel, 246, no. 11 ; Batterel, II., 161 *seq.*

a meaning that might have served the flights of certain extraordinarily endowed spirits,[1] but for the average Christian this Rosary was either wholly unintelligible or apt to mislead. At the instigation of the Archbishop of Sens, the Sorbonne condemned the pamphlet whilst Rome would have preferred to see it suppressed without formal condemnation.

This condemnation was a severe blow to the newly founded monastery of the Blessed Sacrament. The nuns were almost considered to have fallen into formal heresy.[2] As early as 1633, complaints reached Rome about the "new heresy" of which Port-Royal was said to be the seat.[3] The difficulties in which the convent of the Blessed Sacrament became involved caused it to be suppressed in 1647, when the community was united to that of Port-Royal which thereupon adopted the habit of the Sacramentines. At the same time the overcrowding of the Parisian Port-Royal led to the re-occupation of the original Port-Royal which had been abandoned for twenty-two years.[4]

Zamet, who had approved the Secret Rosary, was also hard hit by its condemnation, hence he looked for help and asked for St. Cyran's opinion. The latter declared the "Rosary" to be harmless, whilst Jansenius and Fromondus in Louvain only saw in it the language of love which does not weigh its expressions.[5]

[1] An attempt has been made by Bremond to explain the booklet in the light of Bérulle's and his Oratory's curious phraseology, *loc. cit.*, and in *Bullet. de littérat. écclès.*, 1915, 433–447 (*cf.* Batterel, II., 34, 161); but he too thinks, "que nul prêtre sensé ne songera jamais à reprendre de pareilles formules" (*loc. cit.*, 442). According to Batterel (II., 161) the booklet was composed on the advice of the Oratorian Condren, and the Oratorian Seguenot wrote a commentary on it. Rapin (*Hist.*, 274) considered St.-Cyran to be the author. Agnes Arnauld, however, testified that she herself wrote it four years before she met St.-Cyran. Zamet also calls her the authoress (Bremond, IV., 203; Prunel, 245).

[2] *Mémoires*, I., 596.,

[3] Fagniez, II., 69.

[4] *Mémoires*, I., 596 *seqq.*

[5] The Louvain approbations of July 16 and 23, 1633, are in Pascal-Wendrock, III., 304 *seq.*; Prunel, 247.

St. Cyran, who repeatedly took up his pen in the course of the controversy round the booklet, rose now so high in Zamet's favour that before returning to his diocese the Bishop appointed him confessor to the convent of the Blessed Sacrament.

Little could Zamet know that he had taken a step of incalculable bearing on the history of the Church in France: at last St. Cyran had secured what he had so long desired, a convent which he could turn into a stronghold of " Pilmot ". Soon many of the nuns were all fire and flame for the new spiritual guide. Zamet's direction had been modelled on the moderation and mildness of Francis de Sales.[1] St. Cyran met with a ready hearing from the majority of these excitable women when he explained to them that, according to the conduct of the early Church, the Fathers and the Councils, penance and strictness alone became their state and that they could never do enough to render themselves worthy of sacramental absolution and especially of the Eucharist.[2] Nevertheless the Sisters' weekly Communion did not yet come to an end,[3] though some of them stayed away from the Eucharist for months together, either out of timidity and because they judged their preparation inadequate, or out of a spirit of penance and in order to inflict on themselves a particularly sensible mortification.[4]

Angélique, in particular, was completely dominated by the new confessor. St. Cyran laid it on her as a duty to keep from everyone, even from Zamet, her lawful superior, whatsoever he counselled or commanded her. Submission to such guidance may well have been the fatal turning point in Angélique's life for she could not, by herself alone, weigh St. Cyran's erudition as in a balance and appraise the true value of the texts of the Fathers and Councils with which he confronted her.

[1] Prunel, 228 *seqq.*

[2] Zamet's report for Richelieu, 1638, *ibid.*, 265 *seq.*

[3] Bremond, IV., 134 *seqq.*; Arnauld, *Œuvres*, XXIX., 351 *seq.* St.-Cyran himself said Mass daily (Bremond, IV., 137, note).

[4] Zamet, *loc. cit.*, 266.

Soon she could talk of nothing but the Primitive Church, the canons, the manners of the early Christians, the Councils and Augustine.[1] The community of the Blessed Sacrament entered wholeheartedly into the ways of the new director and when Angélique returned to Port-Royal, in 1635, as a simple nun, St. Cyran dominated through her first of all her sister Agnes, who was now the Abbess, and very soon through the latter the whole of Port-Royal. Zamet protested in vain; even to him Angélique could only speak of St. Augustine, St. Paul and predestination. Things came to such a pass that Zamet was requested to stay away from Port-Royal because of his excessive mildness.[2]

The nun's letters to St. Cyran which have been preserved, give a vivid picture of his influence on Port-Royal and of the confusion which he caused. Already in 1633 one of the nuns writes to him [3] that she had never heard anything so wonderful as the explanation of the truths of the faith by her new confessor. Six months later Angélique writes that since listening to St. Cyran's instructions her sister Magdalen had been striving to confess rather to God than to man, but that just then she found herself in a state of extreme stress: she went to confession in fear and trembling lest she should not be adequately prepared, and after the avowal of her sins she at once left the confessional because she did not dare to receive absolution.[4] Three months later another sister writes [5] that she felt an indescribable torment every time she had to go to Holy Communion because she did not know whether she had done as much penance as was required by the teaching of the confessor in order to recover lost grace. The new Abbess, Agnes Arnauld, thought her heart had become hardened because she had no sense of sorrow and did not deem it a

[1] *Ibid.*

[2] *Ibid.*, 267.

[3] November 8, 1634, in Rapin, *Hist.*, 279.

[4] Letter of March 3, 1634, in Rapin, 274, who errs, however, when he considers Agnes as the writer, for the latter was residing at Dijon at the time.

[5] Rapin, 279.

humiliation to be deprived of the Sacraments.[1] Later on she writes [2] that her spirit was troubled at the thought of receiving Holy Communion in obedience to St. Cyran's suggestion. Through having been deprived of it, the Sacrament of the Altar had become for her an object of terror ; she could not believe herself called to such divine intimacy and she begged her spiritual guide to grant her three months' surcease and time in which to do penance. Angélique herself, at one time, went five months without communicating and one year it was noticed that she stayed away from the Sacrament even on Easter Sunday.[3]

It was only by degrees that St. Cyran dared to reveal even to his intimate friends the views on Penance and forgiveness of sins which inspired his singular guidance of souls. According to him the Sacraments of Confirmation and Holy Order have as much power to blot out sin as Baptism, and the Eucharist possesses it in an even higher degree than the Sacrament of Penance. In his opinion absolution by the priest does not remit sin ; it merely declares that it has already been forgiven, hence it is only valid if the penitent already possesses the perfect love of God. The words of the Council of Trent which assert the opposite must be given a different interpretation, or it must be granted that on this point the Council was mistaken ; as a matter of fact the assembly of Trent was no real Council because it was not held after the manner of the early Councils. That is how the Bishop of Langres, Sébastian Zamet, sums up the opinions of St. Cyran [4] and other accounts agree

[1] *Ibid.*

[2] May 7, 1638, *ibid.*, 280.

[3] Zamet in PRUNEL, 266.

[4] Zamet in PRUNEL, 266. Zamet's memorandum was published against his will. A refutation was undertaken in *Apologie pour feu monsieur l'abbé de St.-Cyran* (1644), by ARNAULD (in conjunction with Lemaitre ?), *Œuvres*, XXIX., 173–390. However, Zamet's accusations are substantiated by other witnesses. The justification of St.-Cyran was to be strengthened by the publication of his *Lettres chrétiennes* (Paris, 1645), which for the most part preach the traditional theories of asceticism (BRUCKER in the *Recherches*, IV., 371 ; *cf.* HANS LINDAU in the *Zeitschr. für*

with it. In the course of a conversation with the Cistercian Abbot Jean Jonault, at the convent of Maubuisson, St. Cyran intimated that God had allowed him to sound to its depths the deplorable state of contemporary Church discipline. He also found fault with the theologians of his time as well as with St. Thomas Aquinas himself whom he accused of having spoilt everything; he lamented the corruption which had made of the Church an adulteress, so that not a trace remained of her primitive purity and complained of the Council of Trent with whose decrees scholasticism had had more to do than the Holy Ghost.[1]

It would have meant a valuable acquisition for St. Cyran had he succeeded in winning for "Pilmot" his countryman, Vincent de Paul, and through him the Congregation of Priests of the Mission. He did succeed in establishing relations with the lowly founder who was affable to all men, but his fifteen years' friendship with Vincent came to an end when St. Cyran remarked to him that Calvin was right and that he had only expressed himself badly; that the Council of Trent had been an assembly of scholastics given to intrigues and factions; that in point of fact for six centuries there had been no Church at all; formerly the Church had been a stream of pure and clear water, now that stream only carried dirt and mud; Christ had indeed built His Church upon the rock, but as there was a time for building so there was one for pulling down; formerly the Church was the Bride of Christ, now she was an adulteress whose Bridegroom felt compelled to cast off the faithless one and to seek another Bride.[2]

Kirchengesch., XXXVI. (1916), 405–423). St.-Cyran's views on the administration of the Sacrament of Penance are nevertheless apparent in his letters (BRUCKER, *loc. cit.*, 342 *seqq.*). For the fact that these writings were trimmed before publication, see *ibid.*, III., 431; IV., 342 *seqq.* Arnauld in DE MEYER, 349, note. V. COUSIN, *Jacqueline Pascal*,[6] Paris, 1869, 39. A summary of the accusations against St.-Cyran in DE MEYER, 490–9.

[1] RAPIN, 309.

[2] MAYNARD (II., 238, 240 *seqq.*) according to ABELLY (*Vie de V. de Paul*, LIV., 2, ch. 38), whose report was confirmed by Vincent himself. *Cf.* Vincent to Dehorgny, June 25, 1648 (COSTE,

Statements such as these, even though made with the utmost caution, before persons he could trust, and denied by St. Cyran whenever they were likely to prove dangerous,[1] were nevertheless bound to come gradually to the knowledge of wider circles

III., 319) : " La seconde raison (for not adhering to Jansenism) est celle de la connaissance que j'ai du dessein de l'auteur de ces opinions nouvelles, d'anéantir l'état présent de l'Église et de la remettre en son pouvoir. Il me dit un jour que le dessein de Dieu était de ruiner l'Église présente, et que ceux qui s'employaient pour la soutenir, faisaient contre son dessein ; et comme je lui dis que c'était le prétexte que prenaient pour l'ordinaire les herésiarches, comme Calvin, il me répartit que Calvin n'avait pas mal fait en tout ce qu'il avait entrepris, mais qu'il s'était mal défendu." The essential principle of all these doctrinal reformers was : " de réduire l'Église en ses premiers usages, disant que l'Église a cessé d'être depuis ces temps-là." Two protagonists of the new teaching had said that for fifteen hundred years the Church had ceased to exist (to Dehorgny, September 10, 1648, *ibid.*, 364). With regard to deferring absolution until after the performance of penance, Vincent said : " En effet n'ai-je pas vu faire pratiquer cela par M. de St.-Cyran ? " (*Ibid.*, 365 ; *cf.* MAYNARD, II., 282, note.) Vincent had been called as a witness at St.-Cyran's trial. His evidence has only come down to us through Jansenist hands (COSTE, XIII., 86–93). Coste considers (I., 402, note) : " Ce document que nous croyons authentique est certainement altéré ou incomplet." The statement is damaging only in one detail, namely, St.-Cyran's words, " Que Dieu détruit son Église depuis 5 ou 600 ans . . . et que la corruption s'y est glissée, même dans la doctrine. . . . Il dit qu'il semble que ceux qui la soutiennent fassent contre l'intention de Dieu." But even this he had only heard him say once and he seeks to interpret St.-Cyran's words here, as on the other heads of the accusation, in an acceptable sense. Vincent obviously did not wish to play the part of an informer, he does not say all he knows of the accused, but merely answers the questions put to him, and this solely as they are put to him.

[1] " J'ai oui dire à feu M. St.-Cyran que, s'il avait dit des vérités dans une chambre à des personnes qui en seraient capables, que, passant en une autre òu il en trouverait d'autres qui ne le seraient pas, qu'il leur dirait le contraire, que Notre-

and to create sensation. Richelieu was no friend of novelties whether in the political or the ecclesiastical sphere, hence, when his suspicion had been roused, he had St. Cyran arrested at his lodgings in the early hours of the morning of May 14th, 1638, and imprisoned in the castle of Vincennes. In the course of the interrogatories which now followed St. Cyran displayed no great eagerness to become a martyr for his opinions; he sought to tone down his own assertions and to represent the accusations against him as mere misunderstanding.[1] For the rest, though Richelieu's action may have been prompted by considerations of a quite different order, he invariably protested that his real motives were purely religious ones and he remained deaf to all pleading. "I have a sure feeling," he declared,[2] "that I have done good service both to Church and State. If Luther and Calvin had been locked up from the beginning, many disorders and disturbances would have been prevented." Condé's intervention on behalf of the prisoner was met with

Seigneur en usait de la sorte et recommandait qu'on fit de même" (Vincent of Paul to J. Dehorgny, September 10, 1648, in COSTE, III., 366). BREMOND (IV., 36 *seqq.*) has attempted to disentangle the psychological difficulties which the character of St.-Cyran has presented and always will present. According to him, St.-Cyran was not quite normal; his piety was unquestionable; his heretically sounding phrases must not be taken literally, they were merely "thrown off" and uttered without pre-meditation. Vincent of Paul also had at first understood him in this way (in his deposition of 1639) and he only came to a different conclusion (in his letters of 1648) when he saw the fateful consequences of these utterances. These results prove that it was not a case of occasional statements. For the rest, we abide by the facts as they have been established beyond controversy by Zamet, Vincent of Paul and others, leaving on one side the psychological question as well as that of responsibility. *Cf.* P. COSTE, *Rapports de St. Vincent de Paul avec l'abbé de St.-Cyran*, Toulouse, 1914.

[1] MAYNARD, II., 260 *seqq.*; BRUCKER, *loc. cit.*, IV., 344.

[2] To the subsequent Archbishop Baumont de Péréfixe; see MAYNARD, II., 253; STE.-BEUVE, I., 493.

the remark : " So you do not know that he is more dangerous than six armies ? " [1]

Richelieu, who had been provoked by Jansenius' sharp criticism of his policy,[2] rightly gauged the peril but the conflagration was no longer to be put out, in fact the Cardinal's violent action did harm by winning many sympathizers and fresh adherents for the prisoner.[3] The nuns of Port-Royal were in constant and close touch with the ladies of the aristocracy and the story of the family of Pascal is there to show to what extent the general revival of religious had prepared the ground in that world, for the extravagances of St. Cyran.[4] Moreover a number of young girls were always being educated at Port-Royal. By degrees the new spirituality became the fashion and large audiences flocked to the convent chapel to listen to the sermons preached during St. Cyran's imprisonment by his lieutenant, Singlin.[5]

The new orientation gained even greater influence when a whole crowd of spiritually eminent men, the so-called " Hermits " of Port-Royal, unreservedly devoted themselves to its furtherance.[6] The first of these hermits was Antoine Le Maître, a nephew of Angélique and the son of her elder sister. At twenty Le Maître was already famous as an orator and a greatly admired advocate ; people flocked to the sessions whenever he was expected to speak and preachers put off their sermons in order to hear him. At twenty-eight he was a Councillor of State. It was then that he met St. Cyran at the death-bed of his aunt D'Audilly and he was so impressed that

[1] MAYNARD, II., 253. For the accusations see DE MEYER, 490–501.

[2] *Cf.* above, p. 75, note 6. *Mars Gallicus* appeared in 1638 in a French translation.

[3] BRUCKER, *loc. cit.* ; MORF, *Richelieu*, 190.

[4] W. KREITEN in the *Stimmen aus Maria-Laach*, XLII. (1892), 281 ; XLIII (1892), 152 *seqq.*, 260 *seqq.*

[5] Angélique on July 4, 1647, to the Queen of Poland (*Lettres*, I., 335).

[6] STE.-BEUVE, I., 368–474 ; KREITEN, *loc. cit.*, 380 *seqq.* ; BREMOND, IV., 244 *seqq.*

he resolved, in 1637, to renounce his brilliant position and his still more brilliant prospects in order to live for God alone. Wholly in keeping with the spirit of St. Cyran, this idea soon grew into a resolve to renew at Port-Royal the life of the early Christian hermits, the so-called Fathers of the desert. His example drew others; in 1647 there were ten hermits, in 1652 there were twenty-five,[1] among them five former army officers. The two leaders of Jansenism, Pierre Nicole and Antoine Arnauld, came from this band and the great mathematician and physicist Pascal was also one of them for a time. The hermits spent their time in prayer and study but, in accordance with ancient monastic custom, they also devoted four hours a day to manual work in the fields or in the garden. They published a vast quantity of books and by means of their "Little Schools" they exercised a certain influence over the young.[2] The poet Racine completed his studies at Port-Royal.[3]

Eight days before St. Cyran's arrest his friend Jansenius died at Ypres without having published his great work on grace. Thus seemingly the year 1638 was a critical one for the rising heresy: however, only seemingly so. St. Cyran's imprisonment did not injure his prestige, on the contrary, for his friends he was henceforth a kind of martyr and confessor. From his prison, by means of almost daily letters, he continued the spiritual direction of Port-Royal.[4] When soon after Richelieu's death he recovered his freedom, all the great

[1] Angélique to the Queen of Poland, July 4, 1647, and May 16, 1652 (*Lettres*, I., 335; II, 110).

[2] COMPAYRÉ, *Hist. crit. des doctrines de l'éducation en France*, I., Paris, 1880, 243 *seq*; CARRÉ, *L'éducation à Port-Royal*, Paris, 1887; CADET, *Les pédagogues de Port-Royal*, Paris, 1887; MOURRET, 375; RAPIN, *Mém.*, I., 335. An appreciation of the methods of Port-Royal by C. DANIEL in *Études*, 1880, I., 117–137.

[3] For the relations of the latter with the "Little Schools" and the Jansenists in general, *cf.* A. GAZIER, in the *Rev. d'hist. litt. de France*, VII. (1900), 32–58; for Racine as the poet of Jansenism, see J. PAQUIER, *Le Jansénisme*, Paris, 1908, 8th lecture.

[4] BRUCKER in the *Recherches*, IV., 342 *seqq*.

ones and the noble ladies flocked to his lodgings to congratulate him. However, he died not long after, on October 11th, 1643, when he was given a pompous funeral. Three Bishops took part in the obsequies and his grave was visited like that of a Saint; pictures of him were disseminated and stories circulated of the miracles which he was supposed to have wrought.[1] Nor was Jansenius' death a blow for "Pilmot". He died a Catholic but survived as the father of a heresy through his book, the publication of which was the real birthday of Jansenism.

The bulky tome which Jansenius had completed at the time of his death, dealt with a question that touches the innermost core of Christianity, namely that of the relation between the natural and the supernatural. Thus it is easy to understand why at an epoch which was still thoroughly Christian, the new doctrines were bound to cause a profound stir, especially in view of their reaction on the Christian life and conduct. For the same reason both the excitement and the whole question itself are bound to be almost unintelligible to those who do not share the Christian mentality and are not impregnated with it. Hence a brief explanation cannot be omitted.

In view of man's nature and the spirituality of his highest faculties, that is his intellect and will, the purpose of his existence can only consist in the possession of God by knowledge and love; his nature is such that only in the possession of infinite Truth, of infinite Good, can mind and will find complete satisfaction and rest. Now according to Christian teaching, God did not leave man in a purely natural condition; though no more than a *servant* of God by nature, he was called to become a *child* of God. In Baptism there is poured into his soul a gift called sanctifying grace which as it were grafts on it a higher spirituality, which gives it a mysterious share in the divine nature itself, somewhat after the manner in which a wild tree is made fruitful by grafting. By this partaking of God's nature, which is something so sublime that reason is not even able to know its bare possibility, man becomes God's adopted child. And even as the spirituality of his soul is ennobled by this grace of sonship, so is his mind enriched with

[1] *Ste.-Beuve*, I., 211 *seqq.*; RAPIN, *Mém.*, I., 39, 123.

higher knowledge, viz. the infused virtue of faith, and his will with the infused virtue of charity. To these are then joined those supernatural virtues by the exercise of which man acts as a child of God and merits eternal bliss through the possession of God. However, in the exercise of these virtues, in fact in any supernatural activity, man is not as autonomous as in the play of his natural faculties. He needs the assistance of grace, that is, such an illumination of the mind and such prompting of the will as are themselves supernatural and proceed from God, though in our experience they need not be distinguishable from the thoughts and acts of the will which spring from nature. Experience shows that we often resist the promptings of grace to follow inspirations of a baser order, whilst at other times we follow the call of grace and reject the allurements of our lower nature. Thus the question arises whether it is due to the innermost nature of grace that at one time we obey it, thus making it efficacious, and at other times reject it, so that it remains merely a sufficient grace. The doctrine of grace, more particularly the relation between grace and freedom, nature and supernature, constitutes the theme of Jansenius' three folio volumes. His object is to explain the relation of nature and grace in man's original condition in Paradise, after the flood, and after the redemption by Christ. For him the whole mighty intellectual structure is based, as it was for his predecessor Baius, on the idea that grace and the supernatural are part of the very essence of man, hence they had of necessity to be imparted to the first man in his creation and their loss, through the fall, implies an injury and a wounding of nature itself.[1] True, in view of Baius' condemnation by the Pope, Jansenius did not risk an unqualified statement of this fundamental idea. Originally the work was to have been described, on the title page, as a defence of Baius, but he deemed it more prudent to call it simply " Augustinus ",[2] after the name of the Father of

[1] *Cf.* our account, Vol. XVII., 367.

[2] *Cornelii Iansenii episcopi Iprensis Augustinus seu doctrina S. Augustini de humanae naturae sanitate, aegritudine, medicina adversus Pelagianos et Massilienses,* Louvain, 1640, Paris, 1641, Rouen, 1643 and 1652. We use the edition of 1652.

the Church who first explained in detail the doctrine of grace in his controversies with the Pelagians and Semi-Pelagians (*Massilienses*). Augustine, according to Jansenius, has so perfected the doctrine of grace, on the basis of St. Paul, that nothing can be added to it ; all that a theologian can do is to make that exposition his own and to explain it in his turn.[1] Even as a young man, Jansenius writes, he could not understand how theologians could go on disputing about the doctrine of grace when St. Augustine had given so luminous an explanation of it.[2] In order to get to the bottom of the matter he had studied it for twenty-two years [3] and during that time had read and re-read the writings of the great African as often as ten, twenty or even thirty times.[4]

Now it is quite true that St. Augustine's prestige among theologians is only equalled by that of St. Thomas. Until well into the thirteenth century, he was the real and unrivalled teacher of the West and in regard to the doctrine of grace, papal pronouncements have proclaimed him as authoritative for all time, but—and this the Jansenists refused to consider—only in regard to the really fundamental questions.[5] But for an accurate understanding of Augustine it must be borne in mind that his teaching on grace has to be taken from his controversial writings against the Pelagians in which he lays

[1] *Iansenii Augustinus*, tom. II., lib. prooemialis ch. 27 (Rouen, 1652, p. 24) : " Quid aliud existimabimus nisi. . . . Augustini ingenium . . . divinitus electum esse, quod instar novi principii perennisque fontis intelligentiam tam profundi arcani tanta ubertate profunderet, ut quidquid de humanae naturae corruptione, de divina gratia, de praedestinatione per modum primorum principiorum in apostolo Paulo clausum erat, educeret, quidquid nobis impervium penetraret atque ita quadam eminenti perfectione doctrinae suae, quidquid posteriorum sciendi sitim extinguere, quidquid omnes eorum quaestiones enodare et adversantium argumenta retundere posset, comprehenderet."

[2] AUGUSTINUS, ch. 2, p. 2.

[3] *Ibid.*, ch. 20, p. 11.

[4] *Ibid.*, ch. 28, p. 25.

[5] *Cf.* E. PORTALIÉ, in the *Dictionnaire de théol. cath.*, I., 2501 *seqq.*

great stress on certain points whilst he leaves in the background other principles likewise held by him.[1] Thus it happens that his language sometimes goes beyond what he really wishes to convey; this is made clear when we compare various statements of his on the same subject; at other times he attaches to certain turns of language a meaning which is not that of a later period.[2] Hence grave misunderstandings of his teaching occurred even in his life-time; Wiclif appealed to him in the fourteenth century and Luther and Calvin, together with the Catholics, in the sixteenth; certain propositions which are found textually in Augustine have been condemned by the Church, though not in the sense of Augustine.[3]

As regards Jansenius' book, we do not find in it what to-day we should expect before all else, viz. an array of all the assertions of the Fathers on the controverted points and the elucidation of obscure texts by clearer ones. Such historical and philological treatment is unknown to Jansenius. His book consists chiefly of doctrinal expositions supported by isolated quotations from Augustine, in fact at times by only a few texts and such as are already found in Luther and Calvin. On the other hand, his argumentation is undeniably clear and

[1] *Ibid.*, 2466.

[2] Thus he says, that through Adam's fall, man had lost "freedom", when he only means the freedom of the state of Innocence in which concupiscence did not incline the will to evil. He speaks of the "necessity" of sinning in fallen man, but by "sin" he only means the involuntary motions of sensuality which do not become formal sins until the consent of the will is given; he calls grace "invincible" but means that grace which God foresees man will not resist, etc. (PORTALIÉ, *loc. cit.*, 2404 *seqq.*). "Le plus souvent" says PORTALIÉ (*ibid.*, 2404), "les difficultés sont purement verbales: on nous oppose *dans le sens actuel* des mots, les formules que le docteur d'Hippone employait alors dans un sens tout différent qu'il a lui-même formellement indiqúe. . . . Il faut le dire franchement, le procédé littéraire d'Augustin, faisant ressortir sa pensée par des expressions qui la dépassent de beaucoup, formulant ainsi des paradoxes troublants, a souvent obscurci sa doctrine, et soulevé l'aversion de beaucoup d'esprits."

[3] PORTALIÉ, *loc. cit.*, 2404.

even inevitable, on the supposition that we grant his premises. However, from the start, Jansenius reads Augustine exclusively with the eyes of Baius and accepts the latter's fundamental view of the mutilation of human nature through the fall of Adam. The will is no longer master of its own decisions; its freedom is only freedom from coercion, not from necessity, and it always obeys the strongest impressions. As for the relation between grace and freedom, Jansenius starts from the saying of St. Augustine that "We must needs act according to that which gives us most pleasure".[1] The sense of the text in Augustine is this: according as, *by a free choice*, we put our happiness, our joy, in either virtue or vice, virtue or vice will be the ruler of our life.[2] But Jansenius takes the words of St. Augustine as meaning that the will is for ever hovering between two attractions, two impulses, and that the stronger of these is always and infallibly victorious and bends the will to itself.[3] If we ask Jansenius how, in these circumstances, there can still be question of guilt and merit, he

[1] "Quod enim amplius nos delectat, secundum id operemur necesse est" (*Expositio in epist. ad Gal.*, n. 49, in Migne, *Patr. lat.*, XXXV., 2141).

[2] Portalié, *loc. cit.*, 2491 *seq.*

[3] According to Jansenius, Augustine's view is: "Quod arbitrium voluntatis . . . antequam divina gratia visitetur, . . . sub cupiditatibus terrenis ita arcte captivum possideatur, ut libertas illa voluntatis velut ferreis vinculis astricta nullo modo possit surgere, ut bonum velit aut faciat; sed ut tantummodo captivo modo versetur in malo. Qua de causa liberum arbitrium toto illo tempore non tam esse liberum quam servum, hoc est, liberum esse iustitiae, peccati autem servum." The will, therefore, enjoys freedom only in the sense in which a bound man possesses the possibility of motion (tom. II., lib. 3, cap. 2, p. 178). For the so-called "delectatio victrix", *ibid.*, cap. 7, p. 186, and often elsewhere, e.g. tom. III., lib. 4, cap. 4, p. 173: "Docet Augustinus quamdiu in hac vita mortali vivimus, esse in homine luctam quandam duarum delectationum, noxiae et beneficae, terrenae atque coelestis; quarum utralibet vicerit, animum secum consentientem ac pronum trahit. Tunc vero hominem a peccato liberari et opus bonum effici, cum coelestis illa suavitas de coelo venerit atque adversariam suam superaverit." *Cf* Portalié, *loc. cit.*, 2488 *seq.*

replies that in order to merit or demerit freedom from external coercion is sufficient. And if we insist how God can punish that which we are unable to avoid, the answer is that God can do it because through Adam's sin man has reduced himself to his present wretched condition so that he is himself to blame for the state he is in. There is a further reason, according to Jansenius, why fallen man cannot help sinning continually: in his opinion every action must spring from the love of God, but without grace this is impossible to fallen man. Accordingly, in all he does fallen man sins grievously; hence, for instance, whether he keeps or breaks conjugal fidelity, he deserves eternal damnation in either case, though in a different degree.[1]

In short, Jansenius' peculiar teaching consists in a denial of the so-called sufficient grace, that is, a grace strong enough to enable us to keep God's commandments yet one that may be rejected, so that, notwithstanding the assistance of grace, the will retains its full liberty. According to Jansenius, a grace which gives a really sufficient help necessitates the consent of the will. From this it follows quite naturally that man only sins because he lacks grace and since he can do nothing to obtain it, it equally follows that his eternal salvation or damnation depends in no wise on himself but solely on God's eternal predestination. A further consequence is that Christ did not die for all men, for had He died for all He would have merited grace for all, and since grace is always efficacious, all would be saved.

A truly appalling doctrine! It makes of man a cripple in his natural faculties and of his interior life a kind of machine robbed of all freedom; the history of the world, the gigantic

[1] "Ita peccato periisse libertatem arbitrii ad faciendum bonum, ut ante gratiam non solum non possit universam legem moralis honestatis implere, sed nec unam quidem nec unum opus eius; . . . ita periisse libertatem abstinendi a peccato, ut nec in illo quidem opere omnis peccati culpam possit effugere; ita inductam esse peccandi necessitatem, ut in omni actu quo legem sibi videtur vel servare vel transgredi, reus alicuius peccati teneatur" (tom. II., lib. 4, cap. 18, p. 258).

struggle between light and darkness, becomes a mere puppet-show and God's final triumph a victory over marionettes. Of God the new teaching makes a tyrant who lays down laws only to withhold from the majority of men even the slightest ability to observe them, until he finally casts the offenders into that everlasting damnation for which He has from the first predestined them! One asks oneself involuntarily how it was possible for Catholics to allow themselves to be, as it were, bewitched by such ideas. The most obvious explanation would seem to be the influence of Calvinism. The outward austerity of the lives of many Calvinists was calculated to make a certain impression on Catholics, all the more so as in the country where Jansenism found its most fruitful soil, viz. in France, an extraordinary religious fervour had got hold of men's minds as a kind of reaction against the previous corruption of manners. The mistake made at the time of the reformation was repeated. Instead of striving for a renewal of the inward man on the basis of traditional doctrine, that doctrine was held responsible for the existing decadence and a search was made for something new and unheard of. But though a few individuals may possibly have been roused to greater fervour by the strictness of the new prophets, on the whole such harshness could only do harm. If a conception of God, such as Jansenius', was put before the world, it was inevitable that the world would turn away from God.

Although he originated a heresy, Jansenius died in peace with the Church and he was not personally a heretic. In more than one place of his writings he protests emphatically that he was an obedient son of the Roman Church to which he had adhered from his youth and in which he wished to die; whatever the Pope commanded, that he accepted and what the Pope condemned, that he too condemned.[1] As a matter of

[1] "Mihi enim constitutum est, eandem quam ab infantia secutus sum, sensuum meorum ad extremum spiritum usque ducem sequi Romanam ecclesiam et beatissimi Petri in Romana sede successorem. . . . Quidquid ab ista Petri cathedra, in cuius communione a teneris vixi et porro vivere et mori fixum est, ab isto principis apostolorum successore, ab isto Christi D. N.

fact in his polemical writings against the Calvinists Jansenius defended the Pope's authority and infallibility, and he was attacked by them for doing so.[1] But we may well ask whether, for all that, Jansenius would not have countered a papal condemnation of his opinions with the same subterfuges as those used by his Baianist teachers and, later on, by his own followers. In his work he discusses the condemnation of Baius by Rome, and endeavours to evade it himself. The great Doctor of the Church, St. Augustine, he writes, has never been condemned by Rome; hence the condemnation of Baius must be explained so as to leave the teaching of Augustine untouched. In this way Augustine, as understood by Jansenius, is substituted for the Church's magisterium; Augustine is decisive, not Rome's definitions. Jansenius was well aware that his work would meet with opposition, in fact he expressed his great distrust of Rome in this respect.[2] One peculiarity of the *Augustinus*

vicario, ab isto Ecclesiae christianae universae capite, moderatore, Pontifice praescriptum fuerit, hoc teneo, quidquid improbatum, improbo, damnatum damno, anathematizatum anathematizo" (tom. II., lib. proem. cap. 29, p. 26). Similarly in the *Epilogus*, tom. III., p. 443. It is therefore of little consequence whether the declaration to this effect contained in the so-called "Testamentum", dictated half an hour before his death, and printed at the beginning of Vol. I., is an interpolation as VANDENPEEREBOOM, CAUCHIE, and DE MEYER (*cf.* the latter's note, p. 16), think, or whether it is not, as CALLEWAERT and NOLS, pp. 202–224 opine. A manuscript of the Anima Library, Rome (*Cod. Preuck.*, C. 43, pp. 385–390) preserves a draft of a letter in which Jansenius intended to dedicate his *Augustinus* to the Pope. Here we read, towards the end: "Quidquid in hoc perplexo disputationum labyrintho sensimus, diximus, scripsimus, . . . ad Sanctitatis Tuae pedes affero, probans improbans, figens refigens quidquid probandum aut improbandum vox apostolica mihi intonuerit."

1 The titles of two controversial pamphlets against him in Yves de la Brière in *Recherches*, VI. (1916), 271.

2 "De croire, qu'il sera facile de faire passer mon ouvrage aux juges, cela peut difficilement tomber en mon esprit, quelques dispositions qu'il puisse y avoir de delà, sachant les extravagances qu'il y a, et les oppositions des esprits (letter of March 25, 1635, in RAPIN, 358). A. Schill thus words his opinion: "Jansenius

which acquired considerable importance in the sequel, is the author's hatred of the theologians of the Jesuit Order, whose views he combats as Pelagian or semi-Pelagian.[1] Herein lies the reason why Jansenism increasingly developed into a struggle against the Society of Jesus.

It would seem that Jansenius had at first intended to have his book secretly printed at the episcopal palace of Ypres,[2] but only on his death-bed did he take a decisive step when, through his chaplain, he entrusted the publication to his friends Libertus Fromondus and Henry Calenus.[3] The matter was in the right hands. As Dean of St. Peter's, Fromondus was the outstanding professor at the University of Louvain, whilst Archdeacon Calenus completely dominated the ignorant Archbishop of Mechlin, Jacob Boonen,[4] to whose diocese Louvain belonged. When permission to print was asked for by Fromondus, the Syndic of the University, Pontan, could not refuse, and after that a publisher was soon found in Louvain.

Though the printing was carried out with the utmost secrecy, the most diverse rumours percolated through to the public. The Jesuits, having got hold of a few sheets,[5] complained to the papal internuncio Paul Richard Stravius, Archdeacon of

was too learned and too shrewd to ignore the opposition in which his doctrine stood to that which the Holy See had enunciated in condemning Baius; Jansenius was too full of hatred of scholasticism in general and Jesuit theology in particular, not to look for every loophole; finally, "Jansenius' intellectual pride and conceit were such that he cherished the hope that, under the name of St. Augustine, he would be able to steer the theologians of his day in a different direction." (*Hist. Jahrbuch*, 1894, 217 *seq.*).

[1] In the opinion of Rapin he wrote not so much a history of the Pelagians as a satire against the Jesuits. DE MEYER, 87, note.

[2] RAPIN, 357.

[3] See JANSENIUS' *Testament* at the beginning of his *Augustinus*.

[4] "(Fromondus et Calenus), a quorum consilio (archiepiscopus) totus pendet." Thus the Jesuit Judoci, July 6, 1641, Angelica Library, Rome, S. 3, 1.

[5] DE MEYER, 87; GERBERON, I., 7 *seq.*; RAPIN, 415 *seq.*

Cambrai and Arras. However it was impossible thus early to realize all the consequences that were to follow from the publication of the new work. Paul V. had forbidden the publication of any book treating of grace and the freedom of the will. Basing himself on this prohibition, Stravius requested the Rector of the University to have the printing of the book stopped pending a further papal decision, and he reported in this sense to Rome.[1] However Stravius himself was not sure whether the University would take action against Jansenius, one of its Doctors and Professors. Moreover Paul V.'s ordinance had been repeatedly contravened with a number of publications which had raised no protest. He thought it unlikely that the Jesuits would keep silence in face of the new book's fierce attacks against them.[2] Accordingly he requested the Council of Brabant to lend the assistance of the civil officials and demanded from Rome a special condemnation of Jansenius' work, of which he forwarded a few sheets.[3] Thereupon the Pope decided that Stravius should prevent the printing of the book and draw the publisher's attention to the fact that the money spent on a prohibited book was money thrown away. The decree for which he had prayed was dispatched to the internuncio[4] who forwarded it to all the Bishops and heads of Orders as well as to the Universities of Louvain and Douai.[5]

Urban VIII.'s decree is dated July 19th, 1640. However, it was too late. The book had been hurried through the press

[1] *Nunziat. di Fiandra*, tom. 25, Papal Secret Archives.

[2] *" Siccome dubito che la sudetta Università sara per moversi per la publicazione e difesa del detto libro, essendo l'autore di quello stato dottore e lettore dell'istessa Università, cosi prevedo che quei della Compagnia di Jesu non patiranno che la loro opinione e dottrina venghi con tanta passione e animosità dal suddetto autore censurata e riprovata." *Nunziat. di Fiandra, loc. cit.*

[3] *June 16, 1640, Angelica Library, Rome, S. 3, 1.

[4] *Decision recorded on the back of Stravius' report of June 16, 1640, *Nunziat. di Fiandra, loc. cit.*

[5] Stravius' *report to Rome, August 18, 1640, *ibid.*

with feverish haste; on July 14th Stravius reported to Rome that it had appeared [1] and that the Dutch Calvinists had ordered a large number of copies. He would forward the bulky work to Rome through trade channels but meanwhile he enclosed Calenus' scandalous approbation.[2] In Rome it was decided to submit the *Augustinus* to the judgment of the Inquisition as soon as it came to hand.[3]

Stravius was right when he did not expect the Louvain professors to take action against Jansenius. The answer of the theological Faculty to the papal prohibition was that it had no knowledge of the book nor of its teaching; that Paul V.'s decree against all writings on grace had not been communicated to it; in any case it had not understood it to be generally binding, seeing that even since its publication many books on the forbidden topic had appeared in Flanders, France and Germany; hence the Faculty was of opinion that it could absolve both the author and the publishers from any disobedience. As for the printer, the Faculty had no jurisdiction whatever over him; hence, all it had been able to do was to request the Rector of the University to forbid the sale of the book, but before the prohibition was carried into effect it would be necessary to hear the publisher who had already lodged a protest.[4]

In a plenary assembly the University declared its readiness to obey, but[5] at the same time it expressed the opinion that on further reflection the Pope himself would no doubt refrain from inflicting on so deserving a man as Jansenius the stain of a condemnation. As for Paul V.'s decree, writings on grace had been published since and some of them had even been dedicated

[1] With the approbation of Calenus and Pontan, and with the privilege of the Council of Brabant, dated April 8, 1639, and the Emperor, dated February 13, 1640.

[2] *Angelica Library, Rome, S. 3, 1.

[3] *Remark on the back of the report of July 14, 1640, *ibid.*

[4] *Reply of September 1, 1640, sent to Rome by Stravius, September 8, *ibid.*

[5] *Reply of September 13, 1640, sent to Rome by Stravius on September 15, *ibid.*

to the papal Legate. Three representatives of the University would further discuss the matter with the internuncio.[1]

In view of this reply Rome decided on the suppression of the *Augustinus* and all writings affected by the decree of Paul V.[2] To be binding, papal decrees needed only to be published in Rome. The prohibition of books on the basis of Paul V.'s decree, which had been issued solely in order to prevent tiresome disputes, implied no stain on the character of the author of the writings in question.[3] Notwithstanding this explanation, the University refused to submit to the prohibition. Its representative had another interview with Stravius and, at the latter's request, stated its views also in writing.[4] They were to the effect that it was not possible to carry out the papal command since nearly every theological book discussed the relation between grace and freedom. It was likewise useless, for Jansenius' work was in everyone's hands and had already been reprinted in Paris. Hence they begged the internuncio to offer to the Pope the University's excuses and to further a book which had received the encomiums of the illustrious University of Paris. Even the opponents, on their own admission, would have raised no objection if Jansenius had not attacked them by name. Thus there was nothing to be got from the University. For the time being Rome did no more than maintain its prohibition,[5] although the Cologne nuncio, Chigi, had drawn attention to the diffusion of the book in the Rhineland and had asked what line of conduct he should adopt.[6] He was told to discuss the matter with Stravius and to act in concert with him.[7]

Meanwhile *Augustinus* made its way through Europe. The Paris reimpression of 1641 had appeared with the approval

[1] *Ibid.*

[2] *Ibid.*, remark on the back of the document.

[3] *Stravius to the University, November 19, 1640, *ibid.*

[4] *January 24, 1641, *ibid.*

[5] *Rescript of February 27, 1641, *ibid.*

[6] *October 21, 1640, *ibid.*

[7] *Remark on the back of the document, *ibid.*

of six Sorbonnists,[1] and as early as 1643 the bulky work was reprinted at Rouen. St. Cyran bestowed the highest praise on it: after the Apostle Paul and St. Augustine, Jansenius was the third who had spoken "most divinely" of grace, and produced "*the* book of devotion of these latter days".[2] In Flanders, the Archbishop of Mechlin, the Bishops of Ghent and Tournai, and the Louvain professors Pontan, Sinnich, Paludan and Van Werm, gave it their support; many priests, both secular and regular, among the latter especially the Oratorians, were its warmest supporters.[3] The Dutch Calvinists gave it high praise. The Calvinist preacher Gilbert Voit, who had at one time opposed Jansenius, extolled the book in the pulpit, whilst another preacher undertook a Dutch translation,[4] seeing that nothing was better calculated to strengthen the Calvinist people in their faith than this book. Hugo Grotius no longer doubted the possibility of uniting Calvinists and Catholics if the teaching of *Augustinus* was likewise that of the Pope. The Calvinist pastor of Leerdam, Jansenius' birth-place, wrote that he thanked God that the late Bishop of Ypres had ended by being converted and had accepted the teaching which he himself expounded in the pulpit of Leerdam.[5]

Through the Jesuit Bivero who was preacher at the Court of the Cardinal-Infante, and through the Abbé de Mourgues who was with Marie de Medici at Brussels, the Fathers of the Society had obtained the prohibition of *Augustinus* from the Lieutenant and his council. However, whilst the new teaching spread ever more and more, Paul V.'s prohibition

[1] De Meyer, 89.

[2] *Ibid.*, 88.

[3] Rapin, 426.

[4] The translation was actually published at the Hague "per servizio della plebe e particolarmente delle donne." *Stravius, September 14, 1641, *loc. cit.*

[5] *Letter to the brother of Jansenius, February 13, 1641; it is also in *Cod. Barb.* 3150, fol. 242 of the Vatican Library. *Cf.* Rapin, 424.

seemed to make it impossible for loyal Catholics to oppose it. In the end some Jesuits of Louvain judged that, in the circumstances, it was lawful not only to hold a public disputation in order to refute Jansenius and his bitter attacks on their Order, but even to bring to the notice of the general public, by means of the press, the propositions in dispute. Stravius tried to dissuade them but he was told that such disputations had not been forbidden by Paul V.[1]

The disputation did take place[2] and the list of theses became a fairly large volume which not only stated the Jesuit teaching on the subject in brief propositions, supported by references to dogmatic sources, but likewise, in the same terse fashion, the views of Jansenius, which it pilloried by showing how they were in contradiction with the Council of Trent whilst they agreed with the condemned proposition of Baius and Calvin.[3] With these Louvain theses the ice was broken: within three months both sides published a whole series of polemical writings.[4] With a view to weakening the impression created by the disputation, the opponents organized a solemn funeral service for Jansenius. In the panegyric pronounced on the occasion not only was the deceased extolled to the sky, but

[1] *Stravius*, April 6, 1641, Angelica Library, Rome, S. 3, 1. Vincent de Paul was of opinion, at a later date, that the prohibitions of Clement VIII. and Paul V. only concerned points which the Church had not defined, and if Jansenius attacked, it was " du droit naturel de défendre l'Eglise et de soutenir les censures fulminées contre ". Letter to Dehorgny, June 25, 1648, in Coste, III., 327.

[2] Rapin, 432; Hermant, I., 137.

[3] The full title is in Sommervogel, *Bibliothèque*, s.v. " Derkennis " and " Jonghe ", II., 1942, IV., 815; contents in De Meyer, 117–120. That the celebrated " five propositions " were already then found in Jansenius' work is shown by Yves de La Brière in *Recherches*, I. (1910), 497–9.

[4] Title in Sommervogel, s.v. " Bivero " and " Derkennis ", I., 1526, nos. 13–15, II., 1942, nos. 11–13. For the *writings see a *letter of Bollandus of July 5, 1641, *Cod. Barb.*, 3150, f. 210, Vatican Library.

a virulent attack was also made on the Jesuits.[1] The Bishop of Ghent described the Jesuit theses as so many calumnies.

In France *Augustinus* was naturally hailed with joy by the friends of St. Cyran. Nevertheless, whilst their master was a prisoner of Richelieu, they provisionally contented themselves with reprinting *Augustinus* first in Paris, in 1641, and subsequently at Rouen in 1643. They even sought to increase its effectiveness by adding some of the writings of the Louvain Franciscan Conrius and by publishing anew the condemnation by the University of Louvain in 1587 of the Jesuit Lessius.[2] All this so complicated the situation that the Jesuits in particular deemed a decision by the Holy See an urgent necessity. The Court preacher of Cardinal Cueva pressed the Infante in that sense and it was all the easier to prejudice Cardinal Richelieu against the author of *Mars Gallicus*, as the sharp eye of the famous statesman quickly saw the danger that lurked in the new teaching. He was anxious for the Sorbonne to condemn *Augustinus*, but its Doctors judged it more prudent to do nothing in the matter since, in their view, the objections to the book were insignificant.[3] Accordingly Richelieu waited for a condemnation by Rome. There was nothing objectionable in the Jesuit theses, he told the French nuncio Grimaldi in his camp before Hesdin, whereas *Augustinus* was full of mischievous and heretical statements. A condemnation seemed necessary ; it was a dangerous thing to have allowed the affair to drift so long ; prompt action was imperative.[4]

However a prompt and, above all, a decisive measure was scarcely to be expected from Rome. The seventy-three years

[1] **Stravius*, May 11, 1641 : "onorevole e gloriosa per il Jansenio, e mordace e piccante contro la reputatione degli Gesuiti." Angelica Library, Rome, S. 3, 1.

[2] De Meyer, 113.

[3] Grimaldi, May 9, 1641, in *De Meyer*, 125.

[4] **Grimaldi*, June 20, 1641 : "che l'Augustinus e pieno di cattive proposizioni et eretiche, e che gli pare si debba dannare . . . ; che il lasciarlo cosi lungamente senza farvi provisione, era un dargliela vinta." Angelica Library, Rome, S. 3, 1.

old Urban VIII. was infirm and his Secretary of State Barberini, did not wish to trouble the frail old man with complicated business, least of all to drag him into a dispute on the doctrine of grace, the difficulties of which had been so painfully experienced under Clement VIII. Accordingly Barberini decided to enjoin silence on both parties, without siding with either of them, and thus to stifle the quarrel. Instructions in this sense were sent to the nuncios of Cologne and Paris, Chigi and Grimaldi, to the internuncio Stravius and to the Archbishop of Mechlin.[1] All writings by both parties were to be confiscated, and the Universities of Louvain and Douai, as well as the heads of Orders, were to be strictly forbidden to publish anything on the subject, so that " this conflagration, which was so disastrous for the whole of Christendom might at last be put out." [2] Stravius in particular was to do his utmost to this end with the help of Chigi, whilst Grimaldi endeavoured to win over Richelieu to the views of the Roman Court. To Grimaldi Barberini wrote[3] asking him to use his influence with the most eminent theologians of Paris, with a view to preventing the outbreak of a paper war in that city.

The Jesuit Provincial, Judoci, was quite ready to agree to a truce. More than once the nuncio Chigi had pointed out to him that this " scratching of pens " was a mistake, for it only helped to fan the flame ; it would have been far better to wait for the remedies prescribed by the Holy See and to practise a little patience.[4] Judoci had judged it necessary to excuse himself in a letter to Cardinal Barberini ; he explained that grace was scarcely mentioned in the theses and that the points which had occasioned such prolonged discussions under Clement VIII. as well as Paul V.'s prohibition, had not even been mentioned.[5] When, therefore, the Bishop of Antwerp,

[1] *To Chigi, April 25, 1641, *to Stravius, May 22 and June 12, 1641, *ibid.*

[2] *To Stravius, June 21, 1641, *ibid.*

[3] *May 9, 1641, in De Meyer, 124.

[4] *Chigi to Rome, May 12, 1641, Angelica Library, Rome, S. 3, 1.

[5] *Letter of June 7, 1641, *ibid.*

acting under instruction of Jacob Boonen, requested Judoci to lay down his arms, the latter agreed at once, with the one exception of the second edition of the theses of Louvain which was about to appear.[1]

However before a week was out Fromondus and Calenus published a pamphlet in which they challenged the Jesuits of Louvain. The introduction sounded pacific enough: they prayed that a stop be put both to writings and scandals. But after that they went on to the attack. With a list of fifty passages from the publications of their opponents they sought to prove that the Jesuits were guilty of calumny when they accused Jansenius of renewing the errors of Baius, of distorting the teaching of the Jesuits, of opposing the Council of Trent and agreeing with Luther and Calvin. They concluded with a challenge to a clean fight with an enemy who would await his opponent with his feet firmly planted in the arena: "You are bound to show that Jansenius misinterprets St. Augustine; but know that all your movements are watched by many eyes, especially by those of the students of the school of St. Thomas, in Belgium, Germany, France, Italy and Spain".[2] The Louvain Jesuits replied[3] that since Jansenius had begun the quarrel he had made a reply necessary. With regard to the Thomists, the Jansenists had indeed sought to shelter behind them, but the dispute in Rome between Jesuits and Dominicans had nothing to do with Jansenius since theologians of both Orders were in agreement on the most important points, such as the freedom of the will, Christ's death for all, and sufficient grace: it was not a question of Jansenius' person but of his teaching.

Such writings presaged ill for the discussions which took place on June 21st, 1641, between Archbishop Boonen and the

[1] *Explanation of JUDOCI, June 10, 1641, *Cod. Barb.*, 3150 f., 244. Vatican Library. *Cf. ibid.*, *BOLLANDUS, July 5, 1641, and JUDOCI, June 22, 26, 28, to the General of the Order.

[2] *Epistola Liberti Fromondi et Henrici Caleni ad PP. Societatis*, Lovanii, Junii 16, 1641.

[3] Title of the letter (2 folio sheets) in SOMMERVOGEL, II., 1942, n. 12.

Jesuit Provincial Judoci. The provincial declared his willingness to impose silence on his subjects but demanded a corresponding promise in writing from the other side. Boonen replied that an oral promise must suffice; however, there is no evidence that it was given: in any case it was not kept. A young Doctor of the name of Sinnich, who had compiled the index to Jansenius' work[1] and who was in the habit of taking advantage of his lectures to attack the Jesuits, published on the very next day a pamphlet in which he attempted to show the agreement between "Augustine of Hippo" and "Augustine of Ypres" concerning God's universal salvific will. The Jesuits remonstrated and after some delay the Archbishop also forbade the booklet which, however, like all the other Jansenist polemical writings, continued to be sold everywhere, even in England, Denmark and Sweden. The time was not far off, Judoci declared,[2] when it would be necessary to oppose to the Jansenists not simple theses but whole volumes.

It became more and more evident that no decisive step could be expected from Archbishop Boonen. At the conference of June 21st he had told Judoci that he had been on terms of friendship with Jansenius, yet of his teaching or his book he had heard nothing during his life-time, nor had he read the book and its refutations; Stravius reported[3] that the Archbishop had strong leanings towards the opinions of his deceased friend, so that he did not trust him. Boonen promised indeed to prevent the publication of further writings, but at the same time mentioned the necessity of the royal *placet*; moreover Calenus was a constant guest at his table. Accordingly Stravius was instructed to admonish the procrastinator[4] whilst Boonen himself received direct instructions to give effect to the Roman decrees. However, Stravius reports to Rome,[5] they say here that Paul V.'s decree was never published in Belgium and could only be enforced with the royal *placet*. The Archbishop

[1] *Stravius, Dec. 5, 1641, Angelica Library, Rome, S. 3, 1.

[2] *Letter of June 28, 1641, Angelica Library, Rome, *loc. cit.*

[3] *June 29, 1641, *ibid.*

[4] *July 11, 1641, *ibid.*

[5] *July 13, 1641, *ibid.*

showed great coldness and indecision so that no salutary remedy to the disputes was to be expected from him. He never ceased, Judoci wrote again,[1] to recommend Jansenius' book; in his opinion it contained nothing contrary to sound doctrine and the Pope's only weapon against it was Paul V.'s prohibition, which was not operative in the Netherlands. By reason of his leaning towards the Jansenist party, which managed him through Calenus, Boonen had taught already four years earlier that perfect contrition was necessary for the reception of the Sacrament of Penance,[2] but owing to the protests of his clergy he had been obliged to cancel his ordinances on the subject. Nor were the Archbishop's own letters to Rome calculated to create a more favourable impression of his zeal. After conferring with men of mark, Boonen wrote to Cardinal Barberini,[3] he thought it best to do nothing until he had consulted the Cardinal-Infante who happened to be away just then. A week later all he had to say about his conversation with the Infante[4] was that the latter had put off answering him for a few days; that for the rest he was seeing to it that no new books appeared and that the old ones were not sold.

In these circumstances help could only come from Rome. On June 22nd, 1641, Judoci wrote[5] that the professors of the University appeared to be paralysed and contented themselves with rejecting Jansenius' teaching before their pupils whilst the opponents strove, with word and pen, to enhance his prestige with the Abbés and the parish priests. If it was too early for a sentence against *Augustinus*, the Pope should at least threaten to carry out the Bull against Baius. A little later Judoci gave it as his opinion[6] that the Holy See would not obtain its object unless it condemned anew

[1] *July 6, 1641, *ibid.*

[2] By decree of March 26, 1637, which Judoci encloses, *ibid.*

[3] *July 13, 1641, *ibid.*

[4] *July 20, 1641, *ibid.*

[5] *To the General of the Order, *Cod. Barb.*, 3150, 236, Vatican Library.

[6] *July 6, 1641, Angelica Library, Rome, S. 3, 1.

certain propositions already reprobated by two Popes. If this was done all disputes would soon terminate, for no Fleming had ever resisted a papal decision, and if at the University anyone presumed were it only to murmur, the greater and better part would rise in opposition, for these men really disapproved of Jansenius' teaching.[1] In the opinion of Bollandus,[2] Jansenism found favour with all the enemies of the Jesuits, hence, since men of evil disposition and conduct always predominate, Jansenius found many supporters; he also said that a celebrated French writer had asserted that Jansenius' writings did more harm to the Church than those of Calvin, with which they were in full agreement and that a certain Bishop had said that Jansenius would destroy more souls than the present war would kill bodies if "His Holiness did not provide a strong remedy and censure Jansenius' teaching as it deserves". Stravius' opinion [3] was to the effect that the Holy See should forbid all polemical writings on the Jansenist question but without mentioning the prohibition of Paul V. Chigi, who had been assured by two Dominicans that the *Augustinus* was nothing but one long satire against the Jesuits and that it was at variance with St. Thomas and the Thomists, demanded the condemnation of the book.[4] Richelieu, too, not only repeated to Grimaldi his previously expressed opinion, but likewise informed Rome, in unmistakable terms, of his wish for "expeditious action".[5]

Discussions on the *Augustinus* had been in progress in Rome for a considerable time. From the first there was

[1] *"Ea namque Belgii catholici erga Sedem Apostolicam est reverentia, ut nemo unquam eius decretis, quae doctrinam concernunt, contradixerit, aut si quis hic in Universitate vel hiscere auderet, sanior et maior Universitatis pars, quae Iansenii doctrinam improbat, non tantum illi adversaretur, sed et de illo beneficiis officiisque exuendo strenue ageret." *Ibid.*

[2] *July 5, 1641, *Cod. Barb.*, 3150, f. 210. *loc. cit.*; also in his *letter of August 2, 1641, *ibid.*, f. 208.

[3] *Letter of July 13, 1641, Angelica Library, Rome, S. 3, 1.

[4] DE MEYER, 123.

[5] *Grimaldi, July 21, 1641, Angelica Library, Rome, S. 3, 1.

no doubt that the book could be forbidden, without lengthy examination, on the basis of Paul V.'s prohibition ; but it was necessary to sift the teaching of the voluminous work which teemed with quotations from St. Augustine, the exact meaning of which had to be ascertained : for these reasons final sentence must needs be delayed.[1] Yet something had to be done, and Boonen's lukewarmness and Richelieu's pressure [2] led to a provisional measure. On August 7th, 1641, the Inquisition issued a decree renewing Paul V.'s prohibition and fixing penalties for its transgression. The decree then expressly condemns, because they had been published without papal leave, works of which it gives the titles, viz. Jansenius' *Augustinus*, the theses of the Louvain Jesuits and all writings for or against the Jesuits which had appeared since that time.[3]

This long overdue decree appeared at an inauspicious moment in so far as the Netherlands were concerned. The Lieutenant had died at the beginning of May and the management of affairs lay completely in the hands of the Privy Council of State which was dominated by President Rooze and Archbishop Boonen, both of whom favoured Jansenism. On September 1st, the Council of Brabant forbade publication of the Roman decree, whilst the University of Louvain declared, on September 28th, that, of course, the Pope must be obeyed

[1] Opinion of the Consultor Rancati addressed to the Assessor of the Holy Office, Albizzi, February 23, 1641, in De Meyer, 227.

[2] According to Albizzi, Boone, who out of friendship for Calenus, carried out badly the papal instructions, was the cause of the decree. (De Meyer, 126.) Gerberon (I., 29 *seqq.*) made Cardinal Cueva responsible for it.

[3] *Bull.*, XV., 99. *Cf.* Yves de la Brière in *Recherches*, I. (1910), 497 *seqq.* On the condemnation of the Jesuit theses, Bollandus says (*Letter of July 5, 1641, *Cod. Barb.*, 3150, f. 210 *seq.*, Vatican Library) : " De thesibus etsi abesse a culpa existimamus, parum tamen solliciti sumus ; telum, quo confixus hostis est, cum eo sepeliatur licet ". For the rest, only the points of conflict between Catholics and heretics were discussed and not anything under dispute among Catholics.

but that before publishing the Roman ordinance it was necessary to come to an understanding with the Archbishop, the Council of State, and the Council of Brabant. This the University did after its own fashion by demanding from the Council of Brabant the annulment of the papal decree and the recall of the publication made by the nuncio.[1] At Louvain itself the decree had been torn from the doors of the church of St. Peter; since the adversaries of Jansenius had also been condemned, it was argued, there could be no question of a dogmatic definition but merely of a police measure, and that was the King's business—papal encroachments must not be tolerated—moreover the Roman Inquisition and the ordinances were not recognized in the Netherlands.[2] In consequence of these remonstrances the Council of State decided to seek further information; meanwhile the Jansenist writings were disseminated as if Rome had never prohibited them, in fact at that very time Fromondus published a book on the freedom of the will, quite in the spirit of Jansenism, and dedicated it, as if he wanted to insult him, to Cardinal Barberini. All this time the Council of State did not move a finger. When a nephew of Jansenius presented a petition in favour of his uncle,[3] he was told that it would be necessary to consult first the Bishops of the country and the University of Louvain. To the petition were appended the approbations which one Bishop and fifty-four priests, secular and regular,[4] had given to Jansenius' work. When, by order of Stravius,

[1] *Stravius, October 12, 1641, Angelica Library, Rome, S. 3, 1. The Oratorians also, "molto affezionati al Jansenio," had appealed to the *conseil*; *ibid.*

[2] *Letter of Bollandus, October 6, 1641, *Cod. Barb.*, 3150, f. 214, Vatican Library.

[3] Contents in GERBERON, I., 38 *seqq.*

[4] e.g. Philip Rovenius, Archbishop of Philippi, 6 Sorbonnists, 9 Dutch mission priests, 8 from Louvain, 3 Belgian priests, 3 Benedictines, 5 Praemonstratensians, 2 Augustinians, 5 Dominicans, 4 Carmelites, 6 Franciscans, 1 Carthusian, 2 Oratorians. For Rovenius (Van Roveen), *cf.* C. VAN AKEN in *Études Relig.*, 1873, I., 161, 343.

the decree of the Inquisition was posted up at the Irish College at Louvain, both the Rector and the internuncio were threatened with legal action. Whilst Louvain proved recalcitrant, the University of Douai submitted and published the ordinance of the Inquisition ; consequently on December 5th, the Pope directed that Douai should be praised and Louvain reprimanded.[1]

In France also a decree of the Inquisition, the very name of which was odious this side of the Alps, was bound to create uneasiness. None the less the Government suffered it to be published since there was question of a dogmatic definition and Rome's command to make it known was not against " the liberties of the Gallican Church ". Moreover, the decree could not excite much attention since, so far, little notice had been taken of the *Augustinus* in France.[2]

As early as August 3rd, 1641, the Assessor of the Holy Office, Francesco Albizzi, wrote to the nuncio Chigi that the decree of August 1st was no more than a provisional measure.[3] In the Netherlands it had proved ineffective, hence the chief opponents of Jansenism, the Jesuits, pressed for a formal condemnation. They found supporters for their plan in the University of Louvain itself, in the persons of the senior of the theological Faculty, John Schinchel and Professors Christian Beusecom and William ab Angelis. Towards the end of 1641 these three men sent to Rome a full account of the agitation.[4] Jansenius, they pointed out, had had to take the University oath against the teaching of Baius on three or four occasions, and both in his lectures and in his conversation he had betrayed no sign that he favoured it, but his book was in contradiction with his oath, hence they could no longer remain silent since novelties were being expounded as Catholic teaching and those who maintained them were becoming increasingly violent and had already attracted some of the

[1] *Stravius, November 9, 1641, and remark of December 5, after this report, Angelica Library, Rome, S. 3, 1.

[2] *Grimaldi, February 15, 1642, in DE MEYER, 226.

[3] *Ibid.*, 127.

[4] **Cod. Preuck.*, f. 505–9, Anima Library, Rome.

younger members of the Faculty. There follows a list of propositions from the *Augustinus* to which are opposed ten Tridentime decrees to the contrary and the Bull against Baius. A formal condemnation of these propositions was indispensable since the decree already issued by the Inquisition seemingly put the opinions of both parties on the same footing, and, as it was, its publication had been put off. It was to be hoped that the younger members of the Faculty, who had been misled by a false interpretation of St. Augustine, would submit to a fresh condemnation of propositions already condemned by Pius V. and Gregory XIII.

Copies of this memorandum were secretly distributed by the Jesuits with the consequence that nine other University professors in their turn sent a violent counter-petition to Rome.[1] Schinchel and his associates, their memorandum states, were enemies of Jansenius though they were but very inadequately acquainted with his work. Envy and a lying spirit prompted the assertion that Jansenius contradicted the Council of Trent, the Popes and the theologians; as a matter of fact he followed in all things Augustine and Thomas Acquinas, and in particular his explanation of the Council of Trent's teaching on grace was based on Augustine and the Thomists, whilst he interpreted the Bull against Baius in the same sense as Bellarmine, Vasquez, and others. It was quite wrong to accuse Jansenius of having entertained the hope that he would be able to force the Apostolic See to revoke the condemnation of Baius; all he had done was that he had not despaired of obtaining something else, namely a statement as to what must be thought of every one of the condemned propositions of Baius, for so far all that one could gather from the Bull of Pius V. was that each of the condemned propositions fell under one or more of the censures enumerated at the end of that document. The memorandum bears the signatures of Fromond, Van Werm, Pontan, Sinnich, three Augustinians and three Dominicans. Meanwhile the examination of the *Augustinus* by the Roman Inquisition progressed but slowly. It was necessary for several persons

[1] *March 6, 1642, *ibid.*, f. 521 *seqq.*

to read the huge work in its entirety since the intention was to pronounce judgment on the book as a whole. Moreover Rome was never in a hurry when there was question of a Bishop otherwise of good repute.[1] Besides this it was also necessary, in the draft of the Bull, to consider the Dominicans, many of whom feared lest the condemnation of certain Jansenist propositions should create prejudice against their own teaching on grace.[2] Nor was the insistence of the Louvain Jesuits favourable to the progress of the affair; according to what some of their Roman colleagues wrote to them, they gave the impression of being far more concerned about their Order than about the welfare of the Church.[3] When the Bull was ready at last, there was some hesitation to make use of so drastic a remedy and to touch so sensibly the honour of a Bishop who had died at peace with the Church. It was the situation at Louvain that finally decided the publication of the Bull. On March 21st, 1642, the members of the University had declared that the decree of the Inquisition of August 1st of the preceding year must indeed be received, but that it was no concern of theirs but rather that of the Archbishop or the internuncio.[4] On the following day the Council of Brabant forbade anew the publication of the decree, whereupon the professors informed the Pope[5] that they had received the decree but were unable to publish it. Explanations like these did not remove the distrust which prevailed in Rome. On June 18th, the Roman Inquisition[6] decided that the patron of the Louvain professors, the nuncio of Cologne, should be informed that in consequence of his report to the effect that the University was ready to submit to the decree

[1] De Lugo to the Jesuit Rector at Louvain, April 25, 1642, in De Meyer, 128, note 4.

[2] De Meyer, 129, note 1.

[3] "Credi autem non potest, quantum id (so much talk about the Jesuits in the Louvain discussions) causae obsit." *Ph. Alegambe to Judoci*, April 19, 1642, *ibid.*, 128.

[4] Gerberon, I., 50.

[5] April 3, 1642, *ibid.*

[6] *Angelica Library, Rome, S. 3, 1.

of Paul V., the Bull containing the dogmatic definitions against Jansenius had not yet been published. In view, however, of the fact that the followers of Jansenius continued to write in his defence, and the University allowed the *Augustinus* to be publicly sold, the Holy See would be forced to lay aside all consideration for Jansenius' honour and publish the Bull. This threat, based on the same motive, was renewed on July 1st.[1] However, not only did these warnings remain ineffectual, but the Jansenists endeavoured to ruin their opponent Schinchel by accusing him to Chigi and Antonio Bichi, Abbot of S. Anastasia, who had succeeded Stravius as internuncio at Brussels and to obtain the postponement of the condemnation.[2] It was with difficulty that Schinchel prevented the Jansenists from securing a majority in the special theological Faculty which consisted of only eight Doctors. In 1641, Sinnich, against all law, forced his way into the special Faculty[3] so that when a vacancy created by death had to be filled, four Jansenists faced three old Doctors. However, Schinchel succeeded in prejudicing against Jansenius[4] the very man whom the majority had agreed to elect, viz. Jacob Pontan, whose favourable judgment had largely contributed to the *Augustinus* being printed. Schinchel now pressed Rome to excommunicate Sinnich in view of his having published a book in favour of Jansenius. Rome refused because there was some doubt about his being the author, but promised to forward before long the Bull against Jansenius which was about to be sent to the press.[5] But only on March 18th, 1643, was information received that the Bull was in the press.[6]

[1] *Ibid.*

[2] GERBERON, I., 52 *seq.*

[3] The Jesuit Cromm *to his Superior, October 10, 1641, *Cod. Barb.*, 3150, f. 215, Vatican Library.

[4] *Bichi, after the decision of the Inquisition of September 3, 1642, was commissioned to support Schinchel in the affair. Angelica Library, Rome, S. 3, 1.

[5] *Resolution of the Inquisition, November 26, 1642, *ibid.*

[6] *" esse sub typo et brevi exemplaria illius transmittentur," *ibid.*

Meanwhile controversy had grown more and more acute. After Richelieu's death the Jansenists were allowed a freer hand. The Jesuits, the nuncio wrote,[1] had had the boldness to qualify the teaching of the *Augustinus* as heretical, whilst others, both among the secular and the regular clergy, defended the book as agreeing with the true teaching of St. Augustine; the chancellor had forbidden all discussion on the subject both in the pulpit and in private. The nuncio drew the attention of the Archbishop of Paris to the decree of the Inquisition of August 1st, 1641, but was told that that ordinance only forbade the publication of books; besides, in the opinion of all theologians, the Congregation of the Inquisition had no orders to give in France. Thereupon the Congregation comforted the nuncio with the prospect of an early publication of the Bull against Jansenius.[2]

At last, on June 10th, 1643, the Inquisition ordered the Bull to be published in the Eternal City. This was done on the 19th. At the same time the nuncio Chigi was instructed to have the necessary number of copies printed in Cologne and to forward them to Bichi, who was to distribute them as directed by Chigi.[3]

The one feature of the Bull[4] which strikes the reader from the first is its reserved and cautious tone. It speaks first of all of Pius V.'s ordinance against Baius which it renews, of its confirmation by Gregory XIII., of Paul V.'s prohibition of all writings on grace which Urban VIII. had himself enforced anew, and lastly of Urban's decree of August 1st, 1641: "But since a careful reading of the *Augustinus* has shown that it contains and defends many propositions which our predecessors have condemned, to the great scandal of Catholics and disrespect for the authority of the Holy See," the above-mentioned papal decrees are confirmed anew and *Augustinus* is once more forbidden. The prohibition extends to some writings which had appeared after the

[1] *April 20, 1643, in De Meyer, 129 *seq.*

[2] *May 20, 1643, Angelica Library, Rome, S. 3, 1.

[3] *Ibid.*

[4] "In eminenti," *Bull.*, XV., 93 *seq.*

decree of August 1st in which, therefore, they could not have been included. Nowhere does the Bull expressly qualify the *Augustinus* as a heretical book, it only speaks of scandals and disputes which it seeks to remove and of the disobedience implied in the publication of both the *Augustinus* and its refutations. The Bull was drawn up by Francesco Albizzi, a lawyer who on the death of his wife had embraced the ecclesiastical state. He was at first employed as *Uditore* at the nunciatures of Naples and Madrid; in 1635 he became assessor of the Inquisition and in that capacity he composed many documents against the Jansenists by which he incurred their open hatred.[1] The restraint of the first Bull may probably be ascribed to the influence of Cardinal Barberini who was at all times averse to sharp measures.

Immediately after its publication the Bull was reprinted by Chigi at Cologne and by Bichi at Antwerp, but with unfortunate misprints. The original Bull was dated March 6th of the year of the Incarnation 1641. Now since the year of the Incarnation begins on March 25th, the computation from the day of the Incarnation is a whole year behind the computation now in use, hence March 6th, 1641—the date of the Bull—is March 6th, 1642 in our computation. Accordingly Chigi changed the date 1641 to 1642 in his reprint.[2] The Antwerp reprint avoided this mistake, but in a footnote it

[1] For Albizzi's work *De inconstantia in iure* see PASTOR: *Allgemeine Dekrete der römischen Inquisition*, Freiburg, 1912, 11 *seq.*

[2] Bichi had written to Albizzi, June 27, 1643: *" Ho ancora osservato in essa (bolla) un errore nella data a quale è da temere che li Janseniani attacheranno per mantenersi nella loro dichiarazione, et è che dice . . . 1641, che cosi sarebbe cinque mesi avanti che fosse dato fuora il primo decreto contro il Jansenio, e dal anno 19 del pontificato si vede che doveva dire anno 1642. Spero però che certo saranno conosciuti questi errori e che quando la mandaranno collo ordine di publicarla, sarà corretta " (Angelica Library, Rome, S. 3, 1). For proof that the Bull was printed by Chigi in Cologne, under instructions of the Inquisition dated June 10, 1643, and that 60 copies were sent to Bichi from there, see *Chigi, July 12 and *Bichi, July 18, 1643, Angelica Library, Rome, S. 3, 1.

was stated that the document had been printed in Rome, in the press of the Apostolic Camera which, as regards the reprint, was inaccurate. The Jesuits of Paris came to know of the Bull even before the nuncio and they allowed themselves to be carried away into publishing it both separately and together with the Louvain theses. This was an encroachment on the rights of the nuncio. And as if this were not enough, several copies lacked the attestation of the official publication of the Bull and in the list of prohibited writings, books were referred to which only became known in Rome after the publication of the Bull.[1] These mistakes were at once most skilfully exploited in an anonymous pamphlet[2] written for the purpose of proving that the Bull was a forgery. There we read that the statement as to the place where the Bull had been printed was false; false also was the date 1641 since the Bull condemned writings published in 1642; the date 1642 was equally false and was but an attempt to cover up the contradiction already noted; equally false was the indication of the official publication which was missing in earlier reprints; false also the date of publication, June 19th, since the Jesuits of Paris had the documents in their hands already on June 24th. The wide margin between the dates of drafting and publication also looked exceedingly suspicious. Moreover the Bull passed no judgment on the teaching of Jansenius, a circumstance which was intelligible enough, for the forgers would not dare to condemn it since that would have implied a condemnation of the teaching of St. Augustine. Moreover in this forgery the Pope was made to say: "From what we hear" the book of Jansenius contains some of the propositions of Baius; this showed that the Pope had no personal knowledge of things. For the rest many a proposition of Baius was capable of an orthodox interpretation, as even a number of Jesuit theologians conceded. After some further arguments the writer concludes that the Bull was a forgery of the Jesuits. They resented the fact that Rome had

[1] De Meyer, 131 *seq.*

[2] *Observations sur une bulle prétendue.* (Arnauld, *Œuvres*, XVI., 1–4.)

condemned some of their writings and in order to revenge themselves against the Holy See they now ascribed to it a Bull of this kind.

The author of the pamphlet was Antoine, brother of Angélique Arnauld, who from now onwards appears as the protagonist of the Jansenists. The latter openly refused to receive the Bull. Towards the end of August a second pamphlet by Arnauld appeared, again without author's name.[1] In it he stated that he had had information from Rome that by command of the Inquisition the *Augustinus* had been examined by eight theologians who had found nothing blameworthy in it ; at most the Bull could only be taken as a sketch of a decree of condemnation which the enemies of Jansenism intended to submit to the Pope. It condemned writings which were not known in Rome on March 6th, 1641, and not even after that date of the following year ; the document was therefore undoubtedly apocryphal. The Jansenists maintained this assertion, hence it made but little difference when, on the representations of the nuncio Grimaldi, the Roman Inquisition attested the genuineness of the Bull and instructed the nuncio on September 5th, 1643, to get it recognized. From the meeting of the Bishops in November of that year Grimaldi obtained nothing whatever ; only towards the end of the year did the Archbishop of Paris make up his mind to publish the Bull and to forbid any discussion of the doctrine of grace in sermons and catechetical instructions. All that the Sorbonne would agree to, on January 15th, 1644, was to inscribe the propositions condemned by the Bull in the registers of the Faculty and to forbid all public discussion of the subject until the Holy See should issue further decisions.[2]

Grimaldi could not, of course, accept such a decision, all the more so as he had secured a royal command ordering the Faculty to receive the Bull. Once more he reported to Rome to the effect that the strife in France was becoming increasingly embittered and that neither side took any notice of the

[1] *Secondes observations sur la fausse bulle* (*ibid.*, 5–9).

[2] De Meyer, 135 *seq.*

prescriptions of the Bull. A third pamphlet by Arnauld,[1] which contains a list of twenty-seven objections to the Bull, also stresses the fact that, notwithstanding every papal prohibition, the Jesuits on their part, had taken up their pens against the *Augustinus* and in one and the same publication they had given both the text of the Bull and the Louvain theses which the Bull condemned. However Grimaldi's insistence had to reckon with the opposition, even in Rome itself, of the delegates of the Louvain University who had arrived there at the beginning of 1644. As a matter of fact the Bull met with as much opposition in Flanders as in Paris. The Bishops and religious Superiors received it indeed, but when the Bishop of Namur published it, he was summoned before the Council because of the missing *placet*.[2] The Jansenist Sinnich was Rector of the University of Louvain, hence Bichi had sent the Bull not to him but to the Dean of the theological Faculty, Schinchel.[3] All the members of the special Faculty expressed their approval,[4] though three Jansenists made use of some curious expressions in doing so; thus Fromond received it with all the respect with which it could be accepted, and van Werm with the reservation "if it was not incomplete." On July 15th and 17th, publication took place before the Doctors and Licenciates; one Doctor offered opposition and one Licentiate first mentioned the word "forgery" on this occasion. On July 16th De Angelis read the Bull to the students. At this point Sinnich stepped in. On July 21st he summoned Schinchel and De Angelis before him and told them that the publication of the Bull was illegal. On the next

[1] *Difficultés sur la bulle qui porte deffense de lire le livre de Corn. Jansenius, etc.* (*Œuvres*, XVI., 10–21). The petty sophistry of the author, again unnamed, appears for example in no. 18: "The Pope is wont to call the Cardinals 'Sons', the Bishops, 'Brethren'. How could he call the Jesuits 'Fathers?' But in the so-called Bull the words occur: 'Theses *patrum* Societatis Iesu!'"

[2] *Bichi, August 14, 1643, Angelica Library, Rome, S. 3, 1.

[3] *Bichi, July 11, 1643, *ibid.*

[4] For what follows, *cf.* GERBERON, I., 70 *seqq.*

day this declaration was approved by a general meeting of the University. The two Professors had refused to accept as judge the party man Sinnich. Schinchel appealed from the sentence of the University to the internuncio. From the latter's judgment, after vain representations to Bichi, the University appealed to the Council of Brabant. That body declared that the nuncio had exceeded his authority since they alone were competent to deal with the matter.

The University now realized the necessity of justifying its conduct in Rome. This it did by casting doubts on the authenticity of the Bull. The reasons alleged are about the same as those adduced by Paris, viz. the long interval between the date of issue and publication of the document, the divergent dates in the various reprints, the erroneous indication of Rome as the place of printing. Lastly, reference was once more made to the famous comma in the Bull of Pius V., the *Comma Pianum* [1] which the Bull of Urban VIII. placed wrongly in the reprint of Pius V.'s Bull.

The Pope's answer came on October 24th, 1643, in three Briefs respectively addressed to the Governor of Belgium, Francis von Mello, to Archbishop Boonen, and to the University of Louvain itself.[2] The arguments by which the authenticity of the Bull had been attacked are described as futile, frivolous and impudent. In the letter to Mello the reason for the delay in the publication of the Bull is stated to have been a desire to safeguard the honour of Jansenius and to give his adherents time for reflection. The Archbishop was asked to proceed against the presumptuous professors, the Governor to help him, and the University to call to mind and to return to, its former loyalty to the Holy See. Even before these Briefs were drawn up, Sinnich and a young lawyer of the name of Paepe

[1] *Cf.* our account, Vol. XVII., 377, note 3.

[2] **Cod. Preuck.*, ff. 568 *seqq.*, printed in FONTAINE, 29 *seq.* On November 29, 1643, the Pope ordered Briefs to be sent to Bichi for the Archbishops of Mechlin and Cambrai, the Bishop of Antwerp, the Universities of Douai and Louvain, and to Francis von Mello. Whether Bichi made use of the Briefs cannot be ascertained from *Cod.*, S. 3, 1, of the Angelica Library, Rome.

set out for Rome, on September 22nd, 1643, as envoys of the University, in order to expostulate with the Pope. On October 7th the University imposed silence on both parties until the return of the delegates. This order furnished the desired handle against Schinchel, for the latter was just then collecting signatures for the Bull. The Brief of October 24th to the University was met with the usual subterfuges. The Faculties of Theology and Canon Law received it, but the lawyers, physicians and artists declared that before doing in like manner, they wished to have the opinion of the Archbishop and the Council of State. Now Archbishop Boonen and President Rooze advocated in the Council of State that a decree should be issued against the Bull, and when the Governor refused to comply with the suggestion, it was decided that nothing could be done in the matter without the King and that the Bull could not be executed without the royal *placet*.

Thereupon Schinchel made a direct appeal to Philip IV., begging his help against the abuse which prevented the execution of the Bull. He prayed the King to use his authority, for surely the monarch did not claim the right to judge papal prohibitions of books. Philip IV.'s confessor, the famous Dominican theologian Johannes a Sancto Thoma,[1] answered that the King certainly had no such pretension. However other letters had also come from Louvain, which stated that the Bull had been obtained by means of false information, and prayed the King to induce the Pope to submit the affair to a fresh and more thorough investigation ; such a request was not against right and equity but was in keeping with the practice of the royal tribunals in Belgium where no Apostolic Letter was carried into affect without the royal *placet*, and the King had asked the Governer for further information.[2]

Thus Schinchel's efforts in Madrid were in vain and in Louvain also his sympathizers seemed to be losing ground. The Jansenists insisted on the orthodoxy of Jansenius' teaching and its agreement with that of St. Augustine. As

[1] About him, see HURTER, *Nomenclator*, III., 915.

[2] *Letter of May 13, 1644, Angelica Library Rome, S. 3, 1

early as February 14th, 1644, a meeting of theologians took place at which the Jansenist party maintained this view. Schinchel and his followers had offered to demonstrate the contrary in the presence of a papal plenipotentiary; but they refused a discussion before the Jansenist Rector and left the room when it was decided to refuse the Bull.[1] Soon after the Sorbonne was severely taken to task by the Faculty of Louvain for its acceptance of the Bull. "The teaching of St. Augustine was at stake, it was rumoured, and the Jesuits were the common enemy whose aim it was to reduce all schools to the wretched condition in which they were in Germany!"[2] The University adopted a particularly bitter tone towards Schinchel who fought the Jansenists in his lectures. Under threat of deposition he was forced to retract, and eight propositions, which he was accused of having taught, were condemned.[3]

Meanwhile the delegates of the University, Sinnich and Paepe, were busy in Rome on behalf of their sympathizers. They were graciously received both by the Pope and by the Secretary of State; Cardinal Barberini even invited them to his table, an honour which drew from the University a special expression of thanks.[4] But it was only on January 28th, 1644,

[1] GERBERON, I., 42; **Cod. Preuck.*, ff. 537–568, Anima Library, Rome.

[2] GERBERON, I., 132–6.

[3] The University was of opinion, *" per Iansenianorum latus suam auctoritatem peti et existimationem gravissime laedi" (*Cod. Preuck.*, f. 469 *seq.*, *loc. cit.*).

[4] The *letter of thanks of March 7, 1644, in *Cod. Barb.*, 3150, f. 188, Vatican Library. For the audience with the Pope a detailed account is in GERBERON, I., 83 *seq.*, but with many improbabilities. Thus, he makes Sinnich say (p. 87) that the mission was not on behalf of Jansenius. On p. 89 he says the contrary. The deputies are said to have bluntly accused Albizzi of deceit (p. 103), to have spoken before the Pope of frauds and knavish tricks, to have convicted him of being in contradiction with the Bull, so that he remained speechless. Against this Barberini (to Bichi, November 24, 1643), relates with satisfaction that the deputies had spoken " cum multa modestia de controversia Ianseniana,

that they presented a first memorial; in it they demanded to be heard by a special Congregation of Cardinals, a request which by itself sufficiently showed that they were not so much concerned about the authenticity of the Bull as anxious for a fresh discussion of *Augustinus*. The Cardinalitial Congregation was granted; the Inquisition, through Albizzi, informed them that it would be composed of Cardinals Spada, Pamfili (the future Pope Innocent), and Falconieri. In their memorials the Louvain delegates endeavoured to show that Jansenius did not in any way teach the condemned propositions of Baius and that he only held them in the same orthodox sense which Vasquez, for instance, attached to them, hence the Pope was ill-informed at the time of the publication of his Bull. The teaching of Jansenius was none other than that of St. Augustine.[1] This last assertion Sinnich sought to prove in a long discourse before the Congregation, on April 28th, and when Cardinal Spada objected that he held the teaching of the *Augustinus* to be the same as that of Baius, Sinnich and Paepe endeavoured to refute this view in a lengthy paper which, together with an excursus,[2] they handed in on June 6th. In this document they maintain that Jansenius wrote his work in order to bring the teaching of St. Augustine into harmony with papal declarations. He realized that in the disputes on grace under Clement VIII. there was a lack of clear understanding of the views of St. Augustine, whose teaching had gradually fallen into oblivion in the Church, its place being taken by contrary notions. That was why he had so earnestly devoted himself to the study of the African Doctor for he was anxious to render a service to the Church.

asserentes se certos, bullam praedictam esse veram et non falsam ". The Procurator-General of the Augustinians knew nothing as yet of the Bull according to GERBERON; he and the Master of the Palace received the Bull only on December 30, 1643, and in January, 1644 (p. 118). As for the statement that Albizzi had drafted the Bull in arbitrary fashion, i.e. that he had mentioned Jansenius by name, against the Pope's wishes, *cf.* DE MEYER, 134, note.

[1] GERBERON, I., 125.

[2] **Cod. Preuck.*, ff. 578 *seqq.*, Anima Library, Rome.

If these questions were going to be discussed, there was every prospect of a repetition of endless negotiations, such as those which had taken place under Clement VIII. In Rome it was felt that the *Augustinus* had been sufficiently discussed previous to the publication of the recent Bull against Jansenius. Accordingly, instead of any answer, a decree of the Inquisition of July 6th, 1644,[1] ordered the original of the Bull to be shown to the two Louvain Professors and an accurate copy to be handed to them. On July 29th they received notification of a decree guaranteeing the genuineness of the Bull. Sinnich protested at once; that was not the question, he declared; they were concerned for the honour of the holy Doctor of the Church St. Augustine and wanted help against his opponents. To Albizzi the Louvain professors further complained that publication of the Bull had not been held back until the report of the Lieutenant and the Bishops was available. Moreover the University of Louvain could not receive the decree without the consent of the King of Spain.[2] It was fatal to the effect which the Papal decision might have had, that it was communicated to the Louvain delegates just as Urban VIII. died. Previous to Urban's demise other deaths had, as it were, made room for the new tendency of Jansenism. Richelieu's death on December 4th, 1642, removed its most dangerous opponent and when the powerful minister was followed to the grave by the man who was in reality the first of his subjects, viz. Louis XIII., the weak King's place was taken by the weaker Anne; as for Richelieu's successor, Mazarin, he had but little understanding for and interest in, religious questions, and during his first years of office he was fully occupied with opponents of a different kind. The death of the two founders of the sect, viz. Jansenius' in 1638 and St. Cyran's on October 11th, 1643, not long after Richelieu, proved favourable to the new movement. From various motives Jansenius during his lifetime had been forced to observe a certain restraint in the exposition of his opinions; now the repeatedly reprinted

[1] Printed in FONTAINE, IV., 33.

[2] Sinnich and Paepe *to the University, July 30, 1644, *Cod. Preuck.*, ff. 393 *seqq.*, *loc. cit.*

Augustinus proclaimed them to the whole world and the aged St. Cyran's place was taken by a far abler man, then in the full vigour of youth and likewise a member of the family whose name is for ever linked with that of Jansenism, namely Angélique Arnauld's youngest brother Antoine, whom his followers surnamed the "great" Arnauld.

Antoine Arnauld was not without real greatness of a kind. In him intellectual gifts of a high order went hand in hand with extensive acquaintance with theology and other branches of knowledge; he was well read in the Fathers and the Councils and had a consummate mastery of his native tongue. To all this he joined strength and tenacity of will. Once he had adopted Jansenism he held on to it with an obstinacy which assumed the proportions of fanaticism. He remained unmoved when he was expelled from the Sorbonne and forced to lie in hiding for a number of years, until at last he had to leave the country. During fifty years and up to the time of his death in 1694, he directed every step of his party in its conduct towards the Holy See and the secular power; in every question affecting it he intervened either with a formal treatise or as an ever-ready polemist. With a love of work which knew no fatigue, he wrote pamphlet after pamphlet, either in order to promote the cause of Jansenism or to deal a blow to the Jesuits whom he hated with deadly hatred. If we take into account his intellectual gifts alone, he might undoubtedly have been a Bishop after the manner of Bossuet or Fénelon, or at least an outstanding scholar. As a matter of fact he did produce one isolated scholarly work of abiding value when, in conjunction with Nicole, he wrote an excellent treatise to prove that the Catholic doctrine of the Eucharist was the teaching of the Church from the beginning.[1] As for the forty-two volumes which include his other works,[2] their interest is chiefly

[1] *La perpétuité de la foi de l'Église cath. touchant l'Eucharistie*, Paris, 1669.

[2] *Œuvres*, Paris, 1793 *seqq.*, vols. 1–4: Letters; 5–9: on the Jansenist translations of Holy Scripture, the Breviary, and the Missal; 10–11: dogmatic writings; 12–15: polemical writings against the Protestants; 16–25: Defence of the Jansenists;

historical. They repel by the arrogant and bitter tone that runs through them ; by the insatiable hatred with which he pursues his opponents, the Jesuits, and the artifices of which his first pamphlets against Urban VIII.'s Bull against Jansenism had given a foretaste.[1] In the last analysis the personality of the " great " Arnauld is little more than the pitiable figure of a man apparently destined for great things but who, once he had been thrown out of his true orbit, wasted his remarkable intellectual gifts in the invention of those subterfuges and trickeries of which, under his guidance, Jansenism was so prolific ; instead of the life-giving sun that he might have been, he became a firebrand wreaking destruction for centuries to come and leaving no trace once its fury was spent.

It is a further proof of the almost demonic influence of St. Cyran, even on superior minds, that he succeeded in drawing even an Arnauld into his orbit. Born in 1612, Antoine Arnauld had at first thought of devoting himself to the law, as his father had done. St. Cyran persuaded him to take up theology instead, and before long he exercised upon the young student, whom he got to read St. Augustine, a far greater influence than his professors at the Sorbonne. Arnauld's trial disputation in 1636 seemed like a prelude to the *Augustinus* of Jansenius, which appeared four years later. Not long after, Antoine put himself completely under St. Cyran's guidance,[2] though, on the latter's advice, he went on with his studies. In 1641 he took his doctorate, became a priest, and after Richelieu's death secured admission into the Sorbonne. Whether the shrewdly calculating St. Cyran initiated the enthusiastic pupil into his views concerning the utter decadence of the Church [3] cannot be ascertained. However, the extent to which Arnauld

26–34 : on ethics, chiefly polemical against the Jesuits ; 36–42 : miscellaneous, among which (vol. 38), the *Logique de Port-Royal*.

[1] *Cf.* above p. 121.

[2] By a letter of December 24, 1638 (*Lettres de M. Arnauld*, I. Nancy, 1727, 1 *seqq.*). *Cf. Arnauld* to d'Andilly, January 15, 1639, October 7 and 12, 1641, to St. Cyran, September 15, 1641 (*ibid.*, 18, 31, 40, 43).

[3] *Cf.* above p. 89 *seq.*

had made his own his teacher's thought is shown by his first important work which proved an event in the religious world of France and rendered its author famous at one stroke. This was the book on frequent Communion.[1] Just as Jansenius' *Augustinus* crystallized the ideas of his followers concerning God's action within the innermost sanctuary of the soul, so did Arnauld's book define their practical conduct in the most sacred and most delicate concerns of piety. With this work Arnauld became the joint founder of Jansenism. As a matter of fact he was far superior to the real founder as regards the extent and power of his influence, because he treated of a more easily intelligible subject and instead of a scholar's ponderous Latin, made use of a French which, though not equal to present-day demands, created a sensation at that period and remained unsurpassed up to Pascal's time.

Arnauld introduces himself as the spokesman of a group of men who thought as he did.[2] These can only have been the followers of St. Cyran, though the latter's name is never breathed.[3] This fact alone betrays his real aim: he would fain extend to the whole Church the principles on the reception of the Sacraments of Penance and the Eucharist which St. Cyran had advocated for Port-Royal. Arnauld, indeed, does not say so in so many words. To judge by the title of his book, his only aim is to expound faithfully the ideas of the Fathers of the Church, the Popes and the Councils on the reception of the Sacraments, for the benefit of those who wish to become truly converted as well as for the use of zealous spiritual directors.[4] St. Cyran, with his views on the Sacraments, wished, in the first instance, to set himself in opposition to the Jesuits, but eventually he found himself sharply at variance with Christian antiquity. In the days of the Apostles it was an understood thing that as often as the Holy Mysteries were

[1] We quote from the text in the *Œuvres*, XXVII., 71–673.

[2] *Préface*, n. 42, p. 145.

[3] De Meyer, 225.

[4] *De la fréquente communion, où les sentiments des Pères, des Papes et des Conciles, touchant l'usage des sacremens de Pénitence et d'Eucharistie, sont fidèlement exposéz*, Paris, 1643.

celebrated, all the faithful communicated[1] and daily Communion was the rule, though it may not have been universally observed, throughout the era of the Fathers. At the close of the Middle Ages frequent reception of the Sacraments had indeed almost completely ceased, but theologians still maintained the doctrine that it was better to approach the table of the Lord often rather than only on rare occasions. Accordingly, the reform Orders of the sixteenth century, and more especially the Jesuits, sought to revive the practice of the frequent reception of the Sacraments, though they betrayed a certain rigorism and their theologians demanded as a condition for frequent Communion, freedom from wilful attachment even to the smallest sins, and their spiritual directors limited the average Christian to weekly Communion. Francis de Sales adopted these views. However, opposition to the relative rigorism of the Jesuit theologians arose in Spain where the Carthusian Antonio de Molina (died 1619) protested against the limitation of frequent Communion in a book which has been frequently reprinted.[2]

It was quite impossible to justify the Jansenist teaching on the administration of the Sacraments by quoting the Fathers, as soon as the latter's views were expounded in the light of their context and by the standards of true scholarship. However an incident of which he made the most enabled Arnauld to dispense with a strictly scientific procedure. A lady belonging to the upper circles of Parisian society, the

[1] 1 *Cor.*, XI, 20 *seq.*

[2] E. DUBLANCHY in *Dictionnaire de théol. cath.*, III., Paris, 515–551. *Cf.* H. LECLERQ, *Dictionnaire d'archéol. chrét. et de liturgie*, III., 2, Paris, 1914, 2458 *seq.* For Molina's doctrine see DE MEYER, 56–60; his book, *Instruccion de sacerdotes* obtained as many as twenty editions in Spain, and was translated into Latin (by the Dominican *Nic. Jansenius*, Antwerp, 1618, 1644), into French, English, and possibly into Italian. Bishop Quiñonez of Valladolid ordered that in his diocese it was to be in every sacristy, secured by a small chain, and every cleric was to read it within six months. *Cf.* N. ANTONIO, *Bibl. Hisp. nova*, I., 145.

Princess Anne de Rohan-Guémené, was a partisan of Port-Royal,[1] whilst the Marquise Madeleine de Sablé had taken a Jesuit for her spiritual director. The two ladies were in the habit of discussing the advantages of frequent or occasional Communion and the Marquise de Sablé persuaded her director, the Jesuit Sesmaisons, to set down in a short paper, for her benefit, the principles governing the matter.[2] Sesmaisons did so by supplying an extract from the book of the Carthusian Molina. Accordingly Arnauld's book took the form of a refutation of that summary. In this way he had the advantage of being able to evade a systematic exposition of the teaching of the Fathers. No need for him to give a connected account of his own views, and he might hit out against his chief opponents, the Jesuits, without fear of having to deal with their great theologians.[3] Accordingly, in the first part of his book Arnauld discusses the teaching of the Fathers and in the third part, the requisite preparation for Holy Communion in such wise that he deals with Sesmaisons' treatise proposition by proposition, opposing to it his own refutation. Between the first and the third part he inserts a lengthy dissertation on the penitential system of the early Church and the words of his opponent are pressed into service in order to introduce and justify it. His real aim, that of checking frequent Communion, is nowhere expressly stated by Arnauld; on the contrary, when Sesmaisons says that all the Fathers approved of the frequent reception of the Sacrament, he asks: "Who does not join in this approval?"[4] He would even encourage Christians to communicate more than once a day if it were possible![5] Once he has taken up such a position he may leave on one side all that the Fathers have written in favour of frequent Communion since he is apparently not opposed to it. On the other

[1] Her conversion, however, was not a lasting one; see LANCELOT, *Mém.*, I., 324 *seqq.*

[2] RAPIN, *Mém.*, I., 29 *seq.*; HERMANT, *Mém.*, I., 211 *seq.*; DE MEYER, 222 *seq.*

[3] D. PETAU, *De poenitentia*, lib. 3, ch. 6 (*Opera*, IV., Venetiis, 1745, 255).

[4] I., ch. 7, p. 197.

[5] *Préface*, no. 8, p. 88.

hand he describes the preparation for the reception of the Holy Eucharist which the Father deemed *desirable*, as an *indispensable* condition, consequently, he lays down conditions for its reception of so exacting a nature that, from his point of view, no one could ever presume to approach it.[1] Arnauld pursues a like purpose in what he says of the stern penitential system of Christian antiquity which punished grave sins with privation of Communion. The Church, he asserts, has not changed her mind with regard to penitential rigour; if in course of time the only penance required was sacramental confession, after which the sinner was at once admitted to the Holy Eucharist, such a custom has only established itself because it favours the general lack of penitential spirit, since everybody wants to confess but no one is prepared to do penance. The contrary practice was the primitive one and that of the Apostles, the Fathers and the universal Church during twelve centuries[2]; in other words, it was of divine institution, hence it could not be altered. For all that Arnauld only desires the restoration of one single point of the ancient penitential system, viz. exclusion from Holy Communion whilst a man undergoes a more prolonged period of penance. But since he starts from the untenable and erroneous principle[3] that in the primitive Church every grave sin was punished with public penance and exclusion from the Holy Table, the majority of ordinary Christians, on his assumption, would be debarred, in practice, from the Eucharist.

[1] He requires an "extreme pureté" (I., ch. 22, 40, pp. 238, 297, 298), or, in the words of the pseudo Dionysius, "un amour divin, pur, et sans aucun mélange" (I., ch. 4, p. 195). He concludes from St. Francis de Sales' writings that the frequent communicant must be "mort à toutes les affections du péché, même véniel, dans le détachement de toutes les choses qui pourraient déplaire à Dieu, etc." (I., ch. 22, p. 242).

[2] II., ch. 46, p. 545.

[3] G. Rauschen, *L'Eucharistie et la Pénitence durant les six premiers siècles de l'Église*, Paris, 1910, 212 *seqq*. (This translation contains notes which are lacking in the German original.) See also J. Stufler in the *Zeitschrift für kath. Theol.*, XXXII. (1903), 546 *seqq*.

These assertions affect so intimately the very core of Catholic thought and practice that it is scarcely possible to give to outsiders an idea of their bearing. From the sixteenth century onwards the chief aim of every successive effort for a renewal of the religious life had been to promote the reception of the Sacraments. The Jesuits saw in their success in this matter both the crown of their labours and the extent of their success. Charles Borromeo ascribed the moral improvement in Milan chiefly to the frequent reception of the Sacraments; he was anxious that his people should take the petition of the Lord's Prayer in which we pray for our daily bread, as also referring to the food of the soul, viz. Holy Communion [1]; he desired the faithful to draw nigh to the table of the Lord at least once a month and in Lent and Advent once a week.[2] Arnauld frequently quotes Borromeo,[3] but the latter's ordinance forbidding any preacher to enter the pulpit who dared even indirectly to speak against frequent Communion, sufficiently shows what treatment the Jansenist teacher would have met with at the hands of the Archbishop of Milan.[4]

Thus the book on frequent Communion runs counter to the essential element of the hitherto prevailing tendency of the reform. As an exposition of a much-discussed theological question its value is nil, but Arnauld is a past master in the use of all the rhetorical tricks which Cicero displays in his judicial orations. No matter what his opponent may say, Arnauld always succeeds in extracting from his assertion some argument in favour of his own thesis. Of course this cannot be done without travestying the opponent [5] for, on the whole,

[1] Goila in *San Carlo Borromeo nel terzo centenario della canonizzazione*, 133.

[2] *Instructiones Praedic. Verbi Dei*, in *Acta Eccl. Mediolan.*, P. IV., Bergamo, 1738, 486.

[3] *Préface*, n. 12, 25–9; ch. 33–44, pp. 93, 109 *seqq.*, 474 *seqq.*

[4] *Conc. prov. III. Acta Eccl. Mediolan.*, I., 92; *cf.* 512.

[5] Thus Sesmaisons' pamphlet had emphasized the fact that since every Communion is an act of worship, it promotes the glory of God. Would any one dare to say, Arnauld asks, that it is an honour for a King if a beggar sits down at his table? (III.,

Sesmaisons' essay is above criticism. But horror of heresy, love of the Church, regard for her traditions, for the Fathers, for Borromeo and St. Francis de Sales are so much to the fore in Arnauld's work, that the generality of readers to whom he addressed himself in his flowing French, were not likely to notice the distortions. In addition to this he repeatedly protests that on no account would he upset any one, or stir up trouble within the Church; all he wishes is to defend himself and those who felt like him. In their love of peace, he goes on to say, the latter had kept silence for five years, notwithstanding frequent provocation, but at last Arnauld could no longer refuse to speak in their defence; love of truth demanded it,[1] and as a Doctor of Sorbonne he had sworn to defend the truth even to the shedding of his blood.[2] He prays that his friends may be suffered to go on in their own way; his book asks for no more; in its pages, he protests, only the voice of the Fathers and Christian tradition will be heard, for he would not presume to expound his personal views.[3]

As a matter of fact it is not easy to ascertain what were Arnauld's own views. He never states them systematically and they are mingled with much that is good and irreproachable. Moreover, if a passage sounds suspicious, it may be taken for granted that the very opposite is stated in another part of the book.[4] Thus Arnauld's explanation on the delay of sacramental absolution until penance had been done implies that the sinner must be justified before he can be absolved and that the priest's power to bind and to loose is limited to the imposition of penance. However, in another place, he expressly states that absolution does not merely declare that sin is

ch. 11, pp. 601 *seqq.*). Sesmaisons allows frequent Communion even to those whose feelings and imaginations are still full of involuntary love of self and the world (si attaché au monde que de merveille). Arnauld makes of "involuntary attachments" "voluntary ones" (III., ch. 10, pp. 592 *seqq.*). In fact he speaks as if Sesmaisons excluded no one from frequent Communion.

[1] *Préface*, n. 42, p. 145.

[2] *Préface*, n. 2, p. 74 *seq.*

[3] *Préface*, n. 45, p. 150.

[4] *Cf.* below, p. 143.

remitted, but actually blots it out.[1] Another fundamental error of the book lies in the assertion that during the preceding five centuries the Church had erred in the administration of Penance, a statement that would mean that she is not infallible. The objection that such an assertion naturally calls forth is met by him with a number of lengthy arguments; according to Arnauld the Church is indeed not liable to error in her teaching, but discipline may decay since all great Churchmen have fought for its restoration.[2] Here and there the book bestows high praise on Jansenius of Ypres,[3] whilst an occasional remark betrays the fact that the writer adheres to the latter's peculiar views on grace.[4] On the other hand the Jesuits, whose principles on the administration of the Sacraments Arnauld had especially in view,[5] are nowhere described as the opponents.

How deeply rooted religion and Christianity must still have been in the soil of contemporary France if a book like Arnauld's could thus excite public feeling! The book on frequent Communion became a general topic of conversation. The first edition was sold out in a couple of days; within six months a fourth edition became necessary,[6] and this was followed by many more.[7] There is a good deal of evidence to show that it was precisely the *beaux esprits* and the great ladies who discussed with particular zest the questions raised by Arnauld.[8] But what was of far greater consequence was the approval which Arnauld met with on the part of the clergy. From the outset he found himself in a position to offer his book to the world with splendid letters of recommendation from fifteen

[1] II., ch. 12, p. 386.

[2] *Préface*, n. 35, pp. 131 *seqq*.

[3] II., ch. 12, 40, 45, pp. 382, 507, 543.

[4] (PATOUILLET), *Dictionnaire des livres Jansénistes*, I., Anvers., 1752, 267 *seqq*.

[5] ARNAULD, *De la tradition* (*Œuvres*, XXVIII., 21).

[6] *Ibid.*, 243.

[7] We examined the 11th edition (Lyon, 1739).

[8] RAPIN, *Mém.*, I., 36; D. PETAU, *De poenitentia*, lib. 1, ch. 2, no. 6.

Bishops and twenty-one Doctors of theology,[1] and the subsequent editions give the text of further similar encomiums.[2] Even Cardinal Bentivoglio expressed his satisfaction with the book.[3] The nuncio Chigi was of opinion that it would be better to refrain from any reply in view of Arnauld's moderate tone ; moreover refutations would only enhance the prestige of the book.[4] " How many adherents has not this teaching won in the space of two or three months," wrote an adversary of Arnauld's ? [5] How many admirers are there who look on the book as a fifth gospel and as a revelation from heaven ? This applause need not surprise us too much. Traces of the ancient public penance survived into the late Middle Ages, the Council of Trent had declared that it was fitting that public penance should be done for public scandals,[6] and both before and after the Council many assemblies of Bishops and in particular Charles Borromeo, had expressed themselves in the same sense. These utterances were very skilfully exploited by Arnauld,[7] hence there was no need to reject his proposals *a priori*, even though it had not entered into any one's head, except his, to make public penance consist chiefly in the deprivation of Holy Communion. More frequent Communion had only come in with the reform Orders of the sixteenth century and thus far it was something new ; hence it was only natural that the advisability of an unconditional approval of the new practice should be examined. Moreover Arnauld's book showed so much zeal against alleged abuses, and he appeared to support his proposals with the authority of the

[1] ARNAULD, *Œuvres*, XXVI., xxvi.

[2] *Ibid.*, xli. ; copy of the approbations, *ibid.*, XXVII., 153 *seqq.*, XXVIII., 599 *seqq.*

[3] See his letter to d'Andilly, March 26, 1644, *ibid.*, XXVIII., 627.

[4] Letter to *M. d'Acquin le père, docteur en médicine*, February and April, 1644, *ibid.*, 590. DE MEYER (243) makes of d'Acquin a Dominican.

[5] ARNAULD, *Œuvres*, XXVI., xxvii.

[6] SESS., 24, ch. 7.

[7] *Fréquente communion*, II., ch. 21–32 on the Council of Trent, ch. 33–44 on Borromeo, ch. 45 on other authorities.

Fathers and the Councils with such skill, that it is not to be wondered at if excitable Frenchmen took his side in considerable numbers.

Moreover the principles which Arnauld attacked were those held by the Jesuits, Now on the occasion of the dispute in England between the Vicar Apostolic and the Jesuits, a certain exasperation against the Society of Jesus had got hold of many French Bishops. St. Cyran had exploited the situation thus created; under the pen name of *Petrus Aurelius* he had written several polemical pamphlets, seemingly in defence of the rights of Bishops, and these he collected and published in one volume in 1632. The book created a sensation; on the part of the French clergy the author was promised a reward if he would reveal his identity. The assembly of the clergy of 1641 had the collected works of Petrus Aurelius sumptuously printed and copies sent to all the Archbishops and Bishops of France.[1] A precipitate step by the French Jesuits added fuel to the prevailing ill-feeling against them. When the polemical writings against which Petrus Aurelius inveighed, came to be generally ascribed to the Jesuits, the Superiors of the three houses in Paris, together with the King's confessor, made a joint declaration, on March 23rd, 1633, that the author was none of their number.[2] Now it was quite true that these writings were not from the pen of a French Jesuit but from that of the English Jesuits Floyd and Wilson (Knott), and in 1643 that fact became generally known through Alegambe's catalogue of Jesuit writers. This admission was promptly taken advantage of by the assembly of the French clergy and brought to the notice of all the Bishops of the realm by means of a circular letter.[3] Old condemnations of the Jesuit writings in question dating from 1631 were once more produced. The judgment of the University of Paris was printed anew in 1643, by order of the clergy, that of the assembly of the clergy of 1631 was reprinted in 1644, and again in 1653; in 1645 the assembly of the clergy republished the work of

[1] Dupin, I., 482 *seq.* [2] In Dupin, I., 477.

[3] November 29, 1643, printed in Arnauld, *Œuvres*, XXVIII., 613–15.

Petrus Aurelius with a panegyric of the author from the pen of Bishop Godeau of Grasse. At that time rumour alone connected St. Cyran's name with the book. Too late was it realized that Petrus Aurelius was an undesirable auxiliary and that the writings on which so much praise had been lavished, advocated the Jansenist doctrine.[1] The assembly of the clergy of 1656 saw itself compelled expressly to repudiate the book of Petrus Aurelius and to order the suppression of the eulogy which had been inserted in the great compilation of *Gallia Christiana*.[2]

It soon became apparent how greatly the Bishop's annoyance was destined to affect the impending controversy round the question of frequent Communion. The Jesuit Jacques Nouet, subsequently known as a valuable ascetical writer, was the first to dare attack Arnauld's book in a course of six sermons, though fifteen Bishops bestowed praise on it. He was promptly accused of having spoken in disrespectful terms of fifteen prelates. The assembly of the clergy of 1643 took up the matter and compelled Nouet to make a retractation [3] which, however, besides the assurance of his submission to the Bishops, stated no more than that he had not made use of the alleged expressions. The assembly of the clergy nevertheless deemed it expedient to bring the recantation to the notice of the Bishops of France in the above-mentioned circular.[4] It was even proposed to adopt Arnauld's book by general agreement, to condemn Nouet's sermons, and to debar him from all pastoral work until he should have made satisfaction.[5]

[1] *Cf.* (PATOUILLET), I., 135 *seqq.*

[2] *Cf.* DUPIN, I., 475 *seqq.*, 483 ; RAPIN, *Hist.*, 211 ; STE.-BEUVE, I., 319 *seqq.*; SOMMERVOGEL, *Bibliothèque*, III., 814–17 ; IV., 1134 *seqq.*

[3] ARNAULD, *Œuvres*, XXVIII., 618.

[4] *Cf.* November 29, 1643, *ibid.*, 613 *seqq.*

[5] *Ibid.*, 605. Nouet's sermons are described as : " téméraires et présomptueux, remplis d'ignorances, faussetés, calomnies, impostures, tendants à renverser les plus saintes maximes de l'Évangile, à fonder l'hypocrisie, semer le schisme," etc., De Meyer overlooks the fact that here there is question of a proposal which was not accepted.

Notwithstanding so unpromising a beginning, the defenders of the Church's teaching were not frightened. Soon there appeared a whole series of polemical writings against the book on frequent Communion,[1] the most important of them being from the pen of "that Father of the History of Dogma", the learned Denis Petau (Petavius) whose book[2] went through three editions in the years 1644 and 1645 alone. Petau puts in bold relief the errors which lie at the basis of Arnaulds exposition but which, for the most part, he merely states casually here and there. In the matter of style Petau was no match for his adversary, but as regards the substance he undoubtedly crushed Arnauld.[3] Among these refutations mention must be made of that by the Bishop of Lavaur, Abra de Raconis, because here, among so many episcopal panegyrists, a Bishop raises his voice in condemnation of Arnauld.[4] A pamphlet by Prince de Condé, Henri de Bourbon (died 1646), also carried some weight by reason of the position of its author.[5] Though none of these refutations rivalled the circulation of Arnauld's book, the oft-repeated protests of so many thoughtful men at least attracted the attention of more serious people to the dangers that lurked in Arnauld's assertions. Apart from some isolated exceptions, the spate of episcopal recommendations abated in 1644. It goes without saying that in the face of these attacks the pugnacious Arnauld did not confine himself to the rôle of a silent spectator. As early as May, 1644, he had ready a voluminous work directed

[1] ARNAULD, *Œuvres*, XXVI., lxxii, *seqq.*; DE MEYER, 251–268, 291–300, 315–322.

[2] *De la pénitence publique et de la préparation à la communion*, Paris, 1644, 1645, 1658. We use the Latin translation appended to PETAU'S chief work *De theologicis dogmatibus*, vol. iv, Venice, 1745, 211–332.

[3] For the answer of the Jansenists that Petau had sacrificed understanding and conscience to the interests of his Order and that in the main he agreed with Arnauld, see DE MEYER, 263 *seq.*

[4] *Ibid.*, 315–321.

[5] *Ibid.*, 296.

chiefly against his most dangerous opponent, Petau.[1] Perhaps no less fatal than Petau's book was the fact that a Protestant preacher, Brachet de la Milletière, who in point of fact became a Catholic not long after, claimed Arnauld's book for the purposes of his theology of mediation and read into it, not without justification, various questionable propositions which were condemned by the Sorbonne. However Arnauld's reply to Milletière is dated the same day as that on which the Sorbonne met in order to examine those theses.[2] The book against Petau was positively devoured by the reading public; the fifth edition appeared a year after its publication.[3] The rhetorician Balzac lamented the poverty of the French language which failed to provide him with words in which to express his enthusiasm for the book[4]: Arnauld's triumph seemed complete.

Petau, on the other hand, did not long keep him waiting for an answer. When faced with certain statements Arnauld had referred to others in which he had asserted the contrary and in the new book he presented the contested points in a milder form. Thereupon Petau added to the third edition of his first book an appendix in which he gave a complete list of the contradictory statements to be found in various parts of Arnauld's work. He then exposed the real opinions of his

[1] *La tradition de l'Église sur le sujet de la pénitence et de la fréquente communion* (*Œuvres*, XXVIII., 39–460). On the immediate cause of this book, *Grimaldi writes on April 1, 1644 (Angelica Library, Rome, S. 3, 1): that the sponsors of the book on Communion had asked Arnauld to write a defence of all the propositions in his book which had been attacked, "che non rimanga luogo a poter dubitare," that the book "contenga cose aliene da sentimenti della Chiesa". Grimaldi writes that the University of Paris had declared "col motivo di contraporsi alle soddisfazioni de' Jesuiti dopo qualche contrarietà di pareri", that it did not intend to approve Arnauld's book, but to let it stand over until a further decision was reached, and they wished that Arnauld would submit himself and his book to the Pope and the Bishops.

[2] *Œuvres*, XXVIII., 529–567. *Cf.* De Meyer, 285.

[3] *Œuvres*, XXVI., xlvi.

[4] De Meyer, 284.

opponent by means of a connected analysis of the ideas which constitute the basis of the book on frequent Communion but which appear only in fragmentary fashion in isolated passages.[1] These explanations of Petau's were also meant only for serious readers; they had hardly any direct influence on the general public. In the later editions of the book on frequent Communion Arnauld, undisturbed by these refutations, maintained unchanged all the old propositions.

Enthusiasm for Arnauld was fanned by the circumstance that the Government seemed resolved to take strong measures against him.[2] Queen Anne, who was not favourably disposed towards the Jansenists, ordered the two heads of the party, Arnauld and De Barcos, a nephew of St. Cyran, to give an account of their teaching in Rome. This was the signal for immediate and violent protests. Parliament pleaded the Gallican liberties, the University declared that it would have to protect the person of Arnauld, and the Sorbonne protested against the proposed injustice to one of its Doctors. The Queen, nevertheless, repeated her command but Arnauld thought[3] "that he would offend against the precept of the Gospel if he refused to flee from the violence of men in order to shelter in the arms of God"; so he hid "under the shadow of God's wings", that is, in the house of Hamelin, an inspector of roads and bridges, in the faubourg Saint-Marceau.[4] In point of fact Mazarin no longer insisted on the execution of the royal command once Arnauld had given a sworn assurance in writing, on March 14th, 1644,[5] that the book on frequent Communion

[1] *De poenitentia publica*, lib. 7, ch. 1–19; a summary of Arnauld's system in eighteen propositions; ch. 20–8: eight contradictions of Arnauld (*De theol. dogm.*, IV., 298–321). Lib. 8 (*ibid.*, 312–332) deals with each of Arnauld's replies.

[2] De Meyer, 270. According to *Grimaldi (April 1, 1644, Angelica Library, Rome, S. 3, 1), the "risoluzione presa dalla regina" had aroused "gran commozione" because Arnauld's friends declared it to be a machination of the Jesuits.

[3] *Œuvres*, XXVI., xli.

[4] Rapin, *Mém.*, I., 34 *seq.*; De Meyer, 270 *seqq.*

[5] *Œuvres*, XXVIII., 36.

was prompted solely by love of truth and zeal for the salvation of souls, and that he submitted it to the judgment of the Roman Church, the Pope, all Catholic Bishops, the Archbishop of Paris and the Faculty of Theology. This assurance would have been more effective had he not lumped the Pope together with authorities which can only demand a conditional assent. The statement that " with all his heart he committed to the Pope as the supreme Vicar of Christ, both his person and his opinions ", was rather surprising, seeing that at that very moment he was seeking security for his person from the attentions of the Pope. However, at that time it was not yet deemed necessary to examine too closely the wording of Arnauld's protestations of obedience. His assurance made an excellent impression.

The Bishops who had eulogized Arnauld's book felt not a little hurt when their protégé was summoned to Rome. On April 4th, 1644, they addressed a collective letter to the Pope [1] in which they definitely sided with Arnauld against the Jesuits: " Certain persons," they wrote, " had laid down principles that were dangerous to papal and episcopal authority, turned the use of the Sacraments into a harmful misuse, and instead of applying the true remedies to the decay of manners, had recourse to attenuations and palliations. When the Bishops sought to remedy these conditions, they had had the impudence to speak disrespectfully of the Bishops in the pulpit. This had occurred in particular in connexion with a book on frequent Communion." They then proceed to condemn in severe terms the conduct of the Jesuits in regard to Arnauld and to defend his book against objections.

Petau had forwarded a memorial to Rome against the book on frequent Communion [2] and the Capuchin Yves also lodged a protest in the same quarter.[3] The Holy See was accordingly compelled to take up the matter. On the other hand the nuncio Grimaldi dissuaded it from condemning Arnauld,[4] as this would

[1] *Ibid.*, 628–633.

[2] SOMMERVOGEL, VI., 614.

[3] *Œuvres*, XXVI., lxxii; DE MEYER, 295.

[4] April 19, 1644, in DE MEYER, 427.

also hit his episcopal friends. Accordingly Cardinal Barberini allowed the affair to drag on, and Urban VIII. died in the meantime.[1] At this moment the main elements of Jansenism had attained their full development almost everywhere. The sect would not sever itself from the Church, though it constituted an opposition and a complete novelty. In the dogmatic sphere the new heresy entirely overlooks that which the Christian professes in the opening words of his most habitual prayer, viz. the doctrine that God is our Father in heaven. In the *Augustinus* of Jansenius God is only an implacably stern Lord and Judge. In the same way the other chief product of the Jansenist heresy, viz. the book on frequent Communion, shows no understanding of the loving-kindness and condescension of our Redeemer. As regards moral conduct and the exercises of a devout life, Jansenism is involved in hopeless contradictions. On the one hand its conception of the unapproachable majesty of God impells man to convulsive attempts to propitiate Him, but since the sect denies free will the scoffers were quite consequent when they countered the Jansenist exhortations to penance with the remark that they wished first to wait for the irresistible grace of Port-Royal.[2] Its exaggerated conclusions drawn from the sublimity of the Holy Eucharist and its exorbitant demands for the reception of absolution are likewise based on the idea that the efficacy of the Sacraments depends almost wholly on the effort of the free will in the preparation for their reception. This constitutes yet another contradiction of Jansenism with itself.[3]

Furthermore the Jansenist teaching on grace leads to an undervaluation of nature; from the first the sect is inclined to sniff the presence of the devil in everything natural. It was assuredly a wonderful thing that a Le Maître should give

[1] *Ibid.*, 427 *seq.*

[2] Rapin, *Mém.*, I., 357.

[3] It is often in contradiction with itself. Thus the chief moralist of the party, Nicole, teaches that it is "an essential Christian duty" even for a just man, always to withstand concupiscence by "prière, recueillement, mortification, pénitence" (*Essais de morale*, V., 250 *seq.*).

up a brilliant post to become a hermit at Port-Royal, or De La Petitière, the best swordsman of France, should practise the trade of a cobbler as an expiation for having fought a duel, or that De la Rivière, a former army officer and a Hebrew, Greek and Spanish scholar, should act as a forester.[1] But these acts of abnegation were based on ideas which closely trench on Manicheism and Buddhism, and a man must be vastly prejudiced in favour of Port-Royal if he can admire Pascal, who deemed a broom a superfluous utensil or a Pontchâtean who never changed his body linen.[2] Nor was Angélique Arnauld very far from holding similar opinions.[3] It was in keeping with this unreasonable fear of nature that everything was excluded from Jansenist worship which might stir the senses [4] Isaac Le Maître, the translator of the Bible, styled the world " a reversed Eucharist ",[5] in as much as the devil lay hid behind every object in this world, demanding worship. His comment on the struggle between Descartes and Aristotle was that one thief was but robbing and slaying another, however, " all the better, for the more dead there are, the fewer enemies remain." [6] In their dislike of scholasticism, but because some sort of philosophy was indispensable, the Jansenists as a body took up Descartes [7] though this did not prevent them from regarding philosophy with the same scorn

[1] *Cf.* Ste.-Beuve, II., 233 *seq.*

[2] Perrens in the *Rev. hist.*, LI (1893), 270. Pascal's Jansenist sister does indeed reproach her brother " que vous mettez les balets (balais) au rang des meubles superflus . . . il est nécessaire que vous soyez au moins quelques mois (!) aussi propre que vous êtes sale (V. Cousin, *Jacqueline Pascal*, Paris, 1869, 253, 338).

[3] She makes the following reproach to Zamet : " Il voulut que tout fût dans un grand ajustement *et propreté* " (Cousin, *loc. cit.*). Ste.-Beuve quotes the passage, but omits the last two words.

[4] It was so already at Port-Royal in St. Cyran's time. (Ste. Beuve, IV., 148.)

[5] *Eucharistie retournée* (Ste.-Beuve, II., 338).

[6] *Ibid.*

[7] See Kohler, *Jansenismus und Cartesianismus*, Düsseldorf, 1905, 5 *seqq.*

with which they treated all mundane knowledge.[1] Strict principles were by no means identical with strictness of conduct even with the Jansenists. True, Port-Royal had its penitents of whom the new sect never ceased to boast.[2] and in the book on frequent Communion,[3] Arnauld was able to point to the parish of Saint-Maurice on the Aveyron, twenty-five miles from Paris, whose pastor, Duhamel, had restored the practice of public penance. Duhamel divided the sinners of the parish into four classes, of whom the last two had to stand during the service, some in the cemetery and others on a hill facing the church, and only for the sermon were they summoned into the sacred edifice.[4] St. Cyran's nephew, De Barcos, imposed on his penitents such penances as wading through rivers with bare feet in the winter time, or he limited marital intercourse.[5] However, on the whole these were exceptions. Of St. Cyran and his friends Vincent de Paul says that he never saw them do an act of penance.[6] Whilst in gaol at Vincennes St. Cyran gave scandal by his daintiness with regard to his food.[7] In the Hôtel Nevers, a rendezvous of the elegant world, the "Patriarchs and Prophets of Port-Royal" did themselves well at a daintily laid table whilst the ordinary Jansenists did penance for the glory of the sect.[8]

The spokesmen of the new sect did not even invariably act on their principles with regard to the reception of the Sacraments. Vincent de Paul says that were he to go by the book

[1] *Cf.* Nicole's preface to Arnauld's "Géometrie" (Arnauld, *Œuvres*, XLVI., 5).

[2] See Rapin, *Mém.*, I., 470.

[3] *Préface*, ch. 39.

[4] Rapin, *Hist.*, 441. For Duhamel see Ste.-Beuve, II., 543 *seq.*

[5] Rapin, *Mém.*, I., 532, 534; *cf.* 222 *seq.*, 470.

[6] Letter to Dehorgny, September 10, 1648, in Coste, III., 372. For St. Cyran's successor at Port-Royal, Singlin, who preached penance but only practised it in that he very rarely said Mass, see Rapin, *Mém.*, I., 448 *seq.* Even among the solitaries not all were penitents (*ibid.*, 473).

[7] Rapin (*Hist.*, 402), learned this from the daughter of the governor of the castle.

[8] Rapin, *Mém.*, I., 403 *seq.*; *cf.* 287.

on frequent Communion, he would never dare to approach the altar, but Arnauld himself, though he demanded a preparation that might have frightened St. Paul, boasted that he said Mass every day.[1] So did St. Cyran; nor did the latter dare to abolish frequent Communion at Port-Royal. There were others, however, even in the first period of Jansenism, who refrained from Holy Communion even at Easter or on their death bed[2], and there were some who never said Mass.[3] At a later period Jansenist priests deemed it a particularly meritorious thing to reduce the reception of the Sacraments to a minimum; people were found who, at the age of thirty, had not yet made their first Communion.[4]

In their infrequent reception of the Sacraments and their dislike of the external splendour of divine worship, the Jansenists approximate to the Protestants and are visibly influenced by them. To the same source, no doubt, must be traced their coldness with regard to the veneration of the Mother of God[5] and their recommendation of indiscriminate Bible reading, a practice which they even represented as obligatory[6] and as a "universal sacrament" in the sense of St. Cyran.[7] Accordingly, from 1650, a French translation of the Bible was in progress at Port Royal, under the direction of

[1] To Dehorgny, in Coste, III., 370.

[2] Rapin, *Mém.*, I., 466, 532, 534.

[3] *Ibid.*, 522, note.

[4] Sicard, *L'ancien clergé de France*, I., Paris, 1905, 467; Rapin, *Mém.*, II., *app.* 520–5.

[5] *Avis de la bienh. Vierge Marie à ses dévots indiscrets* (Lille, 1674), translated from the Latin of the Cologne jurist Wildenfeldt by Gerberon. A small collection of writings grew round this pamphlet (Patouillet, I., 164–176). Already St. Cyran had only the adjective "terrible" for the honour due to the Blessed Virgin Mary (Ste.-Beuve, I., 353). *Cf.* proposition 26 condemned by Alexander VIII., in 1690 (Denzinger, 1316); (Fontaine), *Constitutio "Unigenitus"*, IV., 535 *seq.*; (Patouillet), I., 193, 231, 302, II., 201, 226.

[6] Constitution "Unigenitus", propositions 79–85 (Denzinger, n. 1429 *seqq.*; (Patouillet), I., 183, 280; II., 38, 275, 277, 331.

[7] Ste.-Beuve, I., 447.

Le Maître de Sacy.[1] The New Testament appeared in 1667. It was printed at Amsterdam, not at Mons, as was alleged, but the whole Bible, in four volumes, was only ready in 1717. Owing to the text having been given a Jansenist bias in many places, prohibitions of the Book of Mons were published as early as 1668 by Archbishop Péréfixe of Paris and Pope Clement IX. Together with the Bible, the Jansenists wished to see the liturgical books, that is the Missal and the Breviary, in the hands of the faithful, in the vernacular tongue ; however, in consequence of their Jansenist colouring, these translations were frequently condemned by the Church.[2] It was only in the eighteenth century that attempts were made to restore in the liturgy practices which it was claimed were those of the primitive Church.[3]

On the other hand the attitude of the new sect towards the universal Church became clearly defined in its very first years. Since it did not wish to break openly with the Church, it needs must acknowledge the supremacy of the Pope. Like Jansenius,[4] Arnauld gave public expression to his regard for the Holy See and in this respect the Jansenists of a later period followed suit, but whilst for ever professing respect for the Pope they systematically refused to obey him.

In opposition to the numerous encomiums bestowed by the Holy See on the Jesuits, Jansenism pursued them from the first with deadly hatred.[5] Personal motives may have had a part in this : it is said that as a young man Jansenius had sought admission into the Order and that, to vent his

[1] *Ibid.*, II., 359 *seq.* ; NICOLE, *Essais de morale*, VIII., 2. 442 *seqq.*

[2] (PATOUILLET), I., 199 ; II., 59, 177 ; III., 131, 498.

[3] *Missale s. Ecclesiae Trecensis* (by the younger Bossuet), 1736. *Cf.* (PATOUILLET), III., 126 *seqq.* ; 409 ; LAFITEAU, *Hist. de la Constitution* " *Unigenitus* ", II., 94 ; *Hist.-polit. Blätter*, LXXIV (1874), 730.

[4] *Cf.* above p. 100.

[5] " que les jésuites sont grandement nuisibles à l'Église, pour le bien de laquelle il est nécessaire de les détruire " (ST. CYRAN, *Maxime*, 18, in DE MEYER, 498).

spite, because he was rejected, he joined the ranks of its enemies. In the sequel, the more he approximated to Calvin, walking as he did in the steps of Baius, the more his aversion grew, in fact it did not even stop before Ignatius of Loyola: in a letter to St. Cyran [1] he scoffs and derides the great Founder on the occasion of the latter's canonization by Gregory XV., 1622. When shortly after the question arose at Louvain of limiting Jesuit competition in the scholastic sphere, Jansenius worked against them in Spain in 1624 and 1626.[2] Even after his return he gave himself no rest: "It seems to be God's will," he wrote to St. Cyran on May 19th, 1627, "that I should exert myself everywhere against the Jesuits." He now initiated against the hated adversaries the paper war which, continued by his friends and admirers, has not yet come to an end after all these centuries. A first work of some importance against the Jesuits was completed by Jansenius in 1627, however he did not dare to publish it.[3] St. Cyran had opened hostilities already in the preceding year with an attack on the Jesuit Garasse [4] who had several times got mixed up in a somewhat unfortunate way with the freethinkers of the day; after that he carried on the campaign on a wider scale under the pseudo-name of *Petrus Aurelius*. Meanwhile Jansenius had made up for past omissions with the most violent attacks on the Jesuit theologians in the pages of *Augustinus*. In this he was followed by Arnauld, first in the pamphlets against the Bull of Urban VIII. and thereafter,

[1] Of June 13, 1621, in RAPIN, *Hist.*, 128 *seq.*; *Katholik*, 1875, II., 275.

[2] *Cf.* above p. 75.

[3] RAPIN (*Hist.*, 193) is mistaken in thinking that Jansenius was speaking of his *Historia Pelagianorum* at the beginning of the *Augustinus*. As the passages quoted by RAPIN (*ibid.*, 208), from the letters of Jansenius show, it was a special work against the Jesuits.

[4] ALEXANDRE DE L'EXCLUSSE (St. Cyran), *La somme des fautes et faussetés capitales, contenues en la somme théologique du P. F. Garasse*, Paris, 1626; ANNA PRZYREMBEL, *La controverse théol. et morale entre St.-Cyran et le P. Garasse* (Thèse), Paris, 1917. For Garasse's book, *cf.* PRAT, *Recherches*, IV., 491 *seqq.*

in most effective fashion, in the book on frequent Communion [1] and in many other writings. In the sequel the intrigues and the writings of the Jansenists took increasingly the form of a campaign against the Jesuits.[2]

This opposition was not the result of chance; an observer as dispassionate as Vincent de Paul has said in so many words that Jansenism was born of the desire to discredit the Jesuit Order [3] and historically the new heresy can best be understood if Jansenius is viewed as the antithesis of Ignatius of Loyola, as the contradiction of, and a reaction against, the Jesuits' teaching on grace, their ascetical and moral theology, their principles on the frequent reception of the Sacraments and their strong attachment to Rome.

At the close of the eighteenth century Jansenism seemed to have triumphed all along the line. The Jesuits were out of the fight; even in the seminaries of Italy, the teaching was

[1] *Cf.* above p. 136 *seq.*

[2] In the 18th century says STE.-BEUVE, " le caractère distinctif du Jansénisme se reduit à un point: être ennemi du Jésuite " in PERRENS, LII., 36). " Ils (the Jansenists) sont plus anti-jésuites ou anti-romains que sérieusement jansénistes. Leurs dogmes les occupent beaucoup moins qu'on ne le croirait (BREMOND, IV., 299 *seqq.*). According to the Jansenist GAZIER (d. 1922) there never was a doctrinal Jansenism (I., 1); Jansenism is the opposition of Catholic circles to the Jesuits, who from selfish motives, uphold the omnipotence of the Pope against the Bishops, and who corrupt dogma, morals and ecclesiastical discipline, so that since 1870, there is no faith to be found anywhere on earth (*ibid.*, II., 274).

[3] " Aussi est-ce " (the diminution of the reception of the Sacraments in consequence of Arnauld's book) " ce qu'a prétendu feu M. de St.-Cyran pour désaccréditer les Jésuites. M. de Chavigni disoit ces jours passés à un intime ami, que ce bon Monsieur lui avait dit, que lui et Jansénius avaient entrepris leur dessein pour désaccréditer ce saint Ordre-là, à l'égard de la doctrine et de l'administration des sacrements. Et moi je luí ai ouï tenir quasi tous les jours quantité de discours, conformes à cela." Letter to Dehorgny, June 25, 1648, in COSTE, III., 322.

based on rigoristic books of moral theology. Yet at that very time a reaction was preparing. The Society of Jesus was restored and to-day, apart from some scanty remains, Jansenism has no more than a tenuous existence in the books and in the admiration of a few literary men: the essential tenets of the sect concerning grace, conduct, the reception of the Sacraments, have all been rejected and condemned by the Church.[1]

The Jansenists were not wanting in zeal and strenuous effort. By means of a mass of books and booklets they meant to influence in their favour contemporary public opinion, and the opinion of posterity through voluminous works on their own history. They had at their service scholars like Arnauld and Tillemont and even men of real genius such as Pascal, Boileau and Racine.[2] It may be affirmed, says Rapin,[3] that never was error more skilfully sown among the people or defended in more spirited fashion; its success was due

[1] The most recent condemnation is in Pius XI.'s encyclical "Miserentissimus Redemptor" of May 8, 1928.

[2] The literary skill of "Messieurs de Port-Royal" is demonstrated by the success of their writings and the admissions of their opponents, *e.g.* RAPIN (*Mém.*, I., 22, 36). However recent history of literature only values as stylists Pascal and perhaps D'Andilly. In the opinion of the Jansenist Gazier (in PETIT DE JUVILLE, *Hist. de la langue et de la littérature française*, IV., Paris, 1897, 567) Singlin's sermons have "ni ornement, ni politesse, ni éloquence, ni science humaine". The pleadings of Antoine Le Maître, "ne répondent pas à la réputation du grand orateur," (*ibid.*, 570). Of Nicole he says: "comme écrivain, il arrive à peine au troisième rang" (*ibid.*, 587). Even the "great" Arnauld, "n'est malheureusement pas un grand écrivain . . . c'est écrit trop vite, et le trop d'abondance appauvrit la matière" (*ibid.*, 579, 582). Cf. also the opinion of RAPIN (*Mém.*, II., 196) who esteems their translations but denies them poetic feeling and invention. "Colourlessly and monotonously, uninterrupted by any picturesque expression or flash of inspiration, the chain of their ideas" (the Jansenists') unwinds itself. A haphazard glance at any of Arnauld's writings confirms the praise and blame of this criticism. (*J. v. Kunow* in *Romanische Forschungen of Vollmöller*, XXXIX (1921), 72).

[3] Mém., I., 1.

solely to cleverness and craftiness, not to violence, as in the case of other heresies. For all that the story of Jansenism is that of a great failure. Renewal of the Church, moral strictness, holiness, these were the slogans with which Jansenists justified their enterprise. It must be acknowledged that as regards moral conduct, Port-Royal was above reproach, apart, of course from the obstinacy and rebelliousness which developed at a later period. However, in the seventeenth century, France possessed a vast number of men and women distinguished for real sanctity, such as the Bishops of Marseilles and Cahors, Jean Baptiste Gault (d. 1643), and Alain de Solminihac (d. 1659), the great missionaries Jean Eudes (d. 1680), Grignon de Montfort (d. 1716), the Apostle of Brittany, Michel Le Nobletz (d. 1652), the founder of the Brothers of Christian Schools, Jean Baptiste de Lasalle (d. 1719), the founder of the Lazarists and the Sisters of Charity Vincent de Paul (d. 1660) and his co-foundress Louise de Marillac (d. 1660), as well as other women, such as the two Marys of the Incarnation, one the Carmelite Madame Acarie (d. 1618), and the other the Ursuline Madame Gruyart (d. 1672), Jeanne de Lestonnac (d. 1640), Jeanne Françoise de Chantal (d. 1641), Margaret Mary Alacoque and, lastly, among the much maligned Jesuits, the two missionaries Francis Regis (d. 1640) in the Cevennes and Julian Maunoir in Brittany (d. 1683), the devout Claude de la Columbière (d. 1682), and the eight missionaries martyred in Canada whose leaders were Isaac Jogues (d. 1646) and Jean de Brébeuf (d. 1649).

Before the achievements of such heroes of self-sacrifice and brotherly love, the theologizing nuns of Port-Royal and the handful of penitents among its hermits, sink into insignificance, even as regards mere numbers. Outside convent walls it may be that many lay people, especially in the early days of the sect, felt themselves encouraged to greater fervour by their rigour, but on the religious life of the masses Jansenism could only have a chilling effect. True, the new teachers were not immediately interested in the masses : Jansenism was above all the heresy of the *salon* and the study, the mass of the people was only the hapless victim of its exaggerations.

One result of this exclusiveness was that Jansenism did nothing for popular missions, for the spread of Christianity overseas nor did it make any monastic foundation worth mentioning.[1] But after a number of priests had gone over to the sect, it brought its action to bear on the masses also. To very many the new teaching could not but be welcome inasmuch as it more or less did away with the irksome duty of confession, in fact abstention from the Sacraments became transfigured with the halo of a higher perfection.[2] Large sections of the people were thus first alienated from religious practices and thereby from religion itself. Furthermore the excessive rigorism of the parish priests led to a cleavage between them and their flock ; a small number of particularly devout souls remained loyal to the priests but the latter saw themselves increasingly abandoned by the bulk of the faithful. For many the end could only be the ruin of all religion.[3] The absurdity of the Jansenist teaching which made of God a tyrant and an executioner, and of man a machine and a marionette, the exaggerations of Jansenist moral teaching which was for ever at variance with sound reason,[4] were bound to lead to the following

[1] Towards political life the Jansenists also adopt, for the most part, an attitude of indifference ; *cf.* P. HONIGSHEIM, *Die Staats- und Soziallehren der französischen Jansenisten im 17. Jahrhundert* (Diss), Heidelberg, 1914.

[2] *Abra de Raconis* spoke in this sense already in 1644 (DE MEYER, 317). SICARD (*L'ancien clergé en France*, I., Paris, 1905, 467) says : " Les Jansénistes, avec leur tendence d'esprit à la Tertullien, ne voyaient pas qu'ils faisaient déserter l'église et qu'à force d'épurer les fidèles . . . ils finissaient par n'en avoir rien . . . Sous prétexte de n'ouvrir les trésors spirituels qu'aux âmes vraiment converties, ils finissent dans quelques diocèses par en priver des populations entières."

[3] The opinion that such was the real object of the sect arose already in 1654, see p. 73, n. 2.

[4] " On peut le dire aujourd'hui, sans craindre de passer pour le complice du P. Annat et du P. Le Tellier : c'étaient les Jésuites alors qui défendaient la bonne cause (COUSIN, Jacqueline Pascal,[6] Paris, 1869, 6) ; L'Église se rangea du côté du bon sens et de la liberté (SICARD, *L'ancien clergé en France*, I., 463).

result[1]: in 1641 Jansenius magnified the omnipotence of divine grace at the expense of human freedom; in 1789 the French National Assembly exalted the rights of man at the expense of those of God.

[1] *Goethe* is of opinion that "Voltaire, Hume, Lamettrie, Helvetius, Rousseau and their whole school did far less harm to religion and morality than the stern, sickly Pascal and his school" (*Werke*, edit. Hempel, XXIX., 43). Voltaire would assuredly have been rejected with loud protests had not the ground been prepared for him by Jansenism also. The French envoy to Venice, D'Argenson (d. 1651) lamented already on May 31, 1651, in a letter to the nuncio of Turin, that the new teaching was gaining ground, "avec péril très-grand qu'il ne se forme un athéisme de cette secte, particulièrement pour la noblesse" (in Rapin, II., 122).

CHAPTER II

CREATIONS OF CARDINALS BY URBAN VIII—RELATIONS WITH POLAND—STRUGGLE AGAINST THE CÆSARO-PAPALISM OF THE SMALL ITALIAN STATES, OF VENICE AND SPAIN—THE PORTUGUESE REVOLUTION.

DURING the twenty years of his pontificate Urban VIII. saw the death of twenty Cardinals,[1] among them that of the nephew of each of his two predecessors, viz. Ludovico Ludovisi (November 18th, 1632) and Scipio Borghese (October 2nd, 1633). In nine creations he appointed seventy-eight Cardinals of whom four were reserved *in petto*. After he had bestowed the purple on his nephew Francesco Barberini, on October 2nd, 1623, and, on October 7th, 1624, on his brother Antonio Barberini, as well as on Lorenzo Magalotti and, out of gratitude towards Paul V., on Pier Maria Borghese,[2] a considerable time passed before a further creation. In this respect the Pope was chiefly guided by the view that only outstanding men should be summoned to the supreme senate of the Church.[3] Delay was likewise caused by the various and conflicting proposals of candidates by France and the Emperor.[4] A

[1] See the names in CIACONIUS, IV., 637 *seq.*

[2] *Ibid.*, 531 *seq.*

[3] *Cf.* *Avviso of October 14, 1623, *Urb.* 1093, Vatican Library. See also the *report of the envoy of Este, September 16, 1623, State Archives, Modena.

[4] The French Government first suggested Marquemont, and immediately afterwards the Archbishop of Tours, Bertrand d'Eschaux, but finally, through the good offices of the nuncio Spada, decided to leave the choice between these two to Urban VIII.; see *NICOLETTI, II., 1261, Vatican Library. Urban VIII. had at first only given a vague promise about Marquemont: see *Brief to Louis XIII., November 18, 1623, *Epist.*, I., 1, Papal Secret Archives. It appears from the *Brief to Ferdinand II. of August 31, 1623 (*ibid.*), that the Emperor first suggested G. D. Spinola, whereupon Urban demanded that a German should be nominated, since according to the decrees of the Council of Trent

fairly large creation took place on January 19th, 1626, for fifteen wearers of the purple had died since the election of Urban VIII.[1] Those elected were: one Frenchman, Denis Simon de Marquemont, Archbishop of Lyons; one German, Ernest Adalbert von Harrach, Archbishop of Prague[2]; one Spaniard, Enrico Guzmán de Aros; and nine Italians, viz.: Luigi Caetani, Archbishop of Capua, a man full of zeal for the reform; Bernadino Spada, who had been nuncio in Paris since 1623[3]; the Prefect of the Palace, Laudivio Zacchia, who had been nuncio at Venice under Gregory XV.[4]; Berlingherio Gessi, who had distinguished himself at the time of the acquisition of Urbino[5]; the son of the Doge of Venice, Federigo Cornaro, Bishop of Bergamo; Giulio Sacchetti, Spanish nuncio since 1624[6]; the Uditore di Camera,

all nations were to be represented in the College of Cardinals. The Swiss desired the red hat for their nuncio (see *Brief of September 7, 1624, *ibid.*).

[1] See CIACONIUS, IV., 539 *seq.*; CARDELLA, VI., 249 *seq.*, for further details on those nominated.

[2] For Harrach *cf.* Vol. XXVIII., p. 117 *seq.* The Cardinal's correspondence is preserved in the Archives of Count Harrach at Vienna. *Cf. Archivalien zur neuren Gesch. Österreichs*, I., 4, Vienna, 1913.

[3] His marble bust is in the Spada Palace at Rome. G. B. TARABUCCI writes in his **Relation* of 1643 with regard to Spada: "É un signore desideroso d'honore, di gloria e di riputatione"; the Pope and Cardinal Barberini very frequently avail themselves of his services, "nelle consulte più ardue"; the Cardinal is said to be overwhelmed with work and therefore difficult of access. Gonzaga Archives, Mantua.

[4] For Algardi's wonderful bust of Zacchia, see *Jahrb. der preuss. Kunstsamml.*, XXVI., 170 *seq.*

[5] *Cf.* Vol. XXVIII., p. 58 *seqq.* For Gessi, see besides MIGNE, 991, the **Vita card. Gypsii a se ipso conscripta* in *Barb.* 2552, p. 82 *seq.*, Vatican Library.

[6] G. B. TARABUCCI bestows high praise on Sacchetti in his **Relation* of 1643 (" è uno de'più qualificati soggetti ch'il habbia s. Collegio "), Gonzaga Archives at Mantua, and in the **Relatione dei cardinali papabili* of 1644, in *Cod.* C. 20 of the Boncompagni Archives, Rome.

Giandomenico Spinola[1]; the head of the Dataria, Jacopo de'Cavalieri and Lelio Biscia, Prefect of the Annona. The brother of the Duke of Lorraine, Nicolas François, the President of the Romagna, Girolamo Vidoni, and the Maggiordomo Marzio Ginetti were named *in petto* and only proclaimed on August 30th, 1627. On the same date the nominations took place of the Governor of Umbria, Fabrizio Verospi, Alessandro Cesarini and, at the request of the Kings of France and Spain respectively, those of Pierre Bérulle and Egidio Carillo Albornoz. Five Cardinals were again reserved *in petto*.[2] Two of the latter, Antonio Barberini and Girolamo Colonna, were published on February 7th, 1628.[3] There was to be no other promotion in the immediate future though many vacancies occurred in the Sacred College,[4] but in February,

[1] For Spinola see BOGLINO, *La Sicilia* (1884), 59 *seq.*

[2] *Cf.* for those nominated, CIACONIUS, IV., 556 *seq.*; CARDELLA, VIII., 277 *seq.*, and NOVAES, IX., 234 *seq.* For Ginetti see also the Appendix to *Ciaconius*, Romae, 1791, 6 *seq.* Of Verospi, a **Relatione de'cardinali papabili fatta al princ. del a.* 1630, records his "costumi integri", and his "grandissimo valore" (*Cod.* C. 20 of Boncompagni Archives, Rome). Albornoz became "capo della fattione Spagnola"; G. B. TARABUCCI says of him in his *Relation of 1643: "*A lui sono appoggiati tutti gl'interessi della corona" (Gonzaga Archives, Mantua). The question of reservation "in petto" is treated by MICH. LONGINO in a *Discorso*, dedicated to Urban VIII., *Barb.* 4504 and 5243, Vatican Library. *Cf. Archiv für kath. Kirchenrecht*, LXXXI., 421 *seq.* For Bérulle's Cardinalate see *Lettres de Richelieu*, II., 276 *seq.*, 278 *seq.*, 310, 625; WIENS, *Faucon*, 101. A letter of Bérulle to Richelieu, dated Paris, October 28, 1627, is in FILLON, *Autogr.* 2509. Urban VIII. allowed Duke Nic. François of Lorraine, who was in Minor Orders, to resign his cardinalate in order to marry; see **Bull* of May 5, 1639, Papal Secret Archives, XI., 49, p. 200. A similar case is reported in **Acta consist.* (MS. in my possession); December 1, 1642, *Dimissio pilii card^lis^ Mauritii de Savoia*; 13 *April.* 1643 *Acceptatio* of this *dimissio.*

[3] See CIACONIUS, IV., 565 *seq.*

[4] The *Avviso of April 12, 1627, reports that when the death of Bevilacqua occurred on April 7, there were 12 vacant places in the College of Cardinals. *Urb.* 1097, Vatican Library.

1629, shortly after the death of Cardinal Cavalieri (January 28th) a creation was confidently expected.[1] Cardinal Pietro Valiero died at the beginning of April, and Cardinals Bandini and Peretti in the first days of August. It now appeared certain that the gaps in the Sacred College would be filled in the near future.[2] In the sequel the deaths took place of Carlo Madruzzo, Millini and Bérulle, but it was only on November 19th, 1629, that Urban VIII. proceeded to a fresh creation. On that day two of those reserved *in petto* in August, 1627, viz. the nuncio of Madrid, Giovan Battista Pamfili and the nuncio of Paris, Guido del Bagno[3] together with eight others, were proclaimed; they were Peter Pázmány, proposed by the Emperor; the Viennese nuncio, Giovan Battista Pallotto; the Polish nuncio, Antonio Santa Croce; Richelieu's brother, Alphonse Louis, Archbishop of Lyons; Gregorio Novis, President of the Annona; the auditor of the Rota Luca Antonio Virili; the Milanese Teodoro Trivulzi and the Archbishop of Seville, Diego Guzmán de Naro.[4] With the inclusion of two reserved *in petto*, the supreme senate of the Church was once more complete.

On the occasion of the elevation of the church of St. Charles al Corso to the dignity of a cardinalitial title, on October 6th,

[1] See the *report of Fabio Carandini Ferrari of February 3, 1629, State Archives, Modena.

[2] See the *report of Carlo Camillo Molza, August 13, 1629, *ibid.*

[3] The mortuary chapel of Cardinal Bagno, one of great interest for the history of art, is unfortunately little known. It is next to S. Alessio on the Aventine and contains the statue of the Cardinal by Dom. Guidi; see FORCELLA, VIII., 364; L. ZAMBARELLI, *S. Alessio e Bonifacio*, 22.

[4] See CIACONIUS, IV., 570 *seq.*; CARDELLA, VI., 284 *seq.*; for the Cardinal of Lyons, see DE MUN, *Un frère de Richelieu*, in the *Rev. d'hist. dipl.*, XVIII. (1904), and NAVENNE, I., 163 *seq.* Virili was buried in S. Trinità de'Monti, Rome. (See CIACONIUS, IV., 582); his brother also raised a monument to him in the Abbey church of Farfa adorned with a bust of the Cardinal. G. B. TARABUCCI, in his *Relation* of 1643 praises the ability of Pallotto, but says he was difficult of access. Gonzaga Archives, Mantua.

1627, by Urban VIII.,[1] a decree of the Congregation of Ceremonies dated May 14th, 1630, on the political rank and the style of preconized Cardinals was read in a consistory of June 10th, 1630. By its terms they were to rank immediately after kings, and they alone, together with the ecclesiastical Electors and the Grand-Master of the Order of St. John, were to have a right to be styled "Eminence".[2] On June 15th the Duke of Savoy protested against this decree, for on account of his pretensions with regard to Cyprus, the Duke claimed royal rank for himself.[3] The lengthy negotiations with Poland on the subject of a Cardinal led to the bestowal of the purple, on December 20th, 1632, on the Bishop of Cracow, John Albert, a son of Sigismund III. That excellent prelate was unfortunately carried off by death as early as December 16th, 1634.[4] One Cardinal died in 1630, another in 1631, two in 1632, and a third on October 3rd, 1633.[5] This necessitated a considerable promotion which took place on November 28th, 1633. Accordingly the two prelates

[1] See **Acta consist.*, *Barb.* 2986, Vatican Library.

[2] *Ibid. Cf.* *NICOLETTI, II., ch. 20, p. 1675 *seq.*, Vatican Library. KHEVENHÜLLER, XI., 1410; *Anal. iuris pontif.*, 1855, p. 1921; HINSCHIUS, I., 357. An "Oratio in Eminentiae titulum" in *Barb.* 1807, Vatican Library. Urban VIII. showed at the very beginning of his pontificate that he wished to see special honour paid to the Cardinals; see **Avviso* of September 6, 1623, *Urb.* 1093, *ibid.* Early in November, 1623, the Congregation of Rites deliberated upon a reform of titles; on November 6 it was reported that they had decided on the title of "Eminentissimo" for the Cardinals (*Avvisi of November 1 and 6, 1623); but on November 29, the envoy of Este *reported that: "Il titolo d'Eminentissimi che si doveva dichiarare per li sig. cardinali pare che sia svanito" (State Archives, Modena). Urban VIII., however, did not abandon the idea; *cf.* the *letter of Lorenzo Belli of 1635 in *Barb.* 6443, Vatican Library.

[3] See SIRI, VII., 293 *seq.*; P. BRAYDA, *Il titolo di Eminenza ai cardinali ed i Duchi di Savoia* (*Tre documenti del* 1630), Bene Vagienna, 1922.

[4] See CIACONIUS, IV., 580.

[5] *Ibid.*, 597 *seq.*

reserved *in petto* in 1629, viz. Ciriaco Rocci, nuncio in Switzerland from 1628 to 1630 and after that in Vienna, and Caesare Monti, nuncio in Madrid since 1630, were proclaimed. Six other prelates were likewise raised to the Sacred College; they were: Alessandro Bichi, nuncio in Paris since the autumn of 1630; Francesco Maria Brancaccio, who as Bishop of Capaccio had steadfastly defended the rights of the Church against the viceroy of Naples; Ulderico Carpegna, Bishop of Gubbio; the treasurer Stefano Durazzo; Agostino Oreggi, Secretary of the Congregations of the Inquisition and of Rites and the intimate friend of the younger Cardinal Antonio Barberini, Benedetto Monaldi Baldeschi.[1] The Bishop of Lucca, Marcantonio Franciotti, who was nominated *in petto*, was only proclaimed on March 30th, 1637.

Year by year death was thinning the ranks of the Sacred College. In 1634 it lost three of its members; two died in each of the next three years, viz. 1635, 1636, 1637, four in 1638 and six in 1639; yet the fresh recruits so eagerly desired by the Curia [2] were not forthcoming.[3] Only when a further five Cardinals had died in the course of 1641, did the Pope

[1] See **Acta consist. Urbani VIII.*, 1631–4, original MS. from the library of Cardinal Gentili, bought by me in 1902 in Rome. According to this document the Pope, when proposing the candidates, said: "Qui omnes adeo Curiae et vobis sunt cogniti, ut de illorum erga hanc sanctam sedem meritis plura dicere sit superfluum." For those nominated see CIACONIUS, IV., 584 *seq.*; CARDELLA, VI., 302 *seq.* *Cf.* NANI, 30 *seq.* For Bichi *cf. Rev. hist.*, XXIX., 472 and F. BANDINI PICCOLOMINI, *Notizie di documenti Senesi relat. alla monarchia francese nei tempi del card. Richelieu*, Siena, 1894. Bichi was, as G. B. TARABUCCI shows in his *Relation* of 1643, a favourite not only with the French, but also with the Spaniards. It is further stated here that Carpegna lived a quiet and devout life; Brancaccio was very polite and capable and "partialissimo del card. Antonio Rocci e un amabilissimo signore". Gonzaga Archives, Mantua.

[2] See NANI, 32 *seq.*

[3] *Cf.* also FAGNIEZ, II., 405 *seq.*, for the years 1637–8. In March, 1640, eight red hats were available and there were many candidates for them; see DENIS, *Nouvelles*, I., 11.

at last decide to make a fresh creation on December 16th, 1641.[1] The purple was bestowed on the following candidates: Francesco Maria Machiavelli, a kinsman of the Barberini; Ascanio Filomarino, Archbishop of Naples; the Venetian Marcantonio Bragadino, Bishop of Vicenza; the Genoese Ottaviano Raggi; the Treasurer Pier Donato Cesi; the Dominican Vincenzo Maculano; Francesco Peretti Montalto, the last descendant of the family of Sixtus V.; the Roman Girolamo Verospi, a nephew of Cardinal Fabrizio; Giulio Gabrielli and Virginio Orsini, Rinaldo d'Este, at the request of the Emperor and, lastly, the ruling minister of France, Mazarin.[2] After the death of another five Cardinals in 1642 and that of a sixth at the beginning of 1643, Urban VIII. proceeded to his last creation on July 13th, 1643. In it a

[1] CIACONIUS, IV., 599, and CARDELLA, VI., 1, leave it undecided whether the creation took place on December 10 or 16. **Acta consist.* (*loc. cit.*) give 16th, but the *Nouvelles*, ed. Denis, I., 14, give 13th by mistake.

[2] For those nominated see CIACONIUS, IV., 599 *seq.*; CARDELLA, VII., 1 *seq.* From the *Brief to Duke Francis d'Este of Modena of October 4, 1636 (*Epist.*, XIII–XIV., Papal Secret Archives), it appears that he had already then made a request for the red hat for his brother; later Ferdinand III. warmly supported the request; see the *Brief addressed to him of June 11, 1639, *loc. cit.* For Mazarin's cardinalate see *Rev. des Guest. hist.*, XVI. (1874). On A. Filomarino *cf. Arch. stor. Napolet.*, 1880–1; REUMONT, *Carafa*, I., 299 *seq.* For the grave of Filomarino designed by Borromini in the church of the Holy Apostles at Naples, see WEISBACH, *Baukunst*, 192. An anonymous characterization of the Cardinals refers to Machiavelli's "buona indole et natura", to Filomarino's "buoni costumi", but misses scholarship both in him and Bragadino; Raggi was "di buoni costumi e ingenuo", also "intelligente", but unstable; Cesi, "nel tesoriato è stato tenace, libero nel parlare, di natura gagliarda, intelligente de'negozii e di lettere mediocramente"; Maculano loved his relations more than befitted a religious; Peretti had been made a Cardinal through the favour of the Spanish ambassador; Gabrielli was "intelligente e capace di negotii"; the same is said of Orsini. Papal Secret Archives, XI., 49, p. 239 *seq.*

number of papal diplomatists were rewarded for their services: these were Cesare Facchinetti, nuncio in Madrid from 1639 till 1642, as well as his successor, Gian Giacomo Panciroli; also Lelio Falconieri who had been appointed nuncio in Brussels in 1635 but whom the Government refused to accept; Gasparo Mattei, since 1641 nuncio in Paris and Cardinal Rossetti, the Pope's representative at the Peace Congress of Cologne. The Secretary of State, Francesco Adriano Ceva, Fausto Poli, Maggiordomo and Administrator of the possessions of the Barberini and Antonio Giori, Maestro di Camera, owed the purple to their close relations with the Pope. To these were added besides the Jesuit Juan de Lugo, a man as learned as he was humble, and Achille d'Estampes, known as Cardinal of Valençai, who had rendered great services in the war of Castro, a number of men who had distinguished themselves in the service of the Court and in the administration: they were the Romans Giambattista Altieri, Mario Teodoli, Angelo Francesco Rapaccioli, Vincenzo Costaguti, Paolo Emilio Condinini and the Genoese Gian Stefano Donghi.[1]

[1] See Ciaconius, IV., 617 *seq.*; Cardella, VII., 21 *seq.* For Costaguti as a lover of music see Ambros, IV., 340. F. Poli is sharply criticized in the *" Characterization " quoted above, p. 163, note 2. " Di nessuna letteratura, incapace e giovane e non ha altro merito che di essere accetto a tutti Barberini havendo loro ministrato l'entrate." Of Lugo it is said (*cf. Freib. Kirchenlex.*, VIII.², 284 *seq*; Sommervogel, V., 176 *seq.*, IX., 619 *seq.*): " La nuova del cardinalato li fu portata mentre stava nel refettorio, et all'aviso venne preso, ma si riebbe subito " (Papal Secret Archives, *loc. cit.*). Lugo (see Astráin, V., 82 *seq.*), gained great merit by propagating the use of quinine as an antidote to malaria; *cf.* also the essay by A. Canezza in the *Corriere d'Italia* of October 4, 1925. A very unfavourable opinion of Poli, Ceva and Gori is contained in the **Discorso dei cardinali papabili* of 1644 in *Cod.* 20 of the Boncompagni Archives, Rome. In his uncritical work on Clement XIV., Theiner asserts the existence of a medal of Urban VIII.'s with the legend: " Non vos me elegistis, sed ego elegi vos," which was intended as an allusion to the fact that all the Cardinals who had elected him were dead. This assertion is quite wrong for at the death of

The Popes have at all times found it difficult to satisfy the wishes of the various Governments in the creation of Cardinals. Urban VIII. also experienced this more than once. Repeatedly the Emperor[1] and the Kings of Spain and France were dissatisfied. It was a particularly embarrassing practice of nuncios to try to obtain the purple with the help of the Princes to whom they were accredited. Already Pius IV. had issued a Bull against this abuse,[2] but he failed to root out the evil. Again and again exceptions had to be made, but just as often the requests of Princes had to be rejected. Thus Sigismund III. had vainly sought to obtain the red hat for the nuncio Rangoni.[3] In 1627 he sought to obtain it for the nuncio Lancellotti who had been at Warsaw since 1622.[4] The Pope resisted this demand but yielded in 1629 when he granted the purple to Antonio Santa Croce, Lancellotti's successor.[5] On December 20th, 1632, the Pope gave satisfaction to the new King Ladislaus IV. by raising to the Sacred College the deserving son of Sigismund III., John Albert. When the latter died in 1634, Ladislaus demanded the same honour, in 1640, for Onorato Visconti, nuncio in Poland from 1630 to 1635.[6] The Pope could not see his way to accede to the

Urban VIII. seven Cardinals of Paul V.'s time and one of Gregory XV.'s were still alive; moreover, MARTINORI (78) has been unable to trace any such medal.

[1] As early as 1626, because the Nuncio at Vienna had not been nominated; see Altoviti's *report from Vienna, dated February 4, 1626, State Archives, Florence.

[2] See BIAUDET, 26. [3] *Cf.* our account, Vol. XXVI., 237, 219.

[4] See the *Briefs to Sigismund III. of June 12, 1627, and April 1, 1628, in the *Epist.*, V., Papal Secret Archives. For Lancellotti's nunciature see *Anz. der Krakauer Akad.*, 1893, 110 *seq.*

[5] Urban VIII. did not like doing so for as early as May 11, 1624, he had written to Sigismund that he should rather propose a Pole; see THEINER, *Mon. Pol.*, III., 372.

[6] *Cf.* the *Brief to Ladislaus IV. of November 17, 1640, *Epist.*, XV–XVII., Papal Secret Archives. Italian music spread in Poland through the influence of O. Visconti, see O. F. TENEAJOLI, 'Musica e musicisti ital. in Polonia,'' in *Ars et Labor*, 1906.

request. When Visconti was passed over in the creation of December, 1641, the King was very angry,[1] so much so that when his candidate was also passed over in July, 1643, the situation developed into a formal rupture with the Holy See. In vain Savelli, Protector of Poland, endeavoured to smooth out the quarrel; in 1643 the nuncio of Warsaw, Mario Filonardi, was handed his passports whilst simultaneously the Polish envoy in Rome was recalled.[2] Such a step was bound to hurt the Pope all the more as from the beginning of his pontificate he had bestowed numerous favours upon Poland and had taken the greatest interest in the welfare of that kingdom which was afflicted with the same religious troubles as Germany.[3]

The Pope fully appreciated the religious sentiments of Sigismund III. which prompted the latter to win over to the Church, "with gentle pressure," the Polish nobility, and he placed great hopes on Poland not only with regard to the war against the Turks, who in this way were to be prevented from attacking Austria,[4] but likewise for the reunion of Russia to the Church by means of the union of the Ruthenians.[5] A thousand favours had been bestowed on the Polish King, the Venetian ambassador Angelo Contarini wrote in 1629.[6] In the previous year the Pope had authorized him to levy a subsidy from the clergy for the war against the Turks[7]; it was the Pontiff's thanks for the Catholic zeal of the King who gave further proof of his good disposition by co-operating with Urban VIII. in the reform of the Polish monasteries.[8]

[1] In a *Brief of March 31, 1643 (*Epist.*, XIX., *loc. cit.*), Urban VIII. sought to pacify the Polish king.

[2] See Siri, *Mercurio*, III., Lione, 1652, 493 *seq.*; Ciampi, II., 73-7; Biaudet, 51.

[3] *Cf.* R. Zeno, 177.

[4] *Ibid.*, Pietro Contarini, 217; Ang. Contarini, 295.

[5] See Urban VIII.'s remark made in 1629, in Harasiewicz, *Annales eccl. Ruth.*, Leopoldi, 1866, 323.

[6] See Ang. Contarini, 295. *Cf.* Theiner, *Mon. Pol.*, III., 378.

[7] See Theiner, 381.

[8] See the *letter of thanks to Sigismund III. of August 1, 1626, *Epist.*, III., Papal Secret Archives. *Ibid.*, *Epist.*, V.,

When Sigismund III., whom Rubens glorified as the subduer of heresy,[1] died on April 30th, 1632, the Pope favoured the election of his son Ladislaus.[2] The new ruler of Poland appointed Prince Jerzy Ossolinski as his *obbedienza* ambassador. Ossolinski was instructed to carry out his mission in the same style as the representatives of the King of France and even to surpass them: "Where the French had silver he was to take gold; where they had gold he was to have precious stones; and where they had precious stones he was to use diamonds."[3] On November 20th, 1633, Ossolinski arrived before the Porta del Popolo with a retinue of 300 men, twenty carriages, and ten camels. He was met by Cardinal De Torres, Protector of Poland, and by the Roman nobility with 160 carriages and escorted to his lodgings. Ossolinski's solemn entry was fixed for November 27th. Stefano della Bella, in a copper engraving, has perpetuated the magnificent spectacle which all Rome flocked to see.[4] The procession was headed by mounted men; then came the camels in gorgeous harness carrying the ambassador's luggage; four mounted trumpeters dressed in green velvet followed. Then came Ossolinski's body-guard of Cossacks and thirty-four knights in full armour, behind whom rode the aged shield-bearer of the envoy, also in full armour, with wings on his shoulders, and a group of pages with bows and quivers adorned with silver. The astonishment of the Romans was specially roused by six Turkish horses which followed, whose trappings were studded with emeralds and rubies whilst harness, stirrups and even the shoes were of

*Brief to Sigismund III. of July 2, 1628, with regard to the mission of the new Commissary-General of the Franciscan Province, Prosp. Gabbiati, as "Restaurator s. disciplinae".

[1] See B. ANTONIEWICZ, "Un Rubens ignoré," in *Bullet. de l'Acad. de Cracovie*, Cl. de Phil., 1905, 16 *seq.*

[2] See THEINER, *loc. cit.*, 387 *seq.*

[3] *Cf.* for what follows, L. KUBALA, *Jerzy Ossolinski* (in Polish), 2 vols., Lemberg, 1883; and CHŁĘDOWSKI, II., 119 *seq.* See also the *Avvisi of December 3 and 10, 1633, *Ottob.* 3339, Vatican Library.

[4] *Entrata in Roma dell'ecc. ambasciatore di Polonia* 1633, Roma, 1633, partly reproduced in CHŁĘDOWSKI, II., 128.

pure gold. The members of the embassy, too, were resplendent in cloaks set with diamonds. Ossolinski's *zupan* (Polish coat) of black cloth shot with gold, glittered with diamonds; his sword, set with precious stones, was valued at 20,000 scudi. On December 10th the *obbedienza* audience took place in the Sala Regia at which Ossolinski delivered an address [1] which Urban declared to be worthy of Cicero.

As early as January 3rd, 1634, Rome received within its walls yet another guest from Poland, Prince Alexander Charles. The latter immediately called on the Pope and dined with him on the 17th; on the 22nd he was honoured with the gift of the Golden Rose,[2] but he left the Eternal City on the following day without waiting for the tournament which Cardinal Barberini had arranged on the advice of Marchese Cornelio Bentivoglio. His departure was probably due to disputes over questions of precedence.[3] The fantastic festival was held on February 25th, 1634,[4] without the Prince in the Piazza Navona which had been turned into an arena by means of stands. Mascardi has left us a description. The chariot of Fame opened the proceedings; then the tournament began, at the end of which there appeared on the scene a richly decked galley with Bacchus surrounded by musicians.[5]

Whilst all Rome was still talking of the Polish visitors, reports of a very disturbing nature concerning Ladislaus IV. arrived in the Eternal City. These made it abundantly clear that the King had not inherited the staunchly Catholic sentiments of his mother. In fact he was so lukewarm in his religion [6] that he even thought of marrying Elizabeth,

[1] See CIAMPI, I., 305 *seq.*

[2] See **Diarium P. Alaleonis, Barb.* 2919, Vatican Library.

[3] This is CHŁĘDOWSKI's opinion (II., 133).

[4] Not 1631, as CHŁĘDOWSKI (II., 133) says.

[5] See the monograph dedicated to Cardinal Barberini by *Vitale Mascardi: Festa fatta in Roma alli* 25 *di Febbr.* 1634 *sotto gli auspici del card. Barberini,* pubbl. da L. Passarini, Roma, 1882 (Nozze-Publ.). *Cf.* POSSE, *Sacchi,* 7.

[6] *Cf.* the *report of the nuncio O. Visconti, July 13, 1636, in the *Relacye,* II., 189 *seq.*

the daughter of the Calvinist Winter King.[1] It was not to be expected that he would further the interests of the Church. How little Catholic feeling he had was shown by his attitude towards the dissident Ruthenians as well as towards the Uniats when, on November 12th, 1623, the latter's Martyr, the splendid Archbishop of Polozk, Josaphat Kuncewicz, expired at Witebsk under the axes of the schismatics.[2] However, even the greatest difficulties were unable to shake "the holy work of the Union". Sigismund III. had obeyed the repeated requests of the Pope[3] to protect the Union against the schismatics. Urban VIII. never wearied of urging the Ruthenian Bishops to remain steadfastly loyal to the Union.[4] In 1630 he had the joy of seeing the Archimandrite of Vilna, Meletius Smotrziski, return to the Catholic faith[5] and in the same year the Armenian Bishop of Lemberg, Nicolas Toroszewicz, promised obedience to the Roman Church.[6]

[1] How much the abandonment of this plan was appreciated in Rome appears from *Nani's* report (38).

[2] *Cf.* IAC. SUSZA, *Cursus vitae et certamen martyrii b. Iosaphat Kuncewicii*, Rome, 1665, and Brussels, 1865; N. CONTIERI, *Vita di S. Giosafat*, Roma, 1867; D. GUÉPIN, *St. Josafat Martyr*, Poitiers, 1874 (new edition in 2 vols., *ibid.*, 1897/98); G. HOFMANN, *Der heilige Josaphat*, Rome, 1923. The remains of the Martyr, whom Pius IX. canonized in 1867 and whose process of beatification had been begun by Urban VIII. in 1635 (see THEINER, *loc. cit.*, 11, and HOFMANN, *loc. cit.*), were hidden in a safe place when Russia, in 1875, suppressed Cholm, the last of the Uniat dioceses. The body was translated to the Greek-Catholic Church of St. Barbara in Vienna in 1920; at the identification the cleft of the mortal wound in the skull was clearly visible. The old pontifical vestments were removed to the national museum at Lemberg.

[3] See THEINER, *loc. cit.*, 371 *seq.*, 373, 377, 380.

[4] *Ibid.*, 378, 382.

[5] *Ibid.*, 383 *seq.*

[6] *Ibid.*, 387; *Freib. Kirchenlex.*, VII.², 1731 *seq.*, with further details on the activities of N. Toroszewicz for the union and on his journey to Rome, when Urban VIII., in 1625, confirmed him as Metropolitan of the Uniat Armenians.

Now as before, the Metropolitan Rutski [1613–1635 [1]] whom Urban VIII. had surnamed the "Atlas of the Union" and compared with St. Athanasius, worked unceasingly on behalf of the Union.[2] Difficult days came for the Union with Ladislaus IV., who already in his election capitulation had made extraordinary concessions to the schismatics, to the great injury of the Union.[3] The protests of the Ruthenian Bishops as well as the repeated complaints of the Pope against this action remained without effect.[4] In 1633 Ladislaus once more officially recognized the schism by confirming in their position the opposition Metropolitan and four opposition Bishops and by sanctioning the erection of a schismatical academy at Kiev. Even towards the Arians and the Calvinists he did not take the side of the Church to which he belonged. None the less Urban VIII. still hoped that the King would change his mind when, in April, 1635, Mario Filonardi succeeded Visconti in the Polish nunciature. In addition to promoting the Union of the Ruthenians and the Armenians, Filonardi was instructed to exert himself on behalf of the Catholic restoration in Poland where in recent times, in addition to the Jesuits,[5] the Capuchins had also begun to work for the religious renewal of the people. Before all else, in accordance with the decrees of Trent, the nuncio was to see to the reform of the clergy, to prevent pluralism, and to enforce the enclosure in convents of nuns. As regards politics, Filonardi's Instruction reveals the fact that the Pope counted on Poland to fight against the Turks and the Swedes.[6] However, on September,

[1] See Chotkowski in the *Hist.-polit. Blätter*, CIV., 545.

[2] See Hefele in the *Tüb. Theol. Quartalschr.*, 1853, 391; *Freib. Kirchenlex.*, II.², 4.

[3] *Cf.* Theiner, *loc. cit.*, 398.

[4] *Cf. ibid.*, 402 *seq.*

[5] *Cf.* Zaleski, *Jesuici w Polsce*, II. and IV., 3. See also *Script. rer. Polonic.*, XVII. and XIX.

[6] See the **Instruttione* for Filonardi, in the extract in *Nicoletti, VI., 494 *seq.*, Vatican Library. The *reports of Filonardi are in *Barb.* 6161 (1635–9), 6160 (1635–6), 6162 (1639–1642), 6065 (1635–9), 6067 (1642), *ibid.*

12th of the same year Ladislaus concluded a twenty-six years' armistice with Sweden whilst at the same time he renounced the title of King of Sweden and his claim to Livonia. The Swedish army in Poland was now free to turn against Pomerania. As for the Turks, in view of the war with Russia, Poland had already concluded a peace treaty with them a year earlier.

Urban VIII. worked on behalf of the Union until the end of his reign, and again and again he also recommended it to the King,[1] but the support of the Government was inadequate.[2] At that time the Jesuit Matthias Casimir Sarbiewski sang the advantages of unity of faith in an ode addressed to the nobility of Poland which is one of the gems of the Polish Horace: "Polish knights," we read,[3] "prophesying I foretell the coming destiny. If once again one common faith unites you round the altar of the Virgin, if Poland's entire people greets the noble Queen with incense and hymns, if as in the days of our fathers, devout crowds flock to her image and the ancient battle song resounds, then shall come the time when the waters of the Vistula and the Dniester shall once more peacefully and freely roll down from the snow-capped Carpathians, and no longer shall we fear the eagle of the East, no longer the Danish bear." [4]

(2)

All historians are agreed that Urban VIII. deemed it one of his chief duties to defend the independence of the Church.[5] To this end, as early as December, 1623, he set up a special

[1] See THEINER, *loc. cit.*, 412 *seq.*, 416 *seq.*, 417 *seq.*, 435 *seq.* *Cf. Bull.*, XIV., 318 *seq.* The Ruthenians received the church of SS. Sergius and Bacchus, in Rome; see *Bull.*, XV., 91 *seq.*

[2] See the details in LIKOWSKI, *Die ruthenisch-römische Kirchenvereinigung*, German trans., Freiburg, 1904. On the union of the Ruthenians in North Hungary see FIEDLER in the *Sitzungsber. der Wiener Akad.*, Phil.-hist. Kl. XXXIX., 487 *seq.*

[3] See DIEL in the *Stimmen aus Maria-Laach*, IV., 357.

[4] *Lyrica*, IV., Ode 1.

[5] See R. ZENO, 182.

Congregation of Cardinals whose duty it was to see to it that Gregory XV.'s Bull on ecclesiastical jurisdiction was observed.[1] Such a measure was all the more imperative as the ever-increasing State absolutism was giving rise to endless disputes. This was the case in a most acute form, in Savoy where the aged nuncio Pietro Francesco Costa showed excessive indulgence so that Urban VIII. recalled him in the spring of 1624 and replaced him by the energetic Lorenzo Campeggi.[2] The new nuncio was instructed to recover what had been lost in respect of ecclesiastical prerogatives.[3] The chief question was the right of nomination to episcopal sees, far beyond mere recommendation, to which the Duke laid claim: also the jurisdiction of the Inquisition, the safeguarding of the immunity of monasteries and the taxation of the clergy. The Instruction also draws the nuncio's attention to the heretics in Pinerolo, to the furthering of the Capuchins and the Barnabites, the support of the action of Propaganda in the districts threatened with Calvinist contagion from Geneva and the necessity of stimulating the Archbishop of Turin in the discharge of his duties.[4] The execution of the decrees of Trent

[1] See the *Avisso of December 20, 1623, Vatican Library. *NICOLETTI (II., 862, *ibid.*) places the creation of the Congregation in the year 1625, MORONI (XVI., 208), and REUSCH who follows him (II., 372), in the year 1626. A decree on the subject cannot be found. According to the inventaries, the Papal Secret Archives (X., 1) preserved the minutes (protocols) of the *Congregatio immunitatis* from 1633, but since the removal of the archives to Paris, these have not been seen.

[2] The "uditore" of Campeggi was Bernardino Campello, known also as a writer (*cf.* CRISTOFANI, *Della vita e degli scritti del conte B. Campello*, Assisi, 1873, and *P. Campello della Spina Il castello di Campello*, Roma, 1889). His detailed report on the nunciature of 1627, was published by PAGNOTTI in the *Arch. d. Soc. Rom.*, XVI., 454 *seq.* Campeggi's *reports and the instructions sent to him are in the *Nunziat. di Savoia*, 42–4, 45, 167, 168, Papal Secret Archives.

[3] "*V.S. vada riacquistando il perduto." *Instruttione a Msgr. Campeggi vesc. di Cerano per la Nunziatura di Torino, Cod.* X,V. 14, of the Casanat. Library, Rome.

[4] *Ibid.*

wherever they had not been carried through was to be the principal duty of the nuncio of Turin, as it was that of every other nuncio.[1] Campeggi's successor, Fausto Caffarelli (after 1634), was engaged in several conflicts for the preservation of ecclesiastical jurisdiction,[2] and his successor Cecchinelli in his turn had to fight a bitter struggle against an edict published by the Regent Maria Christina on April 30th, 1643, which encroached on ecclesiastical immunity. In the end the nuncio suggested the proclamation of an interdict but to this Urban VIII. would not consent.[3]

As with Savoy so did conflicts arise with Tuscany, not only over the possessions in the Romagna but likewise over the clergy's exemption from taxation which nearly led to a rupture.[4] In that quarter relations with Urban VIII. were still further adversely affected by the circumstance that the Grand-Duke Ferdinand II. showed himself wholly dependent on Spain.[5] With regard to ecclesiastical affairs it was a fatal thing that the Grand-Duke was badly advised by his confessors, the Jesuit Maurizio da Curtis, Fr. Giovan Francesco Centurione, a Discalced Carmelite, and the Barnabite Francesco Casallo.[6]

[1] *Cf.* Pagnotti in *Arch. d. Soc. Roma*, XVI., 467.

[2] *Cf.* the work of Maggiorotti (p. 26 *seq.*) quoted in note 3.

[3] See A. Bazzoni, *La reggenza di Maria Cristina*, Torino, 1865, 273 *seq.* Maggiorotti, *Il Piemonte dal* 1637 *al* 1642. *I contrasti nella reggenza di Maria Cristina e l'opera dei Nunzi papali*, Città di Castello, 1913, shows (122), that the chief credit for the peace between Savoy and France (June 14, 1642), which was furthered by Urban VIII., belongs not to Cecchinelli, but to his predecessor Caffarelli.

[4] *Cf.* Nani, 38; Reumont, *Toskana*, I., 413.

[5] *Cf.* Reumont, *loc. cit.*, 414.

[6] *Cf.* the account dedicated to Urban VIII., **La Nuntiatura di G. Fr. Passionei in Toscana*, 1634–1641, in *Barb.* 5678 *seq.*, p. 31, Vatican Library. Here we read of P. Centurione: " *Alla libertà ecclesiastica è contrario sopra modo, se bene pare a lui di fomentare la giustizia e sostentando li pareri contrarii alle risolutioni delle Sacre Congregationi di Roma in favor del Gran Duca, crede diffendere l'innocenza. Mostra di amare il Gran Duca con amore tanto straordinario che eccede ancora gli affetti

The result was a number of violations of ecclesiastical liberty and immunity.[1]

A very grievous conflict with the Republic of Lucca arose out of a similar cause in 1638. There can be no doubt of the survival, in that city, of the anti-Catholic spirit which had led it to the verge of apostasy from the Church already in the days of Paul III.[2] Gregory XV. had complained that Lucca allowed German Protestants to reside within its walls, a fact which constituted a danger of heretical contagion.[3] Violations of ecclesiastical immunity were the order of the day at Lucca. Another source of harm lay in the circumstance that the aged Bishop Alessandro Guidiccioni was quite unequal to his task. Urban VIII. was unwilling to proceed against him because Guidiccioni had at one time opposed him and the Pope feared lest action on his part should have the appearance of revenge.[4] When Guidiccioni died in 1637, the Pope gave the see to the excellent Cardinal Marcantonio Franciotti. The latter, a descendant of an old aristocratic family of Lucca, did all he could to improve ecclesiastical conditions in his native city.[5] But the Government of Lucca, which had at one time complained of Bishop Guidiccioni, was not yet satisfied. It created one difficulty after another for the Cardinal and continued to violate ecclesiastical jurisdiction. The disputes became so serious that on September 1st, 1639, Urban VIII. commanded the Cardinal to leave the city to

dei cortigiani non che i termini de'religiosi. È amicissimo del Vettori et conferiscono insieme i studi de'casi più gravi. . . ." Here also indications of the Spanish tendencies of the Grand-Duke. The author declares that: *" Il card. de Medici, zio del Duca, non s' ingerisce nei negocii." The Codex contains all the *Lettre, Cifre* and *Informazioni* of *Passionei*.

[1] See **La Nuntiatura di G. Fr. Passionei*, n. 47 *seq.*, 151 *seq.*, *loc. cit.*

[2] *Cf.* our account, Vol. XII., 498 *seq.*

[3] *Cf.* the *Relation* in the *Studi e docum.*, XXII., 207.

[4] *Ibid.*, 184, note 2.

[5] See *NICOLETTI, VI., ch. 20, Vatican Library; MORONI, XXVII., 145 *seq.*

which he then dispatched Cesare Raccagna, Bishop of Città di Castello, as Apostolic Commissary.[1] When every exhortation had proved in vain the latter saw himself at last compelled to lay an interdict upon the city of Lucca and its territory. The sentence was proclaimed on April 2nd, 1640.[2] The clergy observed the interdict but the Government would not yield even now, for it was aware that both the Grand-Duke of Tuscany and Spain were on its side.[3] Lucca's conduct grieved the Pope all the more as he had bestowed many favours on the city, and in 1633 he had assigned to its people a church of their own in Rome.[4] After prolonged negotiations a satisfactory compromise was reached, whereupon Urban VIII., on March 31st, 1643, raised the interdict.[5]

But most of the Pope's worries and continual annoyances were caused by Venice. The attitude of the Republic of St. Mark in every important political question was as damaging

[1] *Brief to Lucca, October 22, 1639, *Epist.*, XVII., Papal Secret Archives.

[2] The action of Lucca was defended by G. BERALDI : *Difesa per la republica di Lucca,* Colonia, 1640 ; and *Relatione d'alcuni successi occorsi alla republ. di Lucca negli anni* 1638–1640 *dopo la venuta a quel vescovada del s. card. Franciotti,* Colonia, 1640. The name Beraldi and the place of printing are fictitious ; the documents are of no historical value. For a corrective see the *reports in *Cod.* G. VIII., 244, of the Chigi Library, Rome, especially p. 1 *seq.* : *Narratione di quanto è seguito in Lucca contra il card. Franciotti e suoi fratelli* ; 43 *seq.* : *Relatione di Msgr. Raccagna spedito commiss. apost. contro la republ. di Lucca* (1639). This Relation is also in *Barb.* 4, p. 1 ; *cf. ibid.*, 4607, and *NICOLETTI, VI., ch. 20, Vatican Library. See also *Vat.* 8460, p. 1 *seq* : FRANC. MARIA FEBEI, **Memoria sopra l'interdetto contra Lucca* 1641 *cavata dal diario del Febei,* Vatican Library.

[3] See NANI, 39.

[4] The church of St. Bonaventure which was henceforth called Sta. Croce dei Lucchesi ; see A. GUERRA, *Storia del Volto Santo di Lucca,* Lucca, 1881, 174 *seq.* *Cf.* also CANCELLIERI, *Lettera sopra il Tarantismo,* 313.

[5] See **Acta consist.* for March 31, 1643, MS. in my possession ; *NICOLETTI, VI., ch. 20, *loc. cit.*

to Catholic interests as was its ecclesiastical policy. Though fully cognizant of the situation, Urban was nevertheless anxious, after his election, to do everything that could be done without sacrificing the Church's rights, so as to establish tolerable relations with Venice.[1] In conversation with the Venetian ambassador, Renier Zeno, the Pope expatiated on the merits of the Venetian Constitution whilst at the same time he stressed Venice's importance for the preservation of the independence of Italy in opposition to Spanish preponderance, though he also strongly warned the Republic against allying itself with the Protestant Powers.[2] Nor did the shrewd Venetians fail to realize how much they would benefit by being on good terms with the Pope; accordingly, yielding to the strong protests of the Secretary of State [3] and the Pope,[4] they cancelled the proposal of setting up an inscription in honour of Sarpi.[5] For all that the spirit of that sinister personage was still at work in the City of the Lagoons and the new nuncio in Venice, Giovan Battista Agucchi, was to have ample evidence of the fact when he took the place of Laudivio Zacchia towards the end of 1623.[6]

Agucchi's Instruction enumerates the following complaints of the Holy See: Venice's alliance with the German Protestants, especially with the Duke of Halberstadt and with Mansfeld, by which, as well as by its hostility towards the Emperor, the Republic did grave injury to the Catholic religion; the reception of the envoys of Bethlen Gábor and Holland; its friendship with the Turks; the toleration

[1] *Cf.* *Avviso for August 26, 1623, *Urb.* 1093, Vatican Library.

[2] See R. Zeno, 181 *seq.*, 183.

[3] The same called for the intervention of France; see the *Instruction to the nuncio Corsini at Paris, October 23, 1623, in *Cod.* X., VI., 16 of the Casanat. Library, Rome.

[4] See R. Zeno, 183.

[5] See R. Zeno, 183. *Cf.* above, p. 41. See also *Carte Strozze*, I., 2, 83 *seq.*

[6] See the *Brief to Venice, December 16, 1623, *Epist.*, I.[a], Papal Secret Archives. For G. B. Agucchi, *cf. Rev. d'hist. et de litt. relig.*, VII. (1902), 487 *seq.*

of Protestant worship in the houses of foreign envoys and the printing of anti-Catholic writings and lastly the long-standing encroachments on the rights of the Church.[1]

During his stay in Venice, Agucchi displayed the utmost consideration and prudence in defending the rights of the Church whilst the Venetian ambassador in Rome, Pietro Contarini, had recourse to threats in the hope of rendering the Pope more accommodating. In the summer of 1624 he demanded for an utterly worldly young man, whose only recommendation was that he was his kinsman, the wealthy Abbey of St. Zeno at Verona. As was to be expected the Pope refused and when a second request also remained fruitless, Contarini remarked that the Pope must not be surprised if Venice also took no notice of his wishes.[2] The new Doge, Giovanni Cornaro, who entered on office at the beginning of 1625, assured the nuncio that he was anxious to be on the best of terms with the Holy See,[3] but Venice's policy in the question of the Valtellina and that of Urbino was utterly at variance with these promises.[4] Among other things, Agucchi had to complain of the fact that, in order to deceive the people of Venice, the Protestant envoy Thurn was allowed to assist at Catholic services.[5] But the pretensions of the Venetian Government to a right of nomination to ecclesiastical

[1] **Instruttione a Msgr. Agucchio Nunzio destinato alla republ. di Venetia*, MS. in my possession. *Barb.* 6049 contains the **Lettere decifrate di L. Zacchia e G. B. Agucchi*, from October, 1623, to March, 1625; *Barb.* 6055 has the *reports of Agucchi from December, 1623, to December, 1624; *Barb.* 6052, *those of 1627; *Barb.* 6053, *those of 1628; *Barb.* 6082, *those from December 29, 1629, to December, 1630; *Barb.* 6059, *those of 1630; *Barb.* 6055, Agucchi's *reports of 1631, Vatican Library. *Cf.* also in the Papal Secret Archives, *Nunziat. di Venezia*, 44–9 (**Lettere del Nunzio di Venezia*), 273–5 (**Lettere al Nunzio di Venezia*).

[2] See Agucchi's *reports of June 1 and 8, 1624, in *Nicoletti, II, ch. 8, Vatican Library.

[3] See Agucchi's *report of January 2, 1625, *ibid.*

[4] *Cf.* Vol. XXVIII., p. 94 *seq.*

[5] See *Nicoletti, II., ch. 8, *loc. cit.*

dignities as extensive as that granted to Francis I. by the concordat of 1515 must have appeared even more alarming to the nuncio.[1]

In the sequel Agucchi's experiences were so bitter that in April, 1627, he sent a very gloomy report on the situation to Rome. In that message he sketches in broad outline the growth of Venice's Caesaro-papalism. During the last 400 years the Government had been violating the Church's immunity and jurisdiction in consequence of its desire to exercise unlimited domination over all its subjects, including the clergy. The situation had been further embittered by the political teaching of men who were Catholics only in name. The Servite Sarpi, learned, cunning and outwardly of blameless life, had so skilfully defended his Caesaro-papistic ideas, that even good men had been deceived. To this was to be added the weakness of the clergy, especially the regular clergy, who for the sake of their personal interests invariably took the part of the Government and showed excessive indulgence towards the nobility. Small wonder, then, if the Government looked on its usurpation of ecclesiastical jurisdiction as a right and made bold to lay down the law even in purely spiritual matters and to threaten priests in order to compel them to give absolution from censures. Of the Senators still sincerely Catholic one part had died and the other, for reasons of personal interest, did not dare to offer opposition; in this way the reins had passed into the hands of the younger generation which was wholly under the influence of Sarpi's ideas. Private negotiations, such as were customary in other States, were declined at Venice. Without as much as listening to any argument to the contrary, the most weighty decisions were taken on the advice of Fra Fulgenzio, a follower and colleague of Sarpi. The regular clergy stood on the side of the Government, were it only because they were afraid lest the nuncio and the Pope should interfere with their free and easy life. In vain Cardinal Cornaro had appealed to the Doge, his father; in vain he himself had pointed out to the Doge that Urban VIII. could not tolerate the violation of

[1] *Ibid.*

ecclesiastical immunity which had become the rule since the interdict of 1605. Even the request that at least these innovations should cease, remained unheeded. The Doge declared that he was powerless against the Senate. Accordingly, Agucchi's advice was that the dispute should be settled with the Venetian ambassador in Rome, for the latter could not refuse to negotiate.[1] But from that quarter also there was nothing to be hoped for. In vain the Pope complained to the ambassador of the action of the Signoria in ecclesiastical matters and of the interference by Venice with the people of Ferrara and Bologna.[2] The negotiations were all the more hopeless as Urban VIII., the common father of Christendom, would not depart from the duty of maintaining his impartiality in political questions as requested by Venice.

Meanwhile ecclesiastical affairs were managed at the discretion of Fra Fulgenzio by whose advice the politicians, above all the influential Domenico da Molino, decided everything. The Friar was being blindly obeyed though it was known that he had Calvinist learnings, was on terms of greatest intimacy with the Protestant envoys and led an immoral life. Fulgenzio's influence was greater than that of the nuncio and the Patriarch because all papal ordinances concerning benefices passed through his hands. The degenerate Frate openly boasted of his efforts to foment dissension between Venice and the Holy See.[3] In 1629 the bestowal of the See of Padua on Cardinal Cornaro, to which Venice objected, and the nomination of a coadjutor to the ailing

[1] See Agucchi's *report of April 10, 1627, in *NICOLETTI, *loc. cit.* Fulgenzio was " deputato della Republica a rivedere le bolle apostoliche e le provisioni degli ordinandi che si presentarono in collegio per ottener i possessi temporali de'beneficii ecclesiastici ". *Cf.* Agucchi's *report, June 22, 1624, *loc. cit.*

[2] *Cf.* ANG. CONTARINI, 300 *seq.*

[3] See Agucchi's *report of November 20, 1627, *loc. cit.* For the interference of the Venetian Government, especially in the affairs of the Inquisition, *cf.* the **Informatione* of December 25, 1627, in the *Nunziat. di Venezia*, 45, p. 68 *seq.*, Papal Secret Archives.

Patriarch of Aquileia, Gradenigo, led to violent disputes with Rome which Richelieu tried in vain to smooth.[1] Authentic reports prove how tense the situation had become. When in November, 1629, the Venetian ambassador, Angelo Contarini, complained that at the last creation of Cardinals no Venetian had received the red hat, the Pope replied that the Venetians would at least have no opportunity to ill-treat a Cardinal.[2]

At the end of 1629 Contarini was replaced by the haughty Giovanni Pesaro, a circumstance which aggravated the situation. Counting on the anti-Roman feelings of the new Doge, Niccolò Contarini, Pesaro resolved to bring matters to a head.[3] However, the Pope would not yield on the question of Padua. In September, 1630, the political situation made some attempt at a compromise imperative, though all such efforts were unlikely to lead to a successful issue owing to the usurpation of Church property by the Venetians who were in need of money in consequence of the war in Mantua, an action that had given rise to fresh disputes. In April, 1631, Francesco Orizzo became Doge and the Patriarch of Venice died about the same time. In June a compromise was arrived at; instead of Padua, Cornaro received the patriarchal see of Venice.[4]

However, even so there could be no lasting peace seeing that Pesaro gave sanctuary in his palace to every miscreant, sought to corrupt the Pope's servants, surrounded the Vatican with spies and got into a dispute with the Prefect of Rome, Taddeo Barberini, over a question of etiquette in consequence of which a violent scene took place between the representative of Venice and the Pope. On Pesaro's return from the Vatican, a fresh encounter occurred between him and the Prefect of

[1] *Cf.* *NICOLETTI, IV., 732 *seq.*, 742 *seq.*, Vatican Library.

[2] *"Che li signori Venetiani così non harebbono haver occasione di maltrattare i cardinali." Letter from the Secretary of State to Agucchi, November 19, 1629, *ibid.*

[3] See *NICOLETTI, IV., 767 *seq.*, 776 *seq.*, *loc. cit.*

[4] *Ibid.*, 790 *seq.*, 811 *seq.*, 817 *seq.*

Rome, near S. Andrea della Valle.[1] Thereupon the ambassador left the Eternal City on September 20th.[2] Once more it was France which, for political reasons, sought to mediate.[3] When a compromise seemed at last in sight, in March, 1632, it was put in jeopardy by a quarrel between Venetian and Papal soldiers in the territory of Ferrara.[4] Diplomatic relations were only resumed in July, 1632, with the mission of Alvise Contarini. At the same time the nunciature in Venice received a new occupant, Agucchi having died on January 1st, 1632. The latter was at first succeeded by an internuncio, but at the end of June Francesco Vitelli was named nuncio. This new representation should have resulted in better relations, all the more so as the elevation of Cardinal Cornaro to the patriarchal See of Venice and that of his brother to the See of Padua, had given universal satisfaction. However, this time a dispute broke out over questions of frontiers.[5] Owing to his failure in getting the Pope to join the anti-Spanish League, Alvise Contarini became a bitter enemy of the Barberini at the very time when France was working for a settlement of the frontier disputes and various other difficulties between Rome and Venice,[6] an incident sufficiently trivial in itself —the so-called inscription quarrel—led to a diplomatic rupture.[7]

[1] *Ibid.*, 839 *seq.*, 850 *seq.* *Cf.* also SIRI, VII., 441 *seq.*; DENGEL, *Palazzo di Venezia*, 118.

[2] See *NICOLETTI, IV., 859, *loc. cit.*

[3] *Ibid.*, 881 *seq.*

[4] See *ibid.*, 934 *seq.*

[5] *Ibid.*, 948 *seq.*, 953 *seq.*, 1421 *seq.* From September to December, 1632, mutual relations were strained by controversies about the waters of the River Po (see *ibid.*, V., ch. 3 *seq.*).

[6] See *NICOLETTI, V., chs. 15 and 18; VI., ch. 11, *loc. cit.*

[7] The dispute about the inscriptions was carried on in behalf of the Venetians by ALV. CONTARINI (399 *seq.*), NANI (17 *seq.*), the dispatches in DENGEL (*Palazzo di Venezia*, 118 *seq.*), and on the side of the Pope by *NICOLETTI (VI., ch. 11; VII., ch. 5). That on the question of historical fact the Pope's advocates were in the right was subsequently admitted even by Venice; see A. Zon's account in CICOGNA, *Iscriz. Venez.*, IV., Venezia, 1834,

By command of Pius IV., Giuseppe Porta di Castelnuovo had painted a large fresco in the Sala Regia of the Vatican, to commemorate the peace concluded on August 11th, 1177, between Alexander III. and Frederick Barbarossa. The Venetian Cardinal Mula was in charge of the work.[1] This circumstance, joined to inadequate historical knowledge, accounts for the fact that the inscription beneath the fresco described the part played by Venice in that event as far more important than it was in reality: with enormous exaggeration of the facts it stated that Alexander III. had recovered his papal dignity with the help of Venice.[2] The wording was based on the data of Venetian historians which the progress of historical studies had shown to be untenable. But Venice firmly clung to the ancient tradition and when an authority like Baronius pronounced against it, the Republic had pamphlets written against him. However, when the archivist Felice Cantelori, whom Urban VIII. held in great esteem, took the side of Baronius in a pamphlet published in 1632, the Pope had the inscription painted over, whilst in order not to offend Venice, he ordered at the same time the correction of other inscriptions, both in the Vatican and elsewhere, which were at variance with historical truth.[3] The painting-over

574 *seq.* Recently, G. B. Beltrami in the *Arch. d. Soc. Rom.*, III., 1 *seq.*, had discussed the whole affair in detail and also printed Gigli's report which deserves attention because this chronicler, who is not usually favourable to the Popes, takes their side in this matter.

[1] See Vasari, *Vita de' pittori*, XII., Firenze, 1856, 121. *Cf.* our account, Vol. XVI., 419 *seq.*

[2] According to Siri, VIII., 430, the inscription ran as follows: "Alexander Papa tertius Frederici Imperatoris iram et impetum fugiens abdidit se Venetiis, et a Senatu perhonorifice susceptum, Othone imperatoris filio navali praelio a Venetis victo captoque Fredericus pace facta supplex adorat, fidem et obedientiam pollicitus. Ita Pontifici sua dignitas Venetae Reipublicae beneficio restaurata est." It may still be read there, with a few slight alterations; see Taja, 20.

[3] See G. B. Beltrami, *loc. cit.*, 4 *seq.*, 9 *seq.* *Cf. Cod.* I., VI., 205, p. 546 *seq.*, of the Chigi Library, Rome.

of the inscription in the Sala Regia greatly annoyed the Venetians, but their excitement knew no bounds when, at the end of 1635, a new inscription was put up in which the event was described in accordance with facts, the unhistorical praise of the city of the Lagoons being omitted.[1] The Venetians felt they could not allow such a diminution of the fame of their ancestors; threats were uttered against Rome; there was even question of expelling the nuncio. The passionate excitement of the Venetians was reflected in the final report drawn up by Alvise Contarini in 1635, on the termination of his embassy.[2] Spaniards and Dutch fanned the dispute to such an extent that the new ambassador, Vincenzo Gussoni, who was appointed on July 5th, 1635, never took up his post.[3] In his place the secretary of the embassy, Francesco Maria Rossi, who had stayed behind after Contarini's departure, demanded the immediate restoration of the old inscription. When he was given to understand that he should not get excited over a trifle such as a couple of words, all the more so as everyone was master in his own house, he left the Eternal City in obedience to his instructions, at the beginning of 1636, without a farewell audience.[4]

The Government of Venice continued to insist on the restoration of the old inscription and rejected France's offer of mediation.[5] It was hoped to induce Urban VIII. to give way by oppressing the clergy; but all was in vain. The efforts of the nuncio and those of France for a compromise,[6] remained barren until the Turkish peril led to a change.[7] When Urban VIII. announced his readiness to help the Republic

[1] It runs thus: "Fredericus primus Imperator Alexandrum tertium Pontificem, quem diu insectatus fuerat, post constitutas cum eo pacis conditiones et damnatum schisma Venetiis supplex veneratur." See Siri, VIII., 430.

[2] *Cf.* a criticism of this *Relation* in Appendix I., vol. xxvii.

[3] See Barozzi, *Relazioni, Italia,* II., 7.

[4] See Dengel, *loc. cit.*, 119.

[5] See *Nicoletti, VII., ch. 5, *loc. cit.*

[6] *Cf.* the *report in *Ottob.*, 3238, Vatican Library.

[7] See *Nicoletti, *loc. cit.*

to meet the danger which threatened it from the East, the Signoria resolved, on December 11th, 1638, to dispatch an extraordinary ambassador to Rome in the person of Giovanni Nani. The latter met with an extraordinarily friendly reception and found the Pope prepared to give to the Republic all the support within his power in the struggle with the Turks.[1] Meanwhile, thanks to Cardinal Cornaro,[2] who had exerted himself to the utmost in order to bring about a compromise, the new inscription had been painted over; Nani, however, failed to obtain the restoration of the original inscription on which Venice had set its heart [3]; that wish was only fulfilled by Urban VIII.'s successor.

In the relations between Rome and Spain, as in those with Venice, political differences were frequently mixed up with ecclesiastical ones. The principles of Spanish Church policy remained under Philip IV. the same as under his predecessors: obstinate insistence on rights claimed on the ground of a far-reaching Caesaro-papalism and, if possible, their further extension, though without letting things go as far as an open

[1] See NANI, *Relazioni*, 9 *seq*. Towards the expenses of the war Venice was granted a tenth from the clergy.

[2] Cardinal Cornaro *wrote on January 8, 1639, to the Senate, describing the very friendly reception he had received on the part of the Pope. In a *letter of February 12, 1639, he reports on an audience in which Urban VIII. had emphasized his friendly dispositions towards Venice " e professava di esser buon Italiano et che un Papa buon Italiano non può se non amare e stimare sommamente la republica di Venezia." State Archives, Venice.

[3] When Nani left, Urban VIII. regretted his departure, and in the farewell audience, on March 23, 1640, told him that he considered the rupture of diplomatic relations to be very prejudicial to Venice. In point of fact, Nani was given a successor on April 20, 1640, in the person of Angelo Contarini (see BOROZZI, *loc. cit.*, 45). But relations remained strained and occasions of dispute arose thereafter. Urban VIII. judged in 1641, *" che in Venezia non si corrispondeva a nulla per quel che se le faceva, nè si guardava se non al proprio interesse, e con tutte le grazie sempre si stava come fosse da principio." (*NICOLETTI, VIII., ch. 8, *loc. cit.*)

rupture, for that seemed inadvisable both on political and on religious grounds.

Similar calculations also inspired the efforts of Urban VIII. to remain on good terms with Madrid, in so far as this was at all possible. If he granted numerous favours to the Spanish Government, he did so less from inclination than from a cautious instinct of self-preservation, in the interests of the Holy See. The loss of the important revenues which the *Dataria* drew from Spain would have been a serious matter in view of existing financial circumstances. Though the power of Spain had considerably declined, she still held Milan and Naples and from the latter Kingdom she was able to exercise strong pressure on the States of the Church.[1]

During the pontificate of Urban VIII., both Philip IV. and his ministers were at pains to have their Caesaro-papistic pretensions and their practical consequences defended by means of books and pamphlets. In this campaign more than one of their champions went to such extremes that their writings had to be put on the Index. Such a fate befell a work of Jerome de Cevallus in 1624, and one by the Franciscan Salgado de Somoza in 1628.[2] The latter, the most important of Spanish regalists of his time, had defended the so-called *Recurso de fuerza* in a book published in 1626 with Philip IV.'s privilege, but the King of Spain forbade the Bishops to publish the condemnation of the book on the plea that, in accordance with long-established custom, this could only be done within his realm by the Spanish Inquisition.[3] On April 10th, 1634, he wrote to Cardinal Borgia that he had been informed that Rome encouraged the publication of books supporting Roman views on ecclesiastical jurisdiction, whilst such writings as defended the rights of kings were being prohibited; the Cardinal was to expostulate with the Pope and to ask that in matters concerned not with the faith but with questions of jurisdiction, everyone should be allowed to state his own views; if Urban VIII. forbade books that favoured the King, he would

[1] See Ang. Contarini, 293 *seq.*; Alv. Contarini, 379.

[2] See Reusch, *Index*, II, 370 *seq.*

[3] *Ibid.*, 373.

retaliate by prohibiting those written in support of the Pope.[1] Another Spanish lawyer, Juan de Solórzano Pereyra, in a book on the Spanish patronage in America, propounded no longer as a theory but as an established fact, the idea of an Apostolic Vicariate of the Catholic King confirmed by a hundred years' prescription and the silent assent of the Holy See. Since in virtue of the legitimate patronage which Ferdinand the Catholic and Isabella had acquired, ecclesiastical appointments and the administration of the temporalities lay in the hands of the Government, the theory of the royal vicariate threatened to loosen still further the connection between the Church of America and Rome. Accordingly, the fiscal advocate general of the Camera Apostolica, Antonio Lelio, published a refutation of Solórzano's work and demanded its condemnation, whereupon it was put on the Index on March 20th, 1642.[2] However, no notice was taken of the sentence of the Index either in America nor in Spain: the clergy of both these countries continued to correspond with the Holy See almost exclusively through Madrid.[3]

The theory of the *Monarchia Sicula* constitutes a counterpart of the Spanish patronage in America. It rests on a Bull of Urban II. to Count Roger I., of the year 1098, which granted to the latter the rights of a papal Legate. Although this extraordinary concession had been abolished by the Concordat of 1192, the Spanish Court divines erected on it a fantastic structure of ecclesiastical privileges for their kings as heirs to the rights of the Normans and the Hohenstaufen in Sicily.[4] This gave rise to constant conflicts under Urban VIII. as it had done under his predecessors.[5] The tribunal of the *Monarchia Sicula*, with its permament judge who was wholly

[1] See (LLORENTE), *Colección dipl. de varios papeles* [2] (1822), no. 7.

[2] See the excellent account by LETURIA in *Hist. Jahrb.*, XLVI., 30 *seq.*, 53 *seq.* *Cf.* REUSCH, II., 374.

[3] See LETURIA, *loc. cit.*, 54.

[4] See E. KASPAR in the *Quellen und Forsch. des preuss. Instituts*, VII. (1904), 189 *seq.*, 207 *seq.*

[5] *Cf.* our account vol. xviii, 60 *seq.*; xix, 349 *seq.*; xxv, 8 *seq.*

dependent on the Governor, threatened to destroy all legitimate jurisdiction and whatever survived of the ecclesiastical independence of the Bishops of Sicily.[1] The protests of the Bishops of the realm, in 1629, against the illegal procedure of the tribunal and the non-observance of the decrees of Trent on the subject, remained without result.[2] With a view to undermining all episcopal authority the so-called *Lettere di Salvaguardia* were invented. These were issued to persons who represented and accused their Bishop as their personal enemy in so far as the tribunal deemed such action justified. Anyone holding such a "letter" was exempt from the jurisdiction of his Bishop in civil and criminal affairs, so that impunity for crimes was practically legalized. Urban VIII. condemned this abuse and set up a special Congregation composed of Cardinals Ginetti, Gessi, Verospi and Pamfili and five other prelates, with mission to devise a remedy. Great exertions were needed on the part of the Spanish ambassador, Count De Monterey, and the Cardinals devoted to Philip IV., to prevent the Congregation from taking extreme measures against the *Monarchia Sicula*.[3] When on the retirement of the Viceroy, Albuquerque, the Archbishop of Palermo, Cardinal Giovanni Doria, became Lieutenant, he strongly opposed any extension of the competence of the tribunal of the *Monarchia*. In doing so he appealed to the decrees of the Council of Trent; he also relied on the support of the King, but the latter, in a very ungracious letter, met his demands with a negative answer and in the sequel deprived the Archbishop of the Lieutenancy.[4]

In the Kingdom of Naples also violations of ecclesiastical immunity were frequent,[5] especially during the viceroyalty

[1] See SENTIS, *Monarchia Sicula*, Freiburg, 1869, 130.

[2] *Cf.* CARUSO, *Discorso*, 120; SENTIS, *loc. cit.*

[3] See CARUSO, 120–3; SENTIS, 135. The successor of Count Oñate (1626–8) as ambassador was Monterey from 1628–1631.

[4] See CARUSO, 123 *seq.* *Cf.* SAVAGNONE, *Contributo alla storia dell'Apost. Legazione in Sicilia*, Palermo, 1919, 24 *seq.*

[5] *Cf.* the *letter to the Spanish nuncio of January 1, 1628, in *Barb.* 4336, p. 1 *seq.*, Vatican Library, and the *Brief of August 6, 1636, in the *Epist.*, X., Papal Secret Archives.

of the Duke of Medina (1637–1644). The latter inaugurated his rule by imposing fresh taxes. A Theatine who protested against this oppression of the people was banished from the Kingdom.[1] When the General of the Dominicans visited Naples, the Viceroy demanded that he should present him with a valuable painting by Raphael, a fact which, as in duty bound, the Prior of S. Domenico reported to Rome. To punish him for this act, he was escorted to the frontier by a guard of fifty soldiers whilst at the same time the Viceroy forbade all Dominican convents to receive in future any Fathers from other territories, without his permission.[2] With the Archbishop of Naples, Cardinal Filomarino, the Viceroy also promptly picked a quarrel over a question of etiquette. On this occasion the representative of the Catholic King made the remark that a red biretta did not make a Prince. But far more serious were the disputes over ecclesiastical jurisdiction which at one time nearly led to an interdict.[3]

In the Spanish Netherlands ecclesiastical jurisdiction was violated in sundry ways, especially after the departure of the nuncio Fabio de Lagonissa (1634).[4] When after the death of the Archduchess Isabella, the Cardinal-Infant Ferdinand assumed the lieutenancy of the Netherlands, Lelio Falconieri was given the Flemish nunciature in April 1635. The latter was suspected of leanings towards France. Accordingly, the Government of Brussels made so many difficulties against receiving him, that Cardinal Barberini advised him not to enter upon office until the feeling against him should have abated. Falconieri would not follow this advice and, owing to the troubles caused by the war, travelled via Paris, an act by which he still further roused the distrust of the Government of Brussels which persisted in its refusal to receive him, so that in 1637 he was obliged to return to Italy. During this

[1] See *Arch. stor. ital.*, I, Series IX (1846), 321.

[2] *Ibid.*, 325.

[3] *Ibid.*, 326 *seq.*, 335 *seq.* *Cf.* REUMONT, *Carafa*, I., 298 *seq.*

[4] See CAUCHIE-MAERE, *Instructions*, 179.

[5] *Ibid.*, xxxvi. *Cf.* also *v. d. Essen* in *Bullet. de la Commiss. Royale d'hist. Belge*, LXXVIII. (1909), 272.

difficult period the business of the Brussels nunciature was transacted by Richard Paul Stravius, himself a Netherlander, until the arrival, in April, 1642, of a new papal representative in the person of Bichi.[1]

Spanish Caesaro-papalism, which also reacted on the Court of Vienna in consequence of the ties of kinship between the two Courts,[2] rendered the task of the Madrid nuncio all the more difficult as he had to contend not only with the despotism of the authorities of the State, but likewise with the distrust of not a few ecclesiastical bodies.[3] His position became extraordinarily difficult after Cardinal Borgia's protests against the Pope's attitude in the struggle between France and the House of Habsburg, which the former made in the name of Philip IV. in the consistory of March 8th, 1632.[4] In order to heal the estrangement to which that incident had given rise, Madrid decided, in the autumn of 1632, to send two royal commissaries to Rome. The little that transpired concerning the purpose of this mission could not but considerably disquiet the Pope, but he failed in his efforts to prevent its dispatch.[5] The two plenipotentiaries set out towards the end of October, 1633: they were the Councillor of State Juan Chumacero and the Bishop of Córdova, the Dominican Domingo de Pimentel. Their task was not so much to settle the affair Borgia as to constrain the Pope to take up a partisan position in favour of

[1] See CAUCHIE-MAERE, *loc. cit.*

[2] *Cf.* KOCH, *Gesch. Ferdinands III.*, Vol I, 102, on the Emperor's veto of the publication of a papal Bull; see also HINSCHIUS, III., 756. On the disturbance of the cordial relations between the Pope and the Emperor in 1641, see FIEDLER, *Venet. Relationen*, in the *Fontes rer. Austr. Dipl.*, XXVI., 284 *seq.*

[3] After the recall of J. Morosini, the nuncios were: Guilio Sachetti (January, 1624, to end of May, 1626), G. B. Pamfili (May, 1626, to March, 1630), Ces. Monti (March, 1630, to January, 1633), Lorenzo Campeggi (January, 1633, to August, 1639), C. Facchinetti (1639 to January, 1642), G. G. Panciroli (January, 1642, to July, 1643). *Cf.* BIAUDET, 207 *seq.*

[4] *Cf.* Vol. XXVIII, p. 283 *seq.*

[5] See LEMAN, *Urbain VIII.*, 205, 338.

the House of Habsburg against France.[1] In view of the fact that Spain seemed determined to go to extremes, Urban VIII. took every precaution so as to guard against any injury to his dignity. Before the two plenipotentiaries were received in audience, at Christmas, 1633, they were made to show their credentials so as to make sure that they did not intend to offend the Holy See. In the course of the protracted negotiations it became only too evident that what Spain expected from Urban VIII. was the abandonment of his impartiality, a one-sided partisanship in favour of the Habsburgs and a break with France.[2] To this end the most alluring promises were made, but Urban VIII. refused to yield. In order to win him over, Madrid ended by going so far as to sacrifice Borgia. On April 22nd, 1635, the Cardinal received a letter from Philip IV. recalling him to Madrid.[3] In March, 1635, Urban VIII., yielding to the insistent request of the King of Spain, had allowed him to raise a tenth, to the amount of 600,000 scudi, on the benefices of Portugal, Naples, Sicily and the Indies, though with the reservation that these sums were to be spent solely on the support of the Emperor in his struggle against the Protestants and in the event of peace being concluded between them, on the war against the Turks, so as to preclude the possibility of the money being used against France.[4] The two delegates had extorted this weighty concession by broaching, on December 15th, 1634, besides the request for help for the war against the Protestants, the thorny question of the limitation of papal jurisdiction in Spain. They began by submitting an autograph letter of Philip IV., dated October 1st, 1633, praying the Pope to remove the abuses which had crept into the Court of Rome and the Spanish nunciature, to the disadvantage of Spain.[5] They then presented two memorials,

[1] *Ibid.*, 323. For Pimentel, *cf.* MORTIER, *Hist. des Maîtres généraux*, VI., 392.

[2] See LEMAN, 340.

[3] *Ibid.*, 385 *seq.*, 478.

[4] See *Bull.*, XIV., 468 *seq.* The two agents had at first asked for a million ; see LEMAN, 507, note 2.

[5] An authentic *copy is in a codex (pp. 7–8) bought by me in 1902 from the Corvisieri Library.

one dealing with the support of the House of Habsburg in its struggle with the French,[1] the other with certain grievances against the Dataria and the nunciature. Ten such grievances were mentioned, viz. the imposition of pensions on Spanish benefices in favour of foreigners; their excessive amount, especially in the case of curacies; the granting of coadjutorships *cum jure successionis* without regard for canonical limitations; the *resignatio cum reservatione* of curacies; excessive taxes and fees for dispensations and other official documents; the reservation of benefices for the benefit of foreigners; the strictness displayed in collecting such property of Bishops (spolia) as belonged to the Apostolic Camera, as also in collecting the revenues of vacant bishoprics; excessive delays in filling the latter and lastly, the disadvantages of the judicial power exercised by the nunciature.[2]

Urban VIII. commissioned the Secretary for Briefs Maraldi to draw up a detailed reply to this memorial which was then handed to the Spanish envoys.[3] In view of the numerous complaints against the nuncio and his officials, in consequence of which a request had been made that ecclesiastical tribunals should be composed of nationals, a special Instruction was also sent to the Madrid nuncio.[4] Maraldi's reply, which was also communicated to the nuncio, was to the effect that without

[1] **Scrittura presentata alla Stà di N.S.P. Urbano VIII. dalli ambasc. straordinarii del Re cattolico . . . sopra i sussidii che domandano per S.Mtà Catt.* (*Cod. Corvisieri*, pp. 41–7). On p. 2 is a statement that both memorandums were handed in on December 14, 1634.

[2] **Scrittura presentata alla Stà di N.S.P. Urbano VIII. dalli ambasc. straord . . . sopra i pretesi aggravii della Dataria et abusi di essa e della Nuntiatura di Spagna.* (*Cod. Corvisieri*, pp. 11–37).

[3] **Risposta*, etc. (*ibid.*, pp. 51–9). Riganti (*Comment. in Reg. II Canc.*, S. 2, no. 44, p. 237 (ed. Romae, 1744)), quotes a passage of this *Risposta*. The *Risposta* was published together with the memorandums of Chumacero and Pimentel, at Madrid, but copies of it are very rare outside Spain.

[4] **Risposta piena . . . sopra i pretesi aggravii et abusi della Dataria e Nuntiatura mandata a Mons. Nuntio di Spagna solamenie* (*Cod. Corvisieri*, p. 63–81).

doubt the complaints came not so much from the clergy as from laymen who were ill-disposed towards the Holy See; however, since the King made them, they would be answered. This was done calmly and objectively, and most of the contested points, if not all, were justified.[1] Thereupon the delegates withdrew their memorial.[2] Only then did the Pope have the other memorial examined, that is, the one demanding a money subsidy, after which he granted the great tenth asked for. But the grievances against the Dataria and the nunciature still remained to be disposed of. Though there was much exaggeration and one-sidedness, as well as a desire to circumscribe still further the influence of the Holy See, it was undeniable that more than one demand was justified. However, the true aim of the Madrid Cabinet was not so much zeal for the removal of real abuses, as a desire of rendering the tribunal of the nunciature wholly subservient to the King by packing it with Spaniards and making of it but one more tool of the Government, as the Inquisition already was to a great extent.[3] In accordance with instructions from Madrid, the delegates persisted in their demands and in a fresh memorial sought to refute Maraldi's reply.[4]

The negotiations suffered an interruption when the Pope was taken seriously ill at Castel Gandolfo, on May 10th, 1637. On June 6th it became possible to bring him back to the

[1] *Cf.* also the dissertation: **I pretesi ai quali i Regii appoggiano, le presenti novità intorno alla Nunziatura di Spagna,* in *Cod.* 92, p. 108 *seq.*, of the Campello archives, Spoleto, in which some abuses are admitted, especially with regard to the granting of favours and benefices, and remedies are suggested especially against the conduct of certain agents who demanded "emolumenti".

[2] *Letter from Pimentel and Chumacero to Cardinal Barberini, dated February 13, 1635, *Cod. Corvisieri*, p. 83–6.

[3] See the opinion of HERGENRÖTHER in the *Archiv. für kath. Kirchenrecht*, X. (1863), 35 *seq.*

[4] This *memorandum is in *Cod. Corvisieri*, pp. 87–161, undated. According to *Colección de los Concordatos . . . entre los reyes de España y la S. Sede* (Madrid, 1848), 28 *seq.*, it may have been presented in January, 1636.

Quirinal though his condition continued to inspire grave anxiety.[1] The Spaniards felt so sure of his death that they began preparations for the conclave. The way in which Spain's extraordinary envoy, the Marquis de Castel Rodrigo, sought to force the stricken Pontiff to receive him in audience, was universally resented. He failed and negotiations for the conclave continued. Cardinal Carlo de Medici arrived in Rome. He was accompanied by a band of armed men and there were fears of disturbances owing to the fact that the Medici were on bad terms with the Colonna, because the latter refused to the Grand-Duke the title "Altezza".[2] The Barberini had already engaged the services of 300 Corsicans when happily the Pope recovered. By St. Peter's day, Urban VIII. was so much better that, though still in bed but arrayed in pontificial vestments, he was able to receive at the hands of Castel Rodrigo the customary feudal tribute for Naples. By August 6th, the anniversary of his election, the Pope was fully recovered.[3] Thereupon the Spanish envoy began to press for the bestowal of the red hat on the Abbate Francesco Peretti.[4] The latter lacked the qualities that would have justified such an honour. Urban VIII. also explained that as a rule the Popes only took into account the recommendation of Princes when these concerned their own subjects and that he must be as free in the choice of Cardinals as Princes are in that of their advisers.[5] The Spanish envoy's importunity having led to no result, it was decided to exercise even stronger pressure. At the close

[1] See the *reports of Scipio Gonzaga, Prince of Bozzolo, to Ferdinand II. of May 16, June 6 and 13, 1637. State Arch., Vienna. *Ibid.*, Moltmann's *reports to Ferdinand II. of May 2 and July 25, 1637. **Relatione delle cose occorse nel governo di Roma in tempo di Msgr. G. B. Spada*, MS. of the Library of the Campo Santo al Vaticano, Rome, and the reports in *Period. d. Soc. stor. p. la diocesi di Como* XVI., 188 *seq.*

[2] See Reumont, *Beiträge*, V., 139 *seq.*

[3] See the *report of Moltmann to Ferdinand II. of August 8, 1637, *loc. cit.*; *Nicoletti, VII., ch. 7, Vatican Library. Cancellieri, *Lettera sopra il Tarantismo*, 113, 308.

[4] See *Nicoletti, VII., ch. 8, p. 502 *seq.*, *loc. cit.*

[5] *Cf.* the **Instruction* for Facchinetti on p. 195, note 4.

of February, 1638, a fresh memorial on the abuses in the Dataria and the nunciature was handed in, but its exaggerations were such that it was not so much a petition as a libel.[1] Even so Peretti failed to get the red hat, which was explicable enough. The support which the Spanish Government gave to Cardinal Borgia, who entertained hostile feelings towards the Pope, betrayed its real dispositions. These were also evidenced by its opposition to the bestowal of the office of camerlengo, rendered vacant by the death of Cardinal Aldobrandini (July, 1638), on Cardinal Antonio Barberini.[2] The tension between Rome and Madrid was considerably increased by the circumstance that Philip IV. appointed Cardinal Borgia President of the Council of Italy, in consequence of which he demanded for him a dispensation from the duty of residence. When Urban VIII. refused, Olivares told the nuncio that he appealed from an angry Pope to one better advised.[3] Now as before Madrid was exceedingly annoyed at the Pope's attachment to his old principle of the greatest possible impartiality in the struggle between the Habsburgs and the Bourbons. Whilst the Spaniards strove to induce him to abandon this attitude, they permitted themselves the worst encroachments in the ecclesiastical sphere. Both at Naples and in Lombardy, the immunity of the Church was being most grievously violated. After the death of Bishop Landriani, the Governor of Milan, the Marquis de Leganés and his underlings, arrogated to themselves rights which simply did away with all ecclesiastical immunity and jurisdiction. They justified their conduct by appealing to the royal Economate.[4] Perhaps even

[1] See *NICOLETTI, VII., ch. 8, p. 515, *loc. cit.*

[2] *Ibid.*, ch. 8.

[3] *Ibid.*, ch. 9.

[4] See *ibid.*, ch. 9, p. 567 *seqq.* A detailed statement of the interference at Pavia (*cf. Bull.*, XV., 210 *seq.*), which GALANTE (*Il diritto di placitazione e l'economato dei benefici vacanti in Lombardia*, Milano, 1894), describes most one-sidedly and in part incorrectly, is in the **Instruction* for Facchinetti quoted below, p. 195, note 4. The end of the quarrel at Pavia did not come until July, 1642; see *NICOLETTI, *loc. cit.*, p. 586.

worse was the oppression to which the Apostolic Collector in Portugal was being subjected.[1]

In these critical circumstances a change took place in the Madrid nunciature in August, 1639: the Bolognese Cesare Facchinetti replaced the aged Lorenzo Campeggi who died not long after his recall.[2] The Instruction of the new nuncio [3] throws light on the alarming increase of Caesaro-papalism in the dominions of the Catholic King. At Naples, under plea of the *Monarchia Sicula*, exorbitant encroachments were being perpetrated in internal ecclesiastical questions, the Pope's jurisdiction was impeded, that of the Bishops almost wholly absorbed by the tribunal of the monarchy, laymen judged in cases of higher appeals and episcopal nominations were held up. In the Netherlands nominations to abbeys were made without Indult and in the Milanese territory ecclesiastical immunity was desrtoyed by the royal Economate. This was Philip's thanks to Urban VIII. who had bestowed on him more favours than any Pope had ever granted before, to such an extent, in fact, that the Spanish clergy complained bitterly of the tenths imposed on them with papal authorization. As a result of the Church's dependence on the State, ecclesiastical discipline suffered severely. Facchinetti was instructed to take action in this respect and especially to impress on the Bishops both the duty of resistance and that of personally reporting in Rome by means of *ad limina* visits.[4] However, in the ecclesiastico-political field the new nuncio was destined to have the same

[1] *Cf.* p. 196 *seq.*

[2] See the *Brief to Philip IV., of August 8, 1639, in *Epist.*, XVII., Papal Secret Archives. *Ibid.*, XV., a *Brief to Philip IV. of May 12, 1639, according to which Facchinetti was already destined then to go to Madrid on an extraordinary peace mission.

[3] In order to increase Facchinetti's prestige, Urban VIII. nominated him Archbishop of Damietta; see the *Brief to Philip IV., September 6, 1639, *loc. cit.*

[4] **Instruttione data a Msgr. Facchinetti, Nunzio straord. alla Mtà Catt.*, s.d., MS. from the library of Cardinal Gentili, bought by me in Rome in 1902. The date (summer 1639) is ascertained from the fact that the first disputes with Castracani are already mentioned, but not his dismissal, which occurred in August.

sad experience as his predecessor.[1] It looked as if Spain judged that the time had come to avenge herself, by fresh violations of the Church's liberty, for the Pope's impartiality in the struggle between France and the Habsburgs and to compel him even now to forgo his neutrality. The refusal of the red hat to Peretti had embittered the Spaniards; accordingly the cry went up on all sides, and louder than ever, that the Pope favoured France. The utter falseness of the accusation appears from the fact that just then the Pope was offering a firm refusal to the Cabinet of Paris which pressed him to bestow the purple on Mazarin.[2]

A particularly grave attack on the liberty and immunity of the Church occurred in Portugal, in August, 1639. Ever since his entrance upon office in 1634, the Apostolic Collector, Alessandro Castracani, had had a bitter struggle with the ill will of the authorities. A convert Jew of the name of Tommaso Pignero de Vega, who held the office of a royal procurator, on the authority of a doubtful law on Church property, succeeded in depriving the churches of certain annual legacies, the so-called *Capillas*.[3] As in duty bound Castracani opposed

For the intervention of the State in the Netherlands, see CAUCHIE-MAERE, *Instructions*, *passim*, especially 197 *seq*. *Hist.-polit. Blätter*, CXXXVI., 518. For the **Relatio Belgarum rer. sub nuntiatura Dom. della Lionessa*, 1627–1634 (Papal Secret Archives), see GOEMANS, VI., 279, and CAUCHIE in the *Anal. p. l'hist. ecclés.*, 1906.

[1] Facchinetti was informed of the difficulties which he would have to meet immediately on his arrival, by his fellow countryman, the Marchese Malvezzi, then at the Spanish Court; see *NICOLETTI, VII., ch. 12, Vat. Libr. *Ibid.* the information that it was believed that Campeggi's death was due to mental suffering rather than to old age, inasmuch as the Spaniards suspected him of being in collusion with Richelieu.

[2] See *NICOLETTI, VII., ch. 12, p. 672, *loc. cit.*

[3] The **Instruttione a Facchinetti* quoted above, p. 195, note 4, defines the *cappelle* thus: "Cosi chiamano in Portogallo quei beni che vengono lasciati alle chiese con obligo di messe et altre pie opere." For details on the dispute see *NICOLETTI, VII., ch. 10, VIII., chs. 5 and 7 (p. 327 *seq.*, an historical investigation into the

this measure and the Pope supported him.[1] The dispute began in 1636 and reached a point when towards the end of 1638 the Collector was threatened with expulsion from Portugal. Basing his opposition on an ordinance of Urban VIII. of June 5th, 1638, Castracani threatened with ecclesiastical censures those who violated her immunity.[2] From Rome he received instructions to lay the country under an interdict if he were expelled, though he was to hold on to his post as long as possible. Towards the end of 1639 the Jesuits were likewise threatened with expulsion in the event of their encouraging Castracani's resistance. On August 18th Pignero presented himself with a posse of police at Castracani's house and ordered him to leave Portugal. Castracani protested and laid all the churches of Lisbon under an interdict. On

controversy about the *cappelle*.). The office of Collector is here described as " differente nella nominazione, ma nelle prerogative e nelle facoltà equivalente al Nunzio ". Conditions in Portugal were already very difficult even before Castracani assumed office. Concerning ecclesiastical jurisdiction we read in the **Instruction* for Giov. Batt. Palotta, appointed Collector for Portugal in June, 1624: " La giurisdittione eccles. in quel, regno è forse più travagliata che in qualsivoglia ultra parte christiana e l'offese e gli abusi e gli strappazzi sono arrivati a segno d'intolerabilità." The Collector Ant. Albergati (1621–4), had already sent in a summary of the: " aggravi che sono fatti all'immunità della chiesa della corte secolare "; Palotta was to discuss it with the King in Madrid and draw his attention to the danger of the state of affairs: *" caminando questi abusi ad un manifesto scisma et alterandosi per questa via la religione cattolica può con ragione temere il Re di qualche alterazione nel suo dominio." There follows a summary of the pretensions of the " regii ministri " in Portugal to the detriment of the Church (MS. in my possession). Under Palotta's successor, Lorenzo Tramollo (1627–1634), the Pope was obliged to address a *Brief to Philip IV. as " rex Portugalliae ", on November 3, 1629, begging him to cancel the edict of the " Lusit. magistrat. contra libertatem ecclesiasticam " (*Epist.*, VII., Papal Secret Archives).

[1] *Cf. Bull.*, XIV., 560 *seq.*

[2] *Cf. ibid.*, 655 *seq.*

August 19th he was summoned to withdraw his censures or to leave the realm and his house was seized. He was not allowed to leave his room or to say Mass. On 30th he succeeded in escaping into the adjoining Franciscan convent whilst the sentries were asleep, but on September 4th he was forcibly escorted to the frontier. Thereupon he excommunicated all who had been concerned in this act and repaired to Badajoz from whence he reported to the nuncio.[1]

At the same time Madrid sought to paralyse the tribunal of the nunciature.[2] Henceforth Spaniards alone were to issue its decisions, a pretension which led Cardinal Barberini to remark that even St. James had been a foreigner.[3] Facchinetti protested and hinted at the penalties laid down in the Bull *In coena Domini* against those who interfere with the Church's jurisdiction. However, in view of the fact that recourse to the tribunal of the nunciature had been declared a punishable offence, not many people availed themselves of it.[4] The Spanish ambassador, Castel Rodrigo, did his utmost to induce the Pope to agree to the reduction of the Church's nunciature to the rank of a State department, though just then the Pontiff was very angry because of Castracani's expulsion.[5] With this object in mind the ambassador threw out hints

[1] See Castracani's *reports of August 24 and 28 and September 13, 1639, in *Nicoletti, VIII., ch. 7, *loc. cit.* Everybody in Lisbon observed the interdict, except the Dominicans; Urban VIII., therefore, commanded the Procurator General of the Dominicans to punish the disobedient (*ibid.*, p. 374 *seq.*).

[2] At first regret was expressed for the death of the nuncio, but at the same time the intention was betrayed of limiting the powers of the papal representative; see the two Briefs to Philip IV. of October 31, 1639, *Epist.*, XVII., Papal Secret Archives.

[3] See *Nicoletti, VII., ch. 12, *loc. cit.*

[4] *Ibid.*

[5] *" Stimò l'eccesso così scandaloso che altamente si commosse e fatto chiamare il marchese di Castel Rodrigo per palesarvi i suoi giustissimi sentimenti e esaggerò seco con straordinaria indignatione il fatto rimonstrandoli che non solo era stata empiamente l'immunità ecclesiastica, ma che barbaramente violata la ragione delle genti." *Nicoletti, VII., ch. 12, *loc. cit.*

that he might yield in his quarrel with the Prefect of Rome, Taddeo Barberini. But when this proved in vain, he had recourse to threats. Cardinal Barberini told him that he could not believe that the Viceroy of Naples woud be so foolish as to attack the States of the Church; moreover Madrid might bear in mind the fact that the Chair of Peter was not occupied by a feeble woman but by a strong man.[1] Spain's conduct towards the Holy See was something unheard of, Barberini declared; the Spaniards acted as if Urban VIII. were a French soldier, nay, as if he had robbed Philip IV. of Naples and Milan.[2] If the Spaniards wished for a reform of the tribunal, the Pope was willing to remove all real abuses, but he was not prepared to sacrifice one jot or tittle of the Church's jurisdiction. Barberini comforted Facchinetti with the assurance that the Spaniards only harmed themselves; that he prayed, and was getting prayers said to the end that this dreadful situation might soon take a turn for the better.[3] In the affair Castracani the Pope had addressed three sharp Briefs, all dated October 31st, 1639, to Philip IV., the Vicereine Marguerite and Olivares respectively: "The action against the Collector was illegal," he wrote, "by it not only the Holy See but the law of nations had been injured. Castracani must be permitted to return." [4] When Facchinetti handed these Briefs to Olivares, the latter was so upset that, throwing his cap to the ground, he exclaimed: "So I am excommunicated!" [5]

Very different was the conduct of Urban VIII. when on December 16th, 1639, Chumacero, accompanied by the ambassador Castel Rodrigo, handed to the Pope a letter of

[1] "Sopra la cathedra di S. Pietro non sedevan le asserte Papasse Giovanne, ma una santissima intention in un petto forte e rigoroso." *Ibid.*

[2] *" I modi che si usano con S. Pietro sono da disperati. E che più si farebbe se Papa Urbano fosse nell'esercito Francese? o havesse al Re di Spagna tolto Milano e Napoli?" *Ibid.*

[3] See *Nicoletti, *loc. cit.*, p. 692 *seq.*

[4] See *Bull.*, XV., 20 *seq.*, 23 *seq.*

[5] See *Nicoletti, *loc. cit.*, p. 697.

Philip IV. in which the latter stated that in the interests of his subjects as well as those of the Holy See, the Pope must put an end to the abuses of the nunciature. Chumacero spoke in support of the King's demand, insisting in particular on the venality of the tribunal. Urban VIII. having heard him out without interruption, said that he had expected to hear that the King was about to put an end to the encroachments which had occurred in his domains, especially in the action against Castracani ; instead of this he was now informed of fresh and most grievous usurpations, to the injury of the Holy See. If the King really had at heart the honour of the Apostolic See, he should not have suppressed the judicial power exercised by the nuncios for centuries. Under pretext of abolishing abuses the institution itself had been attacked ; all schisms and heresies had invariably begun with alleged reforms. The nuncio had orders to remove abuses, but the only judge in these matters was the Pope. Heretics might seek to destroy the visible Head of the Church, but he had not thought it possible that Catholics would seek to deprive him of his jurisdiction in ecclesiastical matters. When Chumacero obstinately defended the rights of the monarchy, Urban remarked that he had no intention to argue with him but that it was clear that no sovereign had more authentic titles for his rights than the Pope. Chumacero permitted himself the rejoinder that Christ had said that His Kingdom was not of this world ; to which Urban replied with ready inspiration in the words of St. Augustine : *Mundi dixit tenebrarum harum* ! In the course of the discussion Chumacero expatiated on all that Philip IV. had done for religion. Urban replied that thereby the King had only defended his own domains ; the defence of religion was a duty, for without it States must collapse. He himself would not give way ; neither threats of injury nor promises of advantages for his family, would cause him to swerve from the path of duty.[1]

[1] *" Ne tener conto de torti o de vantaggi di sua casa, perchè sapeva per servizio di Dio sprezzar intrepidamente il tutto " (*Nicoletti, *loc. cit.*, p. 704). The whole discussion is given there, pp. 700–4. The *Brief to Philip IV., of January 25, 1640,

Accordingly, towards the close of the stormy year 1639, Barberini wrote to Facchinetti that measures of violence would not induce the Pope to yield.[1]

On the occasion of the forcible action against Castracani, Urban VIII. had foretold that Spain would be punished by heaven.[2] The prophecy was to be verified sooner than might have been expected. In June, 1640, an insurrection broke out in Catalonia which threatened to assume dangerous proportions owing to France's support. Catalonians and Spaniards alike appealed to the Pope. Urban VIII. immediately declared himself ready for friendly intervention and sought to prevail on France to refrain from supporting the rebels—a step that made a deep impression in Madrid.[3] In October Facchinetti seized the favourable opportunity to negotiate a compromise which might satisfy both parties, on the question of the nunciature. By its terms Spain renounced the pretension that the officials of the nunciature

bears out this conversation: " Io. Clunacerum tuum oratorem audivimus. Dum in Lusit. regno a laico magistratu Ecclesiae dignitatem violatam conquerimur, congrua remedia a tua pietate potius expectabamus, quam ut de imminuendis Nuncii facultatibus isthic ageretur." He had always put a stop to excesses and hoped for remedial steps from the King. " Significabit Cæsar archiep. Damiatensis Nuncius." *Epist.*, XVII. to XVIII., Papal Secret Archives.

[1] See *NICOLETTI, *loc. cit.*, p. 708.

[2] See Barberini's *letter of December 17, 1639, in *NICOLETTI, VIII., ch. 7, p. 372, *loc. cit.*

[3] *Cf.* the *Briefs to Philip IV. of October 13 and 20, 1640, in *Epist.*, XVII., *loc. cit.*; NICOLETTI, VIII., ch. 10, p. 496 *seq.*, 501 *seq.*, 520: *" Altri ammiravano i modi pellegrini e discreti, co'quali il Papa offeriva le sue parti al Re. Altri anche più critici confessavano, che S.S. non poteva con più chiare espressioni nell'acerbità di quelle congiunture mostrare il suo affetto verso la corona, la quale doverà perpetuamente restar obbligata a S.B., e finalemente tutti a piena bocca col confessare la rettitudine di Papa Urbano, benedicevano il suo nome e con encomii celebravano la sua generosità veramente paterna." Here p. 532 *seq.*, further details on the failure of the papal mediation because Olivares would not listen to the advice of Urban. Vatican Library.

must be subjects of the King. On his part Facchinetti agreed to every just demand, such as the regulation of taxes, acceptance of any kind of money current in Spain, foregoing the right of granting benefices during a vacancy of an episcopal see and the concession of the faculties of a Legate *a latere.*[1] Facchinetti, who had remained firm on one point, namely, that the nunciature must remained unaltered in all essentials, insisted on the reopening of its tribunal ; if this was done, he promised ratification of the compromise within eight months.[2] However, the Caesaro-papalists would not even now accept defeat. In contravention of what had been agreed upon, they immediately published the compromise which so far only engaged Facchinetti's personal responsibility, and added to the text a note by the royal council which represented the whole transaction as a unilateral act of the State.[3]

[1] See TEJADA Y RAMIRO, *Colección de Concordatos*, Madrid, 1862, 74 *seq. Cf.* HERGENRÖTHER in the *Archiv für kath. Kirchenrecht*, X. (1863), 36 *seq.* According to *NICOLETTI (VIII., ch. 10, p. 535 *seq., loc. cit.*), "infinite giunte" with 26 members, were held under Olivares' presidency, without any agreement being reached. MERCATI (*Concordati*, 282, note 1), has conclusively shown that the so-called "Concordia Facchinetti" was not, as was long thought, a concordat between the Holy See and Spain.

[2] See *NICOLETTI, *loc. cit.*, p. 536.

[3] From the correspondence of FACCHINETTI (*Nunziat. di Spagna*, 83–4, Papal Secret Archives, and *Barb.* 8451, Vatican Library), to which MERCATI (*loc. cit.*) first drew attention, it appears that the nuncio went further than his instructions warranted, and that the enemies of the nunciature *"per imprimere in tutti li vassalli di questi regni, che se dal Conseglio si erano levati gli'impedimenti havean anco riportato a sodisfattione delle riforme, che istampate per ordine loro si leggevano, et per ciò a'piedi della mia riforma posero un atto del Conseglio, nel quale nominando le mie leggi con titolo falso di Concordia (cosa mai non pensata nonche consentita da me, nè pretesa dai deputati) che per ordine di S. Maestà venivano a riferirmi ciò che si era avanti il signor conte Duca di volta in volta risoluto in quelle giunte, davano ad intendere di haver tolto gli ostacoli in gratia quasi della Concordia" (Letter of Facchinetti, November 10, 1640. *loc. cit.*).

However, Rome quickly saw through the manœuvre[1] and skilfully countered it. A Brief of April 6th, 1641, annulled the act on the ground that the nuncio had not been empowered to negotiate, and that the pact had been concluded without the Pope's knowledge.[2] On the other hand Rome was fully aware of the material value of the compromise, as notwithstanding the restrictions it imposed on the nuncio, it saved the independent existence of the nunciature and prevented that institution from becoming a mere tool of the State. Accordingly, on April 27th, 1641, the text of the settlement was despatched to Madrid, with a few modifications and the necessary regulations, as a papal ordinance.[3] On August 12th, 1641, Facchinetti published the Brief and the regulations in the tribunal of the nunciature, whereupon that court began to function once more.[4]

[1] The instructions of the Secretary of State of December 8, 1640, contain this passage: " Chi l'ha fatto stampare, non solo ha mancato alla parola data a V.S., ma ha voluto far vedere, che il tutto dependeva da esso. . . . Si è ancor avvertito, che in alcuni luoghi della stampa si usa la parola Concordia in modo che il Conseglio pretende che V.S. habbia concordato, et pattegiato con la giunta quanto va nella stampa, quasi che non appartenesse alla giurisdittione apostolica il fare la riforma, ma alla regia egualmente " (MERCATI, *loc. cit.*).

[2] See *Bull.*, XV., 108 *seq.*

[3] See MERCATI, *loc. cit.*, 283 note, who first drew attention to the new " *Regolamento* " of the tribunal preserved in *Barb.* 8475, p. 33, as the *Reformacion del Tribunal de la Nunciatura de Espagna*. A passage from the *Brief of April 27, 1641, has been published by PIGNATELLI (*Consult.*, II., cons. 1, no. 15). The Brief and the Regolamento are the " Constitutioni Urbane " mentioned by *NICOLETTI, *loc. cit.*

[4] See Facchinetti's *report of August 21, 1641, on the publication of the Brief and the " ordinationi nella stanza dove in questo tribunale se da l'audienza all'hora consueta a porte aperte presenti molti curiali ". For this reason, he says, he had had the " ordinationi " translated into Spanish and printed, but that document would remain secret until it had been approved by Madrid; the President of Castile had already privately acknowledged the Brief, *Barb.* 8475, p. 27 *seq.*, Vatican Library.

If the Spanish authorities yielded in this dispute over the nunciature, that fact was due to an event which had occurred in the meantime and which compelled the Government to show the greatest consideration for the Pope. On December 1st, 1640, Portugal, following the example of Catalonia, had rebelled against Spain. The Duke of Braganza, a scion of the ancient royal house, was proclaimed King by the nobility. He arrived at Lisbon on December 5th and at once ascended the throne under the name of John IV.[1] One of the causes which had contributed to the revolution was the conduct of the advisers of the Vicereine Marguerite against the Apostolic Collector in Portugal, Alessandro Castracani, which had excited great indignation among the population.[2]

The new King of Portugal protested his devotion to the Holy See, promised to handle ecclesiastical affairs satisfactorily, and decided to send to Rome his nephew, Don Miguel of Portugal, Bishop of Lamego, to do homage to the Pope in his name.[3] Spanish diplomacy did all it could to induce Urban VIII. to refuse the embassy. The demands made by Juan Chumacero in an audience of February 2nd, 1641, aimed at reducing the Pope to the status of a mere tool of the Spanish Government. Urban VIII. was requested to publish a Brief condemning the action of the Portuguese in

[1] *Cf.* besides SCHÄFER, *Portugal*, IV., 475 *seq.*, RANKE, *Osmanen*[4], 477 *seq.*, and A. CANOVAS DEL CASTILLO, *Estudios sobre Felipe IV*, vol. 1, Madrid, 1888, also the interesting *report addressed to Cardinal Barberini by the two officials Famiano Andreucci and Vinc. Mobili, dated Lisbon, December 29, 1640, who had been left behind by the Collector Castracani, in *NICOLETTI, VIII., ch. 10, p. 509 *seq.*, where there are also further details on the suspension of the interdict by the Sub-Collector Battaglini. Vatican Library.

[2] See *NICOLETTI, VIII., ch. 7, p. 368 *seq.*, *ibid.*; FILIPPO CARPINO, *Relazione al card. Barberini dell'inumani trattamenti fatti da'ministri regii secolari della città di Lisbona a Msgr. Alessandro Castracani vescovo di Nicastro e collettore generale apost. in Portogallo li* 18 *d'Agosto*, 1639, MS. of the Corvisieri Library, Rome (lately sold). For Castracani, *cf.* also BRUZZONE in *Cosmo illustrato*, IV., Rome. 1903.

[3] See *NICOLETTI, VIII., ch. 10, 514 *seq.*, *loc. cit.*

throwing off the Spanish yoke, to refuse to give ear to the rebels and to allow Spanish judges to sentence priests who had had a share in the rebellion.[1]

In view of Spain's power and the uncertain issue of the Portuguese rising, the position of the Pope was a particularly delicate one. He proclaimed a jubilee in order to implore the help of God and appointed a special cardinalitial Congregation to advise him as to his future conduct. Chumacero was told that the divergent accounts of events in Portugal rendered an unbiassed opinion impossible and that nothing definite was known of the dispatch of an embassy by the Duke of Braganza ; hence for the moment it was impossible to arrive at a decision. Chumacero, dissatisfied with this answer, resolved to exercise even stronger pressure. In a second audience on March 2nd, he presented a memorial which accused the Pope of injustice and reproached him with acting not as a shepherd but as a hireling ![2] Notwithstanding this provocation the Pope remained calm. In a third audience on March 16th he replied that he would do his duty as a good shepherd but that he must protest against Spain's management of ecclesiastical affairs. He had in mind in particular the expulsion of Castracani which had called forth the indignation not only of the whole Curia but that of every ecclesiastical circle.[3] Madrid realized its blunder and Castracani was allowed to return, though on condition that he would promote the interests of Spain in Portugal. Castracani was willing to agree to this condition though Facchinetti sought to dissuade him. Urban VIII. settled the matter by recalling Castracani.[4] This step was in keeping with his policy of preserving his impartiality for as long as possible in the ticklish Portuguese question ; hence also Chumacero's efforts to get the Pope

[1] *Ibid.*, ch. 11, the *Brief of February 16, 1641, to Philip IV. shows that Chumacero had replaced Castel Rodrigo, *Epist.*, XVII., ch. 10, p. 314 *seq.*, *loc. cit.*

[2] See *NICOLETTI, VIII., ch. 11, p. 549, *loc. cit.* *Cf.* ADEMOLLO, *La questione della indipendenza Portoghese a Roma dal* 1640 *al* 1670, Firenze, 1878, 20.

[3] *Cf.* ADEMOLLO, *loc. cit.*, 20 *seq.*

[4] See *NICOLETTI, *loc. cit.*, p. 556.

to side unreservedly with Spain, which he renewed particularly in the audiences of May 22nd and 25th, were doomed to failure. When Urban VIII., in order to show that he was not hostile to Spain, further strengthened the Portuguese Congregation with four Hispanophil Cardinals, viz. Lante, Roma, Caetani and Bentivoglio, Chumacero demanded that in future its meetings should no longer be held in presence of the Pope, as this would hinder the free expression of opinion ![1]

The Bishop of Lamego had left Lisbon on April 15th, 1641, journeying to the Eternal City viâ Paris. In Rome his arrival was awaited with a good deal of concern. In view of the Bishop's statement that he came to make his visit *ad limina* (namely to report on the state of his diocese) the Pope could not forbid his entering Rome though the Spaniards described his being allowed to do so as a great crime. Cardinal Barberini had done his best to prevent the journey, but Lisbon and Paris insisted on its taking place. On the Spanish side a rumour was spread that Chumacero and the Spanish Crown Cardinals would leave Rome on the Bishop's arrival. Urban VIII., however, did not suffer himself to be intimidated. He consulted the Congregation once more. Its answer was that there could be no question of refusing to receive the Bishop as such.[2] As a matter of fact it was not possible for the Pope to suspend ecclesiastical relations with Portugal without grave risk to his authority in that country.[3] But Urban VIII. entertained no delusions as to the difficulties of the situation. Cardinal Barberini wrote to the Spanish nuncio that he had never seen the Pope look so worried ; the Holy Father prayed a great deal and asked for prayers, but he could not refuse to do his duty as a shepherd.[4]

[1] *Ibid.*, 556, 594. For the Congregation, *cf.* ADEMOLLO, 23, 24.

[2] See *NICOLETTI, VIII., ch. 12, p. 568 *seq.*, *loc. cit.*

[3] *Cf.* STAUDENMAIER, *Gesch. der Bischofswahlen*, Tübingen, 1830, 368.

[4] *" Nel pontificato di S. S^{tà} non ho mai veduto l'animo di S. B. così ansioso come negli affari e mutazioni di Portogallo e singularmente nella missione del vesc. di Lamego, etc." Letter of November 16, 1641, in *NICOLETTI, *loc. cit.*, p. 571.

Meanwhile, towards the end of October, the Bishop of Lamego landed at Civitavecchia where the new French ambassador, the Marquis de Fontenay, had him met by a group of his servants. The Bishop was accompanied by the Portuguese Inquisitor Pantalião Roiz Pacheco, who was to serve as agent for ecclesiastical affairs in Rome. On their arrival in Rome on November 20th, 1641, both lodged at the house of the French ambassador.[1]

On April 23rd, 1642, the Marquis de los Velez appeared in Rome as envoy extraordinary of Spain and demanded the unconditional dismissal of the Bishop of Lamego. Urban VIII. refused to comply with this request since there was question of ecclesiastical business: Rome, he declared was a free city; anyone could approach the Pope, that was why Pacheco also had been received.[2] The Bishop was at first referred to Cardinal Barberini who forbade him to appear publicly as an ambassador and did not hide from him Rome's grave displeasure at the violation by the new King of ecclesiastical immunity, in particular by the arrest of the Archbishop of Braga and other priests who had remained loyal to Spain.[3] In the sequel the Bishop of Lamego was allowed to take up residence in the palazzo De Cupis, in the Piazza Navona, but he was warned not to appear with an escort. When the Bishop refused to comply, the Pope instructed Cardinal Bichi to forbid him formally to do so. This step was necessary not only because the Spaniards would have concluded that the Pope recognized the Bishop as an ambassador, but because there was reason to fear disorders, for the new Spanish envoy, the Marquis de los Velez, did not disguise his intention of picking a quarrel with the Bishop in the street and, if possible,

[1] See *Nicoletti, *loc. cit.*, p. 575 *seq.* Whereas Siri attributes the admission of the Bishop of Lamego to the representations of Cardinal Bichi, Ameyden says that Fontenay had secured it by threatening his departure; see Ademollo, 26.

[2] See *Nicoletti, VIII., ch. 13, *loc. cit. Cf.* Ademollo, 38.

[3] See *Nicoletti, *loc. cit.* For the Archbishop of Braga, Sebast. de Matos de Noronha, who wished to subject Portugal once more to Spain, see Schäfer, IV., 499 *seq.*, 507.

of driving him out of Rome. Meanwhile tempers became more and more heated and writings for and against the admission of the Bishop as John IV.'s envoy began to appear.[1] The Spaniards uttered threats; one of their sympathizers, Theodore Ameyden, went so far as to declare in the papal antechamber that since Spain was the right arm of the Holy See, the Pope was bound to lend support to Philip IV. against the rebels, even to the extent of selling his chalices, if need be, in order to help him to recover Portugal![2]

In view of the delay of a decision the Bishop of Lamego sought to force it. He demanded an audience, as ambassador of Portugal, from Cardinal Lante, Dean of the Sacred College. When he was told that the "Bishop of Lamego" would be received at seven o'clock in the evening, he repaired to Lante's palace only to find that the Cardinal was out. The Spaniards made capital of the incident and complained that the envoy of John IV. had been received by the Dean of the College of Cardinals. This the Pope denied, but the City refused to give him credence. It was no secret that the Marquis de los Velez was resolved to employ force against the Bishop and that he was gathering armed men for the purpose, notwithstanding the prohibition of the Governor, Giovan Battista Spada. Accordingly, in order to avoid a conflict, Urban VIII. forbade the Bishop of Lamego to leave his house for a few days.[3] The Bishop refused to obey; on August 20th, 1642, he left his house with an armed escort. Not far from the Piazza Colonna and near the church of S. Maria in Via, he encountered the Marquis de los Velez who was also accompanied by an armed band. A clash ensued, firearms went off and there were several dead on both sides. The two hostile envoys fled and the police only succeeded in arresting three of the culprits.[4]

[1] *Ibid.*, 19 *seq.* *Cf.* below, p. 210, note 2.

[2] See ADEMOLLO, 35, note 1.

[3] *Ibid.*, 36 *seq.*

[4] Besides the sources used by SCHÄFER (IV., 529 *seq.*), see the report of *Ameyden* in ADEMOLLO, 41 *seq.* (*ibid.*, 42 *seq.*, corrected by the *Diario* of Governor Spada and the report of Gigli), and

The incident excited and disturbed all Rome. The Marquis de los Velez maintained that the police had favoured the Bishop; he felt injured in his honour and would leave Rome. He was told that if any one had a right to feel offended, it was the Pope. However, every attempt to appease him proved unavailing. Together with Cardinals Albornoz and Montalto and the Spanish auditors of the Rota, he left Rome on August 27th. This action of the Spanish envoy called forth universal resentment: more than anyone else Urban VIII. felt justly indignant.[1] He nevertheless preserved his impartiality and the Bishop of Lamego's hopes of success were frustrated. The Congregation laid the blame on the latter; some of its members even advocated his expulsion, in any case he could not be received as the representative of Portugal because he had not obeyed the Pope. An escort was now forced upon the Bishop, but at the same time he was given the written assurance of personal safety which he had asked for.[2]

Whilst at Madrid the nuncio was doing his best to set the incident in its true perspective, the French envoy De Fontenay, who had been angered because the nomination of Michel Mazarin had received no support, presented himself before the Pope to announce his departure. He handed in a memorial from the Bishop of Lamego in which the latter held the Pope responsible for the injury to the Church which must follow from his refusal to receive the homage of the King of Portugal. The Bishop decided to leave Rome at the same time as the envoy since his King had instructed him to return home if after a year's stay he should have failed to accomplish his purpose. He declined the private audience which the Pope offered him as a Bishop. On December 18th, 1642, together

also *NICOLETTI's account (*loc. cit.*) who wrongly reports the conflict as having taken place on August 25. A Spanish *report in *Barb.* 3561, p. 269 *seq.*, Vatican Library. Even if reports differ in many respects, the main facts are as stated in the text. The **Processo* of the quarrel is in *Barb.* 6212, *loc. cit.*

[1] See BIRAGO, *Hist. d. regno di Portog.*, lib. 4, p. 332; ADEMOLLO, 48 *seq.*, 53 *seqq.*

[2] See *NICOLETTI, VIII., ch. 13, Vatican Library.

with the French envoy, he left Rome whilst Pacheco remained behind. The latter was instructed to obtain for King John IV. the right of nomination to vacant bishoprics which now as before the Spaniards claimed as a privilege of their king.[1] Fontenay, whose conduct was disapproved by Paris, returned to Rome on February 10th, 1643, whilst the Bishop took boat at Leghorn for Portugal.[2]

Even before news of the Bishop of Lamego's departure

[1] *Ibid.* *Cf.* ADEMOLLO, 64 *seq.* On the very rare memorandum of R. PACHECO: *Alla* $S^{tà}$ *di Urbano VIII. N.S.* (Roma, 1642) in favour of John IV., see ANTONIO DE PORTUGAL DE FARIA, *Portugal e Italia*, Leorne, 1898, 13. The question whether Urban VIII. should have received the Bishop of Lamego as *obbedienza* ambassador, was answered in Rome in various ways; *cf.* the documents published by SIRI (*Mercurio*, I., Casale, 1646, 602 *seq.*). These and other papers are frequently found in MSS.; see (1) **Discorso col quale si prova che sia licito e ragionevole, anzi necessario che la Sede Ap. ammetta il vescovo di Lamego, amb. di Giovanni, acclamato dai popoli Re di Portogallo, Barb.* 5218, Vat. Libr.; (2) **Discorso* of similar content, *ibid.*, 5219, p. 149 *seqq.*; (3) **Allegatione per il vesc. Lamego*, Library of St. Mark, Venice VII–MCCLXI (*cf. Cod.* 53 of the Corsini Library, Rome); (4) **Agosto*, 1642. *Ultima allegatione giuridica nella quale si prova che Msgr. vescovo di Lamego deve dalla Santità di . . . Urbano VIII. ricerversi come ambasciatore della Maestà di D. Giovanni IV. Re nuovo di Portogallo, Cod.* 6745, p. 226 *seq.*, of the State Library, Vienna.

[2] See ADEMOLLO, 66 *seq.* Nicoletti quotes the following from a *letter of GRIMALDI of February 20, 1643: "Il Nuntio scrivendo al cardinal Barberino gl'insinuò, che fin dal tempo di Richelieu si erano avanzate certe propositioni, che tendevano evidentemente a far credere, che si poteva ritenere la purità della religione cattolica senza haver bisogno della Sede Apostolica e della corte di Roma, e che all'incontro il card. Mazzarino haveva offerto ad esso Nuntio, che seguendo il ritorno dell'ambasciatore Fontanè con qualche honesta soddisfattione, egli havrebbe havuto campo d'adoprarsi in servitio della Santa Sede in cose di maggior rilievo; vero si fu che il card. Barberino usò tutte le diligenze possibili, acciochè l'ambasciatore non partisse da Roma." *Barb.* 4738, p. 409, Vat. Lib.

reached Madrid a great change had taken place there. Not long after the news of Richelieu's death had filled all Spain with joy, the hitherto all-powerful Olivares was dismissed, on January 15th, 1643. His dismissal met with universal approval. "When the apple is ripe," the nuncio Giovan Giacomo Panciroli wrote, "a small shock is enough to cause its fall."[1]

With the fall of Olivares a man disappeared in whom Panciroli rightly saw the chief instigator of the disputes between Spain and the Holy See.[2] But now as before Spain's Caesaro-papistic traditions and fear for her preponderance in Italy, were obstacles to the restoration of good relations.[3] Madrid greatly resented the refusal of the archiepiscopal See of Toledo to Cardinal Borgia. This was due to the circumstance that the latter would offer no apology of any kind for his conduct towards the Pope.[4] Facchinetti and Panciroli, who had so long held the difficult post of the Madrid nunciature, obtained the purple on July 13th, 1643.[5] A year later Urban VIII. passed out of this world.

[1] *"Quando il pomo è maturo, basta ogni picciolo crollo a far che cada" (letter of January 28, 1643, in *NICOLETTI, VIII., ch. 14, p. 709, *loc. cit*). On Olivares' downfall, *cf.* RANKE'S OSMANEN [4], 487 *seq.*; JUSTI, *Velasquez*, II., 198.

[2] See *NICOLETTI, *loc. cit.*

[3] *Cf.* NANI, 37.

[4] See *NICOLETTI, *loc. cit.*, p. 724 *seq.*, 735 *seq.*

[5] *Cf.* above p. 164.

CHAPTER III

Propaganda and the Missions

On the south side of the Piazza di Spagna in Rome there rises a plain but vast building, the façade of which bears the arms of the Barberini Pope and the inscription *Collegium Urbanum de Propaganda Fide.* Among the many monuments of Rome that recall the memory of Urban VIII., this building is one of the most important for within its walls the central authority of the missionary work of the Catholic Church had its first home. The ground for its work was prepared by a noble Spanish prelate, John Baptist Vives, the representative in Rome of the Lieutenant of the Netherlands, the Infanta Clara Eugenia. At the very first sitting of the Congregation of Propaganda of which he was a member, and at a time when a suitable home was still being sought for it, Vives put at its disposal his palace in the Piazza di Spagna. The building was valued at 14,000 ducats and had formerly been the property of Cardinal Ferratini.[1] On June 1st, 1626, Vives made over to Propaganda the house and all its appurtenances, to serve as a seminary for ten priests or clerics from every nation [2]; at the same time he also assigned to the Congregation, for the maintenance of the students, besides various revenues, the whole of his estate, reserving to himself only the usufruct for his lifetime. At his request, on August 1st, 1627, Urban VIII. confirmed this donation, having in mind his duty to provide zealous apostles for the spread of the faith

[1] For Vives see Castellucci in *Alma Mater*, I., Romae, 1920, and in *Le conferenze al Laterano*, Marzo–Aprile, 1923, 191. *Cf.* also Arens, *Handbuch der kath. Missionen* (1920), 16, and especially Schmidlin in the *Zeitschr. für Missionswiss*, XII. (1922), 12. A reproduction of the fine bust of J. B. Vives is in *Alma Mater*, 1927, 15 (*Colleg. Urb. de Prop. fide*). *Ibid.*, 16, a facsimile of the *Bull. Immortalis Dei Filius* of August 1, 1627.

[2] *Cf.* Pollak Frey, 213 *seq.*

among all nations as well as the uprooting of heresies. At the same time the Pope also erected a College, or Apostolic Seminary, under the patronage of the Princes of the Apostles, and under his own name, for the reception and training of pious and learned priests who would spread the Catholic faith among the infidels of the whole world, if need be even at the cost of their lives. As Governors he named three Canons of the patriarchal basilicas of St. Peter, St. Paul and St. Mary Major, with right to appoint or depose the Rectors and other officials of the College, to lay down statutes and to alter them. The College was to be exempt from the jurisdiction of the City authorities and the payment of taxes, and the privileges of all the other Seminaries were likewise conferred upon it.[1]

A second Bull of 1637 confirmed the establishment of a Seminary in the Urban College for twelve youths, viz. Georgians, Persians, Nestorians, Jacobites, Melchites and Copts—two of each nationality. The Seminary was to be under the direction of Propaganda and the Rector and an annual income of at least 850 ducats was assigned to it by Urban VIII.'s brother, Cardinal Antonio Barberini.[2] The

[1] See *Bull. S. Congr. de Prop. fide*, I., 65 *seq.*, and *Ius pontif.*, I., 87 *seq.* *Cf.* SCHWAGER, *Die kath. Heidenmission*, I. (1907), 19 *seq.* See also STANGHETTA, *La scuola di cantori nel Pontif. Collegio Urbano di Roma*, 1627–1925, Roma, 1926.

[2] See *Ius pontif.*, I, 170 *seqq.* *Ibid.*, 180 *seqq.* a Bull of 1639 : the erection of a seminary in the Urban College for seven Abyssinians and six Indian Brahmins, failing these for Armenians. The Urban College was intended above all to educate a native clergy for those nations which had no College of their own in Rome ; see SCHMIDLIN, *Missionsgesch.*, 208. The Bulls require, in conformity with the prospectus of the College (see *Collect. S. Congr. de Prop. fide*, I. (1907), 134), that the pupils should have good health, should be from 15–20 years old, and know either Latin or Italian. On May 18, 1637, Urban VIII. granted to the scholars and interns of the College the special privilege of being ordained, after three years' residence, *ad titulum missionis* (*Ius pontif.*, I., 173 *seq.*). The names of the first students are in the †*Compendio.* mentioned below, 214, n. 4. For the Rectors see CASTELLUCCI in *Alma Mater*, 1921, no. 3, p. 61 *seq.*

latter had become Prefect of Propaganda on the death of Ludovisi in 1632. In his enthusiasm for the spread of the faith, he gave Propaganda the sum of 200,000 ducats and left to it the whole of his estate.[1] To him Propaganda also owes both its church and its splendid expansion which was rendered possible by the purchase of a whole block of houses. The reconstruction of the somewhat ruinous palace was decided upon on October 1st, 1639,[2] that of the erection of the principal façade facing the Piazza di Spagna, on November 12th, 1642. The plan for the latter was drawn by Bernini, whilst Gaspare de'Vecchi directed the erection of the wing facing the Via Due Macelli which was destined to house the students.[3] The foundation stone of the church was laid on May 5th, 1634.[4] Bernini[5] designed the sacred edifice dedicated to the Three Wise Men, the first fruits of the pagan world. Since the year 1633 the feast of the Epiphany of our Lord has always been appropriately celebrated by Propaganda with the so-called feast of tongues.[6] Every year one may hear there speeches in Italian, French, Spanish, Portuguese, English, German, Polish, Russian, Hebrew, Syriac, Arabic, Armenian, Persian, Chinese, Japanese and in divers dialects of India. All the nations are represented and proclaim, each in its own way, the oneness of the Church which by God's providence is founded on diversity—a faithful image of the task miraculously performed by the Apostles on the first Pentecost—the task of loving devotion to the welfare of all nations.

In 1641 Urban VIII. made a change in the government of

[1] See SCHWAGER, 21. *Cf.* ROCCO DA CESINALE, II., 45, note 3.

[2] *Cf.* POLLAK-FREY, 218.

[3] See CASTELLUCCI in *Alma Mater*, III. (1921), 54 *seq.*, 58. *Cf.* BALDINUCCI, ed. by Riegl, 101 ; POLLAK-FREY, 231.

[4] See BERNARDINO LARIZZA (*sacerdote di S. Girolamo d. Carità*, 1636, for a time Rector of Propaganda), **Compendio cronologico dello Collegio Urbano de Prop. fide* (dedicated to Card. Francesco Barberini, *Barb.* 4477, Vatican Library.

[5] *Cf.* HEMPEL, *Bernini*, 159 ; POLLAK-FREY, 216.

[6] *" *Prima Academia fatta nel Collegio d. Propaganda l'epifania*, 1633 ; see *Miscell. Clementis XI.*, vol. 11, Papal Secret Archives.

the Urban College by withdrawing it, in the interest of uniformity, from the three Canons and assigning it to Cardinal Barberini, at whose death it was to pass under the control of Propaganda.[1] Before long Barberini entrusted the Theatines with the task of training the Seminarists.[2] In 1643, in which year the first pupil of Propaganda, the Belgian Jacob Foelich, died for the faith,[3] Urban confirmed the donation made to Propaganda by the Benedictine Abbot of St. Barontius of the so-called Gregorian College in Rome, together with its library and other appurtenances.[4]

Propaganda, whose faculties Urban VIII extended,[5] owes to him not only its new home but likewise its financial consolidation by means of large contributions of money.[6] To all this must be added the magnificent legacies of Cardinals Calamina, Ubaldini, Cornaro, Giustiniani, Capponi and the Secretary of Briefs, Savenier,[7] as well as the considerable sums collected by the Carmelite Dominic of Jesus and Mary, and the founder of the Congregation of the Mother of God,

[1] See *Bull. S. Congr. de Prop. fide*, I., 113 *seqq.*; *Ius pontif.*, I., 202 *seqq.*

[2] See FERRO, *Istoria delle missioni Teatine*, I., 406 *seqq.*; *Ius. Pontif.*, I., 209 *seqq.*; *Alma Mater*, 1927, 30, 55.

[3] *Cf. Alma Mater*, 1927, 35 *seq.*

[4] See *Ius Pontif.*, I., 216 *seq.* *Cf.* **Avviso*, of November 27, 1627, *Urb.* 1097, Vatican Library. In 1639, Urban VIII. had placed two Colleges at Avignon under the care of Propaganda; see *Ius Pontif.*, 1781.

[5] On March 13, 1640, the superiors of Orders were forbidden to open new convents, houses, seminaries, hospices, or chapels under the name of the Propagation of the faith without the permission of Propaganda (*Ius pontif.*, I., 199). *Cf. La Propagande. Notices hist.*, Rome, 1875, 26.

[6] *Cf.* SCHMIDLIN in the *Zeitschr. für Missionswiss*, XIII. (1923), 58; *idem.*, *Anima*, 499 *seq.*

[7] From the *Testamentum Io. Savenier Leod. secret. apost.*, printed Romae typis Prop., 1638. On the great legacy of Cardinal Ubaldini see *Avviso of April 28, 1635, *Urb.* 1103, Vat. Libr.

Giovanni Leonardi, so that by 1633 the annual income of the Congregation had risen to over 6,000 scudi, by 1638 to nearly 12,000, and subsequently to twice that sum.[1]

An important adjunct to the Congregation of Propaganda was its polyglot printing press. As early as 1622 it was decided to found a printing press provided with Greek, Latin, Arabic, Armenian and Illyrian type. Part of the plant already existed in the Vatican Library and in the printing shop set up by Sixtus V.; the remainder was provided by the printer Stefano Paolino. The press of Propaganda was finally set up on July 14th, 1626. It was warmly supported by Urban VIII. who was ever a patron of scholarship. The first catalogue of its publications, drawn up by Giovanni Domenico Verusi, appeared in 1639.[2]

The great hopes which Urban VIII. set on Propaganda from the beginning[3] were destined to be amply fulfilled. One circumstance which greatly contributed to this result was the special attention paid by Propaganda to the various Seminaries in which good priests were being formed both within and outside Rome. Gregory XV. had already decreed the visitation of the Roman Colleges. Urban VIII. in his turn approved the measure[4] and extended it to foreign Colleges. For its execution he made use partly of Propaganda, partly of the nuncios. In 1623 the Generals of Orders were instructed to establish schools of languages for missionaries.[5] In 1624

[1] See SCHMIDLIN in the *Zeitschr. für Missionswiss*, XII. (1922), 14.

[2] *Cf.* M. GALEOTTI, *Della tipografia poliglotta di Propaganda*, Torino, 1866, *App.*, I. and II. *Ibid.*, III., on the share of Ingoli. *Cf.* also MORONI, XIV., 238 *seq.*; F. L. HOFFMANN, in *Bullet. du Bibliophile Belge*, IX., Brussels, 1852; FALKENSTEIN, 212 *seq.*; *Serapeum*, 1867, 106 *seq.*; *Carte Strozz.*, I., 2, 158 *seq.*

[3] *Cf.* the *Instructions for the nuncios of 1624, especially that for Agucchi in Venice (*cf.* above p. 176), and Sachetti in Madrid (*cf.* vol. xxviii, p. 65).

[4] See **Visite*, VIII., 186, Propaganda Archives, Rome.

[5] See SCHMIDLIN, in *Zeitschr. für Missionwiss.*, XII. (1922), 14, note 1.

the Bulgarian College was subjected to a visitation,[1] and the Greek College was given new statutes.[2] On December 18th, 1626, Propaganda reported that the various visitations which it had carried out had brought to light the fact that, with the exception of the Germanicum, the Roman Colleges fell short of what might be expected from them ; accordingly a reform was indispensable.[3]

Visitations seemed the most appropriate remedy and from the first years of Urban's pontificate they were also held in Colleges abroad, as at Vilna,[4] Olomouc,[5] in the Cologne Seminary of the Congregation of Bursfeld,[6] in the English College at Douai.[7] Between the years 1627–8 the visitation of the papal Colleges of Prague,[8] Vienna,[9] Fulda,[10] and

[1] April 9, 1624 ; see **Visite*, I., 1 *seq.* **Visite*, V., 438, for the index of the " alumni Bulgari " since Clement VIII.'s time.

[2] See *Ius pontif.*, I., 34 *seqq.* ; *La Semaine de Rome*, 1909, 452 *seq.*, where further details are found of Urban VIII.'s efforts, which were unfortunately unsuccessful, to increase the revenues of the College.

[3] See **Memorie per i collegii pontif.*, **Visite*, IV.

[4] See **Sommario della visita del collegio pontif. di Vilna*, February 22–3, 1624 (by Urban VIII.'s command), **Visite*, IV.

[5] Visitation by the nuncio C. Carafa, 1624, **Visite*, I., 6. *Ibid.*, 17, **Catalogus alumnorum* since the foundation by Gregory XIII.

[6] **Relatione del seminario di Colonia*, 1616, erected by the nuncio Ant. Albergati, with the consent of Paul V., for the spread of the Faith in Germany ; in a bad way through the negligence of abbots ; reformed by Urban VIII., *Visite*, III.

[7] **Visita del collegio degli Inglesi a Duaci* by the nuncio of the Netherlands, Fr. G. del Bagno, *Visite*, V.

[8] **Visite*, III. and IV. *Cf.* **Visite*, V., the decision of the Congr. de Prop. fide on the erection of a new seminary at Prague ; Bull. of 1627, *Ius pontif.*, I., 78 *seq.*

[9] *Nova institutio collegii Viennen.*, *Ius pontif.*, I., 82. *Cf.* DUHR., II., 1, 627.

[10] **Visitatio collegii Fuld. 4 febr. 16 ab abb. Fuld., subdelegato Nunc. Colon., Visite*, IV. ; *Nova institutio collegii Fuld.* 1628, *Ius pontif.*, I., 105 *seqq.* *Cf.* DUHR, II., 1, 623 *seq.*

Dillingen[1] led to a reform of those establishments. The nuncio Carafa took a prominent part in the reform of the Colleges of Olomonc, Vienna and Prague. In 1625 a College was erected for the Maronites on Mount Lebanon,[2] and in 1627 the Slavonic College at Loreto was restored.[3] In the thirties of the century the Maronite College in Rome,[4] the Carmelite Seminary at S. Maria della Vittoria[5] and the newly erected Arab College at S. Pietro in Montorio[6] were also subjected to a visitation. The Roman College for Catechumens was given a new domicile by Urban VIII. and his brother Antonio.[7] In 1643 the missionary College erected at Cologne by the Premonstratensian Abbot of Steinfeld was placed by the Pope under his own protection and that of Propaganda.[8]

Urban VIII. also took a lively interest in the Catholics of the Turkish Empire and the remaining possessions of Venice, sending them visitors with mission to report to Propaganda. Thus in the summer of 1624 Ottaviano Garzadori, Archbishop of Zara, was named visitor of Dalmatia. He carried out his task with great zeal and visited all the dioceses and all the islands in the course of 1624 and 1625.[9] When

[1] **Visitatio collegii Dilingae*, 1627, *de mandato Congr. de Prop. fide, Visite*, V. *Cf.* DUHR, II., 1, 626.

[2] **Regole del collegio de'Maroniti nel monte Libanon erigendo*, approved by Propaganda, May 2, 1625, *Visite*, VIII., 469 *seq.* *Cf. Bull.*, XIII., 358 *seq.* *Ius pontif.*, I., 50 *seq.*

[3] See *Ius pontif.*, I., 73 *seqq.*; *Mon. Slav. merid.*, XXIII., 373 *seq.* *Cf.* *NICOLETTI, II., p. 1286 *seq.*, Vatican Library.

[4] See **Visite*, VIII., 187 *seqq.* *Cf. Vat.* 7262, 31 *seq.*, Vatican Library.

[5] See **Visite*, XIII., 1 *seqq.* *Cf. Ius pontif.*, I., 133 *seqq.*, and **Visite*, XVIII., 171 *seqq.* (*Visite* of 1639–1640).

[6] *Visite* of 1631; see **Visite*, VIII., 473 *seqq.*

[7] See FORCELLA, IX., 375, 382.

[8] See *Ius pontif.*, I., 217 *seq.*

[9] *Brief of nomination, July 13, 1624. *Cf.* the letter of recommendation to the Doge of June 15, 1624, in THEINER, *Mon. Slav.*, 122. **Diarium visitationis*, in **Visite*, II., 31–131, with the reform decree. **Visite*, III., contains the reports of Garzadori.

at a later date complaints reached Rome from Dalmatia, Propaganda, in 1628, resolved to apply a remedy, urging in particular the erection of a seminary.[1] Reforms were applied by the Pope in 1631 [2] and in 1640 by the Archbishop of Zara, Benedetto Capello.[3] In the summer of 1625 Propaganda received from Archbishop Luca Stella, of Crete (Candia) [1624–1632] a report on his work as Apostolic Visitor in Zante and Cerigo. The Visitor pointed out existing abuses and suggested remedies.[4] Ragusa was visited in 1627,[5] the islands of Zante and Cefalu in 1635,[6] Corfu in 1636 and 1637 by Stella's successor, Alvise Mocerigo, Archbishop of Crete, who likewise displayed great activity in his own diocese.[7]

In 1638 Ingoli, the indefatigable secretary of Propaganda

In *that of Zara, April 15, 1625, he reports that there were only three Greek churches in Dalmatia and that the Greek priests did not overstep their rights. The letter says: "Non essendo al presente lo scisma de'Greci senza molte eresie, non si può in alcuna maniera celebrare in quelle."

[1] See **Visite*, VIII., 234 *seqq.*

[2] *Brief of November 10, 1631, "per la riforma d. chiesa di S. Simeone di Zara," *ibid.*, 278.

[3] **Decreti della visita del arciv. di Zara, Visite*, XVIII., 221.

[4] *Report, dated Crete, February 21, 1625: In Zante "90 Latini & 12000 Greci; le chiese in malissimo stato; dottrina christiana non s'insegna", only "frati convent.", no secular clergy. Cerigo: two churches "mal tenute, pochi Latini" (*Visite*, III.). Extension of the visitation to the Ionian Islands; *cf. Bull.*, XIII., 82 *seq.*, 140. "*Laudo cantato dal clero greco di Candia per il P. Urbano VIII. e l'arcivescovo L. Stella*" in *Bessarione*, XXVI. (1922), 16 *seq.*

[5] **Relatione al Papa della visita della provincia di Ragusa*, 1627 (by command of Urban VIII.), *Visite*, V.

[6] **Visite*, XIV., 143 *seq.*

[7] **Visita di Corfu*, 1636, by the Archbishop of Crete, Mocenigo, with his decrees, *Visite*, XIV., 1 *seqq.*, 35 *seqq.*, 92 *seqq.*; **Visita di Corfu*, 1637 (Rites), *ibid.*, XV., 320 *seqq.*; *ibid.*, XIX., 291 *seqq.*, **Visita delle chiese dei Greci soggette al dominio Veneto et in partic. di quella di Candia di Msgr. Mocenigo* (by order of Propaganda).

and a man of great initiative,[1] summed up in a memorandum the various causes of the retrogression of the Latin Rite in Crete and the other Greek possessions of the Venetians. He mentions the following: the dearth of priests owing to the fact that there was no seminary; non-compliance with the duty of residence by the Italian holders of episcopal sees; the bestowal by the Dataria of canonries (under pressure on the part of Venetian ambassadors) to subjects of Venice who failed to carry out their duties and the increased difficulty for Latins to obtain matrimonial dispensations. Both Propaganda and the Pope took immediate steps for the removal of these abuses. Urban VIII. consented to a native being given the sees of Sitia and Hierapetra seeing that he complied with the duty of residence and that he would be able to do good work by reason of his knowledge of the language.[2] In 1643, with a view to remedying the shortage of priests, Propaganda contributed towards the erection of a seminary in Crete.[3] The diocese of Sitia had been visited by its Bishop in 1638.[4]

Far more difficult than in the Venetian possessions was the condition of Catholics in the vast Turkish Empire, for there they were threatened not only by schismatics and heretics, but likewise by the Mohammedans. From a report by the Bishop of Antivari, Marino Bizzi, on the situation of the Latin Christians in the diaspora of Macedonia, Albania, Serbia and Bulgaria who had remained loyal to the Pope, notwithstanding their many trials, we get a good idea of the difficulties of their position.[5] Bizzi's successor, Pietro Massarechio

[1] Ingoli well deserves a monograph for which the Archives of Propaganda, Rome, contain abundant material.

[2] Ingoli, **Della visita de Candia, Visite*, XVI., 312 *seqq.*

[3] See **Visite*, XXII.

[4] *Ibid.*, XVII., 223 *seqq.*

[5] See **Informatione intorno allo stato della christianità dei regni di Macedonia, Albania, Servia, e Bulgaria in partibus infidelium*, by *Archbishop Marino Bizzi* (*cf.* our account, Vol. XXV., 379), *Ottob.* 2536, p. 282 *seqq.*, Vatican Library. *Cf. ibid.*, 265 *seqq.*: **Modus iuvandi catholican religionem in dioecesi*

(1624–1635) held a synod in 1625 and visited Belgrade and the adjoining Turkish part of Hungary where he beheld on all sides the ruins of churches and monasteries.[1] Massarechio's successor, George Bianchi, in his capacity as Primate of Serbia (1636–9), undertook the visitation of his diocese and of the whole of Serbia. Everywhere he found a great shortage of priests.[2] He also preached and confirmed in Montenegro, held a synod of Serbian priests and appointed as his Vicar-General the excellent Giovanni Zilli.[3] In 1642 Bianchi revisited Serbia.[4]

The Turkish part of Hungary [5] as well as Bosnia was chiefly evangelized by the Franciscans. Thomas Juvcovich, Bishop

Zagrabiensi ac vicinis regnis et provinciis utentibus lingua Illyrica (see LÄMMER, *Analecta*, 45). *Cf.* the *Informatione di Fra Bonaventura di S. Antonio*, 1632, about Albania published by RANKE without indication of source (*Serbien und die Turkei*, Leipzig, 1879).

[1] See **Visita di Samandria et altri luoghi della Ungheria sotto il Turco dell'arcivescovo di Antivari* (the Hungarians like to hear singing in Hungarian, which the Jesuits do; they almost prefer sermons to Mass, which is due to widespread Calvinist influence), *Visite*, XI., 150 *seqq.*; *cf.* 10 *seqq.*; **Ordini sinodali dell'arcivescovo di Antivari, ibid.*, X., 1 *seqq.*: **Relatione della visita di Belgrado et altri luoghi della Ungheria sotto il Turco dell'arcivescovo di Antivari P. Massarecchio.* For Massarecchio, *cf. Illyria sacra*, VII.

[2] See **Visita di servia dell'arciv. di Antivari et primate di Servia* (report from him 1636), *Visite*, XV., 306 *seqq.*; **Visita d'Antivari e della Servia sup. et inf. dell' arciv. G. Bianchi*, 1637–8, *ibid.*, XVI., 234 *seqq.*; **Visita di Antivari di Msgr. Giorgio arciv.* 1638, *ibid.*, XVII., 239 *seqq.*

[3] See **Relatione della visita di Msgr. arcivescovo d'Antivari nella sua diocesi et in altri luoghi di Servia*, 1639, *Visite*, XVIII., 229 *seqq.*

[4] **Relatione della visita della Servia fatta dal arciv. di Antivari*, 1642 ("anime cattoliche in tutta la Servia sono adesso 3522"), *Visite*, XX., 49 *seqq.*

[5] *Cf.* **Instruttione per il P. Benedetto Radzinense nin. conv. per la visita di Scioli di Transilvania e delle parochie d'Ungheria sotto il Turco*, dated January 24, 1633, *Visite*, XI., 183 *seq.*

of Scardona and Bosnia, was a Franciscan.[1] Between 1626 and 1630 he confirmed 34,479 Catholics, but he had to bribe the Turks to make it possible for him to discharge his functions.[2] The Bishop of Drivasto, Jerome Lucich, also a a Franciscan, confirmed 20,000 persons in Bosnia between 1637–9.[3]

In 1625 the Bishop of Alessio reported to Urban VIII. and to Propaganda on the very difficult situation in Albania. In the course of a visitation of his diocese, which was subject to the Turks, he had found that the Catholics were excellent but to minister to them there were only a few secular priests besides the Fathers of two Franciscan convents. The Bishop visited the whole of his diocese, zealously carried out various reforms and restored the ruined churches.[4] Notwithstanding the establishment, in 1634, of a Franciscan mission in Albania,[5] and repeated visitations in 1634, 1637 and 1641, the situation grew steadily worse. In 1637 thirteen towns had only one priest each, every one of whom had to serve an area of 40 miles. Small wonder that the population deteriorated and adopted Mohammedan customs. They observed Friday instead of Sunday; many men had two wives; Christian women who had married Turks declared that they did not know that this was forbidden. The visitation of 1641 also

[1] *Cf. Illyria sacra*, IV., *passim*.

[2] *Report of July 26, 1630, *Visite*, VII., 147.

[3] **Visita di Bosnia di Msgr. Girolamo vescovo di Drivasto, amministrat. apost. di Scardona e vic. apost. nelle chiese del regno di Bosnia*, 1637–1639 (in the diocese of Scardona and the "regno di Bosnia" there were only four secular priests, but 457 frati) *Visite*, XVII., 173 *seqq.*

[4] *Report to Urban VIII., dated Alessio, April 20, 1625, and **Sommario della visita del vesc. d'Alessio dello stato della diocesi* to Propaganda, same date, *Visite*, III.

[5] *Cf. Orbis Seraphicus. Missiones*, II., Quaracchi, 1886, 393 *seq.*; H. Mattrod, *Albanie au XVII. siècle*, in *Bull. de l'Institut pour l'étude de l'Europe Sud-Orientale*, IX., Boukarest, 1922, 56 *seq.*

revealed a state of profound ignorance in consequence of the dearth of priests.[1]

In Bulgaria Catholics were in a much better position. There the Province of Kiprovac enjoyed a certain independence owing to its being the apanage of the mother of the Sultan, hence it had become the refuge of Catholics who there enjoyed full liberty to practise their religion. The Bishops of Sofia, who were all Franciscans, had resided in Kiprovac since 1600. In 1623 Urban VIII. appointed to the see of Sofia Elias Marini, a member of a noble family of Kiprovac. This splendid prelate converted many heretics, such as the Paulicians, and in 1625 he persuaded Propaganda to erect a Bulgarian Franciscan Province (custody). On July 21st, 1631, Marini renounced all parochial rights in favour of the Franciscans, only reserving to himself the privilege of sharing their table. In 1632 he opened a school in the convent, for the religious and secular instruction of youth. In 1638 Urban VIII. granted to him, at his own request, in view of his increasing age, a coadjutor in the person of Peter Deodat, Superior of the Bulgarian Franciscan Province and Bishop of Gallipoli.[2] When Marini died, Peter Deodat, a Bulgarian, succeeded him in the episcopal see of Sofia and Urban VIII. assigned to him an annual pension of 200 scudi. Deodat visited his new diocese [3]

[1] **Visita di Msgr. Sapatense* (*Georg. Grillus de Blanchis*) *in Albania*, 1634, July, *Visite*, XIII., 64 *seqq.*; **Visita di Msgr. vescovo Sapatense* (*Franc. Blanca*), 1637, *ibid.*, XVI., 193 *seq.*; **Visita de'popoli di monti di Albania di fra Gregorio Romano*, 1641, *ibid.*, XIX., 225 *seqq.*; **Visita di Durazzo et altre chiese d'Albania di fra Marco arciv. di Durazzo*, 1641, *ibid.*, XXI., 33 *seq.*

[2] See J. PEJACSEVICH in *Archiv. für österr. Gesch.*, LIX. (1880), 342 *seq.* The *letter of *Fra Benedetto Emanuele Remondi de Milano, min. conv., missionario di Moldavia et Vallachia*, to Cardinal Barberini, dated Pera, September 14, 1636, is interesting; it is accompanied by a *report on his visitation journeys 1635–6, *Visite*, XIV., 294 *seqq.*

[3] **Visita di Moldavia di fra Pietro vescovo di Sofia*, 1641, with suggestions as to how the Catholics of that district should

and held a synod in 1643, after which he went to Rome where the Pope named him Archbishop of Sofia. Reviving the metropolitan dignity of Sardica, Urban VIII. also entrusted to him the supervision of Riparian Dacia, which included Lower Bulgaria and Thrace (East Rumelia). The boundaries of the new archdiocese of Sardica were ill defined, hence a dispute arose with Mark Bandin whom Urban VIII., in 1643, had appointed Archbishop of Martianople, with residence in Bacău. The dispute was composed on February 6th, 1644. It was settled that, besides his own diocese, the Archbishop of Sardica should administer the province of Thrace (Eastern Rumelia, Riparian Dacia, and Valachia), and the Archbishop of Martianople, in addition to his own diocese, the adjoining one of Tomi (Dobrudja) and Moldavia.[1]

For the benefit of the Catholics of Transilvania, Propaganda entrusted to the Bosnian Franciscan Stephen Salines, the duty of making a visitation for which the Government also gave its permission. Salines found 44,000 Catholics and fifty-eight parishes of which twenty-one were without a priest. Transilvania had not had a Bishop for thirty years, so that grave abuses had crept in. Most of the priests were married. Propaganda did its utmost to remove these abuses.[2]

be cared for. " Dall'esempio della Bulgaria, nella quale la congregazione ha eretta una custodia di minori osservanti," the Congregation is advised to do the same for Moldavia and Wallachia; in Bulgaria there were formerly only three priests; now there are forty, " tutti del paese " (Propaganda Archives, Rome). On Moldavia see also EUBEL in *Röm. Quartalschr.*, XII., 113 *seq.*

[1] See PEJACSEVICH, *loc. cit.*, 346 *seq.* *Cf.* also CANDEA, *Der Katholizismus in den Donaufürstentümern* (1917), 97 *seq.*; HUDAL, *Die serbisch-orthodoxe Nationalkirche*, Graz, 1922, 14; **Visita della Vallachia e Bulgaria di fra Pietro Diodato arciv. di Sofia e Sardica.*, 1644, *Visite*, XXV., 207 *seqq.*

[2] See **Visita de'Sicoli di Transilvania* by order of Propaganda by *P. Stefano Salines, prefetto de'padri Bosnei in Transilvania*; **Domande per servitio della religione in Transilvania*; **Discorso del segr. Ingoli* (appointment of a Bishop a pressing need). *Visite*, XVI., 244 *seqq.*, Archives of Propaganda, Rome.

In north-western Greece, the oppression of which by the Turks was a source of grievous sorrow to Urban VIII.,[1] Propaganda provided for a mission in 1639.[2] The Jesuits laboured under severe difficulties in Bosnia,[3] in the Greek islands,[4] in Naxos, Syra [5] and Paros [6]; also at Aleppo, Patras and Athens [7]; and since 1642 at Santorin.[8] Throughout the Levant the French Capuchins vied with the Jesuits. The former were greatly favoured by the French Government, on national grounds.[9] The idea of this mission proceeded from Fr. Joseph who interested Richelieu in it. Accordingly Propaganda bestowed on Fr. Joseph the title of "Prefect of the Eastern Missions", and both he and Fr. Leonard of Paris were given the widest faculties. In concert with Richelieu the undertaking was organized as follows: To the Capuchin Province of Paris were assigned the missions in Greece, Asia Minor and the Archipelago; to the Province of Tours, the missions in Egypt, Cairo, Aleppo and Persia; to the Province of Brittany the missions in Palestine, Beirut and Damascus. Even if this ambitious scheme was only partially realized, important results were nevertheless obtained, thanks to the support of the French Government. In 1634 there were Capuchin missions in Constantinople, Smyrna, Chios, Naxos, Beirut, Aleppo, Cairo, Bagdad and Tripoli.[10]

The Bishop of Santorin, the Dominican Pietro de Marchis, whom Gregory XV. had appointed visitor of Pera and Constantinople, continued his reforming activities under

[1] See the letter in THEINER, *Mon. Slav.*, II., 123.

[2] See BESSARIONE, XVII. (1913), 130 *seq.*

[3] See *Mon. Slav. merid.*, XXIII., 373 *seq.*

[4] See ZINKEISEN, IX., 361 *seq.*

[5] See *Fouqueray*, IV., 348 *seq.*, 358 *seq.*, V., 372 *seq.*, 376 *seq.*, 379 *seq.*

[6] *Ibid.*, V., 381 *seq.*

[7] *Ibid.*, 382 *seq.* *Cf.* GREGOROVIUS, *Gesch. von Athen*, II., 416.

[8] See FOUQUERAY, V., 386 *seq.*

[9] See FAGNIEZ, I., 314 *seq.*, 355. *Cf.* HOLZAPFEL, 529 *seq.*, and L. DE VANNES, *Deux martyrs Capucins*, Paris, 1905.

[10] See FAGNIEZ, I., 357.

Urban VIII.[1] He was able to send in a good report about the island of Syra (Syros) which was wholly Catholic.[2] At Naxos there still remained 400 Latins with two churches in the town, two in the suburbs, and six in the surrounding district. The Archbishop, the Venetian Sebastiano Quirini, knew no Greek, though such knowledge was essential as de Marchis stated emphatically.[3] On the other hand, at Andros there remained only sixty people of the Latin Rite.[4] At Paros there still remained two noble families of that Rite, but owing to the lack of priests the population had gone over to the Greek Rite.[5] At Santorin there were 700 Latins with five churches,[6] but in the sequel conditions deteriorated to such an extent that Pietro de Marchis, who in 1625 had entrusted the care of the Latins of Smyrna to a Jesuit,[7] had to leave the island because of the risk to his life. In 1640 he was made Bishop of Smyrna. In a detailed report to Propaganda he advocates the following reforms: the nomination of a Vicar Apostolic for Smyrna; that of a coadjutor for Chios whose Bishop was eighty years old; for Milo, a Bishop or a Vicar; for Andros, help for the Jesuit mission; for Constantinople, the appointment of a suffragan and the erection of a College. In the

[1] See *_Decreti et ordini di Msgr. Pietro de Marchis, vesc. di Santorino, visit. apost. nelle parti d'Oriente per le chiese di Pera e di Constantinopoli, emendati d'ordine della s. congregazione de prop. fide nell'anno primo di Urbano VIII._, _Visite_, I., Archives of Propaganda, Rome.

[2] *Report dated Syra, July 12, 1624: "L'isola di Sira sola in Levante tutto del nostro rito latino et per la riverenza che hanno alla chiesa Romana et al s. pontefice vien detto l'isola del Papa." Only 70 Greek schismatics there; 167 churches; two bad priests, who must be removed. _Visite_, I.

[3] See the *report from Naxos of March 29, 1624, _ibid._

[4] *Report of June 12, 1624, _ibid._

[5] See the *report from Paros, April 8, 1624 (qui è quasi estinto il nostro rito). _Visite_, I., Archives of Prop., Rome.

[6] *_Relatione dello stato della chiesa di Santorino_, _ibid._

[7] See Fouqueray, IV., 343. For the difficulties which arose for the Jesuits through the establishment of the Capuchins in Smyrna, see _ibid._, V., 360 _seq._

interests of all the isles he deems it necessary that the Christian galleys should put in an appearance there every year, as had formerly been their practice, otherwise the Christians would be too heavily oppressed by the Turks.[1]

One of the points of supreme importance for the missions in the Levant was Constantinople where in 1609 the Jesuits reopened their establishment which the plague had compelled them to close.[2] Their activity in that city was all the more urgently needed as since November 4th, 1620, the Greek patriarchal see was occupied by a man whose hatred for the Catholic Church and the papacy was unsurpassed either by his own co-religionists or by his Dutch friends, viz. Cyril Lukaris.[3] This crafty Cretan, who lacked a really solid

[1] See **Compendio dello stato dell'isole dell'Arcipelago e de'remedii da farsi per bene di quelle chiese* (*Visite*, I.). A legacy of the noble Cardinal Giustiniani made it possible for the Greek islands to be visited regularly. This was carried out in 1635 and 1636 with the help of the Jesuits; in 1638 the Capuchins also took part; see **Della visita dell'isole dell'Arcipelago in virtù del legato del defunto card. Giustiniani* (*Visite*, XIII., 211 *seqq.*); **Relatione della visita dell'isole d'Andro, Sira, etc., fatta dal P. Michael Albertino e suoi compagni Giesuiti*, 1635, *Dec.* (*ibid.*, XIV., 173 *seq.*; *cf. ibid.*, 174: *Letter from the Jesuit Dom. Mauritio, dated, Chios, January 25, 1636; proposals for the cure of souls); **Visita delle isole dell' Arcipelago di Lorenzo Tulina e di due padri Cappuccini*, 1638 (*ibid.*, XVII., 45 *seqq.*); **Visita delle chiese di Scio*, 1643 (*ibid.*, XXIV, 299 *seqq.*); visitation of the isles by Dom. Mauritio, 1643 (*ibid.*, XXV., 8); **Visita dell'isole dell'Arcipelago del P. G. B. Alessio*, 1644 (*ibid.*, XXV., 187 *seqq.*). Urban VIII. paid special attention to the Italo-Greeks in southern Italy and Sicily. A first visitation of these was undertaken at the end of 1629 (see *Visite*, VIII., 302 *seq.*), a second in 1630 (*ibid.*, 318 *seq.*), a third and fourth in 1635 and 1636 (*ibid.*, XIII. and XIV., Archives of Propaganda, Rome).

[2] *Cf.* our account, Vol. XXV., 378.

[3] The extensive literature on this man, who had a more varied career than any other Greek patriarch, has been collected and summarized by Ph. Meyer in HERZOG'S *Realenzyklopädie*, XI.[3], 683 *seq.*, and Emereau in VACANT'S *Dict. de théol.*, IX., 1018 *seq.*

theological formation,[1] had before this opposed the union of the Ruthenians of Poland,[2] and as Patriarch of Alexandria (1602–1620) he had entered into relations both with the Anglicans and the Calvinists. The danger which thereby threatened the efforts of the Holy See on behalf of the union had already alarmed Gregory XV.[3] It was to become even more acute under Urban VIII. for in his new position Lukaris made it the aim of his life to instil into the Greek Church the spirit of Calvin. It goes without saying that in Constantinople he had to reckon with the opposition of the Jesuits. Through the French ambassador, De Césy, they secured his banishment to Rhodes in April, 1623, but already in October he was able to return to his post with the aid of the ambassadors of Holland and England.[4] His first act was to have printed at Wittenberg, under the name of one of his pupils called Zacharias, a catechism destined to spread Protestant ideas among the Greeks. But he failed in his attempt to obtain the support of the French ambassador for his plans [5]; the latter, as a matter of fact, did all he could to get out of the way an agitator who seemed to know no fatigue,[6] and who was all the more dangerous as he sought to mask his dark designs. He proceeded with the utmost caution and reserve; two of his sympathizers who were preaching heresy, he decried in public whilst he allowed them to go on with their work. The English and Dutch ambassadors likewise did their best to disguise the object of their close relations with Lukaris by pretending that they frequented his company out of mere

[1] This is the opinion of Ph. Meyer in the article mentioned in the preceding note.

[2] *Cf.* our account, Vol. XXIV., 136, 139.

[3] *Cf.* **Lettera di Msgr. Agucchi al Nuntio di Francia*, January 25, 1622, *Cod.* X., V., 31, Casanatense Library, Rome.

[4] See FOUQUERAY, IV., 316 *seq.*

[5] *Ibid.*, 319.

[6] *Ibid.*, 319. *Cf.* Urban VIII.'s *Brief to Césy, January 11, 1625, *Epist.*, II., Papal Secret Archives.

courtesy.[1] On May 24th, 1624, Schiattini, who subsequently became Bishop of Naxos, reported that whilst Lukaris pretended to work for the union of the Greeks with Rome he was, in point of fact, bestowing ecclesiastical dignities on priests of Calvinist sentiments.[2] Popular opinion accused Lukaris of the worst immoralities.[3] The Greek Bishops whom he summoned to a synod in July, 1624, accused him of seeking to overthrow the ancient dogmas of the Eastern Church and burdening the Bishops with heavy taxes in order that he might be able to reward his own adherents.[4] At the close of October, 1624, Schiattini reported that the Calvinism of Lukaris, who was on closest terms with the Protestant ambassadors, was plain to anyone not blinded by passion or interest; he had deposed the Greek Bishop of Corinth and replaced him with one of his own supporters.[5]

Lukaris rightly judged that his chief opponents were the Jesuits, whose enemy he had ever been.[6] Already in 1624 he had sought to obtain from the Porte their banishment from Constantinople; he failed because France held a protecting hand over the Fathers; however, their position became dangerous when not only the envoys of England and Holland but the representative of Venice also began to plot against them.[7]

Besides unfavourable reports about Lukaris, Rome also received very optimistic accounts concerning his person. In February, 1625, the Congregation of Propaganda dispatched

[1] See **Lettera del Schiattini* (*hora arcivescovo di Naxia*), dated Constantinople, April 13, 1624, in the **Relatione data al card. Millini alli* 31 *Maggio* 1628 *per recitarla nel s. Officio*, Archives of Propaganda, Rome.

[2] See **Lettera del Schiattini arcivescovo di Maxia*, dated Constantinople, May 24, 1624, *loc. cit.*

[3] *" Si parla anco di lui assai sinistramente intorno al peccato nefando, et hoc rumor populi "; this is stated in the letter quoted in the next note.

[4] See **Lettera di Schiattini*, dated Pera, July 9, 1624, *loc. cit.*

[5] See **Lettera di Schiattini*, dated Pera, October 28, 1624, *loc. cit.*

[6] See PH. MEYER, *loc. cit.*, 687. [7] See FOUQUERAY, IV., 321.

to Constantinople a priest of the Byzantine Rite of the name of Cannachio Rossi, with mission to demand from Lukaris a confession of faith in harmony with the Union of Florence; if he complied the Holy See would not be chary of its favour and assistance.[1] Acting on the advice of the English ambassador,[2] Lukaris put off Rossi for a considerable time when the latter reached Constantinople in July, 1625. A master in the art of deceit, Lukaris played his hypocritical rôle so successfully that Rossi was completely deluded. He assured Rossi of his willingness to accept the Council of Florence and requested him to arrange for an interview with Césy.[3] Césy had frowned on Rossi's mission because he was anxious to have the negotiations exclusively in his own hands. He therefore demanded Rossi's recall as well as that of the Franciscan-Observant, Ambrogio della Pola [4] and the Archimandrite Philotheus of Jerusalem who had also allowed themselves to be completely deceived by Lukaris.[5] So convinced was Rossi of Lukaris' sincerity [6] that at the beginning of 1627 he complained to Propaganda of its refusal to believe in the Patriarch's readiness to accept the Union. Lukaris,

[1] The Instruction for C. Rossi (in Roe, *Negotiations in his embassy to the Ottoman Porte*, 1621–8, London, 1740, 470 *seq.*) is dated February 21, 1625. For his arrival, on July 25, 1625, see Hammer, V., 90. For Rossi's visit to Mount Athos in 1628, where a Catholic school was erected later (in 1636) and maintained until 1641, see G. Hofman, *Athos e Roma*, Roma, 1925.

[2] *Cf.* Roe, 469.

[3] See *Rossi's letter to F. Ingoli, dated Constantinople, November 4, 1626, Archives of Propaganda, Rome.

[4] See Césy's *letter to the Cardinals of Propaganda, dated Pera, November 13, 1626, Archives of Propaganda. The hostile disposition of Ambrogio della Pola against Césy appears in his **Relatione* of May, 1627, *ibid.*

[5] See the *reports of Philotheus to Ingoli, written in Greek, dated Constantinople, December 12, 1626, and September 27, 1627, *ibid.*

[6] *" Il patriarcha Cyrillo è tutto in favor de'cattolici non modo verbis sed etiam operabus." C. Rossi to Ingoli, dated Constantinople, November 16, 1626, *ibid.*

he wrote, was prepared to accept the Council of Florence and Césy alone was to blame if the Union did not progress as rapidly as there was reason to hope.[1]

On January 26th, 1627, Propaganda had unanimously decided to leave further negotiations in the affair Lukaris in the experienced hands of Césy, and if the latter deemed it advisable Ambrogio della Pola and Philotheus were also to be excluded from the discussions; in any case they were to follow the directions of Césy.[2] To the latter's demand that not only the two last named but Rossi also should have nothing more to do with the question of the Union, the Congregation would not agree; on the contrary, it decided, on January 30th, 1627, that Rossi should remain in Constantinople as its representative.[3] This decision was a fatal mistake. Subsequently (June 13th) Propaganda decided to send to Constantinople the Oratorian Orazio Giustiniani of Chios on a secret mission in connection with the negotiations concerning the Union, but the latter declined and the mission did not materialize.[4]

In November, 1627, reports reached Propaganda which left no doubt about Lukaris' duplicity when he assured Rossi of his readiness to accept the Union. In confirmation of Césy's reports the Greek Archbishop of Naxos, Jeremias Barbarigo wrote on August 1st, 8th and 12th both to the Pope and to

[1] *Letter of January 20, 1627, in which it is stated that Cyril was " prontissimo all'unione . . . ; è una colonna inconcussa et immobile che da 300 anni in qua non v'è stata simili soggetto ! " *Ibid.*

[2] **Congregatio partic. in pal. card. Bandini sup. negotio unionis Graecorum, Jan. 26, 1627*; present, Bandini, Klesl, Ludovisi, Magalotti and Barberini; the above resolution was unanimously approved. *Ibid.*

[3] The resolution was passed by the same Cardinals, with the exception of Magalotti who was not present, *ibid.*

[4] **Congregatio partic. in thalamo seu camera prope consistorium cui interfuerunt card. Bandinus, Cleselius, Magalottus et Barberinus, 1627, June 13, ibid.* At the same time O. Giustiniani was chosen as " coadiutor of the episc. Chiensis cum fut. successione ". *Ibid.*,

Propaganda that Lukaris was assiduously spreading Protestant opinions among the Greeks and that he proved himself an avowed enemy of the Catholic Church. He rejected auricular confession, the real presence of Jesus Christ in the Eucharist, free will and the intercession of the Saints. It was also said that he had obtained from the Sultan the removal of the Archbishops of Smyrna and Edessa and the erection in Alexandria, of a College to be governed by a Greek Calvinist; that he sought to induce the Porte to banish the pupils of the Greek College in Rome, in a word, that he was endeavouring to overthrow all that had been built up by Propaganda. These dark manœuvres, Barbarigo further reported, were not only supported in every way, even with money, by the English and Dutch ambassadors, but they were also favoured by the representative of Venice.[1]

The members of Propaganda, above all Ingoli, fully realized the magnitude of the peril and they were of opinion that

an undated suggestion on the negotiations with Lukaris, in consequence of which O. Giustiniani refused the commission; the unnamed author of the proposal remarks that as the Jesuits were unsuitable for it, on account of Lukaris' hatred for them and their too great friendship with Césy, he was proposing Giov. Maria Gallo, Bishop of Santorin, now in Candia, who though a Venetian was primarily "buon ecclesiastico e poi Venetiano",

[1] See the *reports of G. Barbarigo to Propaganda, dated August 1, 1627; to Ingoli, dated Constantinople, August 8, 1627; to Dr. Pietro Arcudio at Rome, dated Galata, August 12. 1627; to the Pope, dated Galata, August 12, 1627, Archives of Propaganda, Rome. The interest of Venice in Lukaris is explained by Césy in a letter in code to Béthune, dated April 27, 1628: "Premièrement il est Candiote et par consequent leur subject et oultre en ceste qualité qui leur est advantageuse ils aymeroyent mieux qu'un patriarche soit heretique que de bonne opinion car arrivant quelque decadence a cest empire ils croyent bien qu'un patriarche catholique portera plustot les volentez des ecclesiastiques et des peuples a recourir a d'aultres potentats qu'à la Republique de Venise. C'est pourquoi ils veulent un patriarche qui depende entirement d'eux et qui soit totalement aliené de l'Église Romaine." *Ibid.*

Lukaris must be opposed by every possible means [1]: Rossi alone persisted in his optimism. Lukaris, so he assured the Prefect of Propaganda, was sincerely in favour of union with Rome; all reports to the contrary were based on calumny; hence he adjured the Congregation to continue its negotiations with him for the Union.[2] It was fortunate that Propaganda did not allow itself to be deceived. The authentic reports which it had received made it clear that the question was no longer whether it was necessary to proceed against that astute personage, but solely how he might be rendered harmless. On November 13th, 1627, the Congregation resolved as follows: (1) The Calvinist Catechism disseminated by Lukaris to be combated by means of a refutation in the Greek tongue; (2) Cardinal Bessarion's letter on union with Rome to be widely diffused; (3) Lukaris to be declared a preacher of the Calvinist heresy; (4) Césy to press for Lukaris' deposition, if possible, by using the name of his sovereign; support to be given him, even money, if necessary, though it would be better to spend the latter in a literary campaign against Lukaris; (5) the French nuncio to influence Louis XIII. in favour of Lukaris' deposition; (6) the Porte to be induced to shut down the latter's printing press at Constantinople; (7) the owners of Greek merchant ships to pronounce against Lukaris; if they refused they should forfeit the protection of the Christians; (8) the French King to be made to see the great danger that would arise out of an alliance of the schismatic Greeks with England, Holland and the German Protestants.[3]

Towards the end of January, 1628, with the aid of the

[1] Ingoli's addition to Barbarigo's *letter to the Pope of August 1, 1627, Archives of Propaganda, Rome. *Ibid.*, an undated *draft of Ingoli's: *Modo di far il processo contro Cyrillo con facilità et senza pericolo.* [2] *Letter of September 10, 1627, *ibid.*

[3] **Congregatio partic. in pal. card. Bandini, Nov.* 13, 1627. Present: Cardinals Bandini, Millini, Ludovisi, Magalotti and Barberini; reading of the letters of the Archbishop of Naxos, of the French envoy and of C. Rossi; there follow the decisions recorded above (Archives of Propaganda, Rome). The *Estratto* in *Söltl*, III., 374 *seq.*, is short and unreliable.

English and Viennese ambassadors, Lukaris succeeded in obtaining from the Porte the arrest and banishment of the Jesuits of Constantinople, a manœuvre in which the Dutch ambassador, who was on terms of close friendship with the Patriarch, secretly concurred.[1] However, Césy worked indefatigably on behalf of the Fathers, notwithstanding the opposition of the representative of Venice, and he secured in the same year the liberation and readmission of men falsely suspected; in the sequel also he watched over an institute that was dear to him and against which Lukaris and the representative of Holland and Venice plotted unceasingly.[2]

Césy's report on the Calvinist propaganda kept up by Lukaris and his confederate, the preacher Antony Leger[3] who had been summoned from Geneva to Constantinople in 1628, was read at a meeting of Propaganda on July 21st, 1628. The Congregation decided that all the missionaries should unite with the Greek Patriarchs of Alexandria, Antioch and Jerusalem in a joint action against Lukaris so that proceedings might be initiated against the sectary. The Venetian nuncio should enlighten the Senators on Lukaris' Calvinism, to press them to put an end to the support which their representative was giving to him and to urge the Turks to depose him. The subsidy of 12,000 thalers for which Césy had prayed should be forwarded, but the Patriarchs who co-operated in the efforts for Lukaris' deposition were to receive the money only when that matter was an accomplished fact. Lastly it was proposed that the Capuchin Fr. Joseph should go to Constantinople under pretext of visiting the missionaries of his Order in the Levant, with a view to promoting the deposition of Lukaris.[4] On July 25th, 1628, Propaganda met once

[1] See Fouqueray, IV., 326 *seq.*

[2] *Ibid.*, 331 *seq.* *Cf.* *Études*, CXIII. (1907), 70 *seq.*, 384 *seq.*

[3] *Cf.* Legrand, IV., 484.

[4] *" Mittendum esse Constantinopolim P. Iosephum Parisiensem Capuccinum praetextu visitationis missionum orientalium sui ordinis, quarum est praefectus, ut non solum negotio depositionis Cyrilli assistat, etc." *Congregatio partic. in pal. card. Barberini, July* 21, 1628, Archives of Propaganda, Rome.

more, this time under the presidency of the Pope who approved the resolutions of July 21st, to discuss the details of the procedure to be adopted against Lukaris.[1] Three methods were considered: a canonical process through the Roman Inquisition, a process through a synod of the Greek Metropolitans and Patriarchs or, lastly, the expedient of gifts of money to the Greeks or to the Turks. The two first were most to Urban's liking but they were difficult of execution and very lengthy, hence the third method was advisable, but in applying it care must be taken to safeguard both divine and human justice as well as the dignity and honour of the Apostolic See. The Roman Inquisition must be consulted on the point and all the relative documents submitted to it.[2]

By this time the credulous Rossi had come to see things in their true light. In a report to Propaganda dated July 25th, 1628, he admitted that he had been deceived by Lukaris

[1] *" Die 25 Iulii coram Smo praesente d. card. Barberino," *ibid.*

[2] The questions were as follows :—

(1) An attentis relationibus, quae de Cyrillo habentur, iure divino ac humano illius depositio per pecuniam promoveri possit.

(2) An expediat et Sedis Apost. dignitati conveniat huiusmodi pecuniae medio uti pro obtinenda depositione praedicta.

(3) Si in praecedentibus articulis affirmativa (sententia) ad evitandum gravissimum in ecclesia Dei malum sustineri possit, an in conscientia tutius sit ac magis Sedi Apost. deceat pecuniam pro depositione praedicta Turcis solvere an potius metropolitis vel aliis Graecis habentibus ius eligendi patriarcham Constantinopolit.

(4) An aliquibus conditionibus licita et honesta reddi poterit dicta depositio.

(5) Et ultimo si canonice et brevi iuxta negotii exigentiam sententia depositionis Cyrilli a s. Officio ferri posset vel a metropolitis synodaliter convocatis promulgaretur, an liceret iure divino et humano atque Sedis Apost. dignitatis conveniret executionem sententiae vel a Turcis vel a Graecis per pecuniam, si aliter illa haberi nequiret, procurare ? et maxime, si pacto cum Graecis conveniri possit, ut Cyrillus depositus ad inquisitionem Melitae vel Messanam ad archiepiscopum duceretur."

who had made great promises with regard to the Union, none of which he had carried out, in fact he had ended by openly persecuting the Catholics and through the agency of the Protestant ambassadors had set such snares against himself that he came near losing his life.[1]

On August 19th, 1628, Urban VIII. instructed Cardinals Millini and Scaglia to proceed against Lukaris,[2] after which the Inquisition began its discussions which were very protracted. It was only on March 23rd, 1629, that the Pope was in a position to inform Propaganda, under the secret of the Holy Office, that the Inquisition had concluded its process against Lukaris. The latter might now be deposed and to that end even money might be spent; these sums were to be handed to Césy's confidential agent.[3] The rest of the acts cannot be found in the Archives of Propaganda,[4] but from an authentic declaration of Cardinal Barberini in 1635 we learn that the sentence of excommunication was not pronounced against Lukaris because, though every care had been taken, the case of the Patriarch was not proved with all the required clearness. The Patriarch, Barberini went on to say, had printed a wholly Calvinist confession of faith, and in public opinion he was a perfidious heretic; nevertheless the proofs which had been collected with the utmost diligence were not enough to condemn him.[5] The judgment

[1] **Lettera di Cannachio Rossi alla Congreg. di Propaganda*, dated Messina, July 25, 1628, Archives of Propaganda, Rome.

[2] See *Bull.*, XIV., 2 *seq.*

[3] *" 22 Martii 1629 in congregatione de Propaganda: S.D.N. sub sigillo s. Officii significavit: (1) Fuisse in tribunali S. Inquisitionis formatum et absolutum processum contra Cyrillum"; (2) After this step, Cyril could be deposed, "etiam soluta pecunia, quia sumus in casu, quo vexationem medio pecuniarum redimere licet."

[4] Information could only be obtained from the archives of the Roman Inquisition which, unfortunately, are not open to the public.

[5] In the Instruction of April, 1635, to the nuncio in Flanders, Lelio Falconieri, the question of the excommunication of the French king, which had been requested by Spain at that time,

passed on the "Confession" which the Dutch ambassador had had printed in March, 1629, under Lukaris' name,[1] is fully justified, for that document is one that the Calvinists could hail with joy. Many of its clauses are evident proof of apostasy from the teaching of the Greek Church.[2]

For lack of authentic information it is not possible to ascertain to what extent Lukaris, that past master in the art of simulation and deceit,[3] gave yet another display of his tricks. At any rate he constituted so imminent a peril for the Union that it was a duty for the Holy See to do its utmost to get him removed from the Patriarchal see. To that end the most diverse suggestions were offered. In view of the Porte's pressure on the patriarchal elections it was only natural

was dealt with and answered in the negative on account of the evil consequences of the excommunication of Henry VIII., Elizabeth of England, and Navarre. There follows the further note: "Finalmente fu detto che in ogni caso per venire alla sentenza della scommunica si voleva giuditio formato, che in fine era dificillissimo mettere in chiaro il fatto come si ricerca. Et a questo proposito fu allegato il esempio di Cirillo, falso patriarca di Constantinopoli, quale haveva publicato in stampa una Confessione piena di Calvinismo e vi corre fama publica che egli sia perfido eretica; con tutto ciò le prove procurate con ogni diligenza non bastano per condannarlo (CAUCHIE-MAERE, *Instructions*, 238).

[1] *Confessio fidei rev. dom. Cyrilli patriarchae Constantinopolitani nomine et consensu patriarcherum Alexandrini et Hierosolymitani aliorumque ecclesiarum orientalium antistitum scripta, Constantinopoli* (actually in Geneva) *mense Martio*, 1629; see LEGRAND, IV., 315 *seq*. *Ibid*., I., 270 *seq*. for the French and English translations. *Cf*. PH. MEYER, *loc. cit*., 688; EMEREAU, *loc. cit*., 1008 *seq*.

[2] See HEFELE in the *Tüb. Theol. Quartalschr*., 1843, 585, 588 *seq*.

[3] See EMEREAU, *loc. cit*., 1014. The Protestant TRIVIER (*Cyrille Lukaris*, Paris, 1877) also says (p. 90), "que la loyauté la plus élémentaire lui fait défaut," and JORGA (IV., 27, note 4), who would like to make a Greek national hero of Lukaris, is obliged to allow this judgment to stand.

to take advantage of that circumstance. The Archimandrite of Constantinople, Euthymius, gave it as his opinion that it would be easy to overthrow Lukaris if it were pointed out to the already distrustful Porte that he was the author of the inroads of the Cossacks into Turkish territory. He proposed his replacement by a man of sound Catholic sentiments, of blameless life and one who spoke Turkish. To bring this about use should be made of the representatives of Venice and Ragusa whom the Turks trusted much more than Césy, though the mutual jealousy of the two diplomatists would have to be reckoned with.[1] In Rome itself it was realized that, notwithstanding all his zeal, Césy could not overthrow Lukaris single-handed. There could be no question of using the Venetian ambassador in the affair, owing to his anti-Roman bias. However, at the beginning of 1628 the nuncio in Vienna had succeeded in interesting the Emperor in the matter[2] and the instructions of Hans Ludwig von Kufstein, who had been appointed ambassador in Constantinople, were in accordance with this policy.[3] However, Kufstein, who became a Catholic in 1629, accomplished nothing[4]; it was reserved to his successor, Rudolph Schmid, to carry the affair to a successful conclusion. Schmid opposed to Lukaris, who had dealings with Bethlen Gábor[5] and the Swedes,[6] a dangerous

[1] **Relatione di Euthimo archimandrita di Constantinopoli intorno alli modi di far un patriarcha cattolico.* Archives of Propaganda, Rome.

[2] By letter, dated Prague, 1628, the nuncio informed Propaganda that the Emperor had commanded that in the instruction for the ambassador about to be sent to Constantinople it should be stated that he was to work against Lukaris, *ibid.*

[3] Further details in KIEWNING, *Nuntiaturberichte*, I., 260, note 1. Kufstein left Vienna on June 20, 1628; see KHEVENHÜLLER, XI., 252 *seq.*; ZINKEISEN, IV., 459 *seq.*

[4] See KIEWNING, II., 46, note 4.

[5] *Cf.* the **Relatio magni archimandriti Constantinopolitani facta s. Congreg. de Prop. fide circa res gestas contra Cirillum patr.* Archives of Propaganda.

[6] *Cf.* KLOPP, *Tilly*, II.[1], 482 *seq.*

rival in the person of the schismatical metropolitan of Beroea, Cyril Contari, who, stimulated partly by personal passion, posed as a defender of the ancient Greek faith.[1] There now broke out a struggle for the Patriarchate which led to an explosion of the long suppressed discontent of the Greek clergy with the heretical conduct of its hierarchical head whose policy it had been, without further delay, to introduce Calvinism among the Greeks. In this struggle the representatives of the European States sought to win the help of the Sultan who needed money, by means of financial contributions. The ambassadors of England and Holland, whose influence was very great,[2] were in favour of Lukaris whilst against them the representatives of France and the Emperor defended the cause of union with Rome. In May, 1630, Lukaris had been forced to resign the patriarchal See for a brief period, but at the end of it he maintained himself in the See until October, 1633.[3] It was of advantage to him that in 1631 his chief opponent, Césy, who had got into grievous financial difficulties, had to be relieved of his post by the French Government.[4] His successor, Count De Marcheville, was instructed to extend his protection to the religious of every nationality throughout the Levant, particularly to the Jesuits in Constantinople. However, the choice of De Marcheville turned out a very unhappy one. He was as arrogant as he was ignorant of the situation; consequently he became at once involved in such difficulties that any action of his was paralysed from the outset. This was all the more disastrous as the Dutch and Venetian representatives continued to support Lukaris in every way and to press for the expulsion of the Jesuits and all Catholic priests. The indiscreet conduct of De Marcheville, who ostentatiously displayed his contempt for oriental manners, involved him in constant conflicts with the Government. At last the patience of the Porte gave out. On May 2nd, 1634, De Marcheville was

[1] See EMEREAU, *loc. cit.*, 1006. *Cf.* FOUQUERAY, V., 353.

[2] *Cf.* JORGA, IV., 25 *seq.*

[3] See EMEREAU, *loc. cit.*

[4] See FOUQUERAY, V., 341 *seq.*

ordered to leave Constantinople, whereupon the representation of the interests of France was temporarily entrusted to Césy whom his financial obligations still detained in Constantinople.[1]

In October, 1633, Lukaris was forced to resign to Patriarchate for a few days ; he then resumed it until March, 1634, and after yet another interruption in April, 1634, he held it until March, 1635.[2] Again it was Cyril Contari who, with the help of Rudolph Schmid, had him deported to Rhodes. However, Contari alienated his own adherent by his arrogance and by sundry mistakes. In June, 1636, he was obliged to resign his dignity in favour of an insignificant protégé of Lukaris who, however, also laid it aside before long. Thereupon, in March, 1637, to the joy of the Calvinists, Lukaris recovered his See.[3] But when Contari returned to Constantinople from his exile in Rhodes, Lukaris' glory came to an end. Schmid, who had obtained subsidies from the Emperor, did not rest until he had overthrown his enemy. He accused him to the Sultan of having urged the Greeks to rebel and of having had a hand in the loss of Azov which had been captured by the Cossacks. After that Lukaris was lost. He was deposed, imprisoned and strangled on June 21st, 1638. The accusation spread by the Huguenots that the Jesuits had brought about the tragic end of their old opponent is an invention of the Greeks. As a matter of fact Lukaris was the victim of a plot hatched by Contari, by a Pasha of the name of Bayram and by the Greek pope Lamerno.[4]

After Lukaris' death the reaction against his tendencies[5] showed itself in its full force. A synod held at Constantinople in September, 1638, condemned both his person and his

[1] See *ibid.*, 346 *seq.*, 351. [2] See EMEREAU, *loc. cit.*, 1006 *seq.*

[3] See EMEREAU, 1007. A **Relazione di Constantinopoli d'ell anno*, 1637, by Paolo Vecchia is in *Barb.* 5192, Vatican Library.

[4] *Cf.* V. SEMNOZ in *Échos d'Orient*, VI. (1903), 97 *seq.*

[5] Of the three refutations of Lukaris' *Confessio*, which appeared in his life-time, that of the Archbishop of Iconium, J. M. CARIOPHYLLIS, is dedicated to Urban VIII. : **Censura Confessionis fidei seu potius perfidiae Calvinianae, quae nomine*

teaching. On December 15th, 1638, in presence of Rudolph Schmid and the Latin Patriarchal Vicar, Angelo Petricca da Sonnino, Contari signed a profession of faith drawn up by Propaganda and forwarded it to Urban VIII.[1] However, the new Patriarch was not destined long to enjoy his dignity. At the instigation of the Metropolitan of Larissa, a favourite of Sultan Murad, he was banished and like his predecessor, strangled. He was succeeded on July 1st, 1639, by the Metropolitan of Adrianople, Parthenius I.[2]

Philippe de la Haye, who was appointed French ambassador in Constantinople in 1639, was instructed to lend support to the Patriarch Contari, to assist the Jesuits and the Capuchins, and to help the Latins to recover their rights to the Holy Places in Palestine of which they had been robbed.[3] When de la Haye reached Constantinople he found the Patriarchal throne occupied by Parthenius who showed himself a friend of the Jesuits and an opponent of Lukaris' innovations.[4] The Metropolitan of Kiev, Peter Mohila, took steps against

Cyrilli patriarchae Constant. edita circumfertur, Romae, 1631. *Cf.* LEGRAND, I., 288. A *paper by the Armenian *Tilenus* on the *Confessio* of Lukaris is in *Barb.* 3506, Vatican Library.

[1] *Cf.* the *Brief to Contari, April 30, 1639, *Epist.*, XV.–XVI., Papal Secret Archives. *Ibid.*, on the same day *letters of praise to the Imperial Resident, R. Schmid, the Polish chancellor and the Polish king on their attitude. ANGELO PETRICCA compiled a *treatise on the sacrament of the altar and the impossibility of a union of the Orthodox Church with Calvinism, and dedicated it to Urban VIII. (see CERVELLONI in *Bessarione*, XVI., 9), and also a **Relazione dello stato della christianità di Pera e Costantinopoli*, in *Barb.* 5166, note 2, Vatican Library. *Ibid.*, a *Brief addressed to him by Urban VIII., April 30, 1639: he was to continue his labours and deliver the enclosed letter to Contari.

[2] See EMEREAU, *loc. cit.*, 1015 *seq.*

[3] See FOUQUERAY, V., 353 *seq.* On Ph. de la Haye and the establishment of the Capuchins in Constantinople through him in the interests of French policy, *cf.* also FLAMENT in the *Rev. d'hist. dipl.*, XV. (1905). A laudatory *Brief to De la Haye of March 9, 1642, is in *Epist.*, XIX., Papal Secret Archives.

[4] See FOUQUERAY, V., 355. *Cf.* JORGA, IV., 30.

the Calvinist teaching which had penetrated into Moldavia. In 1640 he convened a synod at which he condemned the opinions of Lukaris. This condemnation took the form of a solemn declaration by the Greek Church, at a synod held at Jassy, the capital of Moldavia, which lasted from December, 1641, till October, 1642. On March 11th, 1643, Parthenius, who had already refuted and condemned the teaching of Lukaris in a synodal letter of 1642, gave his adhesion to the decisions of Jassy. Thus the Calvinist tendencies of Lukaris had resulted in the Greek Church defining her teaching, and thereby securing an official profession of faith.[1]

Whilst the troubles caused by Lukaris inflicted grievous injury to the cause of the Union of the Greeks, the mission and the union of the Eastern Christians, for whom Urban VIII. had drawn up a special *Professio fidei*,[2] were able to register various successes in the Near East. The Maronites remained steadfast in their loyalty to the Pope. To their College in Rome Urban VIII. added yet another on Mount Lebanon,[3] and in 1635 he erected a third at Ravenna.[4] On May 15th, 1625, he exhorted the Maronite Bishops to fulfil the duty of residence.[5] Towards the close of 1628 he wrote to Patriarch Peter that he prayed for the Maronites, and that he would gladly appeal to the Christian Princes to go to their defence were it not that Germany, Poland and Italy were under arms.[6] In 1631 he recommended the French Capuchins to the Patriarch.[7] On the condition of the Catholics in Armenia

[1] See Emereau, *loc. cit.*, 1015 *seq.* *Ibid.* for further details on the Synod held at Jerusalem in 1672.

[2] See *Ius pontif.*, I., 227 *seq.* [3] See *Bull.*, XIII., 358 *seq.*

[4] See Moroni, XLIII., 120.

[5] See *Epist.*, II., Papal Secret Archives.

[6] *Brief to *Petrus patr. Maronit. Antioch.* of November 25, 1628, in which the Pope praises the Prince of Sidon: "illum bellatorem, qui se ex christianis ducibus progenitum gloriatur." *Epist.*, VI., *loc. cit.*

[7] *Brief of February 28, 1631, *Epist.*, VIII., *loc. cit.* A decision of Propaganda on the election and name of the Patriarch is in *Ius pontif.*, II., 1, 74 *seq.*

the Dominican Gregorio Orsi presented a detailed report on his return to Rome in 1626.[1] Both Patriarch Moses III. of Ecmiadzin [1630–3], and his successor, Philip I., were won over to the Union. The Dominican Paolo Piromalli whom Urban VIII. had dispatched to Armenia in the interests of the Union, taught in the monastic school which Philip had reopened.[2] Piromalli likewise succeeded in inducing the Armenian Patriarch of Constantinople, Cyriacus of Erivan, to acknowledge the primacy of the Pope.[3] In 1635 Urban exhorted the Archbishop of the Armenians in Jerusalem to do the same.[4] Urban founded burses for Armenians in the College of Propaganda and wrote his thanks to Prince Mirza of Mogor in 1631 for the establishment of a Jesuit College in Armenia.[5]

Urban VIII.'s pastoral solicitude embraced also the Tartars, the Circassians and the Georgians. At the close of 1626 the Dominican Giovanni da Lucca [6] and some

[1] **De statu christianae religionis in Armenia aliisque multis ad fidei propagationem proficuis et necessariis relationes sincerae . . . a fr. Gregorio Ursino Romano ord. Praed. in suo ab Armenia in Urbem reditu*, 1626 (to Urban VIII. and the Cardinals of Propaganda), *Barb.* 2642, Vatican Library.

[2] See HERGENRÖTHER in the *Freib. Kirchenlex.*, I.², 1339. From the *Brief to *Philippus patr. Armen.* of July 16, 1640, it appears that Piromalli sent to the Patriarch, at the Pope's request, the Armenian translation of the Acts of the Council of Florence and the Bull of Eugen IV. (*Epist.*, XVII., *loc. cit.*). *Cf. Ius pontif.*, P. II., 159 on the title of the Armenian Archbishop, p. 61 on baptism among schismatic Armenians, p. 68 on matrimonial dispensations and the liturgy.

[3] See BESSARIONE, XII. (1918), 120 *seq.* *Cf.* HENRION, *Hist. des miss. cath.*, II., 309 *seq.*

[4] See the *Brief of May 12, 1635 (the transmission of Pope Eugen IV.'s *Bull.*, translated into Armenian), *Epist.*, XII., *loc. cit.*

[5] See the *Brief to *Princeps Mirza Zulcurna in Mogor* of February 24, 1631, *Epist.*, VIII., *loc. cit.*

[6] See **Itinerario fatto da me fra Giov. da Lucca Domenicano missionario alli Tartari e Circassi, Mengelli, Giorgiassi e Trabisonda* (beginning with his departure from Rome, November 20, 1626),

Theatines[1] were sent to them. No country, however distant from Europe was overlooked by the Pope.[2] It gave him immense satisfaction when in 1627 King Theophilus of Iberia dispatched to Rome the Basilian Nicephorus Erbacius with mission to pay homage to the Pope.[3] After receiving a report by the Theatine Pietro Avitabilis, he told the King of Iberia, Taimaras Kan, in 1631, that he prayed that he might be victorious like Constantine and that he would then submit to Rome[4]; at the same time the Metropolitan Zacharias received a letter of thanks for handing over a church.[5]

In 1624 Urban VIII. wrote to the Carmelites who had been labouring in Persia since the reign of Paul V., encouraging them in their task of spreading the faith and confirming their privileges.[6] In 1629 he recommended them to the new Shah whose favourable dispositions toward Christianity he praised.[7] In 1639 he similarly recognized the merits of the Dominican Thomas Vitalis.[8] The missionary Baldassar di S. Maria stressed the importance of such letters in his report

Barb. 5319 *seq*, Vatican Library. *Ibid.*, 251 *seq.*, his *report on the races mentioned above. *Cf.* Ciampi, II., 51 *seq.*

[1] See **Origine delle missioni de'P. Teatini nell'Oriente, ne'regni della Mengrelia, Georgia, etc.*, 1625–1630, *descritta dal P. Castelli missionario nella Mengrelia,* Archives of the Theatines, Rome, *Cassetta,* 33. *Ibid.*, the *decree of Propaganda on the Theatrines in Georgia, 1635.

[2] *" Non Europae finibus includitur Pontificis sollicitudo." Brief to the " rex Persarum " of October 13, 1637, *Epist.*, XV., *loc. cit.*

[3] See the *Brief of November 22, 1628, *Epist.*, VI., *loc. cit.*

[4] See *Brief to "*potentiss. rex Taimaras Kan, rex Iberiae* ", of June 14, 1631, *Epist.*, VIII., *loc. cit.*

[5] See *Brief to " *Zacharias totius Iberiae metropolita nuncup* ". of June 14, 1631 (" Apparent flores gratiae in Iberia "), *ibid.*

[6] See *Brief of March 9, 1624 (together with faculty for celebrating in Arabic, see *Ius pontif.*, P. II., I., 18 *seq.*, *Epist.*, I.[le]). A *letter of recommendation of the Carmelites and the Persian Christians to the Shah, March 9, 1624, in *Epist., loc. cit.*

[7] See *Brief to the *rex Persarum,* March 8, 1624, *Epist.*, VI., *loc. cit.*

[8] See *Brief to the *rex Persarum,* October 13, 1637, *ibid.*, XV.

of March 21st, 1630.[1] In 1630 Urban granted a number of faculties to the Prefect of the Carmelite Mission in Bassora and in 1632 to the Bishop of Ispahan,[2] whilst in 1638 the generosity of a noble French lady enabled him to provide an endowment for the diocese of Bagdad, or Babylon, which had been erected in 1632. The Carmelite Bernard of St. Teresa was appointed Bishop but the conquest of the city by the Turks entailed the ruin of that mission.[3] In 1636 Elias, Vicar of the Chaldean Patriarch of Mosul, made profession of the Catholic faith.[4] At this time French Capuchins made foundations at Mosul and Diarbekr; the same Fathers had been established at Aleppo since 1627 and at Bagdad since 1629.[5] On the other hand Propaganda strove in vain to win the Chaldean Patriarch of Babylon, Elias, for the union; he remained obstinate in his Nestorian errors.[6] For the Indian

[1] **Lettera del P. Baldassar di S. Maria dello stato delle missione in Persia*, dated *Aspahan*, March 21, 1630, *Visite*, IX., 11 *seq.*, Archives of Propaganda, Rome.

[2] See *Ius pontif.*, I., 125, 146 *seq.* In 1632, Propaganda, that is a *Brief, assigned to the Bishop of Bagdad, Assyria, Mesopotamia, etc., to the Bishop of Ispahan, the rest of Persia and Armenia, except Nakschiwan (*ibid.*, P. II., I., 60). In 1628 Capuchins had also arrived in Persia and Mesopotamia; see Rocco da Cesinale, II., 234 *seq.* *Cf.* J. Lammeyer, *Gesch. der unierten syrischen Kirche auf Grund des syrischen Patriarchatsarchiv*, in the periodical "*Der Aar*", III. (1913), 667.

[3] See *Ius pontif.*, I., 174 *seq.*; Fagniez, I., 363; Lemmens, *Hierarchia lat. Orientis, Orientalia christ.* (1924), 279 *seq.*

[4] See Neher in *Freib. Kirchenlex.*, III.², 43. Since 1629, two of the Franciscans sent out by Propaganda had laboured to bring about the return to the unity of the Church of the Patriarch himself, an obstinate Nestorian; see their report in Lämmer, *Analecta*, 43 *seq.*

[5] *Cf.* besides the account of Lammeyer quoted in note 2, also Rabbat, *Documents inéd. p.s.à. l'hist. du Christ. en Orient*, and with regard to Aleppo, see the essay by O'Connor in the *Americ. Quart. Review*, XLV. (1920), 540 *seq.*

[6] See *Itinerarium P. Francisci Quaresmii*, 604; Lemmens in *Antonianum*, I., 217.

mission field Urban VIII. renewed in 1629 the privileges of the Jesuits, especially with regard to matrimonial questions.[1] Of even greater importance was another decision. In consequence of Portugal's protectorate over the missions, all missionaries had been obliged until then to travel via Lisbon where they were the victims of all kinds of petty vexations. In 1608 Paul V. had exempted the Mendicant Orders from this obligation [2] and on February 22nd, 1633, a Bull of Urban VIII. allowed all religious to journey to the East Indies by any route, so as to facilitate the preaching of the Gospel. At the same time he prescribed the use by the missionaries of the Roman Catechism of Bellarmine, forbade them to engage in any kind of trade and reserved to himself the decision of the major controversies that might arise between the missionaries.[3]

In India the Jesuits continued their apostolic labours and the establishment of new stations, as at Salsette in 1632 and at Kanara in 1643, whilst in Madura, Nobili proceeded with his method of accommodation, but the disputes with archdeacon George continued to stir up trouble among the Christians of St. Thomas.[4] Through Urban's mediation, for the purpose of founding a Mission in Burma (Pegu), the Franciscans were joined by Dominicans, Augustinians and Carmelites and in 1640 by Italian Theatines under Avitabile and in 1642 by French Capuchins under Fr. Ephrem of Nevers.[5] Native Oratorians laboured at Bejapor under Matthew de Castro. In 1637 the latter, together with Archbishop Francis Anthony of St. Felix, was sent by the Pope to India as Vicar Apostolic, bearing letters of recommendation

[1] *Ius pontif.*, I., 111 *seq.*

[2] *Ibid.*, 444 *seq.*

[3] *Ibid.*, 143 *seq.* *Cf.* JANN, *Die kathol. Missionen in Indien*, 191 *seq.*, and for the prohibition of trade see GRETRUP in the *Zeitschr. für Missionswiss.*, XV. (1925), 259.

[4] See MÜLLBAUER, 171 *seq.*, 287 *seq.*; DAHMEN, *Nobili*, Münster, 1924.

[5] See MÜLLBAUER, 259 *seq.*, 350 *seq.* *Cf.* JANN, 195 *seq.*, and ROCCO DA CESINALE, II., 202 *seq.*

to the Superiors of the Mendicant Orders of those parts.[1] The Grand Mogul Djihan who rose to power in 1628, was hostile to Christianity. In 1632 he ordered the destruction of the Augustinian mission at Hugli in Bengal.[2] Sixteen Jesuits and twenty-four Franciscans were at work in Ceylon in 1626 but after 1630 missionary activity was hampered by dynastic quarrels and insurrections.[3]

In Siam a missionary of the name of Margico built a beautiful church at Juthia in 1624. In 1639 the King begged for the services of priests for the Portuguese soldiers in his army, whereupon Jesuits, Franciscans and Dominicans established themselves in that country. In 1629 the Dominicans erected a church at the Court of Cambodia.[4] The Jesuit Alexander of Rhodes penetrated into Cochin China in 1624 and to Tonkin and back to Cochin in 1630, after which Fr. Amaral and four other Jesuits took up the evangelization of Tonkin. Signal successes crowned their labours: in 1640 the Christians in Tonkin numbered 94,000 and 30,000 in Cochin China.[5] Franciscans and Dominicans laboured successfully in the Moluccas. The Franciscans, who had laboured at Sanguir since 1637, baptized two Kings and built a church and convent. In 1630 Fr. Miguel Rangel reopened the mission in Solor and converted the Emperor of Endeh. In 1640 a reaction in favour of Christianity led to the baptism of the principal chieftains of Timor.[6] The Philippines were being christianized by Franciscans, Dominicans, Augustinians and Jesuits. In

[1] See *Brief to "*provinciales et superiores Mendicant. in India Orient.*", of September 30, 1637, *Epist.*, XV., Papal Secret Archives. *Cf.* MÜLLBAUER, 349 *seq.*

[2] *Cf.* MÜLLBAUER, 341 *seq.*, 383 *seq.*

[3] *Cf.* HOLZAPFEL, 543; CIVEZZA, VII., 3, 219 *seq.*; SCHMIDLIN, *Missionsgesch.*, 256.

[4] See SCHMIDLIN, *loc. cit.*, 252 *seq.*

[5] *Cf.* the *Relatione*, addressed to Urban VIII., *della nuova missione delli PP. della Comp. di Gesù nel regno della Cocincina*, Roma, 1631; PACHTLER, *Das Christentum in Tonking und Cochinchina* (1861); SCHMIDLIN, *loc. cit.*, 253 *seq.*

[6] See SCHMIDLIN, *loc. cit.*, 257; BIERMANN in the *Zeitschr. für Missionswiss.*, 1924, 12 *seq.*

1637 the Jesuits also started a mission in the island of Mindanao and in 1638 in the island of Joló.[1]

The Portuguese Jesuit, Antonio d'Andrada, made a bold advance into all but inaccessible Tibet. In 1624 he established a mission at Tsaparang, and in 1626, a church also, with the help of the King of that country. In 1632 his brothers in religion Azevedo, Cacella and Cabral succeeded in penetrating into western Tibet, but the mission was short lived—its last remnants perished in 1640.[2]

In China the Jesuits were enabled to return to the Court of Peking in 1625, thanks to their mathematical skill, and up till 1633 they were also able to found a number of new stations.[3] Since 1629 the Jesuits Longobardi and Terenzio had been members of the commission for the reform of the Calendar, and in this way they had won the favour of the Emperor. Fr. John Adam Schall, who was summoned to the Imperial Court in 1631 from Cologne, took advantage of this circumstance to forward the work of conversion,[4] with the result that in 1636 the number of Christians in the Empire of the Middle was reckoned at 40,000, and at over 67,000 by 1640.[5] As

[1] *Cf.* Astráin, V., 687 *seqq.* In 1626 Urban VIII. ratified the decisions of Propaganda for the Archbishop of Manila; in 1627 all religious with cure of souls were placed under his authority; in 1633 he granted facilities to the Augustinians for the reception of Holy Orders (*Ius pontif.*, I., 60 *seq.*, 71 *seq.*, 155 *seq.*).

[2] *Cf.* besides the report of the discovery in 1627 and the *Litterae annuae* (Romae, 1628), also Huc, *Hist. du Christianisme en Chine*, 209 *seq.*; Wessels, *Early Jesuit Travellers in Central Asia*, 1603–1721, Haag, 1924, 69 *seq.*; Francke in the *Zeitschr. für Missionswiss.*, XV. (1925), 269 *seq.*

[3] See Schmidlin, *loc. cit.*, 272; Thomas, 92 *seqq.*

[4] *Cf.* Huonder in *Freib. Kirchenlex.*, X.[2], 1753 *seq.*; Huc, II., 347 *seqq.*; Thomas, 104 *seqq.* According to Thomas, Schall was accused of having laboured to the detriment of his priestly vocation; but the assertion that he apostatized and married is an invention; see *Stimmen aus Maria-Laach*, III., 280 *seq.*, and Duhr, *Jesuitenfabeln*, 319 *seq.*

[5] See Martini, *Relatio de numero et qualitate christ. apud Sinas*, Romae, 1654, 10.

early as 1626 the Pope granted numerous privileges both to the Bishop of Funai, who was appointed administrator of Macao, and to the members of the Society of Jesus in China.[1] In 1632 Spanish Dominicans and Franciscans of the Philippines founded missions in China, the island of Formosa being their base and starting point.[2] The opinion that the founders of these missions, the Franciscan Antonio Caballero di S. Maria and the Dominican Juan Morales, were the first instigators of the disputes concerning the lawfulness of certain Chinese customs and ceremonies (rites)—an opinion which prevailed for a long time—has been shown to be untenable. Differences of opinion on these questions had arisen before that within the Jesuit Order itself.[3] In 1626 the Visitor, Andrew Palmeiro, forbade the use of the words *Shang-Ti* (viz. "highest Ruler") and *Ti'en* (viz. "Heaven") to describe the God of the Christians, but in 1630 the General Vitelleschi revoked the prohibition. In 1635 the Archbishop of Manila, an Augustinian, denounced the Jesuits to Urban VIII. in connexion with this question of

[1] See *Ius pontif.*, I., 62, 63 *seq.*, 65 *seq.*

[2] See SCHMIDLIN, *loc. cit.*, 274. The Franciscan O. MAAS has published a monograph "*Die Wiedereröffnung der Franziskanermission in China in der Neuzeit*" (Münster, 1926), which makes valuable new evidence available and gives a detailed account of the work of Caballero. The question of the rites, however, is treated in such a way as to evoke a protest by the Jesuit VÄTH in the *Kathol. Missionen*, 1927, 218 *seq.* The latter maintains that the unpublished *Relations* of 1635–6 preserved in the Franciscan Archives of Pastrana, and quoted as reliable by Maas (*cf. Arch. Francisc.*, II., 553, IV., 51), give a false picture of the methods of the Jesuits. A similar work by the Dominican B. BIERMANN, *Die Anfänge der neueren Dominikanermission in China*, Münster, 1927, is more measured though his statements on the Jesuits are questioned on several points by VÄTH in the *Innsbrucker Zeitschr. f. kath. Theol.*, LII. (1928), 420 *seq.*

[3] See HUONDER, *Ritenstreit*, 8, whose opinion is confirmed by the documents of Propaganda; see PIEPER in the *Zeitschr. für Missionswiss.*, XIV. (1924), 3 *seq.* *Cf.* our account, vol. xxv., 353 *seq.*

rites. Although the Archbishop withdrew his accusation within the same year, owing to its having been based on erroneous information, the question of the rites, from being chiefly a matter concerning the Jesuit community, now became one of general interest.[1]

The main reason why in China the question of ritual developed into a quarrel of ritual, was due to a divergence in missionary methods. From the very beginning the Jesuits, basing themselves on the early Christian and medieval policy of adaptation as practised by St. Paul and St. Gregory the Great, had gone to the utmost limits in their concessions to the existing, deep-rooted ideas and customs of the native population. Instead of proclaiming from the first the integral teaching on the nature of God, they proceeded on lines of sound pedagogy, seeking to link up with what they found, especially with the Chinese classics, and to put profane science at the service of the apostolate, a policy which was all the more in order as there was question of a people with a very ancient civilization, which maintained its peculiarities with the utmost tenacity and in its proud over-estimation of itself, despised everything foreign.[2] The Spanish Dominicans and Franciscans, in whom there survived something of the spirit of the *Conquistadores*, would not hear of such discretion. In their zeal for souls they adopted methods which were quite unusual in China and which created no small stir. Crucifix in hand they preached in the open streets and public places, condemned to the deepest hell Confucius who was held in high esteem as a wise man and a learned lawgiver, and proclaimed that every kind of veneration of ancestors was unlawful; the Jesuits' caution with regard to Confucius and the veneration of ancestors they condemned as connivance at idolatry.[3] The inevitable disputes, which were not a little fostered by mutual rivalry, became still more acute in consequence of the strong national divergences between the Portuguese Jesuits and the Spanish Dominicans and Franciscans. The results

[1] See PIEPER, *loc. cit.*, 4 and 11.

[2] See HUONDER, *Ritenstreit*, 18 *seq.*

[3] *Ibid.*, 35 *seq.*

of the activities of the older Orders did not speak in favour of their methods ; instead of attracting the Chinese they repelled them. At Fukien, in 1637, the storm broke with such fury as to endanger also the Jesuit missions. The Superior of the Dominican missions, Juan Garcia, now recognized not indeed the lawfulness of the veneration of ancestors, but at least that his subjects had been too violent in their manner, and the Franciscan, Francis of Ascalona, also realized that the conversion of China was not the work of one day or the result of one bold stroke, but that on the contrary, it required accurate acquaintance with the peculiarities and the language of the people. " If the Jesuits," he declared, " had adopted a different method from the one they have pursued for so many years, it would long ago have been impossible to find a single missionary or a Christian in China." [1]

Strong divergences between the older Orders and the Jesuits existed also in Japan. This circumstance was all the more deplorable in view of the continuation of the bloody persecution which in the end restored to Buddhism its position as the State religion.[2] However, all the missionaries displayed a like constancy in giving their lives for the faith. In doing so they gave proof of a heroism which recalled the early Christian centuries. Soon after his accession, Urban VIII. comforted the Japanese Christians in his answer of June 18th, 1624, to their letter addressed to Paul V. Where the Roman Empire had not penetrated, the Pope wrote, there the Church

[1] *Ibid.*, 39 *seq.*

[2] *Cf.* the work of the Japanese Anesaki, based on research in the archives and discussed by H. HEUVERS in *Stimmen der Zeit*, CIX. (1925), 315 *seq.*, under the heading " *Eine Wende in der japanischen Geschichtschreibung* ". Anesaki examines, in his first chapter, the policy of extermination from the time of the suppression of the rising of Shimabara (1638), in which many Christian peasants had also taken part on account of the tyranny of the Daimio. In chapter 5 the documents found by Anesaki are discussed ; these had been taken from the Christians ; among them are some moving exhortations and preparations for martyrdom.

had sent her messengers with mission to dispel darkness. This angered hell. However, let them not despond; their martyrdom was a triumph, and one day the ships which now merely went out to fetch pearls would pay homage to their martyrs; hence he prayed that they might have, if not earthly happiness, at least heavenly protection and above all devoted priests.[1] On October 14th, 1624, Urban VIII. wrote in the same strain to the Japanese Christians of the five Kingdoms of Iyo, Agui, Bicchu, Bisen and Farima, sympathizing with their sufferings, praising their perseverance and extolling their fortitude.[2] To the Bishop of Japan, that is, of Funai, who resided at Macao, he granted a number of faculties in 1626 and 1627,[3] whilst Propaganda dealt with divers matrimonial problems and some questions in connexion with ordinations.[4] When in 1633 the Pope abolished the Jesuit monopoly in the East Indies, thereby throwing open Japan, he gave permission to all Japanese Christians, in view of the fierceness of the persecution, to receive the Sacraments from any priest whatsoever.[5] In consequence of the terror to which the Christians of Japan had been subjected since 1625, the number of missionaries had become greatly reduced. Terrible details have come down to us of the tortures to which those were subjected who remained steadfast in the faith. In 1627 a new form of death was invented: the Christians were plunged into the boiling sulphur springs of a volcanic mountain near Nagasaki. By this process the victims were flayed alive. In order to prolong their torture they were not completely submerged but were scalded limb by limb, and the torture repeated for as long as possible. Thus towards the end of 1630

[1] See **Epist.*, I^b^., no. 553, Papal Secret Archives. *Cf.* Pagès, *Hist. de la relig. chrét. au Japon*, II., 320, and Delplace, *Le catholicisme au Japon*, II., 200.

[2] See **Epist.*, IV., *loc. cit.* *Cf.* Delplace, *loc. cit.*

[3] See *Ius pontif.*, I., 62 *seq.*, 65 *seq.*, 69 *seq.*

[4] Thus among others with that of marriage without the presence of a priest, by permission of the Pope (*Ius pontif.*, II., 123 *seq.*; *Collect.*, I., 7 *seq*).

[5] See *Ius pontif.*, I., 145.

the martyrdom of three Augustinians, one Jesuit, one Franciscan lay Brother and two Portuguese women lasted thirty-three days ![1]

When the tyrant Fide-Tada died in 1632, he was succeeded by his son Yemitsi with the title of To-Shogun-sama. Yemitsi had persecuted the Christians even whilst only co-regent; he now completed the work of destruction, and in doing so he proceeded with a cruelty perhaps unparalleled in history. To the boiling in the sulphur springs there was now added the so-called water and pit torture; this consisted in the martyr being suspended head downwards in a pit whilst his tortures were prolonged for as long a time as possible by tightly lacing his limbs so as to impede the circulation of the blood and by bleeding at the temples. The majority endured this martyrdom with unflinching fortitude, but one of their number, the Jesuit Provincial, Christopher Ferreira, who had heroically laboured in the mission for twenty-three years, overcome by pain, apostatized after five hours of torture.[2] When news of this occurrence reached Europe, thirty-three Jesuits, led by Father Marcello Mastrilli, set out in 1633 for the purpose of atoning for the scandal with their deaths. Mastrilli was seized and martyred on landing. Notwithstanding the continuation of the cruel executions, courageous missionaries continued their attempts to go to the assistance of the orphaned Christians of Japan, as, for instance, a Dominican in 1637, the Jesuit Antony Rubino with four Fathers, among them a Pole, in 1542, in 1643 the Jesuit Marquez with four brothers in religion. All these were arrested on landing and suffered the martyr's death. The surviving Christians of Japan died partly in prison, partly in the forests.[3] But though under pressure of the persecution,

[1] See SPILLMANN in *Freib. Kirchenlex.*, VI.², 1253.

[2] Ferreira subsequently expiated his apostasy by a martyr's death; see POUPLARD, *Vie du vén. M. Mastrilli*, Paris, 1903.

[3] See SPILLMANN, *loc. cit.*, 1253 *seq.* *Cf.* CHARLEVOIX, *Hist. du Japon*, 9 vols., Paris, 1736; CRASSET, *Hist. de l'Église du Japon*, 2 vols., Paris, 1715; PAGÈS, *Hist. de la relig. chrét. au Japon*, II., Paris, 1869; PROFILET, *Le martyriloge de l'église du Japon* (1549–1649, 3 vols., Paris, 1897); M. CZERMINSKI, *Vie*

the religion of the cross disappeared from the surface, it continued to live in secret. For this reason, during two centuries, the authorities periodically examined all suspects. They were summoned to tread under foot the image of the Crucified or that of His Mother, either in the temple or in the "conversion office"; only those who complied were set at liberty. In the harbours also every fresh arrival was compelled to deny Christianity. The Calvinist Dutch, with their shop-keepers' souls, who now carried on a profitable trade with Japan instead of the Portuguese, submitted to the most humiliating conditions: they were not permitted to hold any religious services even on their own ships.[1]

Whilst in Japan Christianity was being stifled in a sea of blood, in Africa the Church won the empire of Ethiopia when Seltan-Sagad, known as Emperor Socinius, after the defeat, in 1624, of the rebellious Monophysites, made profession of the

du P. Alb. Mencinski S.J. (†1643), Troyes, 1900; *The Month*, CV. (1905), 506 *seq.*; GOFFREDI, *Vita del ven. M. Mastrilli*, Napoli, 1900, also the documents published by TACCHI VENTURI in the *Civ. Catt.*, of May 6, 1911; M. VOLPE, *Ant. Capece S.J.* (†1643), Napoli, 1912; BÖHLEN, *Die Franziskaner in Japan*, Trier, 1912; P. LOR. PEREZ, *Relaciones de fray Diego de San Francisco sobre las persecuciones del cristianismo en el Japon*, 1625–1632, Madrid, 1914; *Arch. Ibero-Americ.*, I., 335 *seq.*, 514 *seq.*, II., 246 *seq.*, XV., 5 *seq.*

[1] It is not established that the Dutch agreed to trample on the Cross, as Carreri asserts; but as SPILLMANN rightly remarks (*loc. cit.*, 1256), it was not necessary to add this to their other concessions as external evidence of their apostasy from the Christian faith. It is remarkable, as DÖLLINGER says (*Kirchengesch.*, 396), that *v. Haren* in his apologetic work *Recherches hist. sur l'état de la religion chrétienne au Japon relativement à la nation Hollandaise* (Paris, 1778), rather glides over these points. Nevertheless v. Haren defends the missionaries and Christians from the reproach that they had fomented risings in the country and had been the cause of the revolution. He asserts that in the two civil wars that arose, the Christians always took the side of the rightful ruler, and as the usurpers remained the victors they revenged themselves on the Christians.

Catholic faith and on February 11th, 1626, did homage to the Pope before the newly appointed Patriarch, the Jesuit Alonso Mendez.[1] In view of the numerous dogmatic, moral, liturgical and canonical heresies and irregularities of the Ethiopians, their union with Rome through the labours of the Jesuits was a notable success. In his letter of January 30, 1627, in which Urban VIII. replied to the letter of the Emperor to Gregory XV., the Pope told him that he wept for joy on hearing that nearly the whole empire obeyed the laws of the Supreme Pontiff and that the Sovereign had raised the trophy of the cross on his castles. He also warned him to be on his guard against the followers of false doctrines and to repress those who sought to foment revolution, assuring him that he himself would request the King of Spain to assist him in this undertaking.[2] The mission in Ethiopia was reorganized, provided with churches, schools, colleges and seminaries for priests, a rich theological literature was created for apologetical purposes, a printing press, with Ethiopian type and other equipment was procured from Rome and even a bold plan for a native University was submitted to the Holy See. When the General of the Jesuits presented the Royal Oath, sealed by the Patriarch, the Pope on March 6th, 1628, expressed to Alonso Mendez his satisfaction at the reconciliation of Ethiopia and his hope that the emperor would dispatch an embassy to do homage to the Holy See.[3] In a letter of February 24th, 1631, Urban VIII. compared the Emperor to Constantine the Great who had subjected the Roman Empire to the Church and

[1] See SCHMIDLIN, *Missionsgesch.*, 233. The letter of Mendez of June 1, 1626, is in LÄMMER, *Analecta*, 117 *seq.* The *Informatio status ecclesiae imperii Aethiopiae oblata Urbano VIII. nomine Alphonsi patriarchae Aethiopiae* from the archives of the Congr. of the Council in *Bessarione*, XVII. (1913), 485 *seq.* *Cf.* BECCARI, *Rer. aethiop. Script.*, XIII., *passim.*

[2] See the *Brief to the *Sultanus Sagad. Aethiopiae imperator*, of January 30, 1627, *Epist.*, IV., Papal Secret Archives. *Ibid.*, *Brief to Philip IV. of January 30, 1627, directing him to support the Emperor of Ethiopia.

[3] See *Ius pontif.*, I., 103 *seq.*

defeated hell with the emblem of the cross.[1] He also wrote to Facilidas (Basilides),[2] the Emperor's son, and to his brother the brave general Zelachrist whose piety he eulogized.[3] However, a reaction was preparing which was destined to destroy all these hopes. A schismatical opposition party arose, including the majority of the governors who disliked the strict moral code of the new religion. They were joined by the prospective heir to the throne Facilidas, at first secretly and eventually quite openly. Whilst on his part Mendez committed several blunders, every means was made use of to alienate the Emperor from the new teaching and ritual and to lead him back to the traditional Alexandrian form of religion. For a time Socinius remained faithful to the Church, but he too became hesitant when he realized the ferment which had spread to the whole country. He persuaded the Patriarch Mendez to make concessions, such as the use of the native rite at Mass, all of which were interpreted as tokens of weakness. When Zelachrist suffered some reverses in the struggle with the rebels, his enemies succeeded in overthrowing him, thus depriving the Mission of its strongest support. The reaction came to a head in an imperial edict of 1632, reintroducing the Alexandrian teaching and liturgy.[4] In the midst of these upheavals Socinius died on September 16th, 1632. His successor,

[1] The *Brief (*Epist.*, VIII., *loc. cit.*), ends with the question, "When will be the day of the baptism ?"

[2] *Brief to *Faciladas primogenit. Aethiopiae imperatoris filius* of February 24, 1631, *loc. cit.*

[3] *Brief to *Zelachristus Aethiopiae imp. frater* of February 24, 1631, *loc. cit.*

[4] See Beccari, *Rer. aethiop. Script.*, especially Vol. VI. *seq.*, and the discussion by Huonder in *Stimmen aus Maria-Laach*, LXXX., 65 *seq.*, who emphasizes the fact that the Jesuits were not exclusively to blame for the breakdown, as was done in many of the reports sent to Propaganda. The Emperor felt offended when he received no replies from either Rome or Madrid (see Beccari, XII, no. 78). But this was certainly not the only or even the chief reason for his change of policy, as Prätorius points out in his review of Beccari's 12th volume (*Deutsche Literaturzeitung*, 1913, 111).

the impious Facilidas, began at once to persecute the Catholic Church. Zelachrist was banished. In 1636 Facilidas likewise ordered the banishment of the Patriarch, the Jesuits and the missionaries. The Franciscans and Capuchins sent by Propaganda, among them the zealous Agathangelus, all suffered martyrdom.[1] However, Rome did not forget the Christians of Ethiopia. In 1639 Cardinal Barberini founded an Ethiopian seminary attached to Propaganda.[2] As late as 1640 the Pope sent the Carmelite Jacob Weemers to Ethiopia,[3] but by then the Mission in that country was definitely lost.[4] In February, 1631, Urban VIII. dispatched Capuchins to Egypt. They were the bearers of a letter to the heads of the various Catholic Churches. The letter made reference to St. Anthony and his

[1] See HOLZAPFEL, 531 *seq.*; ROCCO DA CESINALE, III., 379 *seq.*; FAGNIEZ, I., 365 *seq.*

[2] *Cf.* above p. 213. An *Avviso of January 29, 1633, states that a youth, who claimed to be a son of the King of Ethiopia, had entered the College of S. Pietro in Montorio (*Ottob.* 3339, Vatican Library). The anxiety of the Holy See for the unhappy Ethiopians is also apparent from the reply of the Congregation of the Council on September 20, 1641, in BESSARIONE, XVII. (1913), 488. A decision of Propaganda on the right to consecrate of the Patriarch, who had been driven to Goa, in *Ius pontif.*, P. II., I., 88.

[3] See the *Briefs to *Sultanus Sagad, imperator Aethiopiae*, to *generalis monachor. Aethiopum ord. s. Antonii* and to *archiepisc. Aethiopiae*, of July 28, 1640, *Epist.*, XVII–XVIII., Papal Secret Archives.

[4] SCHMIDLIN (*Missionsgesch.*, 233) believes that in Ethiopia as elsewhere throughout the black continent, missionary ventures were too sporadic and intermittent so that they were doomed to fail in the end, notwithstanding the most heroic exertions. The failure was due not only to the material difficulties of the climate and the caprice of rulers, but also to the lack of method, especially to precipitation which resulted in Christians who were only nominal converts, and the too close alliance with Portuguese policy, which exploited its missionary connexions for selfish purposes. DUENSING (*Gött. Gel. Anz.*, 1911, 705 *seq.*) and LITTMANN (*ibid.*, 1915, 441 *seq.*), see the chief reason of the failure in the fact that the missionaries proceeded with too great violence and did not sufficiently allow for the character of the people.

mastery over the demons and to the Nile, the source of Egypt's fertility.[1] Since 1624 the mission in Morocco had the strong support of Richelieu and Fr. Joseph: it failed none the less; on the other hand the Andalusian Capuchins successfully established themselves in that country.[2]

By command of Propaganda, French Capuchins established themselves on the coast of Guinea. In 1635 Fathers Alexius and Bernardine baptized several chieftains at Cap Verde, Sereno and Joal. In 1637 Fr. Columbinus of Nantes preached with success at the Court of the Moorish King of Besné.[3]

In East Africa, in 1624, twenty Jesuits laboured in eight separate missionary stations; in 1625 twenty-five Dominicans were established in thirteen different localities and their activities extended far into the Gold Coast. In 1628, after the Christians, led by the Dominican Luiz, had defeated Monomotapa Kaprazine and acclaimed his uncle Manuza as his successor, the latter received baptism and granted full liberty to the missionaries. In 1633 he defeated Kaprazine in a second decisive battle.[4] In 1630 a similar revolution in the more northerly Mombasa brought about the rise of Prince Yussuf who had received a Christian education at the hands of the Augustinians. Whilst still only a pretender to the throne, Yussuf had written to Urban VIII., declaring his submission, but in the same year he returned to Islam and massacred all the Christians. In addition to these external vicissitudes, after 1630, certain internal adverse circumstances led to the gradual decay of the Zambesi Mission.[5] In a memorial of that year the Jesuit Borri prayed the Pope to send missionaries to

[1] See the *Briefs to the "Rectores catholici ecclesiae Aegypti" and to the "Rectores eccles. Syriae et Palaestinae" as well as to the "patr. Maronit. Antichenus" of February 28, 1631, *Epist.*, VIII., *loc. cit.*

[2] *Ibid.*, 368 *seq.*

[3] See Schmidlin, *Missionsgesch.*, 229.

[4] See Kilger in the *Zeitschr. für Missionswiss.*, VII., 101 *seq.*

[5] *Cf.* Strandes, *Die Portugiesenzeit in Ostafrika*, Berlin, 1899, 195 *seq.*; Kilger, *loc. cit.*, 103 *seq.*; Schmidlin, *Missionsgesch.*, 231.

Madagascar and to lend support to Prince Andrew who had received Baptism.[1] In 1643 Propaganda dispatched some Carmelites but owing to the opposition of the French they were unable to consolidate themselves in the island.[2]

In January, 1624, at a sitting of Propaganda, Juan Bautista Vives did homage to the Pope in the name of the Christian King of Congo.[3] Vives had taken the place of Antony Nigrita, the envoy of Congo who had come to Rome in the reign of Paul V., where he had lodged at the Vatican, but had succumbed to the Roman climate.[4] Urban VIII. completed the monument which Paul V. caused to be erected to his memory in St. Mary Major. It stands in the atrium of the Sacristy. The black marble bust with its coloured drapery, perhaps carved from the death mask, is a striking reproduction of the negro type whilst it also reveals marked intelligence.[5] The Capuchin Bonaventura, whom Propaganda dispatched to Congo in 1635, having fallen into the hands of the Dutch,[6] six missionaries of the same Order were sent out in 1638, but these only reached their destination after a voyage of several years.[7] In 1640 the Congo mission was assigned to the Capuchins of the Roman Province.[8]

[1] See SCHMIDLIN in the *Zeitschr. f. Missionswiss.*, XII. (1922), 197 *seq.* Borri proposed Madagascar as the metropolis for the austral missions.

[2] See SCHMIDLIN, *Missionsgesch.*, 232.

[3] See *Avviso of January 13, 1624, *Urb.*, 1094, Vatican Library.

[4] *Cf.* our account, Vol. XXV., 368.

[5] See MUÑOZ in *L'Arte*, 1909 ; F. COLONNA DI STIGLIANO in the periodical *Roma*, III. (1925), 163 *seq.* The Pope inspected the memorial ; see *Avviso of August 16, 1628, in POLLAK-FREY, 174.

[6] See DE JUNGHE-SIMAR, 9 *seqq.*, quoted in SCHMIDLIN, *Missionsgesch.*, 227.

[7] See **Compendio della relatione del regno del Congo scritta dal P. Giov. Franc. da Roma, minor Capuccino, inviato colà con altri padri del medesimo ordine con carattere di missionari da Urbano Papa VIII., l'anno*, 1639, *a richiesta di D. Alvaro VI., re di quel reame, Cod.*, 136, p. 728 *seq.*, of the Angelica Library, Rome.

[8] See *Ius pontif.*, P. II, 1, 86.

In South America Franciscans, Dominicans, Augustinians, Mercedarians, Jesuits and secular priests zealously continued their apostolic labours. From Peru both Dominicans and Augustinians were able to inform Propaganda of splendid successes. Between 1636 and 1639 that Congregation repeatedly sent Augustinians to Peru where Paul of Rozas in particular laboured with extraordinary success as apostolic missionary and preacher.[1] In 1642, whilst on a journey to Europe, the Procurator of the Jesuits in Peru, Bartolomeo Tafur, brought with him to Rome the first sample of the chinchona bark of whose remedial virtue against malaria he informed his brethren.[2] Augustinian missionaries also laboured zealously in Darien (New Granada). In 1629 they reported the conversion of 8,000 Indians in Vraba (Uraba), and that of 1,400 in Guaymi (Duchy of Veragua). By 1642 the Dominican Adrian of Uffelde had converted twenty pagan towns of the *Terra firma*.[3]

In 1628 forty-three Jesuit Fathers set out for Paraguay.[4] Ten years later they undertook the evangelization of Marañon (Upper Amazon).[5] In 1624 the Jesuits of Brazil were joined by French Capuchins in ministering to the Catholics of Pernambuco and evangelizing the pagans. In 1644 the Jesuits saved Maranhão for the Portuguese from the Calvinist Dutch.[6] After the conquest by the French of the Lesser Antilles, French religious established themselves there; the Jesuits settled in the island of St. Christopher in 1625, and the Capuchins in 1635, and in the same year the Capuchins and Dominicans

[1] See the important essay of SCHMIDLIN: *Die ältesten Propagandamaterialien zur Amerika-Mission*, in *Zeitschr. für Missionswiss.*, XV. (1925), 183 *seq.*; *cf.* the same author, *Missionsgesch.*, 308, note 2.

[2] Besides CELLI, 371 *seq.*, see A. CANEZZA, *Pulvis Iesuitica*, Rome, 1925, and *Civ. Catt.*, 1926, *fasc.*, 182, p. 533 *seq.*

[3] See SCHMIDLIN, *Propagandamaterialien*, 185 *seq.*

[4] *Ibid.*, 187.

[5] See ASTRÁIN, V., 443 *seq.*, 513 *seq.*

[6] See SCHMIDLIN, *Missionsgesch.*, 330; *cf. Propagandamaterialien*, 187.

went to Guadeloupe and Martinique, the Jesuits joining them in the latter island in 1640.[1]

In Mexico the Augustinian Valdes worked successfully among the Otomi and the Totopec between 1636–1638.[2] From Mexico the Franciscans penetrated into Yucatan, the Jesuits to Sinaloa and Sonora,[3] and isolated members of the Order as well as secular priests into Lower California.[4] The Franciscans laboured for the conversion of New Mexico and established stations there ; by 1631 they had baptized 86,000 Indians.[5] In Florida they had forty-four stations and thirty thousand neophytes in 1634.[6]

In the colony of Maryland, which Charles I. in 1632 gave to Lord Baltimore, for a Catholic settlement, English Jesuits established themselves and likewise laboured among the Indians ; however, the Puritan revolution of 1644 put an end to their activity.[7] Acting on a report of the nuncio of Brussels of the year 1630 on the emigration of the Puritans to North-America, and in answer to his request for help, Propaganda dispatched in the same year both French and English Capuchins to Virginia or New England.[8] In Canada, or New France, the Gospel was being preached by the Capuchins to the Penobscots, by the Recollects, until their dispersal in 1627, to various tribes, and by the Jesuits from 1627–1629 and again after 1632 to the Hurons and other tribes.[9]

With regard to the American missions, Propaganda's

[1] See SCHMIDLIN, *Missionsgesch.*, 295 *seq.*

[2] *Ibid.*, 342, note 3.

[3] See ASTRÁIN, V., 326 *seq.*

[4] *Cf.* SCHMIDLIN, *Missionsgesch.*, 349.

[5] See SCHMIDLIN, *Propagandamaterialien*, 189.

[6] *Cf.* SCHMIDLIN, *Missionsgesch.*, 351.

[7] *Cf.* below, XXIX., ch. 4.

[8] See SCHMIDLIN, *Missionsgesch.*, 352 ; *Propagandamaterialien*, 190.

[9] See SCHMIDLIN, *Missionsgesch*, 353 *seq.*, 356 *seq.* ; *Propagandamaterialien*, 191 ; FOUQUERAY, IV., 491 *seq.*, V., 290 *seq.* ; *Zeitschr. für Missionswiss.*, XIV., 85 ; GOYAU, in *Correspondant*, 1924.

action was more marked than that of the Holy See. The Bulls of Urban VIII. deal chiefly with the Orders and with ordinations and faculties.[1] A measure of general interest was the re-enactment, on April 22nd, 1639, by the Pope of Paul III.'s Bull against slavery,[2] excommunicating anyone who presumed to reduce to slavery, to buy, sell, exchange or make a gift of an Indian, whether he was a Christian or no, to part him from his wife and children, to rob him of his property, to transport him to another country or in any way to deprive him of his freedom or to keep him as a slave.[3] The storm of protests to which this ordinance gave rise in Brazil, showed how deeply rooted Indian slavery was in that country. The Jesuit Peter Claver toiled with superhuman endurance, until his death in 1654, for the conversion and the alleviation of the wretched condition of the slaves who were landed at Cartagena. In the discharge of this sublime office of an apostle of the blacks, to which he devoted nearly forty years of his life, he converted more than 300,000 negroes.[4]

The intense interest with which Rome watched the progress of the missions in the West and the East Indies [5] appears from

[1] In 1625 the Pope decided that the doctors in theology of the Augustinians should be tested by the examiners of the Chapters (*Ius pontif.*, I., 146 *seq.*); in 1626, that all confessors in Peru were to be examined by the Archbishop of Lima and that the people were to make their Easter Communion in their own parishes (*ibid.*, 64 *seq.*); in 1627, that in convents of nuns only women in the habit were to be received within the enclosure; he also issued rules for the conferring of degrees, after five years' study, in the Colleges of the Dominicans and Jesuits (*ibid.*, 155); in 1634, various faculties for the Ordinaries and for the Jesuits (*ibid.*, 160).

[2] *Cf.* our account, Vol. XII., 519 *seq.*

[3] See MARGRAF, *Kirche und Sklaverei seit der Entdeckung Amerikas*, Tübingen, 1865, 148 *seq.*, 220 *seq.* *Ius pontif.*, I., 176 *seq.* *Cf.* STREIT, I., 513.

[4] *Cf.* our account, Vol. XXV., 385 *seq.*

[5] See RANKE, *Päpste*, II.[6], 320, and *Osmanen*[4], 348, 352, 554 *seq.*, for the **Compendio y descripcion de las Indias occident.*, in *Barb.* 3584, Vatican Library, written in 1640 for Cardinal

the reports demanded by Propaganda. Thus a memorial of the year 1625 by the Franciscan Gregory Bolivar, exposes to the Pope existing abuses in the Church of the East Indies, especially among the clergy, and suggests various remedies.[1] The Augustinian Prior, Peter Nieto, of Havana, urged the need of a nuncio for the West Indies as well as that of a native clergy. In 1629 he drew up a memorandum on the necessary reforms.[2] In this document Gregory Bolivar openly complains that in both Indies, but especially in the West Indies, not enough was being done for the conversion of the pagans, notwithstanding that there were six archbishoprics and forty bishoprics ; he laments the lack of suitable priests for the Indians, because both seminaries and religious concentrated their attention for the most part on the parishes of Christians ; also the covetousness of numerous Bishops and the passion for gambling of many priests and the latter's trading in slaves and wine to the grave injury to their reputation, and lastly, the drawback that almost all the parishes were in the hands of religious. On the evidence of these reports, in the years 1625, 1628 and 1644, the Secretary of Propaganda, Ingoli, drew up memorandums on the abuses obtaining in both Indies and on their remedies. He mentions as the chief sources of these abuses the exaggerated claims of the Portuguese and Spanish patronage by which the publication of Papal Bulls was hindered and the nomination to episcopal sees frequently delayed, and lastly the disputes between the secular and regular clergy for which he lays all the blame on the Jesuits whom he hated because of their autonomy.[3] If in this Ingoli goes too far, he is completely right

Barberini, in 6 volumes (only the first and part of the second are in print) ; *ibid.* (Ranke), 557, for a description of the Spanish colonies in 1625, with special regard to their ecclesiastical organization.

[1] See KILGER in the *Zeitschr. für Missionswiss.*, XII. (1922), 19 *seq.*

[2] See SCHMIDLIN, *Propagandamaterialien*, 183.

[3] Ingoli, usually so reliable, was, like Melchior Cano, filled with passionate dislike of the Jesuits ; see KILGER in the *Zeitschr. für Missionswiss.*, 1922, 26.

in his bitter complaints of the interference and the mania for tutelage of the secular power and the repression and exploitation of the indigenous elements. As chief remedies he lays stress on the training of a native clergy, a more extensive employment of secular priests, and an increase of the hierarchy.[1] These directions were destined to be carried into effect in the near future, especially through the missionary seminaries for secular priests and the creation of Apostolic Vicariates.

[1] See KILGER, *loc. cit.*, 21 *seq.*; SCHMIDLIN, *Propagandamaterialien*, 184.

CHAPTER IV.

The Situation of Catholics in Switzerland, Holland, Denmark, Sweden, England, Ireland and Scotland.

(1)

A large part of the Swiss Confederation was likewise missionary territory. Out of thirteen Cantons, seven had remained wholly Catholic, viz. Lucerne, Uri, Schwyz, Ober and Unterwalden, Zug, Solothurn, and Fribourg; four, viz. Zürich, Bern, Bâle and Schaffhausen had fallen away completely from the ancient Church and two others partially, viz. Glarus and Appenzell. The four Protestant Cantons did not tolerate any exercise whatever of Catholic worship. A third of the population of Glarus still remained sincerely attached to the Catholic faith, half of that of Appenzell was also in sympathy with the ancient Church and there, as in all the other Cantons, the Capuchins helped to an extraordinary degree to maintain loyalty to the faith. The Grisons and Valais were completely mixed from the religious point of view.[1]

None of the six ancient bishoprics, viz. Bâle, Constance, Chur, Lausanne, Sitten, and Como, into which Switzerland was divided, had been completely destroyed, but their territories had been greatly diminished by the apostasy of the Protestant sections. In each diocese there was a Catholic, a Protestant, or

[1] *Cf.* R. Scotti (*Vesc. del Borgo di S. Donino*), *Helvetia profana e santa, Relat. del dominio temporale de' potentiss. XIII. cantoni Svizzeri detti della gran lega, e relat. de' vescovati, abbatie et altre dignità subordinate alla nuntiatura Helvet.*, 2 parts in 1 vol., Macerata, 1642. A copy of this important work, dedicated to the Vice-Chancellor Cardinal Barberini, dated Macerata, 1642, was found in the Corvisieri Library, which was sold in 1901. This copy formed part of the legacy of Cardinal Gentili and was entitled: *Relatione della Nuntiatura Elvetica lasciata per modo d'instruttione da Msgr. Scotti, vesc. del Borgo S. Donino, Nuntio ap., a Msgr. Farnese, arcivesc. di Patrano, suo successore, alla partenza per Franza a 2 Maggio, 1639.* At the end is the note, " Di Lucerna li 30 (*sic !*) di Maggio, 1639."

a mixed district; the latter was considered as missionary territory and, accordingly, as subject to Propaganda. The Bishop of Geneva had been compelled to withdraw to Annecy, that is, into Savoyard territory: the Bishop of Bâle had had to seek a refuge outside his diocese, at Pruntrut, which, for the rest, was his own territory and the Bishop of Lausanne had taken up residence at Fribourg which alone had remained faithful to him. The Bishop of Chur lived in a wholly Protestant town, his palace being his own property as a Prince of Empire.

The Bishops found strong support in the papal nuncio at Lucerne. Rome attached great importance to the Swiss nunciature, for its holder occupied a post from which he was able to make his influence felt in France, Germany, and Austria, and because he represented the Pope in a country which, if it were to fall away completely from the Church, could have cut or hindered communications with Germany whilst it might have opened the way for Protestantism into Italy.[1]

The holders of the Swiss nunciature under Urban VIII were Alessandro Scappi, Ciriaco Rocci (June, 1624–May, 1630). Ranuccio Scotti (till May, 1639), Girolamo Farnese (till October, 1643), and lastly the Theatine Lorenzo Gavotti.[2] The nuncios deemed it their chief duty to further in every way the Catholic cause, especially its champions, the Bishops and the Orders. They also had at heart the suppression of such abuses as had crept in. In this respect Scappi[3] and Scotti

[1] See MEJER, *Propaganda*, I., 108.

[2] See BIAUDET, *Nonciatures*, 214 *seq*. *Cf*. also STEINER, *Die Päpstlichen Gesandten in der Schweiz*, Stans, 1907, and BENZIGER in *Zeitschr. f. schweiz. Gesch.*, VI., 127 *seq*. An essay on the papal nuncio's visit to Altdorf, 1628/29 is in *Anz. f. schweiz. Gesch.*, New Series, XIV. (1911), no. 3. The captain of the Swiss Guard, whose office was much coveted, was considered as the Resident of the Catholic Cantons with the Holy See; *cf. Zeitschr. f. schweiz. Kirchengesch.*, X. (1916). 233 *seq*.

[3] *Cf*. DUHR, II., 1, 275. For Scappi's reform of the relaxed Benedictine monasteries of Disentis and Pfäfers see the **Decreta* of November 15 and December 5, 1623, in the *Visite*, III., Propaganda Archives, Rome. *Ibid*., *Visite*, V. for the **Visitatio monast. Campidonen*, November 22, 1626, by Scappi.

showed particular zeal. The latter, on his retirement at the beginning of May, 1639, drew up a detailed memorandum for the benefit of his successor which throws a most interesting light on the religious and political situation in Switzerland,[1] a country that had been but little affected by the great war.[2]

Of the Bishops, Scotti has nothing but good to report. The Bishop of Constance, Truchsess von Waldburg, was a very pious man but lack of money prevented him from building a much-needed seminary. A *grand seigneur* himself, he left the work of visitation to his suffragans. Almost the whole of Constance had been brought back to the Catholic Church by the Jesuits, so that not more than thirty Protestants remained there. The Bishops of Bâle were in a position of great difficulty, not only because Protestantism had made extensive inroads into their diocese but because their temporal territory was hard hit by the upheavals caused by the war, in consequence of which they had lost their revenues. Bishop Wilhelm Rink von Baldenstein (1608–1628) received both consolation and help from Urban VIII.[3] The Bishop's zeal for the Catholic restoration was shown by his action against the only remaining Protestant community, Allschwill, in the Birseck.[4]

Of his successor, Johann Heinrich von Ostheim (1628-1646), Scotti says that his zeal was such as to leave nothing to be desired, but that the troubles of the war had reduced him to destitution. Equally zealous in the fulfilment of his ecclesiastical duty, according to Scotti, was the Bishop of Lausanne,

[1] What follows is from the memorial quoted in n. 1, p. 265.

[2] *Cf.* Hürbin, *Handbuch der Schweizergesch.*, II., Stans, 1908, 371 *seq.* For the "affair Klus" which France settled in order to preserve the Federation as its undivided recruiting field, see F. Fäh, *Der Kluser Handel und seine Folgen*, 1632/33, Zürich, 1884.

[3] *Cf.* the *Brief to the Bishop of Basle, November 25, 1623, and the Brief in his favour, addressed to the Archduke Leopold William of Austria as Bishop of Strassburg, dated May 31, 1625, and *that to the Emperor, May 25, 1628, *Epist.*, I.[a] II., V., Papal Secret Archives.

[4] *Cf.* K. Gauss in the *Basler Jahrbuch*, 1900.

Jean de Versoix, who resided in staunchly Catholic Fribourg. The Bishop of Chur, Joseph Mohr (1627-1635), as well as his predecessor, John Flugi V., and his successor John Flugi VI., had at heart the visitation of their diocese.[1] The spiritual care of the religiously very mixed population of the Grisons, and the protection of the faith there, found valuable support in the Capuchin mission of Brescia.[2] Scotti likewise obtained Capuchins from Milan who, notwithstanding the difficulties arising out of the political circumstances, threw themselves into their task with burning zeal, with the result that many Protestants were converted.[3] In Sitten also, from which the Jesuits had been banished in 1627,[4] a Capuchin convent was founded in Scotti's time. Geneva constituted a perennial danger of religious perversion for the diocese which also suffered from a great dearth of priests, so that Urban VIII. urged the foundation of a Jesuit College.[5] In the Italian districts of the diocese excellent priests of the school of St. Charles Borromeo were still at work.[6]

Scotti singles out for special praise the admirable state of

[1] *Cf.* the essays of Dr. J. Simonet in the *Bündner Monatsblatt*, 1916, 2 *seq.*, 48 *seq.*, 90 *seq.*, 123 *seq.*, and 1925.

[2] *Cf.* Rocco da Cesinale, II., *passim.*

[3] Scotti says so expressly.

[4] See Duhr, II., 1, 303 *seq.*, where there are further details on the intervention of the nuncio Scappi and Urban VIII. on behalf of the Fathers.

[5] A *letter of encouragement to the Bishop of Sitten, Hildebrand II., Jost, of November 25, 1623, in which we read : " Sed ecclesiae vulnera non patiuntur Nos gratulantium plausibus delectari : notissimum istius dioc. miseriae." Arm yourself for the cause of God, " cum haeret. pestilentiae contagio ex finit. Gehennae fluctibus in istius populi viscera irrepserit." The nuncio would stand by him. A *Brief to the magistrates of Sitten, June 22, 1624 : They should give the Jesuits a College in the town. Similar *Briefs to the magistrates of Sitten and to the Swiss, August 17, 1624, *Epist.*, I.[a], I.[b]. A laudatory *Brief to the new Bishop, Adrian III. von Riedmatten, November 21, 1643, *Epist.*, XIX., Papal Secret Archives.

[6] Here as in my other statements, I am using Scotti's report.

the monasteries and convents of Catholic Switzerland. In the Swiss Benedictine Congregation, which included the famous Abbeys of St. Gall,[1] Einsiedeln, Muri, Rheinau, Fischingen, Engelberg, Pfäfers, and Disentis, both Abbots and Monks observed the Rule with the greatest fidelity. The Abbey of Fischingen in Thurgau, the only one that was still relaxed, was reformed by Scotti.[2] All the Abbeys of the Swabian Congregation were likewise reformed but the wars had reduced them to great straits. Among these was St. Blasien which at one time had had an income of 100,000 florins. Scotti draws a gloomy picture of the destitution of the monasteries of Swabia and Alsace, many of whose monks had been driven from their homes by warlike disturbances; some of these escaped into Switzerland. The excellent Cistercian Abbots of Salem and Tennenbach were likewise in exile.

In the Catholic Cantons Scotti busied himself with the reform of the convents of nuns. For their confessors he usually appointed Jesuits. The latter had five Colleges within the area of the Swiss nunciature, viz. at Constance, Freiburg im Breisgau, Fribourg in Switzerland, Lucerne, and Pruntrut. In addition to these they also had establishments at Ensisheim, Colmar, and Lindau. Scotti reports that they did excellent work everywhere, especially at Lucerne and at Fribourg, where they had many pupils.[3] Scotti also recommended to his successor the Somaschans of Lucerne who had settled in one of the suburbs during the pontificate of Clement VIII. But of all religious in the whole of Switzerland the Capuchins were the most popular.

Not only the nuncios but Propaganda paid assiduous attention to the Swiss mission.[4] The same was true of the

[1] Laudatory *Brief to the Abbot of St. Galle, November 14, 1643, *Epist.*, XIX., *loc. cit.*

[2] *Brief of May 24, 1642 to *Abbas Helvet. congreg. ord. S. Benedicti*. Similarly on May 24, 1642 to the Swiss nuncio, *Epist.*, XIX., *ibid.*

[3] *Cf.* DUHR, II., 1, 263 *seq.*, 266, 268 *seq.*, 270 *seq.*, 275 *seq.* (the efforts of nuncio Scappi on behalf of the house at Colmar) 287 *seq.*, 292 *seq.*, 296 *seq.*

[4] *Cf.* ROCCO DA CESINALE, II., *passim.*

Provinces of the United Netherlands, though with this difference that there were no longer any Bishops left in that country and the nuncios could only make their influence felt from Brussels.[1] Philip Rovenius, who was appointed Vicar Apostolic for the Dutch mission in 1614, when he was also given the title of Archbishop of Philippi,[2] could only work from a distance.[3] The oppression of the Catholics of Holland, who were still numerous, continued.[4] In view of the fact that the law of February 26th, 1622, which forbade the exercise of Catholic worship, even in private, under penalty of heavy fines, could not be carried out everywhere in its full stringency, it was enforced afresh in 1624, 1629, and again in 1641.[5] Almost everywhere priests could only give spiritual comfort at night.[6] In 1628 the Bishop of Bruges wrote to Urban VIII. to lament the complete suppression of the old religion in the deanery

[1] *Cf.* CAUCHIE-MAERE, *Instructions aux Nonces de Flandre*, Bruxelles, 1904, *passim*. The nuncio in Paris, Scotti, also attempted to intervene in favour of the Dutch Catholics. He reports as follows: *" Per le notitie ch'hebbero gl'heretici degl'affari de' cattolici d'Olanda, anzi del nome loro, trovatane la nota fra le scritture levate in Utrecht all'arcivescovo Filippense Vicario Apostolico, che con la fuga miracolosamente si salvò, per esser stato scoperto l'essercitio della sua carica, si levò una fiera persecutione contro li medesimi cattolici; onde furono passati da me offitii in voce, lasciandome memoria in scritto, acciò si dessero da Sua Maestà ordini efficaci al suo ambasciatore appresso le provincie unite per la protettione della religione cattolica etc." (SCOTTI, **Relatione della sua Nunziatura*, XI., 71, pp. 91–2, Papal Secret Archives). BLOCK gives a survey of the contemporary material dealing with Holland preserved in the Archives of Propaganda [1625 to 1662], in *Archief. v. d. geschied. v. h. aartsbisdom Utrecht*, XXVII., 329–376.

[2] *Cf.* our account, Vol. XXVI., 123, n. 3.

[3] *Cf.* KNUIF DE JONG, *Phil. Rovenius*, Utrecht, 1925.

[4] As is clearly shown, as against Fruin, in the monograph quoted in the preceding note, Catholics did not enjoy any liberty of conscience and they were being persecuted not for their Spanish sympathies but for their adherence to the old faith.

[5] See HUBERT, 71.

[6] *Cf. Arch. v. h. aartsb. Utrecht*, XII., 432.

of Ardenbourg.[1] In certain Provinces the severe general ordinances against the private exercise of Catholic worship were made stricter still. How greatly afraid the Government was of every manifestation of Catholic life is proved by the firmness with which it rejected, in 1630, the request of the French ambassador who asked that Catholic worship might go on in conquered Bois-le-Duc ; in 1631 all the Catholic churches there were closed.[2] At Groningen, in the same year, a Dominican was condemned to six months' imprisonment and a fine of 1,000 florins.[3] In 1640 all Catholic priests were banished from Leiden on the plea that they did all that they could to bring about the triumph of the Pope and of Spain.[4] At the Hague, where in consequence of the great number of Catholics —there were 6,000 of them—supervision had been somewhat less strict,[5] everything was now done to make it impossible for them to hear Mass in the chapels of the French and Venetian ambassadors.[6] In Seeland and Frisia, according to the report of the envoy Francesco Michiel, the number of Catholics had been greatly reduced by 1638 ; for that reason they were being treated with increased harshness.[7]

In 1639 the Vicar Apostolic Rovenius drew up a memorandum on the intolerable condition of the Dutch Catholics. He stated that the law guaranteed liberty of conscience to all the subjects but that Catholics did not enjoy this freedom since they were prevented from receiving the Sacraments at the hands of their priests. The Government's treatment of

[1] See *Anal. p. s. à l'hist. écclés. de la Belgique*, III., 68.

[2] See Hubert, 71, 90.

[3] See *Arch. v. h. aartsb. Utrecht* VI., 14 *seq.* Other religious also, *e.g.*, the Augustinians were at work in Holland ; see the dissertation quoted below, p. 273, note 5, by Meijer.

[4] See Hubert, 76.

[5] *Cf.* the account of the envoy Fr. Michiel of 1638 in Block, *Relaz. Venez.*, Hague, 1909, 266.

[6] See Hubert, 77 *seq.*

[7] See Fr. Michiel, *loc. cit.* According to the *Descript. episc. Leoward.* A° 1640, the number of Catholics in Friesland was still fairly high. Thus at Groningen 4,000 yearly communicants were recorded and about 1,000 from the neighbouring district ; see *Arch. v. h. aartsb. Utrecht*, IV., 90 *seq.* *Cf.* Hubert, 103 *seq.*

Catholics was as if it told them: "I allow you to live but forbid you to eat."[1] However these representations were just as useless as the suggestion that a cessation of the persecution would be to the interest of the Republic. Whilst all other religious parties were tolerated,[2] those continued to be oppressed who remained true to the faith of their fathers. The oppression made itself especially felt through the imposition of exorbitant fines.[3] In 1642 Rovenius reckoned that the fines paid during the preceding four years amounted to 50,000 florins.[4] None the less the desired end, that is, the destruction of the old religion, was not realized, partly because notwithstanding the insistence of the Calvinist preachers, a strict execution of the edicts was not possible, and because many of the officials allowed themselves to be bribed. The reports of Rovenius to Propaganda and other sources make it quite clear that there could be no question of a radical extirpation of the ancient Church. Whereas in 1616 the secular clergy numbered 200, it had risen to 246 in 1631, and to 300 in 1642. In 1616 there were 16 Jesuits in Holland, in 1631 nearly 50, in 1634 65, and in 1638 there were 70. In 1617 the Franciscans numbered 7; in 1634 they were 25.[5] We even hear of numerous conversions: in 1635 there were no less than 2,500.[6] To what petty devices the Government had recourse, appears from the fact that in 1636, at Utrecht, the immemorial custom of placing a rosary in the hands of the dead was forbidden under penalty of a fine of 50 florins.[7] and in 1644

[1] See the memorandum in *Arch. v. h. aartsb. Utrecht*, II., 1 *seqq*. *Cf*. KNUTTEL, *Toestand d. Nederl. Kathol.* (1892), 141.

[2] *Cf*. LEMAN, *Instructions*, 141.

[3] See WILDE in *Studiën v. Godsdienst, Wetenschap, Letteren*, New Series, LX. (1903), 265 and KLÖNNE in *Katholiek*, XCVII. (1890), 17 *seq*. *Cf*. HUBERT, 97.

[4] See WILDE, *loc. cit.*, 271.

[5] KNUTTEL, *loc. cit.*, I., 61 *seq*. In the Instruction for the nuncio of Brussels in 1635, the number of priests is given as only 150; *cf*. LEMAN, *Instructions*, 172, note 1.

[6] See *Arch. v. h. aartsb. Utrecht*, XVIII., 1 *seq*.; HUBERT, 98.

[7] See KRONENBURG, *Marias Heerlijkheid in Nederland*, VII., Amsterdam, 1911, 164.

all childless Catholic women were forbidden to make a will ! [1]

The differences between the Vicar Apostolic and the regular clergy had long proved one of the difficulties of the Dutch mission. The situation became even more acute when certain Mendicant Friars from neighbouring countries, having penetrated into Holland, frequently committed grave imprudences. Rovenius also became involved in fresh disputes with the Jesuits. Although in 1644 he had arrived at an understanding with the Provincial of the Jesuits,[2] and both the Pope and Propaganda insisted on the arrangement being honoured,[3] fresh conflicts were for ever arising. In a memorial to Propaganda of the year 1649, both Jesuits and Franciscans defended themselves against Rovenius' accusations.[4] Propaganda, on its part, strictly enjoined on the missionaries, especially the Capuchins, not to meddle in any way with political matters during the war between Holland and Spain.[5]

One of Holland's noblest and most gifted sons, the poet Joost van den Vondel, who for a time had professed Arminianism, became a Catholic in 1641. The literary importance, the depth of feeling and wealth of thought of the famous "conqueror of the Parnassus of the Netherlands" have in

[1] See HUBERT, 87.

[2] *Cf. Arch. v. h. aartsb. Utrecht*, IV., 341 *seq.*

[3] See BROM, *Acta der Propaganda voer de Hollandsche Missië, 1622–1698*, in *Arch. v. h. aartsb. Utrecht*, XXXI. (1906), 298 *seq. Ius pontif.*, I., 54 *seq.*

[4] See *Arch. v. h. aartsb. Utrecht*, XXXIII. (1908), 14 *seqq.*, 77 *seq.* The controversy of Rovenius with the Jesuits is treated in detail in the monograph of KNUIF DE JONG quoted above, p. 270, note 3.

[5] See BROM, *loc. cit.*, 333, 336, 365. For the *Congregatio particularis Hollandiae* created in 1637, see *Mededeelingen v. het Nederlandsch Hist. Institut te Rome*, VII., Haag, 1927, xl. Besides the Jesuits, Dominicans, Franciscans, and Capuchins, the Augustinians were also active in the Dutch mission ; see G. A. MEIJER, *Volmachten door Urbaan VIII. gegeven aan Michael Paludanus, prefect der Augustijnen in der Holl. Missië* (1635), in *Arch. v. h. aartsb. Utrecht*, XXXIV. (1909).

recent times met with universal recognition. In a splendid poem written in 1645, he sang the glory of the Church.[1] In 1644 another intellectual giant of Holland, Hugo Grotius, the founder of international law, " the miracle of his century ",[2] whose aim was the reunion of divided Christendom, returned sincerely and humbly to the bosom of the ancient Church.[3]

The Dutch Catholics may also have found some consolation for the insults which the Calvinists were wont to proffer against the Blessed Virgin Mary in the fact that Jan Pieters Sweelinck, the organist at one of the Calvinist churches of Amsterdam and the mightiest predecessor of Sebastian Bach, composed three splendid musical pieces in her honour and that Rembrandt, in a work of art of the first rank, gave expression to the Catholic conception of the greatness and holiness of the Mother of Our Lord.[4]

Throughout seven centuries the kingdoms of the North had shone like a pearl in the ring of Catholic Provinces which encircle the Chair of Peter, until the storm of the Reformation came to destroy the rich religious life which had unfolded itself

[1] *Cf.* the biographies by ALBERDINGK THYM (Amsterdam, 1869), BAUMGARTNER (Freiburg, 1882), and KOLFF (Haarlem, 1896).

[2] Vossius' expression.

[3] F. X. Schulte, the author of the most important work, on the Catholic side, on the religious views of Grotius, says: " Especially the question whether Grotius ' became ' a Catholic, is still ' sub lite ' " (BROERE, *Grotius' Rückkehr zur katholischen Kirche*, Trier, 1871, VI. KROGH-TONNING (*H. Grotius und die religiösen Bewegungen im Protestantismus seiner Zeit*, Köln, 1904) has nothing further to add to this. SOPHIE GÖRRES (*Ist. H. Grotius katholisch gestorben?* in *Hist.-polit. Blätter*, CLIV., 1 *seq.*, 132 *seq.*, 161 *seq.*) has again taken up the question and on the basis of a newly discovered letter of Balde to Grotius dated March 4, 1644, has answered it in the affirmative. The nuncio F. CHIGI had already hinted at the possibility of Grotius' conversion from Cologne in 1641 and 1642; see KLÖNNE, *Amsteldamensia*, Amsterdam, 1894, 183 *seq.*; ORBAAN. *Bescheiden*, I., 296.

[4] See KRONENBURG, *loc. cit.*, 188.

there. Through the absolutism of secular Governments and their lust of gain, the Catholic religion was abolished by force and the preaching of her doctrine and the exercise of her worship punished with the loss of life and property. Church property was confiscated, the sacred edifices were stripped of their ornaments, not a few of them were destroyed and the monasteries suppressed. However painful all this may have been, the Holy See never relaxed its efforts to save what might yet be saved. As it was, the hope which had still been a lively one under Clement VIII., that the most important of the northern Kingdoms, viz. Sweden, would return to the Church, soon vanished completely.[1] But there still remained those in Sweden who secretly professed the Catholic Faith. The attempt of the Jesuit Henry Schacht to administer the Sacraments to them ended towards the close of 1624, as a result of treachery. In 1625 a young Swede who had made his studies in the papal seminary of Braunsberg, was executed for being a Catholic.[2]

Denmark, whither Propaganda sent a few Jesuits and Dominicans, exhibited the same hostility towards Catholics. The Jesuit Colen was banished in 1624 whilst the merchant who had given him hospitality was put to death. A royal ordinance of February 24th, 1624, forbade under pain of death all Catholic priests and religious to reside in the country.[3] The Dominicans who fled from the persecution devoted themselves to the Catholics of Hamburg and Friedrichstadt.[4] In 1626 Propaganda resolved to send two Jesuit missionaries to Norway; however the plan could not be carried out owing to the stringent Danish law which was operative there. In 1637 Propaganda despatched the priest Rhugius to Norway, his native country, together with a Dominican. The latter was

[1] *Cf.* our account, Vol. XXIV., 341, *seqq.*

[2] See PIEPER, 12 *seq.*; METZLER, 15.

[3] See RÖRDAM, *Danske Kirkelove*, III., København, 1889, 104 *seq.*; PIEPER, 9 *seq.*; METZLER, 14 *seq.*; A. LYSANDER, *Jesuiterna i Malmö, 1624*, Lund, 1922.

[4] See PIEPER, 16 *seq.*; DE WEDEL-JARLSBERG, *Une page d'histoire des Frères-Prêcheurs. La Province Dacia : Danmark, Suède et Norvège*, Rome, 1889, 246 *seq.*

promptly expelled whilst Rhugius succeeded in staying until 1642, but he was unable to carry out any of the functions of his ministry.[1] In 1630 Propaganda sent a Scottish priest to Sweden but nothing is known of his missionary activity.[2] In 1644 Sweden was placed under the pro-legate of Avignon. Two Superiors of the mission were appointed and faculties for Denmark and Sweden were also granted to them, but it would seem that owing to the obstacles put in their way they never even reached their destination.[3]

(2)

At the time of Gregory XV.'s death the heir to the British Crown, Charles, was still in Spain for the purpose of personally bringing to a head the negotiations for his marriage with the sister of the King of Spain which had been pending for so long a time. For a while it looked as if he were about to succeed. True, from the first the leading Spanish statesman, Olivares, would not hear of the English wedding ; consequently he kept making ever larger and even impossible demands from the English. To the minister's astonishment and despair, Charles suffered himself to be driven from one concession to another until he ended by granting all that was asked of him. James I. also proved unexpectedly accommodating. By the terms of certain articles to which he secretly swore on July 20th, 1623, an end was to be put to the persecution of English Catholics, and they were to enjoy the free exercise of their religion within their own homes. Even the Infanta ended by overcoming her reluctance to marry the Englishman.[4] The decisive factor in this change of mind was the hope that thereby she might procure for the English Catholics an alleviation of

[1] See PIEPER, 36 *seq.* ; METZLER, 16.

[2] See METZLER, 16.

[3] See PIEPER, 46 *seq.* ; METZLER, 16 *seq.*

[4] *Cf.* our account, Vol. XXVI., 188 *seqq.* ; for the Spanish marriage see also OPEL, I., 517 to 533. Further literature in *Arch. stor. ital.*, LXXI., 1 (1913), 291. See also *Relazione del viaggio di Carlo principe di Galles a Madrid 1625*, in SAGGIATORE, II., 442 *seq.*

their lot and perhaps bring back the whole island kingdom to the old religion.[1] With a view to giving the King of England time to prove the sincerity of his promises, it was decided that the Infanta should only set out for her new home in the spring of 1624, but the wedding was to be solemnized as soon as information should have come in that James I. had signed the secret conditions submitted to him and that the new Pope sanctioned the marriage, for news of Gregory XV.'s death had by then reached Madrid.[2] However, the newly elected Pope fell seriously ill immediately after his enthronization, hence nothing was done until October.[3] As a Cardinal, so Urban VIII. wrote to James I.,[4] he had been Protector of Scotland and as a member of the commission of Cardinals he had been in favour of the matrimonial alliance and still desired its realization. It grieved him that James I., the son of so saintly a mother, had departed from the religion of his ancestors; as for the future, he hoped the King would protect the Catholics: already once before Britain had given a Constantine to the Church of Christ. On the same day the Pope also sent a most friendly reply to the letter which Prince Charles had written to Gregory XV.; the Pope told him, that his letter was the first document to come into his hands after his election.[5]

Meanwhile the Prince had made up his mind to leave Spain,

[1] English concessions on religious questions raised exaggerated hopes. A member of the French embassy in London, Denis Lazzari, even thought that: "per guadagnare l'anima del re non credo che vi fosse molta difficoltà;" that James I. was indifferent in religious matters; if he was allowed to retain the Church's property and the Spanish marriage or the restitution of the Palatinate were promised to him, his indifference would be no obstacle, especially if Buckingham could be won through his wife who secretly professed Catholicism (GARDINER, IV., 281; *Tilliers* in RAUMER, II., 328 *seq.*); see **Relatione fatta alla Congregatione di Propaganda Fide da Dionisio Lazzari*, Corsini Library, at Rome, 35 B. 9, p. 48 *seqq.* *Cf.* LÄMMER, *Zur Kirchengeschichte*, 147 *seqq.*

[2] GARDINER, V., 92.

[3] *Ibid.*, 113.

[4] October 15, 1623, in KUNSTMANN, 198–201.

[5] *Ibid.*, 201–204.

August 29th being fixed for his departure. In order to justify this action in the eyes of his bride, he requested James I. to send him a formal command to return. This he received on August 10th.[1] Meanwhile the Prince sought to induce the Spanish Court to consent to his bride accompanying him at once to England,[2] but to this the Spaniards would not agree. However, Philip IV. suggested that the Prince should prolong his stay until Christmas ; meanwhile the marriage might be solemnized though even so the Infanta would only accompany him to England in the following spring. The seriousness of the situation was apparent, for if in the meantime a son should be born to the Prince of Wales, the Spaniards would have in their hands as hostages not one but two heirs to the British Crown. Once again Charles' thoughtlessness induced him to consent to remain until Christmas.[3]

The Prince's vacillation occasioned a series of unpleasant incidents. There were so many chances of friction between the Spaniards and the English that sharp conflicts were scarcely to be avoided. Thus it happened that when one of the cavaliers in the Prince's suite fell suddenly ill, he asked for a priest, that he might die a Catholic. Now already another companion of Charles, Cottington, when dangerously ill, had been anxious to enter eternity as a Catholic, though when he recovered he judged it easier to go on living as a Protestant. The repetition of such an incident infuriated the English : they gathered before the door of the dying man to prevent the priest from going to him. When the priest nevertheless appeared on the scene, one of the men struck him in the face with his clenched fist. Only with difficulty were the Spaniards restrained from taking a bloody revenge for this outrage. But the incident had a wide repercussion : " What can English Catholics expect from people who behave thus towards foreign ones ? " it was said " What is the worth of English promises ? " Philip IV. insisted on stern punishment whilst Charles, on the contrary, demanded the punishment of the *alcalde* who had arrested the author of the outrage. The King put an end to the

[1] Gardiner, V., 93, 100.

[2] *Ibid.*, 93 *seqq.*

[3] *Ibid.*, 101.

dispute by informing the Prince that if he wished to remain in Spain until Christmas he must dismiss all his English servants.[1] Apart from this incident, Buckingham had made himself very unpopular in Spain in consequence of his immorality and his haughtiness, so much so that people said that they would rather cast the Infanta headlong into a well than hand her over to such a man.[2]

In addition to everything, Olivares, in an unguarded moment, had allowed the remark to escape him that he never seriously contemplated the wedding.[3] The Prince ended by realizing that he had better leave Spain as soon as possible, and on August 20th, he wrote to his father to that effect.[4] The wedding was to be arranged by someone else, perhaps by Philip IV. himself, or by his brother, power to conclude the bargain remaining in the hands of Bristol, the English ambassador, the marriage to take place ten days after the arrival of the papal dispensation. Before setting out for home Charles took a solemn oath by which he bound himself to the marriage contract, on August 28th,[5] and on September 2nd he took his leave.

Meanwhile the conditions of the marriage contract were being examined in Rome. As a Cardinal, Urban VIII., had been definitely in favour of the Spanish wedding, for he hoped that it would lead to an improvement in the situation of the English Catholics. Immediately after his election he discussed the matter with the Spanish ambassador, and as soon as he had recovered from his illness he once more gave it his whole attention.[6] Cardinals Bandini, Millini, Cobelluzio, Scaglia, Pio, and Ludovisi were commissioned to study the question. Subsequently they were joined by Antonio and Francesco Barberini and, during the latter's absence in France, by the particularly energetic Magalotti.[7] It appeared that the

[1] *Ibid.*, 102 *seq.*

[2] *Ibid.*, 114.

[3] *Ibid.*, 111 *seq.*

[4] *Ibid.*, 103.

[5] *Ibid.*, 113 *seq.*

[6] A *letter of Barberini to the Spanish nuncio, October 25, 1623, in *Nicoletti, LII., 7 *seq.*, 253, Vatican Library.

[7] *Nicoletti, LII., 7 *seq.*, 263, *loc. cit.*

alterations insisted upon by Rome had not been taken into account in the Madrid contract. Thus Rome had demanded that the governesses of the royal children must be Catholics, whereas the contract merely stated that they might be Catholics.[1] Rome wished the royal children to be under the care of the Infanta up to their twelfth year; of this the Prince was not merely to give a hope but a firm promise; but in the Madrid contract there was question of the tenth year only, and no mention whatever was made of the further condition that up to that age the entire domestic staff of the royal children was to be composed of Catholics. This last demand was bound to be of very great importance in the event of the premature death of the Infanta.[2] Urban VIII. was particularly alarmed by an alteration in the clause which granted to the Catholics liberty to practise their religion within their own homes and to attend the chapel or public church of the Infanta. The Prince had put in a claim that this could not be included among the points to which he had to swear, though in a document which the nuncio forwarded to Ludovisi, he promised to the Catholics silent toleration in respect to this point. The Cardinals' comment was that they failed to see why the Prince should not swear what he was ready to promise; the Madrid nuncio should do his utmost to secure this point; if he failed he must not deliver the marriage dispensation.[3] A last difficulty, and it was a big one, was the oath which Catholics were required to take on assuming office or on similar occasions. It was inadmissible that Rome should examine every individual oath, nor could the Pope prescribe a form of oath which the English Government would be obliged to adopt. In the end the Cardinals arrived at the conclusion that they would be satisfied with the Prince's promise that no oath would be demanded which was irreconcilable with the Catholic religion.[4] The nuncio was to be instructed not to deliver the dispensation until these two main points had been settled and the King of Spain had guaranteed by oath the

[1] Barberini's *letter, *ibid.*, 257.

[2] *Ibid.*, 258 *seq.*

[3] *Ibid.*, 260 *seqq.*

[4] *Ibid.*, 262 *seq.* Two secondary points, *ibid.*, 265 *seq.*

execution of the marriage contract. A copy of the sworn contract, signed and sealed by both Kings and by the Prince, was to be forwarded to Rome.[1]

When on October 25th, 1623, the nuncio in Madrid, Massimi, was informed of these decisions, the Roman authorities were still ignorant of the events which had occurred there since the latter's last report dated August 26th, nor could they know that their objections would arrive too late. These were nevertheless presented because it was impossible to ascertain with complete certainty whether the marriage dispensation had already been handed over and because the Pope had the matter very much at heart. He would deem his Pontificate an exceedingly happy one, he wrote to Massimi, if at the very outset of his government he could introduce once more the Catholic religion into a country from which it had been so long banished and where at one time it had been so flourishing.[2]

Meanwhile at Madrid the situation had changed considerably. When Charles undertook his journey south, for the purpose of looking for a bride, he had imagined that his personal appearance in Madrid would sweep away every obstacle to his marriage to the Infanta, whilst he would be in a position to intervene effectively on behalf of his sister, the exiled Palatine Electress. Greatly disillusioned and deeply wounded in his pride, he returned to England without a bride. Already on the return journey and whilst still on Spanish soil, he looked for pretexts to put off the wedding for as long as possible. From Segovia he wrote to Bristol, the English ambassador in Madrid, that even before this he had confessed his fear to him lest after the wedding the Infanta should wish to enter a convent, thereby robbing him of a wife. This remark of the Prince was not meant seriously ; all he wanted was to make it impossible for the wedding to take place on the appointed day. To this end the bearer of the letter was instructed to hand it to Bristol only after the papal approval of the marriage should have arrived. Bristol would then have to ask for fresh instructions from London ; three weeks must then elapse before a reply could reach him, so that it would be

[1] *Ibid.*, 266. [2] *Ibid.*, 267.

impossible for the wedding to be solemnized ten days after the arrival of the papal dispensation.[1] However, the plot miscarried because, in answer to a remark of Bristol's, the messenger said that Rome's answer had already arrived, and he handed over the letter much too soon,[2] viz. two months before the arrival of the Pope's answer.

Three days after the Prince's embarkation, Bristol, as a result of careful inquiry, was able to reassure him with regard to his fears,[3] but he realized that London was on the look-out for pretexts for putting off the wedding; accordingly he drew attention to the bad impression which such a step could not fail to create in Madrid, since in the faculties granted for the marriage settlement it was expressly stated that the Prince could not revoke or alter them. However London continued to search for fresh pretexts. Though Bristol had insisted on the fact that the faculty expired at Christmas, James I. deemed it opportune [4] to fix the wedding for the day after Christmas and to lay down retrospectively a supplementary condition for the match, namely the restoration to his daughter Elizabeth and her husband Frederick of their Palatine principality. Through the intervention of Philip IV. Bristol now found himself in the greatest perplexity. Could he appear before Philip IV. to demand that the wedding should take place on the very first day after the expiration of the time limit previously agreed upon? To do so would be an insult. Should he insist on the restoration of Frederick, which had never been mentioned as one of the clauses of the marriage treaty? Surely this was too much like a pretext for getting out of the marriage, quite apart from the fact that a demand of this kind would lead to an indefinite postponement of the wedding. Bristol urged his reasons in a respectful letter,[5] but even before he could receive an answer, his perplexity grew still further as news reached Madrid that Urban VIII. had granted the necessary

[1] GARDINER, V., 118 *seq.*

[2] September 11, 1623, *ibid.*, 120.

[3] September 21, 1623, *ibid.*, 121 *seq.*; *cf.* 133.

[4] October 8, 1623, *ibid.*, 134 *seq.*

[5] October 24, 1623, in GARDINER, V., 140.

dispensation for the marriage. Everything was to be settled within ten days after the arrival of the document, hence it was necessary to act quickly. Bristol made haste to write to London [1] to the effect that he thought he would be interpreting the mind of the King if he delivered the faculty for the marriage by proxy as soon as ever it was asked for, whilst at the same time endeavouring to put off the day of the wedding for as long as possible, pending further instructions. However, such procrastination was not without its difficulties. The Pope's consent to the marriage duly arrived on November 12th, and on the 19th it was in the hands of the King of Spain, who at once took the required oath, namely, that James I. would discharge his obligations. The 29th November was fixed as the last term for the wedding; if it did not take place by then, the marriage treaty would be null and void.[2]

Meanwhile James I. had drawn up the letter which effectively nullified the marriage plans.[3] To Bristol's reminder that the faculty for Charles' proxy at the wedding expired on Christmas Day, he answered by issuing a new one, which was to be good until March, 1624, but at the same time he commanded him not to hand over the document until Philip IV. should have promised in writing that he would procure the restoration of the Palatine either by peaceful means or by force of arms. If Bristol failed to receive a favourable answer within twenty days he was to take his departure.

Naturally enough Philip IV. refused to submit to these demands, since they aimed at nothing less than that James I. need not move a finger for the restoration of his son-in-law, whereas the King of Spain might conceivably be compelled to go to war. James' instructions arrived in Madrid three days before the day fixed for the wedding. The Infanta now gave up her study of English and ceased to style herself Princess of England.[4] On December 30th Bristol was definitely ordered to return to England; he received but scanty thanks from

[1] November 1, 1623, *ibid.*, 148 *seq.*

[2] *Ibid.*, 150.

[3] *Ibid.*, 145.

[4] *Ibid.*, 153.

James for his faithful service.[1] However, though a considerable time passed before James formally cancelled the plans for a Spanish marriage,[2] in reality everything was at an end.

Whilst the negotiations for a marriage with the Infanta were still pending James felt that he must take some steps with a view to bringing his promise of religious toleration for Catholics nearer execution. After prolonged discussions with the Spanish ambassador in London, both parties signed an agreement[3] for a future amnesty for those Catholics who had been condemned to fines for refusing to attend Anglican services. A royal declaration, also to be made at a future date, would suspend all penal laws against Catholics. Further negotiations took place as to the form of the future amnesty and declaration.[4] On August 28th the King put his signature to both ordinances; at the same time he instructed the Keeper of the Great Seal, Williams, to draw up a warrant for the liberation of imprisoned priests and a letter to the magistrates ordering them to take note of the amnesty and granting permission for it to be pleaded in court. The Spanish envoy nevertheless failed to obtain a formal prohibition of the prosecution of Catholics. The Keeper of the Seals was in no hurry to publish the royal command. He knew full well that these ordinances had only been extorted from James I. by the fear lest his son should be forcibly detained in Spain and that as soon as Charles should be back in London, his father would not be greatly interested in them.[5]

[1] *Ibid.*, 159, 232, 236, VI., 92 *seq.* Later on, Bristol was given back all the presents which the Prince had made to the Infanta, as well as thirty-six letters which he had written to her; the latter were all still unopened and unread. ZELLER, *Richelieu*, 269; RAUMER, *Briefe*, II., 340.

[2] GARDINER, V., 116 *seq.*, 178, 201; GOLL, 2, 5. According to KHEVENHÜLLER (May 29, 1624), Gondomar and others still tried to bring about the Spanish match. W. GOETZ, *Briefe und Akten*, II., 1, 540.

[3] August 8, 1623, GARDINER, V., 97–9. *Cf.* ZELLER, *Richelieu*, 270, note 2

[4] GARDINER, V., 124 *seq.*

[5] *Ibid.*, 125–128.

Williams was not mistaken in his surmise. On the Prince's return to London, the priests were indeed released from prison, but no further favour was granted.[1] However, even the mere, cessation from persecution had its effect. The Jesuits alone reckoned at 2,600 the number of those who returned to the ancient Church in the year 1623 alone.[2] On the other hand the embitterment of the Protestants also grew apace, as was shown by their brutality on the occasion of an appalling catastrophe. On October 26th, whilst a Jesuit was preaching on the third floor of the French Embassy, a beam of the floor gave way hurling the congregation of about three hundred below and carrying away in its fall the storey beneath as well. The Protestant populace saw in the catastrophe a judgment of God, for in the old Calendar October 26th corresponded to November 5th in the new, that is Gunpowder Plot day. When the injured and the dead were dug out of the ruins, insults were heaped on them, and dirt and stones thrown at them.[3] A Protestant writer of the time [4] remarked that it was to be feared that under pretext of rooting out Popery, extreme savagery would penetrate into the Church. However, a Jesuit's account of the occurrence lays these manifestations of inhumanity exclusively to the charge of the Puritans.[5] "Those who behaved in this way were not Englishmen; the latter are much too generous by nature; neither were they English Protestants—heresy has not turned them into savages—but Puritans; nor was there question of the whole country, or even of all London, but only a district of the city which the Puritans boast of as their peculiar den."

The hope of the Spanish dowry having thus vanished, the need of money forced the King to convene his Parliament once more. The speech from the throne [6] plainly betrayed James I.'s perplexity as he endeavoured to justify before the public the concessions made by him in the Spanish marriage

[1] *Ibid.*, 142. [2] FOLEY, I., 74.

[3] FOLEY, I., 76–7: *The Blackfriars Accident.*

[4] *Ibid.*, 89. [5] *Ibid.*

[6] February 19, 1624, in LINGARD, IX., 216; GARDINER, V., 183 *seq.*

treaty. He did not even shrink from actual falsehoods when he asserted that there were times when he contemplated applying the penal laws against Catholics less rigorously, but that he had never thought of dispensing from them or of mitigating them. The truth is that he had not only promised a milder application, but non-application. Not long afterwards Buckingham gave to Parliament such an account of the events and negotiations in Spain [1] that the envoys of the Spanish Court declared that if any one in Spain had spoken in such terms of the King of England, he would have risked his head. However, Parliament expressed itself satisfied with Buckingham's account, and turned its attention to the Catholics. The plan for a Spanish marriage and the success of the imperial arms in Germany combined to rouse the House of Lords. On April 3rd it demanded that the penal laws should be applied in their full rigour and that the King should give a promise that "upon no occasion of marriage or treaty or other request on that behalf from any foreign Prince would he slacken the execution of these laws." [2] A further request by both Houses [3] even aimed at increased stringency of the anti-Catholic laws. These demands produced their effect. James I. called God to witness that at no time had he promised any dispensation from the penal laws and that he would never agree to any clause in any treaty which would entail consideration or toleration for Catholics.[4] At the same time the Prince of Wales took an oath which was destined to create more than one difficulty for him, for he swore that should his future wife be a Catholic, he would only grant religious freedom to herself and her servants.[5]

Thus was an end put to every plan for an alleviation of the lot of Catholics. A royal proclamation fixed a date by which all missionaries must have left the country, under pain of death.

[1] February 24, 1624, LINGARD, IX., 217; GARDINER, V., 185, 188.

[2] GARDINER, V., 208 *seq.*

[3] April 23, 1624, LINGARD, IX., 217.

[4] *Ibid.*, 219, GARDINER, V., 222.

[5] April 5, 1624, GARDINER, V., 222.

Judges and magistrates were instructed to apply the anti-Catholic laws as before, the Lord Mayor was to arrest all persons who were seen to leave the Embassy chapels, and the Bishops and the Privy Council were consulted as to the best means of making Protestants of the children of Catholic parents.[1] With the help of certain members of the Lower House a list was drawn up of persons suspected of being adherents of the old religion with a view to proceeding against them. The plan failed, however, owing to certain juridical objections by the Upper House.[2]

The sharp persecution which now began was all the more painful for Catholics, as they had enjoyed comparative tranquillity since the beginning of the preceding year. True, the death penalty was not applied but, as we read in the annual reports of the Jesuits for the year 1624,[3] " it is hardly possible to imagine how many Catholics will be driven into exile by the recrudescence of the persecution and it is impossible to calculate the numerous and heavy losses that are bound to ensue. No more terrible storm has befallen Catholics within the last thirty years. For the present it rages only in some of the counties around London, but within a few months it will have become general. For the time being Catholics are in great fear for their possessions ; however, whilst a few of them prefer property and freedom to their faith, the majority give proof of unshakable constancy, notwithstanding the prospect of spoliation, imprisonment and chains."

As soon as the heir to the throne had reassured the Protestants with regard to the mere possibility of a Catholic Queen, a fresh matrimonial plan was devised for him. During the Prince's stay in Spain, Buckingham was visited by an English Friar who spoke to him of his influence with Marie de Medici and expressed the opinion that she would probably

[1] LINGARD, IX., 219. About this time Urban VIII. encouraged the Carmelites who wished to settle in England, and admonished them to endure all things for the sake of the Faith. *Briefs of April 27 and May 11, 1624, *Epist.*, I., Papal Secret Archives.

[2] LINGARD, IX., 220.

[3] FOLEY, VII., 2, 1100 *seq.*

be willing to give her youngest daughter, Henrietta Maria,[1] in marriage to the heir to the English throne. In Paris the Friar saw the Queen-Mother who agreed to his proposal and sent him on to London with a message for Buckingham. James I. was ready to take up the plan, the Spanish marriage project having failed.[2] On March 15th Buckingham threw out a hint to Parliament but though the suggestion was ill-received, it called forth no open expression of disapproval.[3]

On February 15th, 1624, that clever courtier, Henry Roche, Viscount Kensington and future Earl Holland, came to Paris as James's envoy for the purpose of sounding the Court.[4] He found both Louis XIII. and Marie de Medici favourably disposed towards the marriage; they hoped that better conditions for English Catholics would be the result; closer relations between France and England were also desirable because both Powers were opposed to Spain—England in consequence of the question of the Palatinate and France by reason of the dispute over the Valtellina. An alliance with powerful France against Spain could not fail to appear desirable even in the eyes of English Protestants, in fact, it was calculated to reconcile them, to some extent, to the idea of a Catholic Queen. Notwithstanding the destruction of the Armada, an almost superstitious fear of the uncanny Catholic Southern Power still dominated English Protestants, and this fear became intensified by the circumstance that just then the Catholic Powers enjoyed an obvious preponderance over the Protestant ones. In the opinion of James I., so an English

[1] J. A. TAYLOR, *The Life of Queen Henrietta Maria*, London, 1905; I. M. STONE, in *The Dublin Review*, 3rd Series, XXI. (1889), 321–341; *Henrietta Maria, Queen of England, her Letters*, ed. by Mary A. Everett Green, London, 1857; ERMANNO FERRERO, *Lettres de Henriette Marie à sa sœur* (*Christine of Savoy*), Turin, 1881. The Papal Legate Con, on August 15 (25), 1636, on Henrietta's strict moral conduct and piety, in GARDINER, VIII., 237. J. GOLL, *Die französische Heirat, Frankreich und England, 1624* und *1625*, Prag, 1876.

[2] GARDINER, V., 175. The French ambassador in London, Tillières in GOLL, 80.

[3] GARDINER, V., 199.

[4] *Ibid.*, 215 *seqq.*

statesman of the period wrote,[1] all the Protestant Powers together could not withstand Spain. A reinforcement precisely through Catholic France could not but seem doubly desirable, for if none but Protestants allied themselves against Spain, an impression would be created, so the King of England thought, that the war was one of religion, a circumstance which would virtually compel all Catholics to side with Spain. The anxiety of the Protestants just then was clearly betrayed by the fact that when the adventurer Mansfeld came to London to beg James I.'s help for the Palatinate, he could not show himself in the street without being mobbed by a populace eager to kiss the hem of the garments of the champion of Protestantism.[2]

On May 17th, 1624, James Hay, Earl of Carlisle, who was commissioned to negotiate the marriage treaty, left London for Paris where the Court gave him a cordial reception.[3] True, a hitch occurred at the very start when the Protestant envoys refused to give to Richelieu the precedence which the latter claimed as a Cardinal. However, Richelieu knew a way out: he pretended sickness and in consequence conferred with the envoys from his bed. It was less easy to settle the religious part of the marriage treaty. The King of England had instructed Carlisle and Kensington not to yield on this point; it was better for the English Catholics themselves, he claimed, that they should remain completely in his own hands, for if they were granted their freedom they would become presumptuous and he would be compelled to proceed against them with even greater severity.[4] In accordance with these directions, the English envoys laid stress on the circumstance that in the previous negotiations for the marriage of the Prince with the elder sister of Henrietta Maria, freedom of religion

[1] NETHERSOLE, *ibid.*, 246. "Protestantism," GARDINER, judges (*ibid.*), "could only defend itself by ceasing to be aggressive, and by appealing to the political sympathies of Catholic States." For the political significance of the French marriage see also OPEL, II., 197–201.

[2] GARDINER, V., 222 *seq.*

[3] *Ibid.*, 248 *seqq.*

[4] *Ibid.*, 250.

had only been insisted upon for the person of the Princess and her servants. To this Richelieu replied that the Spanish Princess had been given a guarantee that no Catholic would be molested because of his religion. The Cardinal was told that no one was being persecuted in England for being a Catholic, but if a man went to Mass he incurred the penalty inflicted for such an act solely because he disobeyed the law. Sophisms of this kind were bound to render the French even more cautious. In the end they declared they would be content if James gave a secret promise that Catholics would not be molested on the ground of religion, but they insisted on the concession being made in writing.[1] To this the King would not consent, and the Prince even less so, hence the negotiations seemed doomed to failure. Accordingly, towards the end of June, James I. issued fresh orders for the application of the penal laws, whilst at the same time he looked for a bride for his son at the Protestant Courts of Germany. The Elector, John George of Saxony, a fervent Lutheran, told him that he would not marry his daughter to a Calvinist.[2]

In Paris, on the other hand, an attempt was made to reopen negotiations. Already in June the French Minister, La Vieuville, had dropped the ambiguous remark that some concession should be made which would satisfy the Pope. Carlisle interpreted this as meaning that the French made their big demands only for appearance' sake, that is, out of consideration for the Catholic party and in order to obtain more easily from Rome the necessary dispensation for the marriage, whilst with regard to the execution of the promise, the King might do

[1] GARDINER, V., 250 *seq.* The French perpetually abated their demands. Religious tolerance for Catholics was to be attained first by open treaty, then by secret articles, then by a written promise of the King, and finally by " écrit particulier ". Further details in GOLL. 24, 26, 34, 38. *Ibid.*, 10 *seqq*, 46 *seqq.* for other particulars, as for example the concession of a public church, the position of the French ambassador Tillières, that of Buckingham, Conway, etc.

[2] Cardinal Barberini to the French nuncio Spada, October 2, 1624, in BELLESHEIM, *Scotland*, III., 488.

as he pleased.[1] In other words, both religion and the Princess were to be betrayed, but the proposal emanated neither from Louis XIII. nor from Richelieu. La Vieuville took yet a further step. On his advice Kensington returned to London to represent to James I. the necessity of making at least a written promise in favour of English Catholics, even if he was unwilling to sign a formal treaty. The new French ambassador in London, the adroit Antoine de Ruzé, Marquis of Effiat, supported the plan. He had found his way to the heart of the King by patiently listening to his endless hunting stories, and what was more, he also won over Buckingham. James I. agreed to the proposal.[2]

However Effiat's efforts in London proved in vain. Vieuville's offer to forgo a formal guarantee on the part of James had been made without the consent of his Sovereign. When Louis XIII. heard of the arbitrary conduct of his minister he dismissed him. Richelieu stepped into his place and insisted, as a matter of course, that the matter should be settled in due form.[3] However, James I. and his son insisted on Effiat's concession. Thereupon Richelieu proposed a middle course. He was prepared to forgo a formal treaty clause though he would not be satisfied with a simple promise in writing; on the contrary he demanded a formal and binding document signed by King James, the heir to the throne and one of the Secretaries of State; the promise of freedom for Catholics to practise their religion within the four walls of their houses was to be given on the faith and word of a king, on his word and oath given on the Holy Gospels.[4]

This proposal roused Carlisle's indignation, but his colleague, Kensington, entered into secret communication with Richelieu, who won him over by his affability, assured him of his friendship, and threw the blame for his exigency upon the Pope. At the same time the French Government made a show of going to the assistance of Mansfeld. The effect of these shrewd measures was soon felt in London. Buckingham was anxious to bring off the marriage in order to secure France's help, and

[1] GARDINER, V., 252.
[2] *Ibid.*, 253 *seq.*
[3] *Cf.* ZELLER, *Richelieu*, 263 *seq.*
[4] GARDINER, V., 258 *seq.*

through Buckingham the Prince was also won over: thus James stood alone; soon he too ended by giving way.[1] The King imagined that everything was now settled: Kensington was created Earl Holland and the Privy Council consented to a suspension of the laws against the recusants. However, in view of the difficulty of justifying such concessions before Parliament, the King prorogued the House until February 26th, 1625.[2]

James' satisfaction was premature. His representatives in Paris were informed that a mere letter of their King was inadequate, even though it was signed by his heir and a Secretary of State; that there could be no question of an offensive league with Protestants against Catholics because such action would offend the Pope and render a marriage dispensation unobtainable. This angered the English envoys in Paris and Carlisle advised his Sovereign to speak "in strong terms" to Effiat.[3] But James was unwilling to forgo the prospect of a league and the restoration of the Palatinate; consequently Carlisle and Kensington were instructed to bow to the French demands even though they were denied a written promise of help for Mansfeld. On November 10th [20th] they signed the marriage treaty; all that was now wanting was James' signature and the papal dispensation.[4] Louis XIII. dispatched his secretary, Ville-aux-Clercs, Count of Brienne, to London for the purpose of receiving James' oath as to the concessions to Catholics. On December 12th [22nd] the marriage treaty was signed by James I. and the Prince.[5] The conditions of the treaty were formulated in thirty articles. In regard to religion it was stipulated that the Queen, her children, and her household were to have full liberty to practise their religion; she was to have a chapel in all the royal palaces, and her suite was to include one Bishop and twenty-eight ecclesiastics. Her children were to remain under her care until their thirteenth year, and the King would not attempt

[1] *Ibid.*, 259–262.

[2] *Ibid.*, 263.

[3] *Ibid.*, 267 *seq.*

[4] *Ibid.*, 270.

[5] *Ibid.*, 276, 277.

to seduce her from her faith.[1] In a secret article the Prince, in accordance with his father's promise, on the faith and word of a Prince, both for the present and the time to come, in everything that lay in his power and in view of his wife, guaranteed to all the Catholic subjects of the British Crown the full religious liberty which the marriage treaty assured to them. They were not to be molested for their profession of the Catholic religion, neither in their persons nor in their property so long as they remained obedient and loyal subjects; he also promised that no oath contrary to these conditions would be required of them. The document was signed by Charles and the Secretary of State Conway.[2]

Charles had given his royal word. Whether he ever intended to keep his royal word may be questioned. He subsequently explained that he had only signed the engagement because the King of France wished him to do so in order to deceive the Pope.[3]

Urban VIII. had warned the King of France from the first against the English marriage.[4] However, Louis XIII. held to his plan and dispatched the Founder and Superior of the French Oratory, Pierre Bérulle and De Béthune to Rome for the purpose of obtaining the marriage dispensation.[5] By that time Urban VIII. had resigned himself to what was virtually unavoidable. In April, 1624, he wrote to the King of England and likewise reminded the heir to the throne of his promise not to take any hostile measure against the Catholic religion.[6]

[1] *Art.* 6–9 and 16; see DUMONT, V., 2, 477; LINGARD, IX., 229; BELLESHEIM, *Scotland*, III., 431.

[2] GARDINER, V., 277 *seq.* According to Brienne and Effiat, (letter of December 22, 1624, in GOLL, 90) James promised, "qu'il ne persécutera jamais ses sujets cath. Rom. ni désirera d'eux aucun serment qui parlât ni du Pape ni du spirituel, ainsi seulement un acte de reconnaissance de la domination temporelle."

[3] GARDINER, V., 278.

[4] LINGARD, IX., 229; OPEL, II., 49.

[5] Instruction for Bérulle, July 31, 1624, in BELLESHEIM, *Scotland*, III., 429. It was drawn up by Brienne; see GOLL, 92.

[6] *Briefs of April 13, 1624, *Epist.*, II., 398, Papal Secret Archives.

In the negotiations which now ensued in Rome, the Pope insisted especially on the Catholics not being compelled to take either the oath of supremacy or that of allegiance; at most they were to take an oath which would meet with the approval of the Roman Congregation. He also strongly insisted on the Queen's chapel being a public one and open to all Catholics. Bérulle's suggestion, that only those should be admitted whom the Queen should invite, he declared to be inadequate, for in that case the lower classes would be excluded and other drawbacks would ensue. Bérulle replied that such demands could not be realized, but the Pope met him with the Prince's Spanish marriage treaty in which all these things were conceded, nor would he accept Bérulle's explanation that at that time the Prince was almost a prisoner of the Spaniards, so that it was anxiety to escape from the snares set for him that caused him to promise things which he had no intention of carrying out. On the present occasion, Urban VIII. replied, France guaranteed that he made no such reservations.[1]

On November 21st (December 1st) the commission of Cardinals presided over by Cardinal Barberini, pronounced in favour of the dispensation and on November 24th the Pope spoke cheerfully of his hopes for the future of English Catholics.[2] However, the demands of Urban VIII. went far beyond what had been conceded in London and Paris. The Pope insisted in particular on the religious liberty of Catholics being guaranteed by a public document. These demands so annoyed the English that for a time everything was put in jeopardy. The King made a show of getting once more in touch with Spain when Richelieu announced that the marriage would be celebrated with a dispensation of the French Bishops only. To this James I. would not agree for fear lest the validity of

[1] Cardinal Barberini to the nuncio Spada in Paris, October 2, 1624, in BELLESHEIM, III., 488 *seqq.* On November 19, 1624, a *Brief to Louis XIII. announces the decision that a Bishop must be in the retinue of the future Queen of England. *Epist.*, II. *loc. cit.*

[2] *Briefs to Louis XIII. and "Ioanni Colletono decano cleri Anglicani", *Epist.*, II., 96, 98, *loc. cit.*

the marriage should be questioned at some future time.[1] In the end Urban VIII. had to be satisfied with a sworn promise by Louis XIII. that he and his successors would do everything in their power to hold James and his son to the execution of the marriage treaty.[2] Thereupon the French nuncio, Spada, was authorized to hand over the dispensation. However, the aged King did not live to see the actual wedding; James I. died on March 27th, 1625.

The wedding was accordingly put off until May 1st. Charles had been eager to repair in person to Paris, but he was given to understand that his presence was not desired.[3] In order not to shock either Catholics or Protestants, it was decided that Charles should be represented by a proxy, that the ceremony should be performed in front of the porch of Notre Dame by a Catholic Bishop, and that there should be no religious ceremony after the bride's arrival in England. The Duke de Chevreuse acted as the King's proxy at the ceremony in front of Notre Dame, and Buckingham came over to fetch the Princess to England, where she arrived on June 12th.[4] The clergy in the Queen's suite consisted of the Bishop of

[1] LINGARD, IX., 231; GARDINER, V., 307; GOLL, 58 *seq.* The text of the dispensation is in ROSKOVÁNY, *De matrimoniis mixtis*, I., 21; KUNSTMANN, 204. How keenly the French minister desired the marriage is shown by a remark of Jocher to the Capuchin Hyacinth, February 25, 1625 (GOETZ, *Briefe und Akten*, II., 2, 61), namely, that Richelieu was ready to grant to the rebellious Huguenots anything, even if it were to the detriment of the catholic religion, so long as he secured the marriage and the attack on Spain.

[2] *Lettres patentes* of March 21, 1625, in GOLL, 92. "Nous promettons à Sa Sainteté . . . et jurons sur les S. Évangiles . . . que de tout nostre pouvoir et en tant qu'il nous est et sera, le contenu ésd. articles . . . sera gardé et accomply, tant ce qui nous concerne ensemble nostred. très chère sœur, comme en ce qui depend du pouvoir dud. Roy de la grande Bretagne et Prince de Galles." As early as April 11, 1625, Urban VIII. had *written to Louis XIII. that he would favour his wishes as far as possible. *Epist.*, II., *loc. cit.*

[3] GARDINER, V., 306.

[4] GARDINER, V., 326.

Mende and several French Oratorians under their founder Bérulle. The Oratorian Robert Philippe acted as confessor to the Queen until his death.[1]

On December 24th of the preceding year the courts had been forbidden further to prosecute Catholics under the penal laws. On the 26th an order was issued to set at liberty all Catholics imprisoned for religion. At the same time all proceedings pending in the ecclesiastical courts against those who professed the old religion were stopped and the Lord Treasurer was commanded to refund all fines ; for the future such fines were indeed to be raised, to save appearances, but the money was to be restored at once to those who had paid it.[2] On the day of the wedding the Keeper of the Seals was instructed by the King to put an end to the persecution of the Catholics. Three thousand letters to the judges to this effect were ready to be sent out, but their dispatch was put off until the end of the parliamentary session.[3] On hearing of these measures Urban VIII. felt that he might exhort Charles to return himself to the Catholic Church.[4]

On June 18th, 1625, Parliament met, breathing Protestant and Puritanical hatred against Catholics. On the very day of the opening the Speaker expressed the House's hope that the King would " execute the laws against the wicked generation of Jesuits, seminary priests and incendiaries ever lying in wait to blow the coals of confusion ".[5] The Commons began by keeping a day of penance and intercession and imposing a similar observance on the whole country ; they listened to four sermons on one day and received Communion the day after.[6] On June 22nd a motion was introduced concerning the execution of the laws against priests and Jesuits ; after some discussion it was referred to a committee of the whole

[1] On him, see BATTEREL, I., 222–232.

[2] GARDINER, V., 278. By March, 1625, 17,710 pounds had been paid back ; see GOLL, 50.

[3] GARDINER, V., 326, 329.

[4] *Brief of August 21, 1625, *Epist.*, II., 342*b*, Papal Secret Archives.

[5] GARDINER, V., 339.

[6] LINGARD, IX., 242.

House.[1] On the following day Eliot made a speech on the need of religion, which he called the " tie of all friendship and society ", and on its purity and unity. The loss of unity, he said, constituted a constant danger for the State, hence the necessary laws should be amended or at least seriously carried out. As a result of the debate which now ensued, a petition was drawn up in which the King was requested " to execute the penal laws in all their strictness and to take other measures to prevent the spread of the doctrine of the Roman Catholic Church ".[2]

Charles I. had previously assured Parliament that his French marriage would not benefit English Catholics, though in the marriage treaty he had solemnly promised the opposite. To which of the two parties should he now prove false ? Considerations of expediency proved decisive. From his marriage he had hoped for an alliance against Spain, which, however, did not materialize, whilst large grants of money could only be obtained from Parliament on condition that he proceeded against the Catholics. Domestic difficulties with his vivacious, less than sixteen years old wife, did not dispose him favourably towards France. Shortly after the opening of Parliament, Charles begged the French envoys not to take it in bad part if he held out hopes to his Protestant subjects of the execution of the penal laws, and to shut their eyes if one or two Jesuits were condemned, for the sentences would not be carried out. After that Catholics were the object of yet one more favour. James I. had allowed foreign ambassadors, on their departure from England, to take imprisoned priests with them. Accordingly, when the French envoys left, Charles I. allowed seventeen captive priests to accompany them.[3] The very day after the grant of this concession, on July 11th, he adjourned Parliament until August 1st when it was to meet at Oxford; there he would explain his attitude in regard to the penal laws, meanwhile their actual execution would be his answer.[4] Curiously enough the pardon granted to a Jesuit bore the date of July 12th, the very day after this announcement.[5]

[1] GARDINER, V., 342. [2] *Ibid.*, 342–4.
[3] *Ibid.*, 375–7. [4] *Ibid.*, 373. [5] *Ibid.*, 397.

It was natural that conduct so contradictory should call for comment when Parliament met at Oxford on August 1st. When the pardon of the Jesuit came up for discussion, none ventured to speak at first, out of regard for the King, but at length John Eliot, the outstanding orator of the House, rose to speak. He could not believe, he said, that the pardon proceeded from the King, hence they must try to discover who was the person responsible. The Attorney General sought to prevent an inquiry, but his excuses met with sharp opposition which was only quieted when the House resolved to present a petition to the King.[1] On August 7th the Court deliberated with a view to finding a way out of existing difficulties. Starting from some remarks which had been dropped in the course of private conversations during the negotiations in Paris, it was decided to advance the pretension that neither side had taken the promises of the marriage treaty seriously, but that their only object had been to deceive the Pope.[2] For the first time Charles I. dared to say so openly, though he had ratified the contract two months after the wedding, at a time when there was no longer any need to deceive the Pope.[3] On August 8th Buckingham informed the House of Commons that all its demands touching religion had been granted; if they were keen on the execution of the recusancy laws, their wishes would be complied with.[4] Both the Queen's almoner, the Bishop of Mende, and Bérulle, remonstrated in vain with Buckingham who sought to reassure them with a promise that the laws against Catholics would be mildly applied and that the seeming strictness was necessary in order to satisfy the populace.[5]

Accordingly, orders were issued for a strict execution of the

[1] GARDINER, V., 397–9. [2] *Ibid.*, 417.

[3] LINGARD IX., 266, note. GARDINER also says (V., 418): "For impartial judges it is enough to condemn so monstrous a proposition, that it was now heard of for the first time, and that Charles had already acknowledged by his actions, when his wife was on her way to England, that he considered his engagement to her brother as a reality."

[4] GARDINER, V., 419. [5] *Ibid.*, 422.

laws against Catholics ; a commission was set up to collect the fines which were to go towards defraying the expenses of the war ; parents and guardians were commanded to withdraw their sons or wards from seminaries over-seas ; all priests were to leave the country by a certain date, the recusants were to surrender their arms and not to go beyond a radius of five miles from their domicile. The ecclesiastical courts were likewise instructed to proceed against Catholics.[1] When the King of France protested, Charles I. excused himself with the plea that the marriage treaty had not been seriously meant ; that it had only been a ruse to deceive the Pope.[2] Thereafter it became the practice of the English Court, on this very ground, to consider the promises as non-existent.[3] The next Parliament, which met on January 6th, 1626, four days after the King's coronation, expressed the view that the calamities which of late had befallen the country, must be ascribed to the growth of Popery, hence it desired a further increase of rigour in the laws against Catholics. Accordingly schoolmasters were summoned from the most distant parts of the country to give an account of the sentiments of their pupils and every member of Parliament was called upon to denounce all persons in authority or office who were either personally suspect of leaning towards the old religion, or whose wives and children were thus disposed.[4]

The persecution which now broke out was all the harsher as the negotiations with the Catholic Powers had added fuel to popular hatred of Catholicism, whilst the priest-hunters were anxious to make up for their prolonged inactivity during the preceding year of peace. The prohibition for Catholics to be in possession of arms supplied the latter with a pretext

[1] LINGARD IX., 247. On August 14, 1625, the Privy Council confirmed the proclamation banishing the priests (GARDINER, VI., 3), on October 5 the order for the disarming of recusants followed, on November 3 the commission for the enactment of the penal laws was set up, on November 7 the order on minors and schoolmasters was signed (*ibid.*, 32 *seq.*).

[2] GARDINER, VI., 32.

[3] *Ibid.*, V., 418.

[4] LINGARD, IX., 297.

for searching and plundering every Catholic house; under this plea they were able to upset everything and not even persons belonging to the highest nobility were exempt from domiciliary searches.[1] No capital executions were carried out but in the opinion of a Jesuit report,[2] even the days of Elizabeth were milder, for in that reign only a few were executed and their death procured for the rest both protection and honour. At the present time they envy us so glorious a triumph, hence they reduce us to extremity by robbing us of our property; thus we suffer the greatest hardships but these do not call forth the sympathy of men. James' oath of fidelity was likewise demanded. Consequently Urban VIII. dispatched three Briefs addressed respectively to Louis XIII., to the Vicar General Smith, and to the English Catholics;[3] the latter he implored rather to die than to take the oath. In the following year a check was temporarily put on the activities of the priest hunters,[4] but in 1628 a Jesuit and a layman were executed at Lancaster in pursuance of the penal laws, though probably without the King's knowledge.[5]

At this time an incident occurred which once again drew public attention to the Catholics. Crowds of London Catholics were in the habit of flocking to the chapel of the French ambassador. On February 26th, 1626, the King ordered the arrest of every English subject who came out of the chapel. However, the ambassador's servants would not look on in silence; in the scuffle which ensued two men were wounded. The populace threatened to intervene, but the Bishop of Durham succeeded in restoring order. The ambassador was naturally indignant at this infringement of the law of nations, as he expressed himself.[6] If Charles I.'s measure against those who attended the French Embassy chapel was prompted by a desire to prove himself a good Protestant, the same motive

[1] Yearly report of the Jesuits for 1625, in FOLEY, VII., 2, 1115.

[2] For 1626, *ibid.*, 1123.

[3] *May 30, 1626.

[4] LINGARD, IX., 265; GARDINER, VIII., 130.

[5] FOLEY, II., 24 *seq.*; SPILLMANN, IV., 212 *seqq.*

[6] GARDINER, V., 142 *seq.*

may well have inspired his exploitation of another incident in 1628. An isolated house belonging to the Earl of Shrewsbury served the Jesuits as a retreat where they gathered from time to time in order to strengthen themselves, in silence and solitude, in the spirit of their holy vocation. The dispatch thither of an unusual quantity of food excited curiosity, and ten Jesuits fell into the hands of the pursuivants at a single stroke. Nothing of a compromising nature was found among their papers, accordingly a letter was forged in order to give substance to an alleged Jesuit conspiracy, the object of which it was alleged, was to sow discord between Parliament and Buckingham. An attempt was made to frighten Parliament with the revelation that only a mile away the Jesuits were hatching a conspiracy. However, the Commons attached but little weight to this information,[1] but the incident had a sequel in the following year. A complaint was made in Parliament that only one of the ten Jesuit prisoners had been condemned and that he had received a pardon, whilst the nine others had been released on bail by order of the King. In the eyes of Parliament this was a grave crime against Protestantism. However, the various speakers all laid the blame not on the King but on his officials, and the matter was allowed to drop.[2]

The persecution of the Catholics naturally weighed heavily on the heart of the youthful Queen. She had consented to marry a Protestant in the hope of thereby procuring for her co-religionists freedom to practise their religion: now she saw that all the agreements to that effect were treated as non-existent. The circumstance was hardly calculated to increase the concord between the royal couple, which was none too great. The King, for his part, ascribed the painful situation to Henrietta Maria's French entourage. Accordingly he committed yet another violation of the marriage treaty by sending back to France, in the summer of 1626, the sixty

[1] GARDINER, VI., 238.

[2] *Ibid.*, VII., 57. The sources for the "Clerkenwell Discovery" have been collected by JOHN GOUGH NICHOLLS in *Camden Miscellany*, II. (1852/3). *Cf.* FOLEY, I., 98–141. The faked letter, *ibid.*, 116–121.

servants of the Queen, on the plea that their maintenance was too costly.[1] In a letter to her mother's confessor, the Jesuit Suffren, Henrietta Maria described herself as the unhappiest of women.[2] She complained of being left alone among barbarians; but though they sought to do violence to her conscience, all their efforts would only make her a keener Catholic. Urban VIII. complained of the breach of the marriage treaty to Louis XIII., to Richelieu, to the Spanish ambassador in London, and to the King of Spain. He also sent a letter of comfort to the Queen.[3] Louis dispatched the skilful Bassompierre to London on a special mission. By his wise counsels he successfully reconciled the royal couple, so that at a later date, after Buckingham's assassination, a really tender attachment sprang up between them.[4] Instead of the twenty-eight ecclesiastics who had previously formed part of her Court, the Queen now contented herself with three English chaplains. Six ladies, two of them Protestants, constituted her immediate entourage.[5]

However, Louis XIII. was not satisfied with Bassompierre's settlement of the situation and insisted on the full execution of the marriage treaty. In England the demand was resented as an insult: Buckingham informed Richelieu that the King now considered himself as freed from all the obligations of the

[1] LINGARD, IX., 262 *seqq.*; GARDINER, VI., 3 *seq.*, 38, 56 *seqq.* 134 *seqq.*, 141. For a few complaints against the household, *ibid.*, 135. According to RANKE (*Engl. Gesch.*, II[4], Leipzig, 1877), the Queen was persuaded on one occasion to take part in a procession to Tyburn, the place of execution of the English Martyrs *Cf.* on this LINGARD, IX., 265, note. On the way in which the agreement on the education of the royal children was broken, see GARDINER, VII., 142; *cf. ibid.*, VIII., 137 *seq.*, 140.

[2] September 23, 1626, in FOUQUERAY, V., 51 *seq.* On the poverty of the Queen's household and the King's extravagance, *cf.* the reports of the Venetian ambassadors Giovanni Soranzo, June 21, 1630, and Angelo Correr, August 16, 1635, in BROSCH, *Cromwell*, 118, 130.

[3] September 21, 1626, *Epist.*, II., 325, Papal Secret Archives.

[4] GARDINER, VI., 141 *seq.*, 145, 367; VII., 106.

[5] LINGARD, IX., 264.

marriage treaty.[1] In the sequel war broke out between the two Powers. When in April, 1629, peace was signed between England and France, the treaty was silent on the question of religion.[2] The King nevertheless allowed his Queen to send to France for some Capuchins for the service of her chapel: the priest who had acted as her confessor up till that time as well as an Oratorian were also permitted to remain.[3]

(3)

At the urgent request of the English Catholics and notwithstanding some misgivings, Gregory XV. had appointed a Bishop for England in the person of William Bishop.[4] The extent to which the hopes set on Bishop's appointment were to be fulfilled was to become evident during the pontificate of Urban VIII. From the French nuncio Corsini, Bishop received an Instruction [5] in which the former sums up briefly the dangers of the situation; he exhorts the new Bishop to ascertain the dispositions of the King, for much depended on his good or ill will; above all he should promote concord and charity among the faithful as well as obedience to the civil power; such an attitude became Catholics who were wont to refer all things to the invisible Head of the Church, that is, Christ, and to His representative on earth. In the performance of his office Bishop should do all in his power to compose the disputes between the secular and the regular clergy, an object easily attained if the Bishop respected the privileges of the regulars, especially those of the Jesuits.

[1] GARDINER, VI., 152.

[2] *Ibid.*, VII., 100.

[3] *Ibid.*, 106. *Cf.* CYPRIEN DE GAMACHES, *Mémoires de la mission des Capucins de la province de Paris près la reine d'Angleterre depuis l'année, 1630–1669*, publiés p. Apollinaire de Valence, Paris, 1882; O. KAMSHOFF in *Wissenschaftl.* Beilage to *Germania*, of August 25 and September 1, 1910, nos. 24 and 35, pp. 261–4, 273–5.

[4] *Cf.* Vol. XXVII., p. 157.

[5] Dated July 15, 1623, in BELLESHEIM, *Cath. Church in Scotland* (Engl. trs.), III., p. 435 *seqq.*

Bishop interpreted these exhortations in his own way[1]: his conduct seems to have been inspired by the principle that in order to restore peace it was enough to drive the Jesuits out of England and out of the English Colleges in Rome and Spain. In other respects also he proceeded without the necessary caution. Though he had received episcopal consecration for a missionary country, he imagined that he could do all that lay within the sphere of Bishops living amid the ordered conditions of the Continent; accordingly he erected Chapters and divided England into archdeaconries and rural deaneries—measures that caused a sensation and roused the King, Parliament, and the Protestant Bishops against him. Rome examined these measures. The Instruction for the French nuncio Spada shows clearly that these proceedings, as well as Bishop's attitude towards the religious, especially towards the Jesuits, met with scant approval in Rome.[2] Another difficulty arose for Bishop from the circumstance that the Scottish Catholics protested to Urban VIII. against their being subjected to an Englishman. There was no great need of a Bishop in their country, they maintained, since the Scottish priests received ordination in the continental seminaries; it was no doubt a loss to be deprived of Confirmation, but there were weighty reasons for submitting to this disadvantage. Urban VIII. listened to these representations: Scotland retained its independence. Even in England Bishop's rule was of short duration. After fleeing from one hiding place to another he died on April 16th, 1624. He was succeeded by Richard Smith who was also given authority over Scotland.[3] Smith[4] was a convert and had been educated at the English College in Rome. For a while he taught at the English Colleges of Valladolid and Seville; he then spent some time at Paris where he engaged in controversy and entered into friendly relations with the future Cardinal Richelieu. However, in his

[1] CORDARA, I., 435; FOUQUERAY, V., 53 *seq.*; BELLESHEIM, *Scotland*, III., 436; GILLOW, I., 218; REUSCH., II, 385 *seqq.*

[2] Instruction of January 23, 1624, in LEMAN, 47.

[3] BELLESHEIM, IV., 39.

[4] *Cf.* about him, *National Biography*, LIII., 102 *seq.*

relations between the secular and regular clergy, he adopted the views which, as a sequel to Richer's theories, were held at that time by many Bishops and priests in France, views that encroached even on the prerogatives of the Holy See in so far as they refused to recognize the privileges granted to the Orders by the Popes.[1] Although he was only granted the title of Bishop of Chalcedon, at the beginning of January, 1625, and that of Vicar-Apostolic so far as England was concerned, Smith considered himself as invested with all the rights enjoyed by Bishops on the Continent. Accordingly he set up an ecclesiastical tribunal whose duty it was to prove wills and testamentary dispositions, to watch over pious foundations, baptisms, marriages and even to inspect private houses. For his own support and that of his clergy he imposed a tax on the laity; above all he caused extreme confusion when he declared those confessions to be null which were made to priests other than those approved by himself.[2] These imprudences annoyed the Pope; through the Paris nuncio and the Queen's confessor he caused a decree of the Inquisition[3] to be sent to the Vicar Apostolic to the effect that Smith was not the Ordinary of England, but of Chalcedon in Asia, and that in the Island Kingdom of the North he only enjoyed the restricted faculties which the Pope delegated to him as his representative: priests who held faculties to hear confessions from the Pope himself were not in need of further approval by the Vicar Apostolic.

This did not end the dispute. The Bishop of Chalcedon had written a letter to the Catholics of England and Scotland in which he stated his pretensions,[4] but in 1628 the English nobility, in a reasoned memorial, represented to him[5] that the setting up of a tribunal such as the one erected by him, was treason in English law, hence any one who had recourse to it

[1] On this FOUQUERAY, V., 38 *seqq.*

[2] HUGHES, I., 202 *seq.* (based on the memorandum of Cardinal Albizzi).

[3] December 16, 1626, *ibid.*, 203. A *letter of condolence to Smith, February 21, 1626, in *Epist.*, III., Papal Secret Archives.

[4] CORDARA, II., 108. [5] HUGHES, I., 204–6.

became liable to the penalty of high treason. Thereupon some of the partisans of the Bishop of Chalcedon asserted that this document was a forgery of the Jesuits and when Lord Baltimore, who in all probability had drawn it up, lodged a protest, it was urged that at least the larger and sounder part of the nobility was on the side of the Vicar Apostolic, the authority of the French ambassador Fontenay being likewise quoted in support of that assertion. When questioned by Baltimore, Fontenay denied having made the utterance attributed to him.[1] Excitement grew steadily. A number of pamphlets appeared. Kellison's exposition of the rights of Bishops, published at Douai in 1629,[2] was followed by other learned works on the same subject.[3] The dispute attracted the attention of the Government. On December 11th, 1628, a writ was issued for the arrest of the Bishop of Chalcedon and on March 24th, 1629, a reward of a hundred pounds was put up for his capture.[4] The Vicar Apostolic wrote letter upon letter to Propaganda accusing the Jesuits,[5] and his partisans complained of the conduct of certain members of the nobility whilst the opposition urged that it was precisely the most deserving members of the Catholic body that were being calumniated in Rome and that it was wrong to say that a number of noblemen were adherents of the Bishop of Chalcedon.[6] In Rome the controversy was now taken out of the hands of Propaganda and entrusted to the Inquisition. None the less Bishop Smith, in a letter to Propaganda, expressed his hope that the Congregation would maintain two of its own decrees in his favour, those namely which ordered regulars, on their arrival in England, to show their faculties to him and the Jesuits to dissolve their Sodality of

[1] Baltimore to Lord Petre, August 8, 1631, *ibid.*, 209–211.

[2] BELLESHEIM, *Allen*, 223.

[3] Especially from the Jesuits Knott and Floyd.

[4] *Dictionary, loc. cit.*, 103.

[5] HUGHES, I., 214.

[6] *Ibid.*, 212. In 1630, the Cardinals and Consultors of Propaganda were asked " an attento statu et circumstantiis catholicae ecclesiae, quae est in Anglia, in eadem restitui debeant episcopi ". LÄMMER, *Analecta*, 37.

the Blessed Virgin. He gave as a reason for the enforcement of the latter decree the circumstance that in England priests depended upon the laity for their support, but through their sodalities the Jesuits attracted the bulk of the laity to themselves, that as a matter of fact this was the explanation of the ill-feeling against them and against regulars in general. As for his quarrel with the Catholic laity, the Bishop claimed that less than a third of the faithful and not one in a hundred among the nobility were opposed to him and that it was not true that he had set up a tribunal in opposition to the secular courts.[1] Propaganda replied that Cardinal Caetani would discuss the question of the Sodality with the General of the Jesuits and that the Inquisition had already given a decision on the question of the regulars.[2]

On May 9th, 1631, a decree was published quashing the controversy between the Bishop of Chalcedon and the regulars and the laity and reserving to the Holy See the settlement of all differences that might arise and declaring valid both in the past and in the future, confessions made to regulars.[3] When the decree was communicated to him through the French nuncio, the Bishop was so annoyed that he crossed over to France on the plea that after this his presence in England would be useless. He offered his resignation to Urban VIII.[4] who accepted it. The Pope desired the nuncio to demand a resignation in due form and to deny to Smith permission to return to England. The latter now regretted his step and begged to be allowed to return to his post. His request was refused and England remained without a Vicar Apostolic for a period of fifty-five years.[5]

[1] London, June 14, 1631, in HUGHES, I., 215–220.

[2] *Ibid.*, 220 *seq.*

[3] *Ibid.*, 221; *Ius pontif.*, I., 125 *seq.*; CORDARA, II., 108. In the **Brevia*. VIII., no. 141 *seq.* (Papal Secret Archives), there is a decree to the same effect dated April 3, 1631.

[4] HUGHES, I., 223 *seq.* The year of his flight to France is usually given as 1628 or 1629; however on June 14, 1631, he is still writing from London.

[5] HUGHES, I., 228. For suggestions for the nomination of a Vicar after Smith's death (1655), see BELLESHEIM, *Scotland*, IV.,

The papal decision did not put an end to the strife. The partisans of the Bishop described the Brief as surreptitious and rejected it accordingly, thereby adding to the general confusion. The spectacle of priests calmly brushing aside an unwelcome Brief, so a contemporary Benedictine wrote,[1] was a grave scandal for the laity. As for the latter, they declared that they had submitted to the papal decision about the oath of allegiance, though compliance was liable to result in the forfeiture of their property or in imprisonment, and despite the fact that many of them felt that the oath was not at variance with the faith. Unless the whole controversy was got rid of, it would be impossible to see how things would end. There were far more nobles against Smith than for him. It was of course most gratifying to have a Bishop in their midst, because of his power to bless and confirm, but when he laid claim to judicial and coercive power there could be no question of submission. The partisanships, inventions, artifices, hatreds and jealousies which had been called forth by the Bishop's claims, were beyond description; here there was matter for regret for years to come.

The papal Brief only dealt with Smith's relations with the Orders and left his dispute with the laity untouched, consequently the Catholic nobles presented a petition to the Pope in which they expressed the hope that, in view of prevailing circumstances, they would not be compelled to recognize Smith's authority as that of an ordinary Bishop. An overwhelming majority of the nobility, the petition stated, unanimously shared this hope; of twenty-six members of the highest nobility twelve had signed in person; five had signified their concurrence by word of mouth and allowed use to be

40 *seq.*; *Istruzione per Msgr. Ceva* (since March, 1632, nuncio extraordinary in Paris; see LEMAN, 192), "circa le cose del clero d'Inghilterra: how the English Church should be organized after the resignation of Bishop Smith (*cf.* LÄMMER, *Zur Kirchengesch.*, 131). Cardinal Barberini as Protector of England and Scotland was given special powers on May 18, 1630; see *Bull.*, XIV., 136 *seq.*

[1] November 2, 1631, to Propaganda, in HUGHES, I., 222 *seq.*

made of their names; two others favoured the Bishop, but not the exercise of episcopal authority in mixed questions; the remainder were in part undecided, others were absent or not yet of age; only one declared himself unconditionally in favour of Smith. The gentry produced about 300 signatures.[1]

These disputes provided a pretext for a renewal of violent attacks on the Jesuits in England.[2] The General directed his subjects not to reply to the numerous pamphlets written against them, for thereby they would only pour oil on the flames.[3] How opportune this admonition was, appeared when the Jesuits Knott and Floyd intervened not indeed in the pamphlet strife but in the learned controversy originated by Kellison.[4] Floyd was a highly gifted man and of Knott the papal emissary Con says that even in the opinion of his opponents he was one of the most learned and prudent men in England; moreover the tone of his writings was invariably temperate.[5] Nevertheless the books of the two Jesuits, which for the rest appeared without the knowledge of the General, enkindled a paper war in England and France which was to last for years.[6]

With a view to collecting information on the controversy round the person of the Bishop, Urban VIII. dispatched an envoy to England as soon as the improvement in the situation of the Catholics rendered it possible.

(4)

Though the accession of a Catholic Queen did not bring religious freedom to her co-religionists on the whole their situation under Charles I. was more favourable than in recent years. It is probable that the religious discussions in which Charles had engaged as Prince of Wales during his stay in Spain,

[1] Information for Rome and a protest, October, 1631, in Hughes, I., 224–6; a list of signatories, *ibid.*, 227.

[2] *Ibid.*, 226 *seqq.*

[3] *Ibid.*, 71.

[4] *Ibid.*, 59; Foley, IV., 237, VI., 185; Sommervogel, III., 814 *seqq.*

[5] Hughes, I., 71. *Cf.* Sommervogel, IV., 1134 *seq.*

[6] *Cf.* above p. 305.

had not been without making some impression on him. His views, as manifested in particular in his discussions with the papal envoy Con in 1636,[1] approximated closely to those of the Catholics.[2] He loved to speak of the blessings of confession and himself went to confession. He realized that according to Catholic teaching an Indulgence did not consist in the remission of sin but in that of the penalty due to sin, and he believed that the Church had power to grant such pardons, only according to him it was presumptuous on the Pope's part to claim it for himself alone. He likewise firmly believed in Saints and miracles and in the veneration of images and relics. When the Queen claimed for herself a relic of the true Cross which had been found in the Tower, Charles kept it for himself on the ground that he venerated it no less than she did. He observed the fasts and gave to the poor what remained from the royal table.[3] With regard to dogma he recognized the first four Councils and the first three Creeds and called himself a Catholic inasmuch as he counted himself among the vast body of the faithful. Union with Rome he did not deem necessary since one could save one's soul equally well in the English Church, though reunion was something which everyone should do his best to bring about. However, he made it a point of honour that, as a preliminary condition of reunion, Rome also should make some concessions, such as Communion under both kinds, the use of the vernacular in the liturgy, and above all, the Pope must not claim the right to depose Princes.[4]

These sentiments of the King easily account for the fact that during his reign only a few priests were executed for religion, nor is he to be held responsible for these few exceptions.[5] Whenever a tribunal passed a death sentence, Charles was wont to listen to his wife's prayer for mercy.[6] He also adopted greater leniency towards the lay recusants who refused to attend Anglican services. The law left it to the

[1] See below p. 319.

[2] See A. O. Meyer in *The American Hist. Review*, XIX. (1913–14), 13–26.

[3] *Ibid.*, 18.

[4] *Ibid.*, 15, 19.

[5] Spillmann, IV., 231–272.

[6] Examples, *ibid.*, 231, 243, 248, 301. *Cf.* Lingard, IX., 307.

Government to levy from them a fine of twenty pounds per lunar month or to confiscate two-thirds of their personal estate. The King now allowed the recusants, in place of these penalties, to compound for a fixed annual sum. The amount was determined at the pleasure of the commissioners ; sometimes it was a tenth, at other times a third of their annual income which was thus taken from them.[1] For the Government this leniency was most profitable. In 1619 the fines for absence from church amounted to £6,000, but in 1635 to as much as £35,000. The reason was that the mitigations of the law made it possible to fine a greater number, and individual Catholics found the burden less heavy because a smaller sum was demanded from them.[2]

The number of English Catholics had shrunk to 150,000 out of a population of three millions [3] but the old religion still possessed a great power of attraction. More than one nobleman who outwardly lived as a Protestant, secretly kept a priest so that he might at least die a Catholic.[4] Many Anglican divines abandoned the tenets of Calvinism and approximated

[1] LINGARD, IX., 308.

[2] GARDINER, VIII., 130. Paris was informed through the Abbé Du Perron, that English Catholics were freer than ever before, that the King spoke of Urban VIII. with esteem ; see *NICOLETTI, *Cod. Barb.*, 4734, p. 133, Vatican Library. " In alcuni si vedono lettere d'Inghilterra con aviso, che quel re non usava più tanto rigore contro li cattolici, de'quali in Londra si trovano più di 30m, et un altro buon numero di fuori, tolerandosi che potessero essercitarvi la religione catt., ma però occultamente, onde nelle case di diversi signori si celebrano le messe et altri divini officii " (note, dated February 12, 1628, Angelica Libr., c. 7, 27). Against this *ibid.*, News from Cologne, February 18, 1629 : " D'Inghilterra s'ha avviso, che quel Re faceva descrivere li beni di tutti li cattolici, che sono nel suo regno, con pensiero di volere da loro una nuova contributione."

[3] PANZANI, **Relatione*, part 2 (*cf.* below, p. 313, note 3). According to a report of 1632, RANKE, *Englische Gesch.*, VIII.[3] (*Werke*, XXI.), 129, the number of Catholics was larger than had been thought, " e forse erano li più e specialmente fra la nobilità, ma non apparivano."

[4] PANZANI, *loc. cit.*

to the teaching of the Catholic Church at least on some points. In 1624 Richard Montague, who became successively Bishop of Chichester and Norwich, caused a sensation which found an echo even in the debates of Parliament, by the publication of a book in which he rejected Calvin's teaching on predestination, declared that the Roman Church was not absolutely unchristian, expressed himself in favour of auricular confession and advocated the use of holy pictures in churches, at least by way of ornament.[1] William Laud, who became Archbishop of Canterbury in 1633 and consequently the first prelate in the realm, maintained the doctrine that the Church must of necessity be a visible body; accordingly he insisted on the greatest ceremonial and ritual uniformity within the Anglican Church, though he showed great laxity with regard to divergences of teaching. In his view the Church of England was a branch of the one Church of Christ which was divided into several such branches; although the Catholic Church was not in his opinion, *the true* Church, she was nevertheless *a* true Church.[2] Certain circles actually thought of a reunion of the Christian Churches and the King shared their sentiments. Laud relates that "someone" had seriously offered him a Cardinal's hat, but that he was unable to accept an offer of the kind "till Rome were other than it is".[3] After December, 1634, to the terror of the Protestants, London actually sheltered a papal envoy in the person of Gregorio Panzani,[4] a man who had confidential dealings with the Oratorians as well as many conversations with the Secretary of State Windebank, on the subject of the reunion of the Churches.

As a matter of fact Panzani was entrusted with no such negotiations, nor was he a properly accredited envoy. He was merely commissioned to study conditions and public opinion in London and to report to Rome on the advisability

[1] Gardiner, V., 352.

[2] Chesnay York in the *Encyclop. Brittanica*, XVI.[11], 276 *seq.* *Cf.* Gardiner, V., 356, VII., 301. [3] Lingard, IX., 312, note.

[4] According to *Nicoletti (*Cod. Barb.* 4766, Vatican Library), Panzani d'Arezzo was a secular priest who lived for a long time at the Oratory, Rome.

of giving England a Bishop.[1] This was Panzani's foremost purpose as well as the last. He knew no English and his French was inadequate ; his wordy reports are vague. Gifted with a vivid imagination but not with sound judgment, he was full of prejudices, especially against the Jesuits. Con, who succeeded him, frankly describes him as "a dangerous lunatic".[2] At the conclusion of his mission Panzani drew up a report on the situation in England.[3] In this document he

[1] HUGHES, I., 354. A *Brief of October, 1634, to the English Catholics which announced Panzani's arrival, in *Epist.*, XII., 127, Papal Secret Archives. **Minute di lettere e di cifre scritte da Greg. Panzani in Londra al card. Barberini ed altri* (from November 25, 1635, to May 21, 1636), Chigi Library, Rome, M.I., 23. Panzani left Rome on September 7, 1634 (**Lettere del Greg. Panzani al card. Barberini*, 1634–5, *Cod. Barb.* 8633, Vatican Library). A *letter of recommendation of February 12, 1635, for Panzani to the Queen, whom the Pope called the protectress of the Catholics, in *Epist.*, XII., 235, *loc. cit.* On September 26, 1635, the Pope *rejoices that the Queen had praised Panzani ; gladly had he granted her request by making Du Perron Bishop of Angoulême (*ibid.*, XIII.). Du Perron is praised in a *Brief of January 10, 1632, for setting out for England (*ibid.*, IX.).

[2] "Pazzi maligni," see HUGHES, I., 232. Between Panzani and Con there was "poco concordia" (*Con, January 1, 1637, *Cod. Barb.* 8640, *loc. cit*). Panzani allowed himself a curious ruse towards Windebank, the Secretary of State : "Diedi al Windebanch una finta cifra nella quale fingevo che V. Em. desiderasse che costà venisse il figlio, per rendergli le cortesie che egli mi fa ; et egli giubilò per allegrezza, e spera che circa la prossima Pasqua habbia da esser costà" (to Barberini, August 8, 1635, in HUGHES, *History*, I., 361 ; *Documents*, I., 150). For another ruse also recommended by him see *ibid.*, 150, July 11, 1635.

[3] Printed in an English translation by JOSEPH BERINGTON, *The history of the decline and fall of the Roman cath. religion in England . . . including the Memoirs of Gr. Panzani*, London, 1813. We use the relation from the MS. in *Cod. Barb.* 5222, Vatican Library. Here is a proof of Panzani's unreliability : he states that Lord Baltimore died a few days after signing the protest against Bishop Smith, "and some saw in this a judgment of God." In point of fact Baltimore lived for another eight months

unreservedly takes the part of Bishop Smith, describes the presence of the Jesuits in England as a calamity for the English mission and recommends the appointment of one or more Bishops for the Island Kingdom, this being in accordance with the wishes of the secular clergy and the Queen. On the other hand the King would not hear of the appointment of a Catholic Bishop for England and Cardinal Barberini instructed Panzani to desist from his efforts for such a nomination.

Charles I. could not very well treat openly with a representative of the Pope, hence he referred Panzani to the Secretary of State, Windebank. The King hoped that the conversations would show whether it was possible to come to terms with the Pope on an oath of allegiance so worded as not to hurt the conscience of Catholics. For seven months all Panzani's reports to Rome speak of a formula drawn up with the help of the Jesuits by the younger Lord Baltimore whom Panzani wrongly imagined to be a friend of theirs. In this oath all reference to the Pope and his authority was omitted. Panzani ended by realizing that Baltimore's formula was intended, not for England, but for Maryland and was not only not inspired by the Jesuits but actually condemned by their General. The Secretary of State, Cardinal Barberini, likewise rejected it.[1] A number of Catholics, however, defended it, in particular many Benedictines, especially Preston who wrote under the name of Widdrington. Others pleaded the alleged declaration of the King that the oath only demanded obedience in civil

after signing the document (HUGHES, *Hist.*, I., 232). Other inaccuracies are shown *ibid.*, 355 *seq.* Part I. of the Relation gives a historical summary of the religious development since the schism, Part II. an account of the religious conditions in Panzani's time, Part III. a discussion as to whether a Bishop was desirable for England.

[1] HUGHES, *History*, I., 355–9; *Documents*, I., 151–6. PANZANI remarks in his *Relation*, that during his stay in England the oath of loyalty had only been required of a very few; "anzi alcuni principali consiglieri mi fecero intendere di volerne mutare la forma, levando quello che da V. Santità non è approvato, se bene non parve alla S. V., che io accettassi."

matters, so that it might be taken on the ground of this explanation. However, the majority refused it unconditionally.[1]

Panzani's conversations with Windebank turned for the most part on the question of the reunion of the Church of England with the Roman Church. Just then the Franciscan Christopher Davenport (Francis of St. Clare) had published a book in which he endeavoured to read a Catholic interpretation into the Thirty-Nine Articles with a view to facilitating the reconciliation of Anglicans with Rome.[2] It must have come as a ray of hope to the sanguine Panzani that the book pleased the King. But the reaction was all the more painful when it was disapproved in Rome so that Panzani wrongly concluded that it had been prohibited there. Only with difficulty did the Roman envoy succeed in reopening negotiations.[3] For the rest Windebank seemed to favour a settlement: "If it were not for the Jesuits and the Puritans," he said, "we should perhaps unite with Rome." [4] By way of concessions to the English Church he demanded Communion under both kinds, the use of the vernacular in the liturgy and for the clergy freedom to marry. The King, he declared, would grant

[1] PANZANI, *loc. cit.*

[2] *Cf.* HURTER, *Nomenclator*, IV.[3], 96; REUSCH, II., 406; GARDINER, VIII., 134, 137. Similar documents: **Somnium de Magnae Britanniae cum s. Ecclesia Romana conciliatione*, 1640 (*Cod. Barb.* 1215, Vatican Library). *D. Francisci Mariae de Monaco Drepanitani* (Theatine) *ad Carolum magnum Britanniae, Hyberniae, etc., regem de orthodoxa fide amplectanda sive de fidei unitate libri tres* (*ibid.*, XIX., 35; also in print: Paris, 1647; see VEZZOSI, *Scrittori de'cherici regolari*, II. (1780), 75). That Urban VIII. himself hoped for the conversion of the English King is affirmed by the Venetian ambassador Angelo Correr, September 18, 1636, in BROSCH, *Cromwell*, 143 *seq.*

[3] "Un giorno mi disse (Windebank) che prima haveva determinato volermi aiutare tanto nel negotio del vescovo, quanto in qualsivoglia altra cosa, ma che a adesso vedendo, che in Roma non si portava rispetto al re, al quale piaceva detto libro, non volerne saperne altro." PANZANI, *Relatione* (towards the end).

[4] GARDINER, VIII., 135.

freedom of religion on condition that Catholics took the oath of allegiance.[1]

Panzani saw everything in rosy hues. In March, 1635, he reported that two sermons had been preached before the King in commendation of sacramental confession and that they had been subsequently discussed at the royal table.[2] In July he reported a conversation in the course of which the Earl of Carlisle had declared himself ready to accept whatever Rome taught, except the Pope's power to depose Kings; that Lord Cherbury acknowledged the Roman Church as the Mother of all the Churches and that he would be glad to submit his book *De Veritate* to the judgment of the Pope[3]; that Bishop Montague stated in November, 1635, "that he did not know why the reunion should not be realized"; and that the two Archbishops, the Bishop of London and several others, as well as the most learned among the clergy agreed with Rome in regard to dogma, especially in respect to the authority of the Pope. As for himself (viz. Carlisle), he regarded the Pope as the Vicar of Christ and the successor of St. Peter without whom nothing could be defined for the universal Church, nor a Council convened. "He openly declared," Panzani adds, "that he believed exactly as I do, with the exception of transubstantiation."[4] Equally good news followed at the beginning of 1636. Lord Goring, the envoy wrote, read Catholic books, the Anglican Bishop of Gloucester recited the Roman Breviary and had asked leave to keep an Italian priest to say Mass secretly in his house.[5] Panzani also speaks of this approximation to the old religion in his *Relation* in which he ascribes the prevailing favourable disposition to the aversion of the Protestants for the Puritans which drove them towards Catholicism.[6] This attraction

[1] *Ibid.*, 136. [2] *Ibid.* [3] *Ibid.*, 137 *seq.*

[4] *Ibid.*, 138 *seq.* [5] *Ibid.*, 139 *seq.*

[6] "Certo è che alcuni hanno detto, desiderare essi unirsi in qualche maniera con i cattolici, per humiliare i Puritani." The approach, especially towards the moderate among the Catholics, appears in published works, in conversations, "e nel modo di trattare, non dubitando talvolta nelle publiche prediche

ended in many instances in a complete return to the ancient faith. Thus the Lord Treasurer, Portland, died a Catholic.[1] Walter Montague, who stood in high favour with the Queen, went to Italy in order to enter the Oratory of St. Philip Neri.[2] In Panzani's opinion [3] this improved feeling towards the old religion was in large measure due to the influence of the Catholic Queen. In addition to her private chapel, he writes, she also had a public one in which the Capuchins, who had taken the place of the Oratorians, said Office in choir, clad in their habits, and celebrated Mass. On great feasts the Queen attended with her whole suite. The sight of the chapel and the altars, the splendid services and the sermons of the Capuchins, greatly impressed the Protestants. In addition to the royal chapel there were also several Embassy chapels which served as so many places of refuge for the Catholics as well as numerous oratories in the houses of the gentry. It was commonly said that, relatively speaking, circumstances had never been so favourable to Catholics.[4]

avanti al re e tutta la corte detestare lo schisma con Roma, lodare li cattolici moderati, et esortare il re ad usare con loro clemenza, avvicinarsi alli dogmi cattolici con lodare la confessione auricolare, la riverenza al nome di Gesù, al segno della croce, et alle chiese, non aborrire l'imagini e gli altari all'usanza cattolica, dir bene del sommo Pontifice et Chiesa Romana, conoscere questa per chiesa primaria et nobilissima et quello per patriarcha d'occidente, al quale come tale non vengano d'esser soggietti. Non solegnano ancora il sentir trattare della reunione, etc.," *Relatione*, part 2.

[1] GARDINER, VII., 378.

[2] *Ibid.*, VIII., 138. Buckingham's mother had also become a Catholic and harboured a Jesuit (report of the Venetian ambassador Alvise Contarini, March 12, 1627, in BROSCH, *Cromwell*, 56).

[3] *Relatione*, part 2.

[4] "Se bene è vero che considerati li tempi scorsi, mentre io era in Londra, ognuno per il più confessava che non mai si erano veduti tempi migliori, non è però che l'uso della religione sia libero . . ." (*ibid*). Later it is said: "Mi volevano far credere (probably the Jesuits are meant) che in Londra vi fosse grandissima persecutione, mentre vi vedeva, particolarmente nella quaresima

Windebank's conversations with Panzani were not altogether barren. The Secretary of State proposed the dispatch of a papal agent to the Queen's Court and that of an agent of the Queen to Rome.[1] For the post in Rome the choice fell first on Robert Douglas, but he died suddenly. His place was taken by Arthur Brett [2] who also died in the following April. He was replaced by the Scotsman William Hamilton.[3] From Brett's instructions we are able to gather what was the King's chief object in this mission. It was mainly concerned with the Palatinate on behalf of which Charles I. was anxious to enlist the services even of the Catholic Powers.[4] As papal envoy there came to the Queen's Court the Scotsman George Con [5] who was kindly received by the King. On the occasion of the festival of the Order of the Garter Charles kept the assembled Knights waiting for the beginning of the service until he had finished showing Con his collection of pictures.[6] As a matter of fact the King was a great art lover and the

un esercitio quasi libero della religione." Nevertheless the Queen said: "che non pretendeva essere la più gran regina, ma si bene la più miserabile per non havere il marito cattolico" (PANZANI, December 25, 1636, *Barb.* 8637, Vatican Library).

[1] GARDINER, VIII., 134. [2] *Ibid.*, 138.

[3] *Ibid.*, 144. On Douglas's mission see also *NICOLETTI, *Barb.* 4734, p. 147. Vat. Libr.; on that of Hamilton, who lived in Rome "non con titolo di agente o residente, ma di gentilhuomo della regina (according to a letter of Cardinal Fr. Barberini to Panzani, July 3, 1636), *ibid.*, 4736, p. 85". *Gugl. Hamilton partì da Londra per venire a Roma. Molto pubblica era a Londra la missione del Coneo, piaceva poco agli Inglesi, perchè il Coneo era Scozzese", writes PANZANI on May 28, 1636 (*Barb.* 8637). "Per tutti li corti si parla molto del agente reciproco" (June 10, *ibid.*). Cardinal Barberini announced Hamilton's arrival on July 3, 1636 (*ibid.*, 8637); Con and Panzani are received by the Queen and bring her presents (Panzani, August 10, 1636, *ibid.*).

[4] GARDINER, VIII., 139.

[5] *Ibid.*, 138, 144. For G. Con (Cuneo), *cf.* GABRIELI, *Carteggio*, 202. Panzani announces his departure, December 25, 1636, *Barb.* 8637, Vatican Library.

[6] GARDINER, VIII., 236.

dispatch of valuable pictures occupies much space in the correspondence of Panzani and Con.[1]

In their exchanges of opinion Charles I. and Con soon entered on a formal discussion of the chief difficulty for Catholics, viz. the oath of allegiance.[2] If the Pope was unable formally to approve the oath, the King thought he might at least take up such an attitude as would morally compel Catholics to take it. Con replied that the latter could not do this without injury to their conscience, and when the King opposed to him the opinion of the Sorbonne, Con said that it was a mistake to affirm that that body had given its approval to the oath. " But what was there in the oath," the King retorted, " except that the Pope cannot depose a Prince ? " There was more than that in it, Con replied, for it described the opposite opinion as heretical ; now, a Catholic may not, on his own authority, label an opinion as heretical ; to do so belonged to the Church, and the oath had been devised by people who wished to sow the seeds of endless opposition between Rome

[1] Cardinal Barberini had sent the Queen pictures by Albani, Aless. Veronese and Stella (**Panzani*, April 11, 1635, *Barb.* 8633, Vatican Library) ; also a picture by Leonardo (*id.*, September 12, 1635, *ibid.*, 8635). " *Piacquerà straordinariamente alla regina et al re quel del Vinci e quelli di A. Sarto e di Giulio Romano (*id.* January 30, 1636, *ibid.*, 8636). A " Caterina della Rota " by A. Caracci and a reliquary with a cross after a drawing by Bernini was taken by Con as a present for the Queen (May 15, 1636), and presented on June 25 (*ibid.*, 8639). " *Della statua di Adone (in the Pighini Palace) e d'altro non mi ha mai parlato il re " (Con, January 15, 1637, *ibid.*, 8640). " *Presentai il crocifisso e il quadro di S. Michele mandato dal card. di S. Onofrio alla regina ", a picture also for the King (Con, February 26, 1637) ; the Queen wishes to have a picture by G. Reni for the ceiling of her room (Con, May 1, 1637, *ibid.*) ; the King is enchanted with an antique head (*id.*, July 31, 1637, *ibid.*, 8641), is pleased with a statue (*id.*, August 7, *ibid.*). Rossetti records the Queen receiving a present of a Titian, December 28, 1640 (*ibid.*, 8648).

[2] Con to Card. Barberini, September 16, 1636, in RANKE, *Engl. Gesch.*, VIII.[3] (Works, XXI.), 136 *seqq.* *Cf.* A. O. MEYER in *American hist. Review*, XIX. (1913/14), 20.

and England. Charles replied that in so far as he was concerned, the oath was only meant to demand true obedience without encroaching on the spiritual rights of the Pope over Catholics; the oath was enforced for the purpose of discovering the Anabaptists and other enemies of the royal authority. In that case, Con answered, he regretted that the oath stated its purpose so badly, for its wording was such as to make it seem exclusively aimed at the papal authority; in purely civil questions the King would find Catholics ready to defend the honour of the Prince even with their blood. Charles I. now played his trump card: the oath could not be altered without the concurrence of Parliament! When Con exclaimed that the King was above Parliament, Charles added that though that body might perhaps give its approval, it was nevertheless easier for the Pope than for himself to give affairs a more favourable turn. Towards the end of the long conversation Con begged the King at least to protect the Catholics from the pursuivants and priest-hunters. Charles replied that that institution was just as necessary as that of the *sbirri* in Italy; if it did not exist Catholics would become arrogant. Finally the King referred him to his ministers.[1]

The papal agent subsequently returned to the subject of the oath of allegiance. With a view to avoiding the difficulties connected with a formal abolition of the formula in use, he suggested that the oath might be allowed to stand but that Catholics should be dispensed from taking it provided they declared their readiness to do so as soon as an irreproachable formula should be devised. This suggestion was not acted upon. More than once Con's comments on the evil of schism among Christians and its perils seemed to impress Charles I.[2]; however, no tangible results were obtained.

[1] Letter of January 7, 1637, in RANKE, *Engl. Gesch.*, VIII., 139 *seq.*

[2] *Ibid.*, 136, 140; *cf.* II., 256. "*Il re, come fa spesso, maledisse gli autori di questa disunione," writes Con on January 29, 1638 (*Barb.* 8642, Vatican Library). His conversion is, however, "cosa da desiderare più che di sperare" (Con, November 6,

Con realized that a reunion of Canterbury and Rome was not to be thought of and that there could only be question of bringing back individual Protestants to the old religion, the Queen using her influence to protect them. About this time the devout wife of Endymion Porter, who was frequently employed on confidential missions during the reigns of James I. and Charles I., succeeded in obtaining a not inconsiderable number of conversions in the highest social circles.[1] One conversion in particular caused a great sensation and threatened to entail grievous consequences for the Catholics, namely that of the wife of Lord Newport. Her husband lodged a protest with Archbishop Laud; the latter laid the facts before the next meeting of the Privy Council and the King promised to provide against a repetition of such an occurrence. However, on the advice of Con, the Queen remonstrated with her husband and Charles did not dare to oppose her. Laud made a second appeal to the King who told him to discuss the matter with Henrietta Maria. Instead Laud suggested to the Privy Council that they should forbid all English subjects to attend the Queen's chapel or the Embassy chapels. The Queen, now fully roused, determined to measure her strength with Laud's and so warmly did she fight for the freedom of her chapel that Con counselled her to moderate her zeal. The dispute lasted throughout November 1637; in December Con learnt that secret orders had been issued for a proclamation against Catholics. In vain did he endeavour to induce the King to change his mind. Something had to be done, Charles said; Catholics must be made to see that they lived in England, not in Rome.[2] In the end, however,

1636, *ibid.*, 8630) *Cf.* A. O. MEYER, *loc. cit.*, 16 *seq.* Abbé Du Perron, on his return to Paris from England, on the contrary thought, "*credersi da alcuni più pratici ed intendenti che saria stato facile il ridurre il re medesimo alla religione cattolica tuttevolte che l'arcivescovo di Cantuario e il gran tesoriere havessero voluto congiuntamente addossarsi l'impresa." *NICOLETTI, 153 *seq.*, Vatican Library.

[1] RANKE, *loc. cit.*, II., 236–9.

[2] Con, December 18, 1637, *Barb.* 8641, Vatican Library.

the King struck out of the proclamation whatever might have offended the Queen so that, in Con's opinion, the document was a fatherly exhortation rather than a threat.[1] The proclamation was published on December 20th, and on Christmas Day all the converts, as if to spite the King, received Holy Communion in a body in the Queen's chapel: "You see what has come of the proclamation," Henrietta Maria remarked to Con immediately afterwards.

The Queen's example heartened the Catholics in other directions also. At no previous time had Mass been said so frequently in the Embassy chapels, or with less secrecy in Catholic houses. "Before her coming," Lady Arundel said to Con, "not for a million would I have cared to have a priest at my table; now, you see how general the custom has become."[2] A Puritan nobleman[3] gave it as his opinion that Barberini's courteous attentions did more harm than all former Roman threats and excommunications.

Con left England on a man-of-war on September 9th, 1639,[4] before he could receive a Brief dated September 10th, empowering him to give a spiritual head to English Catholics.[5] His successor, Count Carlo Rossetti, a scion of a noble family of Ferrara, landed in England on August 28th.[6] On his

[1] Con, January 8, 1638, *ivid.*, 8642. On January 22, 1638, *ibid.* "*La proclamatione ha dato più tosto disgusto che sodisfattione alli Puritani"; they called it a "burla" for it did not harm the Catholics at all.

[2] GARDINER, VIII., 236–242. The Venetian ambassador Angelo Correr writes on September 18, 1636, that in England the Catholic clergy had never enjoyed such freedom as at present (BROSCH, *Cromwell*, 144).

[3] "*Il conte d'Arcrum Puritano disse: fa più danno questa cortesia, che non hanno fatto tutte le minacce e scommuniche di Roma." Con, February 12, 1638, *Barb.* 8642, *loc. cit.*

[4] BROSCH, *Cromwell*, 161.

[5] *Bull.*, XV., 4.

[6] *Con, September 2, 1639, *Barb.* 8644, Vatican Library. *Rossetti to Card. Fr. Barberini, September 2, 1639, *ibid.*, 8648. Description of his journey to England: *Scelta di curiosità letterarie inedite o rare dal sec. XIII. al XVII., fondata e diretta da Franc.*

arrival Rossetti wondered at the way in which Windebank spoke to him; for, as he wrote, he spoke like a fervent Catholic and offered to give him any information of which he might stand in need.[1] However, the papal envoy soon perceived that, as a matter of fact, the favour of the Court constituted a serious danger for the Catholics. The Puritans, he reported,[2] disliked the Queen's relations with Rome; eight days later he wrote that discourses against the Catholic religion, and especially against these relations, were the ordinary topic of conversation in London.[3] In point of fact the favour of a King who was getting more and more hated by his people could not avail to soften public opinion in regard to Catholics. In Presbyterian Scotland Charles' religious innovations had already provoked open rebellion and Ireland was in a ferment. In view of his financial straits the King felt compelled, after a prorogation of eleven years, to convene Parliament, a circumstance that boded nothing but evil for Catholics. "An anti-Catholic Parliament is preparing," Rossetti wrote [4]; "the Puritans and Protestants are infuriated against the Catholics and the Court's relations with Rome." At the beginning of the following year he notes that the Puritans were getting more ill-disposed towards those who professed the old faith and that protests were being raised in Parliament against the freedom granted to Catholics.[5] In the King's ante-room he read the following inscription

Zambrini, disp., 212, Bologna, 1885 (see below, p. 328). For Con's early death, Rossetti's eulogy by the Queen and Rigby's arrival in Rome, see *Brief of May 12, 1640, **Brevia*, XVII., 159, Papal Secret Archives.

[1] GARDINER, IX., 87.

[2] December 23, 1639, *Barb.* 8646, *loc. cit.*

[3] "*Oggi pare che d'altro non si parli che contro la religione cattolica e molto più contro questa intelligenza reciproca che passa con N.S. et V.S. insieme questa Ser. Regina" (December 30, 1639, *ibid.*).

[4] "*Si prepara un parlamento contro i cattolici. I Puritani e i Protestanti sono arrabiati contro i cattolici" and the Queen's relations with Rome (January 6, 1640, *ibid.*).

[5] *January 10 and May 4, 1640, *Barb.* 8647, *loc. cit.*

scratched on a window-pane with a diamond: "God save the King; God confound the Queen with all her party; God grant power in this realm to the Count Palatine."[1] He reports that the Archbishop of Canterbury never ceased agitating against the Catholics in order to court popularity with the Puritans[2]; as for the Bishop of Gloucester, Godfrey Goodman, Laud had ordered his arrest because of his opposition to the Archbishop's action against the Catholics.[3] The House of the Clergy had prescribed the so-called "Etcetera Oath" by which a man bound himself to approve the teaching, discipline and government of the Church of England, not to introduce the opposite Popish doctrine, not to consent to any alteration in the government of the English Church by any Archbishops, Bishops, Deans, Archdeacons, "etcetera," or to suffer the Church to be made subject to the pretensions and superstitions of the Roman See. Among the seventeen resolutions there was one aimed at the Catholics which Goodman refused at first to sign. He ended by subscribing but was nevertheless arrested by order of the King.[4]

Soon Rossetti was to experience in his own person how greatly hatred of the King as well as of Catholics had grown. A rumour spread among the masses that persons in the Queen's entourage were plotting the massacre of all Protestants.[5] Archbishop Laud, though an opponent of the Catholics, was suspected, by reason of his love for ceremonial, of being a tool of the Pope. The King's minister, Strafford, was viewed with similar suspicion. In 1640 it was rumoured that the latter planned to bring over to England an army of 10,000 Catholic Irishmen in order to enforce the King's demands. In the eyes of the common people this was synonymous with permitting a horde of rough savages to throw themselves upon the gentle, God-fearing Protestants. A few incidents were exploited by certain crafty agitators in order to confirm the populace in

[1] "*Dio salvi il Re, Dio confunda la Regina con tutta la sua parte, e Dio faccia regnare in questo regno il Palatino," Rossetti, June 8, 1640, *ibid.*

[2] *Ibid.*

[3] *January 15, 1640, *ibid.*

[4] Gardiner, IX., 146 *seq.*

[5] *Ibid.*, 123, 126.

these opinions. In 1639, in view of the King's financial straits, Henrietta Maria begged the Catholics to come to his assistance, whereupon they raised 10,000 pounds—enough to keep the army for at least one week.[1] In the following year she had recourse to the Pope for the same object, through Windebank and Rossetti.[2] In his distrust of the Puritans, Charles I. thought he could rely on the loyalty of the Catholics and he had accordingly given them commands in the army, a privilege from which he had barred the Puritans.[3] In 1640 an apostate priest spread a tale to the effect that the Jesuits were plotting the assassination of the King and Laud.[4] Pym, the outstanding orator of the Long Parliament and eventually its leader, asserted in one of its first sittings that there were those who planned to alter both the laws and religion and that

[1] *Ibid.*, 26.

[2] *Ibid.*, 134 *seq.* Even before this she had received not a few papal letters, thus, on May 30, 1625, a *Brief to accompany the Golden Rose (*Epist.*, II., Papal Secret Archives); on August 9, 1625, a *reply to the Queen's letter of thanks for the marriage dispensation (*ibid.*); February 12, 1626, an *exhortation to be zealous on behalf of the Catholics, after the example of Esther, Clothilda, Aldiberga, and to be mindful of the holiness of Mary Stuart (*ibid.*, III., 103); on May 30, 1626, the Pope *praised her piety in going to church on foot (*ibid.*, 211), on September 21, 1626, he sent her a *letter of comfort (*ibid.*); on February 12, 1632, *he praises her zeal against heretics, exhorts her to protect the Scottish Catholics against them (*ibid.*, X.); on December 31, 1633, he *congratulates her on a happy delivery (*ibid.*, XI.). On May 3, 1642, he *comforts her: "tot vexationes te passam audivimus" (*ibid.*, XIX.); on October 18, 1642, he *congratulates her on a happy turn of events (*ibid.*); on January 31, 1643 *on a victory over the rebels and rejoices on hearing of her desire to return to England; is pleased with her praise of the Bishop of Angoulême which he has heard of (*ibid.*, 237); on October 15, 1643, he *admonishes her to act on behalf of the Catholics, as Parliament was attempting to harm them during the peace negotiations; let the King observe the marriage contract; he recommends the Irish Catholics (*ibid.*, XIX., 414).

[3] GARDINER, IX., 159.

[4] *Ibid.*, 228.

the scheme proceeded from the Papists who were bound by one of the principles of their faith not only to maintain their own religion but to extirpate all others.[1] The inevitable reference to the great Popish plot[2] kept cropping up in subsequent speeches. The Puritan member for Wigan proved its existence by appealing to a letter in which Catholics were requested to fast for the pious intentions of the Queen.[3] When a woman pretended that an Irish priest had told her that "many thousands were in pay to be ready to cut all Protestants' throats", and to begin by killing the King, that piece of gossip was deemed worthy of serious discussion by both Houses of Parliament.[4] The constant repetition of such statements was sufficient proof for the mass of the people and there was nothing the populace heard with greater pleasure than tales of popish plots.[5] Parliament resolved to take the Communion in a body, so as to discover such as might be secret Catholics.[6] In consequence, on November 8th, 1640, the King deemed it advisable to inform the House that he was thinking of driving the recusants out of London.[7]

In these circumstances tumults and acts of violence were inevitable. In the night of May 11th, a band of 500 people, headed by a drum, marched up to Lambeth Palace, threatening to set it on fire, but Laud had already escaped.[8] Posters were stuck on the houses summoning the people to attack the house of the Queen-Mother, Marie de'Medici, whom[9] Richelieu had forced to seek shelter with her daughter in England in 1638[10]; the posters incited the populace to

[1] *Ibid.*, 230.
[2] *Ibid.*, 233; *cf.* 234.
[3] *Ibid.*, 233.
[4] *Ibid.*, 237.
[5] Secretary Nicholas to the King, in *Lingard*, X., 58.
[6] Gardiner, IX., 237.
[7] *Ibid.*, 232. In Holland, too, the opinion was current that Charles I. was favourably disposed towards the Catholic faith and people blamed the Prince of Orange for supporting him (letter of the Venetian ambassador at the Hague, Zuanne Zon, December 24, 1642, in Brosch, *Cromwell*, 186).
[8] Gardiner, IX., 133.
[9] *Ibid.*
[10] *Ibid.*, VIII., 379 *seq.*

destroy her chapel and to ill-treat her priests. Others demanded the death of Laud. On the occasion of a military mutiny at Aylesbury, thirty-two houses were burnt. In the night of May 14th the prisons were forced and the rioters set at liberty.[1] It was inevitable that the safety of the Papal envoy in particular should be endangered, since it was precisely his presence at Court which supplied fuel to the popular hatred of Catholics. Consequently, as early as September, 1639, when the convocation of Parliament was first mooted, Rossetti sought the protection of the Queen. Charles replied that he would insist on the fact that his wife's freedom to communicate with Rome was part of the marriage treaty. However, this statement was an untruth and Coke was not slow in publicly branding it as such.[2] In Rossetti's letters of the following year there is more than one allusion to attempts against himself and against Catholics. On May 4th, 1640 he speaks of a plot to set fire to his house; on June 1st he reports tumultuous gatherings of the populace in front of the Queen's palace and the Capuchin convent in Somerset; eight days later he writes that he had spent the night at the house of the Queen-Mother in consequence of threats to his life.[3] He repeatedly sends similar information; for instance, that on the night of August 31st, 1640, the Scotch wanted to destroy the chapel of the Capuchins and to kill himself; and on October 26th, that they had planned to set his house on fire.[4] During the night of November 4th, 1641, he once again sought shelter in the Queen's palace.[5] However, he suffered no harm as his secretary, Vincenzo Armanni, wrote,[6] and though the populace seemed on the point of using violence, they nevertheless refrained, contenting themselves with stupidly staring at the envoy without going any

[1] *Ibid.*, IX., 133 *seq.* [2] *Ibid.*, 88.

[3] *Barb.* 8647, Vatican Library.

[4] *Ibid.*, 8648. [5] *Ibid.*, 8649.

[6] *Arch. stor. ital.*, 4 series, XI. (1883), 175. From a report of the Venetian ambassador Giustiniani, it appears that it was intended to summon Rossetti before Parliament (Brosch, *Cromwell*, 213, note).

farther. This may have been due, in no small degree, to Rossetti's courageous attitude. On October 19th, 1640, he wrote that he would only leave if it became necessary; on his part Cardinal Barberini encouraged him, on December 1st, to remain with the Queen if at all possible.[1] Meanwhile. as Rossetti's reports prove,[2] the King's position was growing more and more desperate. The ruin of the royal House, hence that also of the Catholic cause, was to be foreseen, Armanni wrote. All the politicians were raising their voices against a King who was both foolish and good, neither loved nor feared, neither esteemed and revered nor obeyed.[3] On April 19th Rossetti writes that Cardinal Barberini approved of his leaving and that the Queen was anxious for him to look to his own safety. In effect, on July 8th, 1641, he set out for Cologne and on September 25th he wrote to thank the Pope for his appointment as nuncio extraordinary in that city.[4]

[1] *Barb.* 8648, *loc. cit.*

[2] January 11 and 18 and February 2, 1641, *ibid.*, 8649.

[3] " *Le voci di tutti i politici gridano contra quel re di sciocca bontà non amato, non temuto, senza stima, senza rispetto, senza ubbidienza." *Arch. stor. ital.*, *loc. cit.*

[4] *Barb.* 8649, *loc. cit.* On Rossetti's journeys, *cf.* G. FERRARO, *Diario del viaggio fatto in Inghilterra nel* 1639 *del Nunzio pontificio Rossetti scritto da Domenico Fantozzi Parma*, Bologna, 1885 (for a MSS. of this, which contains also an account of the return journey, see J. PH. DENGEL in the *Forsch. u. Mitteil. zur Gesch. Tirols u. Vorarlbergs*, I., 266, and an extract from it, *ibid.*, 264–281); G. FERRARO, *Viaggio del cardinale Rossetti fatto nel* 1644 *da Colonia a Ferrara scritto dal suo segretario Armanni Vincenzo*, in *Atti di Romagna*, VI. (1888). According to Ferraro (*ibid.*, 2) both accounts were by Armanni, but the fragment published by DENGEL (*loc. cit.*, 268 *seqq.*) on the journey in the Tyrol, does not in any way correspond with the style of the parallel passage in Ferraro (72 *seqq.*). See also CUVELIER in the *Bullet. de l'Institut hist. de Belge à Rome*, VI., 127 *seq.*, and the same author in *Bullet. de l'Acad. de Belgique*, 1927. The Queen praised Rossetti to the Pope on the occasion of his departure. Brief to the Queen, August 10, 1641, *Epist.*, XIX., Papal Secret Archives.

From Cologne Rossetti kept in touch with England. Armanni, his secretary, passed on the news that reached Rossetti from England to his brother Francesco Maria Armanni at Gubbio.[1] Besides a full report on the circumstances which led to the overthrow of the monarchy, he supplies much information on the position of Catholics; as, for instance, that the King wished to reprieve seven priests who had been condemned to death but that Parliament raised loud protests against such a measure[2]; that anti-Catholic meetings were being held in London; that a procession of several hundred people had paraded through Holborn, where many Catholics lived, shouting: "Where are the houses of the Catholics?"[3] that a crowd of some three or four thousand people who had been summoned to London from the country, were surging round Parliament with printed petitions demanding that Catholics and Bishops should be excluded from the House[4]; that the martyrdom of the secular priest, Thomas Reynolds, and that of the Benedictine, Alban Roe, had fired the Catholics with extraordinary eagerness to suffer themselves.[5]

Fresh measures against the ancient faith were inevitable, were it only because of the intense public excitement. Further fuel was added to this state of mind by the act of a madman. On November 23rd, as a Justice of the Peace of the name of Heywood was walking through Westminster Hall with a list of recusants in his hand, a certain James made a sudden rush at him and wounded him with a knife. The wound was a superficial one but the incident was taken as proof of the existence of a vast popish plot. Various means were suggested for the safety of the House, one taking the form of a demand for a fresh enforcement of the penal laws.[6] An order was

[1] Published by GIUSEPPE MAZZATINTI in the *Arch. stor. ital.*, 4th series, XI., XII., XV., XVIII., XIX.

[2] January 12, 1642, *ibid.*, XI., 187.

[3] February 2, 1642, *ibid.*, 189. [4] March 1, 1642, *ibid.*, XII., 163.

[5] *Ibid.*, 164. Armanni says of Reynolds: "il quale era mio amico, e, nel vero, di grande innocenza."

[6] GARDINER, IX., 239 *seq.*

issued for the weeding out of the army in the North of all Catholic officers. For some time, one protest stated, priests and Jesuits had remained almost wholly untouched by the anti-Catholic laws and during the last seven or eight years no less than seventy-four pardons had been granted to them, signed for the most part by Windebank. Accordingly the Justices of the Peace in the capital and the surrounding districts were directed to give effect to the laws against the recusants, regardless of any order to the contrary. Windebank escaped being called to account by flight.[1]

Priests were once more being executed, though in small numbers. The first capital sentence was pronounced on January 21st, 1641, against John Goodman, brother of the Anglican Bishop of Gloucester. When Rossetti heard of it he informed the Queen, who was assured by her husband that Goodman would not be put to death solely for being a priest. His pardon raised a storm in the Protestant camp. The City of London had agreed to a loan of 60,000 pounds, but withdrew the promise in consequence of the pardon. Thereupon the Lower House appealed to the Lords with a view to both Houses demanding the execution of Goodman.[2]

Charles I. now summoned both Houses into his presence, though not exclusively because of Goodman, but chiefly in order to open his mind on the subject of the so-called root-and-branch party, which derived its name from the fact that its aim was the destruction of episcopacy, root and branch. He promised reforms in this respect but not the complete suppression of the episcopate. As for Goodman's reprieve, they would soon receive a message on the subject.[3] The message was to the effect that Goodman was only to be banished, but both Houses insisted on the full execution of the anti-Catholic laws, beginning with Goodman's death. The King yielded in so far as he left the condemned priest to the judgment of Parliament, whilst expressing the hope that, in view of the disapproval which the action would provoke abroad, the sentence would not be carried out.

[1] *Ibid.*, 243. [2] *Ibid.*, 264 *seq.*; SPILLMANN, IV., 231 *seqq.*

[3] GARDINER, IX., 268.

At this stage Goodman presented a petition to both Houses in which he prayed the King not to insist on his reprieve in as much as he thought his blood would not be shed in vain if it helped to remove the estrangement between King and people.[1] Whether such generosity impressed Parliament, or whether consideration for the King's wishes also contributed, the fact is that Goodman died only in 1645 from the effects of his confinement in the foul dungeon of Newgate gaol.[2]

At the same time as Charles I. abandoned Goodman to Parliament, he promised a proclamation which was actually published. By its terms any priest found on English soil after April 7th, 1641, was to fall under the full rigour of the law. Accordingly, in 1641, William Ward and the Benedictine Barlow [3] were executed solely for being priests. In the following year five secular priests and three regulars suffered a similar fate,[4] but in 1643 only two Franciscans were executed.[5] The arrest of the Benedictine Barlow shows to what extent ceaseless agitation had roused popular hatred of Catholics. On Easter day, 1641, Barlow was in the act of saying Mass when a preacher of the neighbourhood came to hear of it. Instead of holding his own service, the latter told his congregation that instead of preaching and hymn singing they would be better employed if they put an end to the activities of the popish priest. Accordingly 400 people left the church and, led by their minister, succeeded in capturing Barlow.[6]

The fear of a vast conspiracy on the part of the Catholics continued. The chatter of any gossiping woman was deemed worthy of Parliament's earnest consideration and appropriate ordinances. In May, 1641, as a result of such gossip, an order was issued for the arrest of every priest in England and there were many who judged this measure not severe enough.[7]

[1] NALSON, *Impartial collection of great actions of State*, I., 738, 746, in SPILLMANN, IV., 232; LINGARD, X., 4, note.

[2] SPILLMANN, IV., 309.

[3] *Ibid.*, 235 *seqq.*, 238 *seqq.*

[4] *Ibid.*, 242–272.

[5] *Ibid.*, 274.

[6] *Ibid.*, 240.

[7] GARDINER, IX., 374 *seq.*

In November of that year a certain tailor declared that he had overheard a conversation concerning a plot for the assassination of no less than 108 members of both Houses of Parliament, the 18th of the month being the date fixed for the stroke. The House of Lords seriously examined the tailor's story, only to find that it offered no basis for action.[1]

The Queen, as the alleged centre of the conspiracy, was the chief object of popular hatred. Amid the dangers which threatened to overthrow the English throne, Henrietta Maria displayed far greater courage than her husband; she was sprung from a father who did not know what fear was and from a people that never retreated, she told Rossetti.[2] In May, 1640, she sent Windebank to Rossetti to obtain through him the Pope's assistance with troops and money.[3] Already in the previous year, with a view to giving satisfaction to the King, Cardinal Barberini had spontaneously offered money against the Scots.[4] The Queen now turned to him once again in view of the fact that her chief opponents in Parliament were not immune to bribery.[5] The Cardinal contributed 15,000 scudi out of his private purse.[6] However, as a condition of further help, Urban VIII. demanded that Charles I. should first embrace the Catholic faith,[7] and he persisted in this demand when Henrietta Maria renewed her request to Rossetti in December, 1640.[8] The King, however, was not prepared formally to take such a step, but when the Queen renewed her request for 150,000 pounds, and in the event of its being granted, held out the prospect of religious liberty for the Irish Catholics and for those in England, free attendance at her chapels and those of the ambassadors, as well as,

[1] *Ibid.*, X., 72.

[2] *Rossetti, May 17, 1641, *Barb.* 8649, Vatican Library.

[3] GARDINER, IX., 134.

[4] Con, February 4, 1639, *Barb.* 8644, Vatican Library.

[5] January 21, 1641, *ibid.*, 8659; discussion of the letter by S. HERRLICH in *Hist. Zeitschr.*, LVI. (1886), 238–251. *Cf.* BELLESHEIM, *Scotland*, III., 434.

[6] *Rossetti, April 5, 1641, *Barb.* 8649, *loc. cit.*; HERRLICH, *loc. cit.*, 248.

[7] GARDINER, IX., 175.

[8] *Ibid.*, 251, 310.

in the event of the King's victory, the free exercise of religion throughout the realm, Charles I. himself put his signature to a letter addressed to Cardinal Barberini.[1] In point of fact the Cardinal's liberality was not yet exhausted; as we learn from Rossetti's letters written from Cologne, he was prepared, in 1642, to contribute 30,000 scudi and he mortgaged his own Abbeys so as to be in a position to lend help to the Catholics of England.[2]

Henrietta's courage led her adversaries to take several harsh measures against her. Parliament took care that the young hereditary prince should not see his mother too often, for no good could be looked for from her, either for body or soul.[3] Her confessor, the Oratorian Robert Philippe, was cast into prison and only set free on condition that he no longer saw her,[4] in fact there was even a plan to arraign her before Parliament for conspiring against the liberty of the country and for having a secret understanding with the Irish rebels.[5] On the pretext of accompanying her daughter, the bride of the Prince of Orange, to the Hague, the Queen left for Holland in the spring of 1642 and lived there for a time.[6]

By now Charles I.'s contest with the Long Parliament had become so acute that the King declared war on it.

(5)

Urban VIII. only saw the beginning of the Civil War which, after the execution of Charles I., and under his successor, turned England into a republic. However innocent Catholics

[1] *Ibid.*, 383; *Rossetti, June 14, 1641, *Barb.* 8650, *loc. cit.*

[2] *Rossetti, February 22 and July 13, 1642, *ibid.*, 8651, 8652. For Barberini's solicitude for England, *cf.* **Monumenta varia collegii Anglorum de Urbe Francisc. seniore et juniore cardinalibus Barberini protectoribus*, *Barb.* 2606, *loc. cit.*

[3] GARDINER, X., 42.

[4] *Ibid.*, 42, 54, 98.

[5] *Ibid.*, 128.

[6] *Ibid.*, X., 168. "A la fin, la violance du Parlement a esté sy grande contre moy que pour estre en seureté de ma vie, il m'a falu en aler," she wrote on April 4, 1642, to her sister. *Ibid.*

were of political interference there is nevertheless frequent mention of them in the long-drawn struggle between King and Parliament, so much so that the blame for the Civil War is wholly laid on them. In the opinion of a contemporary, all Charles I.'s misfortunes were due to his violent and obstinate attachment " to the infamous Anglican Bishops " who " without a doubt were resolved before all else, with the help of the Jesuits and the Papists, to extirpate all religion both at home and abroad, and to plunge us into ignorance, superstition, and idolatry ".[1] The King was withal considered as the head of a vast Catholic conspiracy ; in fact his army was described as " the northern papist army ".[2] Months before the actual outbreak of the Civil War, Parliament had declared, in a petition, that the King's intention to alter religion was to be traced to the papal nuncio and the Queen's agent in Rome ; that the war in Scotland had been caused by the Catholics and was being supported by them in order to make way for the change of religion, the proof being the contributions of money made by the adherents of the old faith through the nuncio. The rising in Ireland was also said to have been brought about in consequence of an understanding with the English Catholics.[3]

It may be, it is even likely, that the hated Catholic religion was no more than a pretext for Parliament to mask its revolt against a lawful King. Suspicion may have found some foundation in the fact that the Catholic gentry were " among those who showed the greatest eagerness to serve the King ; their loyalty could never be doubted ".[4] Accordingly from Chester Charles I. called the Catholic gentry to arms in the first months of the war, and shortly afterwards he summoned

[1] D'Ewes in GARDINER, *Civil War*, I., 5, note.

[2] *Northern Papist Army*, *ibid.*, 45. *Cf.*, *ibid.*, 284, Newcastle's jest on the inefficiency of the Royalists : " You hear us called the Popish army, but you see we trust not in our good works."

[3] Armanni, April 29, 1642, *Arch. stor. ital.*, 4th series, XII., 171.

[4] GARDINER, *Civil War*, I., 41. For a list of Catholic noblemen who fell for the King and of those who lost their fortune for his cause, *cf.* CHALLONER, *Memoirs*, etc.

all the Catholics of the realm to support him with their money and their blood. In September, 1642, he wrote that the revolt had assumed such proportions that he could no longer inquire into the opinions of those who were ready to serve him.[1] The admission into the army of Catholic officers naturally added strength to the belief in a Catholic conspiracy.[2] When, in November, 1642, Parliament called upon the Scotch for help against the King, it justified its action by pleading that Catholics had been enrolled in the royal army.[3]

The alleged friendliness of Charles I. towards Catholics provided a pretext for various ordinances against both the King and the Catholics. In January, 1643, the leader of the House, Pym, spoke in support of the alliance with Scotland on the ground that in this way they were able to counter the Catholic conspiracy. True the House refused to agree to the proposal, but it decreed that all the children of Catholics were to be brought up as Protestants so as to put an end to the old religion.[4] Someone moved in Parliament that all Papists in arms should be declared traitors, and when one of the members remarked that the chief papist under arms was the Queen, Henrietta Maria was formally arraigned.[5] About the middle of 1643 the King contemplated bringing together all his London adherents for a *coup de main* against Parliament. When the plan was discovered, the Lower House resolved almost unanimously to give its support to the Parliamentary troops, "so long as the papists, who were now openly at war with Parliament," had the support of the King.[6] Not long after certain symptoms showed that,

[1] GARDINER, *loc. cit.*, 41. Charles I. acknowledged himself to be in debt to the Catholic son of the Marquis of Worcester, Lord Herbert of Raglan, for the sum of over 250,000 pounds, *ibid.*, II., 108. [2] *Ibid.*, I., 45. [3] *Ibid.*, 62.

[4] "To oppose that Catholic league which he believed to have been formed in support of the king." *Ibid.*, 95.

[5] May 23, 1643, *ibid.*, 170.

[6] "So long as the Papists now in open war against the Parliament shall by force of arms be protected from the justice thereof." *Ibid.*, 174.

with or without the King's knowledge, a rising in his favour was in progress and that it would have the support of the Irish Catholics. This intelligence did the King's cause untold harm; it now appeared "that there was a determined resolve in the Popish party to extirpate the true Protestant religion" in England, Scotland and Ireland.[1] When Charles I. received Communion at Oxford, he deemed it necessary to declare that he would maintain the Protestant religion "without any connivance at popery".[2] In London this declaration was received with incredulous laughter. When on top of everything, two English regiments returned from Ireland which were erroneously believed to be composed of Irishmen, there seemed to be no longer any doubt that Charles I. had become a party to a dreadful popish conspiracy.[3] John Pym, the most influential man in Parliament, was a bitter enemy of the Catholics. Though personally neither an episcopalian nor a presbyterian, he was for ever talking about religion and acting as champion of Protestantism.[4] In his very first speech in the House he moved that they should swear to unite their forces in the defence of the country against the Catholics. This proposal, the result of the Association of 1584, became the germ of the Protest of 1641 and of the Parliamentary Covenant of 1643, if not of the Solemn League and Covenant itself,[5] that is, the Covenant with the Scots,[6] which led to the final overthrow of the monarchy. If not the Catholics themselves, then at least hatred and enmity towards them, were responsible, to an enormous extent, for the troubles of that period. Day by day Parliament published fresh ordinances; there are very few among them, even when they deal with indifferent matters, which do not state that the war had been instigated and was being continued by the

[1] *Ibid.*, 208. [2] *Ibid.*, 212.

[3] "The belief, which had always been strong, that Charles had made himself the instrument of a terrible Popish conspiracy, was raised to absolute conviction." GARDINER, *Civil War*, I., 288.

[4] *Ibid.*, 300, 303.

[5] Gardiner's opinion, *ibid.*, 301.

[6] On the Solemn League and Covenant, *cf. ibid.*, 269.

papists in order to exalt the papacy on the ruins of Protestantism.[1]

The everlasting talk of popery and Catholic conspiracies, whether sincerely meant or no, could not but be fraught with disastrous consequences for those who professed the old religion. When Parliament began to levy troops, and these undisciplined bands entered on a campaign of plunder and robbery, Catholics were the greatest sufferers. Thus, damage to the amount of 40,000 pounds was done to the property of Lady Rivers of Colchester.[2] Wherever Parliament gained the upper hand, the adherents of the old religion had to endure ill-treatment and spoliation.[3] The City of London granted to Parliament a loan on the property of those whom, characteristically enough, they styled "papists and criminals".[4] When the multiplicity of religious parties prompted Roger Williams to demand toleration for them all, he nevertheless insisted on one solitary exception—Catholic worship must be forbidden as idolatrous, though the penal laws against Catholics should be repealed.[5] Nevertheless at that period there were only isolated cases of Catholics executed for their faith. Nor were any new laws passed against them, though on December 16th, 1642, Parliament published an ordinance for the arrest of all wealthy or dangerous Catholics and the confiscation of their property. This measure was adopted in consequence of a rumour that twenty convicted recusants were in arms against Parliament under Newcastle.[6] The Capuchins who served the Queen's chapel, after enduring many vexations, were at last arrested and banished from the country; the images in the chapel—they were spoken of as idols—were

[1] LINGARD, X., 126 *seq.*

[2] GARDINER, *loc. cit.*, 14; ARMANNI, *loc. cit.*, XII., 345. Armanni writes of the "inestimabili danni" of the Catholics in several counties (XV., 16), October 5, 1642; especially in Essex where all their houses were plundered; many were left without as much as a chair or a bed; their cattle was driven off, their barns stripped.

[3] GARDINER, *loc. cit.*, 41; LINGARD, X., 127.

[4] April 13, 1644, GARDINER, *loc. cit.*, 400.

[5] *Ibid.*, 342.

[6] GARDINER, *loc. cit.*, 88.

destroyed and Rubens' altarpiece was thrown into the Thames.[1] Shortly afterwards the Lower House set up a committee with mission to destroy every trace of what its members might deem a superstition and idolatry.[2] Thereupon the stained glass windows of the churches were smashed and the remaining statues of the Saints beheaded ; this was done in Westminster Abbey and St. Margaret's. The City of London did not wish to lag behind in such heroic deeds. As early as 1642 stormy scenes occurred around the famous Cheapside cross, one of the finest monuments of old London, when some were for overthrowing it whilst others defended it. A concourse, by night, of some 6,000 persons had to be broken up by the military.[3] A year later,[5] in presence of the chief City magistrates, the image of the Crucified—" antichrist "—was thrown into the flames whilst the bells pealed, volleys were discharged, and the spectators celebrated the triumph with acclamations.[4] Even St. Edward's tomb was in danger.[5]

Notwithstanding their loyalty to the King, Catholics could not feel sure of his loyalty to them, for that weak monarch was quite capable of dropping them should his own advantage make it appear advisable.[6] On the other hand, according to Armanni,[7] Parliament, in spite of its hatred of Catholics, was believed to have held out to them the prospect of the repeal of the penal laws on condition that they

[1] March 30, 1643, *ibid.*, 118. *Cf.* Armanni, *loc. cit.*, XII., 164. XVIII., 8, 13 *seq.*, XIX., 172 ; *Rossetti to Barberini, May 17, 1643, *Barb.* 8653, Vatican Library (*ibid.*, for the execution of the Franciscan Heath). May 8, 1643, *Rossetti notes the increase of the persecution of the Catholics in London (*ibid.*) ; on January 3, 1644, the execution of a Franciscan (Arthur Bell) ; *ibid.*, *Barb.* 8654.

[2] April 24, 1643, Gardiner, *loc. cit.*, 154.

[3] Armanni, *loc. cit.*, XII., 164. Yearly report of the English Jesuits for 1645, in Foley, VII., 1146.

[4] On May 14, 1643 (according to Gardiner, *loc. cit.*, 154, the 2nd) ; Armanni, *loc. cit.*, XVIII., 116. *Cf.* Lingard, X., 127, note.

[5] Armanni, *loc. cit.*, 16 *seq.*

[6] Gardiner, *loc. cit.*, 125.

[7] August 30, 1642, *loc. cit.*, XII., 342.

took up arms against the King. A refusal could only spell bitter persecution for them. All that Urban VIII. could do was to send them a comforting letter [1] and to recommend them to Queen Anne of France.[2]

(6)

Soon after the accession of Charles I., Ireland was threatened with the possibility of Spain retaliating for England's unsuccessful attack on Cadiz by effecting a landing on the soil of the Emerald Isle. It was therefore advisable, for the time being, not to provoke the Irish Catholics, and in point of fact, for a period of about three years, Ireland enjoyed a respite from the customary oppression and spoliation. Accordingly, Catholic life asserted itself once more in public. Chapels and convents arose and even a college was opened.[3] In a Brief to Louis XIII.,[4] Urban VIII. exhorted the King to intervene with the husband of his sister, the Queen of England, on behalf of the Irish Catholics. As a matter of fact the hopes which many people had based on the accession of a Catholic Queen, seemed on the verge of realization as far as Ireland was concerned. After the Irish had made a grant to the King of 120,000 pounds, they ventured to present their own requests summed up under fifty-one headings. On the whole all they asked for was to be put on an equal footing with the Protestants. Charles I. promised to grant their requests and confirmed these so-called " graces " with his own signature.[5]

However, even during the three years' truce, there were not wanting forebodings of the coming storm. Falkland, the Viceroy, suppressed the newly erected college, the building being handed over to the Protestants. The scholarly Archbishop of Armagh, Ussher, convened a meeting of eleven

[1] *November 2, 1641, *Epist.*, XIX., 11, Papal Secret Archives.

[2] *October 15, 1643, *ibid.*, 415. *Brief of October 22, 1639, with a present for the English College at Douai, *ibid.*, XVII.

[3] Bellesheim, *Irland*, II., 332 *seqq.*

[4] July 12, 1625, *ibid.*, 732 *seq.*

[5] *Ibid.*, 336; Gardiner, *Hist. of England*, VIII., 13, 17.

other Bishops and together with them published a declaration [1] in which he described the Catholic religion as a superstition and idolatry which it was a great sin to tolerate. On January 31st, 1629, the Viceroy Falkland and the Protestant Archbishops of Dublin and Armagh, requested the Privy Council to allow them to proceed against the Catholics. Thereupon the Viceroy decreed [2] that all chapels, convents and schools of the papists were to be used for other purposes, and priests were forbidden to preach, to hold services or to impart instruction. The day after Christmas 1629, the Anglican Archbishop of Dublin invaded the church of the Franciscans of that city at the head of an armed band and destroyed all he found there.[3] A few days later a decree was issued ordering the sequestration of all chapels, convents, etc., in Ireland.[4] However, consideration for opinion abroad soon enforced a certain amount of mitigation of the latter decree.[5]

Moderation only began with the recall of Falkland, when the government of Ireland passed into the hands of four judges. But these, too, were soon replaced (in 1632) by a new Viceroy in the person of Thomas Wentworth. Wentworth, subsequently Earl of Strafford,[6] was a shrewd politician and a man endowed with unusual energy. His loyalty to his sovereign, which eventually led him to the scaffold, has surrounded him with the glory which never fails to transfigure the victims of iniquitous arbitrariness. As Viceroy of Ireland he successfully promoted industry, improved the fighting forces and

[1] November 26, 1626, in BELLESHEIM., II., 335.

[2] April 1, 1629, *ibid.*, 337.

[3] BELLESHEIM, *loc. cit.*

[4] *Ibid.*, 338.

[5] *Ibid.*, 339. Documents on the persecution of the Catholics in Ireland, 1642–1714, in *Spicilegium Ossoriense*, 2 vols., Dublin, 1877 and 1878. On Ireland at the time of Urban VIII. see GIUNTI, *Vita di L. Ludovisi*, Corsini Library, Rome, *loc. cit.*

[6] *The Earl of Strafford's Letters and Despatches*, London, 1739; for the life of Strafford by JOHN FORSTER (in *Lives of the Statesmen of the Commonwealth*, vol. 1, London, 1836), by ELIZABETH COOPER, 1866 (*cf. Dublin Rev.*, N.S., XXVII. (1876), 469–499), by TRAILL (London, 1889).

increased the revenue. His one motive in all he did seemed to be the desire to provide the King with as large an income as possible ; in pursuit of that object he was utterly unscrupulous in the choice of means. By assuring them that Charles would grant the promised "graces", he induced the credulous Irish Parliament to vote the extravagant sum of 300,000 pounds ; for all that he subsequently represented to the King that the concession of the promised "graces" would endanger the Crown so that it need not be put into effect. Wentworth expropriated the rightful owners of land throughout County Connaught which thus became Crown property.[1] Seeing that he was of opinion that England could never rely on a Catholic Ireland,[2] it was to be expected that he would suppress the traditional religion of the country as soon as he should feel strong enough for such a step.[3] Small wonder, then, if Thomas Wentworth, "Black Tom" as they called him, incurred the hatred of the victims of his violence to such a degree that in 1640 his recall was judged necessary.

But it was too late. Wentworth's violence was only a continuation of what had been done by James I. and the other rulers of Ireland, even under Charles I.[4] His two successors, William Persons, an adventurer who had enriched himself with Irish landed property, and John Borlase, an old soldier, were no better.[5] In the end all that remained to the Irish was "either to turn Protestant, to leave the country or to allow themselves to be strung up in front of their own

[1] BELLESHEIM, II., 346 *seq.* ; GARDINER, IX., 94 *seqq.*

[2] "I see plainly that so long as this kingdom continues popish, they are not a people for the crown of England to be confident of (*Letters*, I., 345). *Cf. Dictionary of National Biography*, LX., 274 ; BELLESHEIM, II., 350.

[3] GARDINER, X., 144. Examples of the sophistry whereby the Irish were robbed of their property, *ibid.*, VIII., 1–28. For a general account see M. J. BONN, *Die englische Kolonisation in Irland*, Stuttgart-Berlin, 1906.

[4] BELLESHEIM, II., 372 *seq.*, who there refutes the fable that at the time of the outbreak of the rebellion of 1641 religious liberty reigned in Ireland.

[5] GARDINER, X., 44 *seq.*

homes ".[1] Much inflammable material had accumulated which, owing to the absence of any prospect of better conditions, was bound to flare up on the slightest provocation,[2] especially in view of what was happening in Scotland where the people were victoriously defending their faith by force of arms.[3] A gentleman of ancient descent, Roger Moore, who had been robbed of almost the whole of his ancestral estates, journeyed all over Ireland where his exhortations to take up arms fell upon willing ears. An attempt to rush Dublin failed but from the end of October, 1641, bands of mostly unarmed men roamed over the country, driving the Protestant interlopers from their domains. Blood flowed, of course, though at first the Irish had not contemplated such an eventuality. At a later date the number of victims was enormously exaggerated, in fact, beyond the limits of all possibility, when grounds were looked for to justify a refusal to restore to the Irish their own property.[4] In point of fact the massacres were started by the Scots who slaughtered 500 Catholics in the Isle of Magee.[5] After the English Parliament's decision, on December 8th, 1641, not to tolerate the Catholic religion in Ireland, the Justices ordered the troops to wipe out the rebels by every means in their power, a command which was pitilessly executed, regardless of age or sex, guilt or innocence. Only the dogs remained, a Protestant Dean wrote, and these

[1] BELLESHEIM, II., 375 *seq.*

[2] " Everything that had been done in Ireland since the flight of the Earls in 1607 (*cf.* our account Vol. XXVI., 213 *seq.*), had been of a nature to lead up to such a catastrophe." GARDINER, X., 43.

[3] LINGARD, X., 41, note. For the plans of the rising see GARDINER, X., 49, 53.

[4] LINGARD, X., 45 *seq.* For the number of the victims see *ibid.*, 401–7 ; BELLESHEIM, II., 377 *seqq.* ; for a proof that (at a gathering at Mullifarvan) the total annihilation of all " heretics " had not been previously arranged, see *Hist.-polit. Blätter*, C. (1887), 122. BONN (*loc. cit.*, II., 23), speaks of a Brief of May 25, 1643, granting absolution for the extermination of all Protestants. In the *Epist.*, XIX.–XXI., Papal Secret Archives, no such Brief is listed.

[5] BELLESHEIM, II., 378.

fed on human flesh. The fact that the Irish lacked arms was an additional motive for the Justices to proceed with the utmost rigour.[1] A subsequent memorandum of theirs betrays the motives of this conduct with the utmost cynicism.[2] Until then, so we read, the Irish had been too numerous to make it possible to carry out the laws; hence their numbers must be reduced by hunger and the sword.

Notwithstanding the cruelty of the English reprisals, nearly the whole island fell into the hands of the insurgents. As soon as these had seized the harbours and some of the wealthy merchants had sided with them, the Irish no longer suffered from a lack of lead and powder, whereas that want was keenly felt by the English, hence the insurgents had the advantage in the struggle.[3] True, even now there was no question of a plan of war or ordered procedure on either side. We read only of skirmishes, sieges and raids for the purpose of destroying the cattle which constituted the country's chief source of wealth.[4] The prosecution of the war continued to bear the stamp of cruelty: "Wherever an English armed troop penetrated, the path of its advance was marked with fire and the gallows."[5] Humane incidents only occurred on the Irish side: "Whenever in the summer of 1642 the Irish forces were led by officers of rank and distinction, they distinguished themselves by acts of humanity in circumstances which were strongly provocative of a contrary action. The garrisons of fortified posts captured by the Irish were uniformly allowed to escape to a place of refuge."[6]

[1] *Ibid.*, 384.

[2] March 18, 1643, in GARDINER, *Civil war*, I., 143 *seq.* "Cynicism," says Gardiner (*ibid.*) of this memorandum, "has seldom gone further than the cool anticipation of slaughter which followed."

[3] *Ibid.*, 133. [4] *Ibid.*, 131. [5] *Ibid.*

[6] "The garrisons of fortified posts captured by the Irish were uniformly allowed to find their way in safety to a place of refuge" (*ibid.*, 132). GARDINER says, in note 1, that he can remember no exception to this, although the letters and documents of that year came exclusively from English sources.

The Catholic clergy of Ireland had no share in the rising of 1641.[1] Not until March of the following year did the Bishops of the Province of Armagh meet in council at Kells, under the presidency of the Archbishop. They laid a three days' fast on their flocks as well as a General Communion; pronounced the penalty of excommunication for murder, robbery, unlawful seizure of landed property or for supporting the enemies of Ireland. They also made provision for the spiritual needs of the army. But the chief object of their deliberations was the main defect in the whole movement, viz. the lack of subordination and unity; hence they realized the necessity of establishing a legislative and administrative council and of the Bishops and nobles maintaining contact and the clergy lending help for the prosecution of the war. They also removed the chief obstacle to the greatly needed unity, namely the fear entertained by many Catholics that they would have to give up Church property in the event of an Irish victory.[2]

In May 1642 a fresh convention of the clergy was held at Kilkenny. It was decided that an oath of federation should seal their agreement and that the clergy should interest themselves in its promotion. No differences or jealousies should be suffered to trouble the harmony of the Catholic clans. Each Province was to have its own Council; a Council General was to be placed over the provincial Councils, and no Province was to conclude a separate peace. Anyone abandoning the Catholic league and abetting the enemy was to be excommunicated; the Bishops were to proceed even against neutrals.[3] Simultaneously with the clergy, the various orders of the nobility also held a convention. Their decisions dealt with the oath of federation, the introductory clauses of which demanded the restoration, for the Church, of the status that had obtained previous to Henry VIII. as well as the setting up of a General Council composed of nine members, for the administration of the country. A general assembly of all Irishmen should decide what further measures should be taken.

[1] BELLESHEIM, II., 386; HASSENKAMPF in the *Hist.-polit. Blätter*, XCVI. (1885), 340–353.

[2] BELLESHEIM, II., 388 *seq.* [3] BELLESHEIM, II., 390 *seq.*

The Protestant reply to these decisions was a prohibition by the Justices on May 28th of all intercourse with the Catholics, and on June 21st, the exclusion from the Irish Parliament of those who refused the oath of supremacy.[1]

The general assembly of all Irishmen met at Kilkenny on October 24th. It elected a Supreme Council of twenty-five members, with Lord Mountgarret as chairman, and four Governors for the four Provinces of Ireland.[2] In reality the assembly at Kilkenny was a Parliament, though it refrained from adopting that title out of consideration for the King who had not sanctioned the gathering.[3] So far from viewing themselves as rebels the Irish were, on the contrary, anxious to take the King's side against Parliament. The Kells' meeting of Bishops began by declaring that the war was a just one seeing that the people of Ireland were defending their religion, their life and property, as well as the rights of the King and the royal family.[4] On the seal of the Catholic League the following motto was engraved: "The Irish united for the cause of God, King and country."[5] After several fruitless efforts they at last succeeded in getting in touch with Charles I.[6] The King hesitated for a few weeks but at length he appointed representatives[7] to confer with the leaders of the Catholics and a conference of both parties took place at Trim on March 17th, 1643. The Catholics stated their grievances and demanded an independent Parliament for Ireland for the purpose of putting order into the situation; to show their gratitude they were prepared to send an army of 10,000 men to the King's assistance.[8]

Already in March 1642 Charles had alluded to their help but his letter had been intercepted, to the very great damage of his cause.[9] The appearance on English soil of 10,000 Irishmen would have roused against him all the Protestants of England.

[1] GARDINER, *Civil war*, I., 131.
[2] BELLESHEIM, II., 391 *seqq.*
[3] GARDINER, *loc. cit.*, 135.
[4] BELLESHEIM, II., 390.
[5] "Pro Deo, rege et patria Hiberni unanimes." GARDINER, *loc. cit.*, 137.
[6] *Ibid.*, 130, 131, 137.
[7] January 11, 1643, *ibid.*, 139.
[8] *Ibid.*, 142.
[9] *Ibid.*, 130.

None the less he was unwilling to drop the negotiations; if Ireland could be pacified, at least for a time, by half-promises, his troops in that country could be released for service in England against Parliament. Accordingly he empowered the Vice-Chancellor Ormond [1] to negotiate a year's truce with the Irish.

Whilst these negotiations were pending there landed in Ireland a papal envoy who was destined to make his weight felt in the deliberations. In April, 1642, the Irish had appealed for help to France and Spain,[2] but especially to the Pope whom they requested to intervene on behalf of their sacred cause by excommunicating the lukewarm in the country itself and by recommending it to the various Princes.[3] Already on a previous occasion Urban VIII. had sent to them letters of encouragement[4] and a subsidy of 20,000 scudi, and on his part Barberini promoted the equipment of five ships with soldiers and munitions.[5] Whilst negotiations for an armistice were in progress, the distinguished Oratorian, Pier Francesco Scarampi, arrived in July, 1643, in the capacity of a papal agent.[6] The papal envoy soon perceived that the chief danger to the cause of the Irish lay in their lack of unity. There were two parties, that of the Old-Irish and that of the descendants of the English who had settled in Ireland from the end of the Middle Ages onwards but who were also Catholics. The Old-Irish were in favour of an energetic prosecution of the war whereas the Anglo-Irish advocated a truce and a compromise, even if by the latter they obtained no more than permission to practise their religion in their own homes.[7] Scarampi wholeheartedly took the part of the Old-Irish. The salvation of Ireland, he argued, would come from arms and intrepid action, not from a truce and from lukewarmness. Peace between the King and

[1] April 23, 1643, *ibid.*, 145. For what he was willing to concede see *ibid.*, 140 (to Ormond, January 12, 1643).

[2] BELLESHEIM, II., 393, 395. [3] *Ibid.*, 393 *seq.*

[4] February 1, 1642, *ibid.*, 387. [5] *Ibid.*, 388.

[6] *Brief of nomination, April 12, 1643, *Epist.*, X., 19, Papal Secret Archives.

[7] BELLESHEIM, II., 400.

Parliament was unlikely, and should it come about, they would join forces for an attack on Ireland. If the English Parliament triumphed, Ireland was lost ; if the King was victorious, his Protestant partisans would deem it sufficient if the country reverted to the miserable pre-war condition. On the other hand, if at the end of the struggle in England, the victorious party was faced with a strong Ireland, powerful by reason of a well-equipped army and its foreign connections, England would take care not to commit any acts of violence or to suppress religious freedom.[1]

Scarampi's arguments did not prevail ; on September 2nd, 1643, a twelvemonths' truce was arranged. With the exception of a few strong places, a strip of coast in the north-east and round Cork in the south, the whole of Ireland was to remain in the hands of the Catholic league. The Scots, who held a strong position at Carrickfergus, were to be free to accept the truce ; if they refused, Ormond and his troops were not to hinder the Irishmen's attack on them. In exchange for these concessions the united Catholics undertook to provide a subsidy for the maintenance of the English garrison at Naas and the transportation of the English regiments to England.[2] When this transportation became a fact, it did the King's cause incalculable harm in consequence of the erroneous notion that he had summoned them to assist him in his struggle against Parliament.[3] Charles, however, only sought to obtain from Ireland the 10,000 men [4] who had been promised to him at an earlier date,[5] but the Irish made it a condition that they should have freedom of religion and a Parliament of their own.[6] This the King could not and would not grant ; the envoys of the Catholic league were graciously dismissed and the negotiations for a treaty of peace were left in the hands of the Viceroy Ormond.[7]

Urban VIII. was annoyed when he learnt of the conclusion of

[1] GARDINER, *Civil war*, I., 261 *seq.* ; BELLESHEIM, II., 401 *seq.*

[2] GARDINER, *loc. cit.*, 264. [3] *Cf.* above, p. 345.

[4] In February, 1644, in GARDINER, *loc. cit.*, 300.

[5] *Cf.* above, p. 345. [6] GARDINER, *loc. cit.*, 392.

[7] *Ibid.*, 409 ; BELLESHEIM, II., 402.

the armistice. He sent the agent of the Irish Bishops in Rome, Edmund Dwyer, to Ireland, with letters [1] addressed to the whole Irish nation, the Supreme Council and the Archbishops of Dublin, Armagh and Tuam. They contain exhortations to constancy and concord, to the end that the struggle might be brought to a happy termination. That the Pope was not disposed to approve the armistice is made plain enough. To the people of Dublin Urban VIII. sent a Brief in praise of their constancy in the faith.[2] When Dwyer returned to Rome with replies to the papal letters, the Pope was no longer among the living. Urban VIII. had spent about 80,000 gold florins for the liberation of Ireland.[3] In other ways also he had shown his solicitude for the Emerald Isle. In Rome itself a distinguished and scholarly friar, Luke Wadding, took great interest in the Irish and in 1642 he became their representative in Italy. In 1625 Wadding, through whose hands nearly all the ecclesiastical affairs of his native country passed, had founded in Rome the College of St. Isidore for the benefit of his brethren in religion.[4] In 1628 he and Cardinal Ludovisi between them made it possible for Urban VIII. to found the Irish College which had already been planned by Gregory XIII., and to whose pupils the Barberini Pope granted in 1631 the privileges enjoyed by the students of Propaganda.[5] Wadding became the first Rector of the College but in 1635 he had to hand over its government to the Jesuits [6] who transferred the institution to

[1] February 18, 1644, in Bellesheim, II., 408.

[2] April 27, 1644, *ibid.*

[3] *Ibid.*, 409. A Jubilee for Ireland granted on May 15, 1640, *Bull.*, XV., 260.

[4] *Cf.* F. Harold, *Fr. L. Waddingi Vita*, in *Epit. Annal. Ord. Min.*, I., Rome, 1682, 7 *seq.*; *Collegium S. Isidori de Urbe et S. Mariae de Plano Capranicae FF. Min. Recoll. Hiberniae fundatio a P. Luca Wadding*, Romae, 1892; G. Cleary, *Father Luke Wadding and St. Isidore's College, Rome. Biographical and historical notes and documents. A contribution to the tercentenary celebrations*, 1625–1925, Rome, 1925.

[5] *Cf.* the controversial work of Card. Marefoschi: *Relaz. d. visita del Collegio Ibernese*, Roma, 1772, 65 *seq.*, 73 *seq.*

[6] See *Ibid.*, 80 *seq.*

a house near the Dominican church of S. Annunziata. Cardinal Ludovisi remained attached to the establishment and in his will he left it his great vineyard at Castel Gandolfo.[1]

(7)

The Catholics of Scotland might well have hailed Charles I.'s French marriage with hopes similar to those of their co-religionists in England. Like them, they too were involved in the troubles arising out of the dispute concerning the Vicars Apostolic. In Scotland, too, there were many who longed for a Superior invested with episcopal authority. This wish was fulfilled by the appointment of William Bishop and Richard Smith, even though Scotland was again temporarily withdrawn from the jurisdiction of Bishop. When Bishop had made himself impossible his place as Prefect Apostolic for Scotland was taken by the Benedictine Silvanus who was, however, relieved by the Abbot of St. James of Würzburg as early as 1627.[2] On the representations of the Scottish missionary, David Camerarius [Chambers], Propaganda decided in 1631 to give to the Scottish mission another Superior in episcopal orders, one reason being the fact that the number of Catholics had risen to 10,000, and another the need of neutralizing the influence of the Protestant Bishop of Lismore. However, the decision was not carried into effect.[3]

On being consulted by Propaganda, the Jesuits declared themselves opposed to the appointment of an ecclesiastical Superior in Scotland[4]; their opinion carried great weight

[1] *Cf.* MORONI, XIV., 175 *seq.* More on the Irish seminaries in BELLESHEIM, II., 357. Briefs of December 24, 1624 (for Louvain), and of July 20, 1636 (for Lille), in *Bull.*, XIII., 266 (*cf.* 273), XIV., 543. At Lisbon there was the Dominican College of the Holy Rosary and that of St. Patrick for the Irish; see *Collegi*, 370, Archives of Propaganda, Rome. At Louvain also there was an Irish Dominican College, see *ibid.*

[2] BELLESHEIM, *Scotland*, IV., 41, *cf.* 81.

[3] BELLESHEIM, IV., 41.

[4] Documents of Propaganda for August 5, 1630, *ibid.*, 43, n. 1.

since the cure of souls in Scotland was for the most part in their hands.[1] Under James I., and as late as 1661, the secular priests never numbered more than five or six [2] so that a Vicar Apostolic would have been like a general without an army. Besides the Jesuits, the principal missionaries in Scotland were the Franciscans who had a mission in the north of the country since 1619.[3] The Capuchins had one even previous to that date. The outstanding figures among these were Epiphanius Lindsay and Archangel Leslie, both of them sprung from noble families and educated in the Scots' Colleges of Louvain and Rome. They were instrumental in bringing back many Protestants to the ancient Church, among them persons of high rank.[4] The same applied to the Jesuits Christie and James Mambrecht; up to 1628 Christie reconciled no less than four hundred persons to the Church.[5]

Special mention must be made of the Franciscan mission in the Hebrides. In these islands, access to which is rendered difficult by rough seas, there existed a remnant of the ancient Church which, as a matter of fact, has maintained itself up to our own days. However, in consequence of the lack of priests, the moral standard of the population had sunk to a very low level. Thousands were now strengthened anew in the faith, in particular by the Franciscan Patrick Hegerty.[6] In 1640, the Bishop of Down, in Ireland, endeavoured to get that zealous priest appointed Bishop of the Hebrides, but Propaganda refused to fall in with his views.[7] Hegerty's confrère, Ward, reconciled 382 Protestants to the ancient

[1] *Ibid.*, 58. For a time they were the only priests in Scotland (*ibid.*, 64).

[2] *Ibid.*, 49, n. 1.

[3] *Ibid.*, 70 *seqq.*

[4] *Ibid.*, 78 *seqq.* For Leslie, *cf.* G. B. Rinuccini, *Il Capuccino Scozzese*, Rome, 1645; *American Cath. Quarterly Review*, XXXIII. (1908), 29–56.

[5] Bellesheim, IV., 48 *seqq.*; yearly report of the Jesuit mission of 1627 to 1773 in W. Forbes-Leith, *Memoirs of Scottish Catholics during the XVIIth and XVIIIth centuries*, London, 1909.

[6] Bellesheim, IV., 69 *seqq.*

[7] *Ibid.*, 42, note 1.

Church but paid for his zeal with fifteen months' strict imprisonment and nine months of lighter detention in London.[1] It is noteworthy that, in spite of adverse circumstances, even some Protestant preachers in Scotland returned to the Church.[2]

In the reports on the activities of the Scottish priests there is constant question of imprisonment, pursuit from place to place and endless privations. A proclamation of the year 1628 describes the priests as "the most pernicious pests in the commonweal"; no one must receive them, or give them food, drink, lodging, or escort.[3] However, death sentences were hardly ever carried out in Scotland. Subsequently to the execution of the Jesuit Ogilvie at Glasgow, in the year 1615, the capital sentence was passed on the latter's brother in religion, John Mambrecht, who was, however, reprieved at the intercession of the Queen, and on the Capuchin Lindsay, who likewise escaped execution.[4] By means of prohibitions of the old religion, confiscation of property, forcible upbringing of Catholic children as Protestants and by banishment, regardless or either age or sex, the Catholics were oppressed to such an extent [5] that an eye-witness reported to Urban VIII. that one could wish for a return of the times of Queen Elizabeth.[6] At the beginning of his reign Charles I. published stringent penal laws against Catholics, with a view to countering the suspicion that he cherished leanings towards the ancient Church.[7] In subsequent years he occasionally mitigated the merciless severity of the law, but the preachers never ceased from pressing for the execution of the proclamations.[8]

Cardinal Francesco Barberini was the Protector of the Scottish Catholics,[9] but all he was able to do was to interest himself in impoverished Scottish families or to give hospitality to pilgrims from that country as, for instance, during the jubilee of 1625. The Pope had granted him extensive faculties

1 *Ibid.*, IV., 69 *seq.*

2 *Ibid.*, 68, 70.

3 *Ibid.*, 37.

4 *Ibid.*, 73, 76.

5 *Ibid.*, 9 *seqq.*

6 *Ibid.*, 9, note 1.

7 *Ibid.*

8 *Ibid.*, 18 *seq.*

9 Since October 2, 1623, *ibid.*, 38.

for the benefit of Scotland.[1] The Congregation of Propaganda appealed to Queen Henrietta Maria [2] to use her influence with her husband "with a view to putting an end to the cruel persecution". The Pope himself addressed a letter to the Queen to the same purpose.[3] According to information soon after received by Propaganda,[4] there was a hope that this request had not been in vain, However, in a letter of December 17th, 1640, a Jesuit gave it as his opinion that what they had endured up till then was only a foretaste of worse to come. "Within the last ten days," he wrote, "orders have been published throughout Scotland, not to sell anything to Catholics or to buy from them. Many are already deprived of their rents and revenues, others have offered three-fourths of their property in the hope of saving the remaining fourth for the maintenance of themselves and their familes. The threat is heard that not a single Catholic shall be allowed to live or to remain in Scotland by the end of the year." [5]

(8)

It was during the pontificate of Urban VIII. that the Catholic Church for the first time secured a firm footing in English North-American territory which was destined eventually to form part of the United States. The event was one of paramount importance. Even previous to England's first attempt at colonization in those territories, the harshness of the penal laws had caused more than one daring Catholic to think of seeking beyond the ocean the freedom which the Mother Country denied them. As early as 1574, Humphrey Gilbert and George Peckham took some tentative steps in this direction. Characteristically enough, letters-patent issued to Gilbert and his companions except them from the law against "fugitives overseas" which had been devised against Catholic recusants. On June 6th, 1582, Gilbert informed Thomas Gerrard and George Peckham of the privilege thus granted and these appealed in their own names to Walsingham

[1] May 18, 1630, *ibid.*

[2] November 16, 1632, *ibid.*, 26.

[3] February 12, 1633, *ibid.*

[4] September 16, 1632, *ibid.*, 27.

[5] *Ibid.*, 62.

with a request that other recusants might be allowed to sail with them.[1] At that time the whole undertaking was represented to Walsingham as a Catholic venture,[2] and as far as Gerrard and Peckham were concerned, the Jesuit Persons, who was then in Rome, shared that view.[3] A Catholic gentleman of the name of Winslade had consulted Persons on the question of the emigration to America of about a thousand Catholics of the poorer classes; some of their more well-to-do co-religionists would be asked to sell their estates and apply the proceeds to the enterprise which should be urged from the pulpit and recommended to Catholic Princes.[4]

Within the next eighty years no less than fifty-nine licences for colonial enterprises in America were granted, but Catholics were everywhere excluded since the law demanded the oaths of supremacy and loyalty, the only exception being Maryland, a foundation of George Calvert, a Catholic.[5]

On completing his studies at Oxford, Calvert acted at first as private secretary to Salisbury. In 1619 he became one of the two Secretaries of State and in that capacity dealt chiefly with foreign affairs. He had been a member of Parliament since 1609; in 1617 he was knighted and in 1620 he acquired the south-eastern portion of Newfoundland in the possession of which he was confirmed by James I. on April 7th, 1623. His colonizing plans probably had something to do with his intention of embracing the Catholic religion. This intention he carried into effect in the following year and on February 12th, 1625, he resigned his office. He was, however, given an Irish peerage with the title of Lord Baltimore; he was also able to retain his extensive estates in the Emerald Isle. But it was impossible for him to remain in the Privy Council since he could not take the oath of allegiance.[6]

In the summer of 1627 Lord Baltimore paid a visit to "Avalon", as he called his estate in Newfoundland, after the

[1] Hughes, I., 146 *seq.*, 148. [2] *Ibid.*, 147. [3] *Ibid.*, 154.

[4] Parson's unfavourable opinion, March 18, 1605, *ibid.*, 153 *seqq.*

[5] *Ibid.*, 151 *seq.*

[6] *Ibid.*, 176 *seq.*; G. F. Bettany in *Dictionary of English Biography*, VIII., 269 *seqq.*

cradle of Christianity in Britain.[1] He paid a second visit thither in the spring of 1628, but finding the climate too rough, he returned to England for the purpose of exchanging "Avalon", by royal decree, for a strip of territory in Virginia.[2]

The plan met with opposition from Virginia: accordingly a piece of land further north was allotted to him which, in honour of Queen Henrietta Maria, he called Maryland.[3] However, Lord Baltimore died on April 15th, 1632, before the seal had been put on the royal grant. A man of lofty character and wide outlook,[4] Baltimore set up an imperishable monument to his name in the charter for his colony of Maryland, a unique document at that period and one that marks an epoch in the evolution of History. Whereas the foundation charters of the other American colonies contain clauses against "the superstitions of the Romish Church", Baltimore's charter for Avalon, though drawn up by him when still a Protestant, only speaks of "God's holy and true Christian religion", which must not be injured. In the grant for Maryland, the King expressly guaranteed to Baltimore unlimited freedom to erect churches and chapels, the right of patronage over all churches to be erected thereafter, and the removal of all the barriers which, in accordance with the English law on *mortmain*, limited the rights of corporate bodies with regard to immovable property.[5] All the liberties and privileges of the realm of

[1] HUGHES, I., 180. [2] *Ibid.*, 200. [3] *Ibid.*, 233 *seq.*

[4] *Ibid.*, 234 *seq.* *Cf.* the testimony of the Protestant bishop Goodman, *ibid.*, 179. The French ambassador Tillières wrote thus about Baltimore, on November 25, 1621: "the third man (after the King and Buckingham) in whose hands affairs presumably rest, is the Secretary of State, Calvert. He is an honourable, reasonable, well-disposed man, courteous to strangers, very respectful towards ambassadors, zealous for the welfare of England, but on account of these virtues wholly without prestige or influence (in RAUMER, *Briefe*, II., ii).

[5] HUGHES, I., 237–243. Churches and chapels were to be consecrated "according to the ecclesiastical laws of our realm of England". But according to the language of the time this did not refer in any way to the Protestant or Anglican communities. *Ibid.*, 237–9.

England were extended to Maryland, hence the English laws against Catholics did not operate there.

Baltimore's death was a heavy blow for Maryland. His son and heir, Cecil Calvert, second Lord Baltimore, had outwardly returned to the ancient Church at the same time as his father, but at heart he was out of sympathy with Catholic thought.[1] Thus during the voyage to the new colony he forbade every outward practice of Catholicism although the only Protestants among the emigrants were the servants and other persons of lower degree, whereas the upper class consisted exclusively of Catholics.[2] His action for the further development of Maryland also betrayed his lack of nobility of character: his one aim was, apparently, by just or unjust means, to get out of his colony as much profit as he could, irrespectively of the means employed. The first Lord Baltimore's second son, Leonard Calvert, who was Governor of Maryland, considered himself as his brother's tool and left to him the responsibility for the execution of the orders of London. Cecil remained permanently in London; after 1637 his plans and intentions for the colony were in the hands of John Lewger, who had been a Protestant minister, became a convert to the faith but remained wholly impregnated with the spirit of Caesaro-papalism.[3] Lewger was entrusted with the legislation of the new colony. A first draft, of which Baltimore himself was the author, was rejected by the free proprietors of Maryland in 1638[4]: a second, drawn up by Lewger, met with better success; its forty-three articles were read and approved in some ten sittings of half a day's duration each between March 12 and 24th, 1638,[5] although they guaranteed to the noble owner of the colony the most exorbitant powers over the colonists. The whole of the territorial property which the English colonists had lawfully appropriated, was declared to be Baltimore's property, which the allodial owners could only hold in fief from him,[6] whilst the coercive powers of his representatives were so slightly limited by law, as to make them almost

[1] HUGHES, II., 671–5.
[2] *Ibid.*, I., 260, 332 *seq.*
[3] *Ibid.*, 350 *seqq.*
[4] *Ibid.*, 380 *seqq.*
[5] *Ibid.*, 388 *seq.*
[6] *Ibid.*, 398.

entirely arbitrary.[1] A third legislative draft, of which only a few fragments were actually enforced, was no better.[2] Lewger's laws were such, so we read in a memorial to the Inquisition at a later date,[3] that it was possible to tear his shirt off any man's back if it was in the interest of the State. With regard to the right of ownership in particular, the secular power was allowed the most arbitrary interference. Thus if an heiress was not married by the time she attained her twenty-fifth year, her inheritance was forfeit.[4] Ecclesiastical jurisdiction was confined within the narrowest sphere of the conscience ; whatever appeared outwardly came under the jurisdiction of the State and could only claim validity in law if the civil power gave its approval.[5] The acceptance of such a scheme by the assembly of free proprietors can only be accounted for by the fact that many concurred in it because they had nothing to lose, or because they were Protestants,[6] and because they were given no time for reflection. However, by degrees, their better judgment asserted itself and the most authoritative voices warned Lord Baltimore against granting to these proposals an approval that would have given them force of law.[7] With regard to the intrusion into the ecclesiastical sphere in particular, the clergy offered a determined opposition.

Up till that time all the priests in Maryland had been Jesuits. The younger Lord Baltimore had requested their co-operation [8] but when they reached Maryland, no provision had been made for them [9] so that, like the rest of the planters, they were compelled to keep themselves. They submitted to circumstances and established themselves so successfully that, in accordance with the laws of colonization, the number of their servants entitled them to 28,500 acres. Four years after the arrival of the Jesuits, one of their number wrote [10] that though their chief object was to save souls, no one had even approximately done as much as they had for the colonization and

[1] *Ibid.*, 402.
[2] *Ibid.*, 427 *seqq.*, 449 *seqq.*
[3] Of the year 1642, *ibid.*, 515.
[4] *Ibid.*, 418.
[5] *Ibid.*, 417.
[6] *Ibid.*, 391 *seqq.*, 419.
[7] *Ibid.*, 405 *seqq.*
[8] *Ibid.*, 246 *seqq.*
[9] *Ibid.*, 255.
[10] *Ibid.*, 264 *seq.*

cultivation of the country. They laboured not unsuccessfully for the spread of Christianity among the Indians.[1]

The Jesuits refused to fall in with Lewger's conception of Canon Law. The latter informed Baltimore of the fact, with the consequence that Baltimore became estranged from them.[2] He sought to apply at least to the Jesuits the laws on property which, on the whole, proved impossible of application in the colony.[3] He forcibly took from the Fathers an estate which a convert Indian Chief had made over to them.[4] The situation of the Jesuits became so straitened that their Superior thought of withdrawing from Maryland.[5] Of this the missionaries would not hear: "As far as I am concerned," one of them wrote,[6] "I would rather labour here for the conversion of the Indians and die of hunger under the vault of heaven, bereft of all human comfort, than through fear of want entertain so much as a thought of abandoning so holy a task." Baltimore sought in vain to persuade the Provincial of the English Jesuits to fall in with his ideas.[7] There can be no doubt that it was at his instigation that an attempt was subsequently made to remove the Jesuits from Maryland. In a petition to Propaganda [8] it was stated that a new colony had arisen in that country and that the number of Catholics was on the increase; accordingly the petitioners prayed for priests to be sent out, provided with ample faculties, but not a word was breathed of the fact that Jesuits were already labouring in Maryland. Thereupon the Congregation sought information about the colony from the nuncio Rossetti [9] and on February 14th, 1642, some further steps were taken in the matter.[10] In the meantime, however, the dispute between Baltimore and the Jesuits had been taken before the Roman Inquisition; a fortnight before publication of the decree of Propaganda,

[1] *Ibid.*, 336, 481.
[2] *Ibid.*, 419.
[3] *Ibid.*, 399.
[4] *Ibid.*, 477, 489.
[5] *Ibid.*, 481, 514, 529.
[6] Ferd. Poulton, May 3, 1641, *ibid.*, 482; *Documents*, I., 121.
[7] Hughes, *Hist.*, I., 501 *seqq.*, 529.
[8] July 6, 1641, Hughes, I., 493.
[9] *Ibid.*, 496 *seqq.*
[10] *Ibid.*, 519.

the former decided that for the time being things should be left as they were.[1] The secular priests destined for Maryland vainly waited for a long time for the extensive faculties for which they had petitioned the nuncio Rossetti. At last they inquired from Richard Smith, Bishop of Chalcedon and former Vicar Apostolic for England, whether the faculties they held in England were available also for British America and asked his permission to start on their voyage.[2] Rossetti sought to dissuade them.[3] In the end the Jesuits themselves took steps in Rome to obtain the required faculties ; two English secular priests set out for the colony which Baltimore had just forbidden two Jesuits to enter.[4]

Meanwhile the straits of the Jesuits in Maryland continued. From one of them Baltimore bought the whole of his property though on the conclusion of the transaction he would neither pay the purchase money nor restore the estate.[1] At last the General of the Order decided [2] that everything should be done so as to secure the goodwill of Baltimore, lest in consequence of a dispute over temporal goods the Indians should forfeit eternal ones. The landed estates already in their possession could not be surrendered without leave of the Pope, since there was question of Church property, but in the future the missionaries must not accept immovable property without Baltimore's permission. The latter, however, was not yet satisfied ; on the contrary, he insisted on the estates which had previously come into the possession of the Jesuits, being surrendered to him. To this the Assistant of the ageing General Vitelleschi replied [3] that he would submit the matter to the Roman Congregation but as far as the Order was concerned, they would act on the principle : " Let us have the souls, the rest you may take for yourself " ; in view of the fact that the Jesuits only sought to spread the faith it could not but be painful to them if the seed of the Gospel so happily scattered were to be

[1] *Ibid.*, 520.
[2] *Ibid.*, 521.
[3] *Ibid.*, 524.
[4] *Ibid.*, 532, 536 *seq.*, 555.
[5] *Ibid.*, 541 *seq.*
[6] October 31, 1643, *ibid.*, 557 ; *Documents*, I., 29 *seq.*
[7] November 5, 1644, Hughes, I., 561 ; *Documents*, I., 32.

stifled by the weeds of such disputes. Not long after Baltimore's order that the two secular priests of Maryland should be maintained not at his but at the Jesuits' expense,[1] the revolution broke out in England and for the time being, provided a radical solution of existing difficulties. Some of the Jesuit missionaries were shipped back to England ; the others fled and perished miserably.[2] In the end Baltimore himself was destined to experience at the hands of the Government difficulties similar to those which he had created for others in his colony.

[1] HUGHES, *Hist.*, I., 561.
[2] *Ibid.*, 562.

CHAPTER V.

THE STATES OF THE CHURCH AND THE WAR OF CASTRO.

(1)

The warlike nature of the period of Urban VIII.'s pontificate made the military weakness of the States of the Church painfully evident.[1] Everything was lacking: trained troops, armaments, and adequate fortresses. Apart from Ferrara, Ancona, and Civitavecchia, the fortifications of the other strong places of the Pontifical States were for the most part obsolete and, to a large extent, in an utterly neglected state.[2] From the beginning of his reign Urban VIII., who was unwilling to depend on the favour of other Powers, showed great keenness for such an improvement of his armed forces as should render them capable of guaranteeing the security of the States of the Church. As early as the beginning of 1624 he planned the construction of a citadel at Bologna, and because the Bolognese saw in the scheme a means of surveillance rather than of security,[3] he resolved to transform Castelfranco, a locality situate on the borders of Modena, into a powerful fortress.

In addition to this, extensive work was in progress in Rome

[1] This weakness had been on the increase in the latter years according to R. ZENO (143).

[2] *Cf.* P. CONTARINI, 201, and a detailed account apparently based on ocular evidence, **Descrittione dello stato ecclesiastico data al S. Marchese di Pianazza* in *Cod.* 1776, of the town library, Trent; this was written at the time of the conflict between Alexander VII. and Louis XIV. and contains interesting retrospects of the period of Urban VIII.

[3] *Cf.* *Avviso of May 15, 1624, *Urb.* 1094, Vatican Library.

since 1624,[1] for the purpose of turning the Castle of S. Angelo, the fortifications of which dated for the most part from the time of Alexander VI. and were inadequate, into an impregnable bulwark.[2] The advanced works were strengthened, the bastions which enclose from the side of the plain the square of the castle properly so called, with its towers at the four corners, were begun, the moats were widened, and barracks, magazines, a gun factory, and mills established.[3] In 1625 and 1627 the Pope personally inspected the constructions then in full swing. They were planned for the accommodation of 6,000 men.[4] " Every day," so we read in a report drawn up in the last days of August 1627, " work proceeds on this royal fortress." [5] Inscriptions of 1628, 1630, 1631, 1636, and 1641, show that the transformation of S. Angelo into " a modern fortress " went on throughout the pontificate of Urban VIII.[6] The work, in the course of which the Barberini Faun now at Munich, was found,[7] was directed first by Giulio Buratti, then by the

[1] See FORCELLA, XIII., 147.

[2] The *legend of the *Pianta di Borgo e di Castel S. Angelo* (*Barb.*, 4409, n. 40, Vat. Libr.), is thus worded : " *Fortezza da S. S.tà resa per cosi dire inespugnabile* ".

[3] See M. BORGATTI, *Castel S. Angelo*, Roma, 1890, 146 *seq.* ; BOSSI, *La Pasquinata* (1898), 39 *seq.*, 74 *seq.*

[4] See the *Avvisi of September 20, 1625, and February 13, 1627, *Urb.*, 1095 and 1097, *loc. cit.* ; P. CONTARINI, 202, and the *Avvisi in FRASCHETTI, 80. A **Discorso sopra il risarcimento del Castel S. Angelo fatto l'a. 1625*, by PIETRO EGIDII, was in the Corvisieri Library, Rome, which, unfortunately, has been dispersed, **Errori notabili nelle nuove fortificazioni di Castel S. Angelo considerati da Franc. Scala da Faenza per rappresentarli a S. S.tà* in *Barb.*, 4344, p. 42 *seq.* Vatican Library.

[5] See the *Avvisi of August 28 and September 8, 1627, *Urb.*, 1097, *loc. cit.* *Cf.* MARTINORI, 73.

[6] See FORCELLA, XIII., 148–150 ; TOTTI, 3–4. *Cf.* *Avviso of August 2, 1628, *Urb.*, 1098, Vatican Library. For the restoration of the passage leading to Castel S. Angelo see BAGLIONE, 178.

[7] *Cf.* A. E. POPP, *Der Barberinische Faun*, in *Wiener Jahrb. f. Kunstgesch.*, new series, I. (1921/2), fasc. 4. For a find of coins of Alaric, in 1633, see KHEVENHÜLLER, XII., 792.

Dominican and future Cardinal Maculano, and lastly by Peter Paul Floriani and Bernini.[1]

The work at Castelfranco, which was given the name of "Forte Urbano", was pushed forward with no less ardour.[2] Although the Duke of Modena and the Bolognese were greatly annoyed at the rise of this fortress, Urban VIII. held fast to a plan which swallowed vast sums of money owing to subsidences of the soil and the fact that the district was fever-infested.[3] The fortifications of Loreto,[4] Ancona,[5] Sinigaglia, Pesaro,[6] Rimini,[7] and those of the Castle of Orvieto[8] were also completed. At the beginning of the forties, the Quirinal was surrounded by a protective wall.[9] At this time also a start was made with the vast constructions on the Janiculum. These works were necessitated by the war of Castro; they were under the direction of the Dominican Vincenzo Maculano, famous for his engineering skill.

Urban VIII. also cherished great plans for Civitavecchia which was declared an open port at the end of 1630, whilst it was also decided to make it a military harbour with a view to the maintenance of communications by sea with some friendly

[1] *Cf.* Baglione, 178; Morus, IV., 187; C. Promis, *Ingegnieri milit. della Marca d'Ancona*, Torino, 1865, 81 *seq.*; Marchese, *Mem. dei pittori, etc., Domenicani*, II., 306; Fraschetti, 80.

[2] The place was raised to the dignity of a town (*Città Urbana*), see *Avviso of July 7, 1635, *Urb.*, 1103, *loc. cit.* *Cf. Bull.*, XIV., 17 *seq.* See also *Barb.*, 4409, n. 85, Vatican Library.

[3] See G. Pesaro, 330; Alv. Contarini, 359; Khevenhüller, XI., 792; Nani, 23; Brosch, I., 397; Martinori, 74. *Cf.* *Avviso of February 14, 1629, *Urb.*, 1099, Vatican Library, Giulio Buratti, **Breve relazione delle spese fatte per la fortezza Urbana dal principio di essa fin alli 27 di Settembre, 1634*, *Vat.*, 6922, p. 87 *seq.*, *ibid.*

[4] *Cf. Guida di Loreto*, Siena, 1891, 27, 30.

[5] See Ciaconius, IV., 518.

[6] See Brosch, I., 398.

[7] See Novaes, IX., 294.

[8] See Pardi, *Guida di Orvieto*, Orvieto, 1896, 36.

[9] *Cf.* below, ch. VI.

Mediterranean Power.[1] Pompous inscriptions and a beautiful medal extolled the work executed at Civitavecchia, viz., the improvement of the harbour, the restoration of the old lighthouse, the construction of a new one and the strengthening of the fortifications.[2] The Venetians watched these undertakings all the more jealously as the Pope's efforts for the furtherance of Ancona's trade filled them with anxiety.[3]

In the production of engines of war Urban VIII. displayed an activity which has been described as feverish.[4] The arms factory erected by Paul V. at Tivoli was enlarged ; its working was exceedingly costly so long as the necessary iron had to be imported from abroad. To the Pope's extreme satisfaction, mines of iron ore were at last found in the Papal States,[5] though their output did not equal the demand, so that a cargo of iron from Granada in Spain at a later date (in 1643) proved very acceptable.[6] For the fabrication of guns even the antique bronze girders of the portico of the Pantheon and an antique door of S. Adriano were melted down, an act which inspired the famous epigram of Giulio Mancini, the Pope's physician:

[1] See besides G. PESARO, 330, and NANI, 22, also GUGLIELMOTTI, *Squadra*, 410 *seq.* ; CALISSE in *Bauer's Zeitschr. für Sozial- und Wirtschaftsgeschichte*, VII. (1899), 191 *seq.* ; BROSCH, I., 398. *Cf.* also CAUCHIE, *Instruct. des Nonces de Flandre*, 246.

[2] See BONANNI, II., 586 ; VENUTO, 232 ; MARTINORI, 73 ; CALISSE, 450 *seq.* ; GUGLIELMOTTI, II., 412 *seq.* ; POLLAK-FREY, 416. Claude Lorrain drew the harbour of Civitavecchia, with the bastions and the lighthouse, from nature ; see FRIEDLÄNDER, *Claude Lorrain*, 172 *seq.*

[3] See G. PESARO, 330 *seq.* ; ALV. CONTARINI, 385.

[4] See BROSCH, I., 398.

[5] See *Avviso of June 23, 1629 (the iron in the new " miniera nella montagna di Cascia " was very good for " corsaletti, morioni, archibugi "), *Urb.*, 1099, Vatican Library. For the " miniere alle ferriere di Monteleone nell'Umbria ", first exploited by Urban VIII., see MARTINORI, 75, and A. MORINI in *Bollett. d. Deput. p. l'Umbria*, IX. (1903), 3.

[6] See the *Brief to Philip IV., dated July 10, 1643, *Epist.*, XIX., Papal Secret Archives.

"What the Barbarians failed to do, that the Barberini have done." [1]

Already in 1625 and 1626 the armaments accumulated in Castel S. Angelo were very considerable for those times.[2] Urban VIII.'s interest in military matters is strikingly revealed by the fact that under the Vatican Library he had fitted out an arsenal in which were stored manual weapons for an army of 28,000 men [3]; a special medal was struck in its honour, and it was considered one of the sights of Rome.[4] In 1631, 100,000 scudi were spent on buying arms from the niece and heiress of the Duke of Urbino.[5] Diplomatists soon discovered that nothing gave the Pope greater pleasure than when they praised

[1] See the *Avvisi of August 23 (a present for the casting of 60 pieces of canon), and September 20, 1625 ("Giulio Mancini, medico secreto" of the Pope, said, "motteggiando, che quello che non hanno fatto i Barbari, facevano i Barberini"), *Urb.*, 1095, Vatican Library. *Ibid.*, 1097, *Avviso of July 22, 1627, on eighty new bronze cannon which were brought to S. Angelo when the smaller ones were removed for the purpose of recasting.

[2] See CERASOLI, in the *Studi e documenti*, XIV., 59 *seq.*, who published the inventory in *Cod. Barb.*, 6310.

[3] See FORCELLA, VI., 148, 153; TAJA, 487 *seq.*; EHRLE, *Maggi-Mascardi*, 10; SCHUDT, *Mancini*, 50; NANI, 23; MARTINORI, 74. RANKE is mistaken when he says (II.[8], 352) that the rooms of the Vatican Library were intended for use as an arsenal. The Armeria which lies below the Library is now used as a mosaic workshop; over the entrance, Urban VIII.'s fine coat of arms may still be seen.

[4] The pen and ink sketch of the *plan in *Barb.*, 4409, n. 33 (Vat. Libr.), is thus headed: *Armeria posta sotto la libreria Vaticana, cosa unica al mondo, fatta d'ordine di N.S. per sicurezza di Roma e d'Italia, dove da diversi parti del mondo vengono principi a vederla. Ibid.*, n. 35: *Porta d'Armeria fuori* with an inscription; n. 36: *Parte di dentro della Armeria*; n. 37: *Prospetto della Armeria.* JOHN EVELYN, who visited Rome in 1644, observes in his *Diary* (129): "I hardly believe any prince in Europe is able to shew a more compleately furnish'd library of Mars for the quality and quantity."

[5] See *Avviso of August 9, 1631, *Ottob.*, 3338, II., Vatican Library.

his military preparations.[1] Urban himself often turned the conversation to this topic. In January, 1625, he remarked to the Venetian envoy, Pietro Contarini, that the States of the Church had plenty of men able to bear arms and that 15,000 could be mobilized at a moment's notice; there was no lack of arms, 15,000 scudi had been spent on them recently; the fortresses which had been neglected were being put in good condition and the battle fleet was being improved; it was his intention to raise the number of his galleys to twelve and to put a stop to the practice which had formerly obtained of using them on occasion for commercial purposes.[2] In 1628 Urban told the envoy of Lucca that he had already spent 800,000 scudi on the fortifications of Castle S. Angelo and that he had other works in view for the security of Rome, and that he would be glad if the envoy would inspect the store of arms and the magazines in S. Angelo. The envoy did so and reported to his Government on the excellent arrangement of everything and how he had seen arms of every kind, among others petards "which must have been invented by devils".[3]

Inventories of provisions of this kind were frequently made throughout the States of the Church.[4] At the beginning of the forties the Venetian envoy reported that there were arms in Rome for 28,000 men, as well as 130 pieces of artillery; that 3,000 infantry and 450 horse were distributed in the various garrisons, and that the recruiting lists bore over 30,000 names. Accordingly, as he often remarked, Urban VIII. felt in a

[1] See NANI, 23.

[2] See the report of January 11, 1625 (State Archives, Venice), translated in BROSCH, I., 396.

[3] See *Studi e docum.*, XXII., 213 *seq.*

[4] *Cf.* above, p. 364, note 2, and below, 366, note 4 *Barb.*, 5067 (Vatican Library): **Descrittione di tutte l'armi offensive e defensive, artiglierie, etc., nelle città e fortezze della Marca, Romagna, Ferrara e Bologna,* 1625; LIII., 75: *Inventario d'artiglierie, armi, etc., che si trovavano nello stato di Urbino dopo la morte di Francesco Maria VI. ed ultimo duca, 1634*; LV., 31: **Descrittione di tutte le armi et munitione di guerra dello stato eccles*[co], compiled by command of Urban VIII., by FED. SOLERTI, in September, 1634.

position to raise within a very short time, an army of at least 20,000 men.[1] He also took keen interest in the navy and in coast protection. Though he failed to raise the papal fleet to twelve ships, those he had were put in better condition so that they proved serviceable against the Berbers.[2] With a view to coast protection, the fortresses of Circello and Nettuno were strengthened in 1625.[3] The excellence of the provisions in this respect is shown by an inventory drawn up in October 1631, of the store of weapons and munitions in the fortresses and watch towers along the Tyrrhenian coast. Terracina, Ostia, Palo, and Civitavecchia could be considered as fortresses. Moreover a great number of watch towers, manned by armed men, had been put up at intervals of two, three, and five miles. A special fort protected the mouth of the Tiber.[4]

The Commander-in-Chief on land and sea was Carlo Barberini, who was succeeded in the same office by his son Taddeo. His Lieutenant for the fleet was Alessandro Filicaja who, in 1627, was succeeded by Battista Naro[5] who, in 1630, was entrusted with the arduous task of preventing the victims of the plague from landing on the coast.[6] In 1630 the risk of the plague being carried into the States of the Church was exceedingly great. In the preceding winter the oriental plague had made its appearance in Upper Italy; from thence it gradually spread over the whole country which was full of troops and sunk in misery; it claimed over half a million victims.[7] From Mantua the disease spread to the Venetian

[1] See NANI, 23.

[2] *Cf.* GUGLIELMOTTI, *Squadra*, 202 *seq.*

[3] See the *Avvisi of March 15 (construction of the fortress of La Barberina at Monte Circello), and April 2, 1625 (departure of Carlo Barberini for Nettuno), *Urb.*, 1095, Vatican Library. *Cf.* also TOMASSETTI, II., 336. A *memorandum on the protection of the coasts from Capo d'Anzio to Terracina with a coloured plan, in *Varia polit.*, 140, p. 155 *seq.*, Papal Secret Archives.

[4] See the *Inventario* published and annotated by F. CERASOLI in the *Riv. Marittima*, 1891, from MS. *Barb.*, 6311.

[5] GUGLIELMOTTI, *Squadra*, 286 *seq.*, 383 *seq.* [6] *Ibid.*, 410.

[7] BELOCH in *Bulletin de l'Institut internat. de statistique*, III. Rome, 1888, 39. *Cf. Miscell. di stor. ital.*, V., 148 *seq.* (Piedmont);

mainland; at Verona half the population succumbed.[1] The victims were equally numerous at Brescia [2] and Bergamo.[3] In July the disease broke out in Venice which had escaped until then, thanks to its insular position. The outbreak was a mild one at first, but by degrees it advanced irrepressibly until it reached a climax in November, with 12,000 dead.[4] At Saluzzo the population dropped from 20,000 to 6,000.[5] Piacenza,[6] Parma,[7] Modena,[8] Florence and Pisa [9] were also severely stricken. At Milan the devastation was appalling. In that city a superstitious belief that certain *untori*—smearers—smeared the walls of houses with some contagious stuff added to the horror of the situation.[10] Among the Orders, the

HAESER, III.[3], 404 *seq.*, 409; *Zeitschr. für allgem. Gesch.*, II., 708 *seq.*

[1] FR. PONA, *Il gran contagio di Verona nel 1630*, Verona, 1727; L. RUOZI, *La pestilenza in Verona l'a. 1630*, Verona, 1838; C. CIPOLLA, *Storia di Verona*, Verona, 1900; BÜHRING, 90; C. FERRARI, *Il censimento d. popolo nel territorio Veronese dopo la peste del 1630*, Verona, 1904.

[2] ROMANIN, VII., 303, note 1.

[3] FINAZZI in the *Miscell. di stor. ital.*, VI., 448 *seq.*, 457 *seq.*; BENAGLIA, *Della carestia e peste di Bergamo*, ed. Rinazzi, Torino, 1869; *Miscell. di stor. ital.*, VI., 409 *seq.*; A. MEASSI, *Carestia e febbre maligna in tempi di peste*, Udine, 1888.

[4] CUSONI, *La peste di Venezia*, Venezia, 1830; ROMANIN, VII., 306; BÜHRING, 91.

[5] C. F. SAVIO, *Saluzzo nel secolo XVII.*, Saluzzo, 1915.

[6] MORANDI E BOSELLI, *La peste del 1630 in Piacenza*, Piacenza, 1867.

[7] E. CASA, *La peste bubbonica in Parma, 1630*, in *Arch. stor. per le prov. Parmensi*, IV. (1903).

[8] RASELLI in *Atti d. Emilia*, VII., 1 (1881), 189 *seq.*; VALDRIGHI, *Contagio di peste bubbonica in Formigine*, Modena, 1897.

[9] FR. RONDINELLI, *Relaz. d. contagio stato in Firenze l'a. 1630 e 1633*, Firenze, 1634 and 1714; *Arch. stor. ital.*, 5th series, XX., 379 *seq.*; *Arch. stor. Lomb.*, XX. (1897). *Cf.* A. FEROCI, *La peste bubbonica in Pisa*, Pisa, 1892.

[10] *Cf.* MANZONI, *I promessi sposi*, Livorno, 1827 (GALLI shows in *Arch. stor. Lomb.*, 3rd series, XXX. (1903), that Manzoni

Camillans [1] and the Capuchins [2] specially distinguished themselves in tending the plague-stricken.

In the Papal States Bologna suffered heavily: in many parishes the mortality rose to 25 and in one to 32 per cent. of the population. The Cardinal Legate Spada did everything in his power to alleviate the misery of the population. The final cessation of the scourge was ascribed to the Rosary, a fact recalled to this day by the great Plague Pillar with the statue of the Madonna del Rosario in the Piazza S. Domenico. In November, 1630, the Magistrates commissioned Guido Reni to make a large banner, now preserved in the picture gallery: the upper part shows the Blessed Virgin surrounded by small angels with rosaries, whilst in the lower half we see the seven Patron Saints of the city, the ethereal figure of St. Francis forming the centre of the group. This magnificent piece of work was long carried in the annual procession of thanksgiving.[3]

Rome, where great watchfulness over public health was exercised from the beginning,[4] owed it chiefly to the precautionary measures of Urban VIII. that it was preserved from the

kept pretty close to the narrative of Cardinal F. Borromeo); CANTÙ, *Ragionamento sulla storia Lombarda del sec. XVII.*, Milano, 1832; *idem*, *Processo orig. degli Untori*, Milano, 1839; RIPAMONTI, *La peste di Milano del 1630*, ed. F. Cusani, Milano, 1841; MANZONI, *Storia della Colonna infame*, Milano, 1840; *Arch. stor. ital. app.*, I., 489 *seq.*; *Arch. stor. Lomb.*, V., 749 *seq.*; also MUTINELLI, IV.; F. NOVATI, *Milano prima e dopo la peste del 1630*, in *Arch. stor. Lomb.*, 3rd series, XXXIX. (1912); *cf. ibid.*, 1923, 388 *seq.*, and LI. (1924). See also BOGNETTI, *Il lazzaretto di Milano e la peste del 1630*, Milano, 1923; BOLLEA, *Untori Piemontesi e Milanesi nella peste di 1630*, in *Bollet. stor. Subalp.*, XXVII. (1925), 198 *seq.*

[1] See the account of S. Camillus de Lelli's life in Vol. XXI., p. 140, note 1. *Cf.* ARATA. *La peste del 1630 in Borgonovo Val Tidone*, in *Boll. stor. Piacent.*, XI. (1919), 5.

[2] See *Katholik*, 1855, II., 517 *seq.*, and V. BONARI, *I conventi ed i Cappuccini Bresciani*, Milano, 1891, 584 *seq.*

[3] *Cf.* LOZZI, *Bibl. ital.*, I., 171; BÖHM, *G. Reni*, 96 *seq.*

[4] See **Editti* of 1624–5, *Editti*, V., 61, Papal Secret Archives.

destroying angel, whose work is recalled by Poussin's picture of the Plague in the Louvre. Already in 1629 a special Health Congregation had been set up with Giambattista Spada as its Secretary.[1] The strictest quarantine was enforced, and in 1629 an observation hospital for suspect cases was established at Ancona.[2] In 1630 two hospitals were opened in Rome, one before the Porta del Popolo, the other on Monte Mario[3]: subsequently a third was added near S. Pancrazio, on the Janiculus.[4] But the Pope did not confine himself to applying all the precautions suggested by the physicians, he also had fervent prayers offered for help from above.[5] For the destitute who came from the Campagna, special hospitals were established in the summer, before all the eight city gates.[6] Communications with Bologna[7] were completely interrupted as early as July and with Florence in September,[8] and a strict guard was kept on the coast.[9] A number of precautionary measures in Rome proved extremely useful. With a view to

[1] See **Lettere, istruzioni, bandi ed altre scritture del 1629 e 1630 relat. alla congregaz. della sanità formata per preservare Roma e lo stato eccl. dalla peste che afflisse l'alta Italia, raccolta da Giov. Batt. Spada segret. di Consulta e della congregaz. med. e dedicate al card. Franc. Barberini prefetto specialmente deputato dalla med. congregazione, Barb.*, 5626, Vatican Library, *ibid.*, 5627; 3. *item* for 1631; *item* 5628 for 1632–4; *item* 5629, *Bandi stampati*, 1629–1634. *Cf.* also **Editti*, V., 61, *loc. cit.* The **Istruttione per Gasparre Mattei in Romagna e Marca per la sanità 1630* in *Varia polit.*, 109, p. 209 *seq.* Papal Secret Archives.

[2] Martinori, 74.

[3] See *Avvisi of April 17 and 24, 1630, *Urb.*, 1100. Vatican Library. *Cf.* **Disegni di Ospedali e lazzaretti fatti da Carlo Rainaldi architetto d'ordine del sig. card. Barberini in occasione della peste, Barb.*, 4411, Vatican Library. *Cf.* Pollak-Frey, 405.

[4] See *Avviso of July 27, 1630, *Urb.*, 1100, *loc. cit.*

[5] See *Avvisi of March 20, June 15, July 3, 10, 17, and 24, 1630, *ibid.* *Cf. Bull.*, XIV., 148 *seq.*

[6] See *Avviso of July 27, 1630, *loc. cit.*

[7] See *Editti of July 1 and 15, 1630, *Editti*, V., 61, *loc. cit.*

[8] See *Avviso of September 11, 1630, *loc. cit.*

[9] *Cf.* *Nicoletti, IV., 358 *seq.*, Vatican Library.

preventing the poor from falling sick—for they were particularly exposed to infection owing to malnutrition—abundant alms were distributed by special commissaries in every quarter of the city. The commissariat was strengthened, all the streets and canals were cleaned ; so also were the prisons. Particular attention was given to the Ghetto, famous for its filth.[1] In consequence of the plague continuing in Lombardy in the following year, from where it spread to the Romagna and Piedmont,[2] these precautionary measures remained substantially unaltered. It was not until March 24th, 1632, that the Pope was able to sing a solemn High Mass in S. Maria in Aracoeli, in thanksgiving for deliverance from all danger of the plague. An inscription on the façade of the church proclaimed all that the Pontiff had done for the city.[3]

The Papal Government exercised the utmost vigilance so as

[1] *Ibid.*, 370 *seq.*

[2] *Cf. Atti d. Romagna*, VIII., 104 *seq.* ; MAZZATINTI, *Archivi d'Italia*, I. (1897), 196 ; R. BERGADANI, *Documenti*, in *Alba Pompeia*, I. (1908), 4 ; G. RODOLFO, *Il combattimento al ponte sul Po il 6 agosto 1630, la pestilenza e la carestia nel 1630 e 1631 a Carignano*, Carmagnola, 1909.

[3] See *NICOLETTI, IV., 382 *seq.*, *loc. cit.* The plague gave rise to many, often very curious suggestions for self-preservation from infection. Of those printed the most noteworthy are, first, the treatises of ALVARIUS CRUCIUS VINCENTIUS : *Providenza metodica per preservarsi dalla imminente peste, Roma*, 1630, and *Consilium prophylacticum a lue pestifera grassante, Romae*, 1631, as well as a pamphlet published by the sanitary authorities in Venice (see on this, *Arch. Rom.*, XXI., 241). The following works have not yet been printed : (1) ANTONE SPONTA, *Trattato della peste e della cura et preservatione d'essa ornato di molti boniss. et optimiss* [!] *rimedii* (dedicated to Urban VIII.), *Barb.*, 4301, Vatican Library; (2) *Antidoton contra pestem in aphorismis iuridicis composit. a Ces. Locatello Romano ad card. Franc. Barberinum*, *Barb.*, 300 ; (3) LEON. FIORAVANTI, *Epilogo del reggimente della peste*, also dedicated to Cardinal Barberini as the " *sopraintend. gen. d. stato eccl.*", *Barb.*, 4262, *loc. cit.* ; (4) treatises by MOD. BRUNELLI in the Angelica Library, Rome (see NARDUCCI, 544–556).

to preserve the States of the Church from epidemics.[1] In October, 1635, the Conservators resolved to erect a statue to Urban VIII., on the Capitol, for having preserved Rome from pestilence and war, added the Duchy of Urbino to the Papal States, and maintained the security of the State in time of greatest need and peril.[2] In June, 1640, Bernini finished the statue, and on September 29th it was unveiled in the great hall of the palace of the Conservators. Previously a High Mass was sung at S. Maria in Aracoeli, in presence of the whole Senate and at the conclusion of the ceremony, bread was distributed to the people.[3]

Urban VIII. showed great zeal in assuring the grain supply of the Eternal City by prohibiting export, reforming the management of the Annona, and improving agriculture,[4] for at the very beginning of his reign he had been obliged to buy

[1] *Cf. Franc. Lucretii viceprotomedici universalis status eccles.* **Perlustrationes factae a 1632 omnium provinciarum ac civit. s. Sedi Ap. subiect.* (autograph), *Barb.*, 2243, *loc. cit.*; continuation, *ibid.*, 2244 (for 1635), and 2245 (for 1636). An *Avviso of September 15, 1635, records that the " Congregatione di Sanità " ordered the cessation of traffic with the Tyrol on account of the plague (*Urb.*, 1103, Vatican Library). **Editti* of September 10, 1636, and May 8, 1637, arranged new traffic prohibitions with Milan, and one on July 27, 1644, with Spoleto. *Editti*, V., 61, *loc. cit.*

[2] See Borboni, 265. *Cf. Cod.* G. III., 78, p. 217 of the Chigi Library, Rome. *Ibid.*, p. 215^b, the *cancellation of the decision of August 28, 1590, not to raise statues to living Popes, dated June 26, 1634.

[3] See Fraschetti, 152; Steinmann, *Die Statuen der Päpste auf dem Kapitol.*, Rome, 1924, 14 *seq.*

[4] *Cf.* De Cupis, 239 *seq.*, 243 *seq.*, 249. With regard to Urban VIII.'s veto on export, Grupp, in *Hist. polit. Blätter*, CXVII., 807, draws attention to the fact that this was customary in almost all States and that Ranke conceals this circumstance in the same way as he omits to say, when discussing the comments of a Venetian in 1627, on the poverty of the peasants and the depression of the cities, that at that time things were no better elsewhere.

wheat in Sicily.[1] In 1640 he established new granaries near the baths of Diocletian and inspected them in person.[2] His biographer is able to bestow on him the eulogy that under him Rome never suffered from a shortage of provisions.[3]

Coats of arms and inscriptions recall what Urban VIII. did for the roads and bridges of the Papal States.[4] At Spoleto he sought to introduce the wool and silk industry[5] and at Viterbo that of wax bleaching.[6] A particularly beneficent institution for Rome which also owed its origin to Urban VIII. was the so-called *Depositeria Urbana* which removed the disadvantages arising from the unregulated mortgage system. In this way the Pope provided for the security of the lenders whilst at the same time he guarded the debtors from injury. The surplus income of the new institution was allocated to the orphanage near S. Euphemia.[7] The Pope was unwearied in his

[1] See the *Brief to *Philippus a Sabaudia Siciliae prorex* of August 20, 1623, *Epist.*, I., Papal Secret Archives. *Cf. ibid.* II., *Brief to Cardinal Soria of November 9, 1624.

[2] See *Avviso of September 22, 1640, Vatican Library; a medal in MARTINORI, 74; inscription: photograph Moscioni 24505.

[3] See *NICOLETTI in RANKE, III., 163*.

[4] See POLLAK-FREY, 2 *seq.* The arms and motto of the Barberini-Pope are preserved on the Ponte Felice near Borghetto; on the bridge at Tivoli (Anno 24), and on the Via Appia Nuova (1635). The road to Viterbo, which Urban VIII. improved, is mentioned by FR. UBALDINI in his *notes on Urban VIII. (*Barb.*, 4901, p. 5, Vatican Library). On the road to Norcia see CIACONIUS, IV., 516; on the new road to Monte Rotondo, see *Avviso of January 16, 1628, Vatican Library. In a Roman antiquary's shop I saw, in 1909, the following inscription which had come from Orvieto: In honorem | Deiparae Virg. | et s. Phil. Nerii | Urbanus VIII. P.M. | annuente | Cong. orat | viam aperuit | plateam stravit. | A. 1628.

[5] See SANSI, *Saggio di docum. d. Arch. di Spoleto*, Foligno, 1861.

[6] See *NICOLETTI, II., p. 1477, Vatican Library.

[7] See the very scarce treatise by N. M. NICOLAI: *Della Depositeria Urbana*, Roma, 1786, 2 *seq.*

support of the poor and the needy of all classes.[1] In 1643 he erected an orphanage near the church of SS. Quattro Coronati.[2] Numerous ordinances of Urban VIII. dealt with the plague of beggars and tramps [3] and with public immorality [4]; however it was not easy to extirpate these long standing evils in a city to which people flocked from every part of the world.[5]

Public security in Rome was very precarious. The nobles and the ambassadors and even many Cardinals, such as the younger Antonio Barberini and Carlo de Medici, surrounded themselves with armed men and took even ex-bandits into their service. Small wonder that tumults and bloody scuffles

[1] See Novaes, XV., 80, note. On the regular alms, *cf.* Totti, 200; *Nicoletti, VIII., ch. 15, Vatican Library.

[2] *Cf. Bull.*, XV., 232.

[3] See **Editti contra gl'otiosi e vagabondi* of December 19, 1623, *Editti*, V., 66, Papal Secret Archives. *Ibid.* **Editti sopra li Zingari*, of September 24, 1631; **Editto sopra li mendicanti che anderanno mendicando per le chiese, strade e luoghe di Roma*, March 7, 1626; **Editto per gli mendicanti*, August 7, 1627; **Editto di proroga*, from August 26 to September 5, 1627; **Eddito sopra i vagabondi, mendicanti et altri che stanno nelli portici e scali delle chiese*, May 17, 1628 (*Editti*, V., 9, *loc. cit.*). In the Consistory of September 20, 1627 (see **Acta consist.*, *Barb.*, 2986, Vatican Library), the Pope pleaded for alms for the hostel for beggars near Ponte Sisto which he had subsidized with a gift of 2,000 scudi; accordingly Cardinals Bentivoglio and Ludovisi gave abundant alms (*Avviso of September 25, 1627, *Urb.*, 1097, Vatican Library). An *Editto of March 3, 1627 (*loc. cit.*), contains "ordini generali da osservarsi nelli hospedali di Roma per sovvenimento de' poveri ammalati".

[4] *Cf.* **Bando che le donne dishoneste non vaddino in carozza ne portino manto*, of October 18, 1624; **Editto delle meretrici e donne dishoneste et loro fautori e ricettatori*, November 27, 1625 (*Editto*, V., 60, *loc. cit*). An *edict against bathing in the nude in the Tiber, 1637 and 1642, *ibid.*, V., 51.

[5] The number of prostitutes did at least not increase, in fact, it remained almost stationary; see *Studi e docum.*, XII., 177.

with the police were of frequent occurrence.[1] The conditions bore a striking resemblance to the wildest periods of the Middle Ages. More than anything, national opposition between Spaniards and Frenchmen, as well as disputes over rank and precedence, gave rise to quarrels and made the task of the Governor of Rome a very thorny one. We get a very striking, and from the point of view of culture, a very interesting picture of conditions in a diary which begins with the entry upon office of Governor Giovanni Battista Spada (January 18th, 1635) and was kept up until his retirement in September, 1643.[2]

The difficulties which this plucky official had to contend with in his efforts to maintain law and order in Rome, are almost past belief. An abiding source of annoyance was the meticulous attention, incomprehensible to a later generation, which that age paid to everything connected with the protocol. The French and Spanish ambassadors had at all times striven for precedence. In addition to this, other disputes of the same kind were the order of the day, as for instance between the ambassadors and the higher officials, especially the Governor, and between the Cardinals and the ancient noble families. At the papal Court, the Master of Ceremonies was a most important personage and he jealously saw to the marks of honour due to the various dignitaries. One curious mark of honour, which was first paid to Cardinal Alessandro Farnese by Marchese Mattei, and which had established itself since, consisted in

[1] *Cf.* **Discorso sopra il fatto tra li Spagnuoli e sbirri occorso in Roma del 1627*, *Vat.*, 7850, p. 233 *seq.* *Ibid.*, 250; **Relazione di un fatto seguito in Roma nel 1636 tra sbirri e gentiluomini per la carcerazione di Evandro Balata*, Vatican Library. **Relatione del seguito tra Spagnuoli e sbirri in Roma l'a. 1629*, *Cod.* VIII., G. 28, p. 319 *seq.*, of the Liechtenstein Library, Vienna.

[2] **Relatione de' casi e contese gravi con cardinali, ambasciatori et altri principi seguiti in Roma dalli 18 Gennaio 1635 per tutti li 18 Settembre 1643 scritta da Msgr. G. B. Spada Lucchese in detto tempo governatore di Roma*, *Vat.*, 10318. **Relaz. d. conclavi I.*, 1–128, Library of the Campo Santo al Vaticano, Rome. *Cf. Barb.*, 4848, 4863, 4975; *Ottob.*, 2710, Vatican Library; EHRLE, *Spada*, 17 *seq.*, 21 *seq.*, 96 *seq.*

having one's carriage stopped when meeting that of a personage of superior rank.[1] If salutations on the occasion of visits had always been an extremely complicated business, driving in town now became subject to a great deal of formality. The new custom added considerably to the already numerous disputes over questions of precedence. Serious incidents were of no rare occurrence in this connexion. Thus in 1634, on such a point as to which carriage should pass first on the occasion of the usual *corso* on September 1st, a duel was fought by Gregorio Caetani and Carlo Colonna. Caetani was killed and Colonna and five of his followers were wounded. The police came too late on the scene.[2] In the summer of 1637, during Urban VIII.'s grave illness, tumults threatened to arise from similar causes.[3] In the summer of 1642, on the occasion of the arrival in Rome of an envoy of the new King of Portugal, a serious street fight took place near the Piazza Colonna.[4] Already previously to this, the privileges claimed by the foreign ambassadors in Rome had led to some very grave incidents. Starting from the point of view that everything was allowed in their own houses, they tolerated there games of chance which had been forbidden elsewhere. This was done even by the imperial ambassador, Prince Bozzolo, whose residence was the Palazzo Cupis, in the Piazza Navona. On November 22nd, 1636, Urban VIII. forbade all games of chance in all places whatsoever, but the French ambassador, Marshal de Cœuvres, took no notice of the prohibition.[5]

[1] I have been unable to discover the document mentioned by RANKE (III., 42), as being in the Barberini library, but without shelf-mark. *Circa il fermar le carozze per complimento e come s'introdusse in uso.* On the other hand I saw a **Discorso sopra l'abuso di fermar le carozze*, in *Urb.*, 1756, Vatican Library. *Cf. Cod. ital.*, 552, p. 148, of the State Library, Munich.

[2] See REUMONT, III., 2, 619. For a similar dispute between the French and Spanish envoys with regard to precedence of their carriages, in March 1642, see *Miscell. di stor. ital.*, XV., 183 *seq.*

[3] *Cf.* below, p. 401.

[4] *Cf.* above, p. 208.

[5] See the **Relazione* of Spada, quoted above, p. 374, note 2, Library of the Campo Santo al Vaticano, Rome.

Besides their palaces, the ambassadors also claimed immunity for the adjoining streets and houses. No prisoners could be marched past their doors. Pretensions of this kind were advanced not only by the representatives of the Great Powers, such as France and Spain, but even by the envoy of little Savoy! The latter had to be satisfied when the Pope roundly told him that he meant to be master in the streets of his own capital.[1] But in 1639 the Great Powers violated this right in flagrant fashion; on that occasion the conduct of the French ambassador nearly led to a rupture between Rome and Paris.[2] The Spanish ambassador, Castel Rodrigo, refused to lag behind his colleagues; on Christmas night, 1639, he had the Prince of Sanza, who was accused of plotting against Spain, seized by a band of hired bandits, in the church of S. Andrea delle Fratte, after which he had the unhappy man executed.[3]

In 1623 the population of Rome numbered 111,727; in 1624 it rose to 113,814; in the jubilee year 1625 to 115,444; in 1626 it reached 116,454 and remained at that level for three years, but in 1629 it sank to 115,549 and kept falling until 1633 when it began once more to rise slowly. In the last year of Urban VIII.'s pontificate Rome counted 110,608 souls.[4] The number of families presents a different picture from that of the population. Here also there is no lack of fluctuation, but it is undeniable that the number of unmarried men who came and went was diminished, whilst that of resident families was on the increase. In 1623 there were 26,854 resident families and 31,758 in 1641.[5]

[1] *Ibid.* [2] *Cf.* Vol. XXVIII., Ch. VI., p. 412.

[3] *Cf.* Ademollo, *Il principe di Sanza*, in the *Riv. Europ.*, XI. (1879), 53 *seq.* See also *Arch. stor. Napolet.*, III, 726 *seq.* The Florentine ambassador wrote on January 14, 1640: "Il Papa e irritatissimo dell'attentato nella sua città e più dell'impotenza di vendicarsi, poiche il processo non approdava nulla" (see Ademollo, *loc. cit.*, 221).

[4] See *Studi e docum.*, XII., 177.

[5] *Ibid.* *Cf.* Ranke, III., 44 *seq.*, where, however, some of the figures are wrongly given.

A survey of the Roman families of the period from the pen of Theodore Ameyden [1] begins with the great nobles, the Colonna, Orsini, Conti, and Savelli as the oldest of them all. These families still lived on their ancient glory but they were heavily in debt and in need of assistance which, in point of fact, Urban VIII. did not withhold.[2] Next to these four noble families stood the Caetani on whom the spirit of Boniface VIII. seemed still to rest; they too had incurred heavy liabilities which Cardinal Luigi strove to pay off. Then came the Cesarini and the Cesi and lastly the Altemps who were related to many Roman families. The old Roman nobility were rivalled by the new papal families: the Bonelli, Boncampagni, Peretti, Aldobrandini, Borghese, Ludovisi, and Barberini. The Peretti and Aldobrandini were already extinct in the male line; the Borghese and Barberini commanded princely wealth which they constantly increased by their parsimony. Ameyden divides the remaining noble Roman families into three classes, fifty being over 300 years old, thirty-five 200, and sixteen 100 years old. Most of them had risen from modest circumstances. Their ancestors

[1] See *Relatione della citta di Roma* in *Cod.* N., II., 50, p. 246 *seq.*, of the Chigi Library, Rome, used by RANKE, III., 41 *seq.*, who gives no indication of source. A second copy is in *Varia polit.* 150, p. 646 *seq.*, Papal Secret Archives. Date of composition: 1649.

[2] *Cf.* ALV. CONTARINI, 358. The author of the "Relatione" quoted in note 1, says in connexion with Savelli: "È costume di quella casa che le donne di rado o mai escono di casa e uscendo vanno in carozza chiusa et incognite, costume lodevole tratto dal antico Romano . . . Ho osservato che li Conti e Savelli espongono nelle loro case i ritratti degli pontefici delle loro famiglie come trofei della loro nobiltà e nelle case degli Orsini non si vede mai la figura di Niccolò III. ne in quella de' Colonnesi la di Martino V. La ragione sarà che le dette famiglie non possono raccontare tanti pontefici quanto ne raccontano le due prime o vero per mostrare che la grandezza loro non dipende da' Papi." Many details may be found in "La storia delle famiglie Romane di Teodoro Amayden con note di C. A. Bertini, 2 vols., Rome, 1910 and 1914.

had been notaries, apothecaries, and even tanners. Nine families, especially such as came from Genoa and Florence, had won great wealth by carrying out the lucrative financial transactions of the Datoria. Italian families were not the only ones that enriched themselves in this way: Ameyden also mentions Portuguese, French, and Flemish ones.[1] The institution of the *Luoghi di Monti*, especially such as were *vacabili* and represented an annual rent, and the existence of offices that could be purchased, at all times attracted to Rome distinguished families from all parts of Italy.[2]

For the purpose of settling frontier disputes in the Papal States, the population of which was reckoned at one and a half million in 1625,[3] Urban VIII. set up a special Congregation in 1627.[4] Another Congregation busied itself with the regulation of watercourses, especially those of the Po and the Tiber.[5] Giovanni Battista Doni dedicated to Urban VIII.

[1] See *Relatione, loc. cit.*

[2] See RANKE, III., 44.

[3] See *Bull.*, XIII., 599 *seq.*; THEINER, *Cod. dipl.*, III, 579 *seq.*; NICOLETTI, II., 1286 *seq.*, Vatican Library; *Acta congreg. sup. controversiis confinium status eccl. 1627–1643. Vat.*, 8311, *ibid.*

[4] See the report of the Venetian *obbedienza* ambassadors in BAROZZI-BERCHET, Roma, I., 228.

[5] See *" Scritture in materia delle acque dello stato pontif." (reports of the Congregatione delle acque and opinions of experts on the Po and the Tiber, beginning in 1626), *Barb.*, 4346, Vatican Library; " Scritture in materia del Reno alli cardinali della congreg. delle acque " (on Ferrara), *Barb.*, 4301, *ibid.*; dissertation by Livio Maria Paselli on the waters of the Rhine " ad istanze di Msgr. Gasparo Carpegna, secret. d. Congre. delle acque ", *Barb.*, 4366; *" Capitoli conchiusi tra la S. Sede e il Gran Duca di Ferrara sopra gli affari delle chiane sotto Urbano VIII.," *Barb.*, 4383, p. 59 *seq.* Floods of the Tiber are mentioned in the *Avviso di Roma of February, 1631, and February 28, 1637 (Vatican Library). Bernini's comedy entitled " *Inondazione del Tevere* " which was acted at the carnival of 1638 at the Barberini palace refers to the latter; see *Chledowski, Rom*, II. (1912), 402 *seq.* For precautionary measures taken, *cf. Ciaconius*, IV., 518; *Armellini, I Papi e il Tevere*, Roma, 1877, 11. *Cf. Bull.*, XIV., 705.

his work on the improvement of sanitary conditions and the colonization of the Roman Campagna; his description of the bands of labourers who year by year came down from the Abruzzi, Umbria, and the Marches, to work in the Campagna, tallies almost exactly with the conditions that obtain to this day.[1] An attempt by Giambattista Sacchetti to carry out the ideas of Doni failed in consequence of malaria carrying off the workers.[2] An improvement was only possible if the marshes were drained. When the mathematician Domenico Castelli presented to Urban VIII. various memorials on the work of draining the Campagna,[3] Benedetto Castelli, a professor at the Roman University, submitted similar plans for the territory of Ferrara and Bologna,[4] together with a scheme for draining the Pontine Marshes.[5] In the spring of 1633 the Pope entrusted the work to a company of Dutch Catholics but their attempts were without permanent results.[6]

[1] I. B. DONI, *De restituenda salubritate agri Romani, Florentiae, 1667* (*Barb.*, 301). *Cf.* DE CUPIS, 250; SOMBART, *Die römische Campagna* (Forschung. by SCHMOLLER, 8), Leipzig, 1888.

[2] See *Arch. Rom.*, XX, 78.

[3] DOMENICO CASTELLI, **Trattato della bonificazione dell' acque di Romagna* (dedicated to Urban VIII., with a plan), *Barb.*, 4242, *loc. cit.*

[4] BENEDETTO CASTELLI, **Discorso sopra la bonificazione del Bolognese, Ferrarese e Romagnolo, Barb.*, 4267, *loc. cit.*; *id.* "Della misura delle acque correnti" (dedicated to Urban VIII.), *Barb.*, 4392, *loc. cit.*

[5] BENEDETTO CASTELLI, **Discorso sopra la bonificazione delle Palude Pontine, Barb.*, 4267, p. 68 *seq.*, *loc. cit.*

[6] "Di questa settimana soo partiti di ritorno in Olanda alcuni deputati Olandesi cattolici, dopo haver aggiustato di venire ad habitare con più di 500 famiglie cattoliche della loro natione a Nettuno, Corneto, Ostia et in altri luoghi della spiaggia Romana, dove vogliono seccare alcune paludi con ridurli alla coltura, disegnando venire quanto prima con un numero de' vascelli non solo carichi de' genti, ma anco obligati di fare in questi luoghi altri bonificamenti, che renderanno l'aria piu salutifera, se gli concedano diverse essentioni et altri privilegii della Camera Ap." (Avviso of March 5, 1633, *Ottob.*, 3339, Vatican Library.)

All these measures, especially the military ones, were very costly. To them must be added the expenditure in connexion with the Valtellina [1] and Urbino, and the sums devoted to assisting the German Catholics, especially Maximilian I., to Propaganda,[2] the vast constructions in Rome, and the papal nephews.[3] All this expenditure upset the State finances.[4] At the beginning of Urban VIII.'s pontificate, these were in a bad way; the debt amounted to between sixteen and eighteen millions,[5] and within the first twelve years of his reign Urban added another thirteen millions.[6] In 1635, out of the total revenue of the State, only 600,000 scudi were available for the expenses of administration, and in 1640, when the debt had grown to thirty-five millions, only 300,000 scudi: 85 per cent was swallowed by interest on the public debt.[7]

On this subject see MORONI, IV., 72 *seq.*; *Brom, Archivalia in Italië*, Haag, 1908, 160; ORBAAN, *Bescheiden*, I, 217 *seq.*; KORTHALS-ALTES, in the *Mededeelingen v. h. Nederl. Hist. Institut.*, 1926, 193 *seq.*

[1] *Cf.* Vol. XXVIII., p. 92 *seq.*

[2] *Cf.* above, p. 215.

[3] *Cf.* Vol. XXVIII., p. 45 *seq.*

[4] Urban VIII. confirmed Costanzo Patrizi Tesoriere of his predecessor, in his office. After his death in 1625 the latter was succeeded by Girolamo Vidoni. Vidoni was made a Cardinal on August 20, 1627, when he was replaced by Stefano Durazzo who received the purple on November 28, 1633. Durazzo was followed by Pier Donato Cesi who also became Cardinal on December 16, 1641. His successor, the Genoese Giovanni Battista Lomellini, died soon after. He was followed by Ang. Franc. Rapaccioli, who was replaced by Paolo Emilio Rondinini during the time he spent with the army in the war of Castro. They were both raised to the Sacred College on July 13, 1643, when another Genoese became Tesoriere, viz. Lorenzo Raggi; see MORONI, LXXIV., 301.

[5] R. ZENO (1623), gives (p. 144) the figures of the debt as 15–16 millions; that of 22 millions given by BROSCH (I., 400), is probably exaggerated. P. CONTARINI (1623–7), speaks (p. 202) of a debt of 15 million gold scudi; the *obbedienza* ambassadors (1624–5) say "più di 18 millioni" (p. 230); ANG. CONTARINI (1627–9), says (p. 258): "tra li di nuove e venti millioni."

[6] See ALV. CONTARINI, 361.

[7] See NANI, 24. *Cf.* RANKE, III., 10.

The Pope began by looking for relief from a reduction of interest, but not long after he raised a fresh loan which swallowed the revenue thus freed. Most of the money was advanced by Genoese bankers.[1] To meet interest Urban was compelled to impose fresh taxes, however much he shrank from such a course.[2] In the first twelve years of his reign no less than ten taxes are mentioned which he either imposed or increased; they were all the more onerous as they were put, for the most part, on the indispensable necessaries of life.[3] Further taxation was rendered necessary when, to fill the measure of misfortune, Urban, towards the end of his reign, became involved, through the action of his nephews, in an exceedingly costly war. This struggle was destined to demonstrate in an alarming manner, the inadequateness of all the military measures hitherto taken for the security of the States of the Church.[4] Military organization had certainly been improved, but the troops were untrained and, moreover, the Italians of that time were anything but soldiers; there was also a lack of capable officers[5]; above all it became apparent that notwithstanding every effort, a State governed by ecclesiastics cannot be turned into a military Power.

[1] See BROSCH, I., 400. On the Monti (see *Bull.*, XIII., 421 *seq.*, XIV., 119 *seq.*, 547 *seq.*), *cf.* COPPI, *Discorso sulle finanze dello stato Pontificio*, Roma, 1855, 15 *seq.* See also Moroni, XL., 156. On Urban VIII.'s coins and medals, see MARTINORI, *Annali d. Zecca di Roma 1621–1644*, Roma, 1919, 27 *seq.* *Cf.* also *Arch. Lomb.*, IV., 295 *seq.*; SERAFINI, *Le monete del Museo Vaticano*, II. (1912), 189 *seq.* On the concession of the Zecca to A. Fr. Farsetti, 1643, see *Raccolta Veneta*, 1 Series I., Venezia, 1866, 47 *seq.*; A. TELLUCCINI, *Castel S. Angelo e l'officina monet. pontif.*, 1642 *seq.*, in the *Riv. ital. numismat.*, XXV., 3.

[2] BOSSI, *La Pasquinata* (1889), 30 *seq.*

[3] See ALV. CONTARINI, 361; RANKE, III., 24. For salt taxes see **Avvisi* of 1625 *passim*; milling taxes, see ADEMOLLO in the *Riv. Europ.*, 1877, II., 424 *seq.*; for a rise in the taxation of meat and wine see *Arch. Rom.*, II., 262, note.

[4] *Cf. Descrittione dello stato eccl. al Marchese di Pianezza, Cod.* 1776 of the town library, Trent.

[5] *Cf.* the report of the Venetian *obbedienza* embassy, *loc. cit.*, 230 *seq.*

(2)

With the acquisition of Ferrara under Clement VIII., and of Urbino under Urban VIII., the Papal States had become a compact territory stretching from the Po to the frontiers of Naples. Such a success early roused the jealousy of the Powers. The most hard hit were two States which, for the rest, were in sharp opposition to each other, viz. Venice and Spain. The Republic of St. Mark feared for its trade, Spain for its mastery of Naples where a rising was preparing against the crushing Spanish taxation.[1] But the Grand Duke of Tuscany and the Dukes of Modena and Parma also cast envious eyes on the States of the Church and on the wealth and power of the Barberini. Disputes were also pending with Francesco, Duke of Modena, over the abbeys of Pomposa and Bodeno, whose revenues Cardinal Barberini enjoyed, the refusal of the purple to an Este and the construction of "Forte Urbano" to which the erection of a citadel at Modena was the reply.[2]

Relations with Duke Odoardo Farnese of Parma,[3] the first

[1] *Cf.* G. Pesaro, 231; Alv. Contarini, 358.

[2] See Alv. Contarini, 384.

[3] *Cf.* the *Brief of Urban VIII. to him on September 14, 1624: "Dilecte fili, nobilis vir, salutem. Poesim, quam Socraticae sapientiae edicta tamquam mendaciorum parentem et obstetricem vitiorum e republica exulare iusserunt, non temere aliqui introducunt in regum praetoria et ecclesias sanctorum. Si enim modesta quaedam superbia pestiferam lascivorum lusuum utilitatem despexerit, potest cantus suavitate humanas aures pelliciens edere oracula virtutis et angelicos choros imitari. Hanc si in isto aetatis constituta vere Nobilitas tua colet, fructus ex ea colligere poterit tibi iucundos, populis salutares. Medicamenta enim libidinum, quae tamquam fellis amaritiem tenerior aetas solet aversari, in nectaris dulcedinem miscens utile dulci poetice convertit. Adolescentia vero Nobilitatis tuae iucundissimo nutrita pabulo salubrium praeceptorum eas vires concipiet, quibus poterit de cupiditatum impotentia triumphare et gentium salutem tueri. At enim quam tibi cohortationem scribimus, eam in laudes vertere persuadet, quam nuper Nobis dicasti, elegantissima illa

among the feudatories of the Church, also became difficult. That ambitious Prince had taken the part of France against Spain but was disappointed in his hope of obtaining the Duchy of Milan through the intervention of Richelieu.[1] Odoardo never forgave Urban VIII. and Cardinal Barberini their opposition to the dangerous plan with regard to Milan. On account of the abruptness displayed by Cardinal Barberini on that occasion, Odoardo looked on him as a deadly enemy of the House of Farnese.[2] Odoardo was in a position to make the Barberini feel his ill will all the more easily as he owned a small State so to speak at the very gates of Rome. This was the Duchy of Castro and Ronciglione which the Farnese had received in fief from Paul III.[3]

Urban VIII.'s nephews took advantage of the Pope's resentment of this proximity to win him over to a plan of

Ode, quae Pindarici fontis haustus non expalluit. Elucet in ea ingenii vis et industriae labor. Quam tamen Nostrae vitae imaginem affingere ibi pro tua in Nos pietate voluisti, eam longe pulchriorem ostentat carminum tuorum elegantia quam speculum conscientiae Nostrae. Complectimur te paternae caritatis bracchiis, dilecte fili, qui contemnens insanias falsas, tanto studio laboras, ut populis tuis antecellas non minus sapientia quam authoritate. Id est verum principem agere et probare se dignum imperio. Servus enim coronatus ille habendus, qui rerum omnium ignarus et luxu perditus, quamvis latissime dominetur, cogitur tamen alienae prudentiae quasi iustiori principatui semper subiici. Solatium quidem vel maximum fuerit paternae caritatis Nostrae, si iis virtutibus animum instruxeris, ut caeteri principes exemplar curandae felicitatis publicae suscipere possint in Nobilitate tua, cuius vita pontificiarum cognationum soboles, cuius principatus Apostolicae munificentiae beneficium est. Quod Farnesiae domui exoptantes gaudium et decus, benedictionem Nostram Nobilitati tuae peramanter impartimur. Dat. ut supra (September 14, 1624)," *Epist.*, I., Papal Secret Archives.

[1] See *Nicoletti, IX., 6 *seq.*, Vatican Library.

[2] See *Nicoletti, IX., 10, *ibid.*

[3] *Cf.* our account, Vol. XI., 316 *seq.* ; *Informatione economica d. città di Castro*, by Benedetto Zucchi, 1638, in *Barb.* 4844, Vatican Library.

theirs for getting the Farnese fief into the Barberini family. If possible the thing was to be done by peaceable means.[1] When Duke Odoardo came to Rome on November 21st, 1639, he met with a most honourable reception not only on the part of the Pope but on that also of the Barberini Cardinals who gave splendid banquets in his honour[2]. The Duke was received in audience by the Pope almost every evening when the conversation turned not only on Urban's poems but on political topics also, on the feudal relations of the Duke, the wiping out of his huge debts, the bestowal of the purple on a young Farnese.[3]

From the first, the Duke of Parma displayed the greatest arrogance towards the Roman nobility and the Barberini whom he detested. The latter were made to feel how greatly superior he thought himself, as a Prince of ancient race, to the upstart nephews; in particular he refused to recognize Taddeo Barberini's privileges arising out of his dignity as Prefect of Rome.[4] The differences to which this gave rise were further embittered when Urban VIII. refused to sanction Odoardo's adventurous plan for wresting Naples from the Spaniards.[5] When the project was betrayed to the Spaniards by an Augustinian friar, the Duke at once threw the blame on the Barberini.[6] The latter's offer that he should give up Castro to them in return for a large sum of money and become connected with them through a matrimonial alliance, was scornfully rejected by the Farnese.[7] In vain the Pope sought to mediate: at the farewell audience granted to the Duke, he made a last effort to induce him not to lend ear to evil tongues. Odoardo left Rome on January 22nd, 1640. In order to hurt Cardinal Francesco Barberini as much as possible,

[1] *Cf.* NAVENNE, *Rome et le Palais Farnese*, I., 165; GROTANELLI, *Ducato di Castro*, 73 *seq.*; DEMARIA, 197.

[2] See NAVENNE, I., 172.

[3] See *NICOLETTI, IX., 16, 22 *seq.*, 25, *loc. cit.*; DEMARIA, 198 *seq.*

[4] See *NICOLETTI, IX., 20 *seq.*

[5] *Ibid.*, 29.

[6] *Ibid.*, 29 and 37.

[7] See NAVENNE, I., 174.

he omitted to pay him a farewell visit.[1] To his representative, Carandini, he gave orders to avoid all intercourse with the nephews and when, out of courtesy, Carandini exchanged a few words with the Cardinal, he was at once recalled.[2]

No sooner had the aggrieved Duke reached home than he gave orders for Castro to be put in a state of defence.[3] Such provocative conduct was most imprudent, for the impecunious Prince was only too dependent on the Pope's favour. In virtue of a papal privilege he had raised loans (*monti*) the interest of which was to come out of the revenues of Castro and Ronciglione. However, this hope was not realized and soon Rome resounded with the laments of unsatisfied creditors. When Urban VIII. refrained from immediate action, he was reproached with excessive regard for the Duke; Julius II. and Sixtus V., he was told, would have acted very differently.[4] In the end the Pope was compelled to take up the affair and to summon the Duke to pay his debts and to put a stop to his armaments. Odoardo answered his liege lord by strengthening the garrison of Castro and by making further warlike preparations, in order, as he openly declared, to render himself for ever formidable to the Popes.[5]

Thereupon Urban VIII. resolved to act. The Farnese were

[1] See *NICOLETTI, IX., 35 *seq.*; NAVENNE, I., 174; RANKE, III.[8], 18, who refers to the *Risposta in forma di lettera al libro di Duca di Parma* (*Inf. polit.*, XLV., State Library, Berlin).

[2] See *NICOLETTI, IX., 37, 40.

[3] *Ibid.*, 36, 55.

[4] *" Sparsa la nuova della rivolta del Duca (fortification of Castro) si udirono maggiori querele del popolo di Roma contro la magnanimità e contro la piacevolezza del Pontefice usata verso il Duca nel suo venire alla corte. Ne mancava chi desiderasse in Papa Urbano il calore di Giulio II. e di Sisto V., e nel card. Barberini l'animo del card. Pietro Aldobrandini in abbassare il Duca, prima che a più alte imprese rivolgesse il pensiero, havendo già alla disubbidienza aggiunto delitto di lesa Maestà." (*NICOLETTI, IX., 55.)

[5] " *Per rendersi, com'egli diceva, una volta per sempre formidabile ai Papi." (NICOLETTI, IX., 56.)

indebted to a privilege of Paul III. for the fact that the great high road between Rome and Tuscany passed from Monterosi, instead as before from Sutri through Ronciglione, as well as for the free export of grain from Castro. On March 20th, 1640, the road was once more made to pass through Sutri, the lucrative export of grain from Castro forbidden and the permission to raise loans withdrawn.[1]

These measures were a big blow for the heavily indebted Duke. But he did not lose heart for he hoped for help from Richelieu. The French Cardinal's interest in the Farnese encouraged the latter in his resistance.[2] In Castro itself a rumour was already current that a French army was on the way[3]; instead of this, at the beginning of August, the Duke received a papal summons to demobilize his troops within thirty days and to raze the fortifications of Castro. When he refused to comply, he was granted a further delay until September 26th, under threat of severer penalties.[4]

Relying on French help, Odoardo had no intention to

[1] NICOLETTI emphasizes the circumstance that the Pope saw himself constrained to take more severe measures in order to uphold his authority: "*Questa dunque (che così curiosamente stata fin hora cercata, e che ha fatto abbagliar tanti scrittori e sciorre tante lingue) fu la cagione, altretanto giusta quanto necessaria, di privare il Duca di Parma de'favori della s. Sede, nell particolare delle tratte de'grani dello stato di Castro, che senz'alcun titolo oneroso egli godeva, e d'intimargli l'estintione de'Monti." This is followed by a detailed account of the historico-judicial aspects of the "tratti de'grani", *ibid.*, 56–9. On April 10, 1641, the Paris nuncio was instructed on the "tratti"; the Camera had cancelled the privilege granted by Clement VIII. on account of abuse; see *ibid.*, 87 *seq.* Chledowski's remark is amusing: "In Rome there was great scarcity & Farnese forbade the export of grain from Castro!"

[2] See *NICOLETTI, IX., 63 *seq.*; DEMARIA, 208.

[3] See *NICOLETTI, IX., 65.

[4] *Ibid.*, 66 *seq.* On August 16, 1641, Urban VIII. commanded Lud. Piccardo to visit Castro and to order all the new military measures to be cancelled (*Bull.*, XV., 134 *seq.*).

give way and continued his preparations.[1] Thus war became inevitable.[2] Accordingly, Urban VIII. convened a special

[1] *NICOLETTI (IX., 68 *seq.*) gives an account of the deliberations which took place at that time on the basis of a diary of September 28, 1641.

[2] For the "War of Castro" *cf.* for the French side, V. SIRI, *Mercurio ovvero historia de'correnti tempi*, III., Casale, 1640 *seq.*, and *Memorie recondite*, Roma, 1676 *seq.* (very prolix and therefore justly criticized by MURATORI (*Ann.*)). The Venetian view is represented by BATT. NANI (*cf.* for him F. N. MOCENIGO, *B. Nani*, Venezia, 1899), *Historia d. republ. Veneta*, I., 1686); the Tuscan by GALUZZI, *Storia del granducato di Toscana*, VII. (1822), the Papal, by *NICOLETTI, IX. (*cf.* app. no. 26). See also *Théâtre europ.*, vol. IV and V. For a description of the conduct of war at that period, which bordered on the comic, see TALLEMANT DES RÉAUX, *Historiettes*, ed. Monmerqué et P. Paris, II. (1862), 241 *seq.* More recent authorities are especially, REUMONT, *Beiträge*, V., 141 *seq.*, and *Toskana*, I., 422 *seq.*; BALAN, VI., 775 *seq.*; G. DEMARIA in *Miscell. di storia ital.*, 3rd series, IV. (1898), 193 *seq.*; CORNA, *I Frati minori di Piacenza durante l'interdetto di Urbano VIII. nel ducato di Parma e Piacenza* (1643), in *Bollet. stor. Piacent.*, IV. (1901), 4. In *Iani Nicii Erythraei Epistolae ad diversos* (2 vols., Coloniae, 1645–9), the events of the war are described day by day (*cf.* CERBONI, *Giano Nicio Eritreo*, Città di Castello, 1909, 95 *seq.*). See also G. ROSALBA, 15 *lettere inedite di F. Testi*, in the *Studi dedic. a Fr. Torraca*, Napoli, 1912. Much that is relevant is still unpublished, thus: GIAMBATT. RINALDUCCI, **Dell'una e l'altra guerra di Castro libri*, XII. (from Urban VIII. to Clement IX.), in CCXXIV., *Cod.* 264 of the Marucelliana Library, Florence, and *Barb.* 5060 and 5061, Vatican Library; **Diario della guerra di Castro* (September, 1641 to July, 1644), 3 vols., in the Communal Archives at Orvieto; **Diario dell'a.* 1642 *nel quale principalmente si narrano gli avvenimenti d. guerra di Castro.*, in *Barb.* 4852, *loc. cit.*; **Li progressi dell'esercito Veneto e collegati contro l'armi pontificie nel papato d'Urbano VIII.*, *Cod.* 6190, p. 1 *seq.*, of the State Library at Vienna. *Letters of A. F. Rapaccioli and others to Cardinal Fr. Barberini on the war, 1641–3, in *Barb.* 6091–3, *loc. cit. Ibid.*, 4341, p. 22 *seq.*: **Fortificazioni fatte ai confini nello stato di Ferrara.* A **Libro di casi militari discussi e risoluti da Virgilio Crispoldi da Riete auditore del campo, nelle guerre di P. Urbano*

Congregation and informed it that the Duke owed his creditors in Rome 1,500,000 scudi, that he refused to pay them, was preparing for war and rousing France. Since it was the Pope's right and duty to see to it that so many Roman citizens obtained their rents, it was his intention to seize the mortgage. Warlike measures, which might lead to intervention by the other Italian Powers, seemed too risky to not a few members, but the majority were of opinion that the defiance of the rebellious vassal could not be tolerated and indulgence would be a disastrous precedent; nor was it likely that Tuscany and Venice would assist Farnese; on the contrary, if they showed they were in earnest, the latter would soon yield, but prompt action was essential.[1] This view finally prevailed, though a few expressed the opinion that as small a body of troops as possible should be employed, perhaps about 800 Corsicans, so as not to rouse the jealousy of the other Italian Princes.[2] However, Urban VIII. deemed it safer to make a display of force and Taddeo Barberini was instructed to collect near Viterbo 12,000 infantry and 3,000 horse and artillery, under the command of Marchese Luigi Lante.[3]

A section of these forces took the Castle of Montalto and soon after Castro itself (October 13th, 1641). The expedition, in the success of which Florence had refused to believe, cost only one fatal casualty.[4] But though France urged him to yield,[5] the Duke remained obstinate, hence he was served with a third summons.[6] Venice offered to mediate, but the Pope declared there could be no discussion between an overlord and his vassal.[7] Accordingly the proceedings continued

VIII. in *Cod.* A. VI., 8 of the Communal Library, Foligno; **Relat. dell'esercito di Urbano VIII. contro il Duca di Parma schierato in Cività Castellana sotto la condotta del card. Antonio Barberini* in *Ottob.* 2175, p. 69 *seq.*, Vatican Library. *Ibid.*, p. 73 *seq.*, **Relatione dell'entrata del Duca di Parma nello stato eccles.*

[1] See *NICOLETTI, *loc. cit.*, 68 *seq.*

[2] *Ibid.*

[3] See *NICOLETTI, IX., 69 *seq.*, Vatican Library.

[4] *Ibid.*, 98b.

[5] *Ibid.*, 93, 135.

[6] *Ibid.* 126.

[7] *"Che ciò si poteva ammettere tra principe e principe, ma non già tra'l supremo e suddito"; neither did he interfere in

their course. On November 26th the Duke's allodial possessions in Roman territory, including the Palazzo Farnese, were sequestrated and ordered to be sold to satisfy his creditors.[1] The action against Odoardo ended, as announced by the Pope in a Consistory of January 13th, 1642, in the obstinately rebellious vassal being excommunicated and in his forfeiting all his fiefs as one guilty of high treason.[2]

Before long the struggle claimed the attention of every chancellery of Europe. The Duke sought to make propaganda in his own favour by means of publications in which the dispute was misrepresented.[3] The Pope was at pains to refute him with circulars addressed to all the nuncios; in these he did not disguise the fact that things had reached such a pass that arms alone could lead to a decision.[4]

the affairs of the subjects of Venice (November 14, 1641). Urban VIII. declared to the Spanish ambassador, "che l'interpositioni de'principi con la S.S. non erano riputate a proposito per la dignità pontificia, ma sariano stato più a proposito col Duca, acciochè facesse il suo debito." (*NICOLETTI, IX., 142, 148.)

[1] See BROSCH, I., 406; NAVENNE, I., 176.

[2] *"Modo lata fuit sententia in qua praefatus Oadoardus declaratus fuit excommunicatus et damnatus in penam criminis laesae Maiestatis, devolutionis, privationis et confiscationis omnium feudorum, civitatum, terrarum, castrorum, locorum et bonorum, eaque fuerunt Camerae Nostrae applicata et incorporata et prout in eadem sententia latius continetur. Haec, quae patere omnibus debent, per Nos in hoc sacro loco Urbis nota esse voluimus uti gesta ad conservandam Sedis Apost. dignitatem" (*Acta consist.*, Urbani VIII., 1630–1643, MS. in my possession).

[3] Farnese published a *Vera e sincera relazione delle ragioni del Duca di Parma contro la presente occupazione del ducato di Castro.* In refutation of this there appeared: *Lettera scritta ad un Signore in risposta del libro stampato sopra le ragioni del seren. Duca di Parma contro la presa di Castro eseguita dall'armi pontificie nell'anno*, 1641, as well as several other pamphlets; see RAIMONDO DI SORAGNA, *Bibliografia Parmense*, Parma, 1866, 67 *seq.*, and LOTTICI-SITTI, *Bibl. generale Parmense*, Parma, 1901, No. 1380–1400.

[4] *Cf.* *NICOLETTI, IX., 121, 157 *seq.* (Instruction for Facchinetti, February 8th, 1642; for all the nuncios, February 22, 1642.)

The grave problem whether Urban VIII. should also proceed against Parma and Piacenza, was maturely examined in Rome. The elder Cardinal Antonio Barberini was of opinion that it would be enough to dismantle Castro. He dwelt on the danger of intervention in favour of Odoardo by the jealous Italian Powers, more especially by the Dukes of Tuscany and Modena who were kinsmen of his.[1] The State Congregation held similar views, but at the decisive meeting Cardinal Francesco Barberini rose and, turning towards the Pope, declared that since the army had been mobilized it was impossible to keep it indefinitely on a war footing; war was unavoidable for the stake was the safeguarding of the interests of the Holy See. The meeting broke up amid the greatest excitement but soon after all but one expressed their approval, in writing, of the plan of proceeding to extreme measures.[2] The step was a fateful one and one that was bound to fill the Italian Powers with anxiety.

What Cardinal Barberini had deemed impossible now became a reality: Venice decided to send 40,000 scudi to the Duke and Florence 30,000.[3] Richelieu also secretly supplied Odoardo with money[4]; by this means the latter was able to complete his preparations.

In a Consistory of August 11th, 1642, Urban VIII. explained that the threatening attitude of the Duke obliged him to see to the security of the frontiers of Bologna and Ferrara; instead of submitting Odoardo, in contempt of the censures, assisted at divine service and armed actively; accordingly he, the Pope, had made up his mind to compel him by force to submit; he had already informed the Princes of his resolve and he now did the same for the Cardinals. Some members of the Sacred College made private remonstrances on the risks

[1] See *Nicoletti, IX., 167. [2] *Ibid.*, 202 *seq.*

[3] *Ibid.*, 247. The elder Venetian Senators were opposed to support being given to the Duke; the younger ones pointed out that it was the Pope's intention to act, even if it were to the detriment of the other Italian States. *Cf. ibid.*, 160, 163.

[4] According to *Nicoletti (IX., 163), Richelieu promised the Duke 30,000 scudi a month. Demaria, 213, No. 3.

of the threatened intervention by the other Powers, but Urban replied that he trusted in the righteousness of his cause.[1]

When France pleaded on behalf of her protégé, the Pope replied that he could not restore Castro after the Duke had scorned the Church's censures and banished the ecclesiastics who observed them; as for the League of Italian Princes with which he was threatened, he trusted he was strong enough to withstand it.[2] Urban assured the Tuscan envoy that he wanted Parma neither for himself nor for his nephews; the Duke was the disturber of the peace and it was wrong to support a rebel against his sovereign.[3] All was in vain; on no account must Urban become still more powerful. On August 31st, 1642, Venice, Tuscany and Modena concluded a defensive alliance which it was left open to Farnese to join.[4] Richelieu had no objection against it, for he hoped, in the capacity of a mediator, to fish in troubled water.[5]

Odoardo sold his jewellery, contracted fresh debts and resolved to start the war on his own account. To the amazement of his friends and heedless of their advice, he undertook, with France's encouragement, the task of recovering Castro.

[1] See *Acta consist.*, MS. in my possession; *NICOLETTI, IX., 250; GROTTANELLI, *Ducato di Castro*, 571, *cf.* CORNA, *loc. cit.* (See above, p. 387, n. 7); *Libri commem. di Venezia. Regesti*, VII., Venezia, 1907, 194 *seq.*; ROMANIN, VII., 335.

[2] *"Uno de'principali motivi che S.S. ha havuto di muoversi è stato il disprezzo che il Duca facea delle censure ecclesiastiche, il mettere sotto sopra tutte le case de'religiosi e l'haver infino levato dalla propria chiesa il suo pastore." Letter to the French nuncio, August 25, 1642, in *NICOLETTI, IX., 360. *Cf.* besides *Bull.* XV., 188 *seq.*

[3] See *NICOLETTI, IX., 255.

[4] See LÜNIG, *Cod. ital. dipl.*, II., 1551. On December 6, 1642, Urban VIII. gave Cardinal Barberini full power to bring an action against the Duke of Modena; see *Bull.*, XV., 217 *seq.*

[5] *"Per quanto comprendo, qui non si ha disgusto che la republica di Venezia, il Gran Duca e Modena siano uniti a difesa di Parma e Piacenza, desiderando il Re di mantenersi in qualità di mediatore." Grimaldi's report, September 19, 1642, in *NICOLETTI, IX., 318.

On September 10th, 1642, he set out with 3,000 horse and as many infantry but without artillery, to invade the Papal States. Forte Urbano did not delay him ; the 18,000 men of the papal army scattered like chaff. Drawing their swords, Marchese Mattei and Marchese Malvasia, who commanded under Taddeo Barberini, sought in vain to rally the fleeing army. On September 13th Odoardo appeared before Bologna and unfurled the banner of a *Gonfaloniere* of the Church, a dignity which was hereditary in his House. In a letter to the Papal Legate, Cardinal Durazzo, and to the Magistrates of the town, he assured them that he made war only against the Barberini, not against the Pope.[1] Leaving Bologna on one side, he continued his march on the following day in the direction of Imola, when the papal army appeared on his left. He ordered his cavalry to attack at once ; this created such a panic that the Pope's men sought safety in flight. Imola also, in order not to run the risk of pillage, opened its gates without opposition and Odoardo's army marched through without a trace of disorder. Cardinal Franciotti of Imola even called upon the Duke who declared here also that he came not as an enemy, but in order to wrest their prey from the Barberini. At one moment Faenza thought of defending itself, but there also the precedent of Imola was repeated. At Forlì Odoardo had to threaten to burn the city before it would admit him After one day's rest he crossed the Apeninnes to re-enter the Papal States from Tuscan Arezzo. By the end of September Odoardo Farnese was encamped on the shore of Lake Trasimeno. In October he advanced as far as Acquapendente where not even the churches escaped pillage.[2] The irresistible progress of the enemy caused consternation in Rome where people recalled to mind the days of Clement VII. Everybody feared another sack. Many of the inhabitants fled, others hid their belongings or took them into the Leonine City, in the conviction that it would be able to withstand attack.[3] The Pope hastened the construction

[1] See GROTTANELLI, *Ducato di Castro*, 577.

[2] *Cf. Arch. stor. ital.*, 5 series, XXXVII., 401 *seq.*

[3] See CERBONI, *G. N. Eritreo*, 95.

of the powerful bastions which began at the Porta Cavallegieri and were intended to protect the crest of the Janiculus as far as the Porta Portese. The work was conceived in accordance with the new science of fortification and advantage was also taken of the terrain.[1] The Pontiff himself took up residence in the Vatican in order that if it became necessary, he might flee into the Castle of St. Angelo. However, Odoardo was no more a statesman than he was a military leader: he lacked the moral courage to carry through his daring undertaking [2]; had he possessed it he would have realized his purpose, for the troops on which the Pope had to rely were worthless. Amusing details are related of the latter's courage. On one occasion, when a cavalry man, having presumed to go too near the enemy, was shot, it was said: "The fool! to have allowed himself to be killed in French fashion"—*Che pazzo! S'è fatto ammazzar alla Francese.*[3] The French envoy, Hugues de Lionne, was negotiating with Cardinal Spada for a compromise by the terms of which Castro would be entrusted to the safe-keeping of the Duke of Modena, under a guaranty of Louis XIII. To this Odoardo was ready to accede but in addition he also insisted on the reimbursement of his heavy expenses.[4] To this the Pope could not assent. At this point Cardinal Antonio Barberini resolved to compel the Duke to beat a retreat. To this end he had recourse to the services of the Frenchman Achille d'Estampes-Valençay, an expert in the art of war. The latter, having collected a considerable

[1] *Cf.* CANCELLIERI, *Tarantismo*, 55; NIBBY, *Le mura di Roma*, Roma, 1820, 338, 364, 368, 381; ROCCI, *Le piante iconografiche e prospettiche di Roma*, Torino, 1902, P. III., Append.; GUGLIELMOTTI, *Fortificazioni*, 388 *seq.*; REUMONT, *Beiträge*, III., 192 *seq.*; *id.*, *Gesch. der Stadt Rom*, III., 2, 743, 868; BORGATTI, *Le mura di Roma*, in *Riv. d'Artiglieria*, XVI. (1899), 400 *seq.*

[2] Opinion of BROSCH (I., 407).

[3] See REUMONT, *Beiträge*, V., 149. *Cf.* also CERBONI, 95 *seq.*

[4] See DEMARIA, 215 *seq.* For a critique of VALFREY's book: *Hugues de Lionne, ses ambassades en Italie* 1642–1656, Paris, 1877, *cf.* ADEMOLLO, in the *Rassegna settiman.*, 1878, no. 19, p. 356 *seq.*

force, constrained Farnese, whose troops were beginning to desert at the approach of the cold season, to break up his camp at Acquapendente and to consent to negotiations. Owing to the fact that the Duke of Tuscany gave him no support, Odoardo's position grew steadily worse. Fresh negotiations for an accommodation which were conducted at Castel Giorgio, near Orvieto, were foiled by the intrigues of Lionne. The aim of that astute negotiator was either to drive the Pope completely into the arms of France or to kindle a general war of the allies against the Holy See.[1] Accordingly when Rome began to prepare for resistance, the French Government laid all the blame on the Pope.

The Paris nuncio, Girolamo Grimaldi, found himself in a difficult situation. The King heaped reproaches on him and on one occasion he roundly told him that he knew very well that Rome wished to enter into an alliance with Spain and was ill-disposed towards France.[2] Relations between Urban VIII. and the Bishop of Lamego became so strained that the French ambassador, Fontenay, left Rome on December 18th, 1642.[3] Louis XIII. endeavoured to justify this step in a conversation with the nuncio in the course of which he complained bitterly of the Pope's attitude towards Mazarin, Lamego and Odoardo Farnese. The nuncio replied that His Majesty forgot the injury done to the Pope in consequence of his having been given the reputation of partiality towards France. The King retorted that the injury he himself had suffered was far greater; he had recalled Fontenay from Rome because he could do

[1] This has been proved by Demaria (217 *seq.*).

[2] See *Nicoletti, IX., 378. Cardinal Barberini answered the nuncio: *" È ben vero che secondo le bravate dell'ambasciatore di Francia e del sig. di Lione se e pensato di trovar modo a poterci buttar dall'altra parte parendo strano il modo tenuto da N.S. in tanti anni di pontificato senza riguardo di continui dispiaceri de' Spagnuoli." Barberini continues "My House is the first which for hundreds of years has never accepted a single 'giulio' from Spain". Letter of January 1, 1643, in *Nicoletti, IX., 381–6.

[3] *Cf.* above, p. 206.

nothing there ; Rome did everything to oblige the Spaniards whereas he himself was badly treated.[1]

There can be no doubt that France was working not for an agreement but for the continuation of a war by which Spain was prevented from levying troops in Italy, and which presented a possibility of mobilizing the Italian Powers against Milan. With this end in view Mazarin took the part of Odoardo Farnese from whom he promised himself more than from Rome. In March, 1642, Fontenay returned to Rome seemingly in order to work for the re-establishment of peace, but in reality to fan the flames of war.[2] Now as before Urban VIII. insisted on Odoardo Farnese seeking absolution from his censures, abandoning his claims to Castro and Montalto and satisfying his creditors. For the rest Cardinal Barberini informed Mazarin that if France wished to mediate, she must make haste for the season was already far advanced.[3] As a matter of fact in the spring of 1643 the league resumed the war with increased forces.[4] Fortunately for the Pope there was a lack of unity among the confederates, as so often happens in coalitions.[5] Odoardo felt hurt because he was not given the supreme command ; accordingly he resolved to act on his own, but his attempt to surprise Montalto failed. The Barberini entered into fresh negotiations with Tuscany. The Grand Duke was prepared to leave the league, provided the Pope gave the purple to his brother and granted certain concessions to himself in the ecclesiastico-political sphere. When Urban VIII. declined such bartering, the Grand Duke broke off the negotiations.[6] On May 26th, Tuscany, Venice and Modena concluded a new treaty by the terms of which two armies were to march simultaneously into the States of the Church, one from Venetian territory into the Romagna, the other from Tuscany.[7] The pretext for their action was the

[1] See *NICOLETTI, IX., 387 *seq.* [2] See DEMARIA, 223 *seq.*

[3] See *NICOLETTI, IX., 460, 466.

[4] See *Libri commen.*, VII., 196.

[5] *Cf.* NICOLETTI, IX., 501 *seq.* [6] *Cf.* DEMARIA, 227.

[7] *Cf.* LÜNIG, *Cod. ital. dipl.*, II., 2039, *NICOLETTI (IX., 510, reports : " In Roma giunse quasi improvisa la nuova di tal

re-establishment of peace in Italy which, it was alleged, had been troubled by the Barberini[1]; in reality everybody pursued his own particular ends and the Duke of Modena in particular cherished the hope of securing Ferrara for himself.[2] On May 29th the Florentine envoy, Niccolini, left Rome without taking leave of the Pope,[3] thereby provoking yet another panic.[4] In June the war broke out anew[5]; however, Odoardo Farnese, who had penetrated into the territory of Ferrara and occupied the important positions of Bodeno and Stellata on the Po, would not hear of a joint action. Venice and the Duke of Modena also acted on their own account. This enabled Marchese Mattei, who commanded under the Cardinal Legate, to enter the territory of Modena and to lay siege to the fortress of Nonantola. However, Raimondo Montecuccoli, who was to become famous at a later date, hastened to its relief and defeated the papal troops. This enabled Duke Francesco of Modena to advance against Bologna, but the danger which threatened that town was averted when the Pope's men succeeded in taking the fort near Lagoscuro in consequence of which the Venetians recalled their troops and Duke Francesco saw himself compelled to retreat.[6]

unione, poichè, sebene vi era penetrata qualche sospizione, tuttavia per le relationi delli due Nunzii di Venetia e di Firenza si credeva che quei principi non sarebbono mai venuti a tal deliberatione tanto più che per la morte del cardinale Richelieu, che si teneva fomentatore del Duca di Parma, era succeduto il cardinale Mazzarini nell'autorità di quello, e questi era Romano, promosso alla purpura da Papa Urbano et intrinseco del cardinale Antonio."

[1] *Cf.* *Nicoletti, IX., 515.

[2] See Pallavicini, *Alessandro VII.*, vol. I., 118.

[3] See Grottanelli, *Ducato di Castro*, 585.

[4] See Cerboni, 96.

[5] The Papal *Commissio auditori Camerae procedendi contra rempubl. Venetam, magnum ducem Hetruriae ac Mutinae et olim Parmae duces nonnullarum terrarum S. Apost. Sedis invasores*, June 26, 1643, in *Bull.*, XV., 273 *seq.*

[6] See Muratori, *Annali, ad* 1643; Reumont, *Toskana*, I., 425 *seq.*

The Tuscan troops had better luck at first; they advanced victoriously into Umbria,[1] but their successes also were neutralized by the lack of unity among the other confederates. This enabled Cardinal Antonio Barberini to stem the advance of the Tuscan troops. The attack on Pistoia, which the Cardinal caused De Valençay to undertake on October 2nd, 1643, failed,[2] and in consequence of the repulse of an advance by the Pope's soldiers against Pitigliano from Castro, the Tuscan troops were at least able to maintain their positions. Odoardo Farnese, for whose sake the whole war was being fought, remained inactive on the Po whilst these events were taking place.[3] All the participants grew increasingly weary of a war which, though not a bloody one, proved exceedingly costly.

The conduct of France sufficiently accounts for the fact that, notwithstanding the hostile attitude of the Viceroy of Naples, Cardinal Barberini kept looking towards Spain; but from Madrid there only came fair words.[4] Yet somehow an end had to be put to the struggle,[5] for Urban VIII.'s resources threatened to give out altogether though he had imposed fresh taxes; in September, 1642, he had even gone so far as to take 500,000 scudi out of the treasure of Castel S. Angelo and by an ordinance of June 16th, 1643, he had commandeered all the silver objects in Rome in return for promissory notes.[6]

[1] *Cf.* GROTTANELLI, *Ducato di Castro*, 795 *seq.*

[2] PIETRO BRACALI, *Relazione dell'assalto e della battaglia dell'esercito de'Barberini contro la città di Pistoia nel giorno due ottobre del* 1643, Pistoia, 1896. This pamphlet, of which only a few copies were printed, was written in honour of the Sanesi-Crocini marriage and is rich in interesting items about the Castro war; its author is Niccolò de'Cancellieri of Pistoia, who addressed it to Pier Colonna, at Pistoia.

[3] See REUMONT, *Toskana*, 8, 426 *seq.*

[4] See *NICOLETTI, IX., 620 *seq.*, 682.

[5] On August 21, 1643, Urban VIII. gave Cardinal Donghi full authority to begin peace pourparlers with Venice and her allies; see *Bull.*, XV., 278.

[6] According to *NICOLETTI (IX, 688), Raggi overcame Urban VIII.'s opposition to touching the treasure of St. Angelo. All the Cardinals at the Consistory of September 22, 1642, voted in

Moreover, since the death of the aged Pontiff was only a matter of time, a settlement could not be further delayed. It came about through French intervention. Louis XIII. had died on May 13th, 1643, and Mazarin had the re-establishment of peace in Italy very much at heart. His representative, Cardinal Alessandro Bichi, who repaired to Venice at the end of 1643, displayed feverish activity.[1]

Bichi's eloquence and Venice's threats ended by inducing Farnese to yield. Rome was in a ferment and loud laments resounded throughout the Papal States. Many accusations were heard to the effect that the Barberini were deriving personal profit from the sums spent on the war.[2] When in the middle of March, 1644, the Venetians defeated the Papal army at Ponte Lagoscuro, on the Po, not far from Ferrara, and Cardinal Antonio Barberini narrowly escaped being made a prisoner,[3] the need of haste was realized. On March 31st, 1644, peace was signed at Venice between the Pope, the Republic of Venice, Tuscany and Modena respectively and on the same day also between the Pope and the Duke of Parma. Urban VIII. saw himself compelled to grant Odoardo Farnese's request for absolution from his censures and to surrender Castro and all the other confiscated property. On his part Odoardo bound himself to surrender his conquests and everything was to be restored to its former condition. France guaranteed the agreement.[4]

favour of 500,000 scudi being borrowed from it (*Acta consist.*, MS. in my possession). The "Chirografo" of June 16, 1643, is in MARTINORI, 103 *seq.*

[1] See *NICOLETTI, IX., 692 *seq.*, 703 *seq.*; DEMARIA, 230 *seq.*; GROTTANELLI, *Ducato di Castro*, 797 *seq.*, who used an account of the negotiations written by Bichi, in the Bichi-Ruspoli archives at Siena. An "Ode" by Fulvio Testi to Cardinal Bichi on the conclusion of the peace of 1644 is in *Barb.* 3888, p. 75 *seq.*, Vatican Library.

[2] See NICOLETTI, IX., 716 *seq.*

[3] *Cf.* BALAN, VI., 778; DEMARIA, 232.

[4] See DUMONT, *Corps dipl.*, VI., 1, 297 *seq.*; THEINER, *Cod. dipl.*, III., 583 *seq.*; ROMANIN, VII., 339; CARABELLI, *Dei Farnesi e del ducato di Castro e di Ronciglione*, Firenze, 1865, 159. The appointment of plenipotentiaries "ad recipienda loca

Thus ended the war of Castro which cost little blood but a vast amount of money, benefited nobody and inflicted grievous injury on all concerned.[1] Perhaps the Pope was the hardest hit. In his fairest provinces, viz. Umbria, part of the Romagna and the territory of Ferrara, large tracts of territory lay devastated, his finances were completely exhausted and his subjects burdened with further heavy taxation.[2] The total expenditure amounted to over 12,000,000 gold scudi.[3] But far worse was the moral damage: a rebellious vassal in conjunction with the Italian Powers had defeated the ruler of the States of the Church and inflicted a most grievous humiliation on his nephews. The Berlin Museum preserves the portrait of a corpulent military captain (so far the name has not been ascertained) proudly trampling on a banner bearing the coat of arms of the Barberini.[4] Urban VIII., who professed great admiration for Countess Matilda, found it all

status eccles. occupata occasione nuperi belli", April 6, 1644, is in *Bull.*, XV., 309 *seq.* In the consistory of May 2, 1644, the Pope said: "Capitulationes initas inter partes, quia vobis innotuerunt, referre omittimus. Gratiae omnipotenti Deo actae sunt, reliquum est, ut negotii executionem curemus, prout diligenter et attente curabimus" (*Acta consist.*, MS. in my possession).

[1] See RICCIUS, *Rer. ital. sui temporis narrationes, Narr. XIX.*, p. 590; REUMONT, *Toskana*, I., 428.

[2] See CALISSE, 456 *seq.*; BERTOLOTTI, *Artisti Veneti* (1884), 77; ADEMOLLO, in *Riv. Europ.*, 1877, II, 426 *seq.*; CERBONI, 26. *Cf.* *"Nota dell'impositioni messe dalla s. mem. di Urbano VIII. nel tempo della guerra passata e prima" in *Cod.* H. II., 40, p. 1, Chigi Library.

[3] See BAROZZI-BERCHET, Roma, II., 53, *"Spese per la guerra contro Parma et la lega da 22 settembre 1642 per tutto luglio 1644 in Roma solamente: sei milioni centocinque mila seicento diciotto scudi" (*Ottob.* 2435, p. 256 *seq.*, Vatican Library). The **Conti di Msgr. Scotti, vesc. di Borgo S. Donino, già governatore della Marca, in tempo della guerra* 1642–3, is in *cat.* 414, p. 44, of K. W. Hiersemann of Leipzig, 1913.

[4] The portrait acquired in 1873 in Florence, supposedly by Ribera, was subsequently ascribed to Velasques, though certainly

the more difficult to recover from this heavy blow, which had shown up before the eyes of the whole world, both the weakness of the States of the Church and the futility of so costly a display of military force. So imbued was he with the memories of the splendour of the Papal States in the Middle Ages that in 1635 he dropped the remark that he would rather lose his life than abandon the rights of the Holy See.[1] Small wonder then that he survived this peace by only four months. During that time Bichi had to remove the manifold and great difficulties which barred the way to the execution of the agreement.[2] When, on July 18th, 1644, Odoardo Farnese

quite wrongly; then to Pietro da Cortona and to others and finally, by Hedberg, to Peter Franchoys of Malines (see *Kunstchronik*, XVIII., 493). Voss (*Monatshefte für Kunstwiss.*, III. (1910), 18 *seq.*: "*Wer ist der Meister des sog. Alessandro dal Borro?*") is inclined to ascribe the picture to Sacchi (*cf.* also Voss, *Malerei des Barock*, 531), but POSSE (*Sacchi*, 4, n. 2) is decisively against this attribution. It is nevertheless ascribed to Sacchi by U. OIETTI (*Il ritratto ital. dal Caravaggio al Tiepolo*, Bergamo, 1928, 9 and table 16). It is a mistake to identify the personage of the portrait with Alessandro dal Borro of Arezzo, who was indeed an opponent of Urban VIII., but an authentic portrait of him in the municipal buildings of Arezzo shows different features and a slim figure. *Cf.* W. BOMBE in *L'Arte*, XII., 374 *seq.*

[1] *Cf.* a conversation which throws extraordinary light on Urban VIII.'s character which the Pope had in July, 1635, with Fulvio Testi whose account has been published by NEGRI (180 *seq.*).

[2] In addition to GROTTANELLI, *Ducato di Castro*, 807, *cf.* especially the full account in NICOLETTI, IX., 730 *seq.* *Ibid.*, details about Malatesta Albani's mission to Mazarin (751–9): * "Circa poi di me potrà assicurare S. Emza, che conducendosi ad effetto questo affare, io di buonissima e prontissima volontà, cedendo a quello che non mai pensai di fare, cioè di accettar già mai il particolar servitio di una delle corone, dopo la vita di S.B. accetterò il servire alla Francia publicamente, et in quei modi, che siano leciti ad un card. italiano, et al medesimo s. card. Antonio, sia con ritenere entrate ecclesiastiche, o altra conveniente dimostratione. Et intanto non lascerò di servire nei particolari

once more took possession of Castro, his supreme feudal lord lay on his death-bed.

Urban VIII. possessed an iron constitution and neither the enormous burden of affairs nor the many commotions which occurred during his reign, were able to injure his health. In 1635 Alvise Contarini stated that, though the Pope was 69 years old, he was free from any disease and perfectly fit in mind and body.[1] Urban VIII. had indeed been seriously ill on two occasions, the first time in consequence of an outbreak of malaria during the conclave, and again in the summer of 1639 when his death seemed imminent.[2] But he made so complete a recovery that even the Spaniards had to reconcile themselves to a considerable prolongation of his pontificate. In February, 1639, Urban told Cardinal Corner that he felt the weight of his seventy years, though on the whole he was quite well.[3] The new Venetian envoy, Nani, also found the

e nel modo che sarà conveniente al carico et al ministerio, che esercito appresso S.B." Mazarin insisted on a written promise by Barberini that after the Pope's death he would enter into the service of France and concluded with the words " che all'hora era tempo, che S.S. procurasse di ricuperar il regno di Napoli, perchè da Francia gli si mandarebbe un armata navale da poter sbarcare 6,000 combattanti " (Nicoletti, *loc. cit.*, 736). Barberini declared his readiness to give " scrittura secreta ad esser del partito francese ", and commended Albani for having refused to agree with the proposal in respect of Naples. Mazarin had Barberini advised to try to detach the Duke of Tuscany from the league. In subsequent discussions Albani demanded that the King should give a written guarantee that in the event of Spain depriving Barberini of his revenues, he would grant him similar ones at once, either in France or in Italy. (Nicoletti, *loc. cit.*, 770–785). At that moment Urban VIII. died.

[1] Alv. Contarini, 366.

[2] *Lettres de Richelieu*, IV., 42 *seq.*, *ibid.*, 289 : Bagno as Richelieu's candidate for the tiara. On the Pope's illness *cf.* above p. 192.

[3] *Letter of Cardinal Corner to the Senate, dated Rome, February 12, 1639. Of the Pope the Cardinal says : " Quanto al suo stato di sanità, io l'ho trovato nell'aspetto invecchiato,

Pope very active.[1] In 1642 a Portuguese astrologer promised him another nine years[2] but this prophecy was not to be fulfilled. In all probability the excitement of the war of Castro hastened Urban VIII.'s death. In the spring of 1644 a Mantuan envoy wrote that though the strong physique of the seventy-six years old man was weakened, his mental vigour remained unimpaired, as could be seen by the promptness of his replies and his undiminished flow of words. However, as much as possible Cardinal Francesco only brought to his notice such affairs as did not trouble his tranquillity; moreover, after a pontificate of twenty years, a thing that had not occurred since Paul III., the Romans were eager for a change.[3] This wish was to be fulfilled sooner than was expected. In June, 1644, such a diminution of strength was witnessed in the Pope that the worst was to be feared. Cardinal Francesco Barberini kept the real condition of the patient secret as long as possible and only when the physician gave him up did he summon Cardinal Antonio Barberini from Ferrara.[4]

incurvato et magrito, ma quanto alla sua vivacità, discorso et spiriti, non mi pare che habbia fatto gran mutatione." State Archives, Venice.

[1] NANI, 35.

[2] See ADEMOLLO, *Indipendenza Portoghese*, 36.

[3] G. B. TARABUCCI, **Stato della corte di Roma nel* 1643, dated Mantua, May 20, 1643, Gonzaga Archives, Mantua.

[4] *" Era già vicino a cominciar il ventesimo secondo anno del pontificato, quando negli ultimi giorni di giugno del 1644 si vide in maniera languido e destituto di forze e di vigore, che fu creduto dalla corte di Roma, che poco gli rimanesse di vita; anzi si divulgò sempre più, che stassi ogni giorno quasi moribondo. Il cardinale Barberini usò tutte le diligenze possibili per tener segreta l'infermità, et in se stesso manteneva la solita et imperturbata franchezza, et il medesimo tenore nel trattare, facendo anche spesso uscir voci da Palazzo, che il Papa andava migliorando, et che fra pochi giorni farebbe il concistorio e crearebbe i cardinali. Quanto poi alla cura del Papa procurò, che fosse esattissima, e che le stanze del pontifice si tenessero ben chiuse, acciochè tolti i suoi più confidenti, niuno potesse penetrare lo stato della vita di S.S. Et in questo particolare fu Urbano in

In view of the fact that there were eight vacancies in the Sacred College just then, Cardinal Barberini sought to induce the Pope to make a last nomination; but Urban VIII. would not hear of it. On the other hand, though mortally stricken, he thought of holding a consistory, because seventeen nominations of Bishops had to be proclaimed and the ceremony of the "closing of the mouth" had not yet been carried out for Cardinal Grimaldi. The Pope clung to his resolution, notwithstanding Cardinal Barberini's advice to the contrary, nor would he listen to the request made in the name of the City of Rome by Monsignor Roscioli, that he would not endanger his precious life. On July 1st, 1644, notwithstanding the great heat, Urban held the consistory as planned; at its conclusion he was taken back to his rooms in an exhausted condition. On the next day the Pope sent for several outstanding theologians, among them Cardinal Lugo, from whom he could expect a candid opinion. He submitted to them a list of all the benefices bestowed on the Barberini family, begging them to examine whether in granting them he had exceeded his powers, for if that were the case, it was his intention to revoke whatever he had illegally conferred on his nephews. The theologians calmed the Pope's conscience, with what arguments cannot be ascertained.[1]

Repeatedly the sick Pontiff gave utterance to his grief over the attitude of the Italian Princes in the war of Castro and the fact that the Barberini were not included in the peace. However, Cardinal Francesco attached no particular importance to this circumstance; on the other hand he would have liked to see his party reinforced by a fresh nomination, but all his efforts were in vain. Even when Cardinal Lugo drew

tutto il tempo del suo pontificato assai ben servito da suoi servitori e familiari, riuscendo pieni di fede, di segretezza e di amore verso la sua persona, onde furono anche largemente rimunerati e ben provisti dal loro benignissimo e liberalissimo principe" (NICOLETTI, VIII., c. 15, p. 751). The details that follow have been published by RANKE (III., 159*–162*).

[1] Nicoletti (in RANKE, III., 160*) only reports what was rumoured.

his attention to the fact that several Cardinals had died since the last nomination, so that the publication of those at least who remained *in petto* was desirable, Urban refused to listen to him: this action was deemed praiseworthy.[1] Urban's remark in the course of his illness, to the *Tesoriere* Lorenzo Raggi, throws light on the dispositions of the Pontiff: he only wished to live for another two months, he said, in order to do penance for his sins, to complete the treasure of S. Angelo which had been grievously affected by the war and to see Rome secured against all attacks by the completion of the ring of walls round the Borgo and the Trastevere.[2] His wish was not granted. On July 23rd the Pope's weakness was such that his death was hourly expected.[3] On the morning of July 29th, 1644, after devoutly receiving the Sacraments, Urban VIII. expired at the age of 76, having preserved all the vigour of his mind to the last.[4]

[1] *Cf.* A. MARCHESAN, *Lettere di O. Rinaldi*, Treviso, 1896, 21. According to this information those reserved *in petto* were Casimir, the brother of the King of Poland, G. B. Spada, *segretario de'brevi de'principi e confidentissimo del s. card. Barberini*, the nuncio in Venice, Vitelli, and the *Tesoriere* Lorenzo Raggi.

[2] Nicoletti in RANKE, III., 163*.

[3] See Fed. Savelli's *report to Ferdinand III., dated July 23, 1644, State Archives, Vienna.

[4] *Cf.* **Avviso* of July 30, 1644 (Vatican Library) in Appendix XXII.; MARCHESAN, *loc. cit.*; COVILLE, *Mazarin*, I., n. 1. NICOLETTI (*loc. cit.*) reports that "when someone suggested to the dying Pontiff the words of the Gospel: 'Deus propitius esto mihi peccatori,' the latter replied: 'Deus propitius esto mihi maximo peccatori." Cardinal Barberini was not present, "et alcuni pensarono, che ciò facesse per non gli aggiunger dolori; altri, per non esser veduto dolersi; et altri credettero più tosto che ciò facesse per liberarsi da pericoli d'imputationi di haver formati Brevi surrettitie per interesse della sua casa." The post-mortem revealed healthy viscera, an extraordinarily small heart, like that of a child, and gravel in the "borsa del fiale". *Cf.* also Cassiano del Pozzo's notes in *Miscell. di stor. ital.*, XV., 185. A. Sacchi painted part of the decorations for Urban VIII.s catafalque in St. Peter's; see POSSE, *Sacchi*, 11.

The love of the Romans for satire is well known, as testified by two world-famed antique marble statues. If already during the war of Castro there had been no dearth of biting satires,[1] now that Urban VIII. was dead, the Romans could not do enough to castigate in pitiless fashion the Pope's weakness for his nephews and to vilify the dead man in every conceivable way.[2] It was natural that the poisoned arrows aimed at the fiscal oppression, which had become heavier still in consequence of the war of Castro, met with most

[1] See FERRANTE PALLAVICINO, *Baccinata overo Battarella per le api Barberine in occasione della mossa delle armi di N.S. Papa Urbano ottavo contra Parma, all'illustriss. e reverendiss. Monsignor Vitellio Nunzio di Sua Santità in Venetia, nella Stamperia di Pasquino a spese di Marforio* 1642. Against this there appeared: *L'Antibaccinata overo apologia per la mossa delle armi di N.S. Papa Urbano ottavo contra Parma di Leopardo Leopardi Romano, Macerata* (without date). Both publications are very scarce; the former is found in MS. in the Boncompagni Archives, Rome, *Cod.* L. 20, as well as "**Franc. card. Barberini somnium ad nepotes suos et alios Parthenio Vasario Graeco authore*". On the *Baccinata* and other pamphlets against the Barberini, *cf.* the *Letter of Alex. Ficher, S.J., in *Barb.* 6027, p. 72, Vatican Library. The *Baccinata* also appeared in a French translation: *La Bassinade c'est à dire bastement de Bassina pour les abeilles Barberini à l'occasion de ce que le Pape Urbain VIII. a prins les armes contre le Duc de Parma*, s.l. et a. (Copy in the State Library, Munich.) Ferrante Pallavicino also wrote: *Il divortio celeste cagionato dalle dissolutezze della sposa Romana. Villafranca* 1643. But there also appeared bitter satires against Odoardo Farnese (*cf.* FRATI in *Arch. stor. ital.*, 5 series, XXXVII., 394 *seq.*) one of which begins as follows:—

Dove avete il cervello, o signor Duca?
Credete aver il Papa capellano?
Non andate a scherzar col sacristano
Che vi sepellirà dentro una buca.

A poem by G. GANDIOSI: *Il pianto d'Italia* is discussed by CIMEGOTTO in *Riv. Abruzzese*, XIV., 3–4.

[2] Ameyden declared that a whole volume could be filled with the satires then current; see *Arch. Rom.*, II., 260, note. *Cf.* FRASCHETTI, 157. A number of satirical *poems of this kind are

applause on the part of the populace. One satirical poem, which derides all these taxes, concludes with the following statement: "Urban VIII. and his nephews have done greater injury to my beautiful Rome than either Goths or Vandals."[1] This was an extravagant assertion.[2] Assuredly the unwarrantable influence and the immense enrichment of the Barberini, are the worst stain on Urban VIII.'s reign of nearly twenty-one years, as he himself felt; but this blame, which is justified, must not make us forget how well he deserved of the Church as Pope, or what he did to further literature and art, to the great material advantage of the Eternal City. Even a Venetian, Giambattista Nani, gave it as his opinion that had

in *Inf. polit.*, XXXIX., 428 *seq.*, 431 *seq.*, State Library, Berlin, among them two epitaphs, one of which begins thus:

PAUCA HAEC URBANI SINT VERBA INCISA SEPULCRO:
QUAM BENE PAVIT APES, TAM MALE PAVIT OVES.

Ibid., 428 *seq.*, a satirical *poem against Urban VIII. complaining chiefly about taxation, with the refrain: *O Papa Gabella.* The 15th strophe runs thus:—

Han fatto più danno
Urbano e nepoti
Che Vandali e Gothi
A Roma mia bella—O Papa Gabella.

A collection of *satires against Urban VIII. is also found in *Cod.* 278 of the Archives of the Spanish Embassy in Rome. Further *satires are in the *Bibl. Communale* of Ancona and in *Cod.* 10806 of the British Museum. A most venomous *satire entitled *Giuco di primiera* is in the town library of Frankfort, II., 42 (in folio), no. 12. Satires against the Barberini in *Vat.* 7098, p. 280 *seq.*, Vatican Library. The sarcastic remark at the expense of his nephews which is often put in the mouth of Urban VIII. (see MORONI, IV., 113), and which Gigli has preserved, is probably one of these satires; see also ADRIAN, *Mitteilungen aus Handschriften*, Frankfort, 1846, 318 *seq.* GROTANELLI, *Ducato di Castro*, 816 *seq.*

[1] See preceding note.

[2] Even Ameyden comments thus on the contemporary satires: Partim probanda, quia vera referant, partim improbanda, quia falsa et calumniosa (*Arch. Rom.*, II., 260, n. 1).

he been less weak towards his relatives, Urban VIII., by reason of the purity of his life, his learning and political wisdom, would have ranked among the greatest Princes of his time.[1]

[1] *Cf.* NANI, *Hist. Venet.*, II., 8.

CHAPTER VI.

URBAN VIII. AS PATRON OF LITERATURE AND ART—ROME A BAROQUE CITY.

(1)

IF all the Popes of the Catholic Restoration were keenly interested in the advancement of learning, it was particularly so with Urban VIII. who stood in the very centre of the learned and artistic life of his time and personally entered into it with his poetical compositions.

Love of poetry was a tradition in the Pope's family, seeing that among his forbears there was one Francesco da Barberino,[1] a contemporary of Dante, to whom a monument has recently been erected in the family's place of origin. Urban VIII. preserved Francesco's moral and philosophical poems, written in pure Tuscan, as a precious heirloom, in the library of the family palace. In 1640 he had the joy to see them published by Francesco Ubaldini. He began to compose Latin and Italian poems in his early youth and some Greek verses of his have also been preserved. With great mastery of form he knew how to express brilliant thoughts in the metre of his favourite poets, Horace and Catullus. The Barberini library preserves Maffeo's earliest poems written in Italian.[2] They date from the eighties of the sixteenth century and owe their production to the influence of Aurelio Orsi, a poet in the service of the Farnese, to whose criticism Maffeo willingly submitted.[3] At that time the thought of

[1] *Cf.* MAZZUCHELLI, II., 1, 25 *seq.*; TIRABOSCHI, VIII., Napoli, 1781, 402 *seq.*

[2] Thirteen *sonnets in all have remained unnoticed up till now. *Barb.* 4009, pp. 1 *seqq.*, Vatican Library.

[3] See Maffeo's *autograph letters from Rome to Aurelio Orsi at Caprarola, of the years 1585 to 1589, *ibid.*, p. 17 *seq.*

becoming a priest had not yet taken shape in his mind, hence it is not surprising to find several love poems among them [1]; but in course of time he turned from profane topics to devote himself to religious subjects. A beautiful sonnet laments the fact of his having allowed himself, in his early youth, to be enmeshed by profane love.[2] The first Latin poems of Maffeo Barberini appeared in 1606, at Perugia, in a collection of poems by members of the Academy of the " Insensati " dedicated to Cardinal Carlo Emmanuele Pio of Savoy.[3] Here we find an ode to Aurelio Orsi as well as poems on contemporary events, such as those addressed to Cardinal Pietro Aldobrandini

[1] The first sonnet **Amante disturbato dal latrar d'un cane, ibid.*, p. 1, and **Bella donna veduta a l'improviso* (*Dolce mio sol*), *ibid.*, p. 5.

[2] *Mentre di basso Amor nel laccio involto
la mia primiera età sforzò, ch'io gissi
quasi in sen de l'oblio spirto sepolto,
fuor ch'a me stesso a tutti ignoto io vissi.

Ma poi che gli occhi ove risplende affissi
ritratto il Paradiso in un bel volto
da quei d'impuro ardore oscuri abbissi,
l'angelica beltà m'hebbe ritolto.

E di desio di gloria acceso il petto
trasse per non segnato ampio sentiero
oltre le stelle il debile intelletto.

E da tal luce scorto, ancora io spero
del bello di là sù sommo e perfetto
lasciar l'imago, e vagheggiare 'l vero.

loc. cit., p. 9.

[3] AURELII URSINI, MAPHAEI BARBERINI, CLAUDII CONTULI, I. B. LAURI, VINC. PALETTARII, M. A. BONCIARII, *Academicorum Insensatorum Carmina ad ill. Carolum Eman. Pium cardinalem, Perusiae*, 1606. A copy of this rare and hitherto unnoticed publication is in the Bibl. Barberini (GGG., II., 41); Barberini's five poems are on pp. 191 *seqq.* According to VERMIGLIOLI (*Scritt. Perugini*, II., Perugia, 1829, 27 and 137) before printing his poems M. Barberini submitted them to G. T. Giglioli and to G. Neri; see *ibid.*, 63 *seq.*, on G. B. Lauro. *Cf.* IANI NICII ERYTHRAEI, *Pinacotheca*, I., 257 *seq.*; *ibid.*, 164 *seq.*, on A. Orsi.

on the conquest of Ferrara and the peace negotiated by the nephew of Clement VIII. (*Pax Allobrogica*). In other poems he bewails the death of Mary Stuart and extols the victories of Alessandro Farnese in the Netherlands. Maffeo's ode on Mary Magdalen was printed at Paris in 1618. Two years later the King's printer, Antonius Stephanus, published, also in Paris, a larger collection of the products of Barberini's muse.[1] After the Cardinal's elevation to the See of Peter, editions of his Latin poems appeared repeatedly, as in 1624, 1627, 1628, 1631, 1633, 1634, 1635, 1637, 1638, 1640, 1642 and 1643.[2] Maffeo Barberini's *Poesie Toscane* were less frequently reprinted.

Two editions of Urban VIII.'s Latin poems deserve special attention. The edition in quarto of 1631, published in Rome by the Jesuits of the Roman College, is remarkable for the great elegance of its production. No less a personage than Bernini collaborated in this publication. The charming ornamentation, in which the Barberini bees appear repeatedly, are his work as well as the beautiful portrait of the author and two other illustrations, one of which, viz. "David overpowering the lion," displays all the genius of the master.[3]

The Paris edition of 1642 is likewise a masterpiece of the printer's art. It is the work of the King's printing press. The title-page shows two allegorical figures; between them we behold the tiara and the arms of Urban VIII., above which two *putti* hold a laurel wreath. Not without reason one of the two figures holds a cross as well as a lyre, for Urban VIII. conceived his poetical work as an act of religion.[4] At the very beginning of the collection we find a burning appeal to youth not to make of paganism the burthen of its song, but rather

[1] MAFFEIUS CARD. BARBERINUS, *Poemata, Parisiis*, 1620.

[2] *Cf. Index bibl. Barberinae*, I., 109 *seq.*; *L'Arte*, XX. (1917), 190. On the Plantin edition see ORBAAN, *Bescheiden*, I., 337.

[3] *L'Arte*, XX. (1917), 190 *seq*. The Barberini Library possessed two copies of this *édition de luxe*, one of them in parchment, destined for the Pope.

[4] MANUCCI in *Atti Ligure*, XLII., 279; TRAVAGLINI, *I Papi cultori della poesia*, Lanciano, 1887, 64 *seq*.

the Christian ideal: "Why do we sing Orpheus descending into the nether world instead of the Saviour ascending into heaven, with the victorious emblem of the cross in his hand? May it be granted to me, like the ancient Fathers, to spread useful thoughts by means of my poems! May Moses be my guide who led the people through the Red Sea!" He then sharply castigates the degradation of poetry when it is made to sing the false gods, Jupiter and Venus; instead, he celebrates St. Helen who, extirpating the worship of the goddess of love, raised the cross. In burning words he calls on the youth of Italy to sound David's lyre.[1]

In conformity with this appeal the reader perceives in every one of the poems a strictly religious spirit, even when the sacred story is not the poet's immediate theme. On the other hand, as has been said already,[2] Urban is not fortunate when he clothes the ancient hymns of the Church in a classical dress. He is much more successful in his own original compositions. Thus the birth and passion of Christ are sung by him in spirited verses.[3] There is deep feeling in his hymn to God,

[1] The Pope also attacked indirectly the abuse of poetry for lascivious ends which then prevailed in Italy. A notorious work of the kind, the "Adonis" of Giovanni Battista Marini, together with other poems by the same writer, was put on the Index by the Pope's command in 1627 and 1628 (see REUSCH, II., 162). As a Cardinal he had withdrawn the favour he had at first shown to Marini. A follower of Marini, Claudio Achillini, specialized in exaggerations and literary tricks; thus, when speaking of the cupola of St. Peter's, he said that Michelangelo had given wings to marble, and in a poem in honour of Urban VIII. he expressed the wish that "every gun might scatter olive balls!" He extols the Pope who *col pletro e con lo scetro in mano diede termini al Merto e metro al regno* (see BAUMGARTNER, VI., 452). One Cl. Achillini, *cf.* GABRIELI, *Carteggio*, 197.

[2] See Vol. XXVIII., p. 16.

[3] Not printed are the **Disticha et epigrammata de morte Christi*, the autograph of which is in *Barb.* 1717, p. 149 *seq.*

In sepulcro Christi.

Insons noster Adam moritur fons vivus amoris,
Noluit et veteris crimina sontis Adae.

and in the dialogue of Christ and His Mother at the beginning of Holy Week. A special poem is dedicated to Mary's wedding ring, preserved at Perugia. In numerous poems he sings the praises of the Saints: John the Baptist, Mary Magdalen, St. Lawrence, SS. Peter and Paul, Pope St. Leo III., King Louis of France, Elizabeth of Portugal, SS. Martina and Bibiana. Charles Borromeo is celebrated together with Cardinals Nobili and Bellarmine. One poem, inspired by Bellarmine's booklet "Of the ascent of the mind to God", explains that heaven can only be reached by means of Jacob's ladder and by walking in the footsteps of Borromeo and Bellarmine. Another paraphrases St. Augustine's saying: "Our heart is restless until it rests in God," whilst his "Thoughts of an old man" breathe profound earnestness.

The collection includes also the poems on contemporary events already published in 1606 at Perugia, to which were added others on the deaths of Cardinals Alessandro Farnese and Pallotto. Among Maffeo Barberini's friends the following receive poetic honours: Aurelio Orsi, Giovan Battista Strozzi, Marcantonio Rossi, Giovanni Ciampoli, Virginio Cesarini, Gabriele Chiabrera, Bernardino Capponi and Flaminio Figliucci. To Clement VIII. he offers comfort amid

Mortis ab imperio moriens nos vita perennis
Eripit; hinc nobis vita perennis erit.
In ligno quondam vicit mors impia, victa est
In ligno. Poterit quid sua dextra? Nihil.

Also the following *poems of which I only give the first line:—

Ad Christum.

p. 149: Quommodo, si Deus es, mortali sanguine victus?
p. 150: Cernite mortales Christum pro crimine vestro.
p. 151: Si Rex es noster, tua sunt ubi regia sceptra?
p. 152: Pro servo Dominus moritur, pro milite ductor.
p. 153: Mors vitae mortem dat morti, vitaque mortem.

The following *epigram on the cross (p. 154) forms the conclusion:—

Una dedit nobis quondam letale venenum
Arbor, bisgemina est hac renovata salus.

his sufferings caused by the gout. To his nephews the Pope addresses religious exhortations. To this series belong the moralizing poems against flattery and pusillanimity. True wisdom, another poem explains, consists in remembering death. The power of truth is exalted in most pleasing fashion. A beautiful hymn beseeches God and the Mother of Our Lord to preserve Italy, already severely tried by war and various cataclysms, such as the eruption of Vesuvius, from the fresh tribulations threatening from the savage enemy who was even then ravaging South Germany with fire and sword.[1]

Maffeo Barberini's enthusiasm for learning is attested by his praise of the library and the collections of Ulisse Aldobrandi. His love of art is shown by the elegant distichs devoted to the Niobedes of the Villa Medici, a picture of St. Sebastian, Guido Reni's pictures in the Vatican, Bernini's fountain of the Barcaccia in the Piazza di Spagna and his group of "Daphne and Apollo". His praise of country life, the glorification of the rose and the flowers of a mild

[1] Te votis adeo : nova
Nos discrimina terrent :
Armis hosticus impetus
Oras Vindelicas premit,
Complens omnia caedibus,
Vicinisque minas parat,
Vincla, incendia, clades.
Tu, Virgo, meritam Dei
Iram comprime : conscios
Urget nos scelerum cohors :
Haec nobis magis, hostium
Quam sint arma, timenda est.
Rerum conditor omnium,
Rex aeterne ter optime,
Qui terram regis ac mare et
Caeli sidera temperas,
Nostras excipe voces.
Obliviscere criminum,
Clemens parce precantibus,
Da natis veniam, Pater,
Tantis pone modum malis.

winter, and lastly the justly famous invitation to Lorenzo Magalotti to visit the Villa Barberini at Castel Gandolfo, breathe a warm appreciation of the beauty of nature.[1]

Some of the poems appear both in Latin and in Greek. The collection ends with an exhortation to the Holy War; it belongs to the last period of the pontificate: Italy, so we read, has been delivered from war and pestilence; even the Gothic King, who was ravaging South Germany and already threatened Italy, has fallen in battle; the Emperor Ferdinand triumphs; may the Lord God now bring the Kings together for a Holy War, in order to break the power of the heretics and the Turks.[2]

Taking them all in all, it cannot be denied that the Latin poems of the Barberini Pope are distinguished not only for their carefully chiselled classical form, but also for their wealth of lofty thoughts and warm feeling, though they suffer greatly from the exuberance of a period which is also characterized by the lavish overloading of the paintings and sculptures of Baroque art.[3] This is even more true of the Pope's Italian poems. They exhibit still more plainly the defects of the period, especially that of excessive ornamentation,[4] though they, too, rise above the majority of the productions of the time. The Italian poems also appeared in Paris

[1] See Vol. XXVIII., p. 53.

[2] Fac, precor, o Deus, ut coeant in foedera reges,
  Fidentesque tua nos tuearis ope;
Haeresis infestas frangat tua dextera vires,
  Dissipet et Turcas Odrysiasque rates.
Tu, Deus omnipotens, iusti sis sanguinis ultor,
  Perde truces hostes, qui fera bella volunt.

This concluding poem is missing in the edition of 1631.

[3] Reumont, III., 2, 615, 702; Ambros, IV., 126, 129; Posse, *Deckenfresko*, 106. How much Urban VIII. polished his poems appears from the pieces collected in **Barb.* 2027 of which, however, only the first is in his own hand, the rest being copies with corrections in the Pope's hand. Vatican Library.

[4] Tiraboschi, VIII., 19; Renazzi, III., 108; Travaglini, *loc. cit.*, 70. *Cf.* also the article, *L'opera poetica di Urbano VIII.*

in 1642 in an *édition de luxe.* The latter collection begins with two sonnets against those who devote their art to the glorification of earthly love. In contrast with these Urban VIII. chooses only spiritual and religious themes. He combats the vices of pride, avarice, lust, anger, gluttony, and sloth, and praises the virtues, especially the queen of them all, charity.[1]

A few sonnets are addressed to the Pope's relatives; to his brother Carlo he expounds the vanity and peril of earthly pleasures; Cardinal Antonio is reminded that virtue is only obtained as the reward of toil; to his nephew Taddeo he depicts the dangers of human life and to a Capuchin novice he points out the duties of his state. A particularly beautiful sonnet is devoted to the death of the Pope's mother whilst another is dedicated to his friend Giovan Battista Strozzi.

Deep religious feeling characterizes the sonnets on the sufferings of Christ, His birth, His goodness, the unspeakable bliss of heaven and the power of grace. In touching accents he implores the Saviour's forgiveness of his sins. The peril of a soul which fails to rise above the things of earth he

in the *Rassegna Settimanale*, 1879, February 16, p. 131 *seq.* CHLEDOWSKI (II., 105 *seq.*), on the other hand ranks the Latin poems higher than the Italian ones. Contemporaries were of a different opinion; see I. NICII ERYTHRAEI, *Pinacotheca*, I., 153.

[1] Sonnet 19, *Lodi della carità* runs as follows:—

Non luce si tra le minute stelle
In bel seren con l'argentato corno
La luna, e 'l sol quando è più chiaro il giorno,
Come alma carità fra le sorelle.
Sembran l'altre virtù saggie donzelle
In atti humili, e con sembiante adorno,
Che stanno a lei, quasi reina, intorno
Ad ogni cenno ubbidienti ancelle.
È viva fiamma, che dal cuor mortale
I più bassi pensier disperge, e madre
D'affetti accesi da pietoso zelo.
All'opre sue non può farsi altra eguale:
Mostrollo all'hor, che fè dal sen del Padre
Scender Dio in terra e l'huom salir'al cielo.

compares to the condition of a caged bird. He emphatically rejects the vain ambition of acquiring fame by means of the poetic craft. Fame is described as a sound that comes and goes; not an array of fine words but good works open the gates of heaven.[1] The ruins of ancient Rome also remind Urban of the transitoriness of all things earthly. As he contemplates, from his beloved Castel Gandolfo, the wonderful panorama of lake and sea, his soul rises to the vision of heavenly beauty.[2] Among the sonnets in honour of Saints, the first rank is justly assigned to those in praise of the Princes of the Apostles, SS. Peter and Paul. Others treat of the stigmata of the

[1] Che fai, Maffeo, che pensi ? a che con arte
Emula all'età prisca si ti cale
Formar' inni canori ? a che ti vale
Vegliar la notte, per vergar le carte ?
La fama è suon ch'in un viene e si parte,
È di fugace rio qual bolla frale
Da permesso l'honor finto immortale,
E invano altrui quel che non ha comparte.
E pur ami l'inganno e 'l dolce errore :
Eternar credi le cose passate
Con cetra armoniosa, e fugir morte ?
Folle speranza ti lusinga il core :
Non alla pompa di parole ornate,
Al ben'oprar del ciel s'apron le porte.

[2] Quì dove il lago Alban le limpide onde
In vago giro accoglie e 'l mar Tirreno
Lo sguardo alletta col ceruleo seno,
Il sol per l'aria i raggi d'or diffonde.
S'ammantan gli arbosci di verde fronde,
Di fiori il prato e 'l ciel di bel sereno,
Dolce mormora l'aura, a cui non meno
In dolci note il rusignuol risponde.
Chi non rinvigorisce, e al cor non sente
Gioia stillar ? O s'erga pronta e ascenda
Per questi gradi al gran Fattor la mente.
Deh squarci homai del van desio la benda
Drizzando al vero ben le voglie intente,
E nel ben ch'è lassù d'amor s'accenda.

Poverello of Assisi and St. Charles Borromeo. The seventy sonnets are followed by two hymns in honour of the Mother of God, of David, the royal psalmist, and by an ode to Countess Matilda. This splendid luminary of the female sex, we read, who loved virtue rather than silk and purple, was the shield of the Roman Church; the praise of her liberality resounds in the Vatican to her everlasting glory.

The extent to which poetry played a vital rôle in the existence of a Pontiff engaged in the most important business of Church and State, appears from the circumstance that in the midst of all the cares of government he never neglected that gracious comforter. At all times he managed to devote an hour to it.[1] In a report of August 23rd, 1634, Fulvio Testi, the envoy of the Duke of Modena, draws a vivid picture of the Pope-poet. Business over, so we read, the Pope rose, and whilst walking up and down the room, he asked the envoy, who was also a poet, how things stood with the muse. When Testi excused his neglect of poetry on the ground of his manifold occupations, Urban remarked: "We too are busy with affairs, but for all that we compose a poem from time to time, by way of relaxation. You shall hear one of our latest Latin poems." The Pope then fetched a sheet of paper from his adjoining bedroom and read to Testi an ode written in the manner of Horace. Testi could afford to be all the more lavish of praise as he was convinced that, as far as Latin poetry was concerned, few if any equalled the Pope. Subsequently Urban VIII. showed him another most beautiful ode, and finally his latest Italian poems.[2] On occasion the shrewd envoy sought to take advantage of the Pope's interest in poetry during the transaction of business.[3]

The numerous editions of his poems, which the Court

[1] An *Avviso of October 26, 1624, reports: S. Stà. invitata dalla solitudine della Villa ha composto a Mondragone alcuni epigrammi in lode delle delitie del Tusculano. *Urb.* 1094, Vatican Library.

[2] See *Opere scelte del conte Fulvio Testi*, II., Modena, 1817, 59.

[3] G. DE CASTRO, *F. Testi e le corti italiane*, Milano, 1875, 88 *seq.*

poets exalted as "a golden book",[1] gratified Urban VIII. exceedingly. When thanking the Jesuits Wangnereck and Laurence Forner, who brought out an edition of his Latin poems in 1640, at Dillingen, the Pope dwelt on the fact that he had always blamed those who considered religious subjects unsuitable to poetry, and who misused this noble art for impure imaginations; accordingly he had sought to make use of it in order to promote religious and moral ideals.[2] Urban wrote in the same strain to Cardinal Richelieu to whom Cardinal Barberini had sent a copy of the Pope's poems. He was not concerned with the acquisition of fame, we read, what he wanted was to foster piety in the hearts of his readers, whilst a few things had also been inserted with a view to

[1] L. Guidiccioni, *Delibatio mellis Barberinae*, Romae, 1639, 31.

[2] "*Eorum opinionem plurimum semper improbavimus, qui censent res sacras minus idoneum esse carminis argumentum nec parum doluimus, poesim praestantissimam artem impuris blandimentis ac dedecorum maculis foedari." Hence, "ex iis quae ad curarum levamentum quandoque exaravimus, dignosceretur, christianam religionem amplissimum patefacere campum ad scribendum poetis, illosque posse mortalium ingenia ad rectam humanae vitae institutionem, ad morum innocentiam, ad veram gloriam cum voluptate excitare" (*Epist.*, XVII.–XVIII, no. 402, Papal Secret Archives). Urban VIII. restates the same idea in a *Brief of the year 1640, addressed to H. Wangereck and Jos. Ilsungh, Diling. acad. moderatoribus: "Cum autem in ejusmodi lucubrationibus illud in primis propositum habuerimus, ostendere, veram poesis gloriam non voluptatum illecebris et perniciosis inanium rerum blandimentis, sed pietatis aliarumque virtutum celebratione magno plurimorum bono quaerendam esse, voti plane compotes efficiemur, si legentium animi, quemadmodum significastis, Musarum castimonia et innocenti carmine invitati a venenato abstinuerint eorum poematum pabulo, quae nil aliud prae se ferunt quam vanitates et insanias falsas" (*Epist.*, XIX.–XXI, no. 405, *ibid.*). *Cf.* also the Brief to Peter Joh. Justinianus, dated January 12, 1635, in which the Pope thanks him for a poem dedicated to him (*ibid.*, XII., 208); printed in *Lettere mem. dell'abbate Michele Giustiniani, Roma*, 1675, 163 *seq.*

exhorting the advisers of the Catholic Princes to bring about peace.[1]

Numerous translations were made of Urban VIII.'s poems. Federigo Morelli translated the ode to St. Louis into Greek.[2] Leone Allacci translated into the same idiom the sonnet addressed to Urban's nephew Carlo.[3] Giovan Francesco Ferranti published an Italian translation of the Pope's Latin poems [4] and Pierre de Reviglias a French one.[5] Some of the poems were translated into Spanish,[6] others into Dutch.[7] Commentaries were provided by a number of writers,[8] among

[1] See ***Epist.*, XIII.–XIV., Papal Secret Archives.

[2] *Ode in s. Ludovicum Francorum regem a Federico Morello Graece reddita*; copy in Barberini Library.

[3] L. ALLATII, *Apes Urbanae*, 15 *seq.*

[4] *Poesie latine tradotte in verso sciolto da Giov. Franc. Ferranti*, Roma, 1642; MS. in *Barb.* 3820, 3850. *Barb.* 1890 contains: * "Urbani VIII. hymni in S. Martinam italicis numeris expressi a Io. Ant. Brolato," with a letter of the author to Urban VIII., dated Vicenza, January 1, 1638, Vatican Library.

[5] *Cf.* the *letters of J. Pierre de Reviglias in *Barb.* 6521, *ibid.*

[6] By Gabriel del Corral; see L. ALLATII, Apes Urb., 114; *cf. Barb.* 1864, *ibid.*

[7] *Cf.* ROOSES, *Rubens*, Stuttgart, 1890, 552. The Pope presented his poems to the great Dutch scholar Erycius Puteanus; see ALLARD, G. Vossius en Erycius Puteanus, Roermond, 1892, 13.

[8] *Poemata Urbani VIII. cum explicatione Henrici Dormalii*, Romae, 1643; **Carmina quaedam Urbani VIII. commentario illustrata a Julio Caesare Capacio, Barb.* 2165, Vatican Library; **Poesie del cav. Maffei Barberini, hoggi N.S.P. Urbano VIII. Compositioni di Tommaso Leva* (with dedication of 1639) *Barb.* 3653, *ibid.*; *Commento et allegoria di Scip. Francucci Aretino sopra le poesie dell'ill. card. Barberini, hoggi Urbano VIII.* Original MS. 1905 in the catalogue of the Roman antiquary Luzzietti. The majority of the commentaries are from the pen of Magno Perneo of Anagni; *Barb.* 3259, 3293. *Explanation of the poem *De Poenitentia*; 3262 and 3297. **Tractatus in Paraphrasim Magnificat ad Urbanum VIII.*; 3264, 3296, 3298, 3299. **Explicatio* of the reformed Breviary hymns; 3295. **Explicatio odarum Urbani VIII.* A **Discorso sulle poesie di Urbano VIII.*, the original presentation copy of which is in *Barb.* 3836, Vatican Library, appeared anonymously.

them the unfortunate poet-philosopher Tommaso Campanella, who owed to Urban VIII. his liberation from the dungeons of the Inquisition [1] as well as financial assistance.[2] John Jerome Kapsperger set the Pope's poetical productions to

[1] See above, ch. I., p. 40.

[2] *Cf.* AMABILE, *Campanella*, I., 314 *seq.*, 321 *seq.*, 336 *seq.* Campanella obtained from Urban VIII. a monthly allowance of 15 scudi and when, towards the end of 1634, he escaped with the Pope's aid from the snares laid for him by the Spaniards, first to Aix and then to Paris, he continued to receive papal support. As for Campanella's *Parole universali del governo ecclesiastico per fare una grege et un pastore* which Ranke made use of (III., 113*), in Inf. polit. of the State Library, Berlin, the date of which he was unable to fix, according to Amabile (II., 370), they were composed as early as March, 1605, but were recast during the reign of Urban VIII. Ranke attaches too much weight to the sentiment there expressed by the greatest Utopian of his time, as B. Croce (*Arch. stor. Napol.*, XX., 4, 1895) calls Campanella, namely that the Pope was supreme in secular matters. In his very full index Ranke omits the following important passage concerning the Pope's universal monarchy : " Si deve forzare il Papa di arrivare a questo per il ben commune degli animi e di corpi di tutti i principati fatti tributarii alla Chiesa facendone un solo." Campanella's inconsistent character is plainly revealed by his relations with Ferdinand II. He made repeated appeals to the latter for assistance, protesting his devotion to the House of Habsburg. But when the poet-philosopher escaped to France, he put himself at the disposal of French diplomacy and inveighed against the Habsburgs as fosterers of heresy ! *Cf.* KVAČALA, *Th. Campanella und Ferdinand II., in Sitzungsber. der Wiener Akad., Philos. hist. Kl. Bd.*, 159, Vienna, 1908. L. BLANCHET (*Campanella*, Paris, 1920) compares (p. 104) the philosopher's attitude as regards religion to that of A. Loisy, whilst G. Gabrieli, in his critique of Vincenzo Spampanato's new edition of the letters of Campanella, defends his " ortodossia dottrinaria " during his last stay in Rome (1627–1634), basing himself especially on the poet-philosopher's friendly relations with Calasanzio and the Scolopi. Campanella's correspondence with Calasanzio is in the Archives of S. Pantaleo, Rome. *Cf.* GIOVANOZZI, *Scolopi Galileiani, pubblicaz. del Gabrieli Osserv. Ximeniano, Firenze*, 1907 ; *Corriere d'Italia* of July 9, 1927.

music [1]; his dedication to Urban VIII. is a classical model of flattery, an art much in vogue with the men of letters of that period. In view of the fact that since Pius II. no Pope had appeared in the capacity of a poet, the numberless poets of the period were enormously excited when Urban VIII. ascended the papal throne. Caspar Scioppius drew up a long list of scholars then living in Italy who, in his opinion, deserved the Pope's patronage [2] and Andrea Vitorelli added more names to the catalogue.[3]

Urban VIII.'s election was sung by Francesco Bracciolini, Lelio Guidiccioni,[4] the Jesuit Stephanus Bubalus de Cancellariis [5] and by Magno Perneo [6]; the latter also sang the coronation.[7] The Pope's *Possesso* was treated by Alexander Rainaldus,[8] the opening of the Holy Door by the Pole John Bronissuchus,[9] the nomination of Cardinals of the year

[1] *Poemata et carmina composita a Maffeo Barberini olim S.R.E. Card., nunc autem Urbano octavo P.O.M., musicis modis aptata a Jo. Hieronymo Kapsperger, Romae,* 1624 (in-fol., 56 pages). *Cf.* AMBROS, IV., 126 *seq.*, who is only acquainted with the copy in the collection of music at the Chiesa Nuova; a second copy is in the Bibl. Vittorio Emmanuele, Rome (32, 10, H. 25). For Kapsperger who, in 1631, also published an *in folio* vol. *Missarum Urbanarum,* lib. I., *cf.* besides AMBROS, IV., 125 *seq.*, 309; also L. ALLATII, *Apes Urbanae,* 159 *seq.*

[2] **Viri docti in Italia, quos Caspar Scioppius novit quique ab Urbano VIII. S.P. ac litterarum patrono ornentur ex animi sententia dignos censet, Barb.* 2645, p. 85 *seq.*, Vatican Library.

[3] *Ibid.*, p. 89 *seq.*

[4] L. GUIDICCIONI, *De Urbano VIII. ad summum pontificatum evecto elegia, Romae,* 1624.

[5] L. ALLATII, *Apes Urb.*, 236.

[6] MAGNUS PERNEUS, **Canticum super electione Urbani VIII., Barb.* 3261, 3291, 3294, Vatican Library.

[7] MAGNUS PERNEUS, **Canticum super coronatione Urbani VIII., Barb.* 3292, *ibid.*, 3652, an anonymous **Canzone* on the coronation.

[8] *Cf.* L. ALLATII, *Apes Urb.*, 22.

[9] JOH. BRONISSUCHUS POLONUS, **In aperitionem portae sanctae et novi anni* 1625 *inchoationem ad S.D.N. Urbanum VIII. P.M., Barb.* 1704, Vatican Library.

1626 by Flaminio Figliucci,[1] the work for peace by Francesco Balducci,[2] the finding of the relics of St. Martina by Andrea Baiano,[3] the ciborium under the dome of St. Peter's [4] by the Burgundian Vernerey [5]; to the latter work of art Lelio Guidiccioni also devoted two poetical encomiums.[6] Nicoletti, Urban VIII.'s biographer, mentions a number of scholars and men of letters with whom the Pope was on familiar terms and whom he was wont to gather round his person in the garden of the Belvedere, at the Vatican, or at the Villa Borghese. He also frequently invited them when he withdrew to his beloved Castel Gandolfo for his annual vacation in the Alban Hills.[7]

[1] Romae, 1626; *cf.* L. ALLATII, *Apes Urb.*, 98.

[2] *La Pace Urbana. Canzone, Napoli* 1632. *Cf. Rime di Fr. Balducci alla S. di Urbano VIII., Barb.* 3860, Vatican Library.

[3] *Andr. Barianus ad Urbanum VIII.* **De inventione S. Martinae virg. et mart. carmen, Barb.* 1964, p. 30; *cf.* 1797, p. 2, *ibid.*

[4] See below, p. 462.

[5] *Urbano VIII. P. O. M. erectis aeneis in Vaticana basilica quatuor columnis non plus ultra,* IOANNES GUILLELMUS VERNEREY BURGUNDUS, *sacrum dicat elogium,* Romae, 1629. There we read:

> " Quid mihi munificos iuvat obiectare Leones ?
> Quidve Pios studio sacrorum Culmen adeptos ?
> Quid mihi Clementes et mansuetudinis arctae
> Subiicere archetypum, pietatis amabilis arcem ?
> Maiora Urbanus spectacula pandit : in uno
> Christoicolae maiora vident et vertice prono
> Orbis adoratis figit merita oscula plantis."

[6] *Ara maxima Vaticana ab Urbano VIII. exstructa,* in Guidiccioni's collected poems, *Romae,* 1633(copy in Ottob. 2420, p. 383), and *De ornato Apostolorum sepulchro,* in his *Delibatio mellis Barberinae, Romae,* 1639, 41. In the collection of poems of 1633 there are some on the Navicella and one addressed to Bernini on his marble busts of Urban VIII.

[7] *Nicoletti, LII., 6, Vatican Library. Besides well-known literary men, such as Chiabrera, Ciampoli, Ant. Querenghi (*cf.* L. ALLATII, *Apes Urb.*, 49). Nicoletti also mentions G. B. Rinuccini (*cf.* on him MORONI, XXIV., 37, XXXIII., 72), Angelo Grillo (see *ibid.*, X., 151), Vincenzo Gramigna, Fabrizio Verospi and the historian Paolo Emilio Santori (*cf.* TIRABOSCHI, VIII., 91).

One of the Pope's intimates was Francesco Bracciolini[1] who had previously been in his service and had accompanied him in his French nunciature, after which he, however, returned to his native place, Pistoia. In 1618 Bracciolini published an heroi-comic poem entitled *Lo Scherno degli Dei*.[2] Remarkable for the finish of its form, the poem pours ridicule on the mythology of the ancients, more particularly on Venus and Cupid. This was wholly in keeping with the ideas of Barberini. So was Bracciolini's castigation of those poets who chose mythological subjects for their own sake, thus misleading the simple-minded who could not grasp the real meaning of such compositions. After the elevation of his one-time patron to the papacy, Bracciolini hastened to Rome where, later on, he was charged to provide poetic themes for the pictorial decoration of the ceiling of the great hall in the Barberini palace.[3] Urban's election was celebrated by him in a special epic poem. The inspiration and composition of this piece are closely akin to the scheme of the ceiling decorations; in both, divine Providence occupies the central plan. Bracciolini had at first intended to entitle his poem *La Divina Provvidenza*, in accordance with the *leitmotiv* of the epic in which, he boasts, he had kept well away from the beaten track of the poetic art. His "unexampled novelty" lay in the fact that, unlike Virgil, Ariosto or Tasso, he did not sing an historical or imaginary hero, but setting aside all that captivates the average reader, and like another Daedalus, soaring to unwonted heights, he introduced directly as actors the virtues and vices which,

[1] *Cf.* MAZZUCHELLI, II., 2, 1958 *seq.*; RENAZZI, III., 113 *seq.*; BELLONI, *Gli epigoni della Gerusalemme Lib., Padova*, 1893: BARDI, *Vite e opere di Fr. Bracciolini, Firenze*, 1892. A marble bust by Algardi perpetuates the features of Bracciolini; *letters from him to Maffeo Barberini, the first from Milan, October 12, 1592, the last, March 16, 1630, as well as some *poems, in *Barb.* 6459, Vatican Library.

[2] MORSOLIN, *Storia lett. d'Italia. Il Seicento, Milano*, 1880, 33 *seq.* BELLONI, *Seicento*, 175 *seq.*; BAUMGARTNER, VI., 456 *seq.*

[3] See below, p. 500.

as mere abstract concepts, had until then spoken only indirectly in the poetic action; this he had done in order to spur the reader more forcibly either to imitation or avoidance. In order to enhance the vividness of the allegorical action, which is described with great mastery of language, he wove into it the most varied episodes of ancient and biblical history which deal with the opposition between virtue and vice.[1] This was done with so much detail that the modern reader finds it irksome to work his way through an epic of nearly 500 printed pages. It is divided into twenty-three cantos, and only in the fifteenth does Bracciolini come to the biography of the "Great Maffeo" whose life and activity he depicts poetically, concluding with the elevation of his hero to the papacy, a consummation brought about by Providence. In the edition of 1628, each canto is preceded by a summary of the contents drawn up by Bracciolini himself.[2] It seems strange that an epic wholly devoted to the praise of a Pope who only cared for religious poetry should be full of mythological allusions. Even the author of a poem burlesquing the old gods could not resist the infinite wealth of imagery of the ancient fables, but he introduces them only as allegories, to illustrate his fundamental thought, and welds them together with religious allegories, as if they were of equal value.[3] Urban VIII. rewarded the epic by granting to Bracciolini the right to charge his arms with the Barberini bees. The poet, who from that time styled himself Bracciolini dell'Api, occupied in Rome the honourable post of secretary to Urban's brother Antonio. As early as 1625 the Pope had created him a Roman citizen.

[1] These particulars from POSSE's *Deckenmalerei*, 109 *seq.*, reproduce exactly what is said in the preface and the appendix by Giulio Rospigliosi (the subsequent Clement IX.) which were added to Bracciolini's new edition of *L'elettione di Urbano Papa VIII.* (Roma, 1628).

[2] *L'elettione di Urbano Papa VIII. di Francesco Bracciolini dell'Api all' ill. et rev. S. il S. Card. Barberini con gli argomenti a ciascuno canto di Giuliano Bracciolini dell'Api*, Roma, 1628.

[3] Opinion of POSSE (*Deckenmalerei*, 107 *seq.*).

Another intimate of Urban VIII.'s was the famous Gabriele Chiabrera, surnamed the Pindar of Italy. Like Bracciolini he was a forceful character and a genuine and extraordinarily productive poet, whom all the Italian Princes held in the highest esteem. The Pope, whilst still a Cardinal, had dedicated an ode to him in which he exalted the prerogative of poetry which enables it to confer immortality on virtue,[1] and he had scarcely been raised to the Apostolic See when he honoured the poet with a special Brief dated November 29th, 1623. In this document, drawn up by Ciampoli, Urban VIII. singles out as Chiabrera's peculiar merit the fact that he had raised lyric poetry from the baseness of unworthy sensuousness to the heights of natural and Christian idealism and had shown to the world that poetic genius was able to fulfil itself without becoming the slave of folly and unclean vices.[2] Urban VIII. was anxious to summon Chiabrera to Rome, but the poet, who dedicated several splendid *canzoni* to his patron on Peter's chair,[3] refused to leave Savona, his native city, whose glory he was. The Pope honoured Chiabrera by himself composing his epitaph.[4]

The lofty purpose which Urban VIII. had before his eyes in furthering poetry, viz. to lead the poetic art into worthier paths, which had also been the aim of Chiabrera, was likewise the guiding principle of the Florentine Giovanni Ciampoli who had early come in contact with Maffeo Barberini.[5] Ciampoli, who in the words of Bentivoglio,[6] had imbibed

[1] *Poemata*, ed. 1631, p. 257.

[2] Baumgartner, VI., 467 *seq.*, who prints the Brief. *Cf.* also the Brief of November 23, 1634, in *Lett. mem. dell'abbate M. Giustiniani* (1675), 251 *seq.*

[3] An unpublished poem, probably of the year 1629, was published by Redi from a MS. in the Barberini Library: Chiabrera, *Canzone in lode di Urbano VIII.*, Roma, 1828.

[4] Tiraboschi, VIII., 283; Baumgartner, VI., 464 *seq.*

[5] *Cf.* Favaro in *Atti d. Istit. Veneto*, 62 (1902/1903), 8 series, V 2, 103 *seq.* *Cf.* also the bibliography in Gabrieli, *Carteggio*, 192. A portrait of Ciampoli is in *La Canonizzazione di S. Ignazi, Roma*, 1923, 59.

[6] *Memorie*, 114.

poetry with his mother's milk, banished from his poems, as his friend Pallavicini remarked, everything unseemly and sought to keep his lyre, even more than Orpheus', attuned to heavenly themes. Though Ciampoli did not wholly succeed in extricating himself from the traditional mythological stock-in-trade, his *poetica sacra* went counter to the old classical form in theory and to its unlimited encroachments in practice.[1] Urban VIII. named him Secretary of Briefs in 1623 and thus a brilliant career seemed to open before him, as previously before Silvio Antoniano. However, his character, no less than his style differed completely from that of his great predecessor; his Briefs were poetry rather than prose.[2] Ciampoli advanced in the Pope's favour especially because as a poet also he was a convinced Christian. He nevertheless wrote verses on the coronation of Urban VIII., the struggle in the Valtellina, the Pope's action for peace, the fall of La Rochelle, the wedding of Taddeo Barberini. One of his poems describes the gathering of the grapes at Castel Gandolfo.[3]

Ciampoli's relations with the Pope were at first so intimate that the nephews grew jealous,[4] hence great was the astonishment of the Court when, in the autumn of 1632, Ciampoli fell into utter disgrace. The reason of his fall has been looked for in his dealings with Galileo. Others thought that a contributory cause was the haughty, arrogant manner with which the chief representative of the bombastic, overloaded style passed judgment on honoured poets such a Virgil and Horace. The real cause of his fall, however, was the fact that Ciampoli, disappointed at being passed over at various nominations of Cardinals, entered into relations with the party of Cardinal Borgia which stood in acute opposition to the Pope. This led to various incidents in the spring of 1632, with the result that in September Ciampoli was relieved of his office of Secretary.[5]

[1] Baumgartner, VI., 466.

[2] Bentivoglio, 117 *seq.*

[3] C. Pulcini, *Msgr. G. Ciampoli*, in *Riv. Abruzzese*, XXXIII., Teramo, 1918, 170 *seq.*, 256 *seq.*, 393 *seq.*

[4] Favaro, *loc. cit.*, 111.

[5] *Ibid.*, 118 *seq.*, 120 *seq.*, 123 *seq.*, 125 *seq.*

Urban VIII. nevertheless softened the blow by bestowing on him the office of President of Montalti.[1]

The ideals of the high-minded Pope were realized in splendid fashion by two poets of the Jesuit Order, the Pole Casimir Sarbiewski, and the Alsatian, Jacob Balde. The two men—the greatest Latin poets of the period—had familiarized themselves with the ancient Roman literature to such a degree, " that Latin, with its rich treasure of metrical forms, had become for them a living language, a handy instrument with which to give expression to the most delicate emotional nuances ". They display such depth of religious feeling, so wide an outlook on history and human life, that their odes have not lost their usefulness to this day.[2]

Balde, the singer of the Catholic League,[3] paid tribute to Urban VIII. in more than one poem whilst Sarbiewski came into personal contact with him.[4] He came to Rome in 1622 and in 1625 he extolled the new Head of the Church in a long panegyric entitled: " The Golden Age."[5] A collection of similar poems in honour of Cardinal Francesco Barberini was

[1] PALLAVICINI, *Alessandro VII.*, I., 74.

[2] Opinion of BAUMGARTNER (VI., 467). BRÜCKNER, in his history of Polish literature (Leipzig, 1905), styles Sarbiewski Poland's greatest Latin poet (p. 176).

[3] WESTERMAYER, *J. Balde*, Munich, 1868.

[4] For Sarbiewski, besides the older works by LANGBEIN (Dresden, 1753), RATHSMANN (Breslau, 1800), KOLANOWSKI (Berolini, 1842), WEICHSELMANN (Laibach, 1864), DIEL in *Stimmen aus Maria-Laach*, IV., 159 *seq.*, 343 *seq.*; V., 61 *seq.*, 365 *seq.*; KULCZYNSKI (Krakow, 1875); KRYSTYNIAKI, *Fasti Sarbevienani* (Chronology of his poetic activity), Lemberg, 1886; WINDAKIEWICZ in *Rozprawy Akademii Umiejetnosci, wydzial filogiczny*, XV., Cracow, 1891; VON RÓZYCKI in the periodical *Der Aar*, III., 2, Regensburg, 1913, 225 *seq.*, 338 *seq.*; F. M. MÜLLER, *De M. C. Sarbievio Polono e Soc. Iesu Horatii imitatore*, *Monachii*, 1917.

[5] *Aureum saeculum Urbano P. O. M. Orbi invectum a° 1625*, *Barb*, 2105, Vatican Library. *Cf. Rozprawy*, XV., 213, of Cracow.

published under the title: "The Gate of Honour."[1] Urban was not slow in recognizing Sarbiewski's merit and made use of him in the alteration of the Breviary hymns.[2] Several odes of the Polish poet testify to the intimacy of his relations with the Pope. If these effusions and his panegyrics are not free from dithyrambic exaggerations, they nevertheless bear witness to the gratitude and admiration which Sarbiewski felt towards his noble patron. In one of his odes he hails the Pope as a kindred-spirit poet who on the triumphal chariot of fame ascends with him towards heaven; the cloud-enfolded earth with its towns, seas, rivers, is left far beneath them; the tops of the highest mountains bow their heads to do them homage; everything proclaims Urban's fame; they rule alone in the vast heights of heaven.[3] Sarbiewski's admiration for his patron appears even more strongly in a panegyric of the latter's *Carmina*, which he compares to the murmur of a rivulet and the roar of a foaming torrent. Urban VIII. must have been particularly gratified by Sarbiewski's "Turkish Odes" in which he summons the Christian Princes of Europe to recover their mastery over the Orient.[4]

When Sarbiewski left Rome, Urban VIII. honoured him with the gift of a gold medal, whilst on his part the poet, in an enthusiastic ode, expressed his gratitude for all he owed to Rome, "the mother of the fine arts." He further extols Rome as a city over which spreads an eternally serene sky; where a beneficent genius empties a cornucopia of splendid gifts; where the Muses are enthroned and the world's choicest men pour out the treasures of their minds.[5]

[1] *Porticus honoris per quam Franc. card. Barberinus ad delubrum honoris poetico opere in Romano Soc. Iesu collegio extructum ingressus est, Barb.* 1941, *loc. cit. Cf. Rozprawy* of Cracow, XV., 216.

[2] See ch. I., p. 16.

[3] See v. ROZYCKI, *loc. cit.*, 227; *cf.* MÜLLER, *loc. cit.*, 68.

[4] v. ROZYCKI, *loc. cit.*, 227; MÜLLER, *loc. cit.*, 72.

[5] "In Rome," so writes VON ANTONIEWICZ in the *Zeitschr. für vergleich. Literaturgesch. und Renaissance Literatur*, new series, II., Berlin, 1889, "Sarbiewski composed his purest, choicest and

Two poets, who were also distinguished for their learning, Antonio Quarenghi of Padua (died 1633) and Giambattista Doni of Florence, were named secretaries of the College of Cardinals by Urban VIII.[1] Another scholar whom Bellarmine used to style the Pico della Mirandola of his time, the Roman Virginio Cesarini, whose Italian and Latin poems were famed for their elegance, was appointed *Maestro di Camera* by Urban VIII.[2] and on the celebrated traveller and Orientalist Pietro della Valle, the Pope bestowed the dignity of a Papal Chamberlain.[3] Agostino Oreggi, equally distinguished for his virtues and learning and who had acted as Maffeo Barberini's theologian, was further employed in this capacity in the Congregations of the Index and Rites. At a later date he became papal almoner, Canon of St. Peter's and finally Cardinal in 1633. Oreggi's theological works were first published in 1637 ; a second edition appeared in 1642.[4]

The number of poems dedicated to Urban VIII. is extraordinarily great ; their worth varies very much and we have no cause to regret that many of them were never printed.[5] In these poems the Barberini crest—bees—are a favourite motif. They are exploited to satiety as symbols of poetic gifts, for the glorification of the Pope, himself *Apis Attica*. The thing began with Francesco Bracciolini's poem on Urban VIII.'s election, in which bees appear as vignettes at the end of each

serenest melodies and all the four subsequent editions of his Latin poems published during the poet's life-time, that of Vilna in 1628 and the three of Antwerp in 1630, 1632 and 1634 (the last two by B. Mont, the first with a frontispiece designed by Rubens) are in large part the splendid fruits of his stay in Rome."

[1] Renazzi, II., 117 *seq*. On Doni's *Lyra Barberini*, *cf*. Ambros, IV., 167.

[2] For Cesarini (died 1624), a special friend of Ciampoli, *cf*. the Monographs by Favorito (*Romae*, 1672) and N. Ratti (1735) as well as Gabrieli, *Carteggio*, 191.

[3] *Cf*. Ciampi, *Pietro della Valle*, Roma, 1880 ; Gabrieli, 205.

[4] Ciaconius, IV., 593 *seq*. ; Cardella, VI., 314.

[5] *Cf*. Appendix 23.

canto. Many other writers produced similar works.[1] Bees also play a great rôle in the learned literature of the period, as appears from the works of Federigo Cesi [2] and Leone Allacci.[3] It is worth mentioning that even Princes, as for instance Odoardo Farnese, sought to win the Pope's favour by writing odes in his honour.[4] We can best get an idea of the output of poetry at that period from the fact that on the occasion of the wedding of Taddeo Barberini to Anna Colonna, over a score of such congratulations were published. Among the authors appear the names of Lorenzo Azzolini,[5] the Dutchman Lukas Holste [6] and Sforza Pallavicini.[7] The last named, who became subsequently famous as the historian of the Council of Trent, was sprung from the Parma branch of the ancient noble family of the Pallavicini. He dedicated to Urban VIII. his extensive collection of religious poems [8] and other

[1] *Cf.* the **Apiarium* of Christophorus Maria Monaldus in *Barb.* 2123, Vatican Library, and BERNARDUS TURAMINUS, *Barbara sacra alle Api Barberine,* Viterbo, 1632. To this category also belong: IGNAZIO BRACCI, *Occulta corrispondenza tra l'arme, e il cognome de'Barberini con l'aggionta di cinquanta epigrammi,* Roma, 1623 (and 1633); LELIO GUIDICCIONI, *Delibatio mellis Barberinae,* Romae, 1639; CHRIST. CRIARDA, *Apis religiosa,* Mediol., 1625, and the scarce poem by JOH. CHRYSAPHULLUS: *Urbanosiridos libri duodeviginti,* Neapoli, 1632.

[2] F. CAESIUS, *Apiarium,* Romae, 1625; *cf.* MORONI, XC., 437 *seq.*

[3] *Apes Urbane,* Romae, 1633.

[4] See the Brief to O. Farnese of September 14, 1624, above, p. 382, note 3.

[5] Urban VIII. raised L. Azzolini to the episcopate; see MORUS, Bibl. *Picena,* I., Osimo, 1790, 279 *seq.*

[6] ORBAAN, *Bescheiden,* I., 301.

[7] *Cf.* ALLATII, *Apes Urbanae,* 63, 64, 84, 99, 106, 111, 116, 127, 132, 133, 144, 149, 157, 159, 161, 174, 182, 185, 203 *seq.*, 223, 234, 237.

[8] The original dedication copy of Pallavicini's *Fasti sacri* is in *Barb.* 4916, Vatican Library; time of composition 1630; see the letter in J. MACCHIA, *Relaz. fra Sf. Pallavicini con Fabio Chigi, Torino,* 1907, 15.

works,[1] among them nine books *De universa theologia*,[2] but he fell into disgrace because of his friendship with Ciampoli. In 1632 he became Governor of Orvieto and in 1637 entered the Society of Jesus. On the completion of his novitiate, in 1639, he taught philosophy at the Roman College ; four years later he succeeded Juan de Lugo as professor of theology on the latter's elevation to the cardinalate.[3] Lugo had dedicated to Urban VIII. the first part of his excellent work : *De Justitia et Jure*,[4] in which he reveals his accurate knowledge of Roman and Canon Law. The Pope, who had not yet made the acquaintance of the scholar, was astonished at their first meeting, by his learning and mental acumen and thereafter frequently consulted him. The humble son of St. Ignatius had to be formally compelled by the Pope to accept the purple.

Among the many learned works dedicated to Urban VIII. a distinguished place is held by the third volume of the classic work of the Jesuit Francis Suarez on the virtue of religion [5] and by the excellent work of the famous liturgist Bartolomeo Gavanti : *Thesaurus Sacrorum Rituum*, a manual which enjoyed the widest diffusion. It describes the Church's sacred ceremonies of Mass and Office, explains their origin and meaning and the manner of carrying out the sacred functions.[6] Besides Gavanti many other scholars were called upon to co-operate in Urban's reform of the Breviary.[7]

The following scholars also presented their works to Urban

[1] **Poesie volgari in lode di Urbano VIII.* in *Cod.* X., IV., 35, p. 267 *seq.* of the *Bibl. Casanat.*, Rome : *ibid.*, p. 271 *seq.* : **Dialogo tra la pace e la guerra* (on the occasion of Urban VIII.'s election) ; p. 413 : *Poesia nel settimo anniversario dell'esaltatione d'Urbano VIII.* ; p. 459 : **Poesia nel quinto anniversario d. esalt. d'Urbano VIII.* (1628).

[2] Romae, 1628.

[3] AFFÒ, *Memorie d. vita e degli studi di Sf. card. Pallavicini*, Venezia, 1780.

[4] Lugduni, 1642.

[5] *De virtute et statu religionis*, III., Lugduni, 1623. The dedication by the Jesuit College of Coimbra of the posthumous work is dated September 13, 1623.

[6] RENAZZI, III., 137 ; *Freib. Kirchenlex.*, V.², 123.

[7] See above, p. 13 *seq.*

VIII.: the Benedictine Angelo Maria Cherubini, his new, enlarged edition of the Bullarium [1]; the celebrated canonist Giovan Battista Coccini, a commentary on the Bull on the election of a Pope [2]; Leonardo Novelli, a dissertation on the Pope's authority [3]; Ignazio Bracci one on the title "Pope" [4]; Ovidio de Amici, a dissertation on the Church's authority in things spiritual and temporal [5]; Michele Lonigo one on the reservation *in petto* of Cardinals [6]; Cristoforo Borri, a report on the Jesuit missions in Cochin China [7]; Constantino Gaetano, a treatise on the States of the Church.[8] Other writings dedicated to the Pope are purely theological; for example: George Conaeus' Defence of Catholic doctrine [9]; Giovanni Falce's work on the characteristics of heresy [10]; the *Index* published in 1640 by Maddaleno Capiferreo, secretary to the Congregation of the Index [11] and Giovan Battista Novati's

[1] Romae, 1634, 4 vols. *Cf.* PHILLIPS, IV., 483.

[2] **Ad bullam Urbani VIII. de electione pontificum glossemata Io. Bapt. Coccini, Barb.* 1616, Vatican Library.

[3] LEONARDUS NOVELLUS, **De auctoritate s. pontificum, Barb.* 1265, *loc. cit., cf.* 975: **Ad S.D.N. Urbanum VIII. de ejus primatu ac suprema poteste tam in spiritualibus quam in temporalibus in universo mundo.*

[4] I. BRACCI, *La etimologia de'nomı Papa et Ponțifex*, Roma, 1630.

[5] See ALLATII, *Apes Urbanae*, 208.

[6] **Barb.* 5243, 453, and *Vat.* 8630. *Cf.* GASPAROLO in *Studi e docum.*, VIII., 25 *seq.* Gasparolo does not note the *dissertations on questions of ceremonies dedicated to Urban VIII. in *Barb.* 2969 and the *dissertation on the *Confessio* of St. Peter's in *Barb.* 4516, *loc. cit.*

[7] *Relatione della nuova missione delli Padri della Comp. di Giesù nel regno della Cocincina*, Roma, 1631.

[8] CONSTANTINO GAETANO, **Del dominio temporale et patrimonio del pontefice Romano*, 1623, *Barb.* 4489, *loc. cit.* On the author see RENAZZI, III., 135.

[9] G. CONAEUS, *Assertionum catholicarum libri III.*, Romae, 1626.

[10] JOH. FALCES DE S. STEPHANO, *Methodus ad cognoscendas haereses*, Romae, 1630.

[11] REUSCH, II., 24 *seq.*

disquisition on the Immaculate Conception.[1] The Augustinian friar Fortunato Scacchi studied the conditions for beatification and canonization.[2] Among the " Lives of Saints " dedicated to Urban VIII. mention may be made of those of St. Yves by Peter Chevet [3]; of St. Bibiana by Domenico Fedini [4]; of Pope Urban I. by Francesco Maria Torrigio.[5] Urban VIII. was extremely gratified when Francesco Maria Fiorentini, who had deserved well of the city of Lucca, dedicated to him his work on Countess Matilda, the importance of which was emphasized by no less a man than Leibniz.[6]

The Barberini Pope was greatly interested in history and antiquities.[7] Agostino Mascardi, author of the *Arte istorica* [Rome, 1636], became his private chamberlain with a salary of 500 scudi a year; at a later date the Pope gave him an appointment at the University.[8] On two occasions he sought to attract to Rome the learned Jesuit Denis Petau who had made himself famous by his " Chronology ", but the plan could not be realized owing to the delicate health of the scholar

[1] I. B. NOVATUS, *De eminentia Deiparae virginis Mariae semper immaculatae*, Romae, 1632.

[2] F. SCACCHI, *De notis et signis sanctitatis beatificat. et cononizandorum, Vat.* 7064, printed *Romae*, 1639. *Cf.* MORONI, LX., 188; LÄMMER, *zur Kirchengesch.*, 68.

[3] *Vat.* 7070, printed *Romae*, 1640.

[4] *Vat.* 7070, printed *Romae*, 1627.

[5] **Barb.* 4486, *loc. cit.*

[6] *Memorie della Gran Contessa Matilda.* Reumont, too, describes these *Memorie* as the most important work on that great woman and her time (*Beilage zur Allg. Zeitung*, 1882, no. 115). *Cf.* also SFORZA, *F. M. Fiorentini*, Firenze, 1879.

[7] The Pope perused at once Benedetto Mellini's *dissertation: *Dell'arco di Portogallo* (the triumphal arch of Marcus Aurelius in the Corso), *Barb.* 4304 and 4305, *loc. cit.* To this class also belong the following writings: **Relazione delle reliquie antique trovate con l'occasione della nuova chiavica scritta da Cipriano Cipriani* (arciprete d. Rotonda), *ibid.* 4301 and 4311, and **Discorso del cavalier Gualdi del conservare le memorie et edificii antichi et in particolare per risarcire il Ponte di Rimini* (1640), *ibid.*, 4309.

[8] RENAZZI, III., 97.

and because in the pursuit of his studies he could not do without the libraries of Paris.[1] The celebrated Leone Allacci was commissioned by Urban VIII. to study the question of Pope Joan: his work appeared in Rome in 1630.[2] Ten years later the history of the Barberini family by Carlo Strozzi was also printed there and its author received a call to Rome.[3] The history of the Order of Malta, with which Cesare Magalotti had been entrusted, remained unwritten.[4] A similar fate befell a far more important and extraordinarily opportune plan of Urban VIII., which was to oppose to Sarpi's tendentious history of the Council of Trent an authentic account based on a comprehensive use of the documents of the papal archives. This task was entrusted to the Jesuit Terenzio Alciati. In the autumn of 1626 the Pope instructed his theologian and private chamberlain Agostino Oreggi to put at the disposal of the scholar all the acts of the great assembly which were preserved in the Papal Secret Archives. In August, 1629, he directed the Augustinians of S. Giovanni a' Carbonari, at Naples, to give Alciati access to the papers left by Cardinal Seripando and all other acts referring to the Council of Trent.[5]

[1] KNELLER in *Freib. Kirchenlex.*, IX.², 184 *seq.*; SOMMERVOGEL, II., 1902; FOUQUERAY, 280 *seq.*; *ibid.*, IV., 266 *seq.*, on the attempt to attract J. Sirmond to Rome. A Brief of thanks to Petavius, of December, 1640, in *Epist.*, XV–XVI., Papal Secret Archives. *Originals of letters of Petavius to Hier. Aleander, Cardinal Francesco Barberini and Urban VIII., in *Barb.* 2185.

[2] *Commentatio in Ioannae Papissae fabulam. Cf.* L. ALLATII, *Apes Urbanae*, 177; DÖLLINGER, *Papstfabeln* ² (1890), 1 *seq.*

[3] On the copy of the Chronicle of Dino Compagni which Carlo Strozzi presented to Urban VIII. and of which the Pope is said to have personally prepared the binding, see REUMONT in *Hist. Jahrbuch*, VI., 151 *seq.* According to RENAZZI (III., 118) Urban VIII. summoned Giambattista Strozzi to Rome and assigned to him a lodging in the Vatican. Strozzi subsequently returned to Florence.

[4] *Cf. Arch. stor. ital.*, 5 series, I., 127 *seq.*; *ibid.*, on another work by Magalotti also dedicated to Urban VIII.

[5] See EHSES in *Röm. Quartalschr*, XVI., 297 *seq.*

Alciati applied himself most conscientiously to his task, and notwithstanding the difficulties created for him by the keeper of the archives, Contelori, he obtained the loan of the original notes drawn up by the secretary of the Council, Massarelli. But Alciati's high aspirations and, no doubt, his inability to master such a mass of detail, prevented him from doing more than collecting these materials. He died in 1631 without having written his history.[1] This does not diminish the credit due to Urban VIII. His action also refutes the assertion, repeated even in our own days, that the Roman Curia was anxious to keep secret the conciliar Acts of Trent.[2]

The Pope's interest in history had a beneficent influence on the deve'opment of historical studies in Rome where men like Ughelli, Wadding, Andrea Vittorelli, Fioravante Martinelli, Francesco Maria Torrigio and the great Oderico Raynald undertook substantial works which have won them lasting fame. Urban VIII. lived long enough to see the beginning of the publication of that gigantic work, the *Acta Sanctorum*, in which it was proposed to give a critical account of the lives of all the Saints based on the most reliable sources. The first two folio volumes, written by the Jesuit John Bollandus and comprising the month of January, appeared at Antwerp in 1643. The *Acta* show the Jesuit Order at the peak of its scholarship.[3] Five years earlier the Jesuit Alexander Donatus had published his description of ancient and modern Rome and dedicated it to Urban VIII.[4] The work is distinguished by thorough philological knowledge and a genuine historical conception. In the first book Donatus expatiates on the

[1] PALLAVICINI, Storia del concilio di Trento, Introduzione, V., 6; EHSES, *loc. cit.*, 305.

[2] Thus RANKE (Päpste, III.[6], 41*.)

[3] Opinion of G. VOIGT in *Hist. Zeitschr.*, X., 19. On the Bollandists, on whose labours Mabillon, the founder of the study of Diplomatics, based his own work, *cf.* BERNHEIM, *Hist. Methode*, 131 *seq.*; *Les Bollandistes et l'hagiographie*, Paris, 1866, and DELEHAYE, "A travers trois siècles," *L'œuvre des Bollandistes*, Brussels, 1920.

[4] ALEX. DONATUS, *Roma vetus ac recens*, Romae, 1638.

circumference, the walls and gates of Rome, and describes the characteristics of the principal epochs of the history of the city; in the second and third books he speaks of the hills and valleys of ancient Rome whilst the fourth extols the new Rome.[1]

The name of Urban VIII. is also linked with another important work. The end of 1634 saw the publication of *Roma Sotterranea* by the Maltese lawyer, Antonio Bosio. The work, which was dedicated to the Pope, was edited by the Oratorian Giovanni Severano.

From the year 1593 Bosio had devoted his life to the exploration of underground Rome, that is the immense network of the burial places of the early Christians. Whereas up till then barely four or five catacombs had been accessible,[2] he explored thirty of them. He lived a life of complete solitude, so much so that legends and calumnies grew round the name of a scholar[3] who, with unparalleled enthusiasm, buried himself in antiquarian material unique of its kind, constituting one of the most precious treasures of the wonderful city round which the axis of the world's history has now revolved for more than two thousand years. The material collected by Bosio, now preserved in the Vallicellian library, shows the vastness of his

[1] See PLATNER, I., XXXVII.

[2] Already then visits to the Catacombs proceeded on lines similar to those in use to-day. Thus we read in the "Wegzeiger zu den wunderbarlichen sachen der heidnischen etwann nun Christlichen stat Rom . . . durch HERMANNUM BAVINCK" (Rome, 1625), p. 55: "It is impossible to go down and to move about without a light. The wax tapers which you see in these churches and in S. Lorenzo cost a quatrin each; thus one gets five for a baiocco or a kreutzer. The money is cast in the box close by." On the removal of relics from the Roman Catacombs between 1638 and 1640 by Cardinal Pallotta see *Röm. Quartalschr.*, XXXIII., 123 *seq.*

[3] On the calumnies against Bosio by Eritreo *cf.* DE ROSSI, *Roma sott.*, I., 43 *seq.*; A. VALERI, *Cenni biogr. di A. Bosio*, Roma, 1900, 65 *seq.*, see also ORBAAN, *Rome onder Clemens VIII.*, Gravenhage, 1920, 234 *seq.*; P. FREMIOTTI, *La Reforma Cattolica del secolo XVI. e gli studi di archeologia christiana*, Roma, 1926.

preliminary labours.[1] The manuscripts also prove that the alterations introduced by Severano were only minor ones, that only a few pages were suppressed and that everywhere the author's ample material was carefully utilized. When Bosio died in 1629 most of the text was ready and nearly all the tables were engraved. Bosio follows a strictly topographical order, describes the various galleries of the cemeteries with their crypts and paintings and puts together all the historical details he has been able to establish. Recent research has shown that nothing which it was possible to ascertain in his day has escaped him. In his designation of the various catacombs he had to rely, for the most part, on tradition, since only in rare instances did he succeed in finding monuments that confirmed or modified it.[2] Notwithstanding this and other shortcomings, his is a wonderful piece of work [3] and one of the most valuable fruits of the scholarship of the era of Catholic restoration in which, after classical Rome, the subterranean Rome of the first Christians was likewise rescued from oblivion.[4] Publication of the gigantic work was made possible by Cardinal Francesco Barberini [5] who followed the example of the Pope as a munificent patron of learning.

Like his uncle, Francesco Barberini had such a mastery of Greek as to enable him, at a later date, to translate the soliloquies of Marcus Aurelius into Italian.[6] The extent of his

[1] *Cf.* besides De Rossi, *loc. cit.*, especially Valeri, 31, 37 *seq.*

[2] De Rossi, *loc. cit.*, K. M. Kaufmann, *Handbuch der Christl. Archäologie*, Paderborn, 1913.

[3] Kraus-Sauer, II., 2, 691; *cf.* Hülsen in *Ausonia*, VI. (1911).

[4] Schlosser, *Die Kunstliteratur*, Wien, 1924, 456.

[5] Valeri, 60 *seq.*, who shows that the work was only published in 1634 though the title-page bears the date 1632, for the Brief with the privilege against reproduction is dated October 6, 1634. Orbaan, *Rome onder Clemens VIII.*, 235, must be corrected accordingly.

[6] Printed in Rome in 1667, MS. in *Barb.* 3897, Vatican Library, *ibid.*, 2068, numerous poems of Card. Fr. Barberini, but not in his hand (*cf.* Mazzuchelli, II., 1, 293 *seq.*); some are printed in Tetius, *Aedes Barb.*

interests is attested by the number of works dedicated to him not only by Italians but by Frenchmen also with whom he had many contacts since his Paris legation. Besides many poems, we come across numerous works of sacred and profane learning and names such as those of Lugo, Lessius, Cornelius a Lapide.[1] In addition to theology, the Cardinal was particularly interested in history.[2] He also paid great attention to the natural sciences, to botany in particular.[3] To the history of art he rendered a unique service when he had copies made of the pictures of the old churches of Rome, with their mosaics and paintings and other works of art, as for instance, the bronze door of St. Paul's.[4] Totti dedicated to the Cardinal his description of the new Rome,[5] Severano the two volumes of his

[1] *Cf.* Appendix 24.

[2] BURGUS dedicated to him his book *De Bello Suecico* (1633); G. CIAMMARUCONE his *Descrittione d. città di Sezza*, Roma, 1641. *Cf. Barb.* 3571; **Elogios de los Papas y cardenales que a tenido la nacion española*, by Balt. Porreño; also a sonnet to the Cardinal. Magnus Perneus wrote *De vita card. Barberini*, *Barb.* 3316 *seq.* Vatican Library.

[3] JESSEN, *Botanik*, 258. A **Botanologia esotica*, dedicated to the Cardinal, is in *Barb.* 4252, *loc. cit.*; *ibid.*, 4278: **Trattazione della coltivazione di alcuni fiori cioè degli anemoni, de' giacinti, de' narcissi, de' tulipani, de' garofani*, by Fr. Mingucci da Pesaro; 4283: **Trattato della coltivazione di alcuni fiori cioè gelsomini e delle rose doppie*, by the same; 4326: **Fiore diversi coloriti dal naturale* by the same, with dedication dated August 21, 1637; 4327: **Ucelli diversi coloriti dal naturale* by the same; 4265: *Giardinetto secreto del em. sig. card. Barberini*, with plan.

[4] The copies are partly in the *Vaticana*, partly in the *Barberini* Library now transferred to the former. *Cf.* PLATNER, I., LIX.; MÜNTZ, *Sources d'archéol. chrét.*: *Mél.*, VIII., 101 *seq.*; SCAGLIA, *I Mosaici antichi di S. Maria Maggiore*, Roma, 1910. The "figure e iscrittioni" on the bronze door of St. Paul's, "copiate d'ordine del card. Fr. Barberini, 1634" in *Barb.* 4378, Vatican Library. The Cardinal had copies of this kind made in France also; see "Disegni e piante di palazzi etc. da alcune città di Francia" executed for the Cardinal by an architect. *Barb.* 4398, *ibid.*

[5] See below, p. 517.

Memorie of the seven principal churches of the Eternal City [1] and Ferreria and Falda, at a later date, their splendid work on the palaces of Rome.[2]

Francesco Barberini was an eager collector not only of books, but of antiques and other rare objects. His collection of ancient inscriptions [3] and coins [4] was especially famous. But his collection of antiques [5] was left far behind by his valuable library. He founded the Barberini library which, next to that of the Vatican, became the first in Rome.[6] Many scholars, among them Aleander, Holste, Doni and Suarez, were commissioned by him to secure further additions to the collection,[7] but its nucleus consisted of the literary treasures

[1] *Memorie sacre delle selle chiese di Roma e di altri luoghi che si trovano per le strade*, Roma, 1630.

[2] P. FERREIRO E G. B. FALDA, *Palazzi di Roma*, Roma, s.a. (*ca.* 1660). *Cf.* CICOGNARA, 3719; BRUNET, II., 1235.

[3] *Cf.* TIRABOSCHI, VIII., 47; RENAZZI, III., III.

[4] *Instruttione sopra le medaglie degli imperatori antichi Romani di Marco Baldanza familiare di N. Sig. Papa Urbano VIII. all em. sig. card. Franc. Barberini* (MS. in 40, *ca.* 250 pages), which passed from the library of A. Manzoni into the possession of Nardechia's antiquarian shop in Rome (Catalogue of 1922).

[5] GIULIO PICCOLOMINI, *Descriz. dell'antichità dell'ecc. casa Barberini* (dedicated to Card. Barberini, 1637). *Barb.* 4817.

[6] See NICOLETTI in *Barb.* 4730, p. 533 (fu stimata una delle più insigni e più celebri che siano in Europa), Vat. Lib.; MABILLON, 131; BLUME, III., 132 *seq.*; REUMONT, V., 167 *seq.*; ORBAAN, *Bescheiden*, I., 271; JENSOVSKY, *La Bibl. Barberini e le ricerche Boeme a Roma*, Prag., 1927. *Cf. Barb.* 3021 (*loc. cit.*).

[7] *Cf.* especially the letters of Giuseppe Maria Suarez (between 1633–1666 Bishop of Vaison, died 1677) to Cardinal Fr. Barberini, 1633–1676 in *Barb.* 6482, *loc. cit.* The literary remains of Suarez, *ibid.*, 2991–2997 (*Adversaria*), 3001, 3010, 3018 (*Lettere*), 3016 (*Omelie*), 3017 (*Epistolae*), 3020 (*Insignia pontif. Avenion.*), 3018 (*Praenestes antiquae libri duo* for *Maffeo Barberini princ. Praen.*), 3022, 3023 (*S. Nili opuscula*), 3026 (*Excerpta*), 3027 (*Opuscula*), 3028 (*S. Augustin.*), 3029, 3030 (*Excerpta de rosa aurea*), 3031 (*De praefecto Urbis*), 3032, 3033 (*Excerpta*), 3034, 3040, 3047, incl. *Adversaria*, 3035 (Ital. MSS.), 3036–3040 (*Carmina*, 3039

gathered by Maffeo Barberini. The Barberini library continued to expand as time went on. Notwithstanding some sensible losses suffered by it, its amalgamation with the Vatican Library in 1902, rendered possible by the munificence of Leo XIII., meant a very great gain for the latter. It includes at this day, 10,659 MSS.—9,902 Latin, 593 Greek and 164 Oriental oncs. The printed works number 31,671, works in several volumes being reckoned as one item.[1] Among its treasures we may mention autographs of Bembo [2] and Galileo.[3] Many printed works bear signed notes by Tasso.[4] Precious treasures also are the collection of drawings by Sangallo,[5] a polyglot of the thirteenth–fourteenth century, the Samaritan Pentateuch, a French Bible with miniatures dating from the end of the thirteenth century, a copy of the forty-two column Bible and a parchment edition of *Orlando Furioso* of 1532. The library was made accessible to the public and a special guardian appointed.[6] In 1636 the post of librarian of the Barberiniana was given to one of the most distinguished theologians, archæologists and critics of the period, Luke Holste, or Holstenius, as he himself spelt his name.[7] Born at

(*Poesie*), 3048 (*Epistolae*) (1617–1677), 3049 (*Lett. Ital.* (*item* 3052), letters in French, among them copies of two letters of St. Francis de Sales, 3053 (*Lettere*), 3054, 3055 (*Opuscula*), 3056 (*Mon. eccl. Vasionen.*), 3167 (Catalogues of Roman libraries). These rich remains are worthy of closer examination.

[1] Information supplied by Mgr. A. Mercati, prefect of the Archives.

[2] *Cod. Lat.*, 2157 and 5963.

[3] *Cod. Lat.*, 6479/6481.

[4] *Cf.* SOLERTI, III., 183 *seq.*

[5] Published by Hülsen.

[6] See TOTTI, 273. For the loan of a MS. to Paris see the publication by Tamizey de Larroche, p. 37, mentioned in n. 4 of p. 444, *ibid.*, pp. 40 and 49 *seq.*, for the dispatch of French books for the Cardinal's library.

[7] See [WILKEN'S] Leben L. Holstenii, Hamburg, 1723; RÄSS, V., 186 *seq.*; BURSIAN, in *Allg. Deutsche Biogr.*, XII., 776; F. WAGNER in *Zeitschr. für Ham. Gesch.*, XI. (1903), 395 *seq.*; FRIEDENSBURG, *ibid.*, XII., 9 (1908), 95 *seq.* *Cf.* also PALMIERI in *Spicil. Vat.*, I., 263; GABRIELI, 204. For Holstenius' literary

Hamburg in 1596, the son of a dyer, Holste had been in touch, even whilst still a student at the University of Leiden, with philologists of mark such as John Meursius, Daniel Heimsius and Philip Cluverius. In 1618 he travelled in Italy with the last named. In 1622 he stayed in England where he worked in the libraries of Oxford and London in the interests of his Dutch friends and the collection of Greek geographers which he himself was planning. In 1624 he went to Paris where, moved by the same inspiration as St. Augustine, he entered the Catholic Church.[1] As librarian of the President of the Supreme Court of Justice, Henri des Mesmes, he came in contact with the most eminent French bibliophiles and scholars. He became a close friend of the librarian of the King, Nicholas Rigault, as well as of Gabriel Naudé, the subsequent founder of Mazarin's library, the Jesuit Sirmond, the librarians Pierre and Jacques Du Puy and Nicholas Claude Fabre de Peirex, councillor of Parliament.[2] Pierre Du Puy, in conjunction with Peirex and Girolamo Aleander, recommended Holstenius to Cardinal

remains, *cf. Zentralblatt für Bibliothekswesen*, XII., 441 *seq.*, XIII, 186, XIX., 321 *seq.* The Barberini family archives, of which the House has retained possession, have not been exploited as regards Holstenius.

[1] In a letter to his nephew, Petrus Lambecius (1646), published by Friedensburg (*loc. cit.*), Holstenius explains the motives of his return to Catholicism. According to this evidence the change of opinion occurred already in 1620, that is, during the period at Leiden. This completely disposes of the idea that Holstenius took this step at the suggestion of his Paris friends or as a result of his relations, at a much later date, with Italy and the Roman curia (*loc. cit.*, 103). In like manner the surmise that Holstenius changed his faith because he had failed to obtain a post he had hoped for in his native town, falls to the ground as a result of the evidence furnished by Friedensburg that, at that very time, his fellow townsmen sought to secure him for a secretarial post which he had to refuse owing to his change of religion.

[2] *Cf.* L. G. Pélissier, *Les Amis d'Holstenius*, in *Mél. d'archéol.*, VI., 554 *seq.*, VII., 62 *seq.*, and *Rev. des langues Romanes*, 1891. G. Naudé has published a *Panegyricus dicatus Urbano VIII. ob beneficia in M.Th. Campanellam collata, Parisiis*, 1644.

Francesco Barberini [1] who assigned to so promising a scholar a permanent post in the Eternal City by entrusting to him the management and completion of his library. Holstenius left Paris in 1626, in company with the nuncio Spada who was returning to Rome, to take up his new post. In Rome he by no means confined himself to the administration and increase of the library,[2] but read widely for himself. The works of the Neo-Platonists and the Greek Fathers occupied him no less than the Greek geographers. History and theology also entered into the ambit of his studies which were rewarded with important discoveries, such as that of the *Liber diurnus*.[3] He also wrote poetry. However, in consequence of this frittering away of his energies, only too many of the works begun by him remained incomplete,[4] which is not to be wondered at in view of the fact that he had to undertake repeated journeys in order

[1] PÉLISSIER, *loc. cit.*, VII., 69 *seq.*

[2] *Cf.* L. HOLSTENII, *Index librorum manuscript. et typis edit. quos Urbanus VIII., Franc. card. Barberinus aliique ad hanc Bibliothecam miserunt vel idem emit Holstenius, Barb.* 3075, Vatican Library ; *ibid.*, 3062, *Index codicum graecorum bibliothecae L. Allatii.*

[3] *Cf.* A. RATTI, *La fine d'una leggenda ed altre spigolature intorno al Liber diurnus Romanorum Pontificum*, Pavia, 1913.

[4] On Holstenius' collection of Lives of the Popes *cf.* GLASSCHRÖDER in *Röm. Quartalschrift*, IV., 125 *seq.* ; Holstenius planned, among other things, an edition of the *Liber pontificalis* and the *Liber diurnus* ; CARINI, *Bibl. Vatic.*, 85. The Barberini Library has the following works by him : 2049, *Epigrammata* ; 2104, poem to Motmann ; 2182, 3063–3074 and 6535, *Adversaria, Opuscula et Varia*. *Cf.* also 6428 and 6419. A small selection of his extensive correspondence has been published by BOISSONADE (*L. Holstenii epistolae ad diverso*, Paris, 1817), PÉLISSIER (see above p. 441, n. 2) and others (see *Riv. d. biblioteche*, 1890, nos. 18–19). The many letters of Holstenius in the Barberini library would well reward fresh study. *Cf.* especially 2177, 2179, 2180, 2181, 2183–9, 3539 (French, German and English letters to Holstenius), 3630 (French letters to Holstenius), 3631 (German and English letters to Holstenius), 6488 (letters to Card. Fr. Barberini, 1636–1642), 6489 (*item* 1643–1660), 6490 (*item* 1646–8),

to secure additions to the Library.[1] Accordingly he only published a Greek-Latin edition of several works of Porphyry with a learned introduction on his life and writings (Rome, 1630), a collection of axioms of the later Pythagoreans (Rome, 1638), notes on Gabriel Naudé's edition of the Neo-Platonist Sallustius' treatise on the gods and the world (Rome, 1638) and on Arrian's book on the chase (Paris, 1644). He also collaborated in the editions of Athanasius and Eusebius published in Paris in 1627 and 1628. To all this must be added theological dissertations and Latin poems.[2] The Pope made provision for the versatile scholar by the grant of ecclesiastical benefices in North-Germany and when the war choked this source of income, he gave him a canonry at St. Peter's.[3] Cardinal Barberini remained at all times a good friend to his protégé who, under Innocent XI, obtained the long-desired post of Custodian of the Vatican Library. When Holstenius died on February 2nd, 1661, Barberini erected a monument to him in S. Maria dell'Anima, with this inscription : " Famous in Rome, more famous in Germany, Holstenius' mind embraced the history and Christian traditions of all peoples and times ; he knew accurately the territories and names of the various countries through which he travelled, also their different languages, besides Greek and Latin, the writers of which he

6491, Card. Fr. Barberini's letters to Holstenius, 1629–1638, 6492 (*item* 1646–8), 6493 (letters of Princes to Holstenius), 6494 (letters of Bishops), 6495, 6496 (various letters), 6497 (letters of Cardinals), 6498, 6499, 6480 (letters of famous personages to Holstenius). The *Fondo* Leone Allacci of the Vatican Library has not yet been exploited and catalogued ; *cf. Arch. Rom.*, VII., 580 seq.

[1] His **Iter per Etruriam*, 1641, has been described by Holstenius himself (MS. F. 192 of Dresden Library) ; extracts in *Arch. stor. ital.*, 5 series, X., 340 *seq.* ; on Holstenius' journey to Lower Italy to visit libraries and his purchases of books for Cardinal Barberini see his *Letters in *Barb.* 6488, Vatican Library.

[2] See Bursian in *Allg. Deutsche Biogr.*, XII., 776.

[3] *Cf.* Friedensburg, *loc. cit.* During the war of Castro, Holstenius was sent to Umbria *per esaminare le fortezze* ; see letters in *Barb.* 6489.

thoroughly explained, and he was versed in ancient philosophy."[1]

It was appropriate that Holstenius should find a resting place in the German national church seeing that he was, as it were, the advocate with Cardinal Barberini of all Germans who came to Rome, obtaining audiences for the rich, and for the poor succour or money for their journey. It was he who, in the spring of 1637, after thoroughly instructing him, induced the Landgrave Frederick of Hesse to return to the Church. With what interest Holstenius watched the destinies of his native land is revealed by his letters and a scheme for a German fleet which he drew up for the imperial Resident Motmann.[2]

Cardinal Barberini kept up relations with numerous foreign scholars.[3] His house in Rome was the rendezvous of literary men of every description. When any celebrities from abroad came to Rome, the Cardinal gave them a most friendly reception and furthered their studies, even if they did not belong to the Catholic Church.[4] The great Dutch philologists Heinsius and Vossius and other learned Netherlanders gave poetic expression to their gratitude for the kindly reception the Cardinal gave them.[5] But the most famous personage received in the Palazzo Barberini was, without doubt, John Milton, whose masterpiece, "Paradise Lost," was to win for him the highest recognition even from Catholics, though, as a Puritan, he combated them most vehemently. Milton arrived in Rome in October, 1638, when Holstenius introduced him to Cardinal Barberini who invited him to his parties.[6]

[1] SCHMIDLIN, *Anima*, 501. [2] *Ibid.*, 477 *seq.*

[3] Numerous *letters to him, mostly on literary topics, from scholars, among them many Jesuits, Cardinals and Bishops, in *Barb.* 6455, 6457, 6458, 6515, 6517, 6521.

[4] Jean Jacques Bouchard also secured the eagerly longed-for post of secretary to Fr. Barberini: *cf.* TAMIZEY DE LARROCHE, *Les correspondants de Peiresc*, III., Paris, 1881, p. v.

[5] See ORBAAN, *Bescheiden*, I., 305 *seq.*, 308 *seq.*, 311 *seq.*, 328 *seq.*; *cf.* 219 *seq.*, 272 *seq.*

[6] *Cf.* T. GUAZZARONI, *G. Milton in Italia*, Roma, 1902, and J. MARTIN, *Milton en Italie*, in *Bullet. italien*, X., No. 4, Bordeaux, 1910, 9 *seq.*

On one such occasion the poet made the acquaintance of the most celebrated singer of the time, Leonora Baroni, of Mantua. Like the rest of the poets of Rome, he too paid exuberant homage to the artiste, singing her praises in Latin and Italian verses. Such was his enthusiasm that from a Puritan it almost turned him into a pantheist. The Roman men of letters extolled Milton in no less florid language. Selvaggi placed him by the side of Homer and Virgil, whilst Salsilli, a member of the *Accademia dei Fantastici,* did not hesitate to award him the triple crown of Latin, Greek and Italian poetry. Milton replied in a poem crammed with mythological allusions. He even accepted an invitation to a dinner in his honour at the English College, but the ecclesiastical atmosphere did not agree with him in the long run; in December he left for Naples.[1]

All the scholars and poets of the city collected round this most cultivated Prince of the Church, whose palace near Quattro Fontane became Rome's first Academy. In an extensive work illustrated by Cornelis Bloemaert [2] and dedicated to the Cardinal, Count Girolamo Teti [3] described not only that magnificent edifice, its works of art, collections of antiquities and its library, but likewise the whole circle of *beaux esprits* who met there. "Nothing so characterizes the scholarly tone which obtained among the *habitués* of the House of Barberini than this work written in studied Latin, in the manner of Cicero, with its wealth of imagery and flowery rhetoric. In its pages the gatherings at the palazzo near Quattro Fontane were compared to Parnassus, on whose peaks the nephews of Urban were enthroned like *alteri Appolines.*" [4] In addition to the librarian Holstenius, one of the intimates of the circle was another official of the library, Carlo Moroni, author of a book on the origin and nobility of the Barberini family [5] and as able a cicerone as he was a courteous one. The

[1] MARTIN, *loc. cit.*, 10.

[2] ORBAAN, *Bescheiden,* I., 133, 272.

[3] *Aedes Barberinae ad Quirinalem a comite Hieronymo Tetio Perusino descriptae, Romae,* 1642.

[4] G. POSSE, *Deckenmalerei,* 103.

[5] *Dell'origine e nobiltà della famiglia Barberini, Roma,* 1640.

collection of coins also had its own learned director in the person of the antiquarian Leonardo Agostino who provided explanations of its treasures.

From the very beginning of his uncle's reign, Cardinal Barberini gathered the most distinguished and most learned writers of Rome in an Academy.[1] On the completion of his palace, its meetings were held in the exedra, adorned with antique statues, which adjoined the gallery painted by Pietro da Cortona. At these gatherings not only were poems recited in praise of the master of the house and the literary men present, or clever epigrams made on works of art, but speeches were also delivered on philosophic, moral or æsthetic themes. Ancient eloquence was recalled, so Teti boasts, when Francesco Bracciolini spoke on the splendours of antiquity and Gaspare de Simeonibus read his *Praelectio contra laudem.*[2]

Among the other Roman Academies it is worth while mentioning one likewise promoted by the Cardinal in the Basilian monastery founded by Urban VIII. in 1631, the secretary of which was the Florentine Giovan Battista Doni. Its members included Holstenius, Allacci, Francesco Arcudio, Vincenzo Riccardi, Pietro Ligaridis and Giovan Battista Rinuccini. The subjects of the discussions were the points controverted between Greeks and Latins.[3] Between 1623–1627 Cardinal Maurice of Savoy likewise gathered the choicest spirits in an Academy at his palace on Monte Giordano.[4] But the most important of all was the Accademia dei Lincei founded by Federigo Cesi, of which Francesco Barberini became a member on October 1st, 1623.[5] Besides history and poetry, the natural sciences were the chief pursuit of its members. When Cesi died in 1630, this particular association broke up but its scientific material was rescued by Cassiano del Pozzo who had

[1] *Cf.* *Avviso of July 17, 1624. Vatican Library.

[2] Posse, *loc. cit.*; on the extensive literary activity of Gaspare de Simeonibus of Aquila *cf.* Allatii, *Apes Urbanae*, 120 *seq.*

[3] See Moroni's account (XXXIII., 71 *seq.*), based on the now scarce History of this Academy by Ignazio de Lazaris (*Roma*, 1682),

[4] See Gabrieli, *Carteggio*, 201.

[5] *Ibid.*, 199.

been Francesco Barberini's companion on his legations to France and Spain in 1625 and 1626.[1] The palace of this scholar in the Via dei Chiavari, which also housed, besides works of art, a museum of natural history, was the meeting place of a circle whose main interest was classical antiquity. Pozzo had been in touch with the Pope whilst the latter was still a Cardinal. His collection of drawings of classical works of art, which is one of the treasures of the library of Windsor, as well as his journals, constitute to this day a rich mine for archæologists. Pozzo was in relation with a number of scholars and artists. Through him Poussin acquired that practical and theoretical knowledge of archæology which largely influenced and furthered his artistic conceptions.[2] Together with Pozzo, Cardinal Barberini took his share in the explanation of the famous mosaic floor with Egyptian motifs which, after its discovery, was first taken to Rome, but in 1640, at the instance of the people of Palestrina, was transferred to the magnificent palace of the Barberini in that locality.[3]

In 1627 Urban VIII. placed Francesco Barberini at the head of the Vatican Library, a position which the Cardinal retained even after his appointment (in 1632) as Vice-Chancellor. However, in 1636, he resigned it in favour of the Pope's brother, Cardinal Antonio. This measure sufficiently shows the importance which the Pope attached to the Vatican Library. One of his first ordinances had been an edict for the preservation of its treasures.[4] The Cardinal was alone empowered to remove any manuscript from the Vaticana, either for his own or another's use.[5] The guardians were enjoined to keep a sharp eye on visitors to the library. A law was also made by which a copy of all books printed in Rome had to be presented

[1] LUMBROSO, *Notizie sulla vita di Cassiano del Pozzo*, in *Miscell. di stor. ital.*, XV, *Torino*, 1876, 129 *seq.*; PREMOLI in *Atti d. Arcadia*, II. (1918), 181 *seq.*, 90 *seq.*; GABRIELI, 197 *seq.*

[2] FRIEDLÄNDER, *N. Poussin*, 13.

[3] *Cf.* SANTE PIERALISI, *Osservazioni sul mosaico di Palestrina*, Roma, 1858; *Miscell. di stor. ital.*, XV. (1875), 176 *seq.*, 178 *seq.*

[4] See *Avviso* of September 23, 1623. Vat. Lib.

[5] BELTRANI in *Arch. d. Soc. Rom.*, II., 197.

to the library.[1] At the same time the Pope made provision for a fitting exhibition of the manuscripts of the Heidelberg library, assigning to them a suitable room to the left of the main hall of the Vaticana.[2] In March, 1624, he himself inspected the collection,[3] the beautiful bindings of which bear witness, even at this day, to the solicitude of the Barberini Pope.

The Vatican Library was considerably enriched by various legacies. The Bishop of Belluno, Alvise Lollini, an old personal friend of the Pope, presented to it his rich collection of Greek manuscripts [4] and Paolo Emilio Santori assigned to it the books and manuscripts left by his uncle, the great Cardinal. The famous Syriac Bible of Sergio Risi, Archbishop of Damascus, was bought for the library.[5] Magnificent printed books as well as manuscripts came from France, the Pope expressing his thanks to the donor in a special letter.[6] In 1628

[1] *Ibid.*, 198.

[2] NICOLETTI (VI., c. 2, *Barb.* 604, Vat. Lib.), writes: "Non si tosto Urbano fu sublimato a qual grado, che desiderando quanto primo di vederla in Roma, ordinò che speditamente vi fosse trasportata e che fossero pagate molte spese fatte da Leone nell'andare in Germania, e tornare con la medesima condotta. Intanto preparolli un nobile e sontuoso luogo in un lato della Biblioteca Vaticana verso la parte di occidente, che prima era rozzo e dishabitato, e quivì con lungo ordine di armarii e di fenestroni di fino vetro per render più luminoso e maestoso il luogo medesimo, collocò la detta libreria, chiamata oggi Palatina, dove per memoria immortale della vittoria, pietà e generosità di Massimiliano Duca di Baviera fece porre questa iscrittione . . . (text in *Forcella*, VI., 147).

[3] See **Avviso* of March 23, 1624, Vat. Lib.

[4] See Mél. d'archéol., IX. (1889), 38 *seq.*; NICOLETTI (*loc. cit.*), remarks on this collection: Se bene per la quantità de' volumi era assai inferiore alla Palatina, tuttavia fu degna per la grandezza dell'animo del donatore e per la qualità de' libri per lo più manuscritti e greci, della stima che ne fece Urbano, e del luogo che assegnolli appresso la Palatina.

[5] CARINI, Bibl. Vatic., 83.

[6] *" Dilecto filio Domino de Noyers Urbanus P. P. VIII. Dilecte fili, salutem et Apostolicam benedictionem. Volumina,

Urban VIII. had the manuscripts and printed books of the Ethiopian Hospice of S. Stefano degli Abessini transferred to the Vaticana together with manuscripts from the Capranica College, from the Minerva and from Assisi.[1] A catalogue of the Coptic manuscripts, dedicated to Cardinal Francesco Barberini, was published by the Jesuit Athanasius Kircher who supplied at the same time interesting information on his own Egyptian studies.[2]

Urban VIII. caused the inventory of the manuscripts of the Vaticana to be proceeded with,[3] Leone Allacci being one of those engaged on the work. However, the latter fell out of favour with the Pope when he resigned his chair at the Greek College against the Pontiff's will and because he had passed some sharp criticisms on Urban's Greek poems ; moreover he had laid himself open to blame in the performance of his duties. Neither his apologia nor his book on the fable of Pope Joan regained for Allacci the Pope's favour.[4] By way of compensation,

quae non ita pridem Parisiis e typographia regia prodierunt, eam quavis ex parte prae se ferunt elegantiam ac splendorem, ut nihil concinnius, nihil ornatius cerni possit. Cum sane tanto operi tua auctoritate praefueris, plurimum tibi debent literarum studiosi, quippe qui tam insignibus monumentis optime de illis promeritus es, et qui omni virtutum genere excellere praedicaris, hoc etiam nomine singularem tibi laudem peperisti. Nobis autem codices, quos una cum epistola detulit dilectus filius Dominus de Chantelon tibi propinquitate coniunctus, gratissimi acciderunt, et in eiusmodi significatione consuetam tuam erga nos observantiam atque humanitatem, quarum merito non minus quam ob eximias alias animi dotes te paterne semper complexi sumus, luculenter agnovimus. Magnifacimus praecipui tui in hanc sanctam sedem obsequii atque affectus officia, tibique a supremo bonorum auctore diuturnam felicitatem precantes pontificiam benedictionem ex animo impertimur. Datum ut supra (31 January 1643). *Epist.*, XIX.–XXI., n. 236, Papal Secret Archives.

[1] *Cf.* BELTRANI, *loc. cit.*, 198 *seq.* ; CARINI, *loc. cit.*, 83 *seq.*

[2] *Cf.* BRISCHAR, *P. A. Kircher*, Würzburg, 1877, 45 *seq.*

[3] CARINI, *loc. cit.*, 82.

[4] See HERGENRÖTTER in *Freib. Kirchenlix.*, I.[2], 549.

Cardinal Francesco Barberini interested himself in him. To the Cardinal, Allacci dedicated his work entitled *Apes Urbanae* which deals with the numerous writers who lived in Rome between 1630 and 1632. By praising Urban's poetical activities in his preface and with a Greek translation of the Pope's ode to Carlo Barberini, Allacci sought to obtain oblivion for his former criticism.[1] To Cardinal Barberini he introduced the learned Cistercian Ughelli and encouraged the latter's *Italia Sacra*.[2] A work similar to the *Apes Urbanae* was published by Giovanni Vittorio Rossi, known as Janus Nicius Erythraeus, who, after a stormy career, retired to Monte Mario where he founded the church of the Madonna del Rosario; there also he found his last resting place.[3] Erythraeus' *Pinacotheca*,[4] unlike Allacci's work, is not a dry list of literary achievements but a lively account of the careers of contemporary writers and artists, though not without partiality and ironical exaggerations.[5]

If the three tomes of the *Pinacotheca* of Janus Nicius Erythraeus describe, in original fashion, the weaknesses of even the greatest celebrities of the period, the four volumes of his letters present a colourful picture of life in the Rome of Urban VIII. His seventeen " Dialogues " complete this work. They are equally important for the history of culture whilst their cold sarcasm reminds the reader of the " Colloquies " of Erasmus. The shadows in the picture of the Rome of the Barberini are even more mordantly described in the satire entitled *Eudemia*, which, under more or less transparent disguises, castigates certain men of letters and other personalities then alive.[6]

[1] See *Apes Urbanae*, 13 *seq.* A Greek poem on the Villa Barberini by L. Allacci was published in Rome in 1640 (Copy in *Bibl. Casanat.*).

[2] Manacorda in *Studi storici*, XII., 4 (1903).

[3] Forcella, XII., 268–9.

[4] The *Pinacotheca* was prepared for the press by Fabio Chigi in 1643; see L. Cerconi, *G. Nicio Eritreo*, Città di Castello, 1909, 15 *seq.*

[5] Orbaan, *Sixtine Rome*, London, 1911, 199.

[6] See the monograph by Cerboni quoted above, n. 4.

Urban VIII. has deserved well not only of the Vatican Library, the bronze door of which is adorned with his arms, but of the Roman archives also. Here practical and historical interests concurred. At that time the archival treasures of the Vatican were kept in two different places, viz. in Castel S. Angelo and in the Secret Archives set up by Paul V., near the Vatican. From that time onwards the prefect of the Vaticana was likewise head of these archives. On the death of Niccolò Alemanni, Urban VIII., on July 9th, 1626, entrusted that important and responsible post to Felice Contelori, but in 1630 he divided the management of the Library from that of the Archives.[1]

The Pope's choice of Contelori was a very happy one, for the latter had been prepared for his task by arranging the Coccini and Barberini libraries; he was, moreover, possessed of immense diligence as well as a shrewd historic sense. It was chiefly he who, after Baronius' death, kept alive in Rome the study of archives.[2] When Cardinal Barberini was named librarian of the Vaticana, Contelori made a valuable report on the library and the adjoining archives.[3] Though he also held the trying post of a Commissary of the Apostolic Camera, which was charged with the supervision of income and expenditure, he still found time for important archival research work which resulted in valuable historical works which may be consulted with profit even at this day. Mention must be made, in the first instance, of the two comprehensive collections of sources for a history of the States of the Church; these were followed by another collection of materials for the war of Parma under Julius III. Contelori's collection of papal Bulls and Briefs, from Leo I. to Julius III., fills four volumes. This keen scholar devoted prolonged and extensive study to the history of the office of the Prefect of Rome and his privileges, the result being a book published in 1631 which caused no small stir. The question of the reconciliation of Alexander III. with

[1] Beltrani, *loc. cit.*, 190 *seq.*

[2] Beltrani, 168. On Contelori's personal library, *cf.* Totti, 234.

[3] Information in *Vat.*, 7763, given by Beltrani, 191 *seq.*

Frederick Barbarossa, which formed the core of the dispute with Venice, was treated by Contelori with equal thoroughness in a book printed in 1630.[1] Contelori also did useful work when he began a catalogue of the existing volumes of *supplicas* from Martin V. up to his own time.[2]

The research work of Contelori would have been impossible had not Urban VIII. effected the transfer to the Papal Secret Archives of the most important relevant documents. He ordered the transfer to the Secret Archives of the registers originally preserved by the Apostolic Secretaries of Bulls issued *per viam secretam*, from the time of Sixtus IV. to that of Pius V., and the registers and minutes of Briefs from Alexander VI. to the year 1567, as well as several bound volumes forwarded from Avignon for the *Segretaria de' Brevi*.[3] He also ordered the transfer thither, from the Library of the journals of John Burchard and Paris de Grassis as well as the original Acts of the Council of Trent.[4] Not content with this he devoted his attention to yet another important category of sources. The correspondence with the nuncios, with Legates and foreign Courts, had until then been incorporated in the archives of the Roman families. To replace these the nuncios were instructed, in 1628, to forward to Rome copies of any documents of this kind in their respective archives. In 1635 a considerable number of volumes of nunciature reports was transferred from the Guardarobba to the archives.[5] Simultaneously with Contelori's nomination, another historian, Giovan Battista Confalieri, was appointed Prefect of the Archives of Castel S. Angelo, of which he drew up an accurate catalogue.[6] In addition to these the Pope established yet

[1] See details in BELTRANI, *loc. cit.*, II., 201 *seqq.*, 263 *seq.*; III., 5 *seq.* See above p. 180.

[2] See EHRLE, *Hist. Jahrbuch*, XV., 252.

[3] *Cf.* MARINI, 37; BELTRANI, II., 208; *Studi e docum.*, VIII., 13.

[4] BELTRANI, II., 208. *Cf.* SICKEL in *Sitzungsber. der Wiener Akad. Hist. Kl.*, CXXX., 121 (1895).

[5] *Cf.* MARINI, 37.

[6] BELTRANI, *loc. cit.*, 191; PALMIERI in *Spicil.*, I., 117. Confalonieri died October 29, 1648; see A. MERCATI, *Sussidi p. la consultaz. d. Arch. Vatic.*, I., Roma, 1926, 221.

another collection of Archives, namely those of the Sacred College, better known under the name of Consistorial Archives, for the purpose of preserving the Consistorial Acts and the processes in connexion with episcopal nominations.[1] In this way a place was created for the safe preservation of documents of high value for practical purposes and constituting an invaluable source for historical research.[2] As director the Pope appointed Giovan Battista Lauro with whom he had become acquainted even before his election through the latter's poetical works.[3]

Yet a fourth set of Archives owe their origin to Urban VIII., viz. the *Archivio Urbano*, destined to house the acts of notaries scattered in the latter's offices. This was a great boon for the Romans because the dispersion of these documents, which had obtained until that time, had been a source of considerable

[1] *Cf. Bull. XIII.*, 402 *seq.*, and our account Vol. I., 387 (where instead of *Arch. Rom. I.*, 189, read : *II.*, 189). Mercati, in *Sussidi*, I., 203 *seq.*, has given a useful account of the contents of the *Archivio concistoriale* which has recently been transferred to the Papal Secret Archives in the Vatican.

[2] *Fu questa erettione stimata di molta prudenza, imperciocchè per il passato le sopradette scritture così importanti conservavansi in un officio venale di notaro con poca sicurezza e minor decore. Vedonsi per memoria scolpite in un marmo queste parole :

Urbano 8º Pontifici Maximo
Quod Archivium sacri Collegii
Camerarius ejusdem
Interregni tempore in Vaticano
destinaverit
Pontifex aperuerit
S.R.Ecc^ae^ Cardinales
Grati animi monumentum posuere
1625
Jo. Baptista Laurus Perusinus
Proth. Ap^cus^ Sacr. Coll. Secretarius.

NICOLETTI, LII., p. 1628. Vat. Lib.

[3] *Cf.* LAUROS' correspondence in J. B. LAURUS, *Centuria selecta, Romae*, 1630.

inconvenience. In 1625 Cardinal Francesco Barberini became the Protector of these Archives which were founded in the teeth of the opposition of the notaries.[1]

The Roman University also received many proofs of Urban VIII.'s solicitude. Immediately after his election he took steps against the abuse of the professors giving their lectures in their own houses.[2] In 1628 he founded a chair of rhetoric which he gave to Agostino Mascardi.[3] When Andrea Argoli retired, the Pope summoned to the chair of mathematics Galileo's foremost pupil, the celebrated Benedictine Benedetto Castelli.[4] Pompeo Caimo, a man distinguished not only as a physician but as a classical scholar, was created a Count before he left for Venice.[5] The Carmelite Paganino Gaudenzi was appointed professor of Greek and the Maronite Abraham Ecchellense taught Arabic and Chaldean.[6] Urban VIII. was anxious to secure for the College of Propaganda the services of Antonio Giggeo, of the Ambrosiana at Milan and editor of the best Arabic dictionary. Giggeo was about to obey the Pope's summons when he was carried off by death.[7] In 1637 the Pope filled once more, for the benefit of his physician Taddeo Collicula, the vacant chair of practical medicine.[8] Among the Protectors of the University he

[1] See the **Avvisi* of July 30 and October 4, 1625, Vat. Lib.; *Bull.*, XIII., 387; *NICOLETTI, *loc. cit.* *Cf. Gli archivi ital.*, VI. (1919), 237.

[2] See **Avvisi* of November 1 and 18, 1623, Urb. 1093, Vat. Lib.

[3] See RENAZZI, III., 97; *Bull.*, XIII, 657 *seq.* For Mascardi, whose book *Le Pompe del Campidoglio per la Stà di N.S.P. Urbano VIII., quando pigliò il possesso*, appeared in 1624 in Rome; see TIRABOSCHI, VIII., 275, and MANUCCI in *Atti Ligure*, XLII., 135 *seq.*, 157 *seq.*, separately, Genova, 1908.

[4] See RENAZZI, III., 87. [5] *Ibid.*, 93. [6] *Ibid.*, 98.

[7] TIRABOSCHI, VIII., 278.

[8] See *Bull.*, XIV., 599; RENAZZI, III., 95, 246 *seq.* From Carlo Cartari's *report, dated February 1, 1658, to Alexander VII., which is based on the *Ruoli*, in the archives of the Roman University, the number of professors appears to have been as

included his nephews, Cardinals Francesco and Antonio. The meetings of the Protectors were occasionally held in presence of His Holiness.[1]

The construction of the University buildings was continued. In 1632 Francesco Borromini was appointed architect.[2] He gave to the University church of St. Yvo the shape of a bee, as a compliment to Urban VIII.[3] The Pope's arms, with an inscription, were likewise affixed to the outer walls of the University. The Barberini bees frequently meet the eyes of the traveller, for the patronage which the highly cultivated Pope bestowed on the arts was even more brilliant than that extended by him to letters.[4]

(2)

With the pontificate of Urban VIII. the efflorescence of Roman baroque reached its climax. The Pope's commissions for monumental works furthered the complete triumph of this tendency and for a period of close on a century assured its almost exclusive prevalence.[5] Just as in Michelangelo

follows: in 1623, 31; in 1625, 31; in 1626, 30; in 1628, 28; in 1629, 1630 and 1631, 33; in 1636, 32; in 1637 and 1639, 36; in 1640, 36; *Cod.* H., III., 62, of Chigi Library, Rome.

[1] RENAZZI, III., 71.

[2] See the Brief of September 25, 1632, in RENAZZI, III., 236; HEMPEL, *Borromini*, 59 *seq.*; GUIDI, *Borromini*, 46.

[3] RATTI, *Notizie d. chiesa interna dell'Archiginnasio Romano*, Roma, 1833, 19 *seq.* On the reconstruction, *cf.* POLLAK-FREY, 159 *seq.*

[4] *Cf.* the opinion of REUMONT, III., 2, 702, and that of ISIDOR DEL LUNGO, *Dino Compagni*, I., 2, 771, and among contemporaries that of A. TAURELLI, *Heros in solio divinitatis sive de rebus gestis Urbani VIII.*, *Bononiae*, 1639.

[5] See ESCHER, *Barock*, 20. According to the **Avviso* of September 11, 1624, Urban VIII. was then thinking of abolishing the "Camerieri secreti di spada e cappa parendogli superflua questa spesa", whilst he held a congregation of the *camerali* for the purpose of paying all the artists who had worked under his predecessors, for which a sum of 100,000 scudi is said to have

Julius II. had been given a titanic genius endowed with unheard-of versatility, so in the person of Lorenzo Bernini the Barberini Pope was granted a master of the first rank for the execution of his plans. Whilst still a Cardinal, Urban had been in relation with a number of artists [1] and already then, thanks to that discernment which was his peculiar gift, he recognized Bernini as the greatest and most gifted of them all, hence, as soon as he became Pope, he admitted him into the circle of his most intimate familiars and loaded him with tokens of his goodwill. On one occasion he went so far as to visit him in his palace in the Via Mercede, an incident which was subsequently immortalized by a fresco on the walls of the palace.[2] At the first audience granted to the artist soon after his election, Urban greeted him with the significant words: "It is a piece of good luck for you, Cavaliere, to see Cardinal Maffeo Barberini Pope, but far greater is our good fortune that the lifetime of Cavaliere Bernini should fall into our pontificate." [3]

Bernini's biographer, the Florentine Filippo Baldinucci, who has preserved this remark, also relates that Urban VIII. expressed a wish that the artist, who until then had devoted himself exclusively to sculpture, should likewise apply himself to architecture and painting. He was given two magnificent commissions in this sphere: for the simple baldacchino erected over the High Altar of St. Peter's under Paul III., he was to substitute a work of monumental proportions whilst

been required (*Urb.* 1094, Vat. Lib.). On Urban VIII.'s staff of architects and their fees see O. POLLAK in *Zeitschr. f. Gesch. der. Architektur*, III. (1910), 207 *seq.*; for Bernini's fees see *Repert. f. Kunstwissensch.*, XXXII., 254 *seq.*

[1] *Cf.* O. POLLAK, *Künstlerbriefe* in suppl. to *Jahrb. der preuss. Kunstsamml.*, XXXIV. (1913).

[2] Via Mercede, No. 11. *Cf.* MUÑOZ, *La casa di Bernini e suoi dipinti*, in *L'Arte*, XIX. (1916), 111 *seq.* At present the house is the property of the *Dames de Sion*. Sir Walter Scott once stayed there. An inscription to that effect, which was affixed to the adjoining house in 1898, is therefore in the wrong place.

[3] See BALDINUCCI, edited by *Riegl*, 79.

he was also instructed to carry out the pictorial decoration of the benediction loggia of the basilica. Bernini gladly undertook to comply with the behest of his high patron and applied himself with the keenest enthusiasm to the study of two branches of art with which he had been unfamiliar until then.[1] Little remains of his pictorial work [2] and the big commission for the benediction loggia was not carried out by him; on the other hand his productiveness in the field of sculpture and architecture was all the greater. His creations in those two spheres are so important that the splendid picture of modern Rome is unthinkable without him.

Bernini's first important creation was destined for St. Peter's.

[1] *Ibid.*, 80 *seq.*

[2] Baldinucci who (p. 235) speaks of 150 pictures by Bernini, only describes two: the master's portrait by himself (to-day in the Uffizi), and the giant canvas: "The Exploits of St. Maurice" for the chapel of the Bl. Sacrament in St. Peter's (to-day in the *Galleria de' Musaici* of the Vatican) which was replaced by a mosaic: reproduction in FRASCHETTI, 232.

TITI (11) ascribes the painting to Carlo Pellegrini. This is confirmed by the accounts for 1636, 1638, 1639, 1640, which O. Pollak found in the archives of the *Fabbrica di S. Pietro*: see *Kunstchronik*, new series, XXIII. (1911/12), 597. From this Pollak argues that the attribution of other pictures, chiefly attempted by Fraschetti, rests on slender grounds. Thus to judge Bernini's activities as a painter we have only his decorative drawings, especially his illustrations for the book of Urban VIII.'s poems published in 1631 (see above, p. 410), and a moving drawing of the aged master, engraved by Spierre and reproduced in Fraschetti (420), who speaks of "the morbid mysticism" (*misticismo morboso*) of the artist. In reality the composition is a magnificent profession of faith in the expiatory virtue of Christ's saving death. Here we behold the crucified Saviour suspended above a sea of blood; above God the Father spreads His hands, Angels are on either side, to the left the Blessed Virgin is seen looking towards her Son from whose five wounds gush forth streams of saving blood by which, as we sing on Good Friday, in Venantius Fortunatus' hymn, *Crux fidelis*, "the earth and the sea, the stars and the whole universe are cleansed."

From the outset of his pontificate and imitating his predecessors, Urban VIII. devoted his constant care to the adornment of "this greatest architectural wonder of the world". It was his good fortune to be able to consecrate "the vastest and most magnificent cathedral of all time",[1] the construction of which had occupied twenty successive Popes for a period of 174 years and to which the most talented artists had given of their best. This most important event falls in the same year as that in which decisive successes over Protestantism were won in Germany. On September 20th, 1626, Urban VIII. celebrated Tilly's victory over the Danes at Lutter, on the Barenberg, with a solemn function in the Anima.[2] Shortly afterwards he fixed on November 18th for the consecration of the new basilica of St. Peter, this being the day on which, according to tradition, Pope Sylvester had consecrated the Constantinian basilica 1,300 years earlier. On November 17th the Pope set out from the Quirinal for the Vatican and in the afternoon of that day the Roman clergy preluded to the solemn function with a procession from St. Marco to St. Peter's.[3] On the morning of the 18th, the Cardinals and the ambassadors assembled in the Vatican: from there they escorted the Pope into the porch of St. Peter's where a throne had been erected. Seated on the throne, the Pope himself blessed the twelve crosses of red mosaic which were to be fixed on the walls of the basilica. At the end of the long function, during which salvoes of guns were fired from Castel Sant Angelo, the Pope said a Low Mass in the new choir of the Canons, after which he returned to the Vatican. The Romans had flocked to the basilica in their thousands not only in order to witness the solemn function, but also to gain the Indulgences which had been granted for the duration of the Octave.[4]

[1] *Cf.* TOTTI, *Roma moderna*, 7. [2] See Vol. XXVIII., p. 17.

[3] See **Diarium p. Alaleonis, Barb.* 2818, p. 305, Vat. Lib., and **Avviso di Roma* of November 18, 1626, *Urb.* 1096, *ibid.*

[4] See the detailed description in **Diarium P. Alaleonis, loc. cit.*, 306–311, the **Avviso* mentioned in the preceding note and *Gigli* in CANCELLIERI, *Mercato*, 180.

Even previous to the consecration of St. Peter's, on June 30th, 1626, at a spot designated by Bernini, that is, about ten feet from the *Confessio* and on the epistle side of the High Altar, a start had been made on the extensive excavations for the first of the four foundations required for the gigantic, cupola-shaped bronze baldacchino which it was intended to erect under Michelangelo's dome and over the tomb of the first Pope, with a view to giving adequate prominence to this all-important spot, both liturgically and spatially.[1]

Before the work was started the Pope had commissioned the Keeper of the Vatican Library, Niccolò Alemanni, to draw up a memorandum on any doubts, objections or dangers that might be urged against excavations on so memorable and sacred a spot. Alemanni dwelt particularly on the possibility of the preservation of the body of St. Peter, whose stay in Rome was denied by the Protestants, being called in question, if no traces of any other sepulchres were found in the proximity of the *Confessio*; he also drew attention to the danger of the Apostle's tomb being damaged by the excavations. After these objections had been dealt with work began on the south-east corner of the altar.[2] Both Christian and pagan sarcophagi were found almost at once. On July 11th Alemanni was taken ill and on the 14th he died. Further deaths, among them that of the Pope's private Chaplain, Franz Schinder, and finally an illness of Urban VIII.

[1] See Böhn, *Bernini*, 58, who rightly describes the *Confessio* as the spiritual centre of the vast structure.

[2] There are several accounts of the work; one by Canon Ubaldi, written in Italian, not very accurately published by Armellini in the periodical: *Il Corrispondente del clero* 1882, and a second time in his book *Chiese di Roma* [2] (1891), 697: a second one, in Latin, the beginning of which is unfortunately missing, was utilized by De Waal in the *Röm. Quartalschr.*, I., 1 *seq.* *Cf.* also D'Achille, *I sepolcri dei Romani Pontefici*, Roma, 1867, 28 *seq.* A new and careful examination of these accounts was published by Lietzmann (*Petrus und Paulus in Rom* [1915], 140 *seq.*). *Cf.* Cecchelli, 11 *seq.* On the memorandum of Alemanni, *cf.* G. Wilpert, *La tomba di S. Pietro*, Roma, 1922, 22.

himself, gave rise in Rome to the fear that all this was a punishment for their having dared to lay hands on the immediate surroundings of St. Peter's resting place. People recalled to mind a passage in a letter of St. Gregory about certain excavations near the tomb of St. Paul. Accordingly, on July 26th, the Cardinals of the Congregation of the Fabbrica di S. Pietro decided to suspend the work.[1] Such was then the state of the science of archæology that the discovery of pagan tombs in immediate proximity to the resting place of St. Peter created a great sensation. However, a memorial by the Oratorian Severano disposed of the scruples to which the discovery had given rise. These were quite unfounded because pagan sepulchres are found in close proximity not only in the Catacombs of St. Agnes, St. Callixtus and elsewhere, but in 1850 a pagan columbarium was found at St. Paul's, in close proximity to the tomb of the Apostle.[2] When the fears occasioned by several sudden deaths had likewise been allayed, Urban VIII. ordered the resumption of work on the foundations: he took, however, the most meticulous precautions so as to prevent every danger of profanation and to make sure that an accurate record was kept of the finds and for their careful preservation. Giovanni Battista Nardone, notary of the Capitol, was commissioned to keep an official record of all the finds whilst the painter Giovanni Battista Calandri was instructed to make a drawing of all the more important ones.[3]

For the purpose of laying down sure foundations for the four corner pillars of the baldacchino, as many pits were excavated, measuring 9·9 feet by 9·9 and 14 feet in

[1] See the quotation from the **Diarium* of the secretary Laurus (*Cod.* T. 3, 10, p. 105, of Bibl. Angelica, Rome), in De Waal, *loc. cit.*, 4.

[2] De Waal, *loc. cit.*, 16; Stevenson in *Nuovo Bull. crist.*, 1897, 319. *Cf.* De Rossi, *Inscript. christ.*, II., 1, 349.

[3] See the report in Armellini, 706. Calandra's drawings have unfortunately not been found so far; they may be in the hitherto inadequately explored archives of the *Fabbrica* of St. Peter's. On Calandra, *cf. Miscell. di stor. ital.*, XV., 212 *seq.*

depth. The objects found in the course of this work were substantially the same. The pits for the columns on the north side yielded but slender results, in particular no pagan remains were found, whereas in those on the south side there appeared at once, under the floor of the old basilica, traces of Christian burial places and at a still lower level, numerous pagan sarcophagi and funeral urns. Part of the ancient presbyterium was also exposed. Near one of the northern foundations large and beautiful marble sarcophagi were found which radiated from the altar like the spokes of a wheel. One of them contained two bodies wrapped in ample garments of many folds, one of which still showed the outlines of a chasuble. The sarcophagi were believed to be those of Martyrs ; accordingly Urban had the bodies carefully buried and an inscription put up. Part of the earth thus dug up was given by the Pope to the Theatines of Naples as a relic for the church which they were building in honour of St. Peter.[1] One of the pagan sarcophagi was that of a certain Flavius Agricola of Tivoli the inscription of which was at once destroyed by order of Urban VIII. because of its revoltingly cynical materialism.[2] As a matter of fact, many of the pagan sarcophagi had been made use of in the Christian era, hence it seems doubtful whether the sepulchre of St. Peter was situate in the heart of a pagan cemetery still in full use between the years 150 and 300.[3] On the other hand, one monument uncovered in one of the pits on the south side and still *in situ*, was certainly pagan. The account of the discovery describes it as a chamber with a simple decoration in stucco and a recess destined to receive dead bodies. Two coins were likewise found on the spot, one buried in ashes and dating from the period of Maximianus [286–305], the other in the mouth of a skull

[1] See the report in ARMELLINI, 713, 717.

[2] See *Cassiano del Pozzo* in *Miscell. di stor. ital.*, XV. (1874), 175 *seq.* ; *Corpus inscript. lat.*, VI., 17975 a 34112.

[3] This is used by CHR. HÜLSEN in the *Neue Jahrb. f. Altertumskunde*, 1918, Part 1, XLI., 285, against *Lietzmann* when he points to similar agglomerations of graves under the floor of ancient Roman churches, as in S. Maria Antiqua.

and identified as a coin of Salonina, wife of the Emperor Galienus.[1]

More important than these finds, though this was not realized at the time, was the fact that the excavations confirmed one of the chief proofs of the existence of the tomb of St. Peter on the site of the *Confessio*, so that the result was the very opposite of what had been feared at first. As already pointed out by Petrus Sabinus at the end of the sixteenth century, St. Peter's tomb beneath the crypt of the old basilica is not in the centre of the apse but further north.[2] This absence of symmetry points to the very important fact of the existence of the grave previous to the erection of the Constantinian basilica, for otherwise the architects would have placed it in the axis of the apse and of the whole building.[3]

Extraordinary difficulty was experienced in procuring the necessary bronze for the baldacchino, the original plan of which underwent some further alterations.[4] The metal secured at great cost from Venice and Leghorn proved insufficient.[5] The existing political situation compelled Urban VIII. to increase his armaments[6]: accordingly, in the autumn of 1625, and on the advice of Bernini, he ordered the removal of the bronze girders of the porch of the Pantheon. So great was the yield of metal that eighty guns were made for the Castle of S. Angelo, whilst another portion was set apart for the baldacchino of St. Peter's.[7] This use of the only untouched

[1] See HÜLSEN, *loc. cit.*, in whose opinion these sepulchral chambers on the sides of the excavations may also have been by the side of the ancient street which passed Nero's race-course.

[2] See DE ROSSI, *Inscript. christ.*, II., 1, 231.

[3] See LIETZMANN, 153 *seq.*, and HÜLSEN in *Neues Fahrb. für Altertumskunde*, 1918, 1 *Abt.*, XLI., 285.

[4] In the first sketch the baldacchino is supported by four colossal angels (see BONANNI, Numismata templi. Vat. tav. 50; FRASCHETTI, 56), the second closely approximates to the plan actually executed; see GURLITT, 349.

[5] See BOSSI, 34 *seq.*; FRASCHETTI, 58.

[6] See Vol. XXVIII., p. 74.

[7] See BOSSI, 40 *seq.*, 46 *seq.*, 53; FRASCHETTI, 58 *seq.*; POLLAK-FREY, 173 *seq.*

monument of antiquity filled the Romans with bitter grief.[1] The enthusiasts for antiquity expressed their disapproval in sharp terms, among them being the Pope's personal medical attendant, Giulio Mancini, who coined the epigram : *Quod non fecerunt Barbari, fecerunt Barberini.*[2] However, the oft-quoted witticism is quite unfair for no work of art was melted down, but only girders which were not even visible, hence no one could justly complain that the monument had been damaged.[3] So little was Urban VIII. conscious of any wrong that in an inscription set up by him in the Pantheon, he boasts " of having made use of a useless ornament for the decoration of St. Peter's and the defence of Rome ".[4] Domenico Bernini, too, praises his father for having advised the Pope as he did.[5] The bronze of the seven ribs of the cupola of St. Peter's was removed in like manner and replaced with lead.

Gregorio de Rossi,[6] a Roman, superintended the casting of the four gigantic columns of the baldacchino, a process which

[1] See GIGLI in CANCELLIERI, *Mercato,* 180.

[2] See above p. 363, BOSSI (57 *seq.*), on the basis of the **Giornale di Urbano VIII.* in *Urb.* 1647, attributes the epigram to the *Agente del Duca di Mantova,* Carlo Castelli (died December 4, 1639) ; but much more authentic than this late evidence is the contemporary one of the **Avviso di Roma* of September 20, 1625 [see above, p. 361, n. 1], which has escaped all students up till now. According to this evidence Castelli did no more than spread the epigram.

[3] Opinion of BÖHN (*Bernini,* 88).

[4] See BOSSI, 51.

[5] See *Vita di G. L. Bernini, Roma,* 1713. *Cf.* BOSSI, 104 ; FRASCHETTI, 64. In his edition of Baldinucci's *Vita di Bernini* (p. 87), RIEGL makes the following comment on Fraschetti's accusation of the latter's want of regard for antiquity : " This was a healthy period which knew no sentimentality ; the bronze girders were of no artistic value ; to spare them simply because they were ' antique ', the age was too sure of itself and too free from all sickly sentimentality." JARO SPRINGER says : " The removal of the bronze girders cannot be described as the ruthless destruction of a work of art." (*Jahrb. der preuss. Kunstsamml.,* XII., 122 *seq.*)

[6] See BAGLIONE, *Nove chiese,* 38. *Cf.* PASSERI, 263.

Bernini was all the better able to watch as Urban VIII. had already in 1623 appointed him master of the papal foundry.[1] The work was completed in 1626, when the Pope inspected the columns and ordered them to be gilded. Each column, together with its base and capital, weighed 27,948 pounds and the total weight of the baldacchino amounted to 186,392 pounds.[2] The work of the erection of the columns began in September, 1626,[3] and on St. Peter's Day, 1627, they were unveiled.[4] Bernini submitted a small model of the roof and when the *Fabbrica* di S. Pietro had approved it, he bound himself, on April 14th, 1628, to execute that part within the space of three years and four months. However, the time limit proved inadequate. On August 11th, 1631, an extension was granted which was again exceeded, so much so that in December, 1632, the Pope pressed for the termination of the work.[5]

At last, in the summer of 1633, Urban VIII.'s wishes were fulfilled; the gigantic work was unveiled on the feast of St. Peter. The cost amounted to the large sum of 200,000 scudi.[6]

Bernini was lavishly rewarded. His monthly salary, which had been 100 scudi at first, had already been doubled in 1627. On February 5th, 1629, after the death, on January 30th, of Maderna who had retained the post of Court and State

[1] Bernini kept this post to the end of Urban VIII.'s pontificate. In 1623 he was likewise given that of *Revisore delle Fontane di Piazza Navona* and that of *Sopraintendente dell'Acqua Felice*; see FRASCHETTI, 41.

[2] See FRASCHETTI, 61; BOSSI, 79.

[3] See Avviso of September 26, 1626, in FRASCHETTI, 61, n. 7.

[4] *The Avviso of June 30, 1627 (*Urb.* 1097, Vat. Lib.), says: "Yesterday feast at St. Peter's: scoperte le 4 grosse et bellissime colonne di bronzo indorato a similitudine di quelle che stavano nel tempio di Salomone, alcune delle quali si vedono di marmo in Basilica Vatic., et vi si deve porre la cuppola con altri ornamenti pur di bronzo attorno l'altare delli SS. Apostoli.

[5] See FRASCHETTI, 62. The **Avviso* of April 8, 1628, mentions an accident: three workmen fell "accomodando la cupola sopra le 4 grosse colonne di bronzo" near the altar of St. Peter's. *Urb.* 1098, Vat. Lib.

[6] See BOSSI, 82; FRASCHETTI, *loc. cit.*

architect, Bernini was also appointed architect of the *Fabbrica* of St. Peter's ; in this way his was a paramount position in the artistic sphere. On the completion of the work he received a further gift of 10,000 scudi, his brother Vincenzo was given a canonry at the Lateran, his son obtained a benefice at St. Peter's and his brother Luigi became head of the *Fabbrica*.[1]

No one protested against the Pope's liberality. The contemporaries were unanimous in their praise of the gigantic baldacchino as a magnificent enrichment of the basilica. A spate of epigrams, sonnets and poems in praise of the master and his patron ensued.[2] Everyone felt that this work, inspired by Urban VIII.'s piety, would vie with the noblest creations of antiquity and that it was one of the most wonderful products of the whole century.[3] The new type of altar (altare alla Romana) was soon reproduced beyond the Alps.[4] So favourable a judgment on this work of genius has long held

[1] See Bossi, 85 *seq.* ; Fraschetti, 63 *seq.* *Cf.* Hempel, *Borromini*, 11. The payments to Bernini as well as all decisions on building plans have been extracted from the Archives of the *Fabbrica* of St. Peter's by O. Pollak ; Dr. Frey is to publish them in the second volume of his work on Urban VIII.'s artistic activities. On Bernini's sketch for the baldacchino of St. Peter's of 1624 or 1638, see Egger, *Architekt, Handzeichnungen Taf.*, 24.

[2] See Bossi, 83 *seq.*

[3] *" È veramente la magnificenza di quest'opera, si come viene giudicata, non inferiore a quelle antiche suntuose de' Romani, così ha fatto meravigliosamente crescere la maestà della basilica Vaticana. . . . La vaghezza, l'ordine e la proportione sono inestimabili, imperciochè per esser macchina così vasta, non impedisce punto il prospetto del tempio, et ella si vede da ogni lato tutta nobile e tutta piena di maestà e di magnificenza, che riempiendo gli occhi di stupore, viene da tutti stimata fra le cose più meravigliose di questo secolo, e che rende tanto più venerabile il sepolcro de' Santi Apostoli e la memoria della pietà di Urbano " (Nicoletti, II., 829, 831, Vat. Lib.). *Cf.* also Totti, 11.

[4] On reproductions of the domed baldacchino see Muñoz in *Vita d'arte*, 1911, 33 *seq.* ; on the most famous of them, due to Bernini himself, in the church of Val de Grâce in Paris, *cf.* M. Reymond in *Gaz. des Beaux-Arts*, 1911, 367 *seq.*

the field. As late as 1739 De Brosses gave it as his opinion that the bronze baldacchino over the High Altar of St. Peter's was the finest work of its kind in the whole world.[1] However, the neo-classic period completely reversed this judgment; no longer was the work looked upon as an artistic triumph, on the contrary, it was belittled and vilified as one of the worst degeneracies [2]; only the most recent art criticism has once more done justice to it.[3] In the first instance, later critics have rightly stressed the difficulty of the undertaking. In view of the enormous proportions, the erection beneath Michelangelo's dome, of an altar which would not break the harmony of the lines, whilst it drew the eye of the visitor as soon as he entered, to what is the true centre of the building, and that without entirely hiding the choir, was a task that might well have baffled an artist of the first rank. Yet notwithstanding the fact that he was but 26 years old and though until then he had not tried his skill as an architect, Bernini applied himself to his task with wonderful courage. His solution of the problem is probably the only possible one.[4] His fundamental conception alone seems an exceedingly

[1] De Brosses, *Lettres familières écrites d'Italie*, letter, XXXIX. (Paris, 1858), Vol. II., p. 6.

[2] See Fr. Milizia, *Memorie degli architetti*, II., 160. Burckhardt (*Cicerone*, 228), still speaks of "the definitely restricting effect of the dreadful baldacchino" and judges that "with his bronze baldacchino Bernini had the temerity to assert the theory that an altar is a piece of architecture of which all the elements have got into motion. His twisted, flower-adorned columns, his soaring baldacchino with its four corner volutes have done more mischief than Borromini's façades". The most recent unfavourable criticism is that of Brinckmann (231).

[3] See especially Muñoz, *Roma barocca*, 133 *seq.*, on whose excellent account our own is based. *Cf.* also Gurlitt, *Barockstil*, 348 *seq.*; Riegl in his editon of Baldinucci, 90; Reymond, 35 *seq.*; Benkard, 11 *seq.*; Sobotka, *Bildhauer*, 32.

[4] Bergner (*Barockes Rom*, 49) justly remarks that those who are dissatisfied with the work should ask themselves how it could have been done better. *Cf.* also Braun, *Der christl. Altar*, II., 439, who points out that a Ciborium in harmony with

happy one. In place of the customary ciborium of the Middle Ages and the Renaissance, he conceived a new type in the shape of a baldacchino resting on four columns which allowed a view of the terminal apse of the choir and, so far from diminishing the impression of length produced by the basilica, enhanced it still further. Its proportions, too, are in complete harmony with those of the huge church.[1] Thus there rose up beneath Michelangelo's dome an epoch-making baroque creation, a marvel in which imposing magnitude is allied to delicacy in the execution of every detail.[2]

The domed ciborium measures 77½ feet to the top of the cross. Its four gigantic bronze columns rise on four marble bases adorned with the arms of Urban VIII.[3] In order to

the colossal proportions of the dome was as impracticable as a baldacchino suspended from the roof of the cupola. For the justification of Bernini see also the remarks of BÖHN, 58 *seq.*; NEUMANN in *Repert. f. Kunstwiss.*, XXXVIII., 21 *seq.*; KUYPERS, *Rom*, Leipzig, 1927, 479, 484; DVORAK, *Gesch. der ital. Kunst*, II., Munich, 1928, 209.

[1] How colossal the dimensions of the baldacchino really are may be gathered from the drawing in DURM, *Baukunst der Renaissance* [2], 889, where it is set side by side with the Palazzo Farnese.

[2] *Cf.* TH. HOFFMANN, *Entstehungsgesch. des St. Peter in Rom*, Berlin, 1928, 274 *seq.*, 277.

[3] "Ogni stemma [see photo. Alinari, 26419], says BOSSI (81, n. 1), è sormontato da un viso di donna di cui lo scudo con le tre api costituisce il corpo, e quella intera figura muliebre sembra sia stata rappresentata nelle varie fasi della gestazione," a statement which CURATOLO (*L'arte di Juno Lucina in Roma*, Roma, 1901, 141 *seq.*), endeavours to substantiate. Female bodies, such as those here represented by Bernini, are nothing unusual in the art of the period; *cf.* FREY, *Barockarchitektur*, 99. The legend, inspired by the expression of the female heads, is first found, as far as I know, in J. C. HARE, *Walks in Rome*, 579, publ. in 1876. The utter unlikeliness of such unseemly allusions being tolerated and the strict watchfulness exercised in this respect, appears from a memorandum in *Barb.* 1196, p. 112. *"Occasione statuarum ex marmore albo repraesentantium angelos nudos imagines Pontificum in sacellis basilicae

recall to mind the venerable columns of the High Altar of old St. Peter's, the shafts are twisted and divided into three sections, the two upper ones being entwined with laurel

Vaticanae sustinentium, in quibus verenda conspiciuntur, quidam dubitavit, . . . an debeant permitti. . . . Porro si in picturis omnis lascivia vitari debeat, quanto magis quicquid ad libidinem provocat ? ut merito hic exclamat Ambrosius Catharinus : quod vero omnium est teterrimum hac tempestate in excelsis templis sacellisque offendas picturis tantae lasciviae ut quicquid natura occuluit turpe nostrum, ibi liceat contemplari ad excitamdam non devotionem sed cuiusvis demortuae carnis libidinem. Quasi, inquit Olaus, historicus septemptrionalis, interior caro non sufficeret sibi in deiiciendo homine in mille tentationes, fragilitate tandem sua collapsuro, nisi et externae augerentur provocationes. Notum est pictores saepe infantem Iesum nudum sculpere aut pingere, sed ob hoc male audiunt a multis non exiguae pietatis et prudentiae viris. Quid enim in hac nuditate esse poterit aedificationis ? Atque utinam nulla hinc oriretur in parvulis destructio, nullum in pusillis scandalum. Viderint ergo pictores, ne suo malo discant, quid sit, quod Dominus ait : Qui scandalizaverit unum de pusillis istis, qui in me credunt, expedit ei ut suspendatur mola asinaria in collo eius et demergatur in profundum maris. Vae homini illi, per quem scandalum venit. Certe si antiquas picturas consulere velint, facile advertent in eis puerum Iesum decenter et honeste depictum esse ac sese multum a maiorum simplicitate degenerasse. His adde quod Guilelmus Durandus Mimatensis episcopus scribit de quibusdam grecanicis [sic] ecclesiis in Rationali divinorum officiorum : Greci, ait, utuntur imaginibus, pingentes illas, ut dicitur, solum ab umbilico supra et non inferius, ut omnis stultae cogitationis occasio tollatur. Prohibet deputatio Tridentinae synodi omnes libros, qui res lascivas seu obscenas ex professo tractant, narrant aut docent, cum non solum fidei, sed et morum, qui eiusmodi librorum lectione facile corrumpi solent, ratio habenda sit ; quanto ergo magis prohibendae sunt huiusmodi picturae non tantum in sacris imaginibus, sed etiam in prophanis. . . ." With regard to Urban VIII.'s attitude in particular, the new statutes for the Academy of St. Luke approved by him on October 1, 1627, lay down that " che nelle opere sacre si osservasse il decreto del concilio di Trento nè si dipingesse cosa che contenesse falsi dogmi o ripugnasse alla s. Scrittura o

wreaths and enlivened with *putti* and the Barberini bees. From the Ionic-Corinthian capitals of the columns, which are joined together by a cornice, the baldacchino rises in the shape of a light cupola the summit of which is crowned with a globe surmounted by a cross whilst a dove, the emblem of the Holy Ghost, hovers in the space within. Four gigantic angels holding garlands of laurels in their hands, stand on the capitals of the columns. In the space between, both in front and behind, the cornice is surmounted by two smaller angels which, in reality, exceed the average height of a man: they hold the tiara and Peter's keys. To them correspond two angels in each of the lateral interstices, holding the emblems of the Apostle of the Gentiles, viz. a sword and a book symbolizing his epistles. At the base, close to the Confessio—on a spot where the soft light of three great lamps burning day and night drew the attention of the pilgrim to the principal shrine of the basilica as soon as he entered,[1] Urban VIII. had put up a form of prayer to the Princes of the Apostles to which he attached precious Indulgences. The formula consists partly of texts of St. Augustine and in part it is the Pope's own composition.[2]

The baldacchino is, in a sense, completed by the decoration of the flat surface of the enormous pillars of the dome. Bernini suggested that the upper niches should be provided with

alle tradizioni della Chiesa, e si fugisse ogni invenzione brutta ed oscena" (see MISSIRINI, 92). That the curious decorations on the marble pedestals were not intended from the first appears from the sketch in *Barb.* 4409 (*Prospetti e piante di tutti gl' edifici eretti si dentro come fuori di Roma dalla f. m. di Urbano VIII. dissegnati da Dom. Castelli*), p. 6.

[1] The reproduction in TOTTI (10) shows that originally there were only three lamps, one of them in silver worth 2,000 scudi and given by the magistrates of Rome in March, 1632; see GIGLI in CANCELLIERI, *Mercato*, 180.

[2] Hence the name *Orazioni Urbane*; see NICOLETTI, II., 382, Vat. Lib. On the Indulgences attached to St. Peter's by Urban VIII., see *Bull. Vatic.*, III., 238 *seq.*, 240 *seq.*, 242 *seq.*; MIGNANTI, II., 100; on money assigned to the *Fabbrica*, see *Bull.*, XIV., 199 *seq.*, 483 *seq.*, 601 *seq.*

loggias from which the most precious of the numerous relics of St. Peter's could be shown to the people, such as Veronica's handkerchief, the large fragment of the cross found by St. Helen, the lance of Longinus and the head of St. Andrew. Larger but empty niches at the base were to be adorned with colossal statues referring to these relics. On December 10th, 1629, the Congregation of the *Fabbrica* of St. Peter's approved the project and entrusted the execution of the statue of Longinus to Bernini, that of St. Helen to Andrea Bolgi, that of St. Veronica to Francesco Mocchi and that of St. Andrew to François Duquesnoy. The latter, a Fleming, was the first to complete his task. When his model had been put up in its niche, the work was greatly admired and the other sculptors were urged to make haste with their task.[1] For all that there was a delay of several years.[2] A crack in the dome gave rise to the rumour that the marvellous structure was about to crash to the ground. The extraordinary favour which Bernini enjoyed with Urban VIII. drew on him the envy of his many enemies. The latter spread a rumour that Bernini was responsible for the crack through excessive drilling into the pillars of the dome which were no longer equal to the weight they had to carry. Injurious pamphlets described

[1] See PASSERI, 81 *seq.*; FRASCHETTI, 69 *seq.* On A. Bolgi fresh information has been published by L. MUSSI in the *Corriere d'Italia* of December 31, 1924. FRASCHETTI (74), gives the information that the sum of 6,000 scudi was paid for each statue. TOTTI, in his *Roma Moderna*, of 1630, mentions on page 530 of the appendix the transposition of the statues of S. Longinus and St. Andrew; critique of the statues in RIEGL, 94 *seq.*, 108 *seq.*; BRINKMANN, *Barockskulptur*, 233 *seq.*, 259, 265 *seq.*; L. DAMI in *Dedalo*, 1924–5, 130; A. PETRONELLI, *Fr. Mocchi*, Piacenza, 1926, 14 *seq.*; CECCHELLI, 26; BÖHN, 18, 62; BENKARD, 11 *seq.*; KNAPP, *Ital. Plastik* (1925), 127 *seq.*

[2] According to the *Diario* quoted by FRASCHETTI (74, n. 2), the last statue, that of Veronica, was only unveiled on November 11, 1640. According to the **Avviso* of November 10, 1640 (*Avvisi*, 90, in Papal Secret Archives), Urban VIII. inspected the statue at once, " opera del Fr. Mocchi scultore Fiorentino, stimata di tutta eccellenza dalli periti dell'arte."

the danger to the dome in such lurid colours that the whole city became greatly alarmed. Ferrante Carli, a deadly enemy of Bernini, is said to have been the author of these rumours. The master remained perfectly calm before the storm; he even wrote a comedy in which he made fun of the rumours then circulating. But when, in the course of the carnival, a fresh attack was preparing against him, he appealed to Cardinal Barberini who took up his cause. Moreover when it was seen that the crack had no further consequences, Bernini was soon again completely master of the situation.[1]

In April, 1638, the loggias were completed and in July the relics were deposited there.[2] The lower niches, which were destined to receive the giant statues, were faced with alabaster and the turn of their arches adorned with the arms of Urban VIII., with appropriate inscriptions.[3] From these niches a staircase leads down to the chapels of the pilasters of the dome which were redecorated by the Pope.[4] These semi-circular chapels correspond to the upper niches; another

[1] See the reports on the envoy of Este of 1636, 1637, and 1638, in FRASCHETTI, 70 *seq.*, and the *Avviso* of January 24, 1637, in FREY, *Barockarchitektur*, 7. On Bernini as *comediografo*, *cf.* *Fanfulla d. Domenica*, 1890, n. 19; as a *caricaturista* Bernini is discussed in *L'Arte*, IX. (1906), 205.

[2] See FRASCHETTI, 72 *seq.*

[3] MIGNANTI, II., 95; FORCELLA, VI., 148; MUÑOZ, *S. Pietro*, *tav.*, 18. The coat of arms beneath the balustrade of the loggia of St. Andrew is by Bernini, according to an order for payment; *cf.* MUÑOZ in *Rassegna d'arte*, 1919, 108. *Cf.* HEMPEL, 13.

[4] *" Fabbricò parimente quattro capelle nella parte inferiore sotteranea dei medesimi pilastroni; chiamata le Grotte, e vi fondò otto capellanie chiamate Barberine, facendole Jus patronati di casa Barberina, e dotandole di buone entrate per la celebratione delle messe quotidiane e pel mantenimento delle suppellettili sacre, alle quale cappellanie gli heredi aggiunsero poi la nona." (NICOLETTI, II., 837. Vat. Lib.; BAGLIONE, 179.) Borromini worked in these chapels, together with Agostino Radio; HEMPEL, 12, table 3. The altar pictures which glorify the four chief relics are by A. Sacchi (see PASSERI, 318 *seq.*; POSSE, *Sacchi*, 55 *seq.*; VOSS, *Malerei*, 531); they are now in the palace of Castel Gandolfo.

staircase within the pillars themselves gives access to the loggias which are provided with a balustrade for the exhibition of the relics.[1] Each niche is adorned with two of the twisted columns which had formed part of the high altar of the old basilica. A gilded grating between them indicates the spot where the relics are preserved whilst sculptured emblems held by angels, and appropriate inscriptions above them, also refer to the relics: the inscriptions run as follows: "They shall call on thy face"; "He opened His side with a lance"; "Hail precious cross"; "In this sign thou shalt triumph."[2]

Urban VIII.'s love for the church which enshrines the tomb of the Prince of the Apostles was not exhausted by the two great works described above. He also took so much interest in the adornment of a number of altars and chapels that Passeri declares that it seemed as if the golden age of painting had returned.[3] In the execution of these works, which continued throughout the pontificate, Rome's first artists vied with each other in giving of their very best. First among them ranks Pietro da Cortona who, between 1628 and 1632, executed the centre piece of the altar of the Blessed Sacrament representing the Holy Trinity, as well as the cartoons for the mosaics of the dome of that chapel and those of the Cappella del Crocifisso.[4] The decoration of the chapel of the Madonna della Colonna occupied not only Andrea Sacchi, Romanelli and Giovan Battista Calandri, but likewise Giovanni Lanfranco.[5] The latter was given a further monumental

[1] Urban VIII. granted a special Indulgence for the veneration of the relics; *cf.* BARBIER, II., 469 *seq.*

[2] MIGNANTI, II., 96.

[3] PASSERI, 312.

[4] TITI, 11; THIEME, VII., 487; POSSE, *Sacchi*, 116. On the picture of St. Mauritius, see above, p. 452, n. 2. Urban VIII. had the monument of Sixtus IV. erected in the chapel of the Bl. Sacrament; see BAGLIONE, *Nove Chiese*, 22, *cf.* CASCIOLI in *Messagero* of November 12, 1926.

[5] BAGLIONE, *loc. cit.*, 33; TOTTI, 530; POSSE, *Sacchi*, 49 *seqq.*; the cartoons by Lanfranco are in the possession of the Barberini family.

commission, viz. a large altarpiece depicting St. Peter walking on the sea which was placed on the altar to the right of the main front pillar of the dome. For this work the Pope bestowed on the artist the Order of Christ.[1] Facing it and above a door, Andrea Camassei painted a fresco of the baptism of SS. Processus and Martinianus, the gaolers of St. Peter.[2] The altar in the tribune of the north transept, where the relics of these Saints repose, was adorned with two columns of porphyry and two great columns of *giallo antico*. The altarpiece was painted in 1639 by Valentin de Boulogne, a pupil of Caravaggio : it represents the martyrdom of SS. Processus and Martinianus.[3] Almost at the same time Poussin painted the " Martyrdom of St. Erasmus " for the second altar.[4] In 1630 Domenichino painted for the second altar to the right of the main entrance [5] the " Martyrdom of St. Sebastian ", " an unusual composition of powerful movement and inspiration and characterized by a dramatic tendency in the manner of high baroque." [6]

In 1626 the Pope transferred to the choir chapel, in which Michelangelo's *Pietà* then stood,[7] the relics of St. John

[1] This picture, of which only a fragment remains, was subsequently replaced by a copy in mosaic (TITI, 13 ; *cf.* POLLAK, *Künsterlerbriefe*, 25) ; it was completed in 1628 ; see **Avviso* of September 20, 1628, which says that on Sunday the *Vicegerente* of St. Peter's consecrated some new altars when two new paintings were unveiled, viz. " Peter's denial " by Guidotti of Lucca and the picture by Lanfranco. *Urb.* 1098. Vat. Lib.

[2] TITI, 13.

[3] Now in the Vatican Gallery, *cf.* BAGLIONE, 337 ; VOSS, *Malerei*, 105, 455. According to the **Abozzi di Fr. Ubaldini* Urban also gave commissions to Caravaggio. *Barb.* 4901, p. 13. Vat. Lib.

[4] Now also in the Vatican Gallery, *cf.* FRIEDLÄNDER, *Poussin*, 34 *seq.*

[5] PASSERI, 30.

[6] VOSS, *Malerei*, 511. The picture, later on replaced by a mosaic, now adorns S. Maria degli Angeli.

[7] BAGLIONE, *Nove chiese*, 23. On the choir chapel, *cf.* LETAROUILLY, *St. Pierre*, I., 40–1.

Chrysostom.[1] The Doctor of the Church is seen in the act of worshipping the cross together with St. Francis and St. Anthony, in the colossal altar picture by Simon Vouet of Paris.[2] Guidotti of Lucca was commissioned to paint Peter's denial [3] and Domenico Passignano the Presentation of Mary in the temple.[4]

Without a doubt the most important of the new altar pictures destined for St. Peter's was that executed in 1625 by Andrea Sacchi for the Cappella Clementina in which repose the bones of St. Gregory the Great. It represents a miracle related by Paul the Deacon: A man had begged for a relic from the treasury of the Church. He was given a linen cloth with which the chalice is purified at Mass. The man seemed to doubt the value of the gift but Gregory convinced him of its worth for when he pierced the cloth with a dagger, blood issued from it.[5] The incident is represented with dramatic force: " In no contemporary painting do we see the immediate effect of a miracle represented with more forceful concentration and greater psychological penetration and in a clearer gradation of the emotions: astonishment in all its degrees up to speechless, frightened recoil on the part of the spectators, in contrast with the calm assurance and dignity of the wonder-worker himself and the self-possessed

[1] **Diarium P. Alaleonis* on May 1, 1626: " Corpus S. Joh. Chrysostomi de mandato Papae remotum de altare ss. reliquiarum sub altare chori novi S. Petri processionaliter intus capsam plumbeam et cipressam: adfuerunt alumni collegii Graecorum " (*Barb.* 2818, p. 282. Vat. Lib.). *Cf.* *Nicoletti, II., 838 *seq.*, *ibid.*; FORCELLA, VI., 149.

[2] TITI, 18; VOSS, *Malerei*, 478.

[3] On Guidotti, see **Avviso* of 1628, above, p. 473, n. 1.

[4] Passignano's picture perished (*cf.* POLLAK, *Künstenbriefe*, 32), and was replaced by another by G. Fr. Romanelli, now in S. Maria degli Angeli (a mosaic copy is in St. Peter's); see BAGLIONE, 323; VOSS, *Malerei*, 267, 549. Voss is mistaken when he says that Possignano's picture dates from 1639–1642, for the **Avviso* of December 22, 1627, speaks of its having been unveiled (*Urb.* 1097. Vat. Lib.).

[5] PASSERI, 312; PISTOLESI, *Vaticano*, I., 220.

attitude (which serves as a gauge for all the tense and excited emotions) of the youthful acolyte in the centre who, kneeling as he is behind the Pope, seems unaware of the sensational occurrence. The figure of the deacon seen from behind, on the right-hand side, with its striking expression of intense surprise, constitutes, by its *bravura* of pictorial treatment, one of the best creations of contemporary Roman art." [1]

Urban VIII. cherished a special predilection for the Archangel Michael [2] who, as a matter of fact, in his capacity as the destroyer of heresy, was a frequent subject for the art of the period of the restoration.[3]

In addition to Sacchi, Romanelli and Pellegrini were also employed on the decoration of the chapel of the Archangel.[4] Cesare d'Arpino was entrusted with the altarpiece—" The Fall of Lucifer," which was executed in mosaic, after his cartoons, by Giovanni Battista Calandra (d. 1644). This work failed to win universal approval so that the Pope gave up the idea of replacing the other paintings in the basilica by mosaics.[5]

To Giotto's *Navicella* Urban VIII. assigned a better position over the main entrance of St. Peter's.[6] The first chapel of the left transept, where St. Peter's chair stood, was set apart as a baptistry. Gregorio Celio decorated its ceiling.[7] Towards

[1] Opinion of Posse, *Sacchi*, 24. *Ibid.*, table 10; a copy of the picture is now in the Vatican Gallery.

[2] See *Nicoletti, II., 389, Vat. Lib.

[3] See below, p. 488, G. Reni's picture. St. Michael is also seen on the façade of St. Michael's church at Munich and, subsequently, on the tomb of St. Ignatius.

[4] See Baglione, *Nove chiese*, 31; Posse, *Sacchi*, 52 *seq.*

[5] Passeri, 167 *seq.*; Baglione, 372; Mignanti, II., 99; Thieme, V., 372.

[6] Fraschetti, 83. *Cf.* **Avviso* of July 25, 1629, *Urb.* 1099, Vat. Lib., and Cascioli, *La Navicella di Giotto*, Roma, 1916, 17 *seq.*

[7] Titi, 20. The **Avviso* of May 8, 1624, says: On Sunday the Pope, accompanied by the Archpriest, Cardinal Borghese, who was convalescent, the Cardinal Vicar Millini, and Cardinal

the end of the pontificate, and as a supreme token of his favour, Urban VIII. gave a significant commission to Bernini: this was the execution of a bas-relief representing the institution of the primacy and destined to be placed over the atrium of St. Peter's. Urban did not live to see the work completed for it was only finished in 1656. The work is perhaps "the most picturesque and realistic relief ever produced previous to modern times".[1]

St. Peter's, which thus increasingly became the real centre of artistic activity in Rome, also owes to Urban VIII. the jubilee door,[2] the pictures in mosaic of the Princes of the Apostles on the lateral walls of the niche in which the palliums are deposited over the tomb of the Apostle,[3] artistic gratings for the choir and the chapel of the Blessed Sacrament,[4] new choir stalls,[5] a portable organ,[6] a magnificent reliquary for the particles of the true cross [7] and, lastly, two magnificent sepulchral monuments.

By reason of the importance which the Barberini Pope

Barberini, carried out the visitation of St. Peter's when he ordered that "che si trasporti il fonte di battesimo nella prima cappella a mano sinistra dell'entrar nella chiesa. *Urb.* 1094, *loc. cit.*

[1] See Baldinucci, edited by Riegl, 103–6. *Cf.* Benkard, 20; Cecchelli, 23.

[2] Forcella, VI., 149; Hempel, *Borromini*, table 2.

[3] Executed by Giov. Batt. Calandra; *cf.* Passeri, 166 *seq.*

[4] Hempel, 13.

[5] Mignanti, II., 89.

[6] According to *a payment of 1636 (communicated by the late Dr. O. Pollak to whom I am greatly indebted for other information).

[7] *April 10, 1629: "Papa donavit crucem argenteam cum ligno crucis basilicae S. Petri (Diarium P. Alaleonis, *Barb.* 2818, p. 443b, Vat. Lib., and *Diarium of Laurus in *Cod.* T. 3, 10, of the Angelica Lib. in Rome). The *inscription on the reliquary is as follows: "Urbanus VIII. suae in sanctissimam crucem pietatis et benevolae in sacrosanctam basilicam voluntatis monimentum extare voluit" (**Nicoletti*, II., 834, Vat. Lib.; *cf.* Barbier, II., 465 *seq.*). In 1634 Urban bestowed the Golden Rose on the basilica (**Nicoletti*, II., 481).

attached to the States of the Church,[1] he held in special reverence Countess Matilda of Tuscany who, by the donation of all her possessions, had assured the Holy See's material security. Whilst still a Cardinal, Urban had written a poem in her honour,[2] as Pope he was anxious to see her mortal remains laid to rest in a worthy monument. From the Abbey of S. Benedetto near Mantua the Countess' body was transferred to Rome where it was at first placed in the Castle of S. Angelo, following its identification by Cardinal Barberini. On March 10th, 1634, it was translated to St. Peter's where her monument was to be erected near a pillar of the right lateral nave, facing the chapel of the Blessed Sacrament.[3] Bernini furnished the plan, but he himself only executed the idealized head of the Countess; all the rest he entrusted to his brother Luigi and to his pupils.[4]

The noble statue of the Countess stands in a niche adorned with her arms and motto: *Tuetur et unit*; the beautiful, youthful figure, expressive of courage and energy, holds a sceptre in the right hand and in the left the tiara and the keys of Peter. The marble relief on the sarcophagus below represents the incident of Canossa. The inscription above it, which is held by two *putti*, was composed by Cardinal Francesco Barberini. It states that in 1635 Urban VIII., urged by a sense of gratitude, had erected this sepulchre for the remains of Countess Matilda when they were removed from the Abbey of S. Benedetto, a well-deserved monument to a champion of the Apostolic See, a woman of virile spirit, outstanding piety and well-known liberality.[5] The effect of the monument,

[1] See above, p. 360. [2] Above, p. 417.

[3] TOSTI, *La Contessa Matilde*, Roma, 1886, 387 *seq.* *Cf.* the special number of *Voce della Verità* on the occasion of the centenary of St. Gregory VII., and INTRA, *Il cenobio S. Benedetto Po*, Mantova, 1897, 16 *seq.*; *cf.* also the *Avviso* in GREGOROVIUS, *Urban VIII.*, 160; *Arch. Stor. Lomb.*, 1897, 312; *Epigrafi relativi al trasporto del corpo d. contessa Matilde nel 1634, in *Regin.* 2018, p. 225 *seq.*, Vat. Lib.

[4] *Cf.* RIEGL, *Baldinucci*, 106 *seq.*; FRASCHETTI, 98.

[5] FORCELLA, VI., 153.

which is characterized by great simplicity and balance, is due to the nobility of its conception.[1] It was only completed in 1637: on March 13th of that year the Pope inspected it.[2]

Long before this, towards the close of 1628, Urban VIII. had decided to have a monument erected for himself within St. Peter's.[3] For its location he selected the niche on the right of the apse; in that on the left he had put up, about the turn of the year 1628–9, the magnificent monument of Paul III. by Guglielmo della Porta.[4] Precious antique marbles from the temple of the sun on the Quirinal were used in the decoration of the two niches.[5] It goes without saying that Bernini, who had carved many busts of his patron and in 1640 the

[1] Böhn, 66. *Cf. Jahrbuch der preuss. Kunstsamml.*, XL., 253 *seq.*; Benkard, 14. A statuette of Countess Matilda after a model by Bernini is in the private possession of Princess Barberini; *cf. L'Arte*, XX. (1917), 188 *seq.*

[2] See **Avviso* of March 14, 1637 (*Urb.* 1105, Vat. Lib.): Yesterday the Pope inspected in St. Peter's " la vaga sepultura fattasi in quella basilica alle ceneri della regina [*sic!*] Matilde, stata vera propugnatrice della S. Sede ".

[3] See **Avviso* of December 27, 1628: " the Pope decided on the transfer of the ' bellissima sepoltura " of Paul III. which then stood against the pilaster of the dome where we now see the statue of St. Veronica [*cf.* data in Vol. XII., p. 453, of this work and the excellent monograph by Steinmann, *Das Grab Pauls III.*, Roma, 1912, 10 *seq.*], " nel nichio " on the left of the tribune in St. Peter's, together with his bronze statue and other ornaments [there was no room in the niche for the figures of Plenty and Peace, they were accordingly transferred to the Palazzo Farnese] because he wishes to erect his own sepulchre in the right-hand niche." *Urb.* 1098, *loc. cit.*

[4] See the *Avviso* of December 6, 1628, in Fraschetti, 155, and *that of January 17, 1629 (*Urb.* 1099, Vat. Lib.): Monday night the Chapter of St. Peter's walked in procession at the translation of the body of Paul III. (" in cassa di piombo foderata d'un altra di cipresso e d'un altra di pietra ") from the niche beneath the dome to that on the left of the tribune and facing the sepulchre which is now being prepared for the Pope.

[5] Bonanni, 92; Lanciani, *Scavi*, II., 249 *seq.*

great statue of the Pope destined for the Capitol,[1] was likewise entrusted with the execution of the monument. By 1639 the work was well forward [2] but the Barberini Pope did not live to see it completed: it was only three years after his death, at the beginning of 1647, that the monument could be unveiled in presence of his successor. Its influence was considerable: for a long time it served as a model for every monumental sepulchre destined to create a strong effect and to dominate a large space.[3] Every artist endeavoured to profit by this new type, the fruit of the genius of high baroque. Only certain particular elements resemble those of the *Cinquecento*: on the one hand, the portrait statue of the dead man, on the other allegorical statues typifying his virtues; the composition differs, account having been taken of the monument that faces it, namely that of Paul III.[4]

Bernini set the monument in a deep, shadowy niche adorned with a gigantic coat of arms of the Barberini from which the figures emerge as if alive. The impression of realism is heightened by the choice of the materials used: coloured marbles and gilt bronze in marvellous harmony.[5] On a base of polished, dark red marble, rests the boldly drawn, jet-black sarcophagus, decorated with gold stripes and with supports of gilt bronze: above it there rises a lofty pedestal of white marble on which is enthroned the Pontiff in the act of giving his blessing. The female allegorical figures on either side of the sarcophagus are not represented in a

[1] See Vol. XXVIII., p. 33.

[2] BAGLIONE (*Nove chiese*, 1639) mentions (p. 35) the bronze statue of Urban VIII. of which the flanking figures "hora si vanno terminando".

[3] See KNAPP, *Ital. Plastik* (1925), 125.

[4] MUÑOZ, *Bernini*, Roma, 1926, 12; also SOBOTKA, *Die Bildhauer der Barockzeit*, edit. by Tietze, Vienna, 1927, 30; *Archiv. für Kunstgesch.*, II. (1914).

[5] POSSE in *Jahrb. der preuss. Kunstsamml.*, XXVI. (1903), 189 *seq. Cf. Baldinucci*, edit. RIEGL, 115 *seq.*; ESCHER, 108 *seq.*; MUÑOZ, *Roma barocca*, 193 *seq.*; *id. Bernini*, 13; WEISBACH, *Barock*, 33; SOBOTKA, *loc. cit.*

recumbent position, as in the Medici tombs of Michelangelo and on the tomb of Paul III., but erect and in close relation to the figure of the dead man. Both are fully clothed, for the stricter outlook of the age of the Catholic restoration would allow nudity in church at most in the *putti*.[1]

On the right of the beholder, the figure of Justice, carved in white marble and over life size, leans against the sarcophagus: it is flanked by two *putti* and gazes sadly towards heaven.[2] The figure of Charity on the opposite side, with a child in its arms, wears an expression of grief but its look of pity is not directed on high but to a little child close by which, pointing upwards, laments the loss of the great Pope. Upon the sarcophagus, with its back turned to the spectator and its head half veiled, a skeleton of gilt bronze crouches whilst with a bony hand it writes in letters of gold on a black scroll the words: *Urbanus VIII. Barberinus Pontifex Maximus*. The initial letter of the name of Urban's predecessor is also seen on the scroll—an amazing inspiration, says Baldinucci, which called forth universal admiration and suggested to Cardinal Rapaccioli the verses in which he declared that Bernini had reproduced the great Urban so vividly and stamped his soul so deeply on hard bronze that, lest the beholder should think that he had the living Pope before his eyes, Death itself appeared on the sepulchre in order to attest his demise.[3]

[1] *Cf*. BRINCKMANN, *Barockskulptur*, II., 266, and the memorandum quoted p. 471, n. 4. The female figures in the painting on the ceiling of the Palazzo Barberini (see below p. 501), are all draped.

[2] "It would have offended every canon of taste," says BENKARD (15), "to give to Urban's sepulchre excessive movement and it is precisely in this adaptation to circumstances that Bernini's greatness reveals itself."

[3] See *Baldinucci*, edit. RIEGL, 112 *seq*. FRASCHETTI (155), wrongly ascribes the verses to Cardinal Panciroli. On the much blamed addition of the skeleton, REYMOND (77) aptly remarks: "Le Bernin, en évoquant l'idée de la mort, ne fait que reprendre la tradition du moyen-âge et se conformer à l'âme des pensées les plus chères au christianisme. . . . Le squelette, fin dernière

The appropriateness of these verses is proved by a glance at the imposing figure of Urban VIII. of jet-black bronze, clad in vestments resplendent with gold, enthroned in majesty above the monument where, unlike Guglielmo della Porta's Paul III., who quietly gives a blessing, Urban throws aside, with violent gesture, his magnificent flowing robes in order to bestow his blessing *urbi et orbi*.[1] The magical shimmer of the gold spread over the folds of the cope reminds the beholder of the gold tone of the contemporary pictures of Rembrandt.[2]

Just as Urban VIII. did not live to see the completion of his sepulchre, so was it not granted to him to behold the realization of yet another plan with which he hoped to crown his work for St. Peter's. It had been Urban's intention to attenuate the disproportion between Michelangelo's dome and the crushing width of Maderna's façade, which was severely criticized by everybody.[3] To this end towers had already been planned by Maderna himself. At last the time had come when they were about to be erected. In January, 1637, Bernini's project triumphed in a competition organized by the *Fabbrica* of St. Peter's.[4] His towers consisted of three light and airy storeys crowned with a dome adorned with

de cette chair, à laquelle l'homme voudrait s'attacher, doit toujours être devant nos yeux, pour nous dire que nous ne devons pas agir en vue de notre corps mortel, mais pour notre âme immortelle."

[1] *" La vaghezza de' marmi pretiosi e de' bronzi e la nobiltà del desegno non solo eccitano lo stupore in chi rimira tutta l'opera insieme, ma vien giudicata una delle cose più cospicue et ammirande, che adornano quella sacrosanta basilica," says NICOLETTI (VII., 767, Vat. Lib.). *Cf.* REYMOND's praise of the work (73 *seq.*). The cost amounted to 25,000 scudi ; see FRASCHETTI, 158.

[2] BENKARD, 16.

[3] See **Discorso* in *Barb.* 4264, Vat. Lib.

[4] See RIEGL, *Baldinucci*, 124, 126 *seq.* ; FRASCHETTI, 161 *seq.* ; EHRLE, *Spada*, 17. On the other tower plans, see BONANNI, *Templi Vat. hist.*, tables 63–6 ; GURLITT, 352. On a *proposal to alter the façade after the model of the Pantheon, see *Barb.* 4264, *loc. cit.*

Urban VIII.'s arms and surmounted by a cross.[1] In 1639 work was in full swing,[2] but it was St. Peter's day, 1641, before the first storey of one of the majestic towers was terminated on the side where the German Campo Santo is situate. However, already at the end of July, to the great delight of Bernini's many enemies, the Congregation of the Fabbrica of St. Peter's ordered work to be suspended.[3] The grief of the master was such that he fell seriously ill. This step was due to the fact that wide cracks had appeared in the façade in the direction of the Campo Santo which gave rise to grave anxiety.[4]

Urban VIII.'s interest in St. Peter's did not make him forget the other churches of the Eternal City. In particular he sought to preserve from ruin the venerable old churches dedicated to the Martyrs of the era of the persecutions. Medals, most of them struck by Gaspare Mola, record these and other artistic undertakings of the Pope.[5]

In February, 1624, in the course of certain restorations undertaken by the Canons of St. Mary Major in the very ancient church of St. Bibiana, near the Porta S. Lorenzo, they found the body of the titular Saint who had been

[1] Drawing in the possession of Prince Chigi, reproduced by FRASCHETTI, 163. *Cf.* BALDINUCCI (Riegl's edition), 128 *seq.*; REYMOND, 79 *seq.*; BRIGGS, *Barockarchitektur*, 34.

[2] The tower towards the Campo Santo "si va terminando" BAGLIONE writes in *Nove chiese* (1639), 15.

[3] EHRLE, *Spada*, 17.

[4] Besides FRASCHETTI, 163, see RIEGL's remarks in his edition of *Baldinucci*, 130 *seq.*; POLLAK, *Künstlerbriefe*, 5, and EHRLE, *Spada*, 21 *seq.* In the museum of the Campo Santo al Vaticano there is a marble tablet found in an antiquary's shop by Mgr. De Waal bearing the following inscription: A.M.D.G. | Urbanus VIII. P.M. | Hoc ad campan. aeris | Opus ab equi. Jo. Lauren^o^ | Bernino pict. scult. et | archit^o^ fieri mand. | Cum assist^a^ Aloysii | Bernini suprast. | ac Petri P. Drei factoris | a die XX m. Maii | A.D. MDCXXXIII.

[5] Besides the great work of BONANNI, *Numismata*, II., *cf.* even now MARTINORI, 70 *seq.*; 72 *seq.*, 76, 78. On G. Mola see *Riv. Europ.*, 1877, III., 256 *seq.*

martyred under Julian the Apostate.[1] Urban VIII., who had written a poem in honour of the Martyr whilst still a Cardinal,[2] resolved to reconstruct the sacred edifice. It was the first task Bernini received at the Pope's hand. In 1625 the work was completed. He had given the church a plain façade and executed the charming marble statue representing the Saint leaning against a column and directing an ecstatic look towards heaven.[3] Pietro da Cortona also executed his first commission for Urban VIII. in this church; his paintings on the left wall of the central aisle completely put in the shade those by his rival Agostino Ciampelli on the one on the right.[4] For the tombs of St. Bibiana, her sister St. Demetria and their mother, St. Dafrosa, who were likewise victims of the persecution of Julian, the Pope, in 1627, had three reliquaries made[5] which he placed beneath the High Altar in a large ancient basin of oriental alabaster.[6]

Yet another church, on the Via Pia and close to San Bernardo, namely that of the holy Pope Caius who had suffered under Diocletian, was rebuilt by order of Urban VIII. by Francesco Peparelli and Vincenzo della Greca and adorned with altars by Giovan Battista Speranza, Andrea Camassei and other artists.[7]

[1] See the *Avvisi* in POLLAK-FREY, 22. In the same year relics were also found under the high altar of SS. Quattro Coronati; see **Avviso* of July 27, 1624, *Urb.* 1094, Vat. Lib.

[2] *Cf.* *NICOLETTI, II., 905, Vat. Lib.

[3] BALDINUCCI (Riegl), 97 *seq.*; FRASCHETTI, 52 *seq.*; BÖHN, 10 *seq.*, 56; BRINCKMANN, *Barockskulptur*, II., 231; BENKARD, 12; LUBOWSKI, 51 *seq.*; POLLAK-FREY, 23 *seq.*, 27 *seq.*; FORCELLA, X., 109.

[4] BAGLIONE, 320; PASSERI, 403 *seq.*; POLLAK-FREY, 28 *seq.*

[5] POLLAK-FREY, 29.

[6] Fr. Maria Torrigio at that time wrote a *Historia del martirio di S. Bibiana which he presented to Urban VIII.; see *Vat.* 7752. Vat. Lib.

[7] BAGLIONE, 179; DONATUS, *Roma vetus*, 399; FORCELLA, XII., 273; POLLAK-FREY, 30 *seq.*; A. PRESENZINI, *G. Camassei*,

The church of St. Sebastian, on the Palatine, in the Vigna of Carlo Barberini, was likewise saved from ruin by Urban VIII. Its reconstruction was carried out by the Florentine Luigi Arigucci.[1] When in 1634 the façade of the church of St. Anastasia, situate at the foot of the Palatine, beneath the imperial palaces, collapsed during a hurricane, the same architect erected a new and plain brick building, in the centre of the gable of which appears the coat of arms of Urban VIII. The church was also given a new roof.[2]

Arigucci, assisted by the Capuchin Michele da Bergamo, also restored, by order of the Pope, the church of SS. Cosmas and Damian created by Felix IV. [526–530] out of the round temple built by Romulus, son of Maxentius, in 307, and two other ancient edifices, but which could not be made use of owing to its dampness. On this occasion the floor was raised by a whole storey, so as to harmonize with the then existing level of the Campo Vaccino, in consequence of which the ancient marble floor with its mosaics (*opus sectile*) disappeared. On the other hand Felix IV.'s mosaics in the apse—which

Assisi, 1880, 69 *seq.* The pen and ink sketches of Dom. Castelli in *Barb.* 4409 (Vat. Lib.) give the plan in no. 57, the façade and high altar in 58, in 59 the remaining altars of the church, and no. 60 the epitaph of Pope Caius. The church was demolished in 1880.

[1] BAGLIONE, 180. Inscription of 1632 in TOTTI, 151. A. UCCELLI (*La chiesa di S. Sebastiano sul colle Palatino e Urbano VIII.*, Roma, 1876), in (p. 61 *seq.*) an extract from a report by the secretary of the Congregation of the *SS. Visite* addressed to Urban VIII., gives the text of an order issued by the Pope on March 9, 1626, for the restoration and decoration of the church for which Andrea Camassei painted the altarpiece; see PRESENZINI, *loc. cit.*, 68 *seq.* *Cf.* also **Barb.* 4409, p. 71 and 72, *loc. cit.*; TRIPEPI, *Papato*, IV., 67 *seq.*, V., 71 *seqq.*; *Anal. Boll.*, XVI. (1897), 248; POLLAK-FREY, 193 *seq.*

[2] BAGLIONE, 180; MARTINELLI, 44; CIACONIUS, IV., 517; F. CAPPELLO, *Notizie di S. Anastasia*, Roma, 1772, 12 *seq.* (*cf.* 26 *seq.*); POLLAK-FREY, 20 *seq.*; see also **Barb.* 4409, p. 80, *loc. cit.*

are among the finest in Rome—remained untouched.[1] Domenico Castelli, whom the Barberini employed by preference, gave to the church a new high altar, a magnificent ceiling and a campanile.[2] Towards the marble shrine designed by Bernini for the relics of St. Frances of Rome which had been rediscovered in 1638 in the church of the same name, Urban contributed 1,700 scudi.[3] He also subsidized the construction of St. Isidore's which Luke Wadding had undertaken [4] and he restored SS. Quiricus and Julitta,[5] S. Lorenzo in Fonte,[6] and the ruinous churches of SS. Peter and Marcellinus near Torre Pignattara and that of St. Urban near the Bosco Sacro.[7] The church of SS. Quattro Coronati, which was restored and embellished by Cardinal Millini,[8] owed a new ceiling to the liberality of the Pope,[9] whilst to Santa Marta he gave a new porch.[10] Restorations were also carried out in the porch of the Pantheon and in 1626, as if to

[1] MARTINELLI, 106; EGGER, *Codex Escorialensis*, Vienna, 1906, 100; POSSE, *Sacchi*, 21; POLLAK-FREY, 158; **Barb.* 4409, p. 65 *seq.*, *loc. cit.*

[2] BAGLIONE, 150; TOTTI, 155; MARTINELLI, 61; CIACONIUS, V., 519; FORCELLA, IV., 59; F. A. POMPA, *La Basilica di SS. Cosma e Damiano*, Roma, 1727, 31 *seq.*; B. MEZZADRI, *Disquisitio de s. mart. Cosma et Damiano*, 1747, 61 *seq.*, 67 *seq.*; LETAROUILLY, 559 *seq.*; POLLAK-FREY, 116 *seq.*; HÜLSEN, *Das Forum Romanum* [2], Rome, 1905, 210 *seq.* *Cf.* **Barb.* 4409, pp. 69–70, *loc. cit.* On D. Castelli see THIEME, VI., 140.

[3] L. RABORY, *Vie de Ste. Françoise Romaine*; LUGANO, *S. Maria Nuova, Roma*, 1923, ill. 9 and 20, with text. *Cf.* FORCELLA, I., 56.

[4] *Cf.* POLLAK-FREY, 158, and above, p. 348.

[5] CIACONIUS, IV., 517.

[6] FORCELLA, IX., 425.

[7] BAGLIONE, 130; TOTTI, 128; MARTINELLI, 139 *seq.*; POLLAK-FREY, 192, 195. In the Consistory of September 16. 1626, the Pope gave orders for the restoration of the churches at Ostia, Porto, Frascati and Magliano (Sabina); see **Acta consist.*, Papal Secret Archives.

[8] MUÑOZ, *Il restauro della chiesa di SS. Quattro Coronati, Roma*, 1914, 72 *seq.*, 75 *seq.*

[9] See *the notes of Fr. Ubaldini on Urban VIII. in *Barb.* 4901, p. 2. Vat. Lib.

[10] BAGLIONE, *Nove chiese*, 47.

crown the temple, the two small turrets were added for which Bernini has been so often blamed and which were removed in 1882.[1]

More extensive works of restoration and embellishment were carried out by Urban VIII. in the venerable old Baptistry of the Lateran—San Giovanni in Fonte. The ambulatory of that octagon was given a magnificent wooden roof and a new pavement and above the central space was erected a cupola with eight circular windows. Cardinal Cueva was at first charged with the supervision of these works; in 1632 he was succeeded by Angelo Giori, a former tutor of the Barberini nephews. Domenico Castelli was the architect. It was likewise decided to give to the Baptistry a rich pictorial decoration. In 1639 the Pope commissioned Andrea Sacchi to execute for the octagon of the cupola eight colossal oil paintings of scenes from the life of St. John the Baptist and to decorate the walls with historical frescoes illustrating the life of the Emperor Constantine, its founder, and his building activities in the service of the Church. However, Urban VIII. did not live to see the completion of this great commission.[2] By order of the Pope the church of S. Salvatore in Campo was reconstructed in 1639, but on another site. This translation was necessitated by the enlargement of the *Monte di Pietà* which was being carried out by Francesco Peparelli.[3]

[1] CIACONIUS, IV., 520; G. EROLI, *Raccolta di iscrizioni nel Pantheon di Roma, Narni*, 1895, 268 *seq.*; FRASCHETTI, 78 *seq.*; POLLAK-FREY, 179 *seq.* LUBOWSKI (p. 80), shares BÖHN's view (p. 64) that the removal of the turrets diminished the effect of the building.

[2] **Barb.* 4409, pp. 74, 75; BAGLIONE, 180 *seq.*; PASSERI, 162, 320 *seq.*; MARTINELLI, 147; LAUER, 326 *seq.*; *Jarbuch der preuss. Kunstsamml.*, XXXIV. (1913), 61; POSSE, *Sacchi*, 79 *seq.*, 91 *seq.*; PRESENZINI, *A. Camassei*, 81 *seq.*; VOSS, *Malerei*, 532 *seq.*, 552; POLLAK-FREY, 132 *seq.*; *cf.* also CIACONIUS, IV., 516; *Bull.*, XIII., 621. Sacchi's paintings have recently undergone an excellent restoration; see STEINMANN in "Cicerone", XVII. (1925), 945 *seq.*

[3] BAGLIONE, 180; CANCELLIERI, *Notizie ist. d. chiese di S. Maria in Julia, di S. Giovanni Calibita*, etc., Bologna, 1823, 23; FORCELLA, VII., 207; TAMILIA, 105 *seq.*

To Urban VIII.'s predilection for the Capuchin Order, of which his brother Cardinal Antonio was a member, that body owed the erection of a new church and convent in Rome. The church hitherto used by the Capuchins, S. Bonaventura on the Quirinal, with which the ancient small church of S. Nicola de Portiis was connected,[1] had long ago become inadequate. Characteristically enough the new Capuchin church was situate in the neighbourhood of the Palazzo Barberini and it eventually became the property of that family.[2] The foundation stone of the new convent was laid by Cardinal Antonio on March 16th, 1626, and that of the church by the Pope himself, in presence of eleven Cardinals, on St. Francis' Day, October 4th, of the same year.[3] The plan of the church, a single nave with five chapels on either side,[4] was drawn up by the Capuchin Michele da Bergamo and Antonio Casone.[5] The Pope showed the greatest interest in the new structure[6] and made such lavish contributions that it was with difficulty that the Capuchins succeeded in preserving the simplicity prescribed by their Rule for their buildings[7]: but they were unable to prevent the High Altar ordered by the Pope from turning out to be more sumptuous than seemed becoming to them; moreover for the side chapels, commissions for valuable pictures were given to the best artists.[8] On the left-hand side the first chapel was adorned with a picture of the

[1] *Cf.* the exhaustive monograph by Ed. D'Alençon: *Il terzo convento dei Cappuccini in Roma,* Rome, 1908. By the same: *Il primo convento dei Cappuccini in Roma, S. Maria de'Miracoli,* Alençon, 1907, and: *De primordiis ord. Fratr. min. Capucinorum,* Romae, 1921, 89 *seq.*

[2] *Cf. Bull. ord. Capuc.*, II., 71 *seq.*

[3] *Cf.* Domenico da Isnello, *Il convento della S. Concezione de'Padri Cappuccini in Piazza Barberini,* Viterbo, 1923, 48 *seq.*, 57 *seq.*, 65 *seq. Cf.* Pollak-Frey, 165 *seq.*

[4] Baglione, 181, 339.

[5] Fr. Michele was given the title of a Papal Architect; see *Bull. ord. Capuc.*, II., 55.

[6] **Avviso* of June 6, 1629. Vat. Lib.

[7] See Dom. da Isnello, 75 *seq. Cf.* Pollak-Frey, 167 *seq.*

[8] Baglione, 181; Passeri, 79 *seq.*, 142 *seq.*, 161, 318; Dom. da Isnello, 79 *seq.*

"Conversion of St. Paul" by Pietro da Cortona[1]: in the second, in which Felix of Cantalice, canonized by Urban VIII., has found his resting-place, Alessandro Turco painted that Saint in the act of worshipping the Child Jesus; for the third, Andrea Camassei painted the descent from the cross; for the fourth, Lanfranco did a Nativity of Christ and in the fifth Sacchi painted the Blessed Virgin Mary appearing to St. Bonaventure.[2] On the right-hand side, in the first chapel, Guido Reni's famous "St. Michael fighting Satan"[3] found its place; in the second Mario Balassi's "Transfiguration"; in the third "St. Francis' Ecstasy" by Domenichino[4]; in the fourth "Christ in the Garden" by Baccio Ciarpi[5] a pupil of Cortona, and for the fifth yet another masterpiece of Sacchi's, the raising of a dead man by St. Antony.[6] For the High Altar Urban VIII. gave a picture by Lanfranco which subsequently perished in a fire, viz. "Maria Immaculata"[7] to whom the church is dedicated. When the building was completed, Urban VIII. said the first Mass in it on September 8th, 1630, and made a gift to the church of the vestments used on the occasion as well as of relics of Saints and a copy of Giotto's Navicella.[8] A further proof of his love for this church is the circumstance that he had a chapel built for himself near the High Altar where he could give himself unobserved to prayer.[9] On more than one occasion he also celebrated Mass publicly in the new church.[10] The spacious convent, which included rooms for the Superiors of the Order and for the holding of General Chapters, was so far advanced by the spring of 1631, that the Capuchins were able to migrate from old St. Bonaventure to the new

[1] One of the most famous and most frequently copied religious paintings; *cf.* Voss, *Malerei*, 547; Dom. da Isnello, 80.

[2] Dom. da Isnello, 80 *seq.*; Posse, *Sacchi*, 99 *seq.*

[3] Passeri, 79; Dom. da Isnello, 82.

[4] Dom. da Isnello, 82 *seq.*

[5] Passeri, 50.

[6] Posse, *Sacchi*, 60.

[7] Dom. da Isnello, 84 *seq.*; Pollak-Frey, 171 *seq.*

[8] Dom. da Isnello, 93 *seq.*

[9] *Id.*, 78.

[10] **Avviso* of July 31, 1632. Vat. Lib.

convent.[1] The church of St. Bonaventure was assigned to the people of Lucca and received the name of S. Croce de'Lucchesi.[2]

Urban VIII.'s nephews vied with him in furthering Christian art. His brother Antonio made himself chiefly responsible not only for the erection of the Capuchin church, but likewise for that of the College of Neophytes near S. Maria de' Monti and the Palace of Propaganda.[3]

The two other nephews proved even more munificent patrons of art. Cardinal Francesco Barberini restored the triclinium (dining hall) of Leo III., the apse of the Lateran basilica, the church of SS. John and Paul and the convent of St. Bartholomew.[4] Above all, the Cardinal had at heart S. Lorenzo in Damaso. There a magnificent tribune, a new High Altar and two organs were erected from plans by Bernini.[5] Domenico Castelli was commissioned by the Cardinal to erect on the Lungara the church of St. James and the convent of Penitents and a convent of nuns near St. Peter-in-chains.[6] He also subsidized the building of S. Carlo al Corso. The Pope himself contributed to the decoration of that church in which the heart of S. Charles Borromeo was deposited in 1626.[7] Cardinal

[1] When the convent was demolished in the spring of 1926, it became possible to examine more closely the vast store-rooms for wheat and wine which the Barberini family had had laid down in the monastery (see DOM. DA ISNELLO, 98 *seq.*).

[2] See ED. D'ALENÇON, *La chiesa di S. Nicola de Portiis*, 36 *seq.*; POLLAK-FREY, 124. [3] See above, p. 213.

[4] BAGLIONE, 181; TOTTI, 452 *seq.*; ROHAULT, 277 *seq.*; *Inventario*, 341. On the Pope's concern for an ancient mosaic in S. Martino ai Monti see CIACONIUS, IV., 527.

[5] BAGLIONE, 181; MARTINELLI, 30; A. FONSECA, *De basilica S. Laurentii in Damaso, Romae*, 1745, 194 *seq.*, 199 *seq.*; FRASCHETTI, 86; LUBOWSKI, 77 *seq.*; POLLAK-FREY, 163. A *poem on the translation of the ancient image of Our Lady into the new chapel "dominica die intra octavam assumptionis 1635", in *Barb.* 1797, p. 3. Vat. Lib.

[6] BAGLIONE, 180. *Cf.* the pamphlet *Per la riapertura d. chiesa di S. Giacomo alla Lungara, Roma*, 1900.

[7] POLLAK-FREY, 35 *seq.* *Cf.* B. NOGARA, *S. Ambrogio e S. Carlo al Corso, Roma* (without date).

Francesco also greatly furthered the erection of yet another church of St. Charles in Rome by the Trinitarians, near Quattro Fontane.[1] The church is one of Bonomini's masterpieces and was completed in May, 1641, but it has only been fully appreciated by modern critics.[2] The Cardinal's interest in painting showed itself especially by his solicitude for the Academy of St. Luke,[3] and his efforts to attract Guido Reni once more back to Rome.[4] Gian Francesco Romanelli enjoyed the Cardinal's patronage in a marked degree.[5] Pietro da Cortona, and later on Maratta, were also employed by the art-loving Prince of the Church.[6] Among the commissions which the Cardinal gave to other painters, mention may be made of " St. Francis of Assisi's Nuptials with Poverty " by Andrea Sacchi, a picture distinguished by the originality of its conception and its deeply religious tone.[7] In 1635 Cardinal Barberini, with the co-operation of the Pope, commissioned Pietro da Cortona to build the upper church of SS. Martin and Luke. The edifice is a Greek cross, largely developed through the addition of semi-circular apses. The crypt with its sumptuous altar of St. Martina was restored by Pietro da Cortona at his own expense and here the master found his last resting-place.[8]

The restoration of S. Agata alla Subura was begun by Cardinal Francesco and continued by his brother Antonio.

[1] BAGLIONE, 181; FORCELLA, III., 261; POLLAK-FREY, 36 *seq.*

[2] *Cf.* HEMPEL, 37 *seq.*, who refutes the objections brought up against this inspired work of Borromini by tracing the story of its construction. *Cf.* also FREY, *Beiträge zur Barockarchitektur* (1924), 81 *seq.*; POLLAK-FREY, 36 *seq.*

[3] PASSERI, 60.

[4] *Id.*, 76.

[5] *Id.*, 320 *seq.*

[6] *L'Arte*, XXVII, 63.

[7] POSSE, *Sacchi*, 75 *seq.*

[8] *Cf.* *NICOLETTI, V., 20, Vat. Lib.; BAGLIONE, 180; MISSIRINI, 101 *seq.* BRINCKMANN, *Baukunst*, 72, 113; POLLAK in *Kunstchronik*, N. S., XXIII. (1911–12), 563 *seq.*; MUÑOZ, *P. da Cortona*, 6 *seq.*; MOSCHINI in *L'Arte*, 1921, 189 *seq.*; FREY, *L'architettura*, 29 *seq.*; POLLAK-FREY, 185 *seq.* See also *Röm. Quartalschr.*, XVII. (1903), 222 *seq.*

This church owes the restoration of its portico, new wooden ceiling, High Altar and other decorations, to the two Cardinals.[1] To the Jesuits Cardinal Antonio presented for the High Altar of the Gesù a golden *paliotto* with scenes from the life of St. Ignatius.[2] For the Dominicans Paolo Marucelli built a new noviciate at S. Maria Sopra Minerva, at the Cardinal's expense. In the same church the Cardinal had the room in which St. Catherine of Siena died, transferred to the space behind the sacristy ; the Pope contributed to the decoration of the room. The sacristy was also restored ; it was enriched with a new altarpiece by Andrea Sacchi representing Christ on the cross surrounded by four Dominican Saints and St. Catherine of Siena—one of the most impressive creations of the master.[3]

Other Cardinals also, together with several religious societies, displayed considerable building activity at that period. New churches arose in rapid succession such as, for instance, S. Maria della Vittoria,[4] S. Giuseppe a Capo le Case,[5] S. Maria della Pietà e Francesco Saverio,[6] SS. Gesù e Maria in the

[1] MARTINELLI, 87 ; POLLAK-FREY, 19 *seq.* ; BAGLIONE, 181 ; CIACONIUS, IV., 564 *seq.* ; FORCELLA, X., 350 ; HÜLSEN E CECCHELLI, *S. Agata dei Goti, Roma*, 1924, 79, 157 *seq.*, 161 *seq.*

[2] *" Il nuovo suntuoso paliotto tutto di lastre di argento massiccio fatto fare dal s. card. Antonio con spesa di più di 5,000 scudi sendovi scolpita alli lati la vita di S. Ignazio Loyola di figure d'argento di basso rilievo " was set up on New Year's Day, 1641. *Avviso* of January 5, 1641, *Avvisi*, 90, Papal Secret Archives.

[3] BAGLIONE, 181 ; POSSE, *Sacchi*, 69 *seq.*, 71. *Cf.* BERTHIER, *L'église de la Minerve à Rome*, Rome, 1910, 283 *seq.* ; POLLAK-FREY, 182 *seq.*

[4] PASSERI, 31.

[5] The laying of the foundation stone of this church, erected by the calced Carmelites, is announced in the **Avviso* of May 31, 1628, *Urb.* 1098, Vat. Lib. See POLLAK-FREY, 144.

[6] The inscription on the façade is of 1633 ; subsequently it became known as Oratorio del Caravita ; see FORCELLA, XI., 525 *seq.*

Corso,[1] Madonna di Loreto on the Ripetta,[2] SS. Domenico e Sisto,[3] S. Francesco di Paola,[4] S. Trinità della Missione [5] and S. Maria Regina Coeli.[6] Cardinal Ginnasio rebuilt the ancient church of St. Lucy in the Via delle Botteghe Oscure and joined it to a College for twelve boys from his native place.[7] S. Niccolò de' Lorinesi, with its rich internal decoration, was likewise entirely reconstructed.[8] The church adjoining the Roman College and dedicated to the founder of the Jesuits, of which Cardinal Ludovisi laid the first stone in 1626, promised to become an exceptionally magnificent sanctuary.[9] But though that munificent Prince of the Church provided the necessary sums with the utmost liberality, the building took a long time to complete. Domenichino furnished the plans and the Jesuit Orazio Grassi worked them out.[10] The façade also was based on a drawing of Grassi; it was probably influenced by Maderna and Grassi's successor, Father Antonio Sasso, introduced several alterations.[11] Though still unfinished, the church was opened on the feast of St. Ignatius, in 1640, that day being the centenary of the foundation of the Society. The Jesuit General, Vitelleschi,

[1] Martinelli, 103; Gurlitt, *Barockstil*, 398; Pollak-Frey, 130; laying of foundation stone, 1633.

[2] Pollak-Frey, 173.

[3] Begun by Vincenzo della Greca in 1628, nave completed in 1630. See Berthier, *Chronique du monastère de S. Sisto et S. Domenico e Sisto à Rome*, II., 199 *seq.*

[4] Pollak-Frey, 127 *seq.*; D. Taccone-Gallucci, *Monografia d. chiesa di S. Francesco di Paola dei Calabresi in Roma*, Roma, 1916.

[5] See Nibby, 141. The church was demolished in 1913.

[6] Laying of foundation stone in 1643.

[7] Forcella *passim.*

[8] Armellini, 389. Forcella, III., 173.

[9] *Ragguaglio della solennità con che illustrissimo signor cardinale Ludovisi pose la prima pietra della nuova chiesa di S. Ignazio nel Collegio Romano della C.d.G., Roma*, 1626.

[10] See Frey, *Beiträge zur röm. Barockarchitektur*, 11 *seq.*, 41; Pollak-Frey, 148 *seq.*

[11] Frey, *loc. cit.*, 41 *seq.*

said the Mass. The church was decorated with the precious tapestries given by its founder, Cardinal Ludovisi, and in view of the fact that the Pope had granted a Plenary Indulgence, there was not a vacant place in the sacred edifice. The afternoon witnessed the baptism of a Jewish family. On the following day Urban VIII. himself came to visit the church of St. Ignatius when he also inspected the *cortile* of the Roman College which had been completed shortly before.[1]

But the most important and sumptuous baroque church of Rome was that of the Theatines, S. Andrea della Valle. Its founder, Cardinal Alessandro Peretti Montalto, who spent 160,000 gold scudi on the edifice, lived long enough to see the completion of the cupola (November 6th, 1622), the largest in Rome after that of St. Peter's. For the completion of the church the Cardinal left at his death (June 3rd, 1623), an annuity of 6,000 scudi to be raised from his revenues for a period of ten years.[2] The Cardinal's relatives, among them the Abbate and future Cardinal Francesco Peretti, also made large contributions.[3] Thus it became possible to carry out Maderna's plan and to have the first Mass said in the church on Palm Sunday, 1625, when Urban VIII. was present with seven Cardinals. For his family chapel there, the Pope commissioned Bernini to carve the statue of St. John the Baptist.[4] Urban did not live to see the dedication of S. Andrea della Valle (in the jubilee year 1650). The façade of travertine was only executed between 1655–1665 by Carlo Rainaldi, who preserved no more than the main lines of Maderna's original design.[5]

[1] See the Avvisi of August 4 and 11, 1640, in POLLAK-FREY, 156.

[2] ORTOLANI, *S. Andrea della Valle, Roma*, 6 *seq.*

[3] **Avviso* of December 4, 1624, *loc. cit.* A *Canzone per la reale fabbrica della chiesa di S. Andrea della Valle*, dedicated to Fr. Peretti, was printed in Rome in 1627.

[4] POLLAK-FREY, 22.

[5] See ORTOLANI's explanations, p. 8 *seq.*, which are directed against A. BONI (*La chiesa di S. Andrea della Valle, Roma*, 1907).

Under Urban VIII., and through the liberality of Cardinal Borghese, S. Maria della Vittoria and St. Gregory on the Coelian Hill received new façades. The plans were drawn up by Giovan Battista Soria.[1] The latter also erected the porch of the new church of the Dominican nuns of S. Catherine of Siena a Monte Magnanapoli.[2] Cardinal Giovan Battista Leni built the façade of S. Carlo ai Catinari[3]; the churches of S. Girolamo della Carità[4] and S. Maria in Publicolis[5] were restored or rebuilt. The crypt of Bramante's Tempietto in S. Pietro in Montorio, was richly decorated.[6] A number of churches were provided with new altars, as St. Sebastian's on the Via Appia,[7] S. Maria sopra Minerva,[8] S. Giovanni de' Fiorentini,[9] S. Agostino and S. Maria in Via Lata. The

[1] Inscription on the façade of S. Maria della Vittoria: *Scipio card. Burghesius* 1626; on that of St. Gregory's on the Coelian Hill: *Card. Burghesius* 1633; *cf.* V. Moschini, *S. Gregorio al Celio, Roma,* 12, 27. The porch of S. Gregorio, also by Soria, was only completed in 1642.

[2] This church, richly adorned with marble and gold, the internal effect of which is very striking, was consecrated in 1640; see Berthier, *loc. cit.,* 593 *seq.* Cardinal Borghese contributed to this building also; see **Avviso* of April 8, 1633, Vat. Lib.

[3] Inscription on the façade (painted): "J. B. Card. Lenius, 1635." *Cf. Memorie intorno alla chiesa de'SS. Biagio e Carlo a' Catinari, Rome,* 1661; Posse, *Sacchi,* 95.

[4] The **Conti per la fabbrica della chiesa e casa di S. Girolamo,* 1633–5 in Archives of the *Compagnia di S. Girolamo della Carità,* Rome. *Ibid.,* *the information that Domenichino's famous "Communion of St. Jerome" (painted in 1614), was transferred to the high altar in 1659.

[5] Forcella, IV., 453.

[6] Inscription of 1628.

[7] The founder was Duke Maximilian of Bavaria; see Forcella, XII., 153.

[8] **Avviso* of October 8, 1625 (*Urb.* 1095, Vat. Lib.): on Sunday "the Madonna della Cappella del Rosario nella Minerva" was deposited in a most beautiful "ornamento" in the form of a baldacchino supported by four columns, at the expense of Costanza Barberini "Priora della Compagnia".

[9] See *Avviso* of July 1, 1634, in Pollak-Frey, 131.

designs for the altars in the two last-named churches are by Bernini.[1] That man of genius likewise superintended the decoration of the magnificent Cappella Raimondi in S. Pietro in Montorio, the Chapel of Maria Leonora Alaleone in SS. Dominic and Sixtus, and the Cappella Poli in S. Maria in Trastevere.[2] The Flemish sculptor François Duquesnoy created a masterpiece with his statue of St. Susanna, completed in 1634 and destined for S. Maria di Loreto, near the forum of Trajan, the church of the bankers' guild.[3] For S. Maria della Vittoria, Domenichino painted, previous to his leaving Rome [1630], "St. Francis worshipping the Child Jesus and its Mother." [4] Lanfranco decorated the Blessed Sacrament chapel at St. Paul's outside the Walls and the chapel of the Papal Master of Ceremonies, Paolo Alaleone, at S. Lorenzo in Lucina,[5] for which Simon Vouet of Paris painted the "Temptation and Clothing of St. Francis".[6] Giacomo Mola, whom Urban VIII. chose for his architect,[7] built and decorated the chapel of Blessed Ludovico Albertoni in S. Francesco a Ripa [8] and Giovanni Baglione his own family chapel in SS. Cosmas and Damian.[9] The cupola of the Cappella Bandini at S. Silvestro, on the Quirinal, was decorated with frescoes from the Old Testament by Domenichino [10] whilst Algardi adorned it with the statues in stucco of St. John and St. Magdalen.[11] Simple but noble lines distinguish Domenichino's frescoes in the four pendentives of the cupola of S. Carlo ai Catinari representing the cardinal

[1] Fraschetti, 42, 89; Reymond, 39 *seq.*

[2] Fraschetti, 88, 89, 90; Reymond, 61 *seq.*, 67 *seq.*

[3] Passeri, 87 *seq.*; Thieme, X., 186, 190; Muñoz in *Annuario d. Accad. di S. Luca*, 1912, and *L'Arte*, XIX. (1916), 137.

[4] Voss, *Malerei*, 513.

[5] Passeri, 132. *Cf.* Baglione, *Nove chiese*, 64 *seq.*

[6] Voss, *Malerei*, 139, 477.

[7] Architectus Cam. Apost et arcis S. Angeli; *cf.* Bertolotti, *Art. Svizz.*, 36, and *Art. Lomb.*, II., 15 *seq.*

[8] Titi (1763), 48.

[9] Voss, *Malerei*, 465.

[10] Baglione, 381; Titi, 281; *Serra, Domenichino*, 78.

[11] Muñoz in *Annuario d. Accad. di S. Luca*, 1913, 38 *seq.*

virtues together with other allegorical figures referring to St. Charles Borromeo.[1]

However, every creation in the field of painting in Rome during the pontificate of Urban VIII. was eclipsed by the frescoes at St. Andrea della Valle. Just as the cupola of this Theatine church vies with that of St. Peter's, so did its internal decoration rival that of the Basilica of the Prince of the Apostles. Here, "in passionate rivalry," Lanfranco and Domenichino gave of their very best.[2] Lanfranco's fresco in the cupola represents the Blessed Virgin Mary soaring upwards, towards Christ, on a sky of clouds supported by angels and having at her right hand St. Andrew with the founder of the Theatines, St. Cajetan, and on her left St. Peter with the other great Theatine Saint, Andrew Avellino.[3] In this work, which is his masterpiece, and on which he began work in 1621,[4] Lanfranco outstripped "all similar attempts of the period immediately preceding, by his conscious calculation of perspective and adaptation to the given architectural proportions and by the grand manner of his pictorial treatment which enabled him so to combine the great masses of figures as to create the illusion of a single picture".[5] At the end of June 1627, the Pope inspected this latest creation of decorative painting.[6] Lanfranco also painted the picture

[1] BAGLIONE, 382; [Cacciari] *Mem. di S. Carlo ai Catinari*, Roma, 1861, 21; SERRA, 80 *seq.*

[2] BAGLIONE, 382; PASSERI, 23 *seq.*, 135 *seqq.*; A. BONI, *La chiesa di S. Andrea della Valle*, Roma. 1908; SERRA, 70 *seq.*; ORTOLANI, *S. Andrea della Valle*, Roma.

[3] C. CESIO, *La cupola del cav. Giov. Lanfranco, dipinta in Roma nella chiesa di S. Andrea della Valle, disegnata et intagliata, Roma*, 1680 (with nine plates).

[4] ORTOLANI, 11, 17.

[5] POSSE, *Sacchi*, 20; *cf. id. Deckenmalerei*, 115, 146.

[6] *"On Monday the Pope inspected the cupola of St. Andrea della Valle, the painting of which" con bellissime figure ("l'ascensione della B.M.V.) was completed", we read in the *Avviso* of June 30, 1627, *Urb.* 1097, Vat. Lib. Consequently the year 1625 given by PASSERI (138) for the unveiling of Lanfranco's "Assumption of Our Lady", a date also accepted by ORTOLANI (17), cannot be correct. Copy in ORTOLANI, figure 5.

for the altar of St. Andrew Avellino ; in it the Saint, struck with apoplexy whilst saying Mass at St. Paolo, in Naples, is seen looking up to heaven from which angels come down towards him.[1]

Almost simultaneously [1624–8],[2] and in consequence of a commission of Cardinal Peretti Montalto, Domenichino painted the frescoes of the choir vault and the pendentives of the cupola of the same church. These mark an epoch "owing to the absolutely natural combination of architectural effect in its entirety and its vigorous, sober presentment of detail and pregnant conception of each dramatic moment". It has been justly emphasized that the master's creation appears even more wonderful when account is taken of the gigantic proportions of S. Andrea della Valle, more especially of the unusual height of the vault of the choir.[3]

The architecture of the building conditioned the division of the work : in the centre of the arch of the cupola, we behold in a magnificent landscape, John the Baptist pointing out the Messias, the Lamb of God, to the future Apostles Andrew and John (John i, 35). Of the triangles of the half-cupola, the middle one shows, also amidst magnificent scenery, the call by Christ of the fishermen Peter and Andrew to be His Apostles ; on the right soldiers leading Andrew to execution ; on the left the martyrdom of the Apostle ; and on top, in the lunette, his ascent into heaven.[4] Between the windows Domenichino painted six virtues : Faith holding a chalice and Host, Hope, Charity, Fortitude, Piety, and Religion with the Cross.[5]

Domenichino's four evangelists in the pendentives of the cupola also rank as masterpieces : Matthew, a powerful

[1] ORTOLANI, fig. 17. [2] BOSSI, *S. Andrea della Valle*, 21.

[3] VOSS, *Malerei*, 510.

[4] SERRA, 74 *seq.* ORTOLANI (in his remarks on fig. 8 *seq.*) is of opinion that the original scheme for the decoration of the choir vault was the work of Maderna. The magnificent stucco decorations are by Algardi. VOSS, *Malerei*, 204–7, gives better reproductions of Domenichino's choir frescoes than ORTOLANI.

[5] SERRA, 73 *seq.*

giant, grasps his gospel in his left hand, whilst on his right an angel holds a cross ; Luke, a bearded old man wrapped in an ample cloak, holds a scroll with the words of his gospel : *Fuit sacerdos* [Zachary] ; Mark, also an old man, reads from a tablet ; a lion crouches at his feet ; the youthful John, with an eagle and an angel who holds up a book before the Apostle is enthroned on clouds ; as he raises ecstatic eyes towards heaven, another angel hands him an inkpot and the Apostle is about to write the Apocalypse in the book held by the first angel.[1]

After his first visit to the church of the Theatines, Goethe wrote : " I can only record the happiness of this day in a few words : I have seen Domenichino's frescoes at St. Andrea." Since these words were penned unnumbered admirers have marvelled at this wonderful creation, one that may well represent the greatest achievement of baroque in the sphere of religious painting.[2]

By far the most important secular building of the pontificate of Urban VIII. is the imposing family palace of the Barberini, on the north-western slope of the Quirinal, which absorbed the palace of the Sforzas bought by the Pope at the end of 1625 for Cardinal Francesco Barberini and subsequently presented by him to his brother Taddeo.[3] Several plans were submitted for the new construction, among them one by Carlo Maderna, the leading architect of the period. However, it was not Maderna but Bernini who was destined to stamp the building, which was practically completed by 1633,[4]

[1] Voss, *Malerei*, 208–9 : Ortolani, figs. 6, 7 ; the three large frescoes on the walls of the choir representing scenes from the martyrdom of St. Andrew are by Mattia Preti (" il cavaliere Calabrese "), 1650–1 ; see Ortolani, figs. 13–15. The frescoes of Carlo Cignani and Alessandro Taruffi over the lateral entrances of the sanctuary were executed at a still later date (1660).

[2] Opinion of Voss in *Thieme*, IX., 401.

[3] Pollak-Frey, 251 *seq.* *Cf.* also V. Ehrle, *La pianta di Roma Maggi Maupin-Losi, Roma*, 1915, 18 *seq.*, 23 *seq.* Rose, *Spätbarock*, 107 *seq.* ; Hempel, 18 *seq.*

[4] P. Ferrerio (*Palazzi di Roma de' più celebri architetti*, plate 7), who is followed by Fraschetti (82), gives 1630 as the

with the seal of his genius.[1] The palace marks a turning-point in Roman architecture. It constitutes "something between a city palace and a suburban villa".[2] The four-square plan is abandoned, the result being an approximation to the ground plan of a villa such as that of the Farnese. The rear is likewise carried out in the villa style; the gardens are laid out both here and on the sides, on lining walls and terraces. The main façade, facing south-east, shows three storeys with wide, round openings between the supporting pilasters, framed, on the ground floor, with engaged Doric columns, whilst in the middle floor they are intended as windows between engaged Ionic columns. The round openings and windows of the upper storey between Corinthian pilasters give an impression of depth, thanks to a trick of perspective. The whole is one of the most magnificent constructions in the baroque style and produces an effect which is as harmonious as it is imposing. The main structure is flanked on either side by vast lateral wings.[3]

On the ground floor of the main building a vestibule opens

year of completion. This is certainly untenable; *cf.* GOLZIO, *Pal. Barberini*, 10 *seq.* The chapel was only completed in the autumn of 1632; see POLLAK-FREY, 329. On the heavy cost of the building, *cf.* besides the letter quoted by POSSE (*Deckenmalerei*, 96, n. 3), of Fr. Niccolini, dated June 8, 1630, the *report of the Florentine envoy dated March 13, 1632, State Archives, Florence, *Med.*, 3351, p. 189. HIER. TETIUS (Perusinus) published an illustrated description: *Aedes Barberinae ad Quirinalem descriptae, Romae*, 1642. The statement that the materials were taken from the Colosseum is wrong; *cf.* BOSSI, 10.

[1] HEMPEL (15 *seq.*, 19 *seq.*, 21 *seq.*, 27 *seq.*), has shown that Borromini executed only secondary parts (Urban VIII.'s arms on the principal façade, some windows at the back). For the rest, as FREY (*L'architettura barocca*, 22) points out, the story of the building of the palace is still so obscure that it is not yet possible to disentangle with any certainty the share of Maderna and that of Bernini in the work.

[2] HEMPEL, 16; GOLZIO, 27 *seq.*, 36, 49.

[3] BALDINUCCI (edit. RIEGL), 102 *seq.*; LETAROUILLY, *Edifices* II., 181 *seq.*; BRINCKMANN, *Baukunst*, 90 *seq.*

in the centre of the magnificent double portico with a passage to yet another portico in the direction of the raised garden at the back. The staircases are at the other end : the one on the right, oval in shape and copied from Vignola's staircase at Caprarola, leads to the library on the top floor ; the large, square staircase on the left serves as the main stairway [1] to the " piano nobile ", the centre of which consists of an immense magnificent hall which takes in two storeys. The ceiling was decorated by Pietro da Cortona with a fresco in the new " illusionistic " style creating the impression of vast spaces. This magnificent fresco was executed according to a scheme drawn up by the Court poet Francesco Bracciolini.[2] and is the fruit of years of toil and scrupulous care.[3] Urban VIII. took the greatest interest in the work which began in 1633 [4] ; when it was completed in 1639, he compared it to the works of Raphael.[5]

The praise was deserved. Pietro da Cortona who, with Bernini, inspired the high baroque movement in Rome,[6] has here produced " one of the greatest and most important creations of all time in the sphere of decorative fresco work.[7] His ceiling is an epoch-making achievement with which he displaced the hitherto preponderant influence of the Bolognese school in Rome. It ushers in a new era of the decorative arts ". In place of sham architecture, the weight of which was suggested by caryatids and pilasters, there succeeds a cunningly painted framework, the material of which is no longer to be imagined as stone, but actually consists of the lighter stucco.[8] The

[1] Golzio, 42 *seq.* On the configuration of Bernini's stairs, *cf.* Rose, *Spätbarock*, 189 *seq.*

[2] Tetius, *Aedes Barb.*, 44 *seq.* *Cf.* above, p. 423.

[3] Posse, *Deckenfresko*, 98 *seq.*, 102 ; O. Pollak in *Thieme*, VII., 489 ; Pollak-Frey, 327 *seq.*

[4] See J. V. Sandrart, *Teutsche Academie*, II.[2], Nürnberg, 1675, 200.

[5] See the report of Fr. Niccolini of December, 1639, in Posse, *loc. cit.*, 102, n. 2. *Cf.* Golzio, 15 *seq.* ; Pollak-Frey, 328.

[6] Voss, *Malerei*, 319.

[7] *Ibid.*, 533 ; *cf.* 537 *seq.*

[8] Posse, *loc. cit.*, 156–7. *Cf.* also Rose, *Spätbarock*, 218 *seq.*, and Weisbach, *Barock*, 43.

subject of the giant fresco is in itself of the greatest interest: with inexhaustible wealth of figures and accessories it blends allegorica and mythological reminiscences with an essentially Christian conception. Contemporary [1] as well as subsequent critics [2] have been alike mistaken when they imagined that the marvellous frescoes exalted the earthly Prince rather than the Vicar of Christ. The exact reverse is the truth: the personality of Urban VIII. recedes before the glorification of the divinely-founded papacy. In keeping with the taste of the period, this fundamental religious notion coalesces, together with allegory and mythology, into a majestic and harmonious whole which forms like a triumphant pæan to the greatness of the Apostolic See and its occupant for the time being.[3] In the centre the figure of divine Providence is seen enthroned in heavenly glory and resplendent with dazzling light; Immortality floating upwards holds a crown of stars with which to crown it; at its behest winged genii carry towards heaven the tiara, Peter's keys, and a poet's laurel wreath shaped like a shield and bearing the Barberini bees.

The representations of the longitudinal and transverse sides are likewise subordinate to the main group. The former show Minerva casting down the Giants, viz. Heresy and Unbelief; at the bidding of Justice, Hercules slays the Harpies whilst Plenty pours out its cornucopia over the earth; human Wisdom and its spring, Religion, overcome the passions of the body; Papal Sovereignty, guided by Prudence, fetters War and holds it in check by the creation of an armed force (Vulcan's smithy).[4]

For the walls, Francesco Ubaldini suggested six frescoes recording the chief events of Urban's pontificate; viz. his election as Pope, the opening of the Holy Door, the furthering

[1] See Domenichino's letter in Bellori, 223.

[2] Voss, *Malerei*, 539.

[3] Posse, *loc. cit.*, 106 *seq.*; 118, whose excellent account serves as a basis to what follows. *Cf.* also Passeri, 406 *seq.* and the detailed description by Fabbrino (45 *seq.*). Reproductions in Posse, 110 *seq.*, 112, 114 *seq.*, and Voss, 243–5.

[4] Posse, 108 *seq.*

of the publication of religious books, the acquisition of Urbino, his solicitude for the welfare of his subjects, and his exertions for the defence of the States of the Church.[1] Eventually, it was decided not to include the walls in the scheme of decoration,

[1] *" Abbozzo per le pitture alle parieti della Sala Barberina. Le attioni principali di Papa Urbano ottavo distinte in sei quadri :

1° La creatione di esso Papa Urbano, con esprimersi la reiteratione dei suffragi. Per ciò si potrebbe ricorrere al poema del Bracciolini maestro di Rosichino nel luogo ove egli tratta di questo, per farvi figure in aria dinotanti le virtù che concorsero a un atto tanto eroico. . . .

2° L'aprimento della Porta Santa co' ritratti de' principi che vennero all'indulgenza dell'Anno Santo, come sarebbe a dire l'arciduca Leopoldo, Vladislao principe di Polonia, etc.

3° La correttione dei riti e de' libri ecclesiastici, la riforma delle ceremonie, la stampa per la Propaganda Fede.

4° L'acquisto dello stato di Urbino. Il Metauro che si sottomette al Tevere. Ha il Metauro per sua insegna un dente di elefante per la vittoria che hebbesi quivi di Asdrubale. Sarebbe etiamdio bello a farvi un gran tronco di quercia d'onde eschino le api per quell' : Et durae quercus sudabunt roscida mella. Nè forse sarebbe fuor di proposito finger angeletti per aria con corone di quercia dette civiche per dimostrare che tale acquisto si fece conservando i cittadini dalla guerra.

5° Il tener lontano la peste, la fame e la guerra dallo Stato ecclesiastico. Si potrebbero queste tre cose esprimere con le tre Furie, ciascheduna con qualche segno a tali calamità appropriato, e che le discacciassero Apollo per la sanità, Cerere coronata di spiche per l'abbondanza, e Mercurio col caduceo per la missione de' Legati e Nuntii.

6° La diffesa dello Stato della Chiesa. Farei Matilda con lo scudo, con la sua arma, con una spada sfoderata avanti la sua sepoltura, la quale Papa Urbano le inalzò nel Vaticano, e la detta Matilda discacciasse i nemici espressi in qualche mostro significante la lega de' principi.

L'introdur Matilda con allusione allegorica non è nuovo, havendolo fatto Dante nel fine del suo *Purgatorio*, etc., per la vita attiva, che, come si ha da san Gregorio Magno, è la propria del Sommo Pontefice. Vedansi le sue prime epistole, etc. *Barb.*, 4901, p. 61, Vatican Library.

as had been done in the Galleria Farnese, but to adorn them instead with a series of gobelins representing scenes of the life and passion of Christ, for which Gian Francesco Romanelli furnished the cartoons.[1] Scenes from the life of Christ were painted by Pietro da Cortona in the chapel of the palace, in the pictorial decoration of which other artists also took part.[2]

In the north wing of the main storey, Andrea Camassei, a protégé of Domenichino, painted the creation of the Angels.[3] He had already executed in another room a representation of Parnassus with Apollo and the Muses.[4] Of much greater significance is the fresco in which Andrea Sacchi,[5] whom Cardinal Antonio Barberini employed at a fixed salary, decorated the ceiling of the great hall in the north wing of the palace. Its subject corresponds to that of the hall of ceremonies, for it was essentially meant to represent the guidance of divine Wisdom, of which the Church stands ever in need; but, as the execution shows, here the grave Roman gave expression to a current of baroque painting contrary to that of the versatile Tuscan Pietro da Cortona, for Sacchi aimed before all else at simplicity and unity in the presentment of his theme. All-embracing divine Wisdom, personified as a noble maiden in a robe of azure and resplendent white mantle, is seen seated on a golden throne surrounded by eleven female figures symbolizing the attributes of Wisdom as described in the Book of Wisdom and pouring out its blessings upon the earth beneath. In contrast with the serene tranquillity of these noble figures, two winged youths are seen floating in the air—they are intended to represent love and fear. This fresco, which conjures up memories of Raphael's Stanza della Segnatura, is justly singled out for praise in the inscription on the artist's tomb

[1] F. Baldinucci, *Notizie de' professori del disegno*, V., 544. *Cf.* below, p. 504, n. 2.

[2] Posse, *Deckenfresko*, 97, 99. *Cf.* Golzio, 19.

[3] Passeri, 159; *cf.* Pollak-Frey, 330.

[4] Posse, *Deckenfresko*, 99. *Cf.* A. Presenzini, *Vita ed opere del pittore A. Camassei, Assisi*, 1880, 62; Pollak-Frey, 330.

[5] Passeri, 313 *seq.*

in St. Mary Major; it is a significant proof of the survival of the classicist movement in baroque.[1]

For the weaving of the gobelins, Cardinal Francesco Barberini established a special factory in 1627. The institution worked until his death [1679] and produced many excellent works, among them being copies in oil on canvas of Raphael's tapestries in the Vatican. The Fleming Giacomo della Riviera (Jakob van den Vliete) was appointed director of the factory.[2] The Cardinal had acquired a special interest in this kind of art, and at a later date he also bought old tapestries.[3] Louis XIII. made him a present of seven tapestries representing the story of the Emperor Constantine,[4] which have not been preserved, but to this day the Palazzo Barberini possesses a series of ten tapestries on which the Cardinal had had depicted some of the events of the life of Urban VIII.[5] such as the conferment of the doctorate on Maffeo Barberini, his activities on Lake Trasimene under Clement VIII., his elevation to the cardinalate, his election as Pope, the annexation of Urbino

[1] In his monograph of Sacchi (38 *seq.*), POSSE has once more drawn attention to this fresco of which he gives an excellent explanation. It may be that it was inspired by Sarbiewski's epode "Of Divine Wisdom" composed by the latter towards the end of his stay in Rome. (*Epodon*, l.c., transl. by SILBERT in "Dom heiliger Sänger", Vienna, 1820).

[2] *Cf.* MÜNTZ, *L'atelier de tapisseries du card. Franc. Barberini à Rome*, in *Gaz. des Beaux-Arts* (Chronique, 1876, 229 *seq.*); MÜNTZ, *Les tapisseries de Raphael*, Paris, 1897, 48, 296, 364: POSSE, *Sacchi*, 69 *seq.*; *L'Arte I.* (1898), 354, XXVII., 66 *seq.* Also GENTILI, *Cenni storici sulle origini e vicende dell' arte degli arazzi in Roma*, Rome, 1915, and H. GÖBEL, *Wandteppiche*, II., 1, Leipzig, 1928, 417 *seq.* Collection of letters referring to the factory in *Barb.*, 4373, Vatican Library. *Cf.* ORBAAN, *Bescheiden*, I., 353 *seq.*

[3] *L'Arte I.*, 355.

[4] ORBAAN, *Documenti*, 496; GÖBEL, *loc. cit.*, 419.

[5] The tapestry was executed in the years 1663–1679. The factory also furnished the following series; (1) 1627–1630, *Serie dei Castelli*, 6 pieces; (2) 1630–1641, *Vita di Constantino*, 5 pieces; (3) 1637–1642, *Giuoco di fanciulli*, 5 pieces; (4) 1643–1656, *Vita di Christo*, 10 pieces.

to the Papal States, the fortification of Rome, the dedication of St. Peter's, the restoration of peace in Italy. One tapestry shows Urban VIII. in the act of receiving envoys; Countess Matilda stands on his left and the City Prefect, Taddeo, on his right; in another the Pope invokes the protection of the Prince of the Apostles against plague and famine.[1]

The Barberini palace, the furnishing of which Cardinal Antonio Barberini the younger pursued with prodigal ardour,[2] contained many other artistic treasures, as we learn from the description of Count Girolamo Teti. First place among these belongs to the picture gallery, one of Rome's largest and choicest. It contained several pictures of the greatest value, such as Raphael's "Fornarina", Sebastiano del Piombo's "Clement VII.", Titian's "Paul III.", Corregio's "Espousals of St. Catherine", as well as works by German painters, for instance, Dürer's "Death of Mary". Italian masters were the most numerously represented; among them Perugino, Michelangelo, Leonardo da Vinci, Sarto, Caracci, D'Arpino, Guido Reni, Lanfranco, and Sacchi.[3] Besides numerous antique statues, among them a river god found in the course of work in Castel St. Angelo, the Faun now at Munich [4] and a bust of Cicero preserved in the museum of the Capitol, one also admired works by more recent sculptors, such as Bernini's marble bust of Urban VIII. and an equestrian statuette of Carlo Barberini by Francesco Mocchi.[5] A special room was

[1] The Barberini family has in its possession all Romanelli's cartoons. Prince Urbano Barberini, who very kindly allowed me to see them, and who gave me some valuable information about them, is thinking of publishing a special work on them based on documents in the family archives of the Barberini (**Libri mastri, Filze di giustificazioni, etc.*).

[2] See the report of Fr. Mantovani of May 12, 1635, in Posse, *Sacchi*, 6, n. 2.

[3] Tetius, 17, 153 *seq.* *Cf.* Orbaan, *Documenti*, 497 *seq.*; G. Incisa della Rocchetta in *L'Arte XXVII.*, 70; de Villa-Urritia, *El Palacio Barberini*, 37 *seq.*; Pelluti, I., *Musei d'Italia*, Roma, 1922, 353 *seq.*; Pollak-Frey, 333 *seq.*, 335 *seq.*

[4] Cassiano del Pozzo in *Miscell. di stor. ital.*, XV. (1875), 177.

[5] Tetius, 169 *seq.*; de Villa-Urritia, 38 *seq.* *Cf.* Golzio, 20.

assigned to an extensive collection of antiques of the pagan and the Christian era, among them being the Roman weapons which Maffeo Barberini had found in the course of his work on Lake Trasimene.[1] To the valuable library founded by Francesco Barberini there was added a valuable collection of antique coins and gems.[2] A special room contained the portraits of famous men, among whom the Florentines were particularly well represented.[3] In the gardens, which were adorned with statues, fountains, rare flowers and laurel trees, there were also housed stags, ostriches, and camels.[4] From Lisbon the Spanish ambassador, Castel Rodrigo, had sent to the Pope a present of orange, lemon, and cedar trees, all of which had until then been unknown in Rome.[5]

Adjoining the palace was a theatre[6] capable of seating 3,000 persons. It was inaugurated in February, 1634, with the presentation of the drama " St. Alexius " written by Cardinal Giulio Rospigliosi, the future Clement IX., and set to music by Stefano Landi. In this play, as in Pietro da Cortona's pictures, classical elements formed a harmonious blend with Christian ones. The excellent music and the splendid staging, the flight of the angels in mid air and the apparition of Religion on a chariot of clouds with which the illusion reached its climax, called forth the enthusiastic applause of the spectators.[7]

[1] TETIUS, 30 *seq.*

[2] *Ibid.*, 23 *seq.*; N. HEINSIUS, *Clar. Belg. ad Magliabech. epist.*, I., 285; BLUME, III., 137.

[3] TETIUS, 18; POSSE, *Sacchi*, 130, n. 2.

[4] TETIUS, 37 *seq.*; POLLAK-FREY, 331.

[5] See the data of Cassiano del Pozzo, *loc. cit.*, XV., 191, *cf.* JESSEN, *Botanik*, 258.

[6] It stood to the left of the palace and had probably been built to the plans of Pietro da Cortona; see GOLZIO, 11, 46.

[7] ADEMOLLO, *Teatri* (1888), 8, 10 *seq.*, 18 *seq.*; GOLDSCHMIDT, *Studien zur Gesch. der ital. Oper*, Leipzig, 1901, 147 *seq.* *Cf.* also GIONA, *I primi melodrami a Roma e il teatro Barberini*, in the *Rassegna internaz. di musica*, 1909, and H. PRUNIÈRES, *L'opéra italien en France*, Paris, 1913, who devotes the first chapter of his book to the development of the opera in Rome at the period of Urban VIII. See also ZUCKER, *Die Theaterdekoration des*

The rapture of the contemporaries over these first musical dramas in the Palazzo Barberini may be gauged by the accounts of Janus Nicius Erythraeus who cannot find words with which to describe the actors dressed in cloth of gold and silver and the changes of scenery and perspective.[1] In the following year, when the melodrama, "The life of St. Theodora," also composed by Cardinal Rospigliosi, was presented, an attempt was made to surpass the success of 1634. Whilst musical drama of a religious kind was being cultivated in the monasteries of Rome, especially by the Jesuits, secular subjects were also acted in the theatre of the Barberini, such as Rospigliosi's comedy "*Chi soffre speri*", in 1639, when Milton was one of the audience.[2]

The memory of the Barberini is kept alive in the Eternal City, not only by the Barberini palace—perhaps Rome's most magnificent,[3] but by many other buildings. We have already spoken of the extensive work on Castel St. Angelo, the fortifications for the protection of the city of Rome and the alterations and reconstruction of the Palace of Propaganda.[4] The school of the Roman mission to the Jews was also given a worthy home. To its protector, Cardinal Antonio Barberini, as well as to the Pope's assistance, was due the new College of the Neophytes erected by Gaspare de' Vecchi [5] near the

Barock, Berlin, 1925. The famous singer, Marcantonio Pasqualini, whose crowning by Apollo has been depicted by Sacchi's brush, was likewise in the service of Cardinal Antonio; see POSSE, *Sacchi*, 107 *seq.*

[1] *Cf.* AMBROS, IV., 187 *seq.*

[2] ADEMOLLO, 25 *seq.*

[3] "If I had to give the preference to one building above all others I would choose the Palazzo Barberini. It surpasses the Vatican by the symmetry of its plan, equals the extent of the Quirinal and the Villas Farnese and Altieri and yields in nothing to the Villas Borghese, Giustiniani, Chigi, Colonna and Pamfili as regards its internal arrangement and its collections of ancient and modern works of art. Moreover, seen from outside, it looks more beautiful and more imposing than all the others." (Confidential letters from Italy of President de Brosses to his friends at Dijon, 1739–1740.)

[4] See above, p. 212 *seq.* and 360 *seq.*

[5] BAGLIONE, 181.

pilgrimage church of the Madonna de' Monti.[1] Mention must also be made of the repairs to the city walls and to the house of refuge for penitents in the Lungara,[2] the extension of the Sapienza, of which Borromini was appointed architect in the autumn of 1632,[3] the alterations in the palace of the Inquisition,[4] the enlargement of the hospital near the Lateran,[5] and that of the grain stores near the baths of Diocletian.[6]

The *Tabularium* on the Capitol was saved from ruin when the Pope transferred elsewhere the salt stores which were situate there. The prisons on the Capitol were enlarged and the decoration of the palace of the Senate was continued.[7] Urban VIII. also carried out extensive restorations and alterations in the Vatican[8]; the *Galleria Lapidaria* was vaulted,[9] and the *Galleria Geographica* restored.[10] On the second floor of the new palace, in 1632, Urban had a passage made to join up with the old one and in honour of Countess Matilda, the supporter of Gregory VIII., he furnished the room which bears her name

[1] See HOFFMANN in *Zeitschr. für Missionswiss.*, XI., 81, who ascribes the building to the year 1634. The inscription in the *Inventario*, 19 *seq.* gives 1635, but an **Avviso* of October 8, 1639, reports that Urban VIII., on that date, inspected the construction of the College of Neophytes *che si fa per ordine del card. S. Onofrio* (*Urb.*, 1107, Vatican Library).

[2] POLLAK-FREY, 2 *seq.*; NOVAES, IX., 294. On the restoration of the city walls, *cf.* NIBBY, *Le mura*, 338, 364, 368, 381; FORCELLA, XIII., 8 *seq.*; *Inventario*, 23, 224, 272, 284, 285, 286, 315, 318.

[3] See above, p. 455.

[4] MARTINELLI, 12; CIACONIUS, IV., 515; on the first floor of the Palace of the Inquisition we read above a door: "Urbanus VIII., P.M."

[5] *Inventario*, 14.

[6] See above, p. 372. *Cf.* BAGLIONE, 182; FORCELLA, XIII., 181; *Inventario*, 349, 350; TOTTI (55), mentions the construction of a staircase in the corn store near Porta Portese which had been restored by Gregory XV.

[7] FORCELLA, I., 51, 55; RODOCANACHI, *Capitole*, 43, 104, 126.

[8] MORONI, 4, 265 *seq.*; POLLAK-FREY, 372 *seq.*; CECCHELLI, 98.

[9] FORCELLA, VI., 152; BARBIER, II., 90.

[10] TAJA, 286, 290; FORCELLA, VI., 150; BARBIER, II., 148 *seq.*, 154; *Mél. d' archéol.*, XX., 295 *seq.*; POLLAK-FREY, 386.

and adorned it with pictures of historical scenes, among them that of Canossa. A pupil of Pietro da Cortona, Gian Francesco Romanelli of Viterbo, executed them and likewise decorated the adjoining room with frescoes.[1] Near the Stanza dell' Incendio, Urban VIII. fitted out a private chapel for himself; its stucco and pictorial decoration had for its theme the Passion of our Lord. The beautiful fresco over the altar is the work of Pietro da Cortona.[2] A second chapel, on the third floor, derived its name from a picture by Romanelli representing the birth of Christ.[3] Besides the above-named painters, Agostino Ciampelli and Agostino Tassi were also employed in the decoration of the Vatican. To this day the friezes of the ceilings of three rooms on the first floor of the Sistino-Clementine part of the palace recall the memory of the Barberini Pope.[4] In 1625 all the frescoes of the Sistine chapel were subjected to a thorough cleaning, the dust being removed by rubbing the figures with bread.[5] The corridor between the Vatican and the Castle of St. Angelo, which had become very ruinous, was also restored.[6]

[1] TAJA, 198 *seq.*, 200; FORCELLA, VI., 151 *seq.*; POLLAK-FREY, 389; in 1907 Pius X. turned the Sala Matilde into a chapel.

[2] TAJA, 271 *seq.*; BARBIER, II., 65; THIEME, VII., 488; POLLAK-FREY, 385.

[3] TAJA, 495; MORONI, IX., 155.

[4] Since 1907 these rooms serve as reception rooms of the Cardinal Secretary of State. On the *Armeria* in the Vatican, see above, p. 364; on the new door of the Vatican Library, p. 451. On other minor works and alterations executed by Urban VIII. in the Vatican see TAJA, 138, 175, 186, 194. In the collection of pen and ink sketches in *Barb.*, 4409, there are reproductions on p. 20, " Porta nel Vaticano " leading into the " Cappella Segreta " (1624); p. 21, a view of the *Cappella Segreta* (cf. p. 26); p. 22, doors in the Vatican; p. 24, " Ristaurationi delle 4. facciate del cortile del Palazzo nuovo edificato da Sisto V."; p. 27, the restored " Galleria Geografica "; p. 30, the door communicating between the old and the new palace.

[5] STEINMANN, *Sixt. Kapelle*, II., 779, 783.

[6] FORCELLA, XIII., 179.

Repairs and decorations were also carried out in the Quirinal[1]; Andrea Sacchi was employed in the private chapel of that palace, besides several other painters. In 1638 Bernini built the small loggia over the main portal.[2] To the left was constructed a bastion and on the right a room for the Swiss guards.[3] The garden of the Quirinal was adorned with new fountains, statues and a sun dial; it was likewise considerably enlarged and surrounded with a strong wall in 1628.[4] The piazza in front of the Quirinal had already been enlarged by Urban VIII. by the purchase of part of the gardens of the Colonna; he also levelled it, in view of the crowds of pilgrims who flocked there to receive the papal blessing. This caused the disappearance of the remains of the temple of the Sun which towered above a large part of the city. In 1634 the Pope gave orders for the removal of the erroneous inscriptions on the statues of "The Horse Tamers" in favour of those seen to-day.[5] The piazza before the church of

[1] *Cf.* MORONI, 4, 234 *seq.* In the collection of pen and ink sketches in *Barb.* 4409 there are reproductions on p. 46 of "Facciata di dentro nel Palazzo del Quirinale" (restored); p. 47. "Facciata d'horologio in Quirinale abbellita, ristorata e ridotta in quella vaga forma che di presente si vede, dalla S. di P. Urbano VIII. con havervi fatto li due corritore che dividono li appartamenti da una e l'altra." *Cf.* BARBIER, III., 305 *seq.* 308; *Repert. f. Kunstwiss.*, 1910, 220.

[2] POLLAK-FREY, 370. On Bernini's loggia, *cf.* FRASCHETTI, 87.

[3] TOTTI, 278 *seq.*; POSSE, *Sacchi*, 66 *seq.*

[4] See the pen and ink sketches in *Barb.* 4409, pp. 45, 48, 49, 50, 51. The inscription above the sun-dial runs thus: "Urbanus VIII. Barberinus. | Recurrentium temporum lex | a luce prima in vesperam, sic tota | decurrit dies currens per anni | circulum."

[5] Besides DONATUS, *Roma*, 399; TOTTI, 281 *seq.*; LANCIANI, IV., 156; POLLAK-FREY, 355 *seq.*, NICOLETTI, II., 875 *seq.*: "*Erano contigui al palazzo Pontificio alcune case ed orti posseduti parte da D. Cesare Estense Duca di Modena e parte dalla famiglia Grimana; onde comprando gli uni e gli altri incorporolli all'antico giardino del Quirinale riducendolo con larga spesa a luogo di amene e vaghe delitie. Ricinse poi tutto l'ambito di esso con forti et alte mura in vece di siepe fragile,

St. Magdalen[1] and that of the fountain of Trevi, were similarly widened. The latter had only three simple spouts. Urban VIII. conceived the plan of erecting here, as for the Acqua Felice and the Acqua Paola, a monumental façade which would provide a " mostra ", that is, the magnificent spectacle of water rushing downwards. Bernini, who was commissioned to carry out the plan, thought of obtaining the required materials by demolishing the tomb of Caecilia Metella. The opposition of the Roman people prevented this ; in fact Bernini's plan

che per avanti lo circondava, e con baloardi si bene intesi, che dalla parte di tramontana sembra al di fuori a guisa di fortezza. Si vede scolpito in medaglia il palazzo Pontificio del Quirinale con queste parole : 'Ad aedium Pontificum securitatem.' Fabricò parimente in un lato di esso giardino verso la parte di oriente un commodo palazzuolo e dispose anco l'habitatione per le guardie di soldati Svizzeri per maestà e sicurezza de' Pontefici. Si leggono in un marmo queste memorie :

URBANUS OCTAVUS PONT. MAX.
SUMMORUM PONTIFICUM COMMODITATI ET OBLECTATIONI ET SECURITATI
VIRIDARII SPATIUM AMPLIORI PROTENDIT ACCESSIONE,
QUAM COMPLANAVIT
HINC VALLIS IMAE SUPERFICIEM ATTOLLENS,
COLLIS INDE SUMMITATEM DEPRIMENS.
AREAS ADDITAS APTE DISTINXIT, IRRIGAVIT FONTIBUS ET DECENTER EXCOLUIT,
IN ANGULO ORIENTALI DOMUM CURARUM INTERMISSIONE RECESSUM CONSTITUIT,
EXCUBIIS MILITUM HELVETIORUM CONTUBERNIA CONSTRUXIT ET DISPOSUIT,
HORTOS AMBITU PARIETUM UNDEQUAQUE CONCLUSIT
ANNO SALUTIS 1628 PONT. ANNO 6°.

Cf. also **Avviso* of May 10, 1625, *Urb.*, 1095, Vatican Library.

[1] See Amici, *Mem. intorno S. Camillo de Lellis*, Roma, 1913, 148 *seq.* *Cf. Arch. d. Soc. Rom.*, V., 656 ; Pollak-Frey, 437.

Besides the inscription here given, I also saw in 1908 the following in the shop of a Roman antiquary : " In honorem | Deiparae virg. | et S. Phil. Nerii | Urbano VIII. Pont. Max. | Annuente | congreg. Oratorii | viam aperuit | plateam stravit | A° sal. 1628."

was never carried out: only the spout of the fountain was given its present position.[1]

In the autumn of 1629 Bernini was appointed superintendent of the Acqua Virgine, a post which his lately deceased father had also held. The latter's last work was the well-known "Barcaccia" in the Piazza di Spagna: this is an oblong barque in a sunk basin from which jets of water are thrown inside and out.[2] This was the first example of a new type of fountain, different from the architectural type hitherto in use,[3] in the development of which the son surpassed the father. In the life-time of Urban VIII., as appears from the shield displaying the Barberini bees, he erected in the Piazza Barberini the famous fountain of the Triton, placed in a straight line with the street ascending from the lower city: three water-spouting dolphins support on their twisted tails a basin in the shape of a shell; on this the Triton kneels whilst through a slender tube he blows high into the air a thin jet of water which bathes his body as it falls back.[4] The arms of the Barberini provided Bernini with a motif for a fountain in the Vatican [5] and for the "Fountain of the Bees" which at one time adorned the bend of the Via Sistina and the Piazza which at that time derived its name from the palace of Cardinal Domenico Grimani. Of

[1] "In quest' anno 1643 la S. di N.S. Urbano VIII. fa rinovare il fonte con disegno del cavalier Bernini (MARTINELLI, 96). *Cf.* FRASCHETTI, 127 *seq.*; BALDINUCCI (edit. RIEGL), 91 *seq.*, 93; GUIDI, 81 *seq.*; POLLAK-FREY, 14 *seq.* As against FRASCHETTI see Voss' arguments in *Jahrb. der preuss. Kunstsamml.*, 1910, 127 *seq.* (who is supported by DOMARUS [BACCI, 45] and EGGER, *Architekt. Handzeichnungen* 10. *Cf.* BENKARD, 24.

[2] That the Barraccia is not by Lorenzo but by Pietro Bernini appears from the documents quoted by O. POLLAK in *Vita d'arte II.* (1909), 458 *seq.*, 515 *seq.* *Cf.* POLLAK-FREY, 12 *seq.*

[3] BALDINUCCI, 35; GUIDI, 41; FRIEDLÄNDER, *Römische Brunnen*, Leipzig, 1922, 8 *seq.*

[4] BALDINUCCI (edit. RIEGL), 91; FRASCHETTI, 123 *seq.* *Cf.* Voss in *Jahrb. der preuss. Kunstsamml.*, XXXI., 107 *seq.*; GUIDI, 43, 71 *seq.*; WEISBACH, *Barock*, 31; BENKARD, 23; COLASANTI, XXXV., dissert., 215.

[5] TOTTI, 22; FRASCHETTI, 122; COLASANTI, dissert., 212.

late the fountain has been once more put up not far from this spot.[1] On the other hand the two interesting fountains erected by Bernini in the Villa Mattei, have disappeared.[2]

Urban's predilection for the fountains which constitute so characteristic an ornament of Rome, is shown by the ordinances of the years 1624, 1629, and 1631 issued for the purpose of ensuring the cleanliness of works of such importance for the health of the people.[3] Nor did he bestow less care on the cleanliness of the streets and on their pavement.[4] New roads were opened from S. Eusebio to S. Bibiana, near the Chiesa Nuova,[5] near S. Caterina de' Funari[6] and along the Ripa Grande.[7] To this day the beautiful street near St. Mary Major bears the name of Urban VIII.[8] The two arches of the bridge of S. Angelo near the right bank of the river were cleared: in this both the safety of Castle S. Angelo and the danger of floods were kept in view.[9] Ponte Molle and Ponte

[1] CANCELLIERI, *Tarantismo*, 10; *Inventario*, 412; FRASCHETTI, 121 *seq.*; GUIDI, 147; POLLAK-FREY, 17.

[2] GUIDI, 42 *seq.*

[3] See *Editti, V., 51, p. 118, 120; V., 74, p. 161, Papal Secret Archives.

[4] See **Avviso* of August 21, 1624; (a beginning had been made of "selciare la piazza del Popolo", the street from St. Mary Major to the Latern and from the latter to the Colosseum; the money to be raised by means of a new tax on the adjoining estates and vineyards), and August 24, 1624 (edict of the Camerlengo on cleaning of streets with a view to public health), *Urb.* 1094, Vatican Library. *Cf.* POLLAK-FREY, 405.

[5] See **Avviso* of February 20, 1627, *Urb.* 1097, *loc. cit.*; TOTTI, 225, 228; HEMPEL, 65; STRONG, *Chiesa Nuova*, 64.

[6] TOTTI, 174.

[7] *Id.*, 55. Urban's coat of arms in the Piazza Marta near S. Ignazio flanked by two cornucopias and surmounted by the Barberini sun and underneath a cartouche with the inscription; "Urb., VIII., P.M.A., XVIII." (1640), no doubt points to some repairs of the streets.

[8] *NICOLETTI, LII., 7, p. 906, Vatican Library. *Cf. Inventario*, 20.

[9] See the inscription of 1628 in TOTTI, 242; *cf.* POLLAK-FREY, 7.

Quattro Capi were also repaired and Ponte Sisto was repaved.[1]

We get a comprehensive view of the appearance of the Eternal City at that period from the plans of Rome, more particularly the large one of 1625,[2] from engravings, etchings, and drawings[3] as well as from numerous travel books.[4] There existed already then professional guides of whom the best known was Johann Hoch, an officer in the Swiss Guards,

[1] Pollak-Frey, 7–8.

[2] Ehrle, *Roma*, *cf.* Huelsen, *Saggio*, 25. On a view dated 1631, see *Mél. d' archéol.*, XX. (1900), 296 *seq.*

[3] Notably those of Stefano della Bella : see below, p. 540.

[4] Among the guides one of the most remarkable was *Italia Antiqua*, by Philip Cluver, published in 1624. A popular Guide to Italy, one which drew attention to everything worth seeing, was the *Itinerarium historico-politicum* of Jakob Grasser of Bâle, also published in 1624. The Jubilee year of 1625 saw the publication of *Mercurius italicus*, with pictures of towns and small maps (new edition Lugduni, 1628 ; on Rome : pp. 260–440). In 1627 Jos. Furttenbach published at Ulm his *Itinerarium Italiae*, a kind of Baedecker with many engravings (see *Bollet. d. Soc. Geog. ital.*, V. [1919], 620 *seq.*). *The Teatro delle città d'Italia, Padova,* 1629, with very pretty illustrations, appeared anonymously. A capital work, the real Baedecker of the period, is Martin Zeiller's *Itinerarium Italiae*, 1640, at Frankfort on the Main, published by Merian (see Friedländer in *Deutsche Rundschau*, 1876, 241 *seq.*). The copper plates are justly esteemed. (*Cf. P. Zeiller, M. Zeiller*, in *Annuaire du Club Alpin, Français*, XIV. [1887]. Only a few travel descriptions deserve to be mentioned. Jean Jacques Bouchard, a frivolous Frenchman with a taste for art who came to Rome in February, 1632, gives a detailed description of the Roman Carnival and of his adventures : some of his information makes a useful contribution to the history of civilization ; see L. Marcheix, *Un Parisien à Rome et Naples en 1632*, Paris, 1897 and 1907. The journey of the archæologist Justus Rycynius (1624), is discussed by Roersch, *De Gand à Rome* in the *Mél. Kurth II.* On the journey to Italy of the two Margraves of Baden (1644), see *Zeitschr. für die Gesch. des Oberrheins N.F.I.* (1866).

who called himself Giovanni Alto.[1] For the benefit of pilgrims during the Holy Year of 1625, a second edition was published of Ottavio Panciroli's *Tesori nascosti dell'alma città di Roma.* Far more important was the new edition of a book by the Servite Pietro Martire Felini on " the wonders of Rome "—*Le meraviglie di Roma*—for here interest in the monuments asserts itself decisively. Much information may be derived from the numerous illustrations showing the contemporary exteriors of numerous churches which subsequently received new façades.[2]

In 1624 Urban VIII.'s personal physician, the Sienese Giulio Mancini, completed his *Viaggio per Roma* (journey through Rome). Here a fine connoisseur, one interested in everything and an acute observer, provides an accurate, topographically ordered survey of the artistic wealth of Rome, though one limited to pictorial works.[3] Until then guide-books had confined themselves to the art of the Renaissance, starting from Giotto, whereas Mancini also gives numerous examples of the art of the early Christian and medieval periods. He enumerates so many works of art and artists that in this respect he surpasses all his predecessors ; he is also very reliable.[4]

Whilst this unique source of information on the history of art, owing to the abundance of the material supplied, remained unpublished for three centuries, a number of publications appeared under Urban VIII. which in part inaugurated a new era, in the literature of which Rome was the theme. In 1638

[1] J. Hoch published a popular illustrated work for Rome travellers entitled *Splendore dell'antica e moderna Roma . . . dato alle stampe da Giov. Alto* (with engraved portrait of Urban VIII.), Roma, 1641. *Cf.* below, p. 538, n. 2.

[2] P. M. Felini, *Trattato nuovo delle cose maravigliose dell'alma città di Roma,* Rome, 1625 (see Schudt, *Mancini,* 30 *seq.,* 123). On p. 161 Felini gives " La facciata della Consolatione come era prima ", on p. 162 the new façade.

[3] On this work, written under Paul V., see our account in Vol. XXVI., p. 438 *seq.*

[4] This is the result of the researches by Schudt in his excellent edition of Mancini's *Viaggio per Roma.* Leipzig, 1923, especially p. 38 *seq.*

there appeared at Naples a work written eighteen years earlier by the painter Gaspari Celio.[1] This work constitutes the first printed guide-book which, leaving aside the hagiographical element, deals exclusively with the monuments. Celio, whose artistic conceptions resemble those of Mancini, though he writes quite independently of him, also devotes his attention chiefly to pictures, but he likewise notes the more important works of sculpture. An alphabetical list of churches is followed by an enumeration of the palaces and the paintings on façades but, contrary to Mancini, he only mentions contemporary works of art.[2] In 1639 the Jesuit Alexander Donatus of Siena published a description of old and new Rome.[3] However, he concentrates on old Rome, and only one of his four tomes, the last, deals with the Christian epoch down to Urban VIII., to whom the work is dedicated. His is an excellent summary, as regards old Rome, of the results of research ever since the epoch-making second edition of Marliani's *Topography* published in 1544, and is distinguished for learning and maturity of judgment.[4]

The year 1639 also saw a new edition of a guide-book by the Westphalian Hermann Bavinck, a chaplain at the Anima,[5] in which the author describes the wonders of the city of Rome, and the seven most famous churches throughout Christendom out of her three hundred and fifty. The same year also saw the publication of a description, by the painter Giovanni Baglione, of the nine churches which most interested the pilgrims.[6] The German Guide starts from the national church of the Anima and departs in many ways from the routine of

[1] *Memoria fatta dal sig. Gaspare Celio delli nomi dell'artefic, delle pitture che sono in alcune chiese, facciate e palazzi di Romai* Napoli, 1638.

[2] See SCHUDT, *Mancini*, 41 *seq.*

[3] A. DONATUS, *Roma vetus ac recens utriusque aedificiis ad eruditam cognitionem expositis*, Romae, 1638.

[4] RICHTER, *Topographie Roms*, Munich, 1901, 19. *Cf.* also J. B. CASALIUS, *De Urbis splendore*, Romae, 1650.

[5] The first had appeared already in 1620: SCHUDT, *Mancini*, 122.

[6] G. BAGLIONE, *Le nove chiese di Roma*, Roma, 1639.

existing guide-books, though he gives no fresh information. On the other hand, Baglione, who dedicated his " Description " to Cardinal Francesco Barberini, produced a much more important work, owing to the fact that he takes equal account of architecture, painting, and sculpture.[1]

Pompilio Totti's description of modern Rome, first published in 1637 and republished in 1639, was dedicated to Cardinal Antonio Barberini.[2] This publication, the most important after Felini's treatise, and which also contains numerous interesting illustrations, spreads the visits to churches, convents, hospitals, oratories of confraternities, colleges, seminaries, palaces, libraries, museums, and villas over a period of six days, each of which is devoted to a visit of two or three *Rioni*. Though here hagiographical interest still remains very great, references to works of art are nevertheless increasingly numerous, though mostly to those of the period.

In 1643 Giovan Domenico Franzini published a new and greatly enlarged edition of Felini's guide-book [3] and the year 1644 witnessed the appearance of a new work on Rome which its publisher dedicated to the antiquarian Cassiano del Pozzo.[4] Its author, Fioravante Martinelli, provides a somewhat dry but wholly new census of everything worth seeing, together with many sidelights on the manners and culture of the period. He spreads the visit of the city over ten days. On the first day he takes the visitor from the old foreign quarter in the streets dell'Orso and Tor di Nona to the Vatican *Borgo*. The second day is devoted to the Trastevere. On the third day he starts from the church of the Florentines, S. Giovanni, near the entrance to the Via Giulia, whence he visits part of the Old City and the Isle of the Tiber. On the fourth day he sets out from the Cancelleria to take the visitor through the *Rioni*

[1] SCHUDT, *Mancini*, 43.

[2] P. TOTTI, *Ritratto delle grandezze di Roma*, Roma, 1637 : the second edition was published in 1639 by Totti's son, Ludovico ; our quotations are from this edition.

[3] SCHUDT, *Mancini*, 126.

[4] F. MARTINELLI, *Roma ricercata nel suo sito e nella scuola di tutti gli antiquarii*, Roma, 1644.

Regola and S. Angelo as far as the Aventine. The fifth excursion starts from the Pasquino and leads to the Palatine and the Celian Hill ; the sixth goes from S. Salvatore in Lauro, through the centre of the town as far as the Forum Romanum and back to the Palazzo di Venezia. The seventh visit starts once more from the foreign quarter near S. Apollinare, and the eighth from the Piazza Nicosia. The former is mainly devoted to the Viminal and the Quirinal, the latter ends at the baths of Diocletian. On the ninth day a start is made from the Piazza Borghese whence the northern part of the city is visited as far as the Porta Pinciana. The tenth day Martinelli devotes to visits to the nine principal churches, and he points out that a pilgrimage to these places sanctified by the blood of Martyrs, and which the Popes had enriched with numberless Indulgences, should be undertaken only after receiving the sacraments of Penance and the Eucharist.[1]

With these guide-books in our hands, and on the basis of Totti's partition into *Rioni*,[2] let us in our turn take a walk through the Rome of that period.

[1] MARTINELLI, 114. The nine principal churches are, according to Martinelli : *St. Peter's, St. Paul's outside the Walls* (on the road to the latter the memorial, recently destroyed in barbarous fashion, of the parting of the Princes of the Apostles and the *Vigna* of St. Frances of Rome on the outer walls of which were depicted the miracles of that Saint), *SS. Vincent and Anastasius alle Tre Fontane* (together with the small churches of *S. Paolo alle Tre Fontane* and S. Maria Scala Coeli), *S. Annunciata della Compagnia del Gonfalone* per amministrare li sagramenti alli coloni delle circovicine tenute, l'a. 1640 ristorata dal card. [Franc.] Barberini protettore (probably the *Annunziatella* mentioned by TOMASETTI, II., 40 and 416), *S. Sebastiano, St. John Lateran, S. Croce in Gerusalemme, St. Laurence outside the Walls*, and *St. Mary Major*. A detailed description of these nine churches is found in the above-quoted work of BAGLIONE, *Le nove chiese di Roma*.

[2] Up to the new order established by Benedict XIV. in 1743 (*cf.* B. BERNARDINI, *Descriz. del nuovo ripartimento de' Rioni di Roma*, Roma, 1744), the boundaries of the Rioni were very ill-defined.

The most interesting for strangers was the *Rione di Borgo* which fell into six subdivisions, viz. Borgo di S. Angelo, Borgo Angelico, Pio, Alessandrino, Vecchio, and S. Spirito. Here St. Peter's and the Vatican, with their choice art treasures, presented sights such as no other city in the world had to offer.

From the bridge of S. Angelo one still beheld, on the left, in the Tiber, between two mills, the remains of the Pons Vaticanus, whilst on the right the river bank, with its medley of houses, grey with age, and their small balconies and verdant terraces, presented a most enchanting view to the painter. The newly fortified Castle of S. Angelo and the arsenal established in the Vatican, gave proof of Urban VIII.'s solicitude for the security of his capital. On entering the Via Alessandrina, so called after Alexander VI., (since the time of Pius V., *Borgo Nuovo*), the finest of the three streets leading up to St. Peter's, the visitor had on his left the imposing pile of the hospital of S. Spirito, which was immediately subject to the Holy See. Its nucleus consisted of the new structure by Sixtus IV. with its two wards of a thousand beds which adjoined a central chapel crowned with a graceful cupola. Annexed to the hospital, which still had its marble gateway and open porticoes beneath, was a home for foundlings and an establishment for the education of 450 boys and 500 girls. Adjoining it was the palace constructed by Ottavio Mascherino under Gregory XIII. for the Commander of the Order of the Holy Ghost who was at the head of the administration of the institution. Both this hospital as well as that of the Lateran, were in excellent condition.[1]

In the main street, viz. the Borgo Nuovo, on the left and facing S. Maria in Transpontina, a church served by the Carmelites, one beheld the prison of the Borgo. From there one reached the small Piazza Scossa Cavalli embellished with a fountain by Paul V. Here stood the classical Renaissance palace of Cardinal Adriano of Corneto, erected towards the end

[1] *Cf.* the account by H. Marchstaller in *Carinthia,* LXXI. (1881), 274.

of the fifteenth century.[1] On the south and facing it rose the palace erected under Sixtus IV. by Cardinal Domenico della Rovere, which at that time belonged to the Madruzzi, a family of Trent ; on the west side, opposite the church of S. Giacomo Scossa Cavalli, stood the palace in which Raphael spent the last years of his life,[2] and further to the right, towards St. Peter's, two small churches which have disappeared and the Rusticucci palace. The piazza of St. Peter's, with Paul V.'s magnificent fountain and Sixtus V.'s obelisk, presented a most picturesque scene, though at that time it had only half its present width.[3] When the pilgrim has inspected the artistic treasures of the basilica of St. Peter's, Martinelli advises him to make the ascent of the dome up to its highest point, so as to get the full impression of the gigantic building, after which he should visit the marvels of the papal palace : the Scala Clementina, the Stanze, the Sala Regia and the Sala Ducale, the Sistine Chapel, the Loggias, the apartments newly restored by Urban VIII., the library, the armoury, the antiques of the Belvedere, and finally the lovely garden. The visit to the Borgo where, near S. Marta, Urban VIII. had established the seminary of St. Peter's, should conclude with an inspection of the collection of antiques of the Cesi and the Hospital of S. Spirito.[4]

The *Lungara*, which leads from the Porta S. Spirito to the Porta Settimiana (Settignana) had by then completely lost its rural character and was built over on both sides, as we see from Maggi's plan. This street, which was included in the *Rione* of the Trastevere, in addition to the Palazzo Salviati and the Camaldolese church of S. Leonardo, included two Barberini

[1] BRADY, *Anglo-Roman Papers*, London, 1890, 9–93, gives the fullest account of the vicissitudes of the palace which, at this time, is the property of the Torlonia.

[2] EHRLE, *Spada*, 55 *seq*.

[3] *Id*., 47 *seq*.

[4] Not far from the Porta Cavallegieri, near the Oratory of St. Peter and on the spot once occupied by the *Schola Francorum*, stood the barracks of the lancers whom Innocent VIII. had chosen for his bodyguard ; see EHRLE in *Roma Aeterna*, VI. (1926), 143 *seq*.

foundations, viz. the churches and convents of S. Maria Regina Coeli [1] and S. Giacomo in Settimiana [2] as well as the Farnesina (Giardino dei Farnesi) and the palace of the Riarii. The street to the right of the Porta Settimiana led to S. Onofrio. Whilst this church rose on the northern section of the Janiculus, on the southern there lay the imposing Acqua Paola and the church of S. Pietro in Montorio, the High Altar of which was adorned with Raphael's " Transfiguration ".

The populous *Trastevere,* with its many towers and churches, was perhaps the most picturesque district of Rome. Among its sacred edifices Martinelli singles out S. Maria della Scala with the convent of the reformed Carmelites, S. Maria in Trastevere with the adjoining palace of S. Callisto occupied by the Benedictines of the Congregation of St. Justina,[3] S. Crisogono, S. Giovanni de' Genovesi, S. Francesco a Ripa and S. Cosimato. The last-named churches as well as S. Maria dell'Orto, were completely surrounded by gardens. The Porta Portese and the Porta S. Pancrazio were rebuilt by Urban VIII. on the occasion of the works of fortification executed in 1643.[4] The cemetery of the Jews was situate near the Porta Portese.[5]

The *Rione di Ripa* on the left bank of the river and facing the Trastevere, which also included the picturesque island of St. Bartholomew, embraced the Aventine and the district between the Tiber and the Gates of St. Paul, St. Sebastian, and the Latin Gate. The churches of St. Sixtus, St. Gregory, SS. John and Paul, St. Anastasia, St. George in Velabro, and the Palatine, which were subsequently included in the Rione Campitelli, were then considered as belonging to the Rione di Ripa. The State salt store was situate at the foot of the

[1] " Chiesa e monasterio ch'ora fabbrica la signora D. Anna Colonna Barberini " says Martinelli (14).

[2] *Cf.* Totti, 48, and above, p. 489.

[3] The illustration in Totti (65), substantially shows the same picture as that which presents itself to the beholder at this day.

[4] Borgatti, *Le mura di Roma,* in *Riv. di Artiglieria,* XVI., 400; Vasi, I., LXVII., LXXV, with picture of the old Porta Portese previous to its reconstruction.

[5] Martinelli, 18.

Aventine where the name of *Marmorata* still recalled the ancient *Emporium*. Apart from some imposing remains of Roman times and some venerable old churches and convents, the whole of this district was occupied by gardens and vine-yards. Houses were only found in the northern section of the Rione, with the churches of S. Maria in Cosmedin [1] and St. Nicholas in Carcere. The ancient round temple opposite S. Maria in Cosmedin had been turned into a church, viz. S. Stefano delle Carrozze (later on S. Maria del Sole); the Garden of the Cenci was near by.[2] The graceful temple of Fortuna Virilis had become the church of the Armenians under the title of St. Mary of Egypt. The medieval house facing it was called House of Pilate by the ignorant populace, Totti informs us. Within the buildings near S. Giovanni Decollato was the burial place of those who had undergone capital punishment.[3]

The palace of the Savelli, built into the theatre of Marcellus, is still included in the Rione di Ripa by Tittone. Later on it was considered as belonging to the *Rione di S. Angelo*, so called after the church of S. Angelo built into the portico of Octavia. The surname " in Pescaria " is due to the nearby fish-market. From there one entered the Jewish Ghetto which was shut off by means of gates. In striking contrast with this filthy quarter, which was also the abode of the tanners,[4] there arose in the Rione di S. Angelo, on the ruins of the Circus Flaminius, the two magnificent palaces of the Mattei; before the older of the two stood the beautiful fountain of Taddeo Landrini. The nearby palace of the Patrizi had passed into the hands of the Costaguti. From there a narrow lane led to the church of S. Ambrogio della Massima, rebuilt in 1606, with its adjoining convent of Benedictine nuns. The remarkable house of Lorenzo de' Manili [5] dates from the Quattrocento and the church of S. Caterina de' Funari from the Cinquecento.

The *Rione della Regola* which followed along the river bank,

[1] In 1639 Urban VIII. presented to the church a mosaic from old St. Peter's (*cf.* Forcella, IV., 308), which is still there.

[2] Martinelli, 33.

[3] *Id.*, 43.

[4] *Id.*, 186.

[5] Pastor, *Rom zur Ende der Renaissance*, 66.

also called " Arenula ", from the sand of the river, likewise abounded in striking contrasts. On the one hand one saw dark, still wholly medieval lanes, on the other the splendid palaces of the Santa Croce, Cenci, and Spada,[1] the latter with a beautiful garden towards the Tiber, the Palazzo Barberini ai Giubbonari near the Monte di Pietà, and, eclipsing everything else, the gigantic palace of the Farnese with its treasures of ancient and modern art. In the piazza in front, which was called after the Duke of Parma, and was adorned with two fountains,[2] there rose the Palazzo Pighini which housed some famous antique statues. Besides numerous old churches of no great size, this quarter was adorned with the magnificent new church of the Barnabites, S. Carlo ai Catinari and S. Trinità de' Pellegrini, in the oratory of which a sermon was preached to the Jews on Saturdays. In the main street, called after S. Maria di Monserrato, the national church of the Aragonians, there also rose S. Girolamo della Carità containing the room of St. Philip Neri, greatly revered by the Romans,[3] S. Caterina della Rota and the English College, and at no great distance from there, the prison of Corte Savella.

The *Rione di Parione* which spread in a northerly direction, also boasted some splendid buildings. The Orsini had two palaces there, one near the Pasquino [4] and another in the

[1] Erected by Cardinal Capodiferro, it first passed into the hands of the Mignatelli and later on into those of Cardinal Spada (TOTTI, 210), who altered and decorated it (see HEMPEL, 49). In the thirties Borromini, Bernini's great rival, erected the magnificent colonnade in the second *cortile*; *cf.* PANOFSKY in *Jahrbuch der preuss. Kunstsamml.*, XL., 249 *seq.*

[2] Water was carried to them in 1626 from the Acqua Paola; *cf.* POLLAK-FREY, 11.

[3] " Camera di molta bellezza e devotione, ornata dal cavalier Pantera (MARTINELLI, 23). The chapel of the confraternity, towards the restoration of which, subsequently to a fire, Cardinal Fr. Barberini contributed, was famous for the *bellissimi oratorii* which were held there during the winter months (TOTTI, 202).

[4] A picture of the statue, which differs from the present one, in TOTTI, 235.

Campo de' Fiori remarkable for its crooked appearance at the back, a peculiarity that made it possible to make out quite clearly the position of the ancient theatre of Pompey, the ruins of which gave its name to the nearby church of S. Maria di Grotta Pinta. The former *Circus* of Domitian—now Piazza Navona—which Gregory XIII. had embellished with three fountains, was almost completely shut in by buildings. Totti extols this Piazza as the finest in Rome, nay, in all Italy and perhaps in the world.[1] The hospital and church of the Spaniards, S. Giacomo, and the palaces of the Pamfili, the Cibo, Princes of Massa, of Urbano Mellini, the Gottifredi and Rivaldi families, of Francesco de Cupis, which was occupied by the imperial ambassador, and that of Cardinal Torres, formed a frame for the piazza. Other famous buildings in this district were the palaces of the Massimi and the elegant houses of the Pichi and Caccialupi, of Bishops Turci and Thomas Le Roy. However, all these buildings were eclipsed by the Cancelleria, the residence of Cardinal Francesco Barberini in his capacity as Vice-Chancellor : S. Lorenzo in Damaso formed part of the palace. The new popular church of the Oratorians, S. Maria e S. Gregorio in Vallicella, the façade of which produced its full effect thanks to the new street that led up to it, rivalled in its magnificence the church of the Cancelleria. A large parish was attached to Chiesa Nuova.[2]

The *Rione di Ponte* was still a densely populated business district and the Strada de Banchi Nuovi was the chief money mart. Sangallo's *Zena* at the terminus of that street already showed signs of incipient baroque. The Quattrocento quarter, to-day unhappily in a very dilapidated condition, shows beautiful middle-class dwellings in the Strada de' Coronari. In the Strada de Banchi Nuovi stood the magnificent palaces of the Niccolini and Alberini (Cicciaporci), and near the bridge

[1] Totti, 234 ; *ibid.*, 232, pictures of Piazza Navona and Piazza Madama. *Cf.* the excellent dissertation by L. De Gregori : *Piazza Navona prima d' Innocenzo X.*, *Roma*, 1926, where there is a reproduction of the drawing by A. Sacchi (inc. F. Collignon), 1634, and of the engraving by Israel Silvestre of 1642.

[2] Illustration in Totti, 235.

of S. Angelo the Palazzo Altoviti which has disappeared.[1] These buildings were rivalled by the former cardinalitial residence of Alexander VI., the old Cancelleria, which subsequently passed into the hands of the Sforza and at the time of Urban VIII. was occupied by Cardinal Sacchetti. The district was as rich in churches as it was in palaces. A number of small churches stood along the Via Giulia laid down by Julius II., which Paul V.'s wall-fountain (Fontanone) worthily terminated at its southern end; these were S. Biagio della Pagnotta, S. Maria del Suffragio, facing the Palazzo Ricci. SS. Faustina and Jovita de' Bresciani, rising on the substructures of the palace planned by Julius II. But these sacred edifices were completely eclipsed by the magnificent churches of S. Giovanni de' Fiorentini, S. Maria della Pace, S. Maria dell'Anima, and S. Agostino. S. Apollinare, the church of the adjoining German College, was famous for its musical performances on feast days. Connected with the church of SS. Simon and Jude was the Orsini palace on the Monte Giordano, the residence, at that time, of Cardinal Maurice of Savoy, a great patron of the arts. The church of S. Simeon the Prophet was connected in the same way with the Palazzo Cesi (Acquasparta) in the piazza Fiammetta, which the French ambassadors rented since 1641.[2] There were many inns along the Tiber, the most famous of them being the "Orso". One of the most picturesque districts of that quarter was that of S. Maria in Posterula, which has recently fallen a victim to the regulation of the Tiber. In the Via Maschera d'Oro the façade paintings of Polidoro Caravaggio and Maturino, representing the story of Niobe, were then still in good condition. To-day they are almost unrecognizable.[3] Totti repeatedly mentions house decorations of the same kind which had become popular under Leo X.; to-day the frescoes on the Ricci palace give us the best

[1] *Cf.* PASTOR, *Rom zu Ende der Renaissance*, 32.

[2] The rent of 1,700 scudi a year seemed unduly high; see AMEYDEN, *Diario*, under date of June 15, 1641, printed in *Il Cracas*, 1888, no. 48, p. 23.

[3] TOTTI, 252.

idea of what they were like.[1] Mention may also be made of the palaces of the Lancelotti and the Altemps ; the latter boasted a splendid chapel and a rich library.[2]

The *Rione di Campo Marzio* became increasingly important as a centre for strangers and foreigners. The largest building there was the Palazzo Borghese. At no great distance, on the Piazza Nicosia, stood the Palazzo Cardelli and the palaces of the Grand-Duke of Florence and Cardinal Gonzaga. There were also two remarkable palaces in the Corso, viz. that of Cardinal Quiñones, contiguous to S. Lorenzo in Lucina, which had been bought by the Peretti,[3] and the palace which Vincenzo Ammanati built for the Rucellai family, which boasted one of Rome's most beautiful staircases. At that time the palace belonged to the Gaetani,[4] from whom it passed into the hands of the Ruspoli. In the Corso, which only now became the real spinal cord of the City,[5] stood the great hospital of S. Giacomo degli Incurabili, surnamed " in Augusta ", after the Mausoleum of Augustus which rose in the neighbourhood. Many foreigners, especially artists, took up residence by preference in the Piazza Trinità de' Monti (Piazza di Spagna) and in the adjoining streets. Here stood the house of Lelio Guidiccioni whose library and picture gallery were held in high repute.[6] S. Maria del Popolo was a kind of museum, more particularly of renaissance sculpture. At that time both the Villa Medici and the Villa Borghese, which Totti includes in the Rione di Campo Marzio, still possessed in their entirety their famous collections of statues. These artistic treasures, as well as the natural charm of the district, specially attracted the artists who flocked to Rome and it was these incomparable villas which directed them towards landscape painting.[7]

[1] See our data Vol. XIII., 378, and *Rom zur Zeit der Renaissance*, 37 *seq.* [2] Totti, 261.

[3] In 1655 the palazzo was sold to Costanza Pamfili-Ludovisi and in 1690 to Marco Ottoboni : at present it is the property of the Duke of Fiano ; *cf.* Baraccioni, *I Rioni di Roma, Torino*, 1905, 212. [4] Totti, 337.

[5] Wölfflin, *Renaissance und Barock*, edited by Rose, Munich, 1926, 242. [6] Totti, 336, 344. [7] Justi, *Velasquez*, I.[3], 310.

The *Rione di Trevi*, which stretched from the Upper Corso as far as Porta Salaria and Porta Pia,[1] had developed into one of the most beautiful quarters of the City. Besides the Quirinal, which was increasingly taking the place of the Vatican as a papal residence, the district included the old palace of the Colonna near SS. Apostoli, the palaces of the Muti-Papazzurri, Bonelli, Aldobrandini, and Cesi, to which was then added the imposing new family palace of the Barberini.[2] The advisers of Cardinals Francesco and Antonio Barberini in all antiquarian matters, Claudio Menidret and Leonardo Agostini, who themselves possessed valuable collections of antiquities, lived in this neighbourhood.[3] To the old churches of SS. Apostoli, S. Maria in Via Lata and S. Marcello, new ones were added ; they were S. Niccolò di Tolentino, S. Isidoro, and S. Maria della Concezione. The Capuchin convent built by Urban VIII. which adjoined the latter church, was reputed one of the sights of Rome by reason of its size ; it possessed a very large garden. Since 1633 a work of art of the first rank and one which contemporaries considered as equalling Raphael's pictures, adorned the high altar of the recently demolished small church of St. Romuald ; this was Andrea Sacchi's " Vision of the Founder of the Camaldolese : The Saint appears pointing out to his devoutly attentive Monks a resplendent ladder amid glittering clouds, by which the members of his Order are seen ascending to heaven. The picture is one of the most solemn and most original creations of baroque art.[4] The whole of the eastern section of the Rione consisted of gardens and villas. The villa Ludovisi with its famous antiques is included by Totti in the Rione di Trevi ; later on it was assigned to the

[1] By the side of the new gateway of Pius IV. one still saw the old walled-up gate ; MARTINELLI, 174.

[2] The " Platea Barberina " is first mentioned in 1640 ; GOLZIO, *Il Palazzo Barberini* (1925), 7.

[3] TOTTI, 275–6.

[4] POSSE, *Sacchi*, 62 *seq.* Sacchi's picture now adorns the Vatican Gallery. A sketch for the picture is in the Dresden collection of engravings ; see *Mitteil. der sächs. Kunstsamml.*, III., Dresden, 1912, 49 *seq.*

Rione di Colonna which owes its name to the column of Marcus Aurelius. Here stood the palaces of the Aldobrandini, Bufallo, Chigi, Spada, and Veralli. Propaganda had its seat near S. Andrea delle Fratte ; Bernini lived in the house opposite. The principal churches were S. Maria in Via and S. Maria in Aquino near the Capranica College. S. Lorenzo in Lucina stood on the border of this quarter. At that time it was included in the Rione di Campo Marzio. For the better religious care of the people, Paul V. had entrusted this, the largest parish of Rome, which was also a collegiate church, to the so-called Minor Regular Clerics (*Chierici Regolari Minori*) of St. Francis Caracciolo who did excellent work there. Five smaller parishes were subject to this church, viz. S. Nicola in Campo Marzio, S. Ivo alla Scrofa, S. Lucia della Tinta, La Madonna dell'Orso, and S. Biagio di Monte Citorio.[1]

Like the Rione di Campo Marzio, that of *S. Eustachio* had acquired an increasing importance, a fact sufficiently explained by its central position. The Roman University was situate in its centre and not far from it, near the very ancient church of S. Salvatore in Thermis, stood the Palazzo Medici which Leo X. had occupied as a Cardinal. The beautiful Lanti and Cenci palaces also dated from the time of that Pope. The Grand-Duke of Tuscany, Ferdinand II., had had the Palazzo Medici (Madama), rebuilt and altered by the Florentine architect Paolo Marucelli.[2] Rallying centres for the French and the Spaniards in Rome were their national churches, S. Luigi and S. Giacomo. At that time the main entrance to the Spanish national church was not from the Piazza Navona but opposite the University. In the neighbourhood of S. Luigi lived the art-loving Marchese Giustiniano, Duke of Bassano, who had established in his palace not only an extensive library,[3] but likewise a valuable collection of antiques, the best pieces of which he rendered available to the general public by means of

[1] Totti, 332–3.

[2] O. Pollak in *Kunstkritik*, new series, IV. (1912/13), 57 *seq.* ; *cf.* Barracco, *Il Palazzo Madama*, Roma, 1904

[3] Totti, 359.

magnificent copper plates executed by Joachim von Sandrart.[1] The Rione S. Eustachio held yet a further attraction for art lovers, viz. the third of the new popular churches, that of S. Andrea della Valle. Here one could admire, besides the magnificent side-chapels of the Rucellai, Strozzi, and Barberini, the epoch-making frescoes of Lanfranco and Domenichino. The Barberini chapel was reputed one of Rome's finest.[2] The Theatines, who owned the church, had likewise begun to build their new convent adjoining the sacred edifice. Three famous scholars lived in the neighbourhood, viz. the Dean of the Rota, Coccini, the archæologist Cassiano del Pozzo and the eastern traveller Pietro della Valle. Besides a choice library, Cassiano del Pozzo owned a valuable collection of antique bas-reliefs, statues, coins, pictures, and drawings. The palace of Pietro della Valle, in the street of the same name, was also rich in antique treasures, but it was rather some objects from the remote Orient, more especially three mummy cases and their pictorial decoration, that called forth the wonderment of the Romans.[3]

The *Rione della Pigna* included an important educational establishment, viz. the Roman College, as well as the principal churches of the Jesuits and the Dominicans, viz. the Gesù and S. Maria sopra Minerva, the latter being the only large Gothic building in Rome. Among the remaining churches mention may be made of the Polish national church, St. Stanislaus, situate in the street of the Botteghe Oscure, the Pantheon, dedicated to all the Saints and the church of the Venetians, S. Marco, embodied in the Palazzo di Venezia; the great church of St. Ignatius, of which the first stone had been laid on August 5th, 1626, was still building.[4] The ground near the imperial forums had been rapidly covered with houses since the days of Gregory XIII.[5] Near S. Maria in Campo Carleo,

[1] *La Galleria Giustiniani del Marchese Giustiniani*, Roma, 1631. *Cf. J*, v. SANDRART'S *Academie*; new edition by Paltzer, Munich, 1925, 383.

[2] TOTTI, 372.

[3] *Id.*, 373.

[4] *Cf.* FREY, *Barockarchitektur*, 12 *seq.*, 41 *seq.*

[5] MARTINELLI, 71.

Francesco Gualdo had established in his house a museum "rich in rare and beautiful objects", to quote Totti.[1]

The chief sights of the *Rione Campitelli* were the palaces of the Capitol and the church of Araceli which Totti describes in detail.[2] This quarter, which also included a forum covered with a thick layer of rubbish and serving as grazing ground, hence called Campo Vaccino,[3] owed to Urban VIII. the new church of SS. Martina and Luke, and the restoration of SS. Cosmas and Damian. Here also there was no lack of palaces of the nobility, such as those of the Serlupi, Patrizi, Paluzzi, and Capizuchi near S. Maria in Campitelli.

The vast *Rione de' Monti*, of which the ancient church of St. Mary Major constituted the centre, had retained its isolated character in its southern section, notwithstanding the new Lateran palace, though the street from the Colosseum to the basilica was now built over; otherwise one only saw gardens and villas, among which Martinelli and Totti single out for special admiration the Villa Mattei on the Celio.[4] The streets leading from S. Croce and the Lateran to S. Martino ai Monti were almost exclusively lined with gardens. The built-over section began at S. Eusebio, S. Martino and S. Pietro in Vincoli. Near S. Maria de' Monti the College of Neophytes had arisen. Close by stood the Villa Aldobrandini and in the direction of the Quirinal there rose a palace famous for its artistic treasures which from the Borghese passed to the Bentivogli and from them into the hands of Mazarin.[5] However, the reputation for being the most beautiful park of Rome went to the Villa Montalto, the property of the Peretti, which spread north of S. Mary Major. There, says Totti, the wealth of vegetation vied with the beauty of the fountains whilst the magnificent apartments were adorned with frescoes and statues.[6]

[1] Totti, 473.

[2] *Id.*, 403-413.

[3] Illustration, *ibid.*, 428.

[4] Martinelli, 437; Totti, 437 *seq.*

[5] Martinelli, 88; illustration in Totti, 504; the palace finally became the property of the Rospigliosi.

[6] Totti, 505.

To the west of St. Mary Major, which marked the boundary of the Villa Montalto, several Orders had established themselves in the street of Quattro Fontane, as for instance, in 1626, the Praemonstratensians at S. Norbert's and the French Trinitarians at St. Denis' in 1619. In the long Via di Porta Pia with which Pius IV. had begun his regularization of the streets, with a view to opening access to the Monti,[1] Urban VIII. founded for the Carmelite nuns the convent della Santissima Incarnazione styled *Le Barberine*, after the Pope's family. The continuation of this street, the Via del Quirinale, showed a whole series of ecclesiastical edifices ; thus, for the Spanish Trinitarians, Bonomini had created his masterpiece, S. Carlino ; to this must be added the hospice of the Spanish Carmelites near SS. Anne and Joachim ; the Villa Bandini ; the Jesuit novitiate of S. Andrea with a very beautiful garden ; the church and convent of the Capuchin nuns of S. Chiara, and, lastly, facing the angle of the Quirinal palace, the convent of the Dominican nuns, S. Maria Maddalena.

Though a wide stretch of the district contained within the walls of Aurelius was not yet built over, it was calculated in 1626 that the built-over area would have increased to the extent of two-thirds within the next half-century.[2] This was chiefly due to Sixtus V. who had been the first to render habitable the higher, airier, and sunnier quarters, viz. the

[1] *Cf.* Wölfflin, *Renaissance und Barock*, 239.

[2] *" Essendo cresciuta la città di Roma quasi due terzi con più nobili edifitii e bellezza et ampiezza della città vecchia da 50 overo 60 anni in quà, cioè dall'arco di Portogallo insino al Popolo, dal Corso insino a Porta Pinciana, a Capo le Case insino a Termini e S. Maria Maggiore stendendosi le habitationi per le strade che vanno a S. Giovanni e parimente a Monte Cavallo, S. Lorenzo in Paneperna et Pantani insino de là dal Coliseo et in Trastevere S. Francesco a Ripa, S.Pietro a Montorio, la Longara et Borgo Pio insino alli bastioni," so we read in a memorial of Mgr. Vives and the " interessati nella piazza della S. Trinità de' Monti ; they prayed that the piazza should be cleaned ; when this was done the air became much better in that locality. *Mem.*, 1652, T. 2, Archives of Propaganda, Rome.

Rione de' Monti, by carrying water there. More and more the hill district began to compete with the narrow, populous quarters in the low-lying region along the Tiber. In the Campo Marzio also there had been an increase in the number of houses, and no longer was the Corso built over only as far as the Arco di Portogallo in the Via Frattina, but the houses spread as far as the Piazza del Popolo ; the same was true of the district between the Corso and Porta Pinciana and Piazza delle Terme. For the Monti, a Saturday market was established under Urban VIII., near the church of the Madonna.[1] Building activity was general and intense. New piazzas, streets, and churches were founded, palaces and monasteries enlarged.[2] The development of the Quirinal was greatly furthered by the fact that the Pope had his residence there, and by the erection of the huge family palace of the Barberini. The approach to the lower town, Via del Tritone, with its continuation, Angelo Custode and Via Rasella, which gave into the main artery opened by Sixtus V., became filled with houses. The new Capuchin convent and the churches of SS. Concezione, S. Niccolò da Tolentino and S. Isidore gave a quite new aspect to a region until then covered with gardens and vineyards. The change which took place here found striking expression in the fact that the name of the street, Capo le Case, was no longer deemed appropriate.[3] Notwithstanding the progress of building on the Monti, the lower town, especially the quarters near the bridge S. Angelo, the Cancelleria, the Campo de' Fiori, and the Piazza Navona, remained the business centre of the city, but it was impossible not to notice the shifting of the centre of gravity towards the Piazza della Trinità which had begun about the middle of the century.[4] When the Spanish ambassador, Albuquerque, took up residence in the Palazzo Monaldeschi, the Piazza della Trinità came to be called Piazza di Spagna.[5] In view of the fact that the hostelries along the

[1] *Cf.* the *Memorial quoted in the preceding note.

[2] *Ibid.*

[3] This is stressed by Totti (297).

[4] *Cf.* our data, Vol. XIII., 398.

[5] De Villa-Urritia, *El Palacio Barberini*, 18 *seq.*

Tiber, in Via dell'Orso and Via di Tor di Nona, were fever-infested,[1] the movement of strangers increasingly directed itself towards that district. Accordingly, a proposal was made in 1626 to establish a third market in the Piazza di Spagna in addition to the ones held every Wednesday in the Piazza Navona and every Saturday near the Madonna de' Monti, but this project was never realized.[2] The Piazza Navona retained its importance, thanks to its favourable position; in 1643 it was looked upon as the true centre of Rome.[3] Here every kind of trader displayed his wares, even those who had old books to sell. Here wandering artists gave exhibitions. At the nearby Pasquino the latest newspapers were on sale as soon as they were delivered at the Milanese Post Office, which had its office there. Here also lived the Stampatore Camerale, the book and paper merchants and the glove makers.[4] In the Piazza Madama, which was contiguous to the Piazza Navona, flowers and plants were sold on Wednesdays. On Thursdays and Fridays there was great animation in the Campo Vaccino, where oxen, cows, calves, pigs, sheep, and chickens were sold. A special horse and donkey fair was held in May near the Baths of Diocletian. On Saturdays the vendors of fruit, vegetables, and kitchen utensils foregathered near the Madonna de' Monti. Every day brisk business was done in the Campo de' Fiori, where horses, donkeys, hay, and grain were on sale. Cobblers and armourers mostly lived here. The two harbours of Rome presented a picture of extraordinary animation. At the Ripetta the smaller ships landed wood, wine, and fruit, whilst the bigger ones unloaded every kind of import at the Ripa Grande.[5] As in medieval Rome so in the era of baroque, traders and merchants had their own streets. The clothes and linen merchants lived near the Customs house (Dogana), not far from S. Eustachio. The goldsmiths lived near

[1] *"Gli Oltramontani, che lasciato gl'allogi dell'Orso, dove s'infermavano o morivano tutti, habitano in questi contorni senza conoscere, benchè all' hora arrivino differenza d' aria da loro paesi" we read in the memorial referred to in n. 2, p. 531.

[2] *Ibid.*

[3] Totti, 236.

[4] Martinelli, 179, 181.

[5] *Id.*, 179, 182.

S. Maria della Pace, the oil merchants near the Palazzo Capranica, the mattress makers near S. Pantaleone. Wood of every kind, also fuel, was on sale in the Piazza Nicosia. The men who let carriages and sedan chairs lived in the Via dell' Orso, from Piazza Nicosia as far as the College of the Celestines; those who let horses, in the continuation of this street, the Via di Tor di Nona, as far as Castle S. Angelo; the merchants of pious objects, the gold and silver smiths and the furriers in the Via de' Coronari, from the Piazza di Tor Sanguigna as far as Via di Panico; the makers of cross-bows in the Campo de' Fiori; the confectioners and soap-makers in the Piazza Capranica; the booksellers and copyists in the Via di Parione, from Pasquino as far as Chiesa Nuova; the vendors of bedding in the Via delle Botteghe Oscure, a name derived from the arches of the Circus Flaminius; the wood merchants, turners, and rope sellers in the Via de' Catinari.

A number of streets owed their names to the artisans who lived in them, as for instance, the Via de' Calderari (coppersmiths), Cartari (paper merchants), Pianellari (slipper merchants), Chiavari (locksmiths), Cappellari (hatters), Calzettari (stocking weavers), Pollaroli (poulterers), Ferravecchi (scrap-iron dealers), Liutari (lute merchants), Cordari (rope sellers), Giubbonari (clothes dealers), Vascellari (crockery merchants).[1]

The Via degli Orefici and the Via del Pellegrino, where trinkets, hats, caps, stockings, tape, straps, and things of that kind were on sale, was a medley of shops of every description. In the Via de' Banchi, which stretched from the bridge of S. Angelo as far as Monte Giordano, there were to be found, besides many banks, shops in which banners, vestments, lace, wearing apparel, and gloves could be obtained.[2] Already then agricultural labourers gathered in the Piazza Montanara and the bakers at S. Andrea della Valle. There was a special vegetable market in the Piazza del Paradiso where there were inns for muleteers. Provisions of every kind were on sale in the most diverse places. Among others, Martinelli mentions

[1] E. Simonetti, *I nomi delle vie di Roma, Roma*, 1898.

[2] Martinelli, 183–8. On the *Via degli Orefici*, see Totti, 224.

the bridge of S. Angelo, the Via di Panico, the district of the Pozzo Bianco near Chiesa Nuova, the Piazzas of St. Peter's, S. Lorenzo in Damaso, S. Croce, S. Maria del Popolo, Piazza Colonna, Sciarra, Rotonda, Giudea and Montanara, and, finally, the districts of Tor de' Conti, the Fountains of Trevi, Tor Sanguigna, the Scrofa and Ripetta, Ponte Quattro Capi and Ponte Sisto; in the Trastevere, S. Apollonia and the region round the Porta Settiminiana.[1]

The life of the small people which spent itself with southern vivaciousness in the narrow streets and the piazzas of the old city, has been splendidly recorded by several painters, such as Michelangelo, Cerquazzi [2] and Pieter van Laar.[3]

Among the many foreign artists which Rome received within its walls at that time was Velasquez, who paid his first visit to the Eternal City in 1630; Cardinal Francesco Barberini gave him many tokens of his favour.[4] That German artists were but poorly represented in Rome at that time is not surprising in view of the Thirty Years' War.[5] All the more numerous were the Dutch who made more or less lengthy stays there, as Van Dyck who painted Maffeo Barberini's portrait shortly before the latter's elevation to the papacy,[6] the brothers Jan and

[1] MARTINELLI, *loc. cit.* *Cf.* MORONI, *Vie voci e viandanti, Roma*, 1894, 55.

[2] Of his interesting popular scenes the Galleria Nazionale of Rome preserves the following: No. 982, "Dentist in Piazza Navona"; No. 984, "Wandering Minstrel"; No. 1058, "Peasants before a public house"; *cf.* THIEME, VI., 298.

[3] His *genre* paintings mark the beginning of Bambocciata painting; see HERMANIN, *Incisioni e disegni*, I., Roma, 1912, 10.

[4] JUSTI, *Velasquez*, I.[3] (1922), 291 *seq.*

[5] Elsheimer of Frankfort (Elsheimer, 1578–1610), who lived in Rome from 1600, belongs to an earlier period. *Cf.* THIEME, X., 483–6.

[6] M. VAES (*Le séjour de Van Dyck en Italie* in the *Bullet. de l'Inst. Hist. Belge*, IV. [1924], 102 *seq.*, proves that the master came to Rome in February, 1622, where he remained until August; in March, 1623, he paid a second visit to the Eternal City. *Cf.* also NOACK, *Deutsches Leben*, 352 *seq.*, and TOMASETTI, *V. Dyck a Roma*, in *Cosmos Cath.*, 1900, 6 *seq.*

Andries Both, Hermann Swanevelt, Cornelis Bloemart,[1] François Duquesnoy.[2] Between 1625 and 1630 the artists from the Low Countries formed a kind of Society, the so-called "Schilderbent" (Painter's Association) which was destined to become an important factor in the artistic life of Rome. German artists were admitted to membership at an early date, as, for instance, the engraver Joachim von Sandrart of Frankfort who had come to Rome in 1628. The leading spirit of this high-spirited and clever group of fellow nationals was Pieter van Laar, surnamed Bamboots, who "depicts with bold brush, in all its rude and manifold variety, the life of the lower classes of Rome in its hovels and taverns built into the ruins of antiquity.[3] Both in regard to numbers and importance, the French artistic colony competed with that of the Low Countries; Jacques Stella and Simon Vouet held an important place in it.[4] To them must be added Nicolas Poussin, Jean Dughet and Claude Lorrain who brought to perfection classical, idealized landscape painting. Italy was their land of predilection, they responded fully to the spell of its beauty and missed nothing of the force of its enchanting colouring.[5]

Poussin, a native of Normandy, lived in Rome from 1624 up

[1] See *Arch. d. Soc. Rom.*, IV., 405.

[2] *Cf.* Bertolotti, *Artisti Olandesi e Belgi in Roma*, Florence, 1880; *Arch. d. Soc. Rom.*, IV., 405; Hermanin in the work quoted above, p. 535, n. 3; Grautolff, N. Poussin, I., Munich, 1914, 365 *seq.*; *Bullet. de l'Inst. Hist. Belge.*, I. (1922), 96 *seq.*

[3] Noack, *loc. cit.*, 7–9. On the Schilderbent, see Vaes in *Bullet. de l'Inst. Hist. Belge*, I. (1914), 303 *seq.*, and Hoogewerff in the periodical *Roma, II.* (1924), 120 *seq.*

[4] Bertolotti, *Artisti Francesi in Roma, Mantova*, 1886; Grautolff, *loc. cit.*

[5] See Gerstenberg, *Die ideale Landschaftsmalerei. Ihre Begründung und Vollendung in Rom*, Halle, 1923, 81 *seq. Cf.* the excellent monographs by W. Friedländer of *Poussin* (Munich, 1914), and *Claude Lorrain* (Berlin, 1921). Also P. Desjardins, *N. Poussin*, Paris; Magne, *N. Poussin*, Bruxelles, 1931, Marc Pattison, *Claude Lorrain*, Paris, 1884; Nolhac, *Cl. Lorrain et le paysage Romain*, in *Etudes ital.*, I. (1919); *id. Souvenirs d'un vieux Romain*, Paris, 1922, 65 *seq.*

to the time of his death in 1665, except for a two years' stay in Paris [1640–1642]. Like Claude Lorrain, who also permanently settled in the Eternal City in the autumn of 1627, he lived in the Via Paolina (Via del Babuino).[1] For a time Claude Lorrain and Joachim von Sandrart were the guests of Marchese Giustiniani.[2] In company with the two French artists, who were fundamentally kindred spirits though they differed profoundly from him in their art and work, Sandrart made numerous excursions "for the purpose of sketching landscapes from life".[3] The impressive loneliness of the Campagna cast a peculiar spell upon the strangers from the North. Where former travellers had seen nothing but hopeless desolation, they discovered unsuspected beauties and created pictures of high poetical conception. Who could forget the solemn stillness of Poussin's picture of the country at Acqua Acetosa in which an angel suggests to the Evangelist Matthew the text of his Gospel? [Berlin Museum.] Who is not carried away by Claude Lorrain's Tiber landscape with Tobias and the Angel? [Prado Museum, Madrid.] The beauty of these works is often equalled by Dughet's landscapes. All these masters beheld a highly idealized picture of the character of the country around Rome, but each of them shows to the spectator a different aspect of it: Dughet its sternness, which is almost threatening; Poussin its historic greatness; Claude its luminous solemnity.[4] Like so many other painters, Claude Lorrain has also perpetuated in a painting and in an etching the life of the Campo Vaccino, "that most Roman of Rome's piazzas". This small picture, now in the Louvre in Paris, is a real "Ricordo di Roma", though not so much for connoisseurs and antiquaries as for those for whom the beauty of the

[1] Claude Lorrain's tombstone in S. Trinità de' Monti was destroyed in 1798 by French soldiers. Thiers had his bones transferred to S. Luigi de' Francesi where Poussin also reposes; see Friedländer, *Poussin*, 20, and *Claude Lorrain*, 30 *seq.*

[2] Sponsel, *Sandrarts Teutsche Academie Kritisch gesichtet Dresden*, 1896, 101.

[3] *Cf.* Sandrart, *Academie*, edit, Paltzer, 31 and 184.

[4] Gerstenberg, *loc. cit.*, 103, 109 *seq.*, 129.

Eternal City consists not in a sentimental romanticizing of ruins but in that ineffable aroma which its atmosphere breathes over great artistic creations.[1]

Only a very small number of Rome pilgrims could acquire such souvenirs, but it may be taken for granted that every one carried away with him etchings, engravings, or woodcuts of the ancient monuments, the principal churches, palaces, fountains, and piazzas, in all their picturesque setting.[2] In many of these prints, to the execution of which Roman engravers had long devoted their energies,[3] the overwhelming impression of the Eternal City is reflected with elemental forcefulness. The etchings were for the most part the work of foreigners. Among Italians mention must be made chiefly of Giovan Battista Mercati whose collection of views of Rome, which he dedicated to the Grand-Duke of Tuscany, appeared in 1629. Here we

[1] FRIEDLÄNDER, *Claude Lorrain*, 37, 131 *seq.*

[2] Engravings of the seven principal churches were particularly popular, such as those published by G. B. de Rossi (see C. E. RAPPAPORT, *Roma aeterna, Catalogue*, XXVII., no. 468) and Jacobus Laurus, 1626 (copy in *Bibl. Hertziana*). Laurus also published *Antiquae urbis vestigia quae nunc exstant, Romae*, 1628 (dedicated to the Cardinal of Savoy), a work which contains a number of interesting views. A very original work was that published by GIOV. RIDOLFO ALTO, *Swizzero da Lucerna, officiale della Guardia Suizzera Pontificia in Roma, interprete dell'ill. inclita natione Alemana*, who, in conjunction with Giacomo Lauro, brought out a book enriched with 166 engravings, under the title: *Splendore dell'antica e moderna Roma, nel quale si rappresentano tutti i principali tempii, teatri, anfiteatri, cerchi, naumachie, archi trionfali, obelischi, etc., etc. Con li più segnalati giardini de gli antichi e moderni Romani. Et in questa ultima impressione . . . in quattro linguaggi Latino, Italiano, Tedesco e Francese dato alle stampe*, Roma, Andrea Fei, 1641. On Giov. Alto (died 1660, 83 years old), *cf.* the article by A. BACCHINI, *Un Suizzero ufficiale Pontificio, "Cicerone" di Roma*, in the periodical *Il Piccolo* of January 3, 1925. See also the essay by H. K. SCHÄFER on Hoch's books of heraldry in the Chigi Library, in *Köln. Volkszeitung*, 1914, no. 147.

[3] See KRISTELLER, *Kupferstich und Holzschnitt* (1905), 267 *seq.*

have excellent views of the Piazza Colonna, the neighbourhood of S. Maria in Cosmedin, and the forum looking towards the Arch of Titus.[1] The number of engravers from the Netherlands is exceedingly great. Mention may be made of Bartholomew Beerenbergh, Willem van Niewlandt [2] and Hermann Swanevelt.[3] But all these are left far behind by Israel Silvestre, a native of Lorraine, who came to Rome in the last year of Urban VIII.[4]

His views are remarkable for their accurate and delicate reproduction of the monuments. He gives an extraordinarily vivid picture of the life and animation of the piazzas in front of St. Peter's and S. Maria del Popolo. He has also perpetuated, in most graceful fashion, the Ripa Grande, the Piazza Colonna, the Vigna Ludovisi and, above all, the forum.[5] Several plates of outstanding beauty show panoramas of the Eternal City.[6] As in the work of Silvestre, so in the etchings of Claude Lorrain, the influence of Callot makes itself felt, more especially in the wonderful view of the Campo Vaccino of 1636.[7] François Perrier, a friend of Lanfranco's, divided his time between Paris and Rome but, like several other artists, he confined himself to etchings of antique statues and frescoes.[8]

[1] G. B. MERCATI, *Alcune vedute et prospettive di luoghi dishabitati di Roma, al serenissimo Gran Duca di Toscana Ferdinando . . . Roma,* 1629 (in 4°, 52 sheets in all). E. RODOCONACHI of Paris possesses a copy of this extremely rare collection.

[2] His view of Torre delle Milizie is reproduced in F. SCHNEIDER, *Rom und der Romgedanke*, Munich, 1926, 18.

[3] *Cf.* WESSELY, *Gesch. der graph. Künste,* Leipzig, 1891, 183 *seq.*

[4] See SINGER, *Künstlerlexicon*, III., Frankfurt, 1898, 279.

[5] See RAPPAPORT, *loc. cit.*, n. 472–5. *Cf.* also Hermanin's catalogue of the collection in the "Gabinetto delle stampe" in Rome; see *Le Gallerie naz. ital.*, III. (1897).

[6] RAPPAPORT, *loc. cit.*, nos. 629, 631–3, 635. The charming panorama of 1642 has been acquired by the Bibl. Vittorio Emmanuele, Rome.

[7] LIPPMANN, *Der Kupferstich,* Berlin 1896, 155.

[8] FR. PERRIER, *Icones et segmenta nobilium signorum et statuarum quae Romae extant* (with engraved inscription, 100 copperplates and two sheets of engraved indices, in fol.), Romae, 1638; *id.*

Often enough the preliminary sketches of artists are of greater interest than their finished etchings inasmuch as they reflect the impression of the moment. Here we meet once more with Claude Lorrain, who, though he paints landscapes for choice, also gives us pictures of certain localities of the city, such as the banks of the Tiber near the so-called Temple of Vesta, and the Piazza of S. Mary Major with its bustling life.[1] Jan Asselyn, Bartholomew Beerenbergh, and Willem van Niewlandt have also left beautiful drawings of Roman scenes.[2]

The drawings of Stefano della Bella are conspicuous for the virtuosity of their technique and the nobility of their conception.[3] The Uffizi Gallery of Florence preserves two valuable albums by him bearing the date 1636: the one contains sketches of horsemen, carters, men tending herds of horses and buffaloes, beggars and lazzaroni, just as the artist drew them for future use in his landscapes; among them there are a few preliminary sketches for the famous picture of the entry of the Polish embassy of 1633.[4] Of incomparably greater value is the album of views of Rome and the Campagna; this forms a collection which has been justly styled a revelation.[5] Whereas at a later date Piranesi expressed with incomparable power the grandeur of the ancient Roman remains, Stefano della Bella reproduces their picturesque beauty with truly Tuscan grace and refinement. He made excellent use of his three years' stay in Rome (1633–1636), and visited every place of pictorial interest. Far more than Dosio, Du Pérac, Giovanoli, Hermann van Swanevelt and Poelenburg, he saw Rome with the eyes of an artist. Only a few plates are devoted to the noisy and brilliant life of the city, but they too are excellent, as, for

Icones et segmenta illustrium e marmore tabularum, quae Romae adhuc extant delineata incisa et ad antiquam formam lapideis exemplaribus passim collapsis restituta, Romae (with 51 plates).

[1] Friedländer, *Cl. Lorrain,* 181 *seq.*

[2] H. Egger, *Römische Veduten, I.,* Vienna, 1911.

[3] *Cf.* De Vesme, *Le peintre graveur,* Milan, 1913, 66 *seq.*

[4] *Cf.* above, p. 167.

[5] E. Magunco, *Stefano della Bella,* in the periodical *Dedalo,* VI. (1925), 209 *seq.*

instance, the harbour of the Ripetta with its many ships, and Castle S. Angelo after the alterations executed by Urban VIII., with its bridge, to the right of which one sees the place set apart for executions whilst in the foreground we get a glimpse of the motley traffic.[1] All Stefano della Bella's love was for the Rome that merged into the Campagna, that verdant wilderness where, among ruins and trees, shepherds tended their flocks and countrymen and huntsmen roamed. Plates of incomparable delicacy and tender poetry depict the loveliness of the Circus Maximus, the Colosseum, the fountains of the Campo Vaccino, the Pyramid of Cestius, the Latin Gate, the Baths of Caracalla, the Aventine seen from the Tiber, the Temple of Minerva Medica, a view of the Villa Medici from the Villa Borghese. The drawings of the lonely road from the Baths of Caracalla to the Celio recall the art of Callot. The picture of the Trofei di Mario clearly shows the changes Rome has undergone: the place was then an almost deserted spot where, besides a few small houses, there was nothing to see but the remains of the Nymphaeum in which a wilderness of flowers had taken root.[2]

If Rome, by the end of the renaissance period, had outstripped all other cities of the world both by reason of the number of its churches with their mosaics, frescoes, pictures, and sculptures, and its palaces, that precious treasure had been considerably increased during the epoch of the Catholic restoration. A crowd of painters and sculptors vied with each other in adorning with the fruits of their art the vast spaces of the new churches and the palaces of high Church dignitaries and those of the aristocracy of blood and finance. Domenichino, one of the pupils of Annibale Caracci, greatly developed the large-scale decorative fresco. He, and his rival Guido Reni, represent the idealistic style of the seventeenth century which spread over a large part of Europe in the wake of the Catholic restoration as the herald of its achievements.[3] These pupils of Caracci were still in possession of all their creative power when, under

[1] *Ibid.*, 215, 219.

[2] *Ibid.*, 216, 218, 219, 221, 223, 224, 225, 227.

[3] Friedländer, *N. Poussin*, 6.

the patronage of Urban VIII and his nephews Francesco and Antonio Barberini, a new race of artists arose. Its forerunner was Lanfranco. The moving spirits of high baroque were the painter Pietro da Cortona and the sculptor-architect Bernini, who vied with each other in respect of versatility and the sublimity of their conceptions.[1] The new style stamped its imprint on the Papal City more deeply than any that had preceded it. Everything came under its spell. Numerous buildings of the Middle Ages and the Renaissance underwent alteration or were decorated at least internally in the baroque style. To this must be added the many new churches, palaces, and other dwellings, the monumental fountains and shady villas with their ornamental waters and statues. Thus the general aspect of Rome differed fundamentally from that of the end of the Renaissance period.

The transformation of Rome into a large modern town was begun by Sixtus V. Until then the city, in consequence of its irregular plan, had preserved that medieval character which the Renaissance had not greatly altered. With his vast scheme for new streets, Sixtus V. had laid down the main lines ; with his obelisks he had introduced an entirely new kind of decoration, whilst by providing plenty of water he had rendered the higher part of the city (the Monti) not only habitable, but a favourite quarter.[2] The Romans were at last able to return to their ancient abode and the town had room in which to expand. The Jubilee years of 1600 and 1625 were milestones in this process of reconstruction and new building, especially as regards churches. The city's wealth and beauty grew steadily; it attracted innumerable foreigners, a circumstance which gave to its life that cosmopolitan character which is observable in the world's great towns. Even more remarkable than the sumptuous palaces of the Borghese and Barberini were the imposing churches of the new Orders—real sanctuaries built for the people. The Gesù of the Jesuits was now rivalled by the Chiesa Nuova of the Oratorians, S. Andrea della Valle of the

[1] Voss, *Malerei*, 519.

[2] *Cf.* our data, Vol. XXII., 208 *seq.* ; Pastor, *Sisto*, V. See also Frey, *Barockarchitektur*, 45.

Theatines, S. Carlo ai Catinari of the Barnabites, which were all adorned with most important works of religious art.[1] Instead of the numerous crenellated towers which, together with the graceful campanili of the early Middle Ages, were still so characteristic a feature of Rome at the end of the Renaissance,[2] the panorama of the city was now dominated by many large and small cupolas, all of which were eclipsed by Michelangelo's dome of St. Peter's.

Urban VIII. worthily continued the patronage which Sixtus V., Clement VIII., and Paul V. had bestowed on the arts, and the bees of his coat-of-arms have become the hall-mark of the high baroque art which then flourished in the Eternal City.[3] His name is intimately linked with those of artists such as Bernini, Pietro da Cortona, and Andrea Sacchi. Besides Carlo Maderna, Domenico Castelli, Vincenzo della Greca, and Bartolomeo Breccioli were also permanently in his service as architects.[4] On occasion other architects were likewise

[1] In his *report of the year 1649 on Rome, *Ameyden* says that the city numbered 3 patriarchal churches and 11 *collegiate secolari*, 10 *basiliche antiche unite a diverse collegiate*, 106 parish churches, 43 monasteries (including those outside the walls), 27 national churches (*le più con hospitali*), and 64 public oratories of lay confraternities. *Varia polit.*, 150, p. 709, Papal Sec. Arch.

[2] One of the biggest towers, the Tor de' Conti, partially collapsed in September, 1630; see JUSTI, *Velasquez*, I.[3] (1922), 293.

[3] Aless. Donato singles out this fact in the dedication of his work, *Roma Vetus et recens*, and writes: "Tu enim ut caetera Pontificatus tui decora sileam, Romae quantum splendoris ac maiestatis adiecisti! Templa passim instaurata et exculta sunt, nova inchoata aut perfecta: palatia Pontificum ornata et munita: restitutae, auctae, erectae quadam Principis aemulatione civium ac dynastarum aedes: refecta moenia; validis munitionibus instructae arces: apertae, stratae, complanatae viae: extructi fontes; substructae ac repurgatae cloacae: elatae valles: demissa iuga: Basilica Vaticana marmoreis operosisque ornamentis illuminata: Moles admiranda ex aere auroque Apostolorum sepulchro imposita, ut iam Roma te non magis praesidem suscipiat religionis quam suae dignitatis propagatorem."

[4] POLLAK-FREY, 341 *seq*.

employed, for instance, Luigi Arigucci and Francesco Contini. Among contemporary painters there were not many who did not get commissions. In this way, notwithstanding the unpropitious conditions of the time, Rome's wealth in works of art grew from year to year, religious works predominating.[1] When the reign of the Barberini Pope came to a close, the transformation, which in the age of the Catholic restoration had made of the seat of the Popes the most splendid capital and the greatest wonder of Europe, had so far progressed that it only needed the activity of his two successors, Innocent X. and Alexander VII., to complete the wonderful baroque city, of the unique charm of which there will soon remain nothing but the memory.

[1] Dvorak in *Kunstgeschichtl. Anzeiger*, 1910, 58.

APPENDIX

OF

UNPUBLISHED DOCUMENTS

AND

EXTRACTS FROM ARCHIVES

APPENDIX.

1. Nuncio Sacchetti to the Cardinal Legate, Fr. Barberini [1]

Madrid, July 2nd, 1625.

Non mancano giornalmente di comparire in questa corte lettere di cattivo ufficio contro le candide attioni di S.S.^{tà}, onde con la venuta di V.S.R. si toglierà ogni diffidenza, correndo qui universalmente concetto ch'ella sia ben affetta a questa Corona, anchorche N.S.^{r} venga stimato dubbioso o almeno inclinato a dar gusto a Francia, anchorchè tanto retto che gli stessi maligni non sanno in qual cosa in particolare attacarlo. E fra l'altre lettere malediche capitone una di un cardinale, il cui nome fin'hora non ho potuto sapere, che per quanto mi vien detto trovasi fuori da Roma, e sotto coperta di zelo di carità dice che il Papa con le sue irresolutioni si dimostra poco amico dal Re di Spagna e manco della religione cattolica, la quale va coll'invasioni nemiche sempre ricevendo aggravii.

Io [2] trovo che Urbano leggendo questa cifra scrisse in margine di suo pugno al card. Magalotti: Vi diremo chi possa essere tal card.^{le} a bocca.

[Copy. Nicoletti II, 1250, Vatican Library.]

2. Pope Urban VIII. to Cardinal Richelieu [3]

[Rome], February 27th, 1627.

" Occlusa tandem sunt in Galliis ora loquentium iniqua et Sorbonensis theologorum senatus temerariam illam censuram damnavit, qua videbatur extra b. Petri ovile princeps quodammodo segregari. Plaudit Roma pietati Ludovici regis. . . . Te vero senatus Apostolicus vocat in societatem regiae laudis consiliisque tuis magnam tanti beneficii partem acceptam refert. Nos certe optatissimum auctoritate tua partum sollicitudini Nostrae solatium fatemur tibique cupimus paternam caritatem rebus potius quam oratione declarare. Iam vero quas non laudes promeritus es iis officiis, quibus pontificii Nuntii dignitatem ab externorum oratorum

[1] See XXVIII, p. 93. [2] Nicoletti. [3] *Cf.* XXVIII, 397.

legibus secerni curasti? Non decebat sane catholicis populis familiaritatem interdici eius antistitis, qui cum pontificiae mentis interpres sit ea semper consilia meditatur, quae habeantur lumina Spiritus Sancti et praesidia regiae Maiestatis."

[*Epist.* IV., p. 35, Papal Secret Archives.]

3. Pope Urban VIII. to Wallenstein, Duke of Friedland [1]

[Rome], February 26th, 1628.

Nobili viro duci Friedlandie.

Dilecte fili, nobilis vir, salutem. Feliciter in Germania agitur cum religione catholica. Haec enim non solum in Caes. M^tis^ solio Imperatorem nacta est rei christianae studiosissimum, sed eos quoque principes ibidem circumtuetur, qui pia Imperatoriae mentis vota gloriose exequantur. Quota harum laudum pars ad Nobilitatem tuam pertineat, non latet Ecclesiam Romanam. Perge, nobilis vir, et Dei omnipotentis patrocinium et fidelium plausus hisce actibus promereri. Nos autem Nobilitatis tuae triumphos Apostolicarum litterarum laudatione non modo prosequemur, sed patrem misericordiarum assidue quoque precamur, ut generosis tuae religionis consiliis addat foelicitatem. Quam impense tui nominis gloriae faveamus et quantam spem in te constituerit pontificia sollicitudo, uberius ex Nuntio Nostro cognoscere poteris, etc.

[*Epist.* V., p. 51, Papal Secret Archives.]

4. The French Ambassador Béthune to [D'Herbault] [2]

Rome, September 23rd, 1628.

Monsieur, Je vous ecrivis par le dernier ordinaire le 20e de ce mois, et vous donnois advis comme depuis vos lettres du 6e du passé je n'en avois receu aulcunes, ce qui me faict desirer avecq plus d'impatience d'en avoir, et advis de ce qui se passe à la Rochelle : est que hier le Pape eust des lettres de son Nunce du 20 qu'il m'a dict avoir esté apportées jusques à Suze par nostre ordinaire, lesquelles il m'a faict voir, ou ledit Sr Nunce luy donne advis que l'armée d'Angleterre avoit donné à travers et avoit esté du tout dissippée par une grande tempeste, et

[1] *Cf.* XXVIII, 178.

[2] *Cf.* XXVIII, 221.

par un postscript à la fin de la lettre l'asseure de la confirmation arrivée de ceste nouvelle et que l'armée estoit du tout ruinée. Sa S^{té} a faict voir la lettre à tous les ambassadeurs qui furent hier à son audience, et le jour de devant à plusieurs cardinaux qui se trouverent assemblez pres l'elle à la congregation du St. Office, lorsqu'elle la receut, ayant voulu, ainsy qu'elle me l'a dict, par ce moyen justiffier ceste nouvelle à cause que je n'en avois point d'advis pour ne sembler qu'elle l'eust inventée, elle luy a esté d'aultant plus agreable que par la dite lettre le Nunce mandoit que la Rochelle estoit preste de rendre les derniers abois, un chacun tenant que dans peu de jours les habitans seroyent contraints de se rendre à la misericorde du Roy. Je ne vous saurois assez representer le contentement que le Pape a faict paroistre universelement de ce bon succez, non plus que celuy qu'en a receu le cardinal Barberin, lequel S. S^{té} me dict depuis son assomtion du pontifficat il n'avoit jamais recogneu une si grande joye dans son visage. Je luy dicts que je ne pensois point estre necessaire de luy tesmoigner par paroles combien l'advis qu'elle m'avoit donné me touchoit et le sentiment de joye qu'elle m'avoit faict recevoir, mais que je luy en exprimerois un qui n'estoit pas commun, qui estoit que j'estimois un plus grand avantaige pour Sa M^{té} la dissipation et ruine de l'armée angloise arrivée par les vents et la mer que si c'eust esté par la puissance de ses armes, pour ce que le bonheur de ce succes ne peult estre attribué qu'à Dieu seul, lequel d'avoir favorable est beaucoup plus advantageux que le secours et assistance de plusieurs armées adjoustant, qu'oultre le bien evident et present qui se recevoit d'une telle et si visible protection de la divine bonté, l'on en pouvoit tirer cet aultre bien que ceux qui combattront pour le Roy et soubs son autorité, en deviendront plus hardis et ses ennemis au contraire plus retenus estimans d'avoir Dieu et les hommes à combattre. Sa S^{té} me respondit qu'elle avoit la mesme opinion que moy et qu'aussy se promettoit elle que Dieu l'assisteroit en la deffence qu'elle esperoit qu'elle estoit pour prendre de la justice d'un prince que l'on vouloit depouiller sans alleguer aucun pretexte contre luy, tenat pour certain que S. M. venant à Lyon et faisant avancer son armée en ces quartiers elle feroit changer de face aux affaires, qu'elle estimoit tant S. M. et les forces de la France qu'en telle compagnie elle ne craignoit rien, que les Venitiens monstroient de leur part de ne vouloir rien espargner pour empescher ceste usurpation que vouloient faire les Epagnols. Je luy dis lors : V. S[té] monstre de se promettre ainsi du Roy et de la Republique mais je ne vois poinct que de sa part elle offre ny asseure aucune chose. Elle me respondit que je me pouvois souvenir qu'elle m'avoit tousjours dict qu'elle vouloit voir la Rochelle prise et V. M. à Lyon devant touttes choses qu'il faillot essayer de retirer M. de Savoye d'avec les Espagnolz dont le moyen seroit de luy asseurer qu'une bonne partie de ce qu'il avoit occupé luy demeureroit et qu'aucun ne pouvoit garantir une telle promesse que Sa M[té] qui seulle la pouvoit faire observer au Duc de Mantoue lequel ne la dediroit d'aucune chose pour n'avoir autre esperance qu'en elle, selon ce que je decouvre de jour en jour par les propos et deportement du Pape. Ilz tesmoignent une tres grande animosité contre les Espagnolz et de laquelle je tiens ma creance bien fondée, c'est qu'elle n'est pas appuyée seulement sur le particulier du Duc de Mantoue ny sur l'injustice que l'on commet en son endroict, mais pour estre tres asseurée S. S. que les Espagnolz la mesprisent et haissent pour estime, qu'elle a une aversion contr'eux. Ce que je vous dis icy pourroit passer pour conjecture sans que le cardinal qui parlant moins que le Pape me declara hier qu'il estoit tres asseuré que les Espagnolz haissoient luy, son oncle et toutte sa maison, et ensuitte me discourut de tous les lieux de l'Eglise confinans avec le royaume de Naples dans lesquels S. S. pouvoit loger des gens de guerre pour faire teste aux Espagnolz, me disant que leurs frontieres n'estoient pas meilleures que celles de l'estat ecclesiasticque, et qu'un cardinal qui luy avoit remonstré que S. S. devoit vivre en respect avec les Espagnolz, considerant le peu de chemin qu'il y avoit de Naples à Rome, il luy avoit respondu qu'il n'y avoit pas moins de Rome à Naples. Bref, je le voy si picque que le Roy prenant resolution, c'est a dire ayant pris la Rochelle, de vouloir entendre à la conservation du Duc de Mantoue et à empescher que de son oppression les envieux de la France ne s'en accroissent l'on feroit entrer le Pape de la partie conjoinctement avec les Venitiens, ce que presupose lesdits Espagnolz auraient à penser à eux, et d'autant plus que la reputation du Roy et l'estime que l'on a de luy est telle, tant pour le continuel employ de la guerre auquel il s'est occupé depuis sept ou huict ans, que pour l'opinion comme certaine que Dieu l'a en une particuliere protection feroient que ses armes seroient grandement redouttées lesquelles tant publicquement on dict qu'elles ne seroient moins justes en cette occasion de l'assistance du Duc de Mantone que contre ceux de la Rochelle, et cela S. $S^{té}$ mesme me l'a dict. Au reste l'on est detrompé des dits Epagnolz, qui avoient tousjours pris la religion pour pretexte et lesquels en ceste consideration trouvoyent plusieurs qui favorisoyent leurs armes de leurs voeux et au contraire accusoyent le Roy, comme nous l'avons veu par les libelles qui ont couru, de se lier avec les heretiques et les deffendre là où maintenant l'on dict publiquement que les armes de S. M. sont aussy justes comme celles des aultres sont injustes.

Comme j'estois arrivé jusques icy de ceste lettre, l'ordinaire est arrivé avecq vostre despesche du 20 qui m'a confirmé la nouvelle de la dissippation de l'armée angloise et ensemble l'obstination que monstrerent ces opiniastres, lorsque l'on leur envoya le herault. Je veulx croire que depuis avoir appris la dissipation de cette flotte en laquelle ilz mettoyent l'esperance de leur secours, ilz auront changé de resolution et que vos premieres me donneront des nouvelles de quelque commancement de traité.

Je vous baise les mains et suis, Monsieur

Votre tres humble serviteur

Bethune.

[Orig., Paris, Archives of Foreign Affairs, *Rome* 41, p. 217 *seq.*]

5. THE FRENCH AMBASSADOR BÉTHUNE TO [D'HERBAULT].[1]

Rome, October 7th, 1628.

Monsieur. Je vous escrivis le 5e de ce mois par l'ordinaire de Rome et le mesme jour au soir je receus vostre lettre du 5e du mois passé par laquelle vous me faisiez sçavoir de n'avoir receu aulcune despesche de moy depuis que vous m'escrivistes le 20e d'aoust et neantmoings je n'ay manqué à tous les ordinaires d'escrire au Roy et à vous, comme j'ay encores une fois faict par Venise et une aultre à l'occasion d'une personne qui alloit en diligence à Lion et que prenoit la voye de la mer ; ce qu'estant, je ne puis assez m'estonner veu

[1] *Cf.* XXVIII, 222.

que les rencontres des empeschements des courriers ne sont pas allans en France, mais venants seulement deça, quelle doncq peust estre l'occasion que mes despesches sont si long temps à arriver jusques à vous? Je ne la puis deviner. Je vous diray que je demeuray fort mortiffié ayant appris qu'un courrier de M. le Duc de Mantoue estoit party de la Rochelle le 14e et qu'il eust esté chargé de lettres de M. le Nunce pour le Pape et non d'aulcunes des vostres pour moy. Par ceste despesche l'on a appris icy la bonne nouvelle de la mort de Bouquinquam, laquelle a depuis esté confirmée par lettres du 22e de Paris, et ensemble ay appris comme ceux de la Rochelle avoyent faict sortir quelques uns des leurs pour traicter de se remettre à l'obeissance du Roy et avecq lesquels il n'avoit esté neantmoings rien conclu, mais seulement leur avoir esté dict qu'ilz retournassent et que dans six jours apres avoir concerté entre eulx la resolution qu'ilz avoyent à prendre l'on les entendroit. Ce commancement joinct avecq la mort de Bouquinquam, laquelle leur fera perdre l'esperance de secours, nous fera bientost icy apprendre, selon le desir que j'en ay, la reddition de ceste place, laquelle est si ardemment desirée du Pape et du cardinal Barbarin, ainsi que je le conneus hier que j'euz audience que j'oserois quasi dire que S. M. ne le souhaite pas davantage. S. S. me dict d'abord que j'entray dans sa chambre que Dieu continuoit ses miracles en faveur du Roy et qu'il paroissoit par la mort de Bouquinquam, mais que pour comble de ses graces il falloit la reddition de la Rochelle. Je luy dis que je l'esperois, apres Dieu, de la necessité où elle estoit reduicte et de ceste mort qui leur feroit perdre l'esperance de ce secours. En suitte je luy parlay des affaires publiques, c'est à dire des affaires de M. de Mantoue afin d'essayer de la porter a quelque resolution qui peust empescher les Espagnolz de s'accroistre si injustement en le ruynant comme ilz pretendent de faire, de laquelle je n'euz du commancement que les mesmes discours cy devant repettez par mes despesches, c'est à dire qu'elle ne se pouvoit fier en personne qu'au Roy, mais qu'avec luy elle feroit paroistre qu'elle n'estoit poinct sans courage et qu'elle n'avoit abondonné jusques icy la deffence de la justice que parce qu'elle ne s'estimoit puissante de la deffendre sans la France. La prudence ne permettant point que par un zele indiscret et sans mesurer ses forces on joignist sa ruyne à celle de celuy qu'on vouloit assister, adjoustant que S. M. venant à Lyon avec intention de se declarer pour la protecttion du Duc de Mantoue et la liberté d'Italye et que pour cet effet elle fist passer une armée, que S. Sté mettroit en mesme temps à la campagne douse mil hommes de pied et douse à quinse cens chevaux et que ce nombre d'hommes avec le nom de S. Sté, qui n'estoient pas seuls capables de deffendre le Duc de Mantoue le seroient joinctz avec les forces du Roy, de donner à penser à ceux qui mettant sous pied la justice, l'honneur et la raison se vouloient accroistre à quelque prix que ce soit. Je n'ay pas neantmoins compris de son discours que son intention soit de joindre ses forces avec celles du Roy qu'apres avoir fait entendre aux Espagnolz qu'en cas qu'ilz ne se voulussent desister de leur entreprise, alors il s'uniroit avec les forces du Roy et celles de Venitiens pour la conservation de la liberté d'Italye. Pour confirmation de son intention à l'ambassadeur de Venise qui entra apres moy, elle demanda combien de gens de pied et de cheval la Republique mettroit en campagne. S. Sté n'estoit jamais passé si avant, aussi vous puis je asseurer que de jour à autre s'accroist en elle l'aversion qu'elle a des Espagnolz. Je luy dis que cependant qu'elle alloit differant de se declarer, il estoit à craindre que Casal se ne perdist. Elle me respondit qu'elle n'estimoit pas que cela fust pour arriver y ayant des vivres et de bons hommes, mais qu'en tout cas l'on pourroit contraindre les usurpateurs de le rendre ne les croyant si imprudens que de vouloir mettre au hasard les estatz qu'ilz avoient en Italye pour se conserver une injuste usurpation, et sur ce que je dis à S. Sté qu'il falloit donc dès cette heure elle mist sur pied ce nombre d'hommes qu'elle m'avoit dit vouloir employer pour une si juste cause affin qu'elle les eust presty quand l'occasion s'offriroit de s'en servir, elle me respondit que bien qu'elle n'eust pas plus de quatre mil hommes maintenant qu'elle avoit fait comme les bons et prudens mesnagers qui voulant bastir preparent et assemblent tous materiaux desquels ilz se veulent servir et qu'aussi elle a tellement touttes choses preparées qu'en un instant elle mettroit en campagne les forces dont elle se vantoit, ce que d'avoir fait plustost n'eust de rien servy sinon à luy faire dependre inutilement de l'argent puisqu'elle n'avoit jamais intention de les employer qu'avec S. M., prenant ouvertement la protection du Duc de Mantoue et la deffence de la liberté les Espagnolz voulans continuer à apprimer l'un et l'autre. J'estime quant a moy, que S. Sté faisant ce qu'elle m'a dict, promettant de nouveau ce que dessus, lorsque S. M. me commanderoit d'en tirer asseurance, c'est autant comme si du commancement elle avoit fait une ligue ouverte avec le Roy ainsi que je l'en avois requis, puisque l'on vient à luy engager par consequence lorsque les Espagnolz ne se voudront desister, qui est, ce me semble, tout ce que S. M. peut desirer, mais il ne faut rien esperer par effect de tout cecy selon mon jugement que la Rochelle prise S. M. estant à Lyon et prenant en son nom la protection du Duc de Mantoue estimant que de Turin le Roy est punctuellement adverty de ce que M. Marini peut descouvrir des intentions de M. de Savoye, cela sera cause que je ne vous diray rien sur ce subject sinon qu'en une rencontre que j'ay eue avec son ambassadeur il m'a semblé qu'il ne seroit pas difficile de destascher son maitre d'avec les Espagnolz pourveu qu'il eust promesse du Roy qu'une bonne partie de ce qu'il a occupé du Montferrat luy demeureroit pour les pretentions que ses predecesseurs et luy ont de longue main comme aussy pour la restitution et payement d'anciennes et nouvelles debtes, m'ayant fait paroistre ledit ambassadeur que ledit Duc estoit demeuré grandement content et satisfait des bonnes paroles qui avoient esté données au comte de Morette et estimant ceste despesche digne de venir promptement à la cognoissance de la S. M., je l'ay adressé a M. d'Avaux pour y avoir encores quinze jours jusques au partement de l'ordinaire par lequel je vous envoyeray un duplicata. Sur ce je vous baise les mains et suis, Monsieur

Vostre tres humble serviteur

Bethune.

[Orig., Paris, Archives of Foreign Affairs, *Rome* 41, p. 925 *seq.*]

6. Cardinal Francesco Barberini to the French Nuncio Guido del Bagno.[1]

Con l'occasione di condurre Mr della Riviere a piedi S. Stà l'altr'hieri rinovò Bettune l'instanze di qualche dichiaratione per le cose di Mantova, già che il Re è disposto a soccorrerlo.

[1] *Cf.* XXVIII, 227. See also Kiewning, I., 331, n. 4.

Rispose S. Beat^{ne} co' soliti termini, senza impegnarsi in dichiaratione alcuna, eccetto di voler armarsi et haver in pronto X^{m} *huomini in caso che le armi regie calino* [1] in Italia, affine che, attaccandosi le mischie, si trovi lo Stato Ecclesiastico con buona difesa e non già per esser contrario alle armi altrui. Aggiunse *ancora che* harebbe parlato più altamente e ferventemente *per disporre* le parti a pensieri di pace. Premé *Bettune che S. S^{tà} armasse, prima che i Francesi venissero,* adducendo che subito giunti potrebbe darsi qualche battaglia con la parte avversa e conseguentemente trovarsi lo Stato Ecclesiastico in bisogno di difesa, oltre l'haver S. S^{tà} accennato altra volta di voler star armata, venendo il Re a Lione. Ma replicò S. Beat^{ne} d'haver presupposto non solo S. M^{tà} o altro capo in Lione, ma anche le genti di lui in Italia, et esser certa non poter venir colta all'improvviso, havendo disposte le cose in maniera che in un mese o minor tempo haverà in punto la detta soldatesca effettiva ogni volta che la voglia. Battè l'ambasciatore per cavar maggior esplicatione dell'animo di S S^{tà}, ma questa si tenne sempre nello stesso tuono di volersi trovar armata e parlar forte per la pace, senza discendere ad altro. Soggiunse bene che in caso di mossa di S. M^{tà} spedirà Nuntio straordinario come ha fatto all'*Imperatore e Re Cattolico.* Replicò S. E. che il Nuntio non harebbe fatto nulla mentre volesse trattenere il Re dall'impresa, e che ciò non li pareva conveniente, mentre gli altri tiravano avanti contro Nivers. Ma S. Beat^{ne} rispose che la *missione del Nuntio* sarebbe *honorevole* per il Re e che porterebbe a S. M^{tà} sensi ragionevoli, e S. S^{tà} *si lascerebbe* intendere parimente con gli altri che si mettessero nella via della ragione e della giustizia e nel cessamento dell'armi acciò gli ufficii di S. Beat^{ne} havessero efficacia.

Quanto poi alla richiesta del card. Richelieu riferitami da V. S. con la sua cifera de 2 passato. cioè di voler *risposta categorica se S. S^{tà} assisterà con 8^{m} fanti et 800 cavalli,* quando le armi *regie siano nel Monferrato* et habbiano fatto qualche effetto, V. S. prevenne saggiamente rispondendoli che *S. Beat^{ne} non harebbe data cotale risolutione* categorica *in modo alcuno,* ma solamente d'armarsi e di farsi sentire altamente per indur le parti alla pace nel modo di sopra

[1] The passages in italics are in code.

accennato e discorso coll'ambasciatore. E questo senso di S. Stà potrà Ella insinuare e farne rimaner capace S. S. Illma con le ragioni scritte altre volte e con quelle che li verran dettate dal proprio avvedimento; perchè in effetto S. Beatne non vuol venir a queste promesse.

Uscì *l'ambasciatore a ritoccar lo sbarco a Civitavecchia e 'l passo per lo Stato Ecclesiastico* a soldatesca francese da inviarsi al Mantovano. Sopra di che non s'impegnò S. Bne in cosa veruna, ma sempre rimise S. E. a parlarne meco. Io così all'improvviso risposi che nulla rilevarebbe questo sbarco, se non s'otteneva prima *il passo dal Gran Duca per il suo*, overo *dal Duca d'Urbino*, benchè questa ultima sarebbe strada molto lunga. E soggiunsi che tali missioni, le quali, quando pur si facessero, sarebbono alla sfilata, poco effetto potriano operare, e meglio senza dubbio saria il mandar denaro al Duca di Mantova, perchè delle genti non le ne mancherebbono. Non premè più oltre l'ambasciatore et il discorso passò senza venirsi alle strette e senza conclusione alcuna. . . .

[*Barb.* 8070 (pages not numbered) towards the end. Vatican Library.]

7. THE FRENCH NUNCIO G. DEL BAGNO TO CARDINAL FRANCESCO BARBERINI.[1]

Rome, April 3rd, 1629.[2]

" . . . Ho scoperto nel card. Richelieu qualche spirito di desiderio della legatione di Francia ad tempus come per benemerito del fatto et incitamento a proseguire la depressione dell'heresia in Francia, della quale speditosi mostra inclinatione di modificare l'autorità de' parlamenti verso il Re e verso le materie ecclesche. Ma io ho fatto sentire che della legatione non può in niun conto concedersi, e me son valso d'un avviso che già mi diede il Sr Sacchetti, che D. Gonzalo haveva detto che una simile harebbe preteso l'infante cardle per li regni di Spagna, che sarebbe cosa perniciosissima alla Sede Apost. e perciò mai si concederà come nè anche quella di Francia specialmente per il rispetto di poter più arditamente negar quella di Spagna."

[*Barb.* 8071, Vatican Library.]

[1] *Cf.* XXVIII, 414.

[2] Decifrato l'11 aprile.

8. Cardinal Francesco Barberini to the French Nuncio G. del Bagno.[1]

Rome, April 14th, 1629.

". . . Ha gradito straordinariamente N. S. l'officio interposto da V. S. per tener dietro il motivo di Richelieu circa il voler la legatione di Francia, poiche l'essempio non solo sarebbe pernicioso in riguardo di Spagna, si come ella ben ponderò a S. S. Illma, ma anco potrebbe destar a medesimi pruriti col tempo nel Imperio e Germania, Boemia, Polonia, e in somma metter scompiglio nel christianesimo cattolico."

[*Barb.* 8071, Vatican Library.]

9. Cardinal Francesco Barberini to Ciriaco Rocci, Nuncio in Germany.[2]

Rome, September 28th, 1630.[3]

". . . La premura che si fa costì in voler disfare et disunir la Lega cattolica, è un gran punto et di gran conseguenza, e con ragione par che il sigr Duca di Baviera e gli altri Elettori se ne mostrino alieni; col qual sigr Duca V. S. può liberamente discorrere, che il desiderio di Nro Sigre e mio sarebbe che la detta unione si conservasse *come quella che ha rimesso in piedi la religione cattolica* in Germania e che tende direttamente a mantenerla e stabilirla; ladove par che gl'altri eserciti mirino più al politico che ad altro, e massime *hora che i moti del Re di Suecia* ed i sospetti *d'altri nemici della religione danno più che mai occasione* di conservar la detta Lega, la quale ha difeso i cattolici senza aggravarli o disgustarli. . . ."

[*Barb.* 7063 n. 13, Vatican Library.]

10. Pope Urban VIII. to Tilly.[4]

Rome, June 18th, 1631.

Dilecte fili, nobilis vir, salutem et Apostolicam benedictionem. Impia illa virgo, quae coelesti sponso nubere noluit,

[1] *Cf.* XXVIII, 414.

[2] *Cf.* XXVIII, 262.

[3] Messo in cifra li 28 settembre 1630.

[4] *Cf.* XXVIII, 276. See also Klopp, *Tilly*, II. (1861), 479.

cum facta esset adultera satanae, Magdeburgensis civitas, experta tandem est ultoris numinis furorem coruscantem in dextera Nobilitatis tuae. Contorqueri voluit Omnipotens per manus catholicorum exercituum fulmina coelestis indignationis, quae incolas et tecta civitatis Ecclesiam aspernantis devorarunt sicut stipulam. Tu vero post tot stipendia et trophaea, triumphalis senex, tanta auctus victoria, potuisti lavare victrices manus in sanguine peccatorum [Ps 57 (58), 11]. O decus dignum, cui coelites plaudunt, quod reges cupiant! mutata est per te rerum facies in septentrione. Ubi enim haeretici, furentes audacia, minitabantur incendia templis, catenas principibus, contumeliam sanctis, nunc in Magdeburgensi clade consternati coguntur formidare impiae potentiae finem. Vive ac triumpha feliciter, nobilis vir, tu laus Israel, tu honorificentia populi nostri, qui convertere Nobis potuisti sollicitudinem in gratulationem et metuentem religionem galea salutis et framea ultionis armasti. Nulla plane natio in hoc Urbis theatro de tuis laudibus conticescet. Diceris enim munivisse semper sanctimonia fortitudinem, nec minus feliciter cupiditates in corpore quam hostes in variis provinciis edomuisse. Iam vero tantarum laudum commemoratione augetur publica spes, quae freta Deo in catholicis castris excubanti, et principibus pii belli auspicibus, videtur non temere in Germania diadema perfecti decoris catholicae religioni a tua virtute polliceri. Eia age, nobilis vir, sequere Deum, qui te hac victoria vocat ad integrum devictae impietatis triumphum. Omnino vero enitere, ne quid in consulentium deliberationibus decernatur, quod dimicantium militum odia irritet et haberi possit victrici religioni inutile aut indecorum. Benedicimus tibi, dilecte fili, intimo paterni cordis affectu atque oramus Deum, cui omnia vivunt, ut in senio Nobilitatis tuae velit ad publicae spei felicitatem inutile robur revirescere. Datum Romae apud S. Mariam Maiorem sub annulo piscatoris die XVIII Iunii MDCXXXI anno pontificatus Nostri octavo."

"Ioannes Ciampolus."

[Orig., State Archives, Brussels.]

In the Epist. Urbani VIII. of the Papal Secret Archives this piece cannot be found, the only information is a marginal note in the Brief to Maximilian I. (cf. above p. 276, n. 1) that a similar one had been sent to Tilly.

11. THE FRENCH NUNCIO ALESSANDRO BICHI TO CARDINAL FRANCESCO BARBERINI.[1]

Paris, June 20th, 1631.[2]

". . . Ho passati nuovi uffici, *acciò S. M^{tà} Christ^{ma} s'interponga per l'accomodamento delle alterationi tra l'Imperatore e il Sveco,* atteso che quelle d'Italia si trovano hormai quasi in tutto accordate. Si continua di darmi certa speranza che, quietata affatto l'Italia, il Re si adoprerà vivamente con inviar anche persona espressa, e fra tanto che *non più daranno aiuto al Sveco. . . .*"

[*Barb.* 8079, p. 29, Vatican Library.]

12. CARDINAL FRANCESCO BARBERINI TO THE FRENCH NUNCIO ALESSANDRO BICHI.[3]

Rome, November 22nd, 1631.[4]

"Dalli discorsi di costà intorno alle cose di Germania e specialmente da quello che V. S. riferisce haver tenuto col Sig^{r} card^{le} Richelieu nella sua prima cifra, *si raccoglie che* la missione del Charnassi e l'intentione di cotesta parte *mira alla separatione di Baviera e di tutta la Lega cattolica dall'interessi dell'Austriaci,* e di far *che lo Sveco* e suoi adherenti *salvino quelli, ma non già questi ; il che non so come possa riuscire senza detrimento della religione cattolica ;* nel qual *punto, riuscire senza detrimento della religione cattolica ;* nel qual punto, *ch'è il principale,* sono e debbono essere uniti tutti, e dannificandosi questa in una parte della Germania, non può essere che anche l'altre non ne patiscano. Quanto all'osservanza delle *promesse del medesimo Sveco in preservatione* della stessa religione cattolica, fin'hora se n'attendono gli avisi di Germania : par che non camini bene, poichè le chiese e le persone ecclesiastiche e tanti prelati Ollandesi [! ?] della Lega cattolica ne son rimasti spogliati e maltrattati insieme con tutti i religiosi, eccetto Cappuccini, come si narra ; ma di questi non è maraviglia, piochè cantabit vacuus coram latrone viator. V. S. dunque ha fatto lodevolmente e conforme al suo zelo, mentre è tornata a raccomandare

[1] *Cf.* XXVIII, 276.

[2] Decifrato li 16 luglio [1631].

[3] *Cf.* XXVIII, 280.

[4] Scritto in cifra li 22 novembre 1631.

gli interessi de' cattolici di Germania, e motivar che l'autorità di Sua $M^{tà}$ $Christ^{ma}$ s'impiegasse per la quiete dell'Alemagna. Avisi freschi di Augusta portano che lo Sveco sia stato rotto e preso prigione dal Tilly. Si aspetta con ansietà di saper, se sia vero. Ma quel che non è, può essere ; onde possono S. $M^{tà}$ e 'l sig^{r} $card^{le}$, con la consideratione della varietà degli humani accidenti, dar luogo maggiormente alla conservatione della quiete universale. . . ."

[*Barb.* 8114, Vatican Library.]

13. Cardinal Francesco Barberini to the French Nuncio Alessandro Bichi.[1]

Rome, December 13th, 1631.[2]

" . . . Torno bene a dirle che gli eretici, com'è lo Sveco, *non osservano promesse,* e si vede chiaramente dalli danni gravissimi et nelle occupationi di città e piazze fatte contro l'Elettor di Colonia, ch'è pur anche fratello di Baviera, contro Magonza e contro Erbipoli, Bamberga, Fulda et altri prencipi della Lega cattolica, temendosi che, passando il Reno non invada anche Treveri, Magonza medesima, Colonia stessa e tutto quel tratto. L'aura della fortuna e la superbia che si scopre in lui naturale, lo farà anche sprezzatore delli offitii e delle richieste di cotesta Maestà, s'ella non lo atterrisce con l'interminatione e con gli effetti anche della sua potenza ; e realmente non si può in Germania, massime rispetto a' nemici della religione cattolica, distinguer i danni delli altri prencipi da quelli dell'Imperatore o delli Austriaci, e tutti ridondano in detrimento della fede cattolica, e conseguentemente anche in disutile del regno medesimo di Francia, almeno a lungo andare. E consideri S. $M^{tà}$ e 'l sig^{r} cardinale i mostruosi progressi fatti da Gostavo in un sol mese, e che la piena, quando è tanto ingrossata, non si può talvolta riparare. . . ."

[*Barb.* 8114, Vatican Library.]

14. Cardinal Francesco Barberini to the Spanish Nuncio Monti.[3]

Rome, March 8th, 1632.

" . . . Hora pendente il termine della convocatione di detta congregatione il card. Borgia alli altri suoi mali termini ne

[1] *Cf.* XXVIII, 480.

[2] Scritto in cifra li 13 dicembre 1631.

[3] *Cf.* XXVIII, 287.

have aggiunto *un pessimo*; et è stato che nel concistoro hodierno, mentre si proponevano alcune chiese, egli senza accennar prima cosa alcuna del suo pensiero a N^{ro} Sig^{re}, si è posto a *recitare ad alta voce un' ambasciata che portava seco scritta in latino*; ma da tutti s'è conosciuto che la spiegatura e frase di essa *non era farina del medesimo cardinale,* della quale scrittura io mando a V. S. la copia B. Sua Santità, benchè meravigliatasi di tale improvvisata, nondimeno, per usar della sua benignità, stette *pazientemente ad udire,* finchè il cardinale proferì quelle parole: *Et adhuc Sanctitas Vestra cunctatur,* e seguitava alla *protesta.* Allhora dunque Sua Beatitudine gli ordinò che tacesse, dicendo e ripetendo più volte: *Taceas.* E proferì queste parole: *Loquerisne uti cardinalis an uti orator?* Rispose: *Uti cardinalis.* Replicò Sua Santità: *Cardinales in concistorio non loquuntur palam nisi praecedente littera super materia vel interrogati et cum petitur consilium, quod etiam sequi non tenemur.* E soggiungendo il cardinale che *parlava anche come ambasciatore,* ripigliò Sua Santità: *Non habes locum in hoc consessu uti orator, et hic oratoris nullae sunt partes. Sed te privatim audivimus et audiemus.* Allhora egli disse che non havea potuto haver *udienza.* Falsità grande, perchè oltre *l'ordinarie che ha sempre commodamente,* ne ha havute egli, anzi anco i cardinali nationali, quante ne han volute delle *straordinarie.* V. S. haverà veduto dai ragguagli che io li ho dati di mano in mano. Haverà egli voluto intendere dell'*udienze strane* e di insolita forma che egli ha *dimandate,* cioè di venire a Sua Santità *conducendo seco ambasciatori Cesarei, cardinali italiani e cardinali spagnoli,* onde il *Mastro di Camera di Sua Beatitudine* li fece intendere che *se Sua Em.^{za} come ambasciatore* voleva venire, venisse pure, ma che la forma *d'udienza di tanti insieme* era *inusitata* e non poteva darsi, e però lo consigliava a venir da sè. Ond'egli il *giovedì seguente ebbe l'udienza solo,* come di sopra ho detto e come ho signato a V. S. in altre mie. E. poi ha fronte di asserire di *non haver potuto havere udienza.* Anzi questo *aggrava l'eccesso* da lui commesso questa mattina, perchè, mentre Sua Beat^{ne} permise *ch'egli venisse a parlarli con sette altri compagni,* molto meno doveva *parlare* in presenza di *tutto il sacro collegio* contro ogni stile et ogni *modestia.*

Procurando dunque pur egli di finir *la sua diceria, Nostro*

Signore soggiunse: *Donec non es egressus, exhortationem ad ferendas suppetias patienter audivimus. Modo taceas: ita iubemus. Mereris, ut praeciperemus te egredi,* e cosa simile. E di più li disse: Quando *actum fuit de subsidio Nobis dando a cardinalibus pro Statu ecclesiastico, tu solus contradixisti, et debebamus in te animadvertere*; *sed te diletimus plus quam mereris.* Egli a ciò *rispose* che prima nelle congregationi haveva *assentito, e Sua Beat*[ne] ripigliò: *Tanto peius, quia recessisti a bono consilio.*

Intanto che egli non si quetava *ai comandamenti di Sua Santità e voleva pur seguitare a dire, il sig*[r] *card*[le] *di S. Honofrio zelante del poco rispetto*, che vedeva portarsi *dal sig*[r] *card*[le] *Borgia al Papa suo fratello*, se li accostò *sgridandoli che tacesse e ripetendo pù volte, Taceas* a fine di cancare maggiori rumori; e perchè forse *Borgia* rappresentarà alterata *la detta attione di Sant' Honofrio*, V. S. avverta bene di risponder, dove bisogna, con dimostrare *lo zelo del cardinal congiunto con una esemplare purità e rettitudine*, e che, *vedendo disobedito un Papa tanto a lui congiunto*, non è gran fatto *che si movesse dal suo luogo* in essecutione delli iterati *commandamenti che Sua Santità faceva a Borgia di tacersi*, benchè ad un sol cenno di S. Beat[ne] *si ritirò subito* da quello a che lo zelo e l'animo *et habito religioso lo spingevano.*

Quando *Sisto 5° santa memoria* parlò al S. Collegio *contro Enrico 3° Re di Francia* sopra *la morte del cardinale di Ghisa* era presente il *card. Gioiosa protettore di Francia*, capo *de' cardinali Franzesi*, e volse solamente allegare con ogni modestia *e con haver prima chiesta licenza al Papa* alcuna *eccettione in scusa del Re*, e nondimeno Sisto quinto li comandò che tacesse, ma anco lo riprese agramente, et alcuni voglion dire che lo facesse uscir di concistoro, e che si ritirò parimente per qualche giorno *da Roma.* Il card. *Santa Severina* una volta che li parve essersi trasportato tropp'oltre *dal suo zelo* sopra una materia che pur era stata proposta dal *Papa in concistorio*, subito in presenza de' cardinali s'andò a *inginocchiare e chieder perdono ai piedi del medesimo Papa.* Ma il cardinal Borgia, trattato più benignamente da Nostro Signore, nè meno si è *degnato di domandar perdono*, sebene privatamente a *me ha detto due parole*, cioè *che lo scusassi*, perchè quelli altri *cardinali nationali* erano stati di parere ch'egli così facesse; tal che ha *raddossata agli altri la colpa.*

Io ancora, vedendo la sua *contumacia*, mi son levato in piede e ho detto alcune cose così: Prima li ricordai che *egomet obtuli Dominationi suae pleraque ex his quae petebat, et ipsa respuit*, e lo replicai due volte essendo vero ch'egli ha ricusato le *missioni* offerte altre volte per negotiare *l'aggiustamento fra le corone.* Inoltre, perchè egli diceva di parlar anco *come protettore*, risposi (si come anco fece Nostro Signore), che *la protettione* non ha annesso *questo uffizio*, ma riguarda *solo le chiese.* Finalmente aggiunsi che *per haec dissidia et dum hoc pacto agimus sacrificamus haereticis*, volendo inferire il gusto che gli heretici haverebbono di sentire *così fatte esorbitanze.* Riferii ancora che di già *hesterna die de ordine SS*^{mi} *erat intimata congregatio super iisdem negotiis et plerique cardinales in concistorio existentes hoc sciebant.*

Il sig^{r} card. Colonna, al quale tocca hora *sonar la campanella*, quando fa di bisogno che entri alcuno de' serventi, la *sono*, perchè, Sua Em^{za} dice, *alcun cardinale li accennò che la sonasse*, e poi anch'egli disse alcune parole a *Borgia*, perchè si quietasse. Al che *il card. Borgia rispose con sdegno*, che egli non parlava *o non voleva parlare con esso lui*, ma concluse: *Obedio Suae Sanctitati, e così si tacque;* ma poi soggiunse che *Sua Santità si contentasse* di ricever la scrittura che li sarebbe data, e *Sua Beatitudine*, benchè potesse con giusta ragione rimetterlo *alla udienza privata*, nondimeno *con eccesso di benignità la prese*, proferendo l'infrascritte parole: *Ad Nos pertinet cura religionis catholicae, cui et incubuimus et incumbimus, et dilectum filium Nostrum regem catholicum amamus, prout ex effectibus ostendimus.*

Questa nell'essentiale è la *vera e semplice serie del successo*, che ha *scandalizato tutti gli huomini da bene. . . .*" [1]

Then follows (p. 89–90). Aggiunta alla cifra di Msgr. Monti, from which we quote this passage: "Il s. card. S. Honofrio stava nel medesimo banco e fra lui e Borgia erano di mezzo tre o quattro cardinali, quando si levò a far tacere il cardinale che faceva renitenza al comandamento del Papa; sia anche per notitia di V. S. ch'egli lo prese per la mano gridandoli che tacesse et obedisse, trasportato dal zelo e della bruttezza

[1] On the back: "A Msgr. d'Antiochia Nunzio. Messo in cifra l'8 marzo 1632. Decif. a Msgr. Nunzio Panzirolo et a Msgr. Nunzio a Napoli li X detto."

di quella disobedienza in faccia del Sommo Pontefice et in esentione de' comandi che S. B. reiterava al medesimo Borgia."

[*Barb.* 8376, p. 85 s., Vatican Library.]

15. P. Savelli to Emperor Ferdinand II.[1]

Rome, April 3rd, 1632.[2]

" Sacra Cesarea Maestà.

Nel concistoro di lunedì passato con occasione di dar parte al collegio de' cardinali della speditione de' Nontii straordinarii S. S^{tà} fece un ragionamento nel quale parve che volesse rispondere al cardinal Borgia, sebene con parole molto modeste, che furono che S. S^{tà} non haveva mancato mai di servire alla causa publica, come haverebbe fatto sempre fin col proprio sangue, e che se non haveva communicato al collegio, quanto era stato operato et opera tuttavia, e che per farlo hora constare, haveva deputato una congregatione de' cardinali, nella quale si erano mostrate tutte le lettere, con che si vedea finalmente che in ordine a tutto questo haveva presa la risolutione di spedire li sudetti tre Nontii straordinarii. Il concistoro fu cominciato ad hora molto solecita e finì anco assai presto, si che più di dodeci cardinali non arrivorono a tempo per intervenirvi, fra quali Sandoval, Spinola et Albornoz, vi fu ben Borgia : dicono che questo si facesse per ovviare che a quanto diceva il Papa, non fosse replicato dalli cardinali Spagnuoli, il che però non fu fatto da Borgia benchè presente.[3]

Dio N. S. guardi V. M. Ces. con ogni augumento di felicità e di gloria.

Roma li 3 aprile 1632.

Di V. M. Ces.

humiliss^{o} e obligatiss^{o} serv^{re}

Paolo Savello." [4]

[Orig., State Archives, Vienna, *Romana*, fasc. 49, pp. 55–7.]

[1] *Cf.* XXVIII, 294.

[2] Cifra ; decoded text herewith.

[3] End of text in code.

[4] Autograph.

16. Instruction of Cardinal Francesco Barberini for the Nuncios Ceva and Grimaldi.[1]

Rome, May 1st, 1632.

" . . . Si divide adunque lo scopo della sua Nuntiatura in due principali capi: cioè il 1°, riconciliare i principi cattolici fra di loro: il 2°, unire le loro armi e forze contro gl'heretici. Ma chi non vede che, quando si conseguisse il 1° di questi capi, ne deriva poi facilissimamente il 2°?, poichè, tolte che fossero le gelosie et i disturbi che corrono fra le due Corone e fra altri principi cattolici per loro puntigli et interessi, non ha dubbio che si congiungeranno a ribattere il nemico della commune religione. Anzi il 2° de' sopradetti capi ha da servire come mezo overo argomento per ottenere il 1°, dimostrando che sempre mai gli avversarii della religione cattolica, o siano stati infedeli o eretici, si son serviti, per avanzare le loro false sette et errori e per opprimere la fede ortodossa, delle discordie e delle guerre, che il demonio, fautore di essi, ha di quando in quando seminate tra potentati cattolici. Di questi esempii sono piene le historie antiche e moderne, e non accade rammemorare la miseranda captività dell'imperio greco, oppresso dal Turco per la sopradetta cagione, poichè ne son fresche le memorie nella Germania e nella Francia medesima, nelle quali provincie, se si considera attentamente, si troverà che i velenosi semi della empietà di Lutero e di Calvino, a guisa di perniciosa zizania, radicarono e si distesero già più d'un secolo, mentre per interessi di stato ardevano parimente le guerre fra le corone Austriache e quella di Francia, le quali tiravan seco le fattioni degli altri principi del cristianesimo cattolico, si che, mentre accesi di sdegno fra di loro attendevano vicendevolmente a oltraggiarsi, non hebbero nè applicatione nè agio di avvertire o di reprimere l'incendio allhora sorgente delle heresie, alle quali conosciute che furono, indarno poi procurarono di por rimedio quelli che per le loro discordie et interessi di stato le havevano lasciate non pur radicare, ma anche germogliare e diventare adult e.

Hora di che altra opportunità si vale Gostavo e i suoi aderenti per avantaggiarsi con tanto danno della religione cattolica, se non della disunione e discordia de' principi che la professano? E se questi, ostinatamente combattendo

[1] *Cf.* XXVIII. 304 *seqq.*

fra di loro, lasceranno che il detto Sveco et i suoi settarii caminino avanti ad abattere hoggi un principe cattolico e domani un altro, come fin hora van facendo, chi non scorge che, crescendo tuttavia così di avidità, di gloria e di dominio come di riputatione e di forze, non si conterrà ne' limiti di Alemagna, ma minaccerà all'Italia, alla Fiandra, alla Francia, alla Polonia et a tutto il cattolico cristianesimo? Et allhora (che Dio benedetto il cessi) si accorgerebbono quei principi, che hora o trascurano le imprese di lui o anche li danno qualche calore per odii o per interessi particolari, quanto era meglio, deposti e sopiti questi, concorrer prontamente a porgere aiuto alli cattolici oppugnati dall'heretico, e procurare di domare o reprimere in casa d'altri l'incendio, prima che lasciar aumentare et approssimare o entrare nella casa propria? E tanto più chiarendosi tuttavia la proterva mente dello Sveco, il quale non stima nessun altro che se stesso e procede con superbia et alterigia anco verso quelli che nel principio delle sue prosperità come amico mostrava di apprezzare et honorare, e senza udirli o tener conto di essi e de loro interessi fa solo quello che giudica di suo proprio profitto. I quali termini orgogliosi e violenti se usa adesso, che farebbe poi quando arrivasse più oltre a ingagliardirsi e crescer di stati, di riputatione e di forze? Si sono vedute le sue propositioni di neutralità, con le quali voleva che gli Elettori cattolici pattuissero seco, et alcune altre capitolationi che offeriva alla città di Colonia ad effetto che stessero neutrali e non si opponessero a lui, nè aiutassero gli altri cattolici. Dalle quali capitolazioni o propositioni si comprova evidentemente quanto di sopra si è detto, perchè contengono così manifesti e gravi pregiuditii della religion cattolica e così dure et inique conditioni, che sono più tosto leggi che un vincitore impone al vinto, che conventioni e patti da stabilirsi con un neutrale. Quali sariano dunque le leggi ch'egli imporria ai soggetti, quando tali sono quelle che ardisce di prescrivere a coloro, con i quali intende ritenere amicitia? E chi eleggerà di rimanere amico o al meno neutrale verso un huomo che disprezza gli amici e tratta coi neutrali come con nemici? Il Re christ^{mo} con gli affari di Pinerolo, de' passi Retici, delle cose di Metz e di Lorena par che habbia preteso di tener somma cura de' passi, per poter sovvenire i suoi alliati in Italia et in Germania, e perchè la Francia e suoi aditi siano liberi da queste bande: e così fatte ragioni allegano i suoi ministri qualvolta si ragiona delli sudetti negotii. E nondimeno comporterà S. M^{tà} che, invece de' cattolici, un heretico vada a poco a poco serrando et occupando i detti passi e rinchiudendo la Francia di maniera, che nè S. M^{tà} possa soccorrer i suoi amici, nè questi ricorrere alla M^{tà} Sua. Che lo Sveco aspiri a tutto suo potere alla occupatione di detti passi, è chiarissimo, e si sà l'animo che hebbe et ha d'impadronirsi dell'Alsatia e di Brisac, per possedere anco il passo del Tirolo, le ambascerie inviate a Svizzeri, tanto cattolici quanto heretici, per metter il piede ne' passaggi delle Alpi, e le occupationi di tanti luoghi lungo il Reno, per le quali il medesimo Re christ^{mo} s'è trovato impedito dal poter mandare aiuti a qualche Elettore e principi cattolici, benchè non le sia mancata la volontà e 'l desiderio di farlo. Similmente s'è manifestamente scorto l'animo suo d'occupar Confluenza e quinci Colonia e quegli aditi che dia paesi di Fiandra portano dentro la Germania, e tutto per chiudervi ogni strada alle due più potenti corone del christianesimo cattolico.

Se dunque è vero, come è verissimo, che lo Sveco e gli heretici hanno fondati i loro disegni sopra la disunione e discordia de' principi cattolici, e col medesimo fondamento attendono a proseguire, non vi è altro rimedio che l'unione delli animi e de' voleri de' medesimi principi cattolici per sovvertire i disegni de' nemici e sottrarre il fondamento ai loro pensieri e machine, su le quali è da credere fabrichino gagliardamente le loro speranze gli Ugonotti di Francia, quali, abbattuti con tanta gloria sua dal Re christ^{mo}, pensano a risuscitare il loro partito con la vicinanza dello Sveco, e fin d'adesso è verisimile che ne concepiscano ardire, e tanto più vedendo in piedi le dissensioni della casa reale. Le quali considerationi maggiormente devono muovere il Re christ^{mo} a giuntarsi con l'Imperatore e co' principi cattolici, sicome dall'altro canto li Spagnuoli devono anch'essi tor le difficoltà della detta unione, considerando l'audacia che s'accrescerà all'heretici de' Paesi Bassi e della Fiandra, se le prosperità di Gostavo camineranno avanti. . . .

. . . .

. . . A molti vien dato a credere che il Papa possa dar monti d'oro per la guerra contro gli heretici e che per poca volontà e non per impotenza nieghi di farlo. Bisogna dunque metter loro avanti gli occhi il piccolissimo dominio temporale e le pochissime rendite della Sede Apostolica a petto di quelle di altri potentati cattolici; l'impegno delle entrate fatto non da lei sola, ma dalli antecessori di S. S^{tà}; le spese gravissime e necessarie dal principio del pontificato fino a questo giorno et che tuttavia continuano; la desolazione estrema della povera Italia per la guerra e per la peste. E con tutto ciò altri pontifici passati in simili occorrenze non hanno fatto più di quello che hoggi fa la S^{tà} Sua. Che il danaro di Castello non si è voluto toccare da altri Papi in simiglianti bisogni, nè si può senza periurio, nè meno senza pericolo, per i grandi richiami de' popoli; e che finalmente la S. Sede per le sudette strettezze, in che si trova, non ha altro sangue che il detto danaro, et è anche poco per ogni necessità propria che gli avvenisse. Similmente quanto alle leghe o confederationi; che S. Beat^{ne} manda a posta i Nuntii per unire i principi cattolici insieme contro li heretici, che questi uffitii gli han sempre fatti i suoi ministri e che ella non ha ricusato mai di impiegarvisi, mentre si fussero fatte propositioni, che sodisfaccessero a' principi cattolici. Se diranno poi della lega proposta a nome di Cesare, si potrà in bel modo far conoscere che molti articoli principali di essa non erano in modo alcuno proportionati o decenti al Sommo Pontefice. Finalmente, per ribatter in generale le calunnie di connivenza o di tardanza di S. Beat^{ne} nel fare uffitii con Francia e con tutti, si può e deve andare insinuando che, sebene senza pompa di legati, che harebbono accresciute notabilmente le spese e ricercavano tempo e de' quali nè meno si curavano alcuni de' principi interessati, nondimeno S. S^{tà} non ha tralasciato, senza pure esserne richiesta, fin dal principio di questi moti d'interporre la sua efficace intercessione col Re chr^{mo} e con gli altri, per mezo de' suoi Nuntii ordinarii, suoi Brevi, sue lettere et in qualunque modo; e che, se ciò non havesse fatto a tempo, hoggi non vi sarieno le aperture di negotiatione che vi sono tra S. M^{tà} Ces^{ea} e il Re christ^{mo}. Doversi considerare che i sospetti, le gelosie e le turbolenze tra i primi prencipi della christianità hoggi son tanto radicate e grandi che il disgombrarle e diradicarle, oltre la lunghezza e fatica, richiede la mano onnipotente di Dio. E quanto al Papa, vi si ricerca una sincera e disombrata confidenza delle parti verso S. Beat^{ne}, la quale ha desiderato e desidera con tutto il cuore una tal filiale fiducia e leale corrispondenza, dolendosi acerbamente che per falsissime sospicioni e congetture senza fondamento alcuni siano andati freddi e dubbiosi con la S^{tà} Sua. E qui esagerar si deve la candidezza e rettitudine delli pensieri della S^{tà} Sua, l'indifferenza paterna verso tutti senza veruna partialità, la svelata apertura del suo cuore et il non haver già mai covati nell'animo designi nè fini chimericamente imaginati da alcuni, eccetto quelli della pace e unione de' cattolici, e del bene e servitio della nostra s. religione, per i quali fini si è adoperata sempre ferventemente dal suo lato fra tante difficoltà e discordie del christianesimo cattolico, nè mai ha voluto troncar il filo delle sue interpositioni, benchè il demonio gli habbia orditi incontro mille impedimenti di diffidenze, di calunnie e di giuditii erronei. Molti de' quali col tempo e colla verità son restati chiariti, et il medesimo potersi e doversi credere et argomentare de gli altri, cioè che sempre saranno trovati mendaci e senza alcuna reale sossistenza.

Questi e simili concetti e ragioni, le quali a V. S. et alli altri Nuntii somministrerà la loro prudenza, si hanno da andar imprimendo e divulgando, come di sopra ho detto, acciocchè i prencipi, i nobili, i popolari, gli ecclesiastici e tutti ributtino e discaccino le contrarie o maligne o ignoranti persuasioni e credano e sentano della persona e della volontà di S. Beat^{ne} quello che è fondato in irrefragabile verità, nota agli occhi del tremendo giudice Dio benedetto, il quale illuminerà il buio delle tenebre e manifesterà i consigli e i sentimenti de' cuori. . . ."

[*Arm.* 3, t. 47, p. 1 s. Papal Secret Archives and *Barb.* 2629, p. 155 s., Vatican Library.]

17. Draft of a Brief of Pope Urban VIII. to Emperor Ferdinand II.[1]

Rome, July 21st, 1635.

Carissimo in Christo filio Nostro Ferdinando Hungariae et Bohemiae Regi illustri in Romanorum Imperatorem electo.

Urbanus PP. VIII.

Carissime in Christo fili Noster, salutem et Apostolicam benedictionem. Ex egregiis Maiestatis tuae conatibus pro

[1] *Cf.* XXVIII, 347.

Ecclesiae catholicae defensione summa cum laude susceptis Nobis semper polliciti sumus, nihil animo tuo sese offere quod vehementius cupias, quam gloriam christianae reipublicae, quae merito magnam futurae suae amplificationis in tua virtute ac pietate spem posuit, quam ut consequeremur, officio Nostro pastorali non defuimus. Monuerunt pluries Maiestatem tuam dilectus filius Noster cardinalis Roccius et venerabilis frater Malatesta episcopus Pisaurensis, ac tibi nomine Nostro insinuarunt, ut caveres, ne quid isthic detrimenti rei ecclesiasticae catholicae in conficiendis pacificationis tractationibus inferretur. Secus tamen non sine gravi animi Nostri sensu accidit, idque praeter exspectationem Nostram; quaedam enim ad nuperae pacis conditiones pertinentia Nobis tuus orator nomine tuo significavit, non undequaque auctoritati tuae ac pietati iure debita constituta fuisse, et in iis sane, quae ad religionem spectant, minus quam ex tuis votis, qui singulari animi magnitudine Ecclesiae dignitatem semper tibi cordi fore declarasti, obtineri potuisse. Fusius hac de re tecum agent venerabilis frater Marius archiepiscopus Avenionensis et venerabilis frater Malatesta episcopus Pisaurensis, quibus a te integram fidem haberi cupimus. Deum precamur, ut religionis causam superno praesidio tueatur, teque caelestibus suis beneficiis affatim ditet. Maiestati tuae Apostolicam benedictionem amantissime impertimur.

Datum Romae apud Sanctam Mariam Maiorem sub annulo piscatoris die XXI Iulii MDCXXXV pontificatus Nostri anno XII.

(Ad improbandas aliquas conditiones pacis eccl. adversantes scriptae fuerant litterae in super. exemplari. Deinde opportunius visum respondere Imperatori sequenti epistola [see next No., et iniunctum Nuntiis, ut eam consignantes simul ei exponerent, pactiones S. S. plur. sollicitudines attulisse.)

[*Epist.* XIII.–XIV. n. 31, Papal Secret Archives.]

18. Pope Urban VIII. to Emperor Ferdinand II.[1]

Rome, July 21st, 1635.

Carissimo in Christo filio Nostro Ferdinando Hungariae et Bohemiae Regi illustri in Romanorum Imperatorem electo.

[1] *Cf.* XXVIII, 347.

Urbanus PP. VIII.

Carissime in Christo fili Noster, salutem et Apostolicam benedictionem. Ex egregiis Maiestatis tuae conatibus pro Ecclesiae catholicae defensione summa cum laude susceptis Nobis semper polliciti sumus, nihil animo tuo sese offere, quod vehementius cupias, quam gloriam christianae reipublicae, quae merito magnam futurae suae amplificationis in tua virtute ac pietate spem posuit. Itaque ubi aliquas nuperae conditiones pacis cognovimus, quas nobilis vir Scipio princeps Bozuli orator tuus Nobis nomine tuo significavit, cum gravi animi Nostri sensu accidit, non omnia auctoritati tuae ac pietati iure debita fuisse constituta, et in iis sane, quae ad religionem spectant, minus quam ex tuis votis, qui singulari animi magnitudine de Ecclesiae dignitae te valde sollicitum praestas, esse firmata. Serio hac de re tecum agent venerabilis frater Marius archiepiscopus Avenionensis et venerabilis frater Malatesta episcopus Pisaurensis, quibus a te integram fidem haberi cupimus. Deum precamur, ut religionis causam praesidio tueatur teque caelestibus beneficiis affatim ditet. Maiestati tuae Apostolicam benedictionem amantissime impertimur.

Datum Romae apud Sanctam Mariam Maiorem sub annulo piscatoris die XXI Iulii MDCXXXV, pontificatus Nostri anno XII.

[*Epist.* XIII–XIV n. 32, Papal Secret Archives.]

19. Protocol of a Cardinalitial Congregation "de redditibus ecclesiasticis" 1642/3.[1]

Sitting of November 11th and 12th, December 3rd, 16th, 23rd and 30th, 1642. Decisions: how much the Pope may take out of Church revenue, signed (on January 18th, 1643) by Cardinal Lugo also.

"Quaesitum est in congregatione facta die 28 Augusti 1643 [?] in palatio coram [?] card. Alterii, an et quale iudicium practicum et prudentiale ferri possit circa quotam aliquam, quam Summus Pontifex possit libere et quasi bona patrimonialia distribuere ex iis quae ratione suae dignitatis percipit, et resolutum fuit ab omnibus, posse ad minus ob rationes

[1] *Cf.* XXVII, 48.

alias consideratas stipendii, laboris et aliorum titulorum assignare centum millia scuta monetae Romanae annua ultra pretia officiorum omnium, de quibus quomodo et quantum possit dispensare ut de bonis patrimonialibus dictum iam fuit in aliis congregationibus, atque etiam id quod ex sua congrua parcius in ea expendendo sibi ad liberam dispositionem reservare potest. Die et mense supradicto."

There follow the autograph signatures of: "Ioh. Bapt. card. de Alteriis, M. A. Maraldus, Valentinus Mangonius, Io. Bapt. de Lugo, Torquatus Cuppis." [1]

[Archives of Foligno, now in the Papal Secret Archives. *Instrum. Miscell.* n. 4196.]

20. The Nuncio Extraordinary F. Chigi to Cardinal Francesco Barberini.[2]

Münster, April 1st, 1644.

"... Quando chiesi la instruttione all'em. sig. card. Rossett con fargli leggere le parole intiere che in tal fine me ne scriveva V. Em. sotto li 26 di Dicembre, mi consegnò la cifra che haveva ricevuta due anni prima di V. Em." Poichè adesso non è più possibile interrogare personalmente il cardinale "come Vostra Eminenza mi ingiunge con i suoi scritti del 27 febbraio e 3 marzo", così mi son rivolto a lui per lettera; temo però, che egli sia già partito da Colonia.

[*Barb.* 6144, Vatican Library.]

21. The Nuncio Extraordinary F. Chigi to Cardinal Francesco Barberini.[3]

Münster, May 27th, 1644.[4]

"La nuova della pace dell'Italia è stata intesa qua con grandissima consolazione particolarmente de' buoni cattolici, poichè si vedevano insolentire gl'heretici con pazze induttioni e con istravaganti conseguenze che a loro prò si sforzavano di cavar da questa guerra, si come hanno fatto ristampare

[1] *Cf.* Moroni on the above-named.
[2] *Cf.* XXVIII, 372.
[3] *Cf. ibid.*
[4] Decifrato il 15 giugno.

in varii luoghi et in altre lingue la Baccinata, il Divortio, il Corriero et altre infamie,[1] che ho procurato sempre di supprimere in questa Nunziatura."

Last Sunday (Trinitatis) I had a Te Deum sung for this peace " in questa chiesa de' Conventuali, dove habito." Opening of the Congress on May 10th.

[*Barb.* 6144, Vatican Library.]

22. Avviso di Roma of July 30th, 1644.[2]

" Essendo la S^{tà} di N. S. caduta ammalata da molti giorni in qua di catarro con dissenterie, martedì mattina si comunicò per viatico, et l'em^{mo} Barberini ne mandò a dar parte alli ss. cardinali, quali poi tutti furono a Palazzo a condolersene con S. Em., et mercoledì notte su le 5 hore furono trasportati in Castel S. Angelo tutti li prigioni criminali di cause gravi, che si trovarono in queste carceri. Hiermattina poi su le 11 hore aggravatasi S. S. nel male, dopo haver ricevuto il giorno precedente l'oglio santo e fatta la raccomendatione dell'anima, rese lo spirito al creatore in età di c^{a} 77 anni." Questa notte sono state spezzate l'anello e la matrice della bolla del papa. Il mattino i cardinali Francesco e Antonio Barberini han lasciato il palazzo per tornare alle loro abitazioni, altrettanto Onofrio, Ceva, Giori, Lugo e Valençay.

[*Avvisi*, 96, Papal Secret Archives, 1644.]

23. Writings Dedicated to Urban VIII.

Ciaconius' survey of such publications (IV. 513 *seq.*) is all the more incomplete as he only considers printed matter. But even here he is very incomplete, as appears from *Allatii*

[1] *Cf.* XXIX, 405.

[2] See above, p. 404. *Cf.* also the letter of *O. Rinaldi*, dated July 30, 1644, on the death of Urban VIII. who had ended by being nothing but " pelle e ossa ", in Marchesan, Lettere di O. Rinaldi, Treviso, 1896, 21. The **Avviso* of August 6, 1644, says : " Lunedi sendo stato posto in una cassa di cipresso e poi di piombo, fu messo nel sepolcro, che la S^{tà} Sua s'era fatto fare in vita sotto la nicchia grande di quella chiesa. Papal Secret Archives, 96, Avvisi, 1644.

Apes Urb.; CERROTTI, *Bibliografia* I. (1893) 507 *seq.*[1] There is an extraordinary number of discourses delivered before the Pope and dedicated to him. I saw a very rare printed work in the Bibl. Borghese (since sold): *Io. Bapt. Spadius, De Urbani VIII. P.O. M. Erato ex Virgilio*, Placentiae, 1627. Little known and rare are the following also: *Le Morali del sig. Fabio Albergati alla S^tà^ di N.S. Papa Urbano VIII.*, Bologna, 1627. By way of supplement I here add a number of works which exist only in manuscript: –

I. *Barb.*, Vatican Library.[2]

1204. Io. Bapt. Catumsyritus (Italograecus), Decem falsa fundamenta M. A. de Dominis, olim ep. Spalat., mox apostati relapsi, et eius disciplui Corydalepti, olim alumni huius collegii graeci Romani, contra veritatem sanct. sacram. Eucharistiae.

1717. Poems, etc. Nr. 8: In summum Urbani VIII. pontificatum panegyricus Benedicti Milani Sublacens. Ivi p. 155–60: Applausus Vissani populi in creationem S. P. Urbani VIII. (six poems of the seminarists). *Ibid.*, pp. 161–70: Georgius Camerarius Scotus [Professor at Padua], Ad Urbanum VIII. P. M. Scotiae quandam protectorem Silva.

1732–3. Silvae Barberinae Stephano Simonino auctore. Cfr. Cat. Bibl. *Barb.* II., 381.

1749. Poem to Urban VIII.

1750. Poem to Urban VIII. by Augustinus Arata, cler. reg.

[1] Here also the data are incomplete, thus there is missing "Laurentii Pignorini presbyt. in Patavi Carmen as Urbanun VII.", s. 1, 1623. On the work "Apis religiosa" by Cristoforo Giarda (Mediolani, 1625), dedicated to the Pope in the Jubilee year, *cf.* PREMOLI, *C. Giarda*, Monza, 1914, 4. The great Armenian-Latin dictionary by the Dominican Paolo Pieromali has been lost; *cf.* MICHELANGELO MACRI, *Memorie* intorno alla vita e alle opere di Mgr. frate Paolo Pieromali Domenicano, arcivescovo di Naxivan, Napoli, 1824.

[2] The following date from the period before the election: *Cod.*, X., 131: Ad Maffeum card. Barberinum de locis dialecticis auctore A. Gallerio Bonon. and X., 132: Compendium moralis Phil. by A. Gallerio, also dedicated to the Cardinal.

1751. Poem on the election of Urban VIII. (according to Catalogue perhaps by Stef. de Bufalo).

1755. Nicolai de Malpas Burgundi Thyara pontificalis (Oratio seu epistola in laudem Urbani VIII.).

1756. Io. Pagani sacerdotis Carmen in laudem Urbani VIII.

1772. De s. Michaele ad Urbanum VIII. carmen.[1]

1782/3. Carmina Dominici Frescobaldis ad Urbanum VIII.

1794. Poems to Urban VIII.

1815. Poems to Urban VIII., ex. gr. by Ant. Liporus (Sardus).

1819. Poems to Urban VIII., ex. gr. by Franc. Boninsegni.

1825, 1829, 1831, 1851, 1869, 1874, 1875, 1877. Poems to Urban VIII.

1890. Poem by Joh. Ant. Brolatus to Urban VIII.[2]

1893. Discorso by Ios. Grisendius on Urban VIII.'s coronation.

1897. Discorso of Ioh. Baptista Donius, Lyra Barberina.

1898. Poem *Duodevicennalia Urbani VIII. ab auctore Steph. Simonimo* (cf. above 1732, 1733).

1905. Poems by Rutilius Cecchius (1625) to Urban VIII.

1909. Poems by Ios. Grisendius to Urban VIII.

1913. Poem to Urban VIII.

1916. Dramatic Allocution to Urban VIII.

1941, 1955. Poems to Urban VIII.

1957. Poems to Urban VIII. by a Jesuit.

1965. Poems to Urban VIII. by Barth. Lagius.

2050, 2060, 2078. Poems to Urban VIII.

2079. Carmina in laudem Urbani VIII. et Franc. card. Barberini by: Laur. Arrighus, Hipp. Nanius, Balth. Bonifacius, Ferd. Bardus, Iac. Tortolettus, Io. Iac. Buccardus, Franc. de Armis, Terent. Alciati, Dom. Orpheus, Hier. Brivius, Phil. Guillerie, Caesar Zarottus, Io. Bapt. Laurus, Fabius Leonida, Tadd. Donnola, F. A. Pupura, ep. Montis Marani, Georg. Porcius,[3] Io. Bapt. Donius, Bonif. Beaminus, De

[1] On St. Michael see Vol. XXIX., p. 475.

[2] On his translation of Urban VIII.'s hymn to St. Martina see Vol. XXIX, 419, n. 4.

[3] The following works by Porcius are in print: "Urbano VIII. panegyrica Ode," Romae, 1633, and "Barberina Clio", Romae, 1634.

Laureis, Thomas Biscia, Io. Ant. Bernabeus, Io. Lud. a Burigliasco, Curtius Castruccius, Sebast. Fantonus, Phil. Baldassarus, Iulian, Blancarius, Io. Bartolettus, Gabriel Nandaeus, Petrus Bertius, Claudius Achillinus, Hier. Serlupius, Laelius Gratianus, Iul. Caesar Stella, Aug. Favoritus, Attilinus Marcellius, A. a Puteo, episc. Burgi s. Donini, Io. Casean Bituntin, Io. Bapt. Stella, Hier. Aleander, Vespas. Crispoltus, Famian. Strada, Gaspar Mustola, Iac. Manaraeus, Rob. Le Chevalier, Gallus, etc.

2080, 2081, 2083, 2104. Poems to Urban VIII.

2015. To Urban VIII. (Sarbiewski's " Aureum Saeculum ", cf. above, p. 427.

2123. Apiarium di Christ. Maria Monaldus (cf. 430, n. 1.

2129. Eclogae by Guy de Souvigny (in French).

2130, 2131. Poems on Urban VIII.

2151. A large collection of poems on Urban VIII., for instance by Hier. Mercatellus, Andr. Tamantinus, Nic. Fagius, Petrus Dubot, Steph. de Bubalo, etc.

2153. Poems by Gauco Gaukema (cf. ORBAAN, *Bescheiden*, I., 307, who quotes various other poems).

3571. Madrigale a Urbano VIII. by Balt. Porreno.

3672. Popeo Tomasini, Il nobiliss. martire Sebastiano (prose and verse).

3709, 3710. Poem to Urban VIII.

3712, 3740. Italian poems to Urban VIII.

3744. Latin poems to Urban VIII.

3749, 3750. Italian poems to Urban VIII.

3754. Spiritual poems.

3759, 3768. *Canzone* to Urban VIII.

3770. Poems to Urban VIII.

3776. Poems to Urban VIII. among them (p. 1–7) " Canzone sopra la fortezza di Castel S. Angelo ridotta a somma perfettione da S. Beat^{ne}."

3677. Poems to Urban VIII.

3779. Franc. Carducci, Latin ode to Urban VIII.

3782. Canzone to Urban VIII.

3786, 3806, 3814. Italian poems to Urban VIII.

3815. Epigr. lat e sonetti in lode di Urbano VIII.

3816, 3825. Italian poems to Urban VIII.

3826. Latin poems to Urban VIII.

3830. La gloria Barberina, Canzone in lode di Urbano VIII. by Giacinto Gigli Romano.[1]

3831, 3835, 3844, 3849, 3875, 3886. Panegyrics of Urban VIII.

3901. Poems to Urban VIII.

4055. Italian poems to Urban VIII.

4260. (1) CARLO PETRUCCI, Trattato sopra alcune eminenze che possono nuocere alla fortezza di Castel S. Angelo. Del modo d'assicurarsi di quelle e ridurlo alla sua intera perfezione. Di alcune varie forme di fortificazione che si potrebbero fare sopra le colline di S. Honofrio sino a S. Pancrazio et includervi tutta ovvero parte di Trastevere (pp. 1–7). (2) By the same: Discorso sopra il porto et fortezza di Civitavecchia (pp. 8–9).

4364. Latin ode to Urban VIII.

5386. Discorso intorno a'tributi, gabelle etc., che si pagano nel regno di Napoli, dell'abbate Giulio Ces. Braccini.

II. Vatican Library.

Ottob. 1729, p. 195 *seq.* Panegirico di Bartolomeo Fortaletti alla S[tà] di N.S. Urbano VIII. 1634 (Italian poem).

2896. Poesie in lode di Urbano VIII.

Regin. 2044. Poem to Urban VIII.

Vat. 6424. Cipriano arciprete di S. Maria n. Rotonda, Relazione di reliquie sotteranee trovate con l'occasione della nuova chiavica fatta dalla ripa del fiume sino alla strada de' Condotti, alla S[tà] di N.S. Urbano VIII.

III. Bibl. Angelica, Rome.

Cod. T. 1, 2. Iconum S. P. Augustini aliorumque sanctorum ac ven. eremitarum quibus medici poeticique flores ex hortis eremitanis decerpti asperguntur (partly in verse) cf. NARDUCCI, 533.

24. WRITINGS DEDICATED TO CARDINAL FRANCESCO BARBERINI.

To complete the data of Ciaconius (IV., 528) which, as a matter of fact, are full enough, there is a good deal of information

[1] Also in Cod. Sessor. 359, p. 137 *seq.* of the Bibl. Vittorio Emmanuele, Rome, with the note " present. al Papa 23 Agosto, 1632 ".

in the "Apes Urbanae" of L. Allacius, but the most important printed works are all given by Ciaconius.[1] Among unpublished works dedicated to Card. Francesco Barberini I noted also the following in *Barb.*, Vatican Library :—

800. Mauritius Roganus episc. Fundanus destinatus, Compendium sacr. oec. concilii Trid. decretor. de mor. ref. et ecclesiastica disciplina.

954. Philippus Rovenius, Tractatus de missionibus ad propag. fidem et conversionem infidelium, paganorum, iudaeorum, haereticorum ac scismaticorum.

979. Franc. Maria del Monaco (Drepanitanus, Theatinus, Adversus nostri temporis usuras irae.

980. Luca Castellino (Ord. Praed.), Disputat. theologicae.

1674. Hier. Ferrarius, Carminium ad Urbanum VIII. et card. Franc. et Ant. Barberinos.[2]

1717. Poems to Card. Fr. Barberini.

1721. Iter Barberinum. Carmen Iacobi Albani Gibbesii Angli, Romae, manu authoris 1648. p. 4 : Ad Franc. card. Barberinum e Gallis ad Urbem reducem carmen ; p. 24b : Ode to the same.

1770. Hercules Barberinus sive virtutes herculeae in Franc. card. Barberino recognitae (Francci Stephanii congreg. Somasc. dat. Romae ex collegio Clementino 1639).

1851. Aemilii Sibonii Vinea card. Franc. Barberini (pp. 17–24) ; also other poems " in laudem Franc. Barberini ".

1895. Poems to Card. Fr. Barberini.

1912. Poems to Card. Barberini by Marcus Barotta " Romanus ".

[1] Missing : *Alvaro Semedo S.J., Relatione della grande monarchia della Cina*, Roma, 1643 (with portrait of the author in Chinese attire).

[2] To Ciaconius' list (IV., 367), of works dedicated to Cardinal Antonio Barberini the Younger, we must add : *Barb.*, 3456 : *Le tableau de la vie humaine du baron St. Germain Ronurou* [*sic !*] ; *ibid.*, 4269 : *Del offitio di commissario generale degli eserciti.* Discorso di Giovan. Batt. Reggi Romano. *Ibid.*, 3738, 3739, poems to Cardinal Antonio Barberini the Younger (Vatican Library). To this also belongs *Malatesta Leonelli, Oblatione* poetica ad Card. Antonio Barberini, Legato di Bologna, Ferrara e Romagna : Opere diverse, Bologna, 1644.

1915. *Discorso* on Card. Fr. Barberini.

1950. Horti Barberini Quirinales illustrati ad ill. card. Fr. Barberinum.

2088. " Hierothriambus Lat." Poem on Card. Fr. Barberini's return from France by Lambert Vossius Belga, Rome XIV. Kal. maii 1627.

2099. Poem on Card. Barberini.

2283. Alberti Moroni S. J. De pontificalibus Urbani VIII. comitiis historia.

2489. Series actorum Urbani VIII. auctore F. Marcellino de Pisis Gallo Matisconensi, praedic. Capucin. prov. Lugdun. (dedicated to Cardinal Fr. Barberini and Urbano VIII.).

3251. Sonetto sopra il dente gigantico donato al card. Fr. Barberini da F. Ughelli (p. 567).

3471. French poems dedicated to Card. Fr. Barberini.

3647. Sonnets to Card. Fr. Barberini by Jac. Guglielmi.

4308. Ottav. Castelli, Sopra i mimi e pantomimi degli antichi.

25. The Elogia and Avvisi of Theodore Ameyden.

In the catalogues of Roman libraries, we often meet with the name of Theodor Ameyden, or Amydenius, or again Amidemenius and even Almaden. The following works of his are found in print :—

(1) Chori publicae de philosophia disputationiis etc., Romae, 1605.

(2) Della natura del vino e del ber caldo e freddo, Roma, 1608.

(3) De pietate Romana, Romae, 1625.

(4) Panegyricus ad Urbanum VIII., Lugduni, 1625.

(5) Relazione della festa fatta alla Riccia, Roma, 1633.

(6) Il can dell'ortolano. Commedia, Viterbo, 1642.

(7) Oratio in funere Elisabethae Borboniae, Romae, 1645.

(8) De officio et iurisdictione Datarii, Venetiis, 1654.

(9) Consultationes duae . . . in materia cambiorum, Piacenza, 1669.

(10) " Relazione di Roma," in *Tesori della corte di Roma*, Bruxelles, 1673.

(11) *La donna frullosa. Commedia dallo Spagnuolo*, 2. ediz. Bologna, 1678.[1]

To these must be added the works not printed in his lifetime, of which only that on Roman Families has recently been published by Bertini, cf. note 4.[2]

In collections of MSS. the work most frequently found is: "Th. Amydenii Summorum Pontificum et S.R.E. cardinalium omnium suo aevo defunctorum Elogia," with a prefatory dedication by his son Philip.[3] For an appreciation of this piece, which covers the years 1600–1655, it is necessary to review briefly the life of the author. Dirk Ameyden was born in 1568 at Hertogenbosch in Northern Brabant, and was therefore a subject of Philip II. He first came to Rome in the Jubilee year 1600, in the train of Cardinal Andrew of Austria. There he went through his humanities with the Jesuits; he then returned home, only to set out once more for the Eternal City. After the death of his uncle Christian Ameyden, in 1605, he succeeded him in the office of Abbreviator, but soon resigned it to act as attorney and agent for the Spanish Government of Milan at the Curia.[4] This appointment was destined to influence very greatly his activities as a historian. A biased judgment is meted out to Popes as well as to Cardinals, according to the angle from which the excited and passionate partisan of the Habsburgs viewed them. True,

[1] Of these works, nos. 2 and the first edition of No. 11 can no longer be found. See Ademollo, *Gigli*, 112.

[2] The **Commento sopra le rime del card. P. Bembo* in the Corsini Library, Rome and the **Discorso sopra l'essere stato interdetta la chiesa di S. Giacomo degli Spagnuoli nel 1628*, in *Barb.* 5275, p. 226 *seq.*, Vatican Library, are not in print.

[3] Among these MSS. I noted: Bibl. Altieri, Rome, X., 62; Corsini Library, Rome, *Cod.* 238; Vatican Library, Vat., 8810, 8747, 9549; Ottob., 2568; Vittorio Emmanuele Libr., Rome, *Cod.* Sessor, CCXLVI. and CCLII.; Papal Secret Archives, Bolognetti, 41.

[4] Besides Schmidlin, *Anima*, 476 (but read "Henzen" for "Henze"), *cf. Freib. Diöz. Archiv.*, I. (1865), 439; Ciampi in *Arch. Rom.*, I., 409 *seq.*; Ademollo, *G. Gigli*, 8, 110 *seq.*; Amayden-Bertini, *Storia di famiglie Romane*, I. (1910), 3rd note; Henzen in *De Katholiek*, CXXIV. (1903), 22 *seq.*, CXXVII.

in 1625, Ameyden published a panegyric of Urban VIII.,[1] but at a later date, according as relations between the Pope and the Habsburgs became more strained, he showed increasing opposition to the Barberini Pope. This is so obvious in his "Vita Urbani VIII.", that Pieper, in his critique of Gregorovius' "Urban VIII.", considers that this biography deserves the same criticism as that which Ciampi (Innocenzo X., p. 263) pronounced upon Ameyden's "Vita d'Innocenzo X": "It is more than a satire, it is a libel" (*Hist. Polit. Blätter*, XCIV., 489). However, Ameyden did not merely take the standpoint of a Habsburg partisan against a Pope like Urban VIII., who strove to fulfil his duties as the common Father of Christendom; the preface to the *Vita* makes it abundantly clear that Ameyden was strongly opposed to the temporal power of the papacy. There he says, for instance: "Efferant encomiis unius principis imperium, qui sub principe vivunt. Ego contra inferam et praesentibus exemplis ostendam, duo illa, quibus respublica continetur, praemium nempe et poenam, apud aristocraticum magistratum suo loco esse, a monarchia exulare. Quid miserabilius quam ad unius tumidi arbitrium sapere, loqui? Quid infelicius quam sub unius impotenti dominatu, latenti immo morienti reipublicae opem ferre non posse? . . . Admittat pluribus commune imperium populares turbas, civiles motus et damnatas dissensiones; non ista quamtumvis perniciosa comparanda sunt cum quibus sub principatu absoluto premimur malis, ubi unius libidini exponimur, rapimur, diripimur, occidimur."

It is clear that Ameyden's work was not meant for the public (non extra privatos parietes prodibit). In the preface he explains its origin and source: "Quandoquidem belli tumultibus e Belgio natali solo eiectum me Roma suscepit et in Urbe domina domicilium et necessitudines contraxi, uxorem duxi, filios procreavi, quorum tu aetate minimus et quem solum ex multis superstitem esse Libitina voluit, ne ociosus

(1904), 421–454; MOLHUYSEN-BLOK, *Nieuw Nederl. Woordenboek*, II., Leiden, 1912, 32 *seq.*; ORBAAN, *Bescheiden*, I., 76 *seq.*, 133 *seq.*; VAES, *Bullet. de l'Institut Hist. Belge de Rome*, I. (1919), 280 *seq.*; Pieper had planned a detailed study of Ameyden, of which I only saw a fragment of five pages which was of great use to me.

[1] *Cf.* above, p. 579.

aut negligens videar fuisse civis, visum est ea annotasse, quae vel ipse observavi vel constans de Summis Pontificibus et S.R.E. cardinalibus huius imperii principibus ferebat fama." Ameyden never thought of investigating the truth of the gossip, the "fama" peculiar to Rome, the classical city of "dicerie" and satire. He busily jotted down everything he heard, and his political standpoint being what it was, he eagerly listened to evil and unfavourable reports, so that it is no wonder that his "Elogia" contain numerous errors, as Pieper pointed out and proved by examples to the point (*loc. cit.*, 489–91). Ameyden was a passionate party man whom Gregorovius wrongly imagined to be well informed (p. 52). The latest Italian research entirely confirms Pieper's judgment of the *Elogia* (v. M. Rosi, in *Arch. d. Soc. Rom.*, XXII., 353; Orbaan, *Rome onder Clemens VIII.*, 38 *seq.*; Hülsen, *Kapitol*, 29; cf. also De Waal, *Campo Santo*, 123, A. 1). The popularity of the *Elogia* to which the numerous manuscript copies bear witness, is due to the preference which the general public always shows for light and spicy reading; but they are not a source for history. First and foremost the author lacks a sense of justice. An acknowledged Dutch authority rightly estimates him as "più caustico chè giusto".[1] Ameyden nowhere attempts any profound analysis; he prefers to deal in anecdotes. The majority of the personages of note whom he describes are dragged down to the plane of everyday life. Nor does he disdain to relate, with much detail, jokes of doubtful quality. Very few of the Cardinals escape his attentions: Baronius is an exception, but even here he cannot refrain from noting the ridiculous rumour that the first volume of the "Annals", was not the work of the celebrated Cardinal at all![2] The greater number of the members of the chief Senate of the Church appear in Ameyden's work as morose or foolish old fellows, or as incapable persons who had risen to eminence through the influence of money or protection. There is scarcely one of whom nothing of the sort

[1] Orbaan (*Documenti*, 33).

[2] Primum (volumen) non a Baronio, sed a cardinali Sirleto scriptum quod apud eruditos constans est fama, quod facile crediderim, cum primum volumen et quoad praxim et quoad texturam historiae reliquis longe praestet (!).

is said. Hence these "Elogia" are of very little historical value; though full of rhetoric they give but few facts and nowhere any real character sketches. It is surprising that such poor work should for so long have passed muster as unquestionably authoritative.

The *Avvisi* of Ameyden are far more valuable and interesting; they have won for him the title of father of Italian journalism.[1] They cover the period of 1640 to 1650 and constitute a sort of Diary. Ranke's attention was drawn to this because there exists a copy in the *Inform. polit.*, 40, 42, 43, 47, of the State Library, Berlin. He made use of it and gave extracts in his *Popes, III.*, 168 *seq.* With regard to the author, he was at first of opinion that he was a Spaniard seeing that he spoke of the "Sacred Spanish Monarchy" with almost religious reverence, as if the Barque of Peter would surely founder without its support; eventually he came to the conclusion (p. 170) that the author may be identical with "Almaden", the author of the *Relatione di Roma.* As a matter of fact, the author's name Deone Hora Temedio in the Berlin manuscript is the anagram of Teodore Ameiden.[2] Ranke might have deduced as much from the work of Cancellieri, *Il Mercato* (Roma, 1811), in which the *Avvisi* of Ameyden are frequently utilized. Cancellieri probably used the collection of Ameyden's *Avvisi* in the Casanatense Library at Rome. They fill three volumes: *Cod.* XX., III., 19 (1640/3), 20 (1644/7), and 21 (1648/9). The year 1650, which is missing here, is in MS. at the National Library, Naples. On the copy among the *Capponi* MSS. in the National Library, Florence, see *Arch. Rom.*, I, 413. The copy in the Alessandrina Library, Rome (*Cod.*, 114*a*), only covers the period August 18th, 1640, to January 1st, 1642.

However interesting the incidents reported by Ameyden in the *Avvisi* may be for the study of civilization, they must be used with great caution as sources of historical information, for here also the author appears constantly as a passionate partisan of Spain and as such he puts in a false light anyone who does not agree with him in all things. The sharp

[1] See Bertolotti, *Giornalisti, astrologi e negromanti in Roma nel sec. XVII.*, Firenze, 1878.

[2] Elsewhere: *Deone hora temi Dio* (*Arch. Rom.*, I, 409).

criticism of him by Ciampi (*Innocenzo,* X, p. 261), and Ademollo, in the monograph, *Giacinto Gigli e i suoi Diarii del secolo XVII,* Firenze, 1877, 110 *seq.*, and in *Independenza Portoghese,* 16, *seq.*, and 42, are fully justified. An example will show how bold Ameyden sometimes is in his statements. He relates that Urban VIII. died without a blessed candle being at hand; at last one was brought from the *Anima,* on which the imperial eagle was stamped, so that the Pope actually died holding the symbol which he had so abhorred throughout his life. Ademollo first drew attention to this malicious invention.[1] From a private letter of Ameyden it transpires that even he did not fail to perceive how little disinterested the religious zeal of the Spaniards was.[2] But he supported them in all things since he was in their service. He could not well relinquish this position, for he had a very numerous family. He married twice but saw all his seventeen children, except one, die before him. It was equally tragic that this jovial Fleming, in whose house comedies were acted, should at the end of his life, have been obliged to leave the Eternal City which he loved so dearly. He published a book without the necessary permission; for this offence the punishment of exile from the States of the Church was inflicted on him in 1654.[3] Alexander VII., who was elected a year later, granted his prayer for pardon, so that he was able to close his eyes in Rome, in 1656.[4] His house in the parish of S. Biagio alla Pagnotta is still extant; it is the fine spacious Renaissance house in Via di Monte Giordano, No. 7–8, over the door of which we read the characteristic inscription: "Unde ea omnia."

26. Andrea Nicoletti's Life of Urban VIII.

The Barberini, like the Boncompagni and the Ludovisi, were anxious to provide an historical memorial for the Pope who had made the name of their House famous throughout the world and raised them to a position of respect and consideration. The nephew of Urban VIII., Cardinal Francesco Barberini, undertook to fulfil this duty of gratitude. It was

[1] See *Il Macinato a Roma,* in *Riv. Europ.*, 1877, II., 439.

[2] See the letter of 1632 in Orbaan, *Bescheiden,* I., 135.

[3] See Ademollo, *Gigli,* 112.

[4] See *ibid.*, 150.

indeed no easy task. The historical presentment of contemporary events always encounters special difficulties owing to personal considerations. Such difficulties were especially certain to be encountered when there was question of the personality of one who, like Pope Urban VIII., had taken so great a part in political life, and who had found himself placed between two great Powers in deadly opposition to each other, during almost the whole of his reign. Yet not only political parties, but numerous individuals still living and occupying the highest ecclesiastical and social positions, were bound to be directly affected by a narrative of this kind. In the conflict between such considerations and historical truth, Cardinal Barberini fell back on the plan which had been adopted in the case of Gregory XIII., namely, to collect all the available material before it was dispersed or destroyed. As the preservation of all the Acts of a deceased Pope in the Papal Secret Archives was only just beginning to be taken for granted, and the abuse of allowing the Pope's family to retain large quantities of documents [1] still prevailed, there was no lack of the necessary manuscript material. This could be supplemented by the reminiscences of the persons concerned. Cardinal Barberini decided to make such a collection of material, probably with the idea that it would serve later on as a source for an historical narrative free from the above-mentioned considerations.

Cardinal Barberini appointed for this work, for which historical research will ever be in his debt, a Canon of S. Lorenzo in Damaso, Andrea Nicoletti, author of a biography, printed in 1610, of Francesca a Jesu Maria,[2] foundress of the Poor Clares of the Strict Observance in Italy, of whom the Cardinal was the special protector.[3] As Nicoletti himself states in the dedication of his biography of Urban VIII.,[4] Barberini placed at his disposal, through his librarian, Carlo Moroni,

[1] *Kiewning*, I., xix, A. 1.

[2] *Vita della ven. Suor Francesca Farnese detta di Giesu Maria*, Roma, 1610.

[3] *Cf.* Moroni, XXVI., 185.

[4] Nicoletti's dedication, at the beginning of the second volume, is as follows: Alla gloriosa memoria del sig^{r} cardinale Francesco Barberini, Vicecancelliere e Decano del Sacro Collegio, Andrea

all the necessary material out of his family archives and his celebrated library, and in addition gave him much oral information. The Cardinal impressed on Nicoletti that he was simply to do his duty as an historian and, whilst avoiding

Nicoletti. Mi recherei a somma gloria, se potessi presentarmi innanzi a V. Em. per presentarle insieme questi nove volumi da me scritti in italiana favella sopra la vita di Papa Urbano VIII. suo zio di san. mem. e sopra l'istoria del suo Pontificato. E fin da quando V. Em. mi fece l'honore di commettermi questo carico, che fu di gran lunga eccedente il mio ingegno e sapere, dubitai che havrei ricoperto l'oro dell'eroiche virtù di quel sapientissimo Pontefice con la creta del mio poco talento; proposi nondimeno, se mai havessi condotta a fine l'opera, di dedicarla a V. Em., poichè l'essere ella stata mio benignissimo principe e benefattore, era anche mio debito il darle questo tributo, e tanto più che le notitie più certe e più sincere per si grande argomento mi furono somministrate per mezzo del sig^r^ can^co^ Moroni suo bibliotecario, non meno dagli archivii e dalla famosa libreria della sua ecc^ma^ casa, ove giacevano quasi in profonda oblivione, che dalla voce viva dell'Em^za^ Vostra, stimata come oracolo di verità.

Ma giacchè V. Em. per divina dispositione ha cambiato il tempo coll'eternità et è stata tolta al mondo per arrichir l'anima sua di un regno più stabile, ho giudicato di dedicare questi volumi (benchè l'opera non sia per ancora compita) alla sua gloriosa memoria, acciocchè facciano ritorno colà, d'onde trassero la nobil materia, alla quale dalla mia penna è stata data una imperfetta forma. E sarà appunto a guisa dei fiumi, li quali havendo havuta la loro scaturigine dal mare, tornan dapoi al mare istesso, ut iterum fluant; cioè a dire se in alcun tempo si divulgheranno, mentre havranno in fronte lo splendore di V. Em., il quale può dar chiarezza alle cose oscure e diffettuose, acquisteranno riputatione e pregio a se stessi e maggior veneratione al nome et alle attioni di Papa Urbano.

Nè dovrà parer inusitato ch'io dedichi quest'opera alla mem. di V. Em., poichè mi vaglio di due nobili esempii: l'uno dell'eruditissimo Padre Pietro Possini della Comp. di Gesù, il quale in questi ultimi tempi nel dare alla luce l'opera di Giorgio Pachimero da lui tradotta dal greco al latino, introduce quel famoso istorico come risorto al mondo, il quale dedica la vita dell'imperatore Michele Paleologo alla santa mem. di Papa Urbano VIII.;

all flattery and rhetorical exaggeration, to keep to facts rather than fine words.[1]

Nicoletti devoted himself to his task with the greatest zeal. With justifiable pride he could say, as his work neared its conclusion, that he had consulted the most authoritative persons and the most authentic sources, viz. Briefs, Consistorial Acts, diaries, letters from nuncios and Princes (IX, 3). The material which he thus obtained was so abundant that his *Vita di Urbano VIII.* grew to nine large volumes of approximately 15,000 pages. At the beginning of 1666 he was compiling the seventh volume (see VII, 584). Cardinal Barberini, who died December 10th, 1679 at the age of 82, did not live to see the completion of the work. Nicoletti dedicated it to his memory, seeing that the Cardinal had given the impulse to the task and had been Urban VIII.'s chief minister. The dedication states that the biography was not

l'altro è di V. Em. istessa nel traslatare dall'idioma greco al Toscano la vita di Marc'Aurelio Antonino imperatore che dedicolla alla rationale et immortale anima di se medesima, quasi che V. E. essendo in grado segnalato arrichita di tutte le virtù christiane, non isdegnò di proporre all'animo suo anche le virtù morali di un principe gentile per imitarle.

Aggiugnasi a ciò l'essere stato V. Em. il più congiunto di sangue a Papa Urbano e il ministro principalissimo del suo Pontificato; onde si come furono comuni gli affari, con la subordinazione però che il braccio destro riceve tutto il suo potere dal capo, così ciò che si dice della grand'anima di Urbano, ridonda in gloria ancora di V. Em.

Finalmente se nell'aspetto e visione d'Iddio come in lucidissimo specchio si vedono anche le cose di quaggiù, spero che V. Em. rimirerà queste mie fatiche con quella benignità, con la quale rimirò sempre le cose mie, e tanto più che contenendo queste, oltre la vita di Papa Urbano, gl'interessi e la riputatione della Sede Apostolica, di cui V. Em. oltre ogni credere fu sempre zelantissimo, m'impetrerà da Dio la sanità, se sarà per sua gloria, e che mi si somministrino gli altri aiuti per dar compimento all'opera, e che dopo questa fragil vita possa riveder Vostra Em. gloriosa in celo, sicome per le sue virtù è stata ammirata in terra.

[1] Ranke, III., 163.

yet completed; in fact, the manuscript shows many pages left blank for additional matter and notes on small pieces of paper have also been stuck in. Only the right-hand pages are written on, whilst the left bear numerous corrections. Most of these are by Nicoletti himself who, with the exception of the last volume, wrote the whole book himself. Nevertheless other hands are to be seen, among them that of Cardinal Pallavicini [1] to whom Nicoletti submitted his work. Each of the seven volumes is divided into chapters, the contents of which are tabulated in an index. Yet another hand has added an alphabetical index of names and subjects.

Ranke was the first to use Nicoletti's work. He remarks (III, 158) that it contains "the family recollections of the personality and acts of Urban VIII., but that which gives it body and accounts for its bulk, is the inclusion of the entire diplomatic correspondence of the whole of the twenty-one years of Urban's reign. This biography is primarily a compilation of the reports of nuncios". Ranke rightly points out that "the official flavour cannot be denied [2] in view of the source and first conception of the work, but that the author is entirely trustworthy when he is only quoting". Kiewning came to the same conclusion (1., XXVIII). He compared the reports of the nuncios in the Vatican with Nicoletti's version and found them "quite accurate". Kiewning also rightly notes that even when the nuncio's reports are available, Nicoletti's work cannot be dispensed with, since he adds many important notes from his personal recollection. Still more valuable are the passages which rest on communications made by Cardinal Barberini; but these are not numerous. An example will show their special interest. In describing the Conclave in the first volume of the *Vita*, Nicoletti gives, almost word for word, the report from the *Conclavi de' Pontefici Romani* (1667), p. 397, *seq.* In the margin he adds notes supplied by Cardinal Barberini on October 19th, 1665. The first addition deals with the conversation

[1] *Arch. Rom.*, XXII., 355.

[2] Ranke gives as an instance Nicoletti's remark on Urban VIII.'s attitude at the conclusion of peace between England and France. But, as Kiewning (I., 299), shows, the example is badly chosen, though in itself Ranke's remark is justified.

of the Spanish ambassador, the Duke of Pastrana, at the Conclave of Gregory XV., with Francesco Barberini concerning Cardinal Maffeo Barberini. Pastrana said that the French sympathies of Maffeo would stand in the way of his election, seeing that these were such that he could only speak of France with tears of tenderness. To this Francesco answered: " che il cardinale suo zio non era così tenero che piangesse per alcuna cosa e molto meno per la Francia; che egli in quel ministerio aveva servito alla Sede Apost. et al Pontefice suo principe, e che in tanto era restato affetionato a quella corona in quanto aveva ricevuto honori segnalati, ma che nel rimanente se dal Papa fosse stato mandato Nuntio in Spagna, la casa Barberini non havrebbe speso tanto come nella Nuntiatura di Francia, che nel rimanente esso cardinale suo zio haveva soddisfatto alle parti di ministro della Sede Apost. e che, o riuscisse o non riuscisse la sua esaltazione, esso Francesco sarebbe sempre stato buon servitore della corona di Spagna e di Sua Eccellenza, con altre parole piene di modestia dal che si raccolse che l'ambasciatore haveva voluto vedere, conoscere e sentire esso Francesco Barberini, a lui per il passato totalmente ignoto."

Cardinal Francesco Barberini told Nicoletti that at the Conclave of the year 1623 Maffeo's conclavist Ceva had acted most skilfully. He gave the following instance: " Mentre si era dato principio alla pratica per (Maffeo) Barberini, alcuni vecchi (cardinali) la sentirono con amarissimo animo, e specialmente uno di essi passando avanti alla sua cella ad arte e mostrando di discorrer con un altro, alzò la voce, acciò Barberini lo sentisse e prorompesse in qualche atto indecente e risentito che potesse scandalizzare il conclave et in questa guisa da se medesimo si precludesse la via al pontificato. Disse dunque (the name of the Cardinal follows but unfortunately it has been made quite illegible) queste parole come per ischernire e provocare: Vogliono far Papa questo matto." When Maffeo heard this he wanted to reply with equal passion but Ceva prevented him by force from doing so. " Urbano fatto Papa alludendo a questo successo disse più volte di esser molto tenuto al Cueva, quale poscia inalzò al cardinalato."

The important part of Nicoletti's work is the very full collection of the correspondence of the nuncios. Ranke remarks that he could not incorporate in his own work such immense material. He therefore confines himself to reproducing in Appendix III, 159 *seqq.*, Nicoletti's report of the last days of Urban VIII. In his book on the Osmanlis (4th ed., p. 471, *seq.*, and 564, *seq.*), Ranke quotes two lengthy passages from Nicoletti, the second of which is especially interesting as it is a report of January 18th, 1643, on the effect of the death of Richelieu on the Spaniards. Ranke's opinion on the trustworthiness of Nicoletti is borne out by KIEWNING (see above), BROSCH (in *Cambridge Modern History,* IV., Cambridge, 1906, 928), and P. NEGRI (*La guerra per la successione di Mantova,* Prato, 1924, 14), the latter rightly qualifying Nicoletti's work as an " erudita e indigesta compilazione ". W. N. WEECH (*Urban VIII.*, London, 1905), gave a summary of it, which of course is of little value in a work that depends on an accurate verbal reproduction of the documents.

Everyone will gladly bear witness to the enormous industry of Nicoletti though he had not received the historian's call. He lacks altogether the capacity for mastering, digesting, and arranging his vast material. He sets to work in mere chronological order, giving us, as it were, the annals of the long reign of Urban VIII., for the story of which he provides inexhaustible data. Scarcely any event of the reign remains unnoticed. The sections dealing with the building activities of the Pope are also valuable, but the most important part will always be the full quotations from the diplomatic correspondence.

At the re-numbering of the Barberini MSS. the volumes of Nicoletti also received fresh shelf-marks. To facilitate reference I give the new marks :—

Volume	I	(42 chapters) :	*Barb.*	LII.	6	now	4730
,,	II	(24 ,,) :	,,	LII.	7	,,	4731
,,	III	(16 ,,) :	,,	LII.	8	,,	4732
,,	IV	(18 ,,) :	,,	LII.	9	,,	4733
,,	V	(21 ,,) :	,,	LII.	10	,,	4734
,,	VI	(20 ,,) :	,,	LII.	11	,,	4735
,,	VII	(13 ,,) :	,,	LII.	12	,,	4736
,,	VIII	(15 ,,) :	,,	LII.	13	,,	4737
,,	IX	(9 Guerra di Castro.) *Barb.* LII. 14 (now 4738). *Barb.* LII. 15 (now 4739) contains the Indexes, *Barb.* LII. 16–24 (now 4740 to 4748) Nicoletti's minutes.					

INDEX OF NAMES IN VOL. XXIX.

Acarie [Mary of the Incarnation], 63, 154.
Agathangelus (Capuchin), 257.
Agazzari, Agostino, 11.
Agostini, Leonardo, 527.
Agostini, Paolo, 12.
Agucchi, Giovan Battista, 40, 176–9.
Alacoque, Marguerite Marie, 154.
Alaleone, Paolo, 495.
Albizzi, Mons. Francesco, 116, 121.
Albizzi, Antonio, 36.
Albornoz, Cardinal, 159, 209.
Albricio, Luigi (S.J., preacher), 7.
Albuquerque, Duke of (ambassador), 187, 532.
Alciati, Terenzio, 13, 434 *seq.*
Aldobrandini, Cardinal Pietro, 194, 409.
Aldobrandini, Ulisse, 413.
Aleander, Girolamo, 439, 441.
Alemanni, Niccolò, 451, 459.
Alexander III., Pope, 182, 451.
Alexander VI., Pope, 360, 361, 452, 519, 525.
Alexander VII., Pope, 544.
Alexander [Charles of Poland], 166.
Alexius (Capuchin), 258.
Algandi (sculptor), 495.
Allacci, Leone, 419, 430, 434, 446, 499 *seq.*
Allegri, Domenico, 12.
Allegri, Gregorio, 11.
Althan, Count, 29.
Altieri, Cardinal, 164.
Alto, Giovanni *see* Hoch, Johannes.
Alvarez, Ferdinand, 39.
Amaral, Fr. (S.J.), 257.
Ameyden, Theodore, 377.
Amicis, Ovidio de, 432.
Andrada, Antonio, 248.
Andreucci, Famiano, 204.
Andrew (prince of Madagascar), 259.
Angelis, William (Abbot), 116, 124.
Anne (Queen of France), 144, 339.
Antoniano, Silvio, 426.
Archangel, Fr. (English Capuchin), 82.
Arcudio-Francesco, 446.
Argoli, Andrea, 454.
Arigucci, Luigi, 484, 543.
Aristotle, 147.
Armanni, Francesco Maria, 329.
Armanni, Vincenzo, 327, 338.
Arnauld, Angélique, 79, 83 *seqq.*
Arnauld, Agnes, 79, 87.
Arnauld, Antoine, 78, 93, 123, 130–153.
Arnauld, Antoine (sen.), 78.
Arnauld, Henri (bishop of Angers), 78.
Arpino, Cesare d', 475.
Arundell, Lady, 322.
Ascalona, Francis of (Franciscan), 251.
Asselyn, Jan, 540.
Avellino, Andrew, Bl., 9.
Avitabilis, Pietro, 244, 246.
Azevedo, Fr. (S.J.), 258.
Azzolini, Cardinal, 430.

Bach, J. S., 274.
Baglione, Giovanni, 415, 516, 517.
Bagno, Guido del, Cardinal, 160.
Bajano, Andrea, 422.
Baius, M., 67 *seqq.*
Balassi, Mario, 488.
Baldassarre, di S. Maria, 244.
Balde, Jacob (S.J.), 427.
Baldenstein, Wilhelm Rink von, 267.
Baldeschi, Benedetto Monaldi, Cardinal, 161.
Baldinucci, Filippo, 456, 480.
Balducci, Francesco, 422.
Baltimore, Lord, 260, 306, 353, 355.
Baltimore, Lord (junior), 314, 355-9.
Balzac, 143.
Bandin, Mark (archbishop of Mastianople), 224.
Bandini, Cardinal, 160, 279.
Barbarigo, Jeremias (Greek archbishop of Naxos), 231 *seq.*
Barbarossa, Frederick, 452.
Barberini, Anna, 430.
Barberini, Antonio (brother of Urban VIII.), 390, 487.
Barberini, Antonio, Cardinal (nephew), 22, 34, 157, 159, 194, 213, 279, 373, 393, 397 *seq.*, 400, 415, 447, 455, 488, 490, 503, 505, 507, 527, 542.
Barberini, Carlo (brother of Urban VIII.), 366, 415, 450, 484.
Barberini, Costanza, 6.
Barberini, Francesco, Cardinal (nephew), 4, 6, 34, 46, 54, 109, 121, 157, 188, 200, 207, 215, 236, 257, 279, 313 *seq.*, 327, 332 *seq.*, 346, 351, 382, 385, 390, 395, 397, 400, 437, 439, 441, 452, 455, 477, 488, 490, 498, 504, 516, 527, 535, 542.
Barberini, Taddeo (nephew of Urban VIII.), 22, 180, 366, 385, 388, 392, 415, 430, 498.
Barberino, Francesco (poet), 408.
Barcos, de, 144.
Barlow, Fr. (O.S.B.), 331.
Barnes, Fr. John (O.S.B.), 40.
Baroni, Leonora, 445.
Baronius, Cardinal, 182.
Bassompierre (French envoy), 302.
Battaglini, 204.
Bavinck, Hermann, 516.
Bayram (Turkish pasha), 240.
Beerenbergh, Bartholomew, 539 *seq.*
Bell, Arthur (Franciscan), 338.
Bella, Stefano della, 166, 540 *seq.*
Bellarmine, Cardinal, 24, 47, 117.
Benedict XIV., Pope, 25.
Bentivoglio, Cornelio Marchese, 168.
Bentivoglio, Cardinal, 30, 139, 206, 425.
Bergamo, Michele da, 484 *seq.*
Bernard of St. Teresa, 244.
Bernardine, Fr. (Capuchin), 258.
Bernini, Domenico, 463.
Bernini, Lorenzo, 20, 214, 362, 371, 410, 457 *seqq.*, 462, 464, 466, 470, 476 *seq.*, 480, 488, 493, 510, 512, 528, 543.
Bernini, Luigi, 465.
Bernini, Pietro, 512.
Bernini, Vincenzo, 465.
Bérulle, Cardinal, 77, 159 *seq.*, 293 *seq.*, 298.
Besné, King of, 258
Bessarion, Cardinal, 233.
Béthlem, Gabor, 176, 238.
Béthune, Philippe de, 293.
Beusecom, Christian, 110.
Bianchi, George, 221.
Bichi, Alessandro, Cardinal, 161, 398, 400.

Bichi, Antonio (nuncio), 119, 121, 124, 207.
Biscia, Lelio, Cardinal, 158.
Bishop, William (bishop), 303 *seq.*, 349.
Bivero, Fr. (S.J.), 106.
Bizzi, Marino (bishop of Antivari), 220.
Blacas, d'Aulps, Duke, 54.
Blaise, Jacques (bishop of St. Omer), 27.
Bloemaert, Cornelius, 445.
Boileau, Despréaux Nicolas (poet), 153.
Bolgi, Andrea, 470.
Bolivar, Fr. (Franciscan), 263.
Bollandus, J. (S.J.), 435.
Bonaventura (Capuchin), 259.
Boncompagni, Cardinal, 46.
Bonomini (architect), 490, 531.
Boonen, Jacob (archbishop of Mechlin), 102, 110–127 *passim*.
Borghese, Pier Maria, Cardinal, 157.
Borghese, Scipione, Cardinal, 157, 494.
Borgia, Francis, 9.
Borgia, Gaspare, Cardinal, 185, 189 *seq.*, 194, 210, 426.
Borlase, John (Irish viceroy), 341.
Borri, Fr.(S.J.), 258, 432.
Borromeo, St. Charles, 136.
Borromeo, Frederick, Cardinal, 28.
Borromini, Francesco (sculptor), 455, 508.
Bosio, Antonio, 436 *seq*.
Bossuet, Jacques (bishop of Meaux), 130.
Both, Andrew (painter), 536.
Both, Jan (painter), 536.
Bozzolo, Duke of, 375.
Bracci, Ignazio, 432.
Bracciolini, Francesco (poet), 421, 423, 429, 446, 500.
Bragadino, Marcantonio, Cardinal, 163.
Braganza V. [John IV.] (King of Portugal).
Bramante, 494.
Brancaccio, Cardinal, 161.
Brébeuf, Jean de, 154.
Breccioli, Bartolomeo (architect), 543.
Brett, Arthur (English agent in Rome), 318.
Brienne, Count of, *see* Ville-aux-Cleres.
Bristol, Earl of, 281–3.
Bronissuchus, John, 421.
Brosses, de, 466.
Buckingham, Duke of, 279, 286, 288, 291 *seq.*, 298, 301.
Buratti, Giulio (architect), 361.
Burchard, John, 452.
Bus, Cesare de, 63.
Bzorio, Abraham (O.P.).

CABALLERO, Antonio di S. Maria, 249.
Caballo, Francesco, 14.
Cabral (Jesuit missionary), 258.
Cacella (Jesuit missionary), 258.
Caetani, Antonio, Cardinal, 12, 14, 206, 377.
Caetani, Gregorio, 375.
Caetani, Luigi, Cardinal (archbishop of Capua), 158.
Caffarelli, Fausto (nuncio), 173.
Caimo, Pompeo, Conte, 454.
Calamina, Cardinal, 215.
Calandra, Giovanni Battista, 460, 472, 475.
Calenus [van Caelen], Henry, 76, 102, 110–14.
Callot, Jacques, 537 *seqq*.
Calvert, George, *see* Baltimore.
Calvert, Leonard, *see* Baltimore.
Calvin, 89 *seqq.*, 155.
Camassei, Andrea, 473, 483, 487.
Camerarius, David [Chambers], 349.
Campana, Francesco Maria (Dominican), 7.
Campanella, Tommaso (Dominican), 40, 48, 420.
Campeggi, Lorenzo (nuncio), 172, 195.

Camus, John Peter (bishop of Belley), 65.
Cancellariis, Stephanus Bubalus de. (S.J.), 421.
Canigiani, Alessandro (bishop of Aix), 65.
Cano, Melchior (Dominican), 263.
Cantalice, Felix, Bl., 9.
Cantelori, Felix, 182.
Capello, Benedetto (archbishop of Zara), 219.
Capiferro, Maddaleno, 432.
Capponi, Bernardino, 412.
Capponi, Luigi, Cardinal, 215.
Caracci, Annibale, 541.
Caracciolo, Francis, St., 528.
Carafa, Pier Luigi (nuncio), 30, 31.
Carandini, Ferrari Fabio, 385.
Caravaggio, Michaelangelo, 473.
Carli, Ferrante, 471.
Carlisle, Earl of, 290, 291.
Carpegna, Ulderico, Cardinal, 162, 163.
Casalla, Francesco, 173.
Casimir (brother of king of Poland), 404.
Casone, Antonio (architect), 487.
Castelnuovo, Giuseppe Porta di, 182.
Castelli, Benedetto, 49 n., 50, 59, 379, 454.
Castelli, Domenico, 379, 485 *seq.*, 489, 543.
Castracani, Alessandro (apostolic collector), 196 *seqq.*
Castro, Matthew de (oratorian), 246.
Cavalieri, Jacopo de', Cardinal, 158, 160.
Cecchinelli (nuncio), 173.
Celio, Gaspare, 516.
Celio, Gregorio, 475.
Centini, Felice, Cardinal, 37.
Centini, Giacinto, 37, 38.
Centurione, Giovanni Francesco (Carmelite), 173.
Cerquozzi, Michaelangelo, 535.
Cesarini, Alessandro, Cardinal, 159.
Cesarini, Virginio, 45, 412, 429.
Cesi, Federico, 446.
Cesi, Giovan Federico (duke of Acquasparta), 46.
Cesi, Pier Donato, Cardinal, 103.
Césy, de (ambassador), 228 *seqq.*
Ceva, Adriano, Cardinal, 104.
Cevallos, Jerome de, 185.
Chantal, Madame de, 82, 154.
Charles (Prince of Wales), 276–295.
Charles I. (King of England), 297–349 *passim.*
Cherubini, Angelo Maria (O.S.B.), 432.
Chevet, Peter, 433.
Chevreuse, Duc de, 295.
Chiabrera, Gabriel, 412, 425.
Chigi, Fabio (nuncio), 105, 109, 116, 119 *seq.*, 139.
Christie (Jesuit), 350.
Chumacero, Juan, 189, 199 *seq.*, 205.
Ciammacurone, G., 438.
Ciampelli, Agostino, 483, 508.
Ciampoli, Giovanni, 45 *seq.*, 50, 412, 425, 431.
Ciarpi, Baccio, 488.
Cigmani, Carlo (artist), 498.
Claver, St. Peter, 262.
Clement VII., Pope, 392.
Clement VIII., Pope, 382, 412, 543.
Cluverius, Philip, 441.
Cobelluzio, Cardinal, 46, 279.
Coccini, Giovan Battista, 432, 529.
Colen, Fr. (S.J.), 275.
Collicola, Taddeo, 454.
Colomba, da Rieti, 10.
Colombière, Claude de la, 154.
Columbinus, Fr. (Capuchin), 258.
Colonna, Anna, 430.
Colonna, Carlo, 375.

Colonna, Girolamo, Cardinal, 159.
Colonna, Pier Francesco (duke of Zagarolo).
Con, George (papal agent), 309, 318–322.
Conaeus, George, 432.
Condé, Prince de, 143.
Condinini, Emilio, Cardinal, 164.
Condren, Charles de (oratorian), 85.
Confalonieri, Giovan Battista, 452.
Conrius (Irish Franciscan), 76, 108.
Contari, Cyril (metropolitan of Beroea), 239 *seq.*, 241.
Contarini, Alvise (ambassador), 180, 183, 401.
Contarini, Angelo, 160, 180.
Contarini, Niccolò, Doge, 180.
Contarini, Pietro (nuncio), 177, 385.
Contelori, Felice, 13, 435, 451.
Contini, Francesco, 543.
Conway (Secretary of State), 293.
Cornaro, Federigo, Cardinal, 158.
Cornaro, Giovani, Doge, 158, 177, 180, 184, 215.
Cornaro, Marcantonio (bishop of Padua), 180.
Corner, Cardinal, 401.
Corneto, Adrian, Cardinal, 519.
Correr, Angelo, 302, 315.
Corsini, St. Andrew, 9.
Corsini, Ottavio (nuncio), 303.
Cortona, Pietro da (painter), 487 *seqq.*, 500, 503, 508, 542 *seq.*
Cospéau, Philippe (bishop of Nantes), 78.
Costa, Pietro Francesco (nuncio), 172.
Costaguti, Vincenzo, Cardinal, 164.
Cottington (English envoy), 278.
Cremonini, Cesare, 41.
Cueva, Alfonso della, Cardinal, 108, 114, 486.
Cupis, Francesco de, 524.
Curtis, Maurizio da (S.J.), 173.
Cyriacus of Erivan (Armenian patriarch of Constantinople), 243.

D'Andilly, Arnauld, 78.
Davenport, Christopher (Franciscan), 315.
Deodat, Peter (bishop of Gallipoli), 223.
Descartes, 147.
Digby, *see* Bristol, Earl of.
Dietrichstein, Cardinal, 29.
Djihan, Grand Mogul, 247.
Domenichino, 488, 495 *seqq.*, 529, 541.
Domenico of Jesus and Mary (Carmelite), 27, 215.
Dominis, de Marcantonio (bishop), 40, 41.
Donatus, Alexander (S.J.), 510.
Donghi, Gian Stefano, Cardinal, 164.
Doni, Giovanni Battista, 378 *seq.*, 429, 439, 446.
Doria, Giovanni, Cardinal, 187.
Dosio, 540.
Douglas, Robert (agent in Rome), 318.
Dubois, Engelbert (bishop of Namur), 124.
Dubois, Susanna, 64.
Dughet, Jean, 536 *seq.*
Duhamel, 148.
Du Pérac, 540.
Du Perron (bishop of Angoulême, 311.
Duquesnoy, François, 470, 495, 536.
Durazzo, Stefano, Cardinal, 161, 392.
Dwyer, Edmond (Irish agent in Rome), 348.

Effiat, Antoine de Ruzé, Marquis of, 291.
Elias IX. (Nestorian Patriarch in Mossul), 245.

Eliot, John (M.P.), 297.
Elizabeth (Queen of England), 351.
Elizabeth (wife of Frederick Palatine, Elector), 281.
Elsheimer (artist), 535.
Ephrem of Nevers (Capuchin), 246.
Erasmus, 450.
Erbacius, Nicephorus Basilian, 244.
Erythraeus, James Nicius, 450, 507.
Eschaux, Bertrand d' (bishop of Tours), 157.
Estampes, Achille d', Cardinal, 163.
Este, Francesco d' (duke of Modena), 163.
Este, Rinaldo d', Cardinal, 163.
Estrées, Annibale d' [Marquis de Coeuvres], 375.
Eudes, Jean, St., 64, 154.
Euthymius (archimandrite), 238.

FACCHINETTI, Cesare, Cardinal, 164, 195, 197, 199 *seqq.*, 210.
Falce, Giovanni, 432.
Falconieri, Lelio, Cardinal, 128, 164, 188.
Falda, 439.
Falkland (Irish viceroy), 339, 340.
Farnese, Alessandro, Cardinal, 374.
Farnese, Girolamo (nuncio), 266.
Farnese, Odoardo (duke of Parma), 382–400, 430.
Fedini, Domenico, 433.
Felini, Pietro Martire, Servite, 515, 517.
Felix IV., Pope, 484.
Fénelon, François de Salignac de la Mothe, 29, 130.
Ferdinand II. (grand-duke of Tuscany), 173, 528.
Ferdinand (archduke of Bavaria), 27.
Ferdinand, Cardinal-Infante, 188.
Ferdinand II. (Emperor), 27.
Fère, Maria de la, 64.
Ferrante, Giovan Francesco, 419.
Ferratini, Cardinal, 212.
Ferreira, Christopher (S.J.), 253.
Ferrerio, 439.
Ficher, Alexander (S.J.), 405.
Fide-Tada (Japanese persecutor), 253.
Figliucci, Flaminio, 412, 422.
Filicaja, Alessandro, 366.
Filomarino, Ascanio, Cardinal, 163, 188.
Filonardi, Mario (nuncio), 106, 170.
Fiorentini, Francesco Maria, 433.
Floriani, Peter Paul, 362.
Floyd, John (S.J.), 140, 309.
Flugi, John V. (bishop of Chur), 268.
Flugi, John VI. (bishop of Chur), 268.
Foelich, Jacob, 215.
Fontenay, Marquis de (ambassador), 207–210, 306, 394.
Forner, Laurence (S.J.), 418.
Fourier, Pierre, 63, 65.
Francesco (duke of Modena), 382, 396.
Franciotti, Marcantonio, Cardinal, 161, 174.
Franzini, Giovan Domenico, 519.
Frederick (Elector Palatine), 281.
Frederick (Landgrave of Hesse), 444.
Frescobaldi, Girolamo, 12.
Fromondus, Libertus, 76, 82, 102, 110, 115, 117.
Fulgenzio, Fra Servite, 178 *seqq.*

GABRIELLI, Giulio, Cardinal, 103.
Gaetano, Constantino, 432.

Galilei, Galileo, 42–62, 426.
Gallo, Giovanni Maria (bishop of Santorin), 232.
Gandiosi (poet), 405.
Garasse, François (S.J.), 151.
Garcia, Juan (O.P.), 251.
Garzadori, Ottaviano (archbishop of Zara), 218.
Gaudenzi, Paganino (Carmelite), 451.
Gault, Jean Baptiste (bishop of Marseilles), 154.
Gavanti, Bartolomeo Barnabite, 13, 431.
Gavotti, Lorenzo (nuncio), 266.
Gazier, Augustine, 151, 152.
Gentili, Cardinal, 162, 195.
George (archdeacon), 246.
Gerberon, Gabriel, 149.
Gerrard, Thomas, 352 *seq.*
Gessi, Berlingherio, Cardinal, 158, 187.
Gibieuf (oratorian), 77.
Giggeo, Antonio, 434.
Giglioli, G. T., 409.
Gilbert, Humphrey, 352.
Ginetti, Marzio, Cardinal, 159, 187.
Ginnasio, Domenico, Cardinal, 491.
Giori, Angelo, Cardinal, 480.
Giori, Antonio Maestro de Camera, 164.
Giotto, 475–480.
Giovanoli, 540.
Giustiniani, Cardinal, 215, 216.
Giustiniani, Marchese, 528, 537.
Giustiniano, Orazio (oratorian), 231.
Godeau (bishop of Grasse), 141.
Gondi, Jean François de (archbishop of Paris), 83, 123.
Gonzaga, Cardinal, 44, 526.
Goodman, Godfrey (bishop of Gloucester), 324.
Goodman, John (brother to above), 329, 331.
Goring, Lord, 316.
Gradenigo (Patriarch of Aquileia), 180.
Grassi, Orazio (S.J.), 42, 45, 47 *seq.*, 491.
Grassis, Paris de, 452.
Greca, Vincenzo della, 483.
Greca, Domenico della, 543.
Gregory the Great, 460.
Gregory VIII., 508, 519.
Gregory XIII., 348, 529.
Gregory XV., 2, 19, 24, 28, 172, 174, 216, 276 *seq.*, 303.
Grignano, Ludovico, 13.
Grillo, Angelo, 422.
Grimaldi, Girolamo (nuncio), 108 *seq.*, 113, 124, 394, 400.
Grimani, Domenico, Cardinal, 512.
Grotius, Hugo, 106, 274.
Gruyart, Madame, 154.
Gualdo, Francesco, 530.
Guerrero, Ferd. (bishop of Manila), 249.
Guevara (Franciscan), 48.
Guicciolone, Diego (hermit), 37.
Guidi, Domenico, Cardinal, 160.
Guidiccioni, Alessandro (bishop of Lucca), 174.
Guidiccioni, Lelio, 22, 526.
Guidotti of Lucca, 474.
Guiducci, Mario, 46.
Gussoni, Vincenzo, 183.

Hamelin, 144.
Hamilton, William (agent in Rome), 318.
Harrach, Cardinal, 29, 158.
Harrison (English archpriest), 28.
Hay, James, *see* Carlisle.
Haye, Philippe de la, 241.
Heath (Franciscan), 338.
Hegerty, Patrick (Franciscan), 350.
Heinsius, Daniel, 441, 444.
Helvetius, Claude Adrien, 156.
Henry IV. (King of France), 69, 79.
Henry VIII. (King of England), 237, 344.

Henrietta Maria (Queen of England), 32, 289, 301 *seq.*, 321 *seqq.*, 332 *seqq.*, 352, 354.
Heywood, J. P., 329.
Hoch, Johann, 514.
Hesse, Frederick, Landgrave of, 444.
Hesse, George. Landgrave of, 7.
Hohenzollern, Frederick, Cardinal of, 40, 47.
Holste or Holstenius, 430, 439 *seq.*, 446.

INGOLI, Francesco (secretary to Propaganda), 27, 29, 219, 232, 263.
Innocent X., 544.
Innocent XI., 443.
Isabella (archduchess), 28, 188.

JAMES I. of England, 276–296, 341, 350, 353.
James (would-be assassin of Heywood), 329.
Jamson, Jacob, 67, 68.
Jansenius, Cornelius, 62–94.
Joan, Pope, 449.
Jognes, Isaac (S.J.), 154.
Johannes a St. Thoma, 126.
John of God, St., 10.
John, Albert, Cardinal (son of King of Poland), 161, 165.
John IV. (King of Portugal), 204, 205, 208, 210.
John George of Saxony, 290.
Jonault, Jean (abbot), 89.
Joseph, Fr., 225, 234, 257.
Judoci (S.J. provincial), 109.
Julius II., 385, 455, 525.
Julius III., 451.
Julian the Apostate, 483.

KAPRAZINE (Emperor), 258.
Kapsberger, John Jerome, 420.
Kellison (writer), 306.
Kensington (Secretary of State), 291.
Kepler, 49.
Kircher, Athanasius (S.J.), 449.
Klesl, Cardinal, 29.
Knott (Jesuit), 309.
Kufstein, Hans Ludwig von, 169.
Kuncewicz, Josaphat (archbishop of Polozk), 169.

LAAR, Pieter van [Bamboots], (painter), 535, 536.
Ladislaus IV. (King of Poland), 105, 166, 170–1.
Lagonissa, Fabio de (nuncio), 188.
Lairuel, Servais, 65.
Lamego, Miguel (bishop of), 204, 207–210, 394.
Lamerno (Greek pope), 240.
Lancellotti, Orazio, Cardinal, 28.
Landriani (bishop), 194.
Lanfranco, Giovanni (painter), 472, 487–8, 495 *seqq.*, 529, 539.
Lante, Cardinal, 206 *seqq.*
Lante, Luigi, Marchese, 388.
Lanuvio, Girolamo, 12.
Lapide, Cornelius a, 438.
Lasalle, St. John de, 154.
Laud (archbishop of Canterbury), 312, 321, 324, 326.
Lauro, Giovan Battista, 453.
Leganés, Marquis de, 194.
Leger, Antony (Calvinist preacher), 234.
Le Gras, *see* Marillac.
Leibnitz, 43.
Lelio, Antonio, 186.
Le Maître de Sacy, Isaac, 147, 150.
Le Maître, Antoine, 92, 146.
Leni, Giovan Battista, Cardinal, 494.
Lenobletz, Michel (missionary), 154.
Leo I., 451.
Leo X., 325, 528.
Leonard, Fr. (Capuchin), 225.
Leonardi, Giovanni, 216.

Leopold (archduke, brother to Emperor Ferdinand II.), 7, 8, 43.
Leopold, William (archduke), 267.
Le Roy, Thomas (bishop), 524.
Leslie (Archangel, Capuchin), 350.
Lessius, Leonard (S.J.), 438.
Lestonnac, Jeanne de, 154.
Lewger, John, 355.
Ligaridis, Pietro, 446.
Lindsay, Epiphanius (Capuchin), 350–1.
Lionne, Hughes de, 393.
Lodron, Paris de (archbishop of Salzburg), 21.
Lollini, Alvise (bishop of Belluno), 448.
Lomellini, Giovanni, Battista (treasurer), 380.
Longobardi (S.J.), 258.
Lonigo, Michele, 432.
Lorrain, Claude (painter), 536 *seqq.*
Lucca, Giovanni da, 243.
Lucich, Jerome (bishop of Drivasto), 222.
Ludovisi, Cardinal, 6, 157, 214, 279, 348–9, 491, 493.
Louis XIII. of France, 288, 291, 300, 339, 394, 398.
Louis XIV., 360.
Lugo, Juan de, Cardinal, 164, 403, 431, 438.
Luigi, Cardinal, 377.
Luiz, Dominican, 258.
Lukaris, Cyril (patriarch of Constantinople), 227–242 *passim.*

MABILLON, 435.
Macchiavelli, Francesco Maria, Cardinal, 162.
Maculano, Vincenzo, Cardinal, 59, 60, 163, 362.
Maderna, Carlo (architect), 491, 498, 543.
Madruzzo, Carlo (bishop of Trent), Cardinal, 160.
Magalotti, Cesare, 434.
Magalotti, Costanza, *see* Barberini.
Magalotti, Lorenzo, Cardinal, 156, 231, 233, 279, 414.
Maggi, 520.
Malvasia, Marchese, 392.
Malvezzi, Marchese, 196.
Mambrecht, James (S.J.), 350.
Mambrecht, John (S.J.), 351.
Mancini, Giulio (physician), 363, 463, 515, 516.
Manili, Lorenzo de, 522.
Mansfeld (military leader), 291 *seq.*
Manuza (African ruler), 258.
Manzoni, Alessandro, 439.
Maraldi (Secretary for Briefs), 191.
Maratta, 490.
Marca, Jacopo della (bishop), 9.
Marcheville, de (French ambassador), 239.
Marchis, Pietro de, 225, 226.
Marchstaller, Jerome (abbot), 8.
Marcigo (missionary), 257.
Margaret (vicereine of Portugal), 199, 204.
Maria (infanta of Spain), 276 *seqq.*
Maria, Christina (Regent of Savoy), 173.
Marillac, Louise de, 154.
Marini, Elias (bishop of Sofia), 223.
Marini, Giovanni Battista (poet), 411.
Marion (advocate general), 79.
Marliani (topographer), 516.
Marquemont, Denis Simon de (archbishop of Lyons), 158.
Marquez, Peter (Jesuit Martyr), 253.
Martin V., Pope, 452.
Martinelli, Fioravante (historian), 435, 517, 520 *seqq.*, 530, 534.
Marucelli, Paolo (architect), 491, 528.

Mascardi, Agostino, 433, 454.
Mascardi, Vitale, 168.
Mascherino, Ottaviano (architect), 519.
Massarelli (Secretary to Council of Trent), 435.
Massarechio, Pietro (bishop of Antivari), 220.
Massimi, Innocenzo de' (nuncio in Madrid), 281.
Mastrilli, Marcello (Jesuit), 253.
Matilda (Countess of Tuscany), 399, 477.
Mattei, Gaspare, Cardinal (nuncio at Vienna), 164.
Mattei, Luigi (Marchese), 374, 392, 394.
Maturino, 525.
Maunoir, Julian (S.J. missionary), 154.
Maximianus (Emperor), 461.
Maximilian I. (duke of Bavaria), 8, 19, 27–8, 380, 494.
Mazarin, Cardinal, 129, 144, 163, 196, 394, 395, 398.
Mazarin, Michel, 210.
Medici, Carlo de', Cardinal, 193, 373.
Medici, Marie de' (Queen of France), 106, 287 *seq.*, 327.
Medina, Duke of, 188.
Mellini, Urbano, 524.
Mello, Franz von, 125.
Mendez, Alonso (S.J.), 255 *seqq.*
Menidret, Claudio, 527.
Mercati, Giovan Battista, 538.
Mesures, Henri des, 441.
Meursius, John, 441.
Michele da Bergamo (Capuchin), 484, 487.
Michelangelo, 456, 535.
Michiel, Francesco, 271.
Milletière, Brachet de la, 143.
Millini, Giangarzia, Cardinal, 160, 236, 279, 485.
Milton, 444 *seq.*, 507.
Mocchi, Francesco, 470, 505.
Mocenigo, Alvise (archbishop of Crete), 219.
Modena, Francesco, Duke of, 360, 382, 391 *seqq.*
Mogor, Prince Mirza, of, 243
Mohila, Peter, of Kiev, 241.
Mohr, Joseph (bishop of Chur), 268.
Mola, Gaspare, 482.
Mola, Giacomo, 495.
Molina, Antonio de (Carthusian), 133 *seq.*
Molino, Domenico, 179.
Monaldus, Christophorus Maria, 430.
Montague, Richard (bishop of Chichester and Norwich), 312, 316.
Montague, Walter (oratorian), 317.
Montalto, Francesco Peretti, Cardinal, 163, 209.
Montalto, Alessandro, 493, 497.
Montecuccoli, Raimondo (military leader), 396.
Monterey (Spanish ambassador in Rome), 187.
Monti, Cesare, Cardinal, 162.
Moore, Roger, 342.
Morales, Juan (O.P.), 249.
Morandi, Orazio (abbot), 36.
Morelli, Federigo, 419.
Moroni, Carlo, 445.
Morosini (nuncio in Madrid), 189.
Mortaigne (Jesuit), 26.
Moses III. (patriarch), 243.
Mothe, Daniel de la (bishop of Mende), 296, 298.
Motmann (auditor of the Rota), 444.
Mountgarret, Lord, 345.
Mourgues, Abbé de, 106.
Mula, Cardinal, 182.
Murad, Sultan, 241.

NANI, Giovanni (Venetian envoy), 184, 401, 406.
Nardone, Giovanni Battista, 460.
Nari, Gregorio, Cardinal, 160.
Narni, Girolamo da (Capuchin), 21.

Naro, Battista (papal commander-in-chief), 366.
Naro, Diego Gusmán de, Cardinal, 160.
Naudé, Gabriel, 441.
Neri, Philip, 523.
Neri, G., 409.
Nero, Francesco del (Capuchin), 7.
Newport, Lord, 321.
Nicolas, François (brother of Duke of Lorraine), Cardinal, 159.
Niccolini (Florentine envoy), 396.
Nicole, Pierre, 93.
Nicoletti, biographer of Urban VIII., 422, and appendix, 26 (vol. xxix).
Nieto, Peter, 263.
Niewlandt, Willem van, 539 *seq.*
Nigrita, Antony (Prince), 259.
Nobili, Cardinal, 24.
Nobili, Roberto de', 246.
Novelli, Giovan Battista, 432.
Novelli, Leonardo, 432.

Ogilvie (Jesuit Martyr), 351.
Olier, 64.
Olivares (Spanish minister), 199 *seqq.*, 210 *seqq.*
Orange, Prince of, 326, 333.
Oreggi, Agostino, Cardinal, 161, 429, 434.
O'Reilly, Hugh (primate of Annagh), 344.
Orizzo (Doge of Venice), 180.
Orleans, Antoinette of, 65.
Ormond (vice-chancellor), 346, 347.
Orsi, Aurelio, 409, 412.
Orsi, Gregorio, 243.
Orsini (family), 523.
Orsini, Virginio, Cardinal, 163.
Ossat, Cardinal D', 80.
Ossolinski, Prince Jerzy, 166 *seq.*
Ostheim, Johann Heinrisch von (bishop), 267.

Pacheco, Pantalião Roiz, 207, 210.
Paepe (jurist), 127 *seq.*
Pallavicini, Ferrante, 40, 426.
Pallavicini, Sforza, Cardinal, 430 *seq.*
Pallotto, Giovan Battista, Cardinal, 28, 30, 160, 412.
Palmeiro, Andrew (S.J.), 249.
Palotta, Giov. Battista (collector in Portugal), 197.
Paludan, Louvain (Professor), 106.
Pamfili, Giovan Battista (later Innocent X.), 128, 160, 187.
Pamfili, Ludovisi Costanza, 526.
Panciroli, Gian Giacomo, Cardinal, 164, 211.
Panciroli, Ottavio, 7, 515.
Panzani d'Arezzo, Gregorio (papal agent), 312.
Paolino, Stefano (painter), 216.
Parthenius I. (metropolitan of Adrianople), 241 *seq.*
Pascal, Blaise, 93, 147, 153.
Pascal, Jacqueline, 147.
Passeri, 471, 496.
Passignano, Domenico, 474.
Patrizi, Costanzo (treasurer of Urban VIII.), 380.
Paul III., 174, 383, 386, 400, 456, 480, 481.
Paul V., 40, 103, 251, 363, 451, 519, 525, 528, 543.
Pázmány, Cardinal, 14, 160.
Pazzi, St. Mary Magd., 10.
Peckham, George, 352, 353.
Peirex, Nicolas Claude Fabre de, 441.
Pellegrini (painter), 475.
Peparelli (architect), 483, 486.
Péréfixe, Hard. de Beaumonts (archbishop of Paris), 150.
Peretti, Francesco, Cardinal, 160, 493.
Peretti, Abbate Francesco, 193–4.
Pereyra, Juan de Salórzano 186.

Perneo, Magno, 421.
Perrien, François, 539.
Persons, William (Irish viceroy), 341.
Persons, Fr. (Jesuit), 353.
Perugino, Pietro, 505.
Pesaro, Giovanni (Venetian envoy), 180 *seq.*
Petau (Petavius), 142 *seqq.*, 433.
Peter, Maronite (patriarch), 242.
Petitière, de la, 147.
Petricca da Sonnino, 241.
Petrucci, Girolamo (Jesuit), 13, 16.
Petrus, Aurelius (St. Cyran), 140 *seqq.*, 151.
Petrus, Sabinus, 462.
Philip I. (patriarch of Ecmiadzin), 243.
Philip IV. of Spain, 189, 190, 199, 200, 278 *seqq.*
Philippe, Robert (oratorian), 296, 303, 305, 333.
Philotheus (archimandrite of Jerusalem), 230 *seq.*
Piccolomini, Ascanio, Cardinal, 59.
Pignatelli, Cardinal, 203.
Pignero de Vega, Tommaso, *see* Vega.
Pimentel, Domingo de, 189.
Pinthereau (Jesuit), 71.
Piombo, Sebastiano del (painter), 505.
Piranesi (painter), 540.
Piromalli, Paolo (Dominican), 243.
Pio, Cardinal, 279.
Pius IV., 165, 182.
Pius V., 452, 519.
Poelenburg (painter), 540.
Pola, Ambrogio della, Franciscan, 230 *seq.*
Poli, Fausto, Cardinal, 164.
Polidoro (painter), 525.
Pontan (syndic of Louvain), 102, 106, 117, 119.
Porta, Guglielmo della, 478 *seqq.*
Porta, Giuseppi (painter), 182.
Porter, Endymion, 321.
Portland (Lord treasurer), 317.
Poussin, 473, 536 *seqq.*
Pozzo, Cassiano del, 446 *seq.*, 517, 529.
Preston, Thomas [Roger Widdrington] (O.S.B.), 314.
Puteanus, Erycius, 419.
Puy, Pierre Jacque Du, 441.
Pym, John, 335 *seq.*

Quarenghi, Antonio, 429.
Quirini, Sebastian (archbishop of Naxos), 226.

Raccagna, Cesare (bishop of Città di Castello), 175.
Racine (poet), 93, 153.
Raconis, d'Abra de (bishop of Lavour), 142.
Raphael (painter), 500, 503 *seq.*, 521, 528.
Raggi, Lorenzo, 404.
Raggi, Antonio, Cardinal, 163.
Raglan, Lord, 335.
Rainaldi, Carlo (architect), 493.
Rainaldus, Alexander, 421.
Rancati (Abbot), 13.
Rangel, Miguel (Dominican), 257.
Rangoni (nuncio in Poland), 165.
Rapaccioli, Cardinal, 164, 480.
Rapin, 153.
Raynald, Oderico, 435.
Régis, Francis, 154.
Rembrandt, 274, 481.
Remondi da Milano (Franciscan), 223.
Reni, Guido, 368, 488, 490, 541.
Reviglias, Pierre de, 419.
Reynolds, Thomas, 329.
Rhodes, Alexander of (S.J.), 257.
Rhugius (priest), 275 *seq.*
Ricasoli, Canon, 36.
Riccardi, Niccolò (Dominican), 7, 13 *seq.*, 46, 48.

Riccardi, Vincenzo, 446.
Riccioli, J. B., 43.
Richelieu, Cardinal, 91, 108, 109, 129, 180, 210, 225, 257, 289, 294, 300, 304, 383, 386, 418.
Richelieu, Alphonse Louis (archbishop of Lyons), 160.
Richer, Gallican, 304.
Riedmatten (bishop of Sitten), 267, 268.
Rieti, Columba of, 10.
Rigault, Nicolas, 441.
Rinucci (friend of Galileo), 45.
Rinuccini, Giovanni Battista, 446.
Risi, Sergio (archbishop of Damascus), 448.
Rivers, Lady, 337.
Riviera, *see* Vliete.
Rivière, de la, 147.
Rocci, Ciriaco, Cardinal, 161, 266.
Rocheposai, Henri Louis (archbishop of Poitiers), 72–3.
Rodrigo, de Castel (Marquis), 193, 199, 376, 507.
Roe, Alban (O.S.B.), 329.
Roger I. of Sicily, 186.
Rohan-Guémené (Princess), 134.
Roma, Giulio, Cardinal, 206.
Romanelli, Gian Francesco, 472, 475, 490, 503, 508.
Romillion, J. B., 63.
Rondinini, Cardinal, 164, 380.
Rooze (president), 114, 126.
Roscioli, Mgr., 403.
Rospigliosi, Giulio, Cardinal, 506, 507.
Rossetti, Carlo, Cardinal (Cologne nuncio), 32, 164, 322, 324–330, 332, 333, 357, 358.
Rossi, Carmachio (Greek priest), 230–5.
Rossi, Giovanni Vittorio, *see* Erythraeus.
Rossi, Gregorio de, 463.
Rossi, Marcantonio, 412.
Rosso, Francesco Maria, 183.
Rovenius, Philip, 270–3.
Rovere, Dom. della, Cardinal, 520.
Rozas, Paul de, 261.
Rubino, Antony (S.J.), 253.
Rutski (metropolitans), 170.

Sablé, Marquise de, 134.
Sacchetti, Giambattista, 379.
Sacchetti, Giulio, Cardinal, 158, 189, 525 (appendix i, vol. xxix).
Sacchi, Andrea (painter), 22, 472, 474, 475, 488, 490 *seq.*, 503, 510, 527, 543.
St. Cyran (Du Vergier), *passim*, 69–131, 148, 149, 151.
Sainte-Beuve, Charles Augustin, 73, 147.
Sales, Francis de, St., 82, 133.
Salgado de Samoza, 185.
Salines, Stefano, 224.
Salisbury, 353.
Salsilli (poet), 445.
Sandrart, Joachim von, 528 *seq.*
Sangallo (sculptor), 524.
Santa Croce, Cardinal, 160, 165.
Santarelli (S.J.), 7.
Santori, Paolo Emilio, 422, 448.
Sanza, Prince, 376.
Sarbiewski, Matthias Casimir (S.J.), 16, 170, 427–8.
Sarmiento de Acusta [Count Gondoman], 284.
Sarpi, Paolo, 40.
Sarto (painter), 505.
Sasso, Antonio (S.J.), 491.
Sauvage (Jesuit), 73.
Savelli (family), 522.
Savelli, Giulio (nuncio in Vienna), 166.
Savenier (secretary), 215.
Savoy, Carlo Emmanuele, Cardinal of, 47, 409, 446, 525.
Scacchi, Fortunato, 12, 433.

Scaglia, Cardinal, 236, 279.
Scappi, Alessandro (nuncio), 266.
Scarampi (oratorian), 346.
Schacht, Henry (S.J.), 275.
Schall (Jesuit), 258.
Scheiner (Jesuit), 43.
Schiattini, Raphael (archbishop of Naxos), 239.
Schinchel, John, 116, 117, 119, 124, 126 *seqq.*
Schinder, Francis, 459.
Schmid, Rudolf (imperial envoy), 238, 240, 241.
Schioppius, Caspar, 421.
Scotti, Ranuccio (nuncio), 266, 267.
Seltan-Sagad [Socinius] (emperor of Ethiopia), 254 *seq.*
Selvaggi (poet), 445.
Serafino, Cherubino (Franciscan), 37.
Seripando, Cardinal, 434.
Sesmaisons (Jesuit), 134 *seq.*
Severano (oratorian), 436, 438, 460.
Shrewsbury, Earl of, 301.
Sigismund III. (King of Poland), 165–9.
Silvanus (Benedictine), 349.
Silvestre, Israel (engraver), 539 *seq.*
Simeonibus, Gasparedi, 446.
Singlin (chaplain of Port Royal), 92, 148, 153.
Sinnich (professor at Louvain), 105, 117, 119, 124, 125, 128 *seq.*
Sirmond (Jesuit), 441.
Sixtus IV., 452, 519, 520.
Sixtus V., 37, 216, 385, 530, 532, 542, 543.
Smith, Richard (bishop), 27, 302, 304–9, 314, 349, 358.
Smotziski (archimandrite of Vilna), 169.
Soldati, Francesco de', 36.
Solminihac, Alain de (bishop of Cahors), 154.
Soranzo, Giovanni (venetian envoy in London), 302.
Soria, Giovan Battista, 494.
Sourdis, Cardinal de, 66.
Spada (nuncio in Paris), Cardinal, 36, 128, 157, 295, 368, 442.
Spada, Giovanni Battista (Governor of Rome), 208, 369, 374.
Spada (family), 523.
Speranza, Battista, 483.
Spinola, Cardinal, 158.
St. Felix, Francis Anthony of (Vicar Apostolic), 246.
Stefani, Inquisitor, 51 *seqq.*
Stella, Jacques, 536.
Stella, Luke (bishop), 219.
Stephanus (painter), 410.
Strada, Faminio, 16.
Strafford, Earl of, 340.
Stravius (internuncio), 102–19, 189.
Strozzi, Giovan Battista, 412, 415.
Strozzi, Carlo, 434.
Suarez, Francis (Jesuit), 431.
Suarez (librarian), 13, 439.
Suffren (Jesuit), 302.
Swanwelt (painter), 536 *seq.*
Sweelink, Jan Pieters (organist), 274.

Taimaras Kan (King of Iberia), 244.
Tarabucci, G. B., 158 *seqq.*
Tassi, Agostino, 508.
Tegrimi, Tegrimio (bishop), 12.
Teodoli, Cardinal, 164.
Teophilus (King of Iberia), 244.
Terenzio (Jesuit), 258.
Testi, Fulvio, 400, 417.
Teti, Girolamo, 445, 446, 505.
Thibault, Philippe, 65.
Tiene, Gaetano da, 10.
Tillemont, 153.
Tillirèes (French envoy in London), 290, 354.
Tilly, 458.
Toroszewicz, Nicholas (bishop), 169.

Torres, Cardinal, 524.
Torrigio, Francesco Maria, 433, 435.
Totti, Ludovico, 438, 518, 525, 530.
Turci (bishop), 524.
Turco, Alessandro, 487.
Trivalzio, Teodoro, Cardinal, 160.

UBALDINI, Cardinal, 215.
Ubaldini, Francesco, 500.
Ughelli, 435, 450.
Urban II., 186.
Urban VIII., *passim*.
Ussher (Protestant archbishop of Armagh), 339.

VALDES (missionary), 261.
Valençai, Cardinal, *see* d'Estampes.
Valentin de Boulogne, 473.
Valiero, Pietro, Cardinal, 160.
Valle, Pietro della, 429, 529.
Van Dyck, 535.
Van Werm, 106, 117.
Vasquez (S.J.), 117.
Vecchi, Gaspare de', 214, 507.
Vecchietti, Girolamo, 40.
Vega, Tommaso Pignero da, 196 *seq*.
Velasquez, 535.
Velez, Marquis de loz, 207 *seq*.
Vernerey (poet), 422.
Verospi, Fabrizio, Cardinal, 159.
Verospi, Girolamo, Cardinal, 163.
Versoix, Jean de (bishop), 268.
Verusi, Giovanni Domenico, 216.
Vidoni, Girolamo, Cardinal, 159.
Vieuville, La (French minister), 290.
Vignola, 500.
Ville-aux-Cleres, Count de Brienne, 292.
Vincent de Paul, 64, 89, 148, 152, 154.
Virili, Luca Antonio, Cardinal, 160.
Visconti (Dominican), 51.
Visconti, Onorato (Polish nuncio), 165, 170.
Vitalis, Thomas (Dominican), 244.
Vitelleschi (Jesuit General), 249, 358, 491.
Vitelli, Francesco (nuncio in Venice), 181 *seq*.
Vittorelli, Andrea (historian), 421, 435.
Vives, Mgr., 531.
Vives, Juan Baptista (Spanish prelate), 212, 259.
Vliete, Jacob van den, 504.
Voit, Gilbert (Calvinist preacher), 106.
Vondel, Yoost van den (poet), 8, 273.
Vossius, J. G., 444.
Vouet, Simon (painter), 474, 495, 536.
Vulponi, Jacopo (oratorian), 13.

WADDING, Luke, 13, 348, 435, 485.
Walsingham, Lord, 352, 353.
Waldburg, Truchsess von (bishop of Constance), 267.
Ward, Mary, 24–34.
Ward, William (priest), 331.
Ward (Franciscan friar), 350.
Wangnereck (Jesuit), 418.
Wentworth, Thomas, *see* Strafford, Earl of.
Weemers, Jacob (Carmelite), 257.
Wigmore, Winefred, 30–2.
Widdrington (English Benedictine), *see* Preston.
Williams (Great Seal), 281.
Wilson (Jesuit), 140.
Windebank (Secretary of State), 312, 314, 325, 330, 332.
Winslade (gentleman), 333.
Wladimir (son of King Sigismund of Poland), 5.

YEMITSI, Mikado, 253.
Yussuf (King of Mombasa), 258.
Yves (Capuchins), 145.

ZACHARIAS (metropolitan of Iberia), 244.
Zacchia, Laudivio, Cardinal, 158, 176.
Zamet, Séb. (bishop of Langres), 82–8.
Zanconi, Domenico, 37, 38.
Zeiller, Martin, 514.
Zelachrist (Ethiopian General), 256 *seq*.
Zeno, Renier (Venetian ambassador), 176.
Zilli, Giovanni, 221.